Set the Night on Fire

Set the Night on Fire

L.A. in the Sixties

Mike Davis
and
Jon Wiener

VERSO
London • New York

First published by Verso 2020
© Mike Davis and Jon Wiener 2020

Chapter 1, "Setting the Agenda," was originally published in
New Left Review 108, Nov–Dec 2017.
Chapter 21, "Riot Nights on the Sunset Strip," was originally published in *Labour/
Le Travail* 59, Spring 2007, and then in *In Praise of Barbarians*, by Mike Davis
(Chicago: Haymarket Books, 2007).

3 5 7 9 10 8 6 4 2

Verso
UK: 6 Meard Street, London W1F 0EG
US: 20 Jay Street, Suite 1010, Brooklyn, NY 11201
versobooks.com

Verso is the imprint of New Left Books

ISBN-13: 978-1-78478-022-7
ISBN-13: 978-1-78478-024-1 (UK EBK)
ISBN-13: 978-1-78478-023-4 (US EBK)

British Library Cataloguing in Publication Data
A catalogue record for this book is available from the British Library

Library of Congress Cataloging-in-Publication Data
A catalog record for this book is available from the Library of Congress

Typeset in Fournier by MJ&N Gavan, Truro, Cornwall
Printed and bound by CPI Group (UK) Ltd, Croydon CR0 4YY

For Levi Kingston and Geri Silva whom I admire
more than words can express and for Alessandra
whose love saved me.

—MD

For Judy
my Angeleno.

—JW

The time to hesitate is through
No time to wallow in the mire …
Try to set the night on fire.

—The Doors, "Light My Fire"

The song was number one in 1967. In many ways the Doors were the quintessential LA group of the sixties.

In 1968, Buick offered them $75,000 to use the song in a commercial. When lead singer Jim Morrison found out, he called the company and said he would personally smash a Buick on TV with a sledgehammer if they used the song. Jim Morrison died in 1971; since then, drummer John Densmore has made sure that the Doors' songs are not sold for commercials.

Densmore told us in an interview for this book: "The seeds of civil rights and the peace movement and feminism were planted in the sixties. And they are big seeds. Maybe they take fifty or a hundred years to reach fruition. So stop complaining, and get out your watering can. That's my rap."

Contents

III. The Explosion

IV. Vietnam Comes Home

V. The Great High School Rebellion

VI. There Is Only the Gun

VII. Reigns of Repression

VIII. Other Liberations

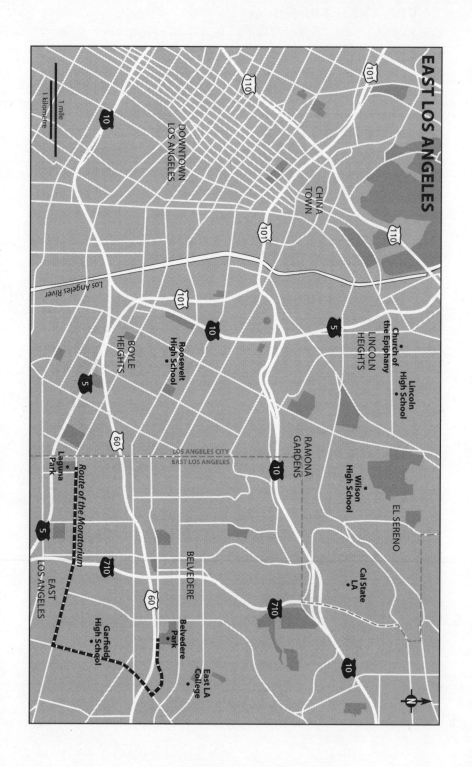

EAST LOS ANGELES

1 mile
1 kilometre

DOWNTOWN
LOS ANGELES

CHINA
TOWN

Los Angeles River

BOYLE
HEIGHTS

Roosevelt
High School

LINCOLN
HEIGHTS

Church of
the Epiphany

Lincoln
High School

RAMONA
GARDENS

LOS ANGELES CITY
EAST LOS ANGELES

Laguna
Park

Route of the Moratorium

Wilson
High School

EL SERENO

Cal State
LA

BELVEDERE

EAST
LOS ANGELES

Garfield
High School

Belvedere
Park

East LA
College

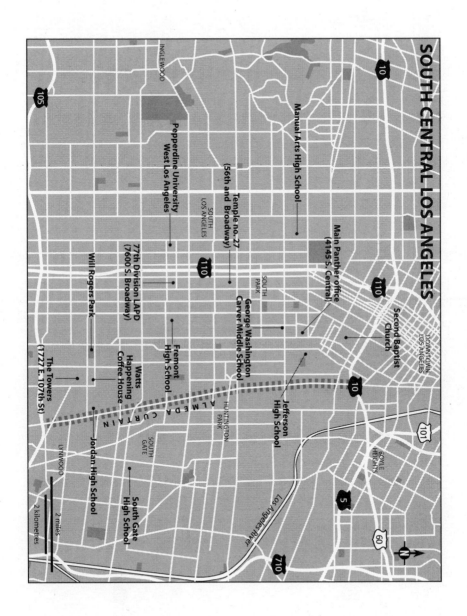

SOUTH CENTRAL LOS ANGELES

10

105

110

10

110

101

5

60

710

INGLEWOOD

Manual Arts High School

Pepperdine University
West Los Angeles

Temple no. 27
(56th and Broadway)

SOUTH
LOS ANGELES

Main Panther office
(4145 S. Central)

SOUTH
PARK

George Washington
Carver Middle School

Second Baptist
Church

DOWNTOWN
LOS ANGELES

BOYLE
HEIGHTS

77th Division LAPD
(7600 S. Broadway)

Will Rogers Park

Fremont
High School

Watts
Happening
Coffee House

Jefferson
High School

A L M E D A   C U R T A I N

HUNTINGTON
PARK

The Towers
(1727 E. 107th St)

LYNWOOD

Jordan High School

SOUTH
GATE

South Gate
High School

Los Angeles River

2 kilometres

2 miles

N

Introduction

A Movement History

I n August 1965 thousands of young Black people in Watts set fire to the illusion that Los Angeles was a youth paradise. Since the debut of the TV show *77 Sunset Strip* in 1958, followed by the first of the *Gidget* romance films in 1959 and then the Beach Boys' "Surfin' USA" in 1963, teenagers in the rest of the country had become intoxicated with images of the endless summer that supposedly defined adolescence in Southern California. Edited out of utopia was the existence of a rapidly growing population of more than 1 million people of African, Asian, and Mexican ancestry. Their kids were restricted to a handful of beaches; everywhere else, they risked arrest by local cops or beatings by white gangs. As a result Black surfers were almost as rare in L.A. as unicorns. Economic opportunity was also rationed. During the first half of the Sixties, hundreds of brand-new college classrooms beckoned to white kids with an offer of free higher education, while factories and construction sites begged for more workers. But failing inner-city high schools with extreme dropout rates reduced the college admissions of Black and brown youth to a small trickle. Despite virtually full employment for whites, Black youth joblessness dramatically increased, as did the index of residential segregation. If these were truly golden years of opportunity for white teenagers, their counterparts in South Central and East L.A. faced bleak, ultimately unendurable futures. The history of their revolts constitutes the core narrative of this book.

But L.A.'s streets and campuses in the Sixties also provided stages for many other groups to assert demands for free speech, equality, peace and justice. Initially these protests tended to be one-issue campaigns, but the grinding forces of repression—above all the Vietnam draft and the LAPD—drew them together in formal and informal alliances. Thus LGBT activists coordinated actions with youth activists in protest of police and sheriffs' dragnets on Sunset Strip, in turn making "Free Huey" one of their demands. When Black and Chicano high school kids "blew out" their campuses in 1968–69, several thousand white students walked out in solidarity. A brutal LAPD attack on thousands of middle-class antiwar protesters at the Century Plaza Hotel in 1967 hastened the development of a biracial coalition supporting Tom Bradley, a liberal Black council member, in his crusade to wrest City Hall from right-wing populist Sam Yorty. In the same period the antiwar movement joined hands with the Black Panthers to form California's unique Peace and Freedom Party. There are many other examples. By 1968, as a result, the "movement" resembled the music of LA free jazz pianist Horace Tapscott's Pan Afrikan Peoples Arkestra: simultaneous solos together with unified crescendos. Historians of Sixties' protests have rarely studied the reciprocal influences and interactions across such broad spectrum of constituencies, and these linkages are too often neglected in memoirs, but they provide a principal terrain of our analysis.

Periodization is often fraught for historians, who understand the necessity of temporal frameworks but also their artificiality. The Sixties in L.A., however, have obvious bookends. We start in 1960 because that year saw the appearance of social forces that would coalesce into the movements of the era, along with the emergence of a new agenda for social change, especially around what might be called the "issue of issues": racial segregation. In L.A. those developments overlapped with the beginning of the regime of Sam Yorty, elected mayor in 1961. 1973, on the other hand, marked not only the end of protest in the streets but also the defeat of Yorty and the advent of the efficient, pro-business administration of Tom Bradley.

There were also three important turning points that subdivide the long decade. 1963 was a roller-coaster year that witnessed the first:

the rise and fall of the United Civil Rights Committee, the most important attempt to integrate housing, schools and jobs in L.A. through nonviolent protest and negotiation. Only Detroit produced a larger and more ambitious civil rights united front during what contemporaries called the "Birmingham Summer." In California it brought passage of the state's first Fair Housing Act—repealed by referendum the following year in an outburst of white backlash. 1965, of course, saw the second turning point, the so-called Watts Riots. The third was in 1969, which began as a year of hope with a strong coalition of white liberals, Blacks and newly minted Chicanos supporting Bradley for mayor. He led the polls until election eve, when Yorty counterattacked with a vicious barrage of racist and red-baiting appeals to white voters. Bradley's defeat foreclosed, at least for the foreseeable future, any concessions to the city's minorities or liberal voters. Moreover, it was immediately followed by sinister campaigns, involving the FBI, the district attorney's office, and both the LAPD and LA County Sheriffs, to destroy the Panthers, Brown Berets and other radical groups. This is the true context underlying the creeping sense of dread and imminent chaos famously evoked by Joan Didion in her 1979 essay collection, *The White Album*. If "helter skelter" was unleashed after 1970, the Manson gang were bit players compared to the institutions of law and order.

For the past half century, a number of stereotypes have framed our recollections of this age of revolt, but the Los Angeles experience confounds most clichés. In the standard narrative, for instance, college students, organized as Students for a Democratic Society (SDS), the Student Nonviolent Coordinating Committee (SNCC), and the Free Speech Movement (FSM) in Berkeley, were the principal social actors, and the great engine rooms of protest were found at huge public university campuses in places such as Berkeley, Madison, Ann Arbor, Austin and Kent, along with some historical Black colleges and several Ivy League schools. In Los Angeles, however, it was junior and senior high schools that were the principal battlefields, and the majority of protestors were Black and brown. Indeed, as many as 20,000 inner-city teenagers and their white Westside allies participated in walkouts and demonstrations between 1967 and 1970. Members of college radical groups as well as the Black Panther Party played significant roles as advisors to these protests, but the "indigenous" teenage leadership was most important. These struggles recruited hundreds of kids to groups like the Panthers and Brown Berets and gave birth to a unique high school New Left formation, the "Red Tide."

The terrain of college protest in Los Angeles also differed from that of the mainstream. Of the two flagship local universities, the University of Southern California was a citadel of campus Republicanism, birthplace of Nixon's so-called "USC Mafia" (and as it turned out, the alma mater of several Watergate conspirators). UCLA, for its part, saw only episodic mass protests, most notably during Nixon's invasion of Cambodia in spring 1970. The real homes of sustained student activism were the three inner-city community colleges (LA City College, Southwest College and East LA College), along with Cal State LA and Valley State (later Cal State, Northridge). The latter was the site of a 1969–70 uprising by the Black Student Union and SDS that was quelled by police batons, mass arrests, and a staggering 1,730 felony charges against Black students: repression on a scale that rivaled or exceeded the more famous battles at San Francisco State.

Historians and political scientists have generally conceded that the one hundred or so ghetto insurrections of the 1960s should be regarded as genuine protests, but they have usually described them as leading to mere chaos and demoralization. Conventionally, "rioters" have been portrayed as the opposites of organizers and builders. This does not describe events in Los Angeles. The 1965 explosion unified and energized a generation of young Black people, ended gang conflict for a number of years, and catalyzed the extraordinary "Watts Renaissance," the city's most important arts and literary movement of the decade. "Black Power" became an aspiration shared by thousands, and in 1967 this grassroots unity found expression in the emergence of L.A.'s Black Congress—the more radical successor to the United Civil Rights Committee. It included SNCC, the Black Student Alliance, the Che-Lumumba Club of the Communist Party, the Black Panthers, and the powerful US organization (or Organization Us) led by Ron Karenga. (The Congress would later be destroyed by a violent conflict between US and the Panthers, instigated and fueled by the FBI's secret COINTELPRO program.)

Contests over public space were also extraordinarily important in Los Angeles. In part this was the legacy of earlier decades when the LAPD's notorious Red Squad had been the enforcer of the anti-union "open shop" doctrine, and when the city council supplied draconian anti-picketing and anti–free speech ordinances. The Sixties saw a renewal of this unsavory tradition. The LAPD, aided by the LA County Sheriffs, conducted an unending siege of bohemian Venice, tried to drive "teenyboppers" and hippies off Sunset Strip, regularly broke up peaceful "love-ins" and rallies in Griffith and Elysian Parks, suppressed lowriders on Whittier Boulevard, harassed kids selling the "underground" *LA Free Press*, raided coffeehouses and folk clubs, and invoked "obscenity" as an excuse to crack down on artists, poets and theater groups. No other major city outside of the Deep South was subjected to such a fanatic and all-encompassing campaign to police space and control the night. Along with minorities, many young whites were also routinely victimized, leading hatred of the LAPD to grow into a common culture of resistance.

The cops, however, had a formidable opponent in the ACLU of Southern California, the national organization's most hard-charging and activist affiliate. When national ACLU director Roger Baldwin and a majority of the national leadership publicly embraced anti-communism in the late 1940s, A. L. Wirin, ACLU SoCal's legendary chief counsel, pointedly challenged the ban on representing Communist Party members in trial proceedings, taking on several cases in private practice. Moreover, in 1952 the local branch chose as its new director Eason Monroe, a state college professor from San Francisco who had been fired for refusing to sign a loyalty oath. A decade later, Monroe charted a novel course for the affiliate by not only defending the local civil rights coalition in court but also joining in its leadership. Significantly, it was an ACLU team, led by UCLA professor John Caughey and his wife LaRee, that launched the legendary 1963 lawsuit to force integration of L.A.'s de facto Jim Crow school system—an effort that would reverberate for three decades. No other ACLU branch claimed such a large role in the decade's protest movements.

Understanding Los Angeles in the Sixties also requires rewriting the histories of gay liberation and the women's movement. Indeed, New York City was not the origin and center of everything. Los Angeles had the first gay street protest in America—over police raids on the Black Cat tavern in Silver Lake, two years before the Stonewall Uprising; it had the first gay church—the Metropolitan Community Church, now the largest gay institution in the world; and it had the first officially recognized gay pride parade—on Hollywood Boulevard in 1970. L.A. also witnessed the nation's first police raid on a women's health clinic, following which the organizers were put on trial for "practicing medicine without a license."

Finally, the course of events in Los Angeles challenged the myth that the "Old Left" was irrelevant in the Sixties and that the New Left had invented itself ex nihilo. The Communist Party, for its part, never appears in the standard narrative except as an unattractive corpse. But in Los Angeles its most unruly and dissident branch remained very much alive under the charismatic and eventually heretical leadership of Dorothy Healey. Despite the party's devastating losses following Soviet secretary Nikita Krushchev's 1956 "Crimes of Stalin" speech, Healey was determined to resurrect what she could of the 1940s Popular Front and to reach out to the new radicals on campus, in the ghettos and in the barrios. Still under the threat of a prison sentence, she found a niche at KPFK, the new 75,000-watt Pacifica Radio FM station, in 1959, where her *Communist Commentary* impressed even hostile listeners with its intelligence and wit—although it almost cost the station its license. In 1966 she ran in the primary for county tax assessor and received a staggering 85,000 votes. By then the local Communist Party had confidentially rebuilt many of its links with progressives in the Democratic Party and had assumed an important role in the Peace Action Council. Its youth members, relatively unconstrained by a party line or adult control, played innovative roles in the early Sixties, including participation in Southern Freedom Rides, and later, more influentially, as the Che-Lumumba Club—which would become the political base of Angela Davis. For two generations Healey defined radicalism in the public eye.

A mea culpa. When we began research for this history, we assumed that our canvas was at least Los Angeles County, if not the entire metropolitan region, including Orange County and the "Inland Empire." However, we eventually had to confront the runaway inflation of both the project's word count and its cost of publication. As a result we decided to confine the narrative within the Los Angeles city limits, albeit with some necessary excursions to unincorporated East L.A., the segregated white suburb of Torrance, and a few other essential locales. The result is a book that our publishers still think is too long, but that many readers will find frustrating because it doesn't deal with such important topics as the school integration battles in Pasadena and the San Gabriel Valley; police abuse in Pomona, Riverside and San Bernardino; GI organizing at Camp Pendleton; or the rise of the New Left at Cal State Fullerton. We also realize that some readers may be shocked that the campus New Left is not center stage in the story, while others will be unhappy that, for the counterculture, we focus only on its politicized aspects. And because our goal was to write a "movement history" of Los Angeles, we look at the city from the vantage points of its flatland neighborhoods and bohemian beaches, where the working-class heroes of this story lived. We invite younger historians and activists to enlarge and revise our account of this crucial but misunderstood decade.

1

Setting the Agenda (1960)

E. P. Thompson, one of the auteurs of the New Left, characterized the 1950s as the "apathetic decade" when people "looked to *private* solutions to *public* evils." "Private ambitions," he wrote, "have displaced social aspirations. And people have come to feel their grievances as personal to themselves, and, similarly, the grievances of other people are felt to be the affair of other people. If a connection between the two is made, people tend to feel—in the prevailing apathy—that they are impotent to effect any change."[1] 1960 will always be remembered as the birth year of a new social consciousness that repudiated this culture of moral apathy fed by resigned powerlessness. "Our *political* task," wrote the veteran pacifist A. J. Muste that year, "is precisely, in Martin Buber's magnificent formulation, 'to drive the plowshare of the normative principle into the hard soil of political reality.'"[2] The method was direct action, nonviolent but unyielding.

First behind the plow were Black students in the South, whose movement would name itself the Student Nonviolent Coordinating Committee (SNCC). The lunch counter sit-ins in February began as quiet protests but soon became thunderclaps heralding the arrival of a new, uncompromising generation on the frontline of the battle against segregation. The continuing eruption of student protest across the South reinvigorated the wounded movement led by Dr. King and was echoed in the North by picket lines, boycotts and the growth of the Congress of Racial Equality (CORE).[3] Separately, the Nation of Islam grew rapidly, and the powerful voice of Malcolm X began to be heard nationally. Meanwhile, as the United States continued to install ICBMs in Europe, the growing revolt against nuclear weapons, as historian Lawrence Wittner put it, "signaled an end to the Cold War lockstep among sizable segments of the American population ... the peace movement by 1960 had been reestablished as a significant social movement." The same could be said for student activism and radical scholarship at some of the major Cold War universities. Progressive campus organizations such as SLATE at UC Berkeley (the precursor of the Free Speech Movement) and VOICE at the University of Michigan in Ann Arbor dramatically broke the ice of student apathy, while journals like *Studies on the Left* (founded in 1959 in Madison) and *New University Thought* (Ann Arbor/Detroit 1960) gave voice to what everyone was soon calling the "New Left."

A young generation was waking up in Southern California as well, despite the stunted character of political and intellectual life in most of the region, and the year 1960 previewed the social forces, ideas, and issues that would coalesce into "movements" over the course of the next decade. This chapter follows month by month the emergence of a new agenda for social change and introduces some of the key actors and organizations. "Agenda" in this case meant something more than a simple menu of issues and causes. Indeed, events and protests in 1960 also delineated the "issue of issues": the dynamic tectonics of racial segregation that were shaping the future of Southern California. With the benediction of federal lenders and the full complicity of the real estate and construction industries, racially exclusive suburbanization was creating a monochromatic society from which Blacks were excluded and in which Chicanos had only a marginal place. The legal victories for civil rights won in the late 1940s and early 1950s had yet to yield edible fruit. In a booming regional economy, irrigated by billions of dollars of military spending, minorities possessed little more than low-skill toeholds in the region's three major industries: aerospace/ electronics, motion pictures, and construction. Los Angeles schools, meanwhile, segregated more students than any Southern city, and as far as most residents of South Central L.A. were concerned, the LAPD might as well have flown a Confederate battle flag outside its new "glass house."

January: The US Commission on Civil Rights

In the summer of 1959 a psychologist named Emory Holmes bought a house in the northeastern San Fernando Valley from an engineer known only as "Mr. T." The transaction would have been utterly unremarkable except that Holmes was Black, "Mr. T" was white, and the home was in a previously all-white neighborhood in Pacoima. According to an investigation by the National Association for the Advancement of Colored People (NAACP), the Holmes' family was welcomed in the following manner:

—A group of people with spades and shovels started digging up their garden, claiming a local paper had advertised a free plant giveaway.

—A drinking water company started delivery—though no order had been received for same.

—A television set repairman called at 11 pm one night without having been sent for.

—A taxi came to the house at 11:30 pm one night without having been called.

—An undertaker called at the home to pick up the body of the dead homeowner.

—Delivery of a Los Angeles newspaper was stopped, without any request from the Holmes.

—A veterinary doctor came to the house, saying that he was answering a call for a sick horse.

—A sink repairman paid an unsolicited home call.

—A termite exterminator showed up, though not requested.

—An unsolicited pool company agent called to install a pool.

—Someone painted on the walls of the house the epithet: "Black cancer here. Don't let it spread!"

—Tacks were found in the driveway.

—A window was broken by a pellet from an air gun.

—Rocks were thrown at the house.

—A second undertaker showed up.

All of this happened during the first two weeks, and the harassment (the Holmeses cited one hundred separate incidents) continued relentlessly for months. However, they were luckier than the seller, "Mr. T," whom white homeowners tracked in vigilante fashion. He was fired from his job as a direct result of the sale, and the LAPD had to be called in when a demonstration in front of his new home in Northridge threatened to turn into a mini-riot. Although "massive resistance" to integration was not an organized movement as in the South, it was a spontaneous reality everywhere in L.A.'s booming "Ozzie and Harriet" suburbs. As the NAACP underscored in testimony to the US Commission on Civil Rights on January 25 and 26, 1960, more than 10,000 people, many of them workers at the new GM Van Nuys Assembly Plant, were squeezed into the segregated Black part of Pacoima. Meanwhile there were only "15 to 18 Negro families [presumably all undergoing experiences similar to the Holmes family] in the entire San Fernando Valley, living in so-called "white neighborhoods." Although apartment owners in the valley groaned about high vacancy rates, only one was found who was willing to rent to Blacks.[4]

In its Los Angeles hearings, the Commission on Civil Rights, established by Congress in 1957 after the Montgomery bus boycott, focused principally on the housing problems of minorities.[5] Mayor Norris Poulson welcomed the commission with the assurance that Los Angeles had an "excellent record in the treatment of minority groups and in the lack of intergroup tension or friction." He also patted himself on the back for establishing an advisory committee on human relations whose major priority was to work with minority newcomers "to raise their appreciation for sanitation."[6] After this comic relief, the commission accepted several hundred pages of dense reports and two days of testimony about housing segregation from the Community Relations Conference of Southern California, an umbrella group that included the NAACP, CORE, the Urban League, the Jewish Labor League, American Friends Service Committee, and the LA County Commission on Human Relations.

Assembly member Augustus Hawkins, the sole representative of Black Los Angeles (13.7 percent of the city's population) in any elected office, told commissioners that because Blacks were unable to buy homes financed by the Federal Housing Administration (FHA) or Department of Veteran Affairs (VA), growth was accommodated through the widespread construction of rental units or second homes on single-family lots, resulting in overcrowding and blight. He also talked about hugely discriminatory fire and car insurance rates where such insurance was even available in inner-city areas. Eloise Kloke, regional director of the President's Committee on Government Contracts, testified about the racial consequences of the suburbanization of employment: "We find where Government contractors are located in geographical areas in which Negroes are unable to obtain housing, Negroes are found within the work force not at all or in very small numbers." In a submission, the Community Relations Conference cited the example of a medium-sized LA manufacturer that relocated to Placentia in Orange County. A single Black employee had succeeded in buying a home in the area, only to have vandals break into his house, cut up all the carpets and pour cement in the plumbing. This was soon followed by a Molotov cocktail hurled against the front window.[7]

The definitive presence at the hearings, however, was Loren Miller, publisher of the *California Eagle* and the nation's leading legal expert on housing discrimination.[8] In the late 1940s and early 1950s, Miller had won a stunning series of legal victories—including (with Thurgood Marshall) the landmark case of *Shelley v. Kraemer* before the Supreme Court—that had overthrown the legality of the restrictive covenants that excluded Blacks, but also sometimes Chicanos and Jews, from more than 90 percent of housing tracts in Los Angeles. But these constitutional victories, Miller emphasized, so far had not opened a single suburb to Black homebuyers or altered the relentlessly discriminatory practices of realtors, developers, and savings and loan institutions. He told the commission of a study by FHA housing analyst Belden Morgan in 1954 that found that "approximately 3,000 of the 125,000 housing units built from 1950 to 1954 in the Los Angeles area were open to non-Caucasian occupancy." More recent research by the Los Angeles Urban League concluded that less than 1 percent of new housing between 1950 and 1956 was occupied by minorities. In addition, "most of the housing that is open to non-Caucasian occupancy is located in subdivisions built expressly for Negro occupancy." Miller reminded commissioners the contemporary ghetto was as much the deliberate product of federal policy as the organic result of local racism. Since the 1930s the FHA had underwritten exclusive practices and was continuing to subsidize mortgages in racially-restricted developments while allowing lenders to limit loans in minority areas.[9]

The result of government-sanctioned discrimination during the 1950s had been the creation of a super-ghetto: 75 percent of Los Angeles County's Black population concentrated in the metropolitan core between Olympic Boulevard on the north and Artesia Boulevard on the south.[10] Alameda Street, the old highway and railroad route to the harbor, was called the "cotton curtain" because Blacks could not live or be seen at night in any of the dozen or so industrial suburbs to its east. A clan of white gangs, the "Spookhunters," patrolled racial boundaries, attacking Blacks with seeming impunity. Meanwhile the western edge of Black residence was roughly Figueroa Street on the south, but northward, at Manchester Boulevard, it began to bulge westward, ultimately as far as Crenshaw in the latitude of Slauson Avenue. South Central L.A. also had an internal physical and socio-economic boundary: The Harbor Freeway, parallel to Main Street and completed as far south as 124th Street by 1958, "had created a massive structural and symbolic barrier between the Eastside and Westside [Black] communities."[11] By 1960, the old "main stem" on Central Avenue was in decline, middle-class Blacks were moving as far west as Crenshaw, and Western Avenue had become the business and entertainment axis of the Black community.

Thus Black Los Angeles expanded, with continuous friction and controversy, through white flight and "block busting" on its southern and western peripheries where the housing stock dated primarily from 1910 to 1940. The chief hot spots of white resistance were the city of Compton (south of Watts), where a racial transition had already begun, and all-white Inglewood, where police and residents were mobilized to defend the city's eastern and northern boundaries against Black homebuyers. (Only the Crenshaw area, with its mixture of Jews, Japanese-Americans and Blacks, qualified as a true multiracial community.)

Apart from South Central Los Angeles, there were also historical Black neighborhoods in Pasadena, Santa Monica, Venice, Long Beach, and Monrovia in the San Gabriel Valley—each of which could be accurately described as a ghetto. The rest of the older secondary cities—like Torrance, Hawthorne, Burbank and, above all, Glendale— were zero-Black-population "sundown towns," where the local police enforced illegal curfews on Black shoppers and commuters. Meanwhile in the eastern San Gabriel Valley, tens of thousands of acres of citrus groves had been bulldozed over the previous decade to create huge new commuter dormitories such as West Covina (which by 1960 already had a population of 50,300) and La Puente (pop. 25,000). It was a mirror image of the segregated San Fernando Valley, as were the hundreds of racially exclusive new home tracts in the southwest (the South Bay) and southeast quadrants of LA County.[12] According to John Buggs of the LA County Commission on Human Relations, segregation was rapidly increasing: between 1950 and 1959 the percentage of nonwhites in thirty-four of the fifty-four county cities had declined; in twelve cases, the decrease was absolute.[13]

While realtors and white homeowners within the Los Angeles city limits confronted the threat—albeit still very small in 1960—that growing minority political clout might eventually pry open housing markets, the county suburbs were building invulnerable walls through home rule. Indeed, as political scientist Gregory Weiher illustrated in a 1991 study, after restrictive covenants had been ruled unconstitutional, the separate municipal incorporation of new suburbs (a practice upheld by California and federal courts) became the most effective method for excluding minorities.[14] Lakewood was the pioneer. Faced with annexation by Long Beach in 1953–54, this mega-development of 17,500 new homes, Southern California's counterpart to the Levittowns erected on the East Coast, had struck a deal to lease municipal services (police, fire, libraries, water, sewage, and so on) from the county. The so-called Lakewood Plan, subsequently reinforced by a law allowing municipalities to keep a portion of locally generated sales taxes, spurred thirty similar incorporations between 1954 and 1970. Through their control over land use, these "contract cities" could ensure residential homogeneity (for example, by excluding apartment construction), while attracting sales tax generators like malls and auto dealerships that enabled many to eliminate local property taxes.

"Promiscuous incorporations," wrote two UCLA researchers, also prevented "the equalization of tax resources among local units of government. Areas possessing high property valuations, such as Commerce, Industry, and Irwindale, have incorporated as cities and have sought to withdraw from arrangements that distributed their taxable resources so as to assist less favored communities." The Lakewood Plan quickly became the utopia of pioneer "public choice" theorists like Charles Tiebout, Robert Warren and Vincent Ostrom, who argued that a large number of competing local governments created a "quasi-market" that optimized consumer choice in public goods. Residents could, in theory, "vote with their feet" for the municipality with the best schools, the lowest taxes and the highest likely appreciation of home values. But minorities had no "foot vote" and could rarely use home equity to buy up into preferred housing; thus their capacity for wealth accumulation through homeownership was extremely limited. The political fragmentation of metropolitan Los Angeles, in other words, was an insidious and largely unassailable form of disfranchisement; one member of a 1959–60 commission studying Southern California's urban issues aptly called it "apartheid."[15]

February: Don't Mess with Lena

At the beginning of February four Black college freshmen reignited a faltering Southern civil rights movement by sitting at a Woolworth's lunch counter in Greensboro, North Carolina, and politely trying to order coffee and donuts.[16] Two weeks later, as the sit-in protests spread wildfire-like across the Carolinas, Tennessee and Virginia, Lena Horne and her husband Lennie Hayton stopped by the Luau restaurant in Beverly Hills for a late-night meal with Lena's old friend Kay Thompson, a big band singer who had recently won new fame with her *Eloise* children's books (modeled after Thompson's goddaughter, Liza Minnelli). Decorated like a stage set for *South Pacific*, the Luau on North Rodeo Drive was a popular hangout for the movie colony.

In the midst of a two-week run at the Cocoanut Grove, the 46-year-old Horne was one of the most famous entertainers in the world. Queen of the nightclub circuit, she moved seamlessly between the Moulin Rouge in Paris and the Sands in Vegas, thrilling audiences with her definitive interpretations of American standards. Since her teenage days in the chorus line at the Cotton Club in New York, moreover, her spectacularly integrated love life (including liaisons with Joe Louis, Orson Welles, Artie Shaw, and Frank Sinatra, among others) had been the bread and butter of Hollywood gossip columns.

But despite occasional exposés, few white Americans realized that this regal woman—who never forgave Sinatra for once being rude to Eleanor Roosevelt—was also a militant Black progressive whose close friends included Paul Robeson and Harlem Communist leader Ben Davis. Because of her stubborn refusal to disavow these connections, she had been blacklisted by MGM, cheated out of Broadway roles that been written for her, and only appeared on television because Ed Sullivan, otherwise a noted conservative, had been willing to battle his network bosses. Within the year she would be fundraising for the young Southern activists behind the sit-ins, now coalesced as SNCC.

Back at the Luau, Thompson was late, so Hayton went to phone her while Horne waited for the food. At a neighboring table, a few feet below hers and hidden by a screen, a drunken 38-year-old white businessman named Harvey St. Vincent was impatient with the service. A waiter explained that he would be back as soon as he had served "Miss Horne's table." (Her fifteen-year marriage to Hayton, a white arranger, was still something of a public secret.) St. Vincent exploded. "Where is Lena Horne, anyway? She's just another nigger." When she leaned over the partition and confronted him, he answered, "Well, all niggers look alike to me and that includes you." According to one account, he also called her a "nigger bitch."

Horne promptly hurled an ashtray at him, followed by a storm lamp and various other objects. St. Vincent was coldcocked, dazed and bleeding when the police arrived. Horne was fiercely unapologetic, and her defense of Black dignity was applauded in some mainstream newspapers as well as the Negro press. A few weeks later the Reverend

Martin Luther King Jr. visited LA churches to extoll nonviolence as "the most potent weapon of oppressed people in a struggle for freedom," but not a few civil rights activists must have wondered if the occasional flying ashtray wasn't a good idea as well.[17]

March: The Jive with Jobs

Johnny Otis, the "godfather of rhythm and blues," seemed to be everywhere in 1960. He had his own weekly TV and radio shows, a famous band that showcased local talent, and a popular column in the *Sentinel*, the largest of the city's three Black newspapers. In the early Fifties, however, his integrated concerts and dances had become the target of such intense LAPD harassment that he was forced to move them to an obscure venue in the eastern San Gabriel Valley. As an inadvertent result, the El Monte Legion Stadium became legendary as the birthplace of Chicano R&B. In 1958 "Willie and the Hand Jive" hit the top ten, introducing Otis to a new generation of teenagers. All the same, he was almost as ubiquitous as a civil rights activist as he was as a musician, songwriter, and R&B impresario. Recently he had picketed a downtown Woolworth's in solidarity with the Southern lunch counter sit-ins, and he would soon file as a candidate in the race for the Sixty-Third District of the California State Assembly, with the support of Loren Miller's *Eagle*.[18]

On the evening of March 14, he was at home with his four children, playing chess with a friend. His dog began to bark, and then the phone rang. "Listen, you nigger, if you keep on writing about niggers taking white men's jobs, this is just a sample of what you're going to get. Look out on your lawn." There was a burning cross, Mississippi style. Otis grabbed a shotgun. Meanwhile in Compton, fifteen minutes later, rocks shattered the front windows of John T. Williams's home, terrifying his three children. Williams, one of the great unsung heroes of the 1960s labor movement, was a Teamsters activist who had taken up the cause of Andrew Saunders, a veteran union member and beer truck driver recently arrived from Newark. Under the Teamsters constitution Saunders had the right to transfer into Los Angeles Beer Local 203 (and had been assured so over the phone), but when officials discovered he was Black, they sent him home. The Teamsters' beer locals (bottlers as well as drivers) were already notorious for their opposition to Anheuser-Busch's concession, after a nine-month consumer boycott by the NAACP, to allow Blacks to apply for jobs at its huge Van Nuys brewery.[19] Williams, along with two other Black Teamsters, Richard Morris and Willie Herrón, strongly spoke up for Saunders at union hearings, which Otis attended and then wrote about in his *Sentinel* column. A few days before the attacks on Otis's and Williams's homes, Saunders received a death threat from the "White Citizens' Council."[20] Although Saunders, unlike Emory Holmes, had the backing of courageous activists, his case demonstrated that resistance to equal employment opportunity in Los Angeles could become just as violent as opposition to open housing.

The jobs battlefield, however, was more complex than in the case of housing. Minorities sometimes had to fight unions as well as employers, and victories often proved hollow, as when Blacks and Chicanos were hired only to be segregated in low-skill and dangerous jobs. For example, there were approximately 1,500 Black autoworkers in L.A. circa 1960, but less than 40 craftsmen. The only Black studio employees were janitors and messengers. Even in factories or firms where minorities held skilled jobs, they were almost never seen in clerical or sales positions—an iron ceiling that especially affected minority women. Likewise, in public employment—the Postal Service, for example—integration tended to stop at the managerial level. Minority job markets, moreover, were ethnically segmented. Blacks were janitors, Mexicans dishwashers; Mexicans had an important foothold in the freight industry, Blacks none. Although their numbers were roughly equal in auto, rubber, building labor, meatpacking and the longshore, Mexicans, who had entered the manufacturing workforce earlier than Blacks, were more likely to hold skilled jobs or belong to craft unions. On the other hand, Blacks constituted a much larger percentage of the civil service workforce.[21]

Statutory relief was stubbornly elusive. In 1946, after Congress refused to renew the wartime Fair Employment Practices Committee (FEPC), Augustus Hawkins had mobilized councils of the Congress of Industrial Organizations (CIO) and chapters of the NAACP to support an initiative outlawing job discrimination by both employers and unions. Proposition 11, denounced by business groups, the Farm Bureau and the *Times*, was rejected by a stunning two-thirds majority of white voters.[22] (Twenty years later the same proportion of the white vote would strike down the state's new fair housing law.) Three further attempts to pass a law failed in the state senate. Meanwhile the Los Angeles City Council in the 1950s repeatedly rejected proposed municipal FEPC ordinances, although a major effort by a coalition of Jewish, Black and Mexican-American groups in 1958 came within one vote of success. They were opposed by the Chamber of Commerce, the Merchants and Manufacturers Association, and, again, the *Times*, whose political editor, Kyle Palmer, linked the proposed ordinance with the union shop as minority attacks on majority democracy.[23]

Without government oversight of hiring practices, only unions had the power to keep the door open to workers of color, but the 1949 national purge of the left wing of the CIO had been locally disastrous, removing many of Los Angeles's most forceful advocates of fair employment and housing. Although the Packinghouse Workers' large LA local remained a paragon of equality, Jim Crow had undiminished support in major craft unions such as the Machinists (who represented Lockheed and Vultee Aircraft workers), the super-nepotistic motion picture crafts, and the skilled construction trades. The Oil Workers, for their part, refused to implement their own nondiscriminatory constitution. Even the San Pedro local of the otherwise-left-wing International Longshore and Warehouse Union (ILWU) was accused of systematic discrimination.[24] As for the rapidly growing and increasingly powerful Teamsters, A. Philip Randolph, the legendary leader of the Brotherhood of Sleeping Car Porters and architect of the wartime March on Washington Movement, had told a 1958 conference in Los Angeles that the conduct of its locals made Southern California "one of the worst spots in the United States for racial discrimination by unions."[25]

Finally in 1959 there was a dramatic breakthrough in Sacramento, when "Big Daddy" Jesse Unruh, a Los Angeles state assembly member who chaired the crucial Ways and Means Committee, threw his weight behind FEPC legislation with the full support of recently elected Governor Pat Brown. The bill that Gus Hawkins and his Bay Area counterpart Byron Rumford had been pushing uphill for fourteen frustrating years finally become law. Unruh, a dirt-poor white Texan who had enrolled in USC after leaving the Navy in 1945, was brilliant, ruthless and genuinely committed to equal rights.[26] After passage of the FEPC, confident that he could prevail over the conservative Senate, he authored a bill in his own name that straightforwardly banned discrimination by "all business establishments of every kind whatsoever." The NAACP feared the bill was too radical to have any chance of passage, but Unruh, in a masterful demonstration of how to wield power in Sacramento, won the day. Still, it remained to be seen whether the nascent state FEPC could grow the teeth needed to actually enforce the new laws.[27]

Meanwhile the biggest industry in Los Angeles County was bleeding tens of thousands of entry-level semiskilled jobs. Blue-collar workers everywhere felt the tremors of the so-called Eisenhower Recession of 1958, but in Southern California the primary reason for layoffs was the advent of the Space Age. The metamorphosis of airframe manufacture, with its Detroit-like assembly lines, into the high-tech aerospace industry created an insatiable demand for engineers and technicians while sharply reducing the need for welders and assemblers. The transition was wrenching. Between 1957 and 1963, 80,000 workers were laid off in aircraft assembly while 90,000 new jobs were created in electronics and missiles. The rapid change in skill sets and required education raised new "nonracial" barriers to minority entry into the industry, as did the seniority system protecting older whites. Although minority engineers and technicians now faced few obstacles to employment (indeed they were migrating into L.A. from all parts of the country), it was little solace to those who had been fighting so long for a place on a North American or Lockheed assembly line. Affirmative action's time had not yet come, and Black workers found themselves chasing a mirage of jobs about to be restructured, eliminated by automation or moved to segregated suburbs.

April: Game Theory

Santa Monica in 1960 was still the three-shift company town of Douglas Aircraft. The huge factory complex at the Santa Monica Airport, which at its peak in 1943 had employed 44,000 workers, was the bread and butter of the city where Route 66 met the Pacific Ocean. Douglas was also the mother (the Air Force was the father) of "Project RAND," a secret weapons planning and strategy group that after the war moved out on its own to become the RAND Corporation. Rand's core mission for the Air Force was to make nuclear warfare, including a possible preemptive strike on the Soviet Union, feasible. To accomplish this it was given the resources to hire the best minds in mathematics and decision theory and put them to work in an atmosphere that was casually academic rather than oppressively military or corporate. Indeed, Albert Wohlstetter, RAND's meister of nuclear strategy, encouraged his younger colleagues, such as 29-year-old Daniel Ellsberg, to embrace the exhilaratingly Southern Californian lifestyle. RANDites surfed, sailed, listened to jazz, sent their kids to progressive private schools, collected contemporary art, and lived in modernist "Case Study" homes in the hills. At their own Laurel Canyon home, the Wohlstetters regularly entertained such stimulating company as Saul Bellow, Ludwig Mies van der Rohe, and Mary McCarthy.

But these were just the sunny fringe benefits of a RAND job; it was the work itself that provided a unique, addictive and bizarre excitement. Sworn to the highest level of secrecy, the RAND people played Armageddon for weeks and months at a time. These Strangelovian games were organized around actual or probable crises—for instance, a Soviet blockade of Berlin or a Chinese invasion of Taiwan—with the goal of clarifying the criteria for the use of nuclear weapons. New mathematical models were used to explore the logical structure of strategic decision-making. "By the mid-1950s," writes journalist Alex Abella in his history, "RAND became the world center for game theory." John von Neumann, Kenneth Arrow, John Nash—the giants of "rational choice" and game theoretics, worked at RAND during the 1950s in the quixotic quest for a solution to the "Prisoner's Dilemma" (a problem first formulated by RAND researchers in

1950). The essence of the dilemma was that two rational opponents might choose *not* to cooperate, even if doing so could avoid nuclear war. Daniel Ellsberg, one of many at RAND struggling with the grim implications of game theory, became so pessimistic about the future that he didn't bother to subscribe to the life insurance offered by the corporation.[28] The Cuban Missile Crisis was just around the corner.

Meanwhile another game, "the Game" in fact, was being played down the street from RAND in the brick three-story building that housed the Synanon Foundation. Its founder, Chuck Dederich, a former executive and recovered alcoholic, had been very active in AA, but became disillusioned by its refusal to help drug addicts as well as by what he regarded as the collusive and formulaic nature of its group sessions. Synanon in contrast was a racially integrated therapeutic commune organized around hours-long group confrontations, emotionally explosive and often terrifying to newcomers, that aimed to destroy self-deception while fostering a tough, "intimate honesty" between participants. No hint of violence was tolerated in the Game, but participants were otherwise free to use language as a sledgehammer. Dederich, who was both the autocrat and loving father inside 1351 Oceanfront Avenue, was frank about the perils of the process. "The Game is a big emotional dance and it's like a dream. It's random. Some dreams are nightmares."[29]

In the event, Synanon seemed to work, as former addicts successfully helped newcomers through the torture of cold turkey withdrawal, and hundreds of vulnerable people, ranging from celebrities to San Quentin parolees, managed to live together in some harmony. In the later 1960s, the community would turn to activism. "Synanon residents marched with Cesar Chavez," recalled activist-historian Frank Bardacke, "boycotted non-union table grapes, and supported a variety of leftish causes. The foundation was committed to environmentalism."[30] But whether seen as therapy or an alternative way of life, Synanon was an anathema to civic leaders who feared that Santa Monica would be deluged with addicts rather than tourists. They prosecuted, sued and then re-sued the foundation for years, with Synanon always winning a last-minute reprieve from eviction, but never exoneration from accusations of being a cult or criminal conspiracy. In contrast, the city council had no qualms about pipe-smoking RANDites sitting around a seminar table and quietly discussing how many millions of casualties would be "acceptable" in the event of a nuclear exchange.

May: The Independent Student Union

On May 2, just minutes before his long-delayed appointment in San Quentin's gas chamber, Caryl Chessman's lawyers made a final, desperate appeal to Federal Judge Louis Goodman in San Francisco to stay the execution. Goodman reluctantly agreed to hear their arguments and asked his secretary to quickly get Warden Fred Dickson on the phone. The secretary dialed the wrong number. By the time he reached the warden, Chessman's face was already turning purple from cyanide fumes and Dickson refused to stop the process. The *Los Angeles Times*, which had earlier lauded the gas chamber as a "sanitary disposal mechanism," termed Chessman's execution a "breath of fresh air," but millions around the world thought it was miscarriage of justice.[31]

Since his original conviction in 1948 for kidnapping (a capital crime under California's Little Lindbergh Law), Chessman, representing himself, had won a sensational series of last-minute reprieves from the gas chamber and published a best-selling memoir, *Cell 2455, Death Row* which was made into a 1955 film. Although he protested his innocence to the last breath, the real issue in the case became the barbarous nature of the death penalty itself. After losing a last appeal in 1959, Chessman was supposed to die the following February, but Governor Brown, stalked by young protestors (including his own seminarian son Jerry) and inundated with clemency appeals from around the world, blinked at the last moment and stayed the execution for two months. This only unleashed fury from the Right as Republican legislators, seeing an opportunity to revenge themselves for their epic defeat in 1958, called for the governor's impeachment. Brown, worried about collateral damage to his proposed Master Plan for the colleges and upcoming State Water System bonds, punted the issue to the legislature in the form of a bill to abolish the death penalty. He knew it had no chance of passage.

The Chessman protests in February coincided with the Southern sit-ins, while the execution in March was followed within two weeks by the so-called "HUAC riots" in San Francisco, when police used batons and fire hoses to violently disperse Berkeley students (including Albert Einstein's granddaughter) peacefully demonstrating against hearings of the House Un-American Activities Committee. Meanwhile, the Cuban Revolution was turning leftward (in March President Eisenhower had given permission to start training exiles for an invasion), and the international "Ban the bomb" movement was burgeoning (over Easter 100,000 Britons rallied in support of the Aldermaston peace march). Together these events catalyzed the birth of a new student activism on California campuses, with Berkeley, of course, as the nominal capital.[32]

In Southern California the foremost example was LA City College, where a spontaneous anti–death penalty rally in the winter, the first protest on campus in twelve years, led to the formation of a multi-issue activist group, the Independent Student Union.[33] While continuing to work on the Chessman case, the LACC students quickly joined the CORE-coordinated demonstrations at local Kress and Woolworth's stores, and by August they were sponsoring three weekly picket lines. On May 7, after extensive leafleting to unions and on campuses across L.A., the ISU led a nine-hour-long "Ban the bomb" march of 300 people from MacArthur Park to the Santa Monica Civic Auditorium—a distance of seventeen miles—where Nobel laureate Linus Pauling spoke. (The public that spring was skittish about the Bomb. Two weeks after the march, a Los Angeles company announced that it had stopped selling trampolines [a recent fad] and was moving instead into the more lucrative market for fallout shelters.) Meanwhile a rally of 300 sit-in supporters at Exposition Park in late May led to the formation of the Southern California Committee on Integration, with Walter Davis, who was organizing an ISU group at Cal State LA, as one of the leaders. In late October, still picketing the retails chains every Saturday, the LACC group mobilized 200 protestors outside a tribute dinner for a local member of HUAC.[34]

This was an impressive record of protest, especially for students on a junior college campus at the end of the 1950s. But LACC was an ethnic salad bowl of inner-city students, and, despite a reactionary administration, perhaps the most likely campus for the inauguration of a new generation of protest. A nearby coffeehouse, Pogo's Swamp, provided a home for freewheeling political debate under the gentle eye of its manager, Levi Kingston, an LA native (from the Pueblo del Rio projects) who had seen the world as a merchant seaman. The ISU, unlike later student groups, was solidly multiracial, and two of its most charismatic leaders, both South Central locals, had recently joined the Communist Party: Carl Bloice, the speaker at the first Chessman rally, and Franklin Alexander, the ISU president. Bloice would soon move to the Bay Area and eventually become the editor of the *Peoples' World*, while Alexander, after the 1965 Watts Rebellion, would become a leader of the Che-Lumumba Club (joined by Angela Davis in 1968). Other ISUers, if not party members, had heroic red diapers. Paul Rosenstein, a key figure in the LA Peace and Freedom Party in 1967–68 and much later mayor of Santa Monica, was the son of a renowned International Brigader. Likewise, Ellen Kleinman (Broms), soon to be a Freedom Rider, was the daughter of the last American prisoner released from Franco's prisons.

Two leaders of the future Black Power movement were also habitués of Pogo's Swamp. Ron Everett, whom Ellen Kleinman remembers whistling Beethoven's Ninth on picket lines, was vice president of the LACC student body (the next year he would become its first Black president) and a spellbinding orator. Intensely interested in African languages and cultures, he went on to UCLA, and then, as Malauna Ron Karenga, founded the controversial US organization. His roommate, Ed Bullins, became a celebrated avant-garde playwright and a central figure in the Black Arts Movement. (He also served a stint as minister of culture in the Black Panther Party.) However short lived, the ISU was both a stepping-stone to the civil rights battles of 1961–63 and a sign that the anti-communist ice age was beginning to thaw on campuses.

June: Fire Rings

A specter haunted Los Angeles in the summer of 1960: beach fire rings. Captain Robert Richards of the Venice Division of the LAPD warned the press that the five rings at Playa Del Rey Beach would "sooner or later" be the scene of a riot. He cited instances of unsupervised teenagers gathered around beach fires, drinking and necking. When told to leave, he reported, "they become angry and vandalize property." The county had already taken action against such anarchy by closing its beaches at night. Surf fishermen protested, and sheriffs replied that they would only enforce the law against "loiterers," that is to say, juveniles and young adults.[35] Los Angeles, it seemed, had too many beaches, too many deserted roads, too many spaces where young libidos and imaginations ran wild. Black and Chicano kids, of course, were used to being denied access to public space, but white teenagers were now seen as a comparable problem, not as individual, alienated delinquents like those depicted in *Rebel without a Cause*, but as rowdy crowds and defiant mobs.

Captain Richards's warning seemed prescient when in August 3,000 young people in San Diego, angry at the closure of the only local drag strip, blocked off a main street to race their '40 Fords and '57 Chevys. The arriving police were greeted with a hail of soft drink bottles and rocks; it took baton charges, tear gas, and Highway Patrol reinforcements to finally quell the hot-rodders. One hundred sixteen were arrested. The city's ultra-conservative daily paper immediately discerned "a family relationship" between the riot, the Southern sit-ins, and the supposed targeting of youth by Communists. According to one syndicated columnist, the Reds were also encouraging kids to organize "sex clubs" on their high school campuses. Los Angeles meanwhile braced for its turn, and in 1961 ten so-called "teen riots" erupted in a six-month period, three of them involving thousands of youth. These were not trivial events. The subsequent political activism and youth culture of the sixties would be built upon this substratum of rebellion against curfews, closed beaches, disciplinary vice principals, draft boards and racist cops. Indeed, spontaneous anti-authoritarianism would define the temper of an entire generation.

July: The Democrats Come to Town

The 1960 Democratic National Convention at the new LA Memorial Sports Arena is best remembered for the dramatic battle between Kennedy and Johnson for the nomination, both of whom were almost upstaged by an emotional last-minute rally for Adlai Stevenson. But it was also the occasion of a bitter breach between Jesse Unruh, who had already endorsed JFK, and Governor Pat Brown, who was running as a favorite-son candidate.[36] (Henceforth, every California Democrat had to choose which camp they belonged to: Unruh or Brown.) It was also a unique opportunity for the nuclear disarmament and civil rights movements to strut their stuff on television and, for the latter, to directly confront the candidates about their plans to dismantle segregation.

On July 10, the day before the opening of the Convention, 3,000 supporters of a nuclear test ban marched from MacArthur Park to Exposition Park, to hear Nobelist Linus Pauling, fresh from an interrogation by the Senate Internal Security Subcommittee, and General Hugh Hester. Hester had won a Silver Star in the First World War and was a quartermaster to MacArthur in the Second, but the nuclear arms race, he told the crowd, had turned him into an "atomic pacifist." The sponsoring groups included the American Friends Service Committee, which later during the Vietnam War would play an inestimable role in supporting conscientious objectors and draft resisters; SANE, the largest mainstream peace group, internally wracked since May by accusations that it had been infiltrated by Communists; and the Emma Lazarus Federation of Jewish Women's Clubs, the reliable old guard in any peace or civil rights demonstration. A new group also announced itself at the demonstration: the Young Socialist Alliance, the youth wing of the Socialist Workers Party (the main Trotskyist group in the United States). YSA members would become indefatigable, if sometimes sectarian, builders of the local and national anti-war movements from 1965 onward.

The big event, however, was a rally of 7,500 people at the Shrine Auditorium, which Loren Miller described in the *Eagle* as the largest Negro political gathering since the 1940s. The *Eagle* had polled a sample of the community, finding universal opposition to LBJ and some support for Kennedy. Stevenson, however, remained far and away the most popular choice. When Kennedy arrived at the Shrine, the crowd, which had been jeering the names of Truman and Johnson, continued to boo, very disconcertingly, as he entered the auditorium. In contrast, "tumultuous, whistling standing ovations were given to Senator Hubert Humphrey [far down the list in the delegate count] and later, Adam Clayton Powell and Martin Luther King." Powell, Harlem's outlaw congressman, stole the show, as he almost always did with urban Black audiences. After the speeches and lofty promises, 5,000 people marched down Figueroa to the Sports Arena, where Democratic Party chairman Paul Butler declared, "We dedicate ourselves to the elimination of all discriminatory practices at the earliest possible moment without violence." Black voices chanted, "No! No! Now—not later!"[37]

August: Moving Mountains and Neighborhoods

In August the California Division of Highways began to excavate the tonnage equivalent of the Panama Canal in the Sepulveda Pass between West Los Angeles and the San Fernando Valley. This segment of the San Diego Freeway—supplanting Sepulveda Boulevard and its infamous "Dead Man's Curve"—would uncork the worst traffic bottleneck in Southern California and humanize (for a few years at least) the drive between the aerospace plants around LAX and the homes of engineers and technicians in Sherman Oaks and Reseda. If the giant Caterpillar earthmovers were symbols of liberation to middle-class commuters, they had more sinister significance for the communities they divided or destroyed. Ground zero of residential displacement in Southern California was the star-shaped ring of freeways around downtown that sliced the Eastside into half a dozen pieces, consuming 20 percent of its land area and forever enshrouding its playgrounds and schools in carcinogenic pollution. The great stacked interchanges, still engineering wonders of the world in the early 1960s, had been sited on residential and park land to avoid any conflict with adjacent railroad yards or the huge Sears Roebuck distribution center in Boyle

Heights. In any event, inner-city residential property was easier to condemn, cheaper to buy and risked less of a political backlash.[38]

Affluent neighborhoods, on the other hand, had dismaying clout. Although the Division of Highways wanted to construct freeways down Olympic Boulevard, across Beverly Hills, and through Laurel Canyon, wealthy homeowners and celebrities eventually nixed the latter two projects and forced planners to reroute the Santa Monica Freeway southward to avoid country clubs and exclusive white neighborhoods. Instead of tony white Cheviot Hills, "Sugar Hill," the elite Black neighborhood in West Adams, was sacrificed to the bulldozers, while angry Black and Chicano residents of Santa Monica's Pico neighborhood protested throughout fall 1960 against the demolition of most of their homes by a final alignment. By its opening in 1965 the Santa Monica Freeway had displaced 15,000 people; all the freeways, perhaps 150,000.[39] The priorities of suburban mobility translated into housing disasters for segregated inner-city populations, whose own transport situation simultaneously deteriorated with the extinction of metropolitan rail transit. 1960 was the last full year of operation for Pacific Electric's famous Red Cars along their remaining route from downtown L.A. to downtown Long Beach. They would trundle down the tracks for the last time in April 1961. The streetcars would disappear a few years later, and their diesel-powered replacements never fully compensated for the loss of faster electric transit routes to work and shopping.

September: Toxic Bohemia

Stinking, muck-filled canals; tired pumpjacks dribbling oil; abandoned bungalows; semi-derelict arcades; kids shooting heroin in the alleys; "hobo jungles"; beatnik coffeehouses; outlaw bikers—Mayor Norris Poulson said it was finally time to clean up Venice, L.A.'s dilapidated Coney Island. The city would begin by chasing the bums off the beach and scouring the toxic canals. The first goal dovetailed nicely with the LAPD's war on nocturnal beach parties and nonconformists, while the second—so the street maintenance department told the mayor—would just require flushing out the canals with seawater.

When the ocean gates were opened, however, the reaction of the seawater with the bacteria and organic matter in the stagnant canals produced, the *Times* reported, a "vile gas ... peeling paint off of many homes and changing colors of others." Within a few days, the gas had seeped through kitchen and bathroom vents and was discoloring interior walls and furniture. At least 150 homes were damaged, and stunned residents found it difficult to accept official reassurances that chemicals that dissolved paint would not harm their children and pets. They sued the city.[40]

The gas attack, however, was not an unmitigated disaster. Venice's toxic pollution raised the costs and slowed the pace of redevelopment, thus keeping rents down and making it the most affordable beach community in California until the early 1970s. Lawrence Lipton's *The Holy Barbarians*, published in June 1959, had advertised Venice as the counterpart of San Francisco's North Beach or Greenwich Village, a paradise of sexual promiscuity, mind-expanding drugs, and stream-of-consciousness poetry. In fact, as John Arthur Maynard shows in his history of the Beats in Southern California, Venice bohemia in the 1950s had never involved more than thirty or forty people, most of whom had passed from the scene by 1960. But Lipton was a superb booster, and the *Holy Barbarians* became something of a self-fulfilling prophecy.[41] In the early Sixties the Venice West coffeehouse, owned by John and Anna Haag, became a hub for a growing radical community of artists, folk singers, communist carpenters, runaways, blacklisted writers, war resisters, and, of course, scribblers of all kinds. Police harassment, as we shall see, was unremitting, but so was community resistance. Venice's new golden age was still to come.

October: The Immovable Object

This month local American Federation of Teachers leader Henry Zivitz accused the LA County Board of Education of blatant discrimination for refusing to assign or transfer Black teachers to schools in majority white areas. "Our present policy," he asserted, "helps to perpetuate a de facto segregation of teachers to the degree that in vast areas ... the number of Negro teachers may be counted on the fingers of one hand, while in other areas, the concentration of Negro teachers bears a disturbing relationship to the concentration of Negro students." His charges echoed those made a year earlier by the Black educator Wilson Riles to the California Advisory Committee to the US Commission on Civil Rights. According to Riles, in the midst of an acute teacher shortage, there were hundreds of fully credentialed Black teachers who could not find jobs. Rather than hiring experienced Blacks to teach in suburban schools, California was giving thousands of provisional credentials to unqualified whites, half of whom had not yet completed college. "Out of the 108 school districts in Los Angeles County," Riles had reported, "only 12 employ Negroes." (One district, Hermosa Beach, also refused to hire Jews.)[42]

As for school integration, the school board insisted that the racial composition of schools was strictly a reflection of housing patterns; in any event, it no longer collected data about such matters. But as UCLA history professor John Caughey would repeatedly point out: "On the residential segregation of minorities largely brought on by court-enforced restrictive covenants, the school authorities superimposed its set of enrollment regulations that implacably resulted in segregated schooling." Although a small minority of schools would meet latter-day standards of "racial balance," including Dorsey High School in the Crenshaw District, the overall racial isolation of students was extreme: more than 90 percent of Black students and two-thirds of Mexican students were assigned to segregated schools.[43] The campaign for integrated schools in Los Angeles would not be launched until 1962, but the subsequent battle would continue for decades and precipitate an angry white backlash accompanied by flight from public education.

November: Downtown in Question

Contractors in November began pouring concrete for the 50,000-seat Dodger Stadium in what was once the Chavez Ravine barrio. In February the LA Housing Authority, which had originally cleared the area for public housing, had quit-deeded it to the city council, who in turn leased it to Dodger owner Walter O'Malley for ninety-nine years. Epic resistance by residents had ended the previous year when the Arechiga family, the last holdouts, were dragged literally kicking and screaming from their home. Meanwhile the 5,000 or so low-income residents of Bunker Hill, L.A.'s famously noir slum on a hill, awaited the final court decree that would allow the Community Redevelopment Agency to begin condemnations and evictions. Opponents of the project claimed that "the city government by one means or another—mostly illegal and arbitrary—has tried to keep Bunker Hill as a slum for the purpose of keeping prices low" for eminent domain purchases.[44] Whatever the case, the hope of transforming the neighborhood and its Victorian cliff dwellings into a shining acropolis of expensive apartment buildings and modernist office towers had become a cargo cult to the old LA dynasties and institutions (including the University of Southern California), whose fortunes were sunk in declining downtown real estate. Their high command was the notorious "Committee of Twenty-Five," headed by insurance executive Asa Call and backed to the hilt by *Times* publisher Norman Chandler.

But a future "downtown renaissance" anchored by Bunker Hill redevelopment seemed mortally threatened by the simultaneous ground-breaking of Century City—an immense high-rise office and residential center being constructed by Manhattan mega-developer William Zeckendorf and Aluminum giant Alcoa on the former back lot of Twentieth Century Fox, just south of Beverly Hills. Despite the *LA Times*-engineered conservative counterrevolution of 1953, economic and cultural power in the eyes of many observers was inexorably shifting away from the WASPish and Republican central city toward the Jewish and more liberal Westside. From the perspective of the old power structure—or at least its reactionary majority—downtown was becoming dangerously encircled by minority neighborhoods, and any weakening of the color line, whether by increased minority political clout and/or residential integration, would only hasten the decline of their power.

December: The Eastside

Among large American cities outside the South, Los Angeles until 1970 had the highest proportion of white Protestants. It was not an accident: Los Angeles industrial boosters in the 1920s did not favor a large "trouble-making" labor force of immigrant Slavs, Jews and Italians as in eastern cities. Employment preference at the new auto and rubber branch plants, as well as in the skilled trades, went to sober working-class Protestants with a mortgage. The exceptions were sweatshop industries like garment, food processing and furniture, as well as fishing and casual labor. In the first half of the twentieth century, the city's only truly multiethnic districts were San Pedro and Boyle Heights. The latter was L.A.'s "Brooklyn" (even subsuming a neighborhood named Brooklyn Heights) and had no majority ethnicity. The biggest population groups were Jews and Mexicans, followed by Japanese, Blacks, Armenians, Yugoslavs, Italians, Molokans (a persecuted Russian religious sect), and Oakies. In contrast to other parts of L.A. and to nearby white suburbs, Boyle Heights had gloriously integrated schools, playgrounds, swimming pools and even a local cemetery. Edward Roybal, the *only* Mexican to be elected to the Los Angeles City Council between 1881 and 1985, had been the candidate of a 1949 popular front that included Jews and Blacks, as well as Mexicans.

By 1960, however, the Eastside had decanted most of its Jewish population to the Westside, and Boyle Heights, although still surprisingly diverse, was majority Mexican and would become progressively more so over time. Despite the concerted voter registration efforts over the previous decade of the Community Services Organization (one of its organizers was Cesar Chavez), Los Angeles's Mexican population (260,389) possessed only marginal political clout. When Roybal went to Congress in 1962, it would be twenty-three years before it again had representation on the city council (Richard Alatorre in 1985).[45] Freeway construction had displaced significant numbers of Mexican voters in Roybal's district, leaving it with a Black political majority who subsequently elected Gilbert Lindsay, the future "emperor of downtown," and kept him in office for the next twenty-seven years. Moreover, the impact of the Mexican-American vote was sabotaged by political boundaries: 70,000 Eastsiders lived on the other side of Indiana Street (where the pueblo grid became the Jeffersonian) in a county enclave called East Los Angeles.

Unincorporated East L.A. had insignificant influence over a county government administered by five supervisors with huge electoral districts. Incorporated, however, East L.A. might become a power base for Chicano political aspirations—an idea that caught fire in the spring and summer of 1960. One prominent advocate for cityhood, Father William Hutson of the Catholic Youth Organization, even suggested that it might aid the United States in the Cold War: "In a time when *Fidelismo* is making strides among Latin Americans ... the incorporation of East Los Angeles would make the residents better Americans."[46] In August the Committee to Incorporate East Los Angeles, led by attorney Joseph Galea, submitted a petition signed by 7,000 property owners to the LA County Board of Supervisors; in December the board heard contending arguments. The enemies of cityhood included business owners along Atlantic and Whittier Boulevards (majority Anglo) who feared higher taxes, as well as white homeowners from a new tract in the area's northwest corner (West Bella Vista) who were unwilling to accept Mexican-American dominance.[47]

What blindsided proponents, however, was the decision of labor leaders, led by IBEW Local 11, to oppose cityhood without even hearing the arguments for incorporation. "We state without qualification," Galea and another community leader told a press conference, "that COPE, as the strategic right arm of political action for the AFL-CIO, has in Southern California consistently supported those interests that have opposed the development of Mexican-American leadership and the expansion of Mexican-American influence. We would like to feel that this is not due to racial bias or prejudice. However, it's a little hard to try to figure otherwise."[48] In the event, cityhood was narrowly defeated in April 1960.

Ruben Salazar later wrote in the *Times:* "At a time in Southern California when new cities are popping up like toadstools after a rain, East Los Angeles—which perhaps had better reasons to incorporate than other areas because of its supposed homogeneity —turned down incorporation by 340 votes."[49] (Over the next half century there would be three more closely fought but failed attempts at incorporation.) In contrast to Los Angeles's Black community, with its national civil rights organizations and incipient alliances with liberals on the Westside, Mexican-Americans (10 percent of the population) had no municipal representation, few allies, and a solitary voice (the young Salazar) in the English-language media. After 1965, ethnic competition for War on Poverty funds destroyed what little remained of the Black-Mexican political alliance. Eastsiders, spurned by city hall and Sacramento, would wander in the political wilderness for the next generation.

Part I

A New Breed

2

Warden of the Ghetto:
LAPD Chief William H. Parker

During its January 1960 hearing, the US Commission on Civil Rights tepidly attempted to open a window on the police abuse of minorities in Los Angeles. Chief William H. Parker, notorious for his explosive behavior under questioning, immediately slammed it shut: "There is no segregation or integration problem in this community, in my opinion, and I have been here since 1922." But long-suffering Los Angeles, he testified, was being inundated by barely civilized poor people from other regions. He suspected that Southern states in particular were sending their thriftless unemployed westward. "I attended a conference of mayors," he submitted, "in which I had certain mayors tell me flatly that they would pay fares for certain people to move them into Los Angeles." The result? "The Negro [in Los Angeles] committed eleven times as many crimes as other races." As for Mexicans, "some of those people [are] not too far removed from the wild tribes of the district of the inner mountains of Mexico. I don't think you can throw the genes out of the question when you discuss behavior patterns of people." But Parker did not totally discount a civil rights problem in Los Angeles: "I think the greatest dislocated minority in America today are the police ... blamed for all the ills of humanity." "There is no one," he complained, "concerned about the civil rights of the policeman."[1]

When Councilman Edward Roybal voiced the outrage of the Eastside about the "wild tribes" remark, Parker denied that he had ever said it. His lie was exposed when a tape of the testimony was played to the city council, but the chief refused to apologize. Police critics, as he always reminded the public, were deliberately or ignorantly doing the laundry for gangsters and Communists.[2] In this controversy, as during every other during his seventeen-year tenure (1950–66), he could count on the city's press (the Chandler family's *Times* and *Daily Mirror* as well as the Hearst-owned *Examiner* [later *Herald-Examiner*]) to automatically editorialize in his support. Although his blood enemies ranged from J. Edgar Hoover to Governor Pat Brown, Parker was politically invulnerable thanks to lifetime tenure, a Hollywood publicity machine, and a blackmail bureau that rivaled Hoover's.

Parker, who had earned a law degree while walking a beat, was adroit at conflating boss control of the police with civilian oversight. In 1934 he orchestrated, on behalf of the Fire and Police Protective League, a charter amendment that established a board of rights, composed of ranking LAPD officers, with exclusive jurisdiction over police misconduct. A subsequent amendment in 1937 gave chiefs life tenure and made it virtually impossible for the city to fire them. These were promoted as reforms that would once and for all remove political corruption from police administration. Joe Domanick, in his history of the LAPD, however, characterized the amendments as the equivalent of a coup d'etat: "A quasi-military organization had declared itself independent of the rest of city government and placed itself outside the control of the police commission, City Hall, or any other elected public officials, outside of the democratic system of checks and balances."[3]

As chief, Parker liked to flaunt his power in the face of an impotent and captive police commission. Before the Second World War the LAPD, especially its infamous Red Squad, had been the military arm of the open shop, of Harry Chandler and the anti-union Merchants and Manufacturers Association. Parker changed the balance of power. He continued to feed the conservative Republican appetite for political intelligence on their enemies, but he seldom broke strikes and absolutely never took orders. He had his own expansive dark agenda as well as an independent and largely impregnable political base. He replaced boss rule with cop rule and used the police commission to rubber-stamp his authority.

In June 1959, Herbert Greenwood, a Black attorney appointed to the commission by Mayor Norris Poulson, resigned in disgust, telling reporters that Parker "runs the whole show." He cited the example of Ed Washington, a spectator at a fight the year before who "was told to move along by an officer and apparently didn't move fast enough ... the officer applied a judo hold and broke the man's neck." When Washington's death was brought before the commission, Parker testified that the death was an accident and that there was "no need to make an investigation." Except for Greenwood, the commission dutifully accepted the chief's word.[4] But even sycophants were sometimes unsettled by the actual man behind the mask of Old Testament rectitude.

Parker was "Whisky Bill": an "obnoxious, sloppy, sarcastic drunk," who regularly relied on his driver, future LAPD chief Daryl Gates, to rescue him from disgraceful situations. According to Domanick,

> He slurred his words, stumbled in and out of cars, and sometimes had to be literally carried home. Awkwardly prancing about shaking his arms doing a Sioux Indian dance he'd learned in his youth in South Dakota, or regularly throwing up after downing his pre-dinner bourbons in his house, among friends, was one thing. Showing up late, hung-over, and still drunk to review the Rose Parade with the mayor, and then giggling uncontrollably, quite another.[5]

But, like a movie star, he had a professional publicity bureau to safeguard his public image.

Dragnet had started as a radio show during the administration of Parker's immediate predecessor, temporary chief William Worton (a Marine general with extensive experience in intelligence and espionage). Parker was initially wary of the show but also saw the opportunity to publicize his views on law and order. So when Jack Webb, the originator and star of the show, won network approval to produce both television and radio versions, Parker offered unlimited LAPD cooperation in production if Webb allowed the department's

Public Information Division (PID) to vet the scripts. Parker kept Webb on a short leash—forcing him, for instance, to never use the word "cop," which the chief regarded as derogatory. In addition, adds Domanick, "the advisors closely examined the script to guarantee that the LAPD officers on *Dragnet* were ethical, efficient, terse and white." It quickly became one of the top television programs of the 1950s and the template for a succession of television procedurals (twenty-five shows in all) and movies that exalted not only the LAPD macho ethos but also its icy and unnerving attitude toward the general citizenry.[6]

In addition to Hollywood, the PID—a unit of twenty permanent assigned officers—worked closely and often intimidatingly with the press: the Hearst-owned *Examiner* published an annual LAPD supplement lauding the chief and his men. *Look* magazine was persuaded to do a photo essay on the skirt-clad LAPD women, in which their marksmanship and homemaking abilities were equally stressed. There were even LAPD fashion shows. The PID also solicited articles on topics like the wonderful architecture of the LA Police Academy.[7] Parker, who insisted on an above-average IQ as an admission requirement for the academy, also made good use of literary talent on the force. Just as he himself had been the speechwriter for Chief James Davis in the 1930s, he now made a young second-generation cop, Gene Roddenberry, his chief speechwriter and script consultant. In 1957 Roddenberry resigned to write full time for television, and legend claims that Chief Parker was the model for *Star Trek*'s Mr. Spock— half alien, half human, with no sense of humor.[8]

An FBI agent assigned to monitor and report on Parker's activities once described him as "a psychopath in his desire for publicity." Undoubtedly. But the chief was also shrewdly selling the need for the LAPD. In several speeches published in academic journals during the mid 1950s, Parker expounded a surprisingly pessimistic doctrine of law enforcement, emphasizing that crime moved in cycles determined by socioeconomic factors beyond the power of the police to control: "Lacking the ability to remedy human imperfection, we must learn to live with it. The only way to safely live with it is to control it. Control, not correction, is the key." He added that "police field deployment is not social agency activity …[it] is concerned with effect, not cause." The public, however, chronically underestimated the prevalence of crime and placed naïve belief in sociological solutions such as the probation and youth services agencies that Parker scorned. The result was an unwillingness to properly finance and support tough policing. Parker's remedy was that police reformers must intervene in the "creation of a market for professional law enforcement."[9]

Generating this demand meant using the media to show that crime lurked in every crevice of urban society and was only held at bay by a "thin blue line" of hard-as-nails cops. Police critics, if they so dared, would have to pass through a gauntlet of irrefutable crime statistics scientifically amassed by police analysts. (Parker's belief in letting no crime, however trivial, go unpunished anticipated the contemporary "broken windows" school of policing.) What went unsaid, of course, was that the easiest way to generate politically dramatic indices of criminality was through the use of dragnets, racial profiling, random traffic stops, raids on gay bars, warrantless home break-ins, and the promotion of ordinary misdemeanors to felonies whenever possible. The relentless, virtually industrialized policing of the southern and eastern districts of the city, as well as gay Hollywood, automatically became its own self-justification. Mob invaders from the East and Red conspirators were just the frosting on Parker's cake. White-collar crime, meanwhile, was scarcely acknowledged.

The Scalp Collection

Parker, like his archenemy J. Edgar Hoover, was also a master extortionist. He had learned the black arts during his three years as an administrative assistant to corrupt and brutal Chief James Davis, for whom, according to Domanick, "he gathered information on the professional and personal lives of elected and appointed officials and prominent citizens."[10] One ranking veteran of the Parker era said that his boss employed a "Soviet model of intelligence—to collect as much as possible about any number of suspicious individuals because commanders never knew when the information could be useful."[11] One of his first acts in office was to expand the intelligence squad into a full division and later, in 1956, to establish a clearinghouse that shared with other law enforcement agencies the LAPD's thousands of dossiers on subversives as well as mobsters, drug dealers and gamblers.[12] Carlton Williams, the *Times*'s city hall correspondent and chief hatchet man for the Chandlers in local politics, also had access to the files and frequently used them against his paper's opponents.[13]

Parker bugged everything: the city jail, all LAPD phone calls, city council offices, the hotel rooms of candidates, and private residences.[14] He also made the sledgehammer LAPD standard equipment. His men routinely raided homes and businesses without warrant, knocking down doors and smashing everything inside. In a 1955 case, *People v. Cahan*, California Supreme Court Justice Roger Traynor expressed amazement at Parker's warrantless empire of surveillance and his force's enthusiasm for the destruction of suspects' property. Parker raged against having his "hands tied" by the ruling against the LAPD in this case, but he continued, if more clandestinely, his illegal surveillance of politicians and suspected criminals.[15]

His scalp collection was impressive. At the beginning of his tenure, he had put a silver stake through the heart of public housing by exposing, in a televised hearing, Frank Wilkinson, the public relations officer of the LA Housing Authority, as a supposed Communist.[16] In 1957 he attempted to destroy the political career of a woman named Ethel Narvid who worked for liberal Valley council member (later congressmember) James Corman. Parker claimed he had evidence that she was a Communist, but Corman, who had the moral backbone missing in many other members of the council, ignored the chief and made her his deputy. The significance of this otherwise-obscure episode, Domanick argues, is that it was a "sign of how closely Bill Parker was monitoring and influencing local political affairs that he would invest himself trying to defeat a staff member of a freshman on a fifteen-member city council."[17]

He stalked bigger game the following year, during one of the most important elections in state history. Challenging generations of Republican control over the governorship, Democrat Pat Brown was locked in a bitter contest with US Senator William Knowland, an archconservative who was also sponsoring a right-to-work amendment on the ballot. In Southern California, Democratic National Committee member Paul Ziffren was Brown's crucial liaison with Hollywood moguls and Jewish political donors. Two years earlier, Ziffren had urged Brown, then attorney general, to investigate Parker's intelligence division for its rampant disregard of constitutional rights.[18] The LAPD's revenge was to pass on to the Knowland camp—probably via the *Times'* Carlton Williams—information that Ziffren, an entertainment lawyer originally from Chicago, was associated with mob members. In Parker's universe, of course, this might simply entail knowing Frank Sinatra, whom Parker considered "totally tied to the Mafia."[19]

But Brown and the Democrats swept the elections, taking control of both houses in Sacramento for the first time in a century, with a well-known enemy of Parker, LA Superior Court Judge Stanley Mosk, elected state attorney general. Mosk subsequently repulsed several attempts by Parker to repeal the Cahan decision and restore wiretapping on a broad scale. The chief spied on both Brown and Mosk, but the governor was beyond his reach. Mosk wasn't. "In July 1963 detectives observed that Mosk boarded a plane for Mexico City with a twenty-three year old woman who was not his wife. Either one of the department's detectives flew to Mexico or arranged with private detectives to set up a camera and focus it on the window of their hotel room." In short order Mosk abandoned plans to run for the US Senate. Brown appointed him to the California Supreme Court as compensation.[20]

Thanks to James Ellroy and other pulp writers, Chief Parker still rules postwar Los Angeles in the imagination. Indeed, he's the only public figure from the 1950–66 period, aside from celebrity gangsters Bugsy Siegel and Mickey Cohen, that anyone today is likely to know about. Yet an important and proud chapter in Parker's biography remains obscure: his service during the Second World War as the designer of the Police and Prisons Plan for the Normandy invasion. Army Captain Parker subsequently accompanied Patton's Third Army to Paris (earning a Purple Heart en route) and then helped denazify police forces in Germany, where he served under Orlando Wilson, another police reformer with an authoritarian style. (In 1960 Chicago

Mayor Richard Daley appointed Wilson as the city's superintendent of police.) Parker, in other words, had the exhilarating experiences of administering martial law and rebuilding police institutions from scratch. In his study of Black radicalism and the LAPD, historian Bruce Tylor suggests that martial law remained Parker's favored paradigm, at least for policing South Central L.A.[21]

The LAPD not only enforced law within the ghetto; it enforced the ghetto itself. Glenn Souza, who graduated from the police academy in 1959, described the department as "completely segregated and by any definition extremely racist," attesting, "Dwight D. Eisenhower was President and Chief William H. Parker was god." Assigned to the University Division (south of USC), he was amazed at the scope of LAPD power over the Black community: "We were a mercenary army unofficially empowered to arrest anyone at any time for any cause." One cause was violation of the unwritten curfew that excluded Black people from white residential districts after dark. Souza reminisced:

> Black people could not venture north of Beverly or much west of La Brea after dark without a strongly documented purpose. In Hollywood Division, a Negro was an automatic "shake" or field interview with the resultant warrant check or match-up to some vague crime report. A favored location for these shakes was the call box at Outpost Canyon and Mulholland Drive. If there was absolutely no way to arrest the suspect, he was told to start walking.[22]

Almena Loman, a community journalist and newspaper publisher, once summed up the universal experience of law-abiding Blacks in dealings with the LAPD: "They're rude, overbearing, and they make the simple act of giving you a ticket an exercise in the deprival of your dignity and adulthood."[23] In July 1960 the NAACP and the ACLU, with attorney Hugh Manes as spokesperson, backed Councilman Roybal's efforts to revive an initiative from the 1940s to establish a civilian police review board.[24] Parker was infuriated by the proposal and unleashed his supporters. The vice president of the Police and Fire Protective League, Captain Ed Davis (a future LAPD chief, 1969–78), denounced it as "shocking" and "an opening wedge for machine politics," while an angry letter to Roybal warned that his proposal would turn the City of Angels into the "City of Demons."[25]

Parker himself reserved a signature rant for a coroner's jury in 1960 that found one of his men guilty of "criminal homicide" in the death of a 16-year-old Black high school student. "The same forces and philosophies backing the Castro regime in Cuba," he warned, were behind the finding.[26] Meanwhile he simply ignored the charge made by Miller's *Eagle* that the police protected the "Spook Hunters"—white gangs based in the industrial suburbs east of Alameda that also had affiliates in Inglewood and neighborhoods west of Vermont. "The Spooks," said the paper, "lately have been going after junior high school kids, terrorizing Negro youngsters at Mt. Vernon, John Muir and John Adams junior highs. They're not arrested, say the Negro teenagers."[27]

Bugging the Mayor

1961 was an election year, and Parker, universally acknowledged as the most powerful public official in the city, was serene in the certainty that Mayor Poulson, who had been hoisted into office in 1953 by the *Times* and the Committee of Twenty-Five, would be back for another term. There was no love lost between the chief and the mayor. In 1950 Parker had bugged Congressman Poulson's hotel room while he was meeting with a lobbyist who later turned out to have left-wing sympathies, and the appliance that he gave Poulson as a gift soon became known as the "Red refrigerator." As the "downtown mayor," however, Poulson had learned to sing in the chief's choir and never criticize him in public.[28] Neither took seriously the wild card candidacy of Sam Yorty, a washed-up former congressman who had moved from the far left of the Democratic Party to its extreme right. His current stock among Democrats was particularly low since he was supporting Nixon and had just published a pamphlet (*I Cannot Take Kennedy*) denouncing JFK for, among other things, his religion. Bookmakers put him barely in third place in a field of nine.

But Yorty retained a constituency among what Nathanael West and Edmund Wilson in the 1930s had denominated the "Folks," the now-elderly Midwesterners who had flocked to Los Angeles in the early twentieth century and then politically oscillated between the Ku Klux Klan in 1920s and Upton Sinclair's socialistic EPIC movement in the 1930s. Many were once again Republicans, but the mayoralty was nonpartisan, and Nebraska-born Yorty, although perhaps no William Jennings Bryan, was a persuasive, folksy speaker who could articulate liberal and conservative values in the same breath. He also enjoyed support from anti-communist AFL unions, who still considered him a labor candidate. Nonetheless, the addition of geriatric Iowans and trade union conservatives still left Yorty far behind Poulson, who enjoyed endorsements from establishment figures across the political spectrum as well as from all the major newspapers.

Yorty's evolving strategy during the campaign was to build a broad coalition of city hall outsiders, with emphasis on three issues: ending trash separation (an issue that appealed to housewives), supporting an additional council seat for the Valley, and firing the police commission (it was widely believed that he intended to get rid of Parker as well).[29] Most of the Black elite continued to back Poulson, but Celes King, who had been one of the famous Tuskegee Airmen and now owned an important bail bond agency, came out for Yorty, as did a majority of rank-and-file Black voters.[30] On the Eastside he had ardent support from one of the wealthiest and most powerful figures in the community, Dr. Francisco Bravo, the owner of health clinics and a bank. Parker meanwhile responded true to form: spying on the campaign and aiding Poulson with information about Sam's alleged criminal connections.[31] Then on Memorial Day, a carousel operator in Griffith Park accused a Black youth of boarding without a ticket; when the young man contested this, he was wrestled to the ground by white police officers and put into a squad car. A crowd of Black youth surrounded the car, liberated the suspect, and were soon scuffling with the police. One officer opened fire; the crowd replied with bottles. As LAPD reinforcements arrived with their sirens screaming, the teenagers shouted back: "This is not Alabama!" Black voters agreed and saw the election largely as a referendum on Parker.[32]

Yorty's victory was an equal shock to Downtown Republicans and Westside Democrats, introducing an unexpected element of populist instability into municipal politics. The Committee of Twenty-Five types were unsure of Yorty's support for Bunker Hill redevelopment, and with Norman Chandler's retirement a few months earlier (in favor of his son Otis), they no longer had a veteran general who could keep city hall in line. Westside Democrats, meanwhile, feared that Yorty's popularity in the Valley could tip the 1962 gubernatorial election to Nixon. Although he would one day become Los Angeles's equivalent to Alabama's George Wallace, in the immediate aftermath of the election, Yorty remained true to his campaign promises to sack the police commission (most resigned) and restrain police abuse in minority communities. "I expect Parker," the new mayor avowed, "to enforce the law and stop making remarks about minority groups. We're not living in the South."[33] He denounced the chief's "Gestapo-like" methods and appointed Herbert Greenwood, the former police commissioner and Parker foe, to the city housing authority.

But Yorty's challenge to L.A.'s alpha wolf was short lived: by spring he was in lockstep with Parker's war against the Black Muslims (the subject of the next chapter) and singing only praises of the chief and his policies. In February 1963 the mayor's archfoe on the council, Karl Rundberg (Pacific Palisades), startled the members with the claim that he had been present when "Parker entered the mayor's office with a briefcase. When Parker came out of that two-hour meeting, they have been sweethearts ever since. I'd like to get that file Parker has on him and make that public." Rundberg believed that the dossier detailed Yorty's hidden stake in the rubbish business, but others were convinced it contained an account of "assignations with women on Sunset Boulevard."[34]

In a cool note to the council, Parker dismissed the story and began planning a suitable revenge against Rundberg. That summer Bill Stout, a local TV commentator who often substituted for Walter Cronkite on *CBS Evening News*, broadcast accusations that Rundberg in his earlier career in St. Louis had passed bad checks and represented corrupt stock manipulators. Stout said that he had received the information from a community group advocating Rundberg's recall; the councilman countered that it had actually come from Yorty and his éminence grise, executive assistant Robert Coe.[35] It's not hard to figure out where they got it.

3

L.A. to Mississippi, Goddamn:
The Freedom Rides (1961)

In April 1947, shortly after the Supreme Court outlawed segregated seating on interstate bus routes, sixteen members of the Congress of Racial Equality and its mother organization, the radical-pacifist Fellowship of Reconciliation, boarded buses to test the implementation of the ruling in the upper South. CORE had been started in 1942, the brainchild of James Farmer, a charismatic Black FOR organizer from East Texas. With a handful of others, he proposed planting the seeds of a freedom movement that would employ non-violent direct action against segregation and inequality.[1] Although the philosophy of CORE was Gandhian (*satyagraha*), its methodology —sit-ins, jail-ins, wade-ins, boycotts—derived as much from the IWW and the CIO as it did from the Indian freedom movement. The primary organizer of the 1947 project was Bayard Rustin, then an assistant to FOR executive director A. J. Muste—a living legend of the American Left. Splitting into two teams to test both Greyhound and Trailways, the CORE riders avoided major violence, but twelve were arrested for defying the "back of the bus" rule. They called it a "Journey of Reconciliation." Fourteen years later Farmer revived the tactic, renaming it the "Freedom Ride."

The 1961 Freedom Rides relentlessly tested the mettle of civil rights activists against mob violence, police brutality, and a federal government unwilling to enforce federal laws. They also transformed CORE from a tiny pacifist sect into a major actor in the civil rights movement: the only one organized to launch direct action campaigns in both the North and the South. (SNCC and the SCLC, of course, were regional cadres, while the NAACP, with notable local exceptions, was primarily committed to political lobbying and judicial activism.) The Rides, of course, were more than just the Riders: they centrally involved Black campuses and communities in almost every Southern state, as well as tens of thousands of active supporters north of the Mason-Dixon Line, who marched in support demonstrations, organized hundreds of meetings, and raised funds to meet the extortionate bails set by segregationist judges. They also constituted a reservoir of volunteers to keep the Rides on the road. Los Angeles ranked second among CORE's "fodder cities" in the North (New York was first), sending five separate contingents of Freedom Riders southward in the summer of 1961. These forty-nine volunteers (twenty-six Black, twenty-three white) were vital reinforcements who braced the movement after the battlefield moved from Alabama to Mississippi, where segregationist officialdom tried to destroy it with mass arrests (nearly 300 of them) and imprisonment under appalling conditions.[2] CORE's chapters in Southern California shared in this aura of courage and, for the next two and a half years, became the spearhead of a protest movement that culminated in the United Civil Rights Committee's campaign of 1963 (see chapter 5).

A Los Angeles CORE chapter, the first on the West Coast, was founded soon after the end of the Second World War by Black draft resister Manuel Talley and a few other pacifists. Talley was a talented organizer and forceful speaker, but also a polarizing personality. Although the group won some victories against discriminatory restaurants, the pro- and anti-Talley factions soon split into separate chapters. Moreover, L.A. CORE, which adopted an anti–Communist membership clause in 1948, was completely overshadowed in the early Cold War period by the activities of Black progressives around the CP and the CIO. (Dorothy Healey estimated that there were 500 Black CP members in the LA area in 1946.) The national office thought Talley's skills might be better applied as a Western field organizer; and indeed, he founded several new chapters before another feud led to his resignation.[3] In any event Talley was frustrated by CORE's lack of impact in the Black community, and he created as an alternative the National Consumers Mobilization to boycott products and firms associated with discrimination. He wrote Martin Luther King, for example, to offer support for the Montgomery bus boycott by organizing a parallel movement against Los Angeles Transit Lines, a subsidiary of National City Lines, which also owned the Montgomery system. King undoubtedly sensed that his correspondent was a general without an army, and he politely declined Talley's offer.[4] In 1962 Talley regained activist stature in L.A. as a leader of the Citizens Committee on Police Brutality and later as L.A. CORE's spokesperson on the same issue.[5] (He died in 1986.)

Los Angeles CORE was briefly revived in the mid 1950s when two experienced activists, Henry Hodge from St. Louis and Herbert Kelman from Baltimore, moved to the area. After a few arrests, the group successfully integrated Union Station's coffee shop and barber shop, but a campaign to pressure the major downtown department stores to hire Blacks in non-menial positions quickly ran out of steam, leaving a demoralized residue of ten or twelve members.[6] But the Southern sit-ins gave the chapter a powerful shot of adrenalin. CORE field secretary James McCain visited L.A. in March 1960 to rally troops for the Woolworth's protests and assess the potential of the local chapter. In addition to the Independent Student Union (ISU) people, some of whom became Freedom Riders and CORE activists, the Woolworth's campaign energized civil rights supporters at UCLA, where Robert Singleton, a Black economics major, led the campus NAACP group (later to become the Santa Monica CORE chapter), and Steven McNichols led PLATFORM, a student political party similar to SLATE at Berkeley. For several years they had been organizing protests against racial exclusion in Westwood student housing. Other members of the proto-CORE group included Robert Farrell (a navy midshipman and future member of the LA City Council), Ronald La Bostrie, Rick Tuttle (a future UCLA administrator and city controller) and at Santa Monica College, Singleton's wife, Helen. Like so many other Black Angelenos, Farrell and La Bostrie had Louisiana roots, and they belonged to Catholics United for Racial Equality—a citywide group struggling uphill against the reactionary policies of Cardinal James McIntyre.

After Kennedy's inauguration in January, 1961, the Southern movement began to lose national attention. In March, Martin Luther King, not invited to a meeting at the Justice Department that included other civil rights leaders, asked the White House for an appointment, but the new president had no time to see him. Confronted with an escalating crisis in Berlin, and in the final preparations for the CIA invasion of Cuba, the administration regarded civil rights as an annoyance rather than a priority. James Farmer, newly appointed national director of CORE, agreed with King and the SCLC that the Kennedys had to be prevented from sweeping their civil rights election promises under the carpet of continual Cold War crises. He proposed a Freedom Ride through the Deep South to test a recent Supreme Court decision that extended nondiscrimination in interstate travel on trains, buses and airplanes to include terminals and waiting rooms, as well. In a situation where the law was now crystal clear but its application was bound to elicit violent reactions in hard-core segregationist states, Farmer calculated that Washington would be forced to act. The Ride would help sustain the energy of the student movement while redirecting it to a higher level of contestation involving governors and federal officials, as well as mayors and local business. Everything, however, depended on the volunteers' willingness to risk their lives by riding into the heart of segregationist darkness.

The thirteen Riders, led by James Farmer, left Washington on May 4 in two groups, one on Trailways and the other on Greyhound, just as in 1947. Unlike the "Journey of Reconciliation," however, which ventured no further South than North Carolina, their tickets were stamped "New Orleans," via the Klan strongholds of Alabama and Mississippi. Outside of Anniston, Alabama, the Greyhound bus, its tires slashed, was forced off the road and then firebombed by pursuing Klansmen. According to Raymond Arsenault's history, "Several members of the mob had pressed against the door screaming, 'Burn them alive' and 'Fry the goddamn niggers,' and the Freedom Riders had been all but doomed until an exploding fuel tank convinced the mob that the whole bus was about to explode."[7] As the attackers retreated, the passengers crawled out of the bus—only to be attacked with pipes and clubs.

Meanwhile the Trailways contingent, also badly beaten in Anniston, found themselves headed toward Birmingham with some Klansmen as fellow passengers. In Alabama's largest city the police commissioner Eugene "Bull" Connor met with the Klan to choreograph a welcome for the Freedom Riders. He gave Imperial Wizard Bobby Shelton and his carefully selected thugs fifteen minutes to set an example that would deter all future attempts at integration. Through a Klan informant, the FBI knew all about Connor's sinister plan, but it made no effort to warn CORE or any of the local civil rights leadership. Nor did J. Edgar Hoover bother to inform anyone in the Justice Department.

The massacre that followed (on Mothers' Day 1961) was such an enthusiastic affair that Klansmen armed with lead pipes and baseball bats hospitalized not only the Riders but also news reporters, Black bystanders and, mistakenly, even one of their own number. President Kennedy, a Cold Warrior first and foremost, was reportedly furious at James Farmer—not Bull Connor or Alabama Governor John Patterson—for embarrassing the administration on the eve of his Vienna summit with Khrushchev. "Can't you get your goddamned friends off those buses?" he shouted at his White House civil rights advisor. "Stop them!"[8]

Huddled together at the parsonage of Reverend Fred Shuttlesworth, the embattled headquarters of the Birmingham Freedom Movement, the CORE group vowed not to surrender and instead went downtown to catch the next Greyhound to Montgomery. But Governor Patterson stopped the departure, going on television to warn that he was unable to protect the Freedom Riders from Klan ambushes along the route. Bobby Kennedy finally convinced the group to fly to New Orleans, but they ended up spending the night on the plane at the Birmingham airport as one anonymous bomb threat after another was called in. Connor and his Klan allies gloated over their victory.

It was a miracle that several of the volunteers hadn't been burned or beaten to death. Farmer, whom many in the NAACP regarded as irresponsible for concocting what Roy Wilkins had called a "joy ride," now wavered in face of the near certainty that any attempt to resume the Ride from Birmingham would be a virtual death sentence for participants. But Diane Nash, the key strategist of the Nashville sit-in movement and cofounder of SNCC, urged him not to lose nerve and capitulate to white violence now that the very premise of nonviolent social change was at stake. Student reinforcements, she assured Farmer, were coming from Nashville under the leadership of John Lewis and were ready to sacrifice their lives if necessary. Although their first attempt to board buses in Birmingham was thwarted when Connor jailed and then deported them across the state line to Tennessee, the kamikaze contingent soon regrouped and clandestinely returned to Birmingham. One of their members was twenty-year-old Susan Hermann, a white exchange student at Fisk University in Nashville from Whittier College (her family lived in Mar Vista, just east of Venice Beach). After much arm wrestling between Alabama officials and the Justice Department, they were allowed to board a Greyhound for Montgomery, the state capital.

There another ambush awaited them, with the Klan again given ten minutes of police noninterference to commit maximum mayhem. When Bobby Kennedy's representative at the scene, Assistant Attorney General John Seigenthaler, attempted to rescue Hermann and another young woman from the mob, he was beaten unconscious with a pipe. In an escalation that took Washington by surprise, the city and state police then allowed several thousand whites to besiege the injured Freedom Riders and their local supporters in the sanctuary of Ralph Abernathy's First Baptist Church. A hastily cobbled-together task force of federal marshals sent to protect the church was attacked, and came close to being overrun, before Governor Patterson, aware that the Army was on alert at Fort Benning, finally sent in troopers to quell the mob. He had cut a cynical deal with the Justice Department: the bus carrying the CORE and SNCC volunteers would be escorted safely through Alabama and handed over to the Mississippi State Police. The Riders were unaware that Kennedy had also promised not to interfere with Mississippi authorities as long as they prevented white violence. Thus, upon arrival in Jackson, the Nashville contingent was arrested and then imprisoned after refusing bail. This became the routine for the rest of the summer: a grim endurance contest between waves of arriving Freedom Riders and their Mississippi jailers. To meet this new challenge, Martin Luther King and James Farmer convened a meeting in Atlanta where SCLC, CORE, SNCC and the Nashville freedom movement formalized their alliance as the Freedom Ride Coordinating Committee. The rides would continue, and in mid June King flew to California to raise money and publicize the FRCC's demand for a summit conference with President Kennedy.[9]

Surprise Packages

As the organization's historians point out, "the joint sponsorship arrangement notwithstanding, the major responsibility for recruiting, financing and coordinating the Riders fell upon CORE." This commitment was symbolized by Farmer's decision to join his young comrades in prison. Meanwhile the strong New Orleans chapter provided a regional base of operations, while CORE field secretaries in Atlanta, Montgomery and Jackson acted both as troubleshooters and emissaries to local Black communities. They also continued to test terminal facilities for compliance with the decision of the Supreme Court—until the Interstate Commerce Commission in September finally did what it always had the power to do and banned Jim Crow in facilities under its jurisdiction.[10]

Recruits for the June Freedom Rides came from divinity schools in the North and traditional Black colleges in the border South. West Coast CORE chapters were meanwhile nominated to serve as a strategic reserve—"surprise packages" of activists to be shipped to Mississippi when the need arose. CORE membership, as Farmer had originally hoped, grew explosively over the summer, as did the pool of potential Freedom Riders—their deployment primarily limited by training and legal resources.[11] One example of CORE's popular charisma was in the San Fernando Valley, where two Berkeley students, Ken Cloke and Pat Kovner (a Freedom Rider in August), had spent the beginning of the summer break assembling a surprisingly large and active chapter, many of them grads from Reseda High School, where Cloke had been student body president two years earlier.

At the beginning of June, CORE opened up an office around the corner from LA City College on Melrose Avenue. Ed Blankenheim, a white Marine veteran turned pacifist who had been on the Greyhound burned outside Anniston, was sent out by Farmer to interview volunteers and plan an LA-origin Freedom Ride that would proceed by train to New Orleans, then by bus to Jackson. But L.A. CORE was also debating how to respond to the area's own simmering racial crisis. One provocation quickly followed another. Three of the Black youth arrested during the Memorial Day incident in Griffith Park, which Chief Parker had blamed on "the publicity coming out of the South in connection with the Freedom Rides," were indicted for "lynching" and "assault with intent to commit murder," while white youth who pelted sheriff deputies with sand-packed beer cans during a far larger "riot" at Zuma Beach a few weeks later were charged with no more than misdemeanors. (Even petty theft could become a capital offense in South Central: in February a fourteen-year-old trying to steal some candy had been shot to death in a darkened theater by an off-duty officer from the [Watts] Seventy-Seventh Division.) Also in early June, Edward Warren, president of the Watts branch of the NAACP, was arrested for remonstrating with LAPD officers who almost caused a riot by their rough arrest of two women on Central Avenue. In Sacramento, meanwhile, a white Democratic assemblyman from Compton, Charley Porter, had bottled up the Hawkins Fair Housing Bill in the Ways and Means Committee, where it languished and died.[12]

On June 18, Martin Luther King spoke at the Sports Arena on behalf of the Freedom Ride Coordinating Committee. In the morning Council Member Roz Wyman, the Westside Democratic power broker, introduced him to Jewish business and political leaders at the Hillcrest Country Club; he then attended a service at the People's Independent Church of Christ, a congregation led by Reverend Maurice A. Dawkins, a friend of King's with an ambition to play a similar role in Los Angeles. On the way to the arena, King and his entourage had no idea of what to expect. The event had been heavily publicized on radio and from the pulpit, but none of the organizers were prepared for the enormous turnout that Sunday afternoon. The arena (site of the Democratic Convention the year before) comfortably seated 12,000 people, and with reluctance the fire marshals agreed to allow 6,000 more to stand. But somewhere between 25,000 and 40,000 showed up—a Billy Graham–sized audience—so the Freedom Rally had to be split into two sessions. King himself was amazed, declaring from the podium, "I believe I can say without fear of contradiction that we are participating today in the greatest civil rights rally ever held in the United States." On the stage with him were Governor Pat Brown (who introduced him), Dick Gregory (as MC), Sammy Davis Jr., Mahalia Jackson, and a dedicated civil rights activist whose role has now been largely forgotten, singer-songwriter Bobby Darin. (Bobby McFerrin's father Robert, a famous baritone, was scheduled to sing the National Anthem, but he couldn't squeeze through the crowd to reach the stage.)[13]

Twenty-three hundred miles away there was considerable anxiety at the Justice Department about what King would say. In Mississippi the Freedom Riders were being transferred to Parchman Farm, perhaps the scariest prison in North America, where discipline was enforced with wrist breakers and cattle prods, while in Washington Bobby Kennedy was cajoling a delegation from the FRCC to accept a "cooling-off period." In fact he wanted them to give up direct action in exchange for a Southern voter registration program funded by private foundations and protected by the Justice Department. (In the event, the promise of protection proved a cruel deception, one of the most ignominious of the Kennedy administration.)[14] King's response in his Sports Arena address was uncompromising: "We cannot in good conscience cool off in our determination to exercise our Constitutional rights. Those who should cool off are the ones who are hot with violence and hatred in opposition to the rides." The crowd overwhelmingly agreed, and for some it became a personal summons to Mississippi. "By the end," ISUer Ellen Kleinman reminisced years later, "the combination of the voices of Mahalia Jackson and Martin Luther King Jr. had been so overwhelming that I decided that I, too, would become a Freedom Rider. It was a turning point, the moment at which my political talking also became serious political walking."[15]

Those who immediately "walked the walk" were eleven L.A. CORE members who arrived in Jackson by train from New Orleans on June 25 and quickly vanished into Parchman's maximum security wing. They included four LACC students, a seventeen-year-old from

Fremont High, two artists, a housewife, the (nonviolent?) professional boxer John Rogers and his wife, and a teacher at a parochial
school near Watts. The last, Mary Hamilton, became an important
leader of CORE in the South, taking on dangerous assignments in
Gadsden, Alabama, and Plaquemines Parish, Louisiana, as well as
winning a landmark Supreme Court case stemming from her refusal
to answer an Alabama judge unless he addressed her as "Miss."[16] The
second LA contingent, seven young Black activists with three others,
arrived in Jackson by train on July 9 to share cells with Riders from
Montgomery, along with teenage members of the Jackson Nonviolent
Movement arrested the same day. One of the LA crew, 29-year-old
Roena Rand, would go on to lead the large but tempestuous CORE
chapter in Washington, DC.[17]

The third LA Freedom Ride—involving four Blacks and eight
whites—was sponsored by the religious flagship of the Central Avenue
corridor, the Second Baptist Church. Dr. Raymond Henderson had
been at the pulpit of this famed church, long associated with the
NAACP, since 1940, and his passionate endorsement of the Rides
was a snub to Roy Wilkins, the organization's executive secretary.[18]
Despite the popularity of the movement among the NAACP's Youth
Councils, Wilkins agreed with the Kennedys that the CORE-initiated
movement had become an "extremist" threat to moderate reform. He
also believed that CORE was infested with Communists and other
left-wingers.[19] Henderson was less worried. The Jackson-bound riders
included two middle-aged Los Angeles lawyers, Jean Kidwell Pestana
and Rose Schorr Rosenberg, whose leadership in the left-wing National
Lawyers Guild and travels in the socialist bloc were widely publicized
by Mississippi's mini-KGB, the State Sovereignty Commission, with
the help of McCarthyism's poet laureate, the conservative columnist
Fulton Lewis Jr.[20]

"The notion that the Freedom Rides were part of a Communist
plot," explains Raymond Arsenault, "first emerged in Alabama in
mid-May when Bull Connor, Attorney General MacDonald Gallion,
and others played upon Cold War suspicions of a grand conspiracy to
subvert the Southern way of life. Later, after the focus of the Rides
moved to Jackson, the Communist linkage became the stock-in-trade

of Mississippi politicians and editors attempting to discredit the campaign."[21] This fusion of McCarthyism and white supremacy was serendipity for hardline Dixiecrats while allowing groups like the John Birch Society to exploit Northern racism. (As we shall see later, the Birchers—with Chief Parker's unofficial sanction—had spectacular success infiltrating the LAPD and winning its rank and file to their ideas.)

By the end of July, scores of Freedom Riders, having served the thirty-nine days that CORE requested, were bailing out of Parchman and leaving the state. Mississippi's leaders, as well as the Justice Department, assumed that the movement had run out of steam and would soon dissipate. However, Farmer, as we have seen, had prepared for such a contingency and now called for more CORE reserves from the West Coast. With the help of veteran activist Henry Hodge, Santa Monica CORE, led by Robert and Helen Singleton, dispatched a contingent that arrived in Jackson on June 25. Nine of the fifteen LA Riders were, like Bob Singleton, UCLA students, and they included Michael Grubbs, the nephew of famed historian John Hope Franklin.[22] By now, the arrest and processing of Riders had become routine, and the volunteers were well informed of the treatment they could expect. But while waiting in the Jackson Jail to be transferred to Parchman, Helen Singleton was "most amazed but not amused" to find a portrait of LAPD Chief Parker on a wall. It was a recruiting poster extolling the opportunities offered by the LAPD.[23]

In early August Birmingham's Reverend Fred Shuttlesworth came to L.A. In 1956 he had crawled out of the rubble after his parsonage was bombed by the Klan; more recently he had saved Freedom Riders from the Klan. He addressed almost a thousand people at Will Rogers Park in Watts, then, in a demonstration of Southern stamina, marched several hundred of them nearly ten miles to the Federal Building downtown to demand protection for civil rights workers in the Deep South.[24] The spirit of that summer was also manifest in a successful boycott, organized by the *Sentinel* and the *Eagle* together with CORE and the NAACP, against the annual *Times*-sponsored charity football game on August 17 between the LA Rams and the Washington Redskins. The DC team, owned by the venomous bigot

George Preston Marshall, was the last Jim Crow holdout against integration in the NFL, and the *Sentinel*'s sportswriters—"Brock" Brockenbury and Brad Pye—had long blasted the *Times* and the Rams for bringing "these Washington Redskins here every year to insult their Negro customers in the first game of the season." In the event, most Black Rams fans stayed away from the game, and some joined the interracial protest of 500 people (including the great blues shouter, Jimmy Witherspoon) outside the Coliseum. The LA protest, moreover, catalyzed demonstrations at other "Paleskin" games, increasing the discomfort of Marshall's rival owners and reinforcing threats from Secretary of the Interior Stewart Udall to deny the team use of the new DC-owned Washington Stadium. In December, pro sports' leading racist George Wallace finally capitulated and drafted Heisman Trophy winner Ernie Davis.[25]

Meanwhile the fifth and last LA Freedom Ride (with seven white and four Black participants) had set out for Jackson, via Houston and New Orleans. Once again the composition of the group reflected the important, even central, role played by red diapers in L.A. CORE. Bev Radcliff and Ellen Kleinman, already mentioned, were ISU activists, while Steven Sanfield (the night manager at the famed Larry Edmunds Bookshop in Hollywood) and artist Charles Berrard were close to the Southern California CP. Steve McNichols, also mentioned earlier, was with UCLA and Santa Monica CORE. Adding a different ideological tincture, Robert Farrell and his close friend Ronald La Bostrie represented the civil rights current among L.A.'s Black Catholics. Marjorie Dunson, slightly older, was a Jamaican citizen. En route to Mississippi by train, the contingent planned to meet up with young activists from Texas Southern University who had been struggling to desegregate the coffee shop at Houston's Grand Central Station. Their Ride ended there.

In Houston's Jim Crow jail, Ferrell, Berrard and La Bostrie, along with two local protestors, were welcomed "as heroes and treated accordingly" by Black male prisoners; likewise for Dunson, and for Marian Moore, one of the leaders of Houston's Progressive Youth Association. With her Mediterranean complexion, Kleinman's race confused her jailers, who initially put her in the Black female section.

Sent back to the white women's wing, she and Pat Kovner (who had helped found CORE in the Valley) became the subject of a hair-raising plebiscite by their fellow inmates, who decided by one vote not to beat them up. The four white male Freedom Riders, however, were greeted as "fuckin' nigger lovers" and spent two terrible days as punching bags for the sadistic racists and anti-Semites in their part of the jail. McNichols from UCLA suffered the worst beatings, which permanently damaged his spine. As Ferrell would recall years later, "he was never the same physically ... he was a damaged man." Their lawyers were shocked at their battered state—reminiscent of the wounded on the first Freedom Rides—and bailed them out in time to prevent them being murdered. Ironically they would have been safer in Jackson, where Riders, however mistreated, were usually kept apart from other prisoners.[26]

In September the last of the LA Riders were released from Parchman, although trials and legal battles would continue until 1962. CORE, meanwhile, supported the vigorous picketing of the LA Greyhound terminal that had been initiated by John T. Williams and other members of the Teamster Rank-and-File Committee for Equal Job Opportunity. The demonstrations continued through the fall until the company, profiting from contracts to carry mail and servicemen and therefore vulnerable to federal anti-discrimination law, finally agreed to hire their first Black driver.[27] L.A. CORE, while continuing to support the Southern struggle, turned its attention principally to housing integration, the issue that would most define the civil rights movement in Southern California for the next three years. The returning Riders, toughened by jail and profoundly inspired by the courage of their counterparts in the South, were eager to unleash nonviolent direct action on a new scale in Los Angeles. But another force was rising in Black communities throughout the North—one that rejected integration, Christian leadership and nonviolence. Although CORE would return to center stage in 1963, it was Malcolm X and the Nation of Islam that would transfix Los Angeles in the approaching year.

4

"God's Angry Men":
The Black Muslims (1962)

In 1958, after a number of guards were injured in a riot at the Deuel youth prison, east of Oakland, authorities took the unprecedented step of transferring the identified instigators, some as young as sixteen, to San Quentin. One of the juveniles was James Carr, an incorrigible LA gang member and armed robber, who was feared throughout the California Youth Authority for his ferocity. George Jackson, a prison revolutionary whose letters would later be published as the bestseller *Soledad Brother*, and with whom Carr would form a close friendship, unequivocally categorized him as *the* "baddest motherfucker." Quentin, as Carr expected, was day after day of relentless combat with guards and other prisoners, but there was also a surprising subculture of Black solidarity: the Nation of Islam (NOI). Carr was indifferent to religious doctrine but impressed by the moral discipline and militant spirit of the Muslims. "Booker North," he wrote admiringly in his autobiography, "was the most important Muslim leader in San Quentin. He was a fantastically effective proselytizer out on the mainline. Every month he would convert ten or fifteen dudes to Islam. They put him in the Adjustment Center—where the state's most violent death row inmates were held—on permanent status. But Booker went right on rapping, usually in the exercise yard." According to Carr, some guards egged on white supremacists to attack Booker in the yard, and when he fought back, guards in the tower shot and killed him.[1] But other brothers took up his work, and the Muslims continued to fight for the right to hold prayer meetings, have Muslim visitors, receive religious publications and keep the Koran in their cells.[2]

They were a new species, unlike any Black group that prison officials or city police had previously dealt with. They cultivated a charismatic gravitas, edged with uncertain menace. Coldly polite in dealings with whites, they were warm toward other people of "dark humanity." Inside prisons, moreover, they were often miracle workers, arbitrating conflicts between Black inmates, promoting literacy and Koran study, and above all, organizing disciplined resistance to degrading routines and brutal treatment. In the community, they were seen as family builders and exemplars of a self-help ethos that they believed someday would be the foundation of a new nation. They also had an impressive record of turning addicts and alcoholics into sober cadre. The widespread belief among whites that they were Black terrorists or dangerous cultists was belied by their careful avoidance of confrontation, obedience to the law, and ban on weapons at meetings and mosques. Even the Fruit of Islam, the NOI's elite bodyguards in black suits and red bow ties, acted principally as a deterrent to violence. But there was a line that could not be crossed: Muslims asserted a legitimate right of self-defense and expected members to aid one another without hesitation or fear of death. "I don't even call it violence when it's in self-defense," said Malcolm X. "I call it intelligence."

As Elijah Muhammad's chief missionary, Malcolm helped to organize temples (they weren't called mosques until 1975) across the country, but his true second home after Harlem was Temple No. 27 in South Central Los Angeles—"Malcolm's Temple," as it was called within the Nation.[3] He arrived in L.A. in spring 1957, writes biographer Manning Marable, "determined to establish a strong NOI base on the West Coast. He also wanted to establish the NOI's Islamic credentials by engaging in public activities with Middle Eastern and Asian Muslim representatives in the region." Accordingly he attended several events sponsored by representatives of Islamic countries, scandalized an interfaith meeting by attacking the wealth of many Black churches, and preached to the converted and unconverted alike at the Normandie Hall.[4] He also acquainted himself with the community's major

Afrocentric institutions, including the Pyramid Cooperative Grocery, Alfred Ligon's Aquarian Book Shop, Adele Young's Hugh Gordon Bookshop (supported by both Communists and Pan-Africanists), and the weekly *Herald-Dispatch*, owned by Sanford and Pat Alexander.[5]

Returning to the city the following spring, Malcolm apprenticed himself to the Alexanders in the hope of learning as much as possible about newspaper publishing. Pat Alexander, the editor and dominant personality, was a fabulist and demagogue who used the paper as a megaphone for hallucinatory claims about Jewish conspiracies against Black people. She believed, for example, that the Jews, "the smart elements in this country," had "brought forth the idea, with which they did a great deal of damage to black Americans, of integration" and that they were responsible for the "danger and threat and the dirty, filthy deception of the political left." Later she alleged that German Jews, expelled by Hitler, had introduced German shepherds to Southern police forces and trained them to attack only Black people. The constant core of her grievances, however, was the considerable number of Jewish furniture and appliance stores, pawnshops, liquor stores (she claimed, preposterously, that there were 3,500) and other businesses in the ghetto, whom she saw as colonial exploiters, regardless of their support for civil rights. They refused to advertise with her for obvious reasons, but in Alexander's eyes this was only further proof of a Jewish plot against Black ownership and economic independence. But the *Herald-Dispatch*, even if more extreme than the NOI in its anti-Semitism, was otherwise a good fit for the ideas of Elijah Muhammad.[6]

Thus the little paper began to publish and syndicate weekly columns from both Elijah Muhammad and Malcolm. Malcolm's column was called "God's Angry Men," and he frequently extolled the rich heritage of Black nationalism, reassuring his readers that the NOI was continuing the work of Marcus Garvey's Universal Negro Improvement Association. He also attacked Martin Luther King, in a language almost identical to Garvey's philippics against W. E. B. Du Bois some four decades earlier.[7] After the new owner of the nation's largest-circulation Black paper, the *Pittsburgh Courier*, dropped the "Mr. Muhammad Speaks" column, the *Herald-Dispatch* soon "became in effect the official Muslim organ," and the Nation assigned a sales quota to each member: thirty copies each week. As a result circulation soared to 40,000, and a regional edition was started in Chicago. But Pat Alexander never relinquished editorial control, and after Malcolm inaugurated the NOI's own paper, *Muhammad Speaks*, in 1961, the *Herald-Dispatch* lost much of its national importance for the movement. Conflicts with Chicago increased, and in 1964 Alexander blamed the Muslims for firebombing her offices.[8]

The organization of Temple No. 27, meanwhile, was not without difficulties; Malcolm's FBI files paraphrase him as saying that "he was very disgusted by the way he was received in Los Angeles, and [it] was one of the worst places in the United States to convert people to Islam."[9] He therefore brought out three of his experienced lieutenants from Temple No. 7 in Harlem as interim leaders. Twenty-four-year-old Johnny Morris, a jazz columnist for Miller's *Eagle*, was apprenticed as assistant minister and changed his name to John X.[10] He would later take over the temple leadership (as John Shabazz) with invaluable help from the temple secretary, Ronald Stokes, a Korean War veteran from Roxbury. Malcolm became warm friends with the energetic and efficient Stokes, but there were other ghosts of his Boston past whom he was perhaps less happy to see. One was Hakim Jamal, who had just hoboed his way to Los Angeles, bringing the same drinking and drug problems that were already evident when he was just fourteen and briefly met Malcolm in a club. Hakim, whose romantic liaisons with famous and wealthy women would one day become serial tragedies, irked Malcolm by bragging to other people that they were cousins. In fact there was no kinship beyond the fact that Hakim had married a remote relative (at best a second cousin) of the Little family.[11]

In July 1959, while Malcolm was meeting with Egyptian President Nasser in Cairo, a New York television station broadcast a sensationalist five-part series, *The Hate That Hate Produced*. It depicted the Muslims as the Black Ku Klux Klan.[12] A one-hour version of the program (produced by Mike Wallace and Louis Lomax) was soon shown nationally, and during the resulting furor several national civil rights leaders, long attacked by Muhammad and Malcolm for their espousal of integration and alliances with whites, especially Jewish liberals, struck back at the Nation. Thurgood Marshall, for example, told a Princeton audience that "the Black Muslim movement is run by a bunch of thugs organized from prisons and jails and financed, I am sure, by Nasser or some Arab group." And Martin Luther King, erroneously comparing men to institutions, declared that "Black supremacy is as bad as white supremacy."[13]

Meanwhile, Black radicals were divided in their opinions about both the movement and its stellar salesman, Malcolm X. In her oral history Dorothy Healey contrasts the attitude of James Jackson, the editor of the *Daily Worker* "who had an absolute hatred against Malcolm X and all that he thought Malcolm X represented," to that of pioneer Black nationalist turned Communist, Cyril Briggs, who "kept insisting on how important they were." Briggs, who had lived in L.A for years, was a Pan-Africanist elder of the highest rank—founder of *Crusader* magazine and the African Blood Brotherhood in 1918–19—but it is unclear whether he and Malcolm ever met. Healey, who acknowledged Briggs's "great influence on my thinking, even though I didn't always admit it," attempted at a "very stormy National Committee meeting" to stop Jackson from publishing any more attacks on Malcolm X, but she was a minority of one, as she would be again ten years later when she supported the Che-Lumumba Club's collaboration with the Black Panther Party.[14]

Black artists, musicians and professionals, on their side, were deeply intrigued by Malcolm, and he obliged them through informal meetings and soirees. Band leader Johnny Otis, who had met Malcolm in his earlier incarnation as "Detroit Red," was part of a group of Black progressives—known as Attack—who would gather for discussions whenever the Muslim leader was in Los Angeles. "He didn't proselytize at the get-togethers," Otis recalled. "His talks with us dealt with standing together, respecting our traditions, defending our communities, treating our women with love and care, being responsible toward our children and not taking abuse from the racists in our society."[15] One outspoken participant in these conversations was the *Sentinel*'s editor, Wendell Green, who had been one of the Tuskegee Airmen during the Second World War and would end his career as the LA representative of the Southern Christian Leadership Conference. Another was a Caribbean immigrant and trade union activist named Mervyn Dymally, who, in alliance with Jesse Unruh, would become a major figure in California politics for almost a half century, representing South Central L.A. in Congress for twelve years.[16]

It was inevitable that Chief Parker and Malcolm X would collide over the activities of the NOI in L.A. But the LAPD would have to provide the pretext. As a frustrated FBI informant reported in 1958: "He is not likely to violate any ordinances or laws. He neither smokes nor drinks and is of high moral character." When in 1960 Hoover unleashed COINTELPRO, the FBI's notorious counterintelligence program, against the NOI, the initial focus was Elijah Mohammad's innumerable affairs with young women members.[17] Given the animosity between Hoover and Parker, it is unlikely that the bureau's large trove of surveillance on the NOI was ever shared with the LAPD. The department, on its side, apparently had yet to develop its own informants inside Temple No. 27—though events there would soon provide ample cover for it to do so. The basic briefing given to the LAPD rank and file was a histrionic memo prepared by the San Diego Police Department in 1959. The Fruit of Islam, it asserted,

> are almost psychotic in their hatred of Caucasians and are comparable to the Mau Mau or kamikaze in their dedication and fanaticism. It has been reported that many temples have gun clubs in which this militant group are trained in weapons ... It has been stated locally, that the members of this cult will kill any police officer when the opportunity presents itself, regardless of the circumstances or outcome.[18]

The *Times*, without the slightest evidence, later expanded these allegations with the claim that the NOI was "dedicated to the extermination of the white race."

Why hadn't the Nation attacked the police already? For Parker and other cops, the law-abiding behavior of Black Muslims was construed as a clever disguise for diabolical schemes. The first skirmish took place in September 1961 when forty police arrived to disperse a "riot" involving a handful of Muslim newspaper sellers and two white "store detectives" outside a Safeway supermarket on Western Avenue near Venice Boulevard. The security men, claiming that the Muslims were blocking shoppers, had drawn their guns when the newspaper sellers refused to leave or submit to citizen arrests. In the scuffle that followed, the two whites suffered a few bruises as well as derision from the crowd, while five of the Muslims were arrested. They were subsequently acquitted by an all-white jury (a rare occurrence in NOI trials) after the manager confirmed that he had given permission for the paper sales.[19] In essence this was a trivial incident that should have raised little alarm, but Parker read it as an omen of a showdown to come. "Following the parking lot melee," Marable writes, "the LAPD was primed for retaliation against the local NOI." Parker "instructed his officers to closely monitor the mosque's activities."[20]

The following April (1962) cops observed two men taking some clothing out of the open trunk of a car, parked about a block and half from Temple No. 27. One worked at a dry cleaner where he acquired unredeemed or damaged clothes to sell to fellow Muslims, who, of course, had to conform to a rigid dress code. The other was examining an item for sale. It was past eleven in the evening, and a service at the mosque had just ended. Neither man ran away, or, for that matter, acted suspiciously, yet the two officers approached them as if they were burglary suspects. After frisking them and finding nothing, the cops called in a license check. The car was clean. Refusing to give up, the cops decided to interrogate them individually. "Let's separate these niggers," one said to the other. When one of the Muslims expressed outrage, he was put in a choke hold and slammed face first on the hood. The other man broke loose to come to his aid, and a brawl developed. Meanwhile, the congregation leaving the mosque saw the commotion, and some of them ran down the street to see what was happening. At this point, according to oral histories gathered years later by Jonah Edelman, a security guard from a local bar, probably a little addled, attempted to help the cops by firing a warning shot in the air. When that failed to back up the gathering group of Muslims, the panicky guard fired again and wounded Roosevelt X Walker, a young sanitation worker. A Muslim wrestling with one of the cops, meanwhile, pried the officer's gun away and shot him in the shoulder, but an off-duty cop arrived just in time to rescue his colleagues and call for aid.[21]

Walker, meanwhile, staggered back to the mosque, where Malcolm's friend Ronald Stokes assisted him while John X (Shabazz) went to call an ambulance. At this point, furious LAPD reinforcements began to arrive—but they went first to the temple, rather than the fight scene up the block. The situation was especially chaotic because Muslim escorts were simultaneously trying to evacuate women from the mosque while husbands were arriving to pick them up. People inside had no idea what had happened up the street. Some began to chant, "Why? Why?" According to trial testimony from the wounded Walker, Stokes and others were trying to carry him outside when they were attacked by two white cops screaming, "You niggers get up against the wall." One swung his billy club, but the other—Officer Donald Weese—just opened fire. Stokes put up his hands, Walker later explained, and said to the officer that was shooting, "Stop. Stop. Don't shoot any more." His hands were in the air when he was shot to death by Weese. Four others were wounded.[22]

In testimony before the grand jury, Weese was asked if he actually had intended to kill Stokes and the other unarmed Muslims. His answer was scornful: "The fact that I shot to stop and the fact that I shot to kill is one and the same thing, sir[.] I am not Hopalong Cassidy. I cannot distinguish between hitting an arm and so forth, sir. I aimed dead center and I hoped I hit."[23] The following year, during the trial of fourteen indicted Muslims, defense attorney Earl Broady (himself a retired LAPD officer) asked Weese: "'Did you see any of these men commit a crime when shot?' 'Yes,' Weese said, 'they were fleeing.' 'Do you consider that a crime?' There was no answer."[24]

Another Korean War vet, William Rogers, was running from the scene when he heard someone shout "that's my nigger." "Then I felt an explosion in my back and fell. The next thing I knew an officer was beating me over the head." He blacked out, and when he regained consciousness he found that his younger brother, Robert, was lying next to him, shot four times. "I put out my hand and we held hands … My brother said, 'They got me, too.' Then someone came by and kicked our hands apart. I was told to get up but I couldn't move. My brother said he couldn't move either." William Rogers was permanently paralyzed.[25]

Inside the Temple, meanwhile, Shabazz was shouting at members not to resist, but nonviolence spared few from police fury. Fifteen were lined against a wall in the men's cloakroom and systematically tormented. "We ought to shoot these niggers," one cop taunted. "We got them lined up and we ought to kill every one of them." Another chipped in: "We just killed some of your brothers outside." There was an obscene obsession with Black men's genitals as they were prodded, kicked, and their pants torn off. Two of the wounded Muslims, moreover, had been shot in the groin. The final tally was Stokes dead, seven other Muslims seriously wounded, fourteen ultimately arraigned on felony counts, and the mosque ransacked and all of its documents seized. On the police side of the ledger, one officer was wounded (shot in the left elbow) and seven were injured, none seriously.[26]

Word of the attack reached Malcolm, in Harlem, by morning. Marable says that "the desecration of the mosque and the violence brought upon its members pushed Malcolm to a dark place." Two former members of the Fruit of Islam, Charles 37X and James 67X, told him that as soon as Malcolm found out that Stokes had been murdered, he began to organize a deadly retaliation.

Members eagerly volunteered, and a team was selected to fly to L.A., presumably, to enact Parker's self-fulfilling prophecy of Muslims as cop killers. But Elijah Muhammad ordered Malcolm and his comrades to stand down. "Malcolm," writes Marable, "was stunned; he acquiesced, but with bitter disappointment."[27]

In Los Angeles, bitter surprise was also the reaction among members of Temple No. 27 when they were told to avenge themselves by going into the streets to sell at least fifty copies each of *Muhammad Speaks*. Hakim Jamal recalled the rank-and-file reaction: "Shock was on every face I looked into. Black men, hundreds of them, ready to kill the devil. Many with guns and many more with enough hate, enough belief in Allah to face anything. We were betrayed!" Some members, according to Jamal, assuaged their anger by going down to Skid Row and sadistically beating up white winos. When Malcolm arrived in L.A., he was told about the forays:

> Some of us smiled at him when the story was being told. We expected a pat on the head or a wink. I have never seen him so angry. He got up out of his chair and tried to explain to us that what we were doing was small time gangsterism. Chopping down a few helpless bums on the sly—it was cowardly and it was useless. Malcolm understood our need to act ... The pain on his face when he spoke of Brother Ronald was clear. But he wouldn't have gone with us to Fifth St. If he had gone into action, then it would have been real action, not that.[28]

Jamal, of course, was unaware at the time of Malcolm's original plan, and he left the NOI with a number of others who were embittered by the failure to retaliate.

Malcolm, hardly naïve about media, was nonetheless appalled by the way the attack was depicted. "The press," he told a radio interviewer, "was just as atrocious as the police. Because they helped the police to cover it up by propagating a false image across the country, that there was a blazing gun battle which involved Muslims and police shooting at each other. And everyone who know Muslims knows that Muslims don't even carry a finger nail file, much less carry guns."[29] At Stokes's funeral on May 5, Malcolm repeatedly praised the Black organizations and leaders (obviously referring to the L.A. NAACP and CORE) that were protesting the attack despite the hysteria about the NOI in the press, commenting, "Our unity shocked them and we should continue to shock the white man by working together." He invoked the example of the Bandung Conference of 1955, where twenty-nine countries had participated in the first Afro-Asian meeting in Indonesia, to oppose neocolonialism; if the colored fourth-fifths of humanity could unite against oppression, Malcolm asked, regardless of religious or ideological differences, why should Black Americans not do the same? He also set aside his usual polemical jihad against Christianity to invoke Jesus as a great revolutionary, the prophet of slaves, outcastes and—pointedly—Black people.[30]

Malcolm spent much of May speaking to large crowds at church meetings and Sunday rallies, repeatedly emphasizing that the Muslims were not at war with the police, but rather that the police were at war with the Black community as a whole. During one meeting at the Second Baptist Church to which he had not been invited to speak because he was "too inflammatory," he took the floor anyway, with the audience roaring their approval. "It wasn't a Muslim who was shot down," he told the congregation. "It was a Negro. They say we preach hate because we tell the truth. They say we inflame the Negro. The hell they've been catching for 400 years has inflamed them."[31] To the horror of many white liberals, even the local NAACP agreed. Whatever their opinion of NOI theology, a broad spectrum of community leaders—from veteran journalist Wendell Green to rising political star Mervyn Dymally and young CORE activist Danny Gray—stood by Malcolm's side and endorsed his call for unity against police violence. Almena Lomax, perhaps the most distinguished Black woman journalist in the country, as well as the founder of the well-regarded *Los Angeles Tribune* (whose writers were Japanese-American and white, as well as Black), wrote that the "Stokes killing and subsequent events have done more to arouse and unite the Negro community than anything of recent times."[32] In many ways it was a trial run for 1963's all-encompassing coalition, the United Civil Rights Committee.

Some Black leaders, however, did not share this ecumenical spirit. Martin Luther King, briefly visiting in mid June, was concerned that the association of civil rights movement with the Muslims could damage support for the Southern struggle. In his two talks in L.A., he equivocated. On one hand, Black supremacy was equally as despicable as white supremacy; "On the other hand I am more concerned with getting rid of the conditions that brought this sort of organization into being than I am with the organization itself."[33] Tom Bradley, now retired from the LAPD and practicing law while he prepared to run for the city council from a mixed district, also felt that he would lose white liberals if he were seen as "soft" on the NOI. That summer, in a forum sponsored by the Valley chapter of the ACLU, he debated Hugh Manes, the organization's chief advocate of a civilian police review board. Bradley claimed that the department had "taken giant steps" on the race problem, refusing to criticize Parker. Manes categorically disagreed, responding that "the history of Los Angeles in 30 years had not indicated the police department is aware of the Constitution." The Muslims, despite their rhetoric, were "strictly law abiding," and the April LAPD attack raised fundamental civil libertarian issues: "The rights of Muslims affect the rights of all of us." The audience, mostly white liberals, booed Manes.[34]

No one, however, was more alarmed by Malcolm's attempt to build an inclusive movement against police injustice than Elijah Mohammad himself. In public pronouncements, they appeared to be on exactly the same page. The Messenger, for instance, had told a press conference in Chicago that "in these crucial times we must not think in terms of one's religion, but in terms of justice for us Black people. This means a united front for justice in America."[35] Marable, again using Farrakhan as a principal source, says that this was mere lip service to the ideal of unity; in fact Elijah Muhammad pulled hard on the leash, "ordering his stubborn lieutenant to halt all [united front] efforts ... he vetoed any cooperation with civil rights groups even on a matter as outrageous as Stokes's murder."[36] His strategy could be interpreted either as patience or passivity. The civil rights movement, he believed, would eventually collapse in the face of white resistance, leaving Black people with no choice but to flock to the NOI. Anything that encouraged hopes of reform or belief in the possibility of integration was pandering to the great lie that the Nation existed to expose.

Malcolm, on the other hand, found it almost unendurable not to be in the thick of battle, whether that meant tooth-for-tooth retaliation or leading mass protests. Farrakhan recalled that Malcolm "was fascinated by the civil rights movement ... [and] speaking less and less about the teachings of [Muhammad]."[37] In Taylor Branch's opinion "the Stokes case marked a turning point" in Malcolm X's "hidden odyssey."[38] In Los Angeles, he took the first steps toward abandoning Elijah Muhammad's folk eschatology and moving toward a distinctive strategy of Black liberation that visualized the American struggle as part of a worldwide revolt.

The temple shootings also marked a watershed for Mayor Sam Yorty, who now became Chief Parker's cheerleader. In suppressing what the

Times now called the "Black Muslim riots," the mayor backed the chief "100 percent." He also denounced the proposed civilian police review board, sponsored jointly by the NAACP and the ACLU, as "communist inspired." (As a result, Almena Lomax observed, "the Mayor's stock in the Negro community right now is on a par with a snake's belly for the reason that he has reneged on his campaign promise to do something about police brutality.")[39] He and Parker, together with Sheriff Peter Pitchess, flew to Washington to ask the attorney general to add the NOI to his list of subversive organizations. Yorty, sounding more like a warden than a mayor, believed that with such a listing "their meeting places could be closed, their literature seized and their activities otherwise curtailed."[40] Undoubtedly, Smilin' Sam was the last person that Bobby Kennedy wanted to see in his office, but Parker was an old friend from his days as a Senate counsel (as well as a fellow Catholic), so he listened patiently and then arranged for Parker to meet the following Monday with top FBI and Justice Department officials to share information about the "Muslim threat."[41] The chief undoubtedly rattled off his favorite statistics—including the preposterous allegation that Blacks committed two-thirds of crimes in Los Angeles—and expounded on his "through the looking glass" theory, as John Buntin put it, that "race relations in Los Angeles seemed bad because race relations were so good that the city had become the target for agitators."[42]

Meanwhile the fourteen Muslim "agitators" comported themselves with quiet dignity in a long trial that began in May 1963. The prosecutor was Deputy District Attorney Harold Kippen, who the summer before had sent two of the 1960 Griffith Park "rioters" to prison. The defense team—Loren Miller and Earl Broady—had been carefully chosen by Malcolm for both legal prowess and unimpeachable respectability (both would later be appointed judges). The initial coroner's jury took only half an hour to rule the shooting of Stokes a justifiable homicide, even though Weese testified that he had had his hands up, trying to surrender. The grand jury which then prepared the original indictments was all white, as was the trial jury. The cops on the witness stand misidentified their supposed assailants and contradicted each other's accounts. The case against Shabazz for attempted murder was based solely on the testimony of the security guard and quickly fell apart as other witnesses acknowledged that he never left the temple. In the end the jury spent a record eighteen days in heavily guarded deliberation.

Shabazz was acquitted along with a few others, but the majority of the defendants received one- to ten-year prison terms. When asked in court about the officers' intentions, Shabazz testified: "I was aware of documents circulated in police stations all over California which constituted anti-Muslim propaganda." The police, he said, "were looking for an excuse to kill us."[43] Six years later the LA Black Panthers would say the same thing.

5

"Not Tomorrow—but Now!":
L.A.'s United Civil Rights Movement (1963)

n his book *Why We Can't Wait*, Martin Luther King proclaimed 1963 "the year of the Negro Revolution." James Baldwin, A. Philip Randolph, and Roy Wilkins echoed the phrase, as did *Newsweek*, *Time*, and the *New York Times*. On the hundredth anniversary of the Emancipation Proclamation, the civil rights movement crossed the Mason-Dixon Line to become a truly national uprising. Its fulcrum, still Southern, was the great struggle in Birmingham—the "most segregated city in America" according to King—where a united Black community, including its children, confronted police dogs, fire hoses, jail beatings and church bombings.[1] Solidarity demonstrations in the North, however, soon led to emulation, as protest groups, often with CORE in the vanguard, embraced the Birmingham strategy of a "package deal"—demanding immediate progress toward integration on multiple fronts.

In his celebrated essay "The Meaning of Birmingham," Bayard Rustin wrote that

unlike the period of the Montgomery boycott, when the Southern Christian Leadership Conference had to be organized to stimulate similar action elsewhere, the response to Birmingham has been immediate and spontaneous. City after city has come into the fight, from Jackson, Mississippi, to Chestertown, Maryland ... frustration has now given way to an open and publicly declared war on segregation and racial discrimination throughout the nation. The aim is simple. It is directed at all white Americans—the President of the United States, his brother, Robert, the trade-union movement, the power elite, and every living white soul the Negro meets. The war cry is "unconditional surrender—end all Jim Crow now." Not next week, not tomorrow—but now.[2]

If not "now," a growing number of national leaders began to recognize, the likely alternative might be an abandonment of nonviolence by the Black community. Thus James Nabrit Jr., the president of Howard University, warned in June that unless Washington took immediate action to enforce equal rights, the country would explode, "including the wholesale killing of people." The SCLC's George Lawrence called the situation a "powder keg," emphasizing that it "was no longer just a Southern thing. [It was] exploding all over the country."[3] And in July, United Auto Workers President Walter Reuther predicted, at an Urban League convention in Los Angeles, that the failure to meet Black demands would lead to "civil war."[4] Although some of this apocalyptic rhetoric was generated in support of a new civil rights bill, the warnings were for the most part accurate and predicted the ghetto insurrections that rocked US cities for six consecutive summers beginning in 1964.

Los Angeles became a major, if unsuccessful, arena for the application of the "Birmingham strategy." At the end of May the SCLC organized a huge rally for King at Wrigley Field, the 22,000-seat baseball stadium east of USC that had been the old home of the Los Angeles Angels minor league team. The city's leading equal rights advocates—including the ACLU, NAACP, CORE, Jewish Labor Committee, and the UAW—joined together as the United Civil Rights Committee (later Council) (UCRC) to challenge discrimination in housing, jobs, policing and schools. Similar freedom movements, some far more militant, emerged in Detroit, Philadelphia, Cleveland, Chicago and San Francisco, and on a smaller scale in Seattle and other cities. This was a unique moment—too often forgotten in a civil rights hagiography that neglects the role of CORE and James Farmer, not to mention Black nationalists like Albert Cleage in Detroit and

Cecil Moore in Philadelphia—when mass protest over discrimination in the North was synchronized with the life-and-death struggle of the nonviolent Southern civil rights movement in cities (to invert Atlanta's slogan) that were *"not* too busy to hate," and did so with relentless ferocity. Behind their liberal facade, as King emphasized in his Wrigley Field speech, many Northern urban power structures and political machines were just as unyielding as Birmingham's, and de facto segregation was, if anything, more intractable than de jure. If civil rights supporters had any illusions on this score, they quickly vanished in a long summer of protest.

Operation Windowshop

The Birmingham campaign and the "Negro Revolution" it launched were responses to a string of defeats. 1962 had been a dismal year for the Southern freedom movement. SNCC's voter registration campaign in Mississippi, another exercise in almost-suicidal courage by young organizers and the Black farmers who sheltered them, barely survived a reign of terror that included assassinations, church bombings, ambushes, vicious beatings, "criminal anarchy" prosecutions, and a food blockade that brought tens of thousands of poor sharecroppers to the edge of starvation. Meanwhile the year's most ambitious attempts to break down urban segregation—CORE's campaign in Baton Rouge and the Albany Freedom Movement in Georgia (which SCLC more or less usurped from SNCC)—filled the jails for months but failed to win significant concessions from local elites or protection from Washington. Neither movement, moreover, received any sustained attention in a national media obsessed with the space race and the Cuban Missile Crisis. In Malcolm X's estimation, "when Martin Luther King failed to desegregate Albany, Georgia, the civil-rights struggle in America reached its low point. King became bankrupt almost, as a leader."[5] The Kennedy administration's only significant intervention in the Deep South was to send 300 federal marshals to register James Meredith at Ole Miss, as ordered by a federal judge. In nightmare scenes, more insurrection than riot, armed mobs murdered two people and wounded 200 of the marshals and national guardsmen defending Meredith. Thousands of regular troops finally quelled the uprising, but it was a strategic victory for the segregationists who had raised the cost of federal police action to a level that the White House was unwilling to pay.[6]

In the North, on the other hand, CORE, mantled by the heroism of the Freedom Rides, succeeded in laying foundations for a score of direct action campaigns that would reach their crescendo in the summer of 1963. The problem for the still tiny and decentralized organization was deciding where to focus its new energies: public accommodation, employment, housing, or education? Local chapters made different choices. L.A. CORE vigorously supported John T. Williams and other Black teamsters in their ongoing fight to break down job barriers in the trucking industry and at Greyhound. Token hirings (two at Greyhound in 1962, for example), however, tended to take the steam out of the struggles.[7] Although it continued to fight job discrimination, most notably in campaigns against the Bank of America in 1963 and several local restaurant chains in 1964, the group's strategic focus shifted toward what the LA County Commission on Human Relations called "the keystone supporting the arch of segregation and discrimination": racial exclusion in L.A.'s fast-growing suburbs.[8] Banks and savings and loan associations, such as Howard Ahmanson's behemoth Home Savings, were the ultimate decision makers, but developers and, most vocally, realtors were the public guardians of the white suburb. In October 1961, for instance, Charles Shattuck, former president of the National Association of Realtors and senior statesman of Los Angeles brokers, told an assembly committee that the Los Angeles Realty Board didn't allow Black brokers to join because it wanted to "preserve neighborhoods" and would not "be a party to the salt and peppering of the whole community." Moreover, he added acidly, "the Negro lacks social privileges because he has not earned them."[9] Shattuck, whose brother Edward was a patriarch of California Republicanism, had unwittingly thrown a gauntlet at CORE's feet.

The first target of "Operation Windowshop," as CORE called it, was a new 567-home subdivision—Monterey Highlands—in the foothills of Monterey Park, a small city east of downtown near Los

Angeles State College. A Black physicist, Robert Liley, down payment in hand, had tried to purchase a mid-market $25,000 house for his young family but was told the tract was sold out. CORE then sent a white couple, who were immediately offered a choice of available homes. The ensuing campaign lasted from February through April 1962, culminating in a thirty-five-day sit-in at the tract office whose participants included three veterans of the Freedom Rides. Montgomery Fisher, the developer, preferred to commit financial suicide rather than yield to protest and was foreclosed by his lenders. The new developer (actually, the original landowner) quickly turned over the keys to Liley and his wife. Although the effort had been exhausting, CORE received encouraging support from the tract's white residents, some of whom were faculty at Cal State LA, as well as from Monterey Park councilman Alfred Song, a Korean-American lawyer who later became the first Asian in the California Assembly.[10]

Such allies were sorely missed when CORE tried, in the fall, to open the Sun-Ray Wilmington tract, in the LA harbor area, where a Black postal worker and his wife, the McLennans, had been turned away. The house they had been told was sold was subsequently offered to a white CORE "tester," Charlotte Allikas, who immediately put down a deposit to hold the home. "We decided to conduct a 'Dwell-In,'" she explained, "to ensure the McLennans a chance to renegotiate their loan." A CORE crew, led by Mari Goldman, housing chair, and Woodrow Coleman, vice chapter chair, occupied the property twenty-four hours a day until they were arrested.[11] After their release, they returned to the house, camped on the lawn (a "dwell-out") and were arrested again. Two of the jailed activists were Freedom Riders Ronald La Bostrie and Charles Berrard, who may have been reminded of their previous encounters with "Southern hospitality" when Sun-Ray neighbors repeatedly harassed, assaulted, and stoned CORE members. But the Superior Court proved to be surprisingly sympathetic to the McLennans. Their counsel, ACLU senior attorney A. L. Wirin, won a rare ruling from Judge Alfred Gitelson that enjoined the developer from discriminating.[12] (Gitelson would later become the bête noire of the New Right for his historic 1970 decision in *Crawford v. Board of Education* that LA schools practiced segregation and must integrate immediately.) Although the builder-developer retaliated in early 1963 by suing CORE, the McLennans eventually moved into their (tarnished) dream home.[13]

Simultaneously CORE was probing the defenses of one of the country's largest suburban builders, Don Wilson. With 50,000 family homes under his belt by fall 1962, Wilson was a major presence throughout Los Angeles and Orange Counties, but the signature of his Gardena-based firm was most indelible in the South Bay.[14] Roughly bordered by LAX in the North, the Harbor Freeway in the East, and the Port of Los Angeles in the South, this area included much of L.A.'s aerospace and oil industry, as well as some heavy industry—steel and aluminum—in Torrance. Wilson's formidable political clout in county and local government was often employed to rezone undeveloped industrial parcels into more valuable residential land: an alchemy that converted cow pastures, auto junkyards and former marshes into lucrative ticky-tacky.[15] His Leave-It-to-Beaver communities were anointed, almost tongue-in-cheek, with names seemingly more appropriate to Beverly Hills or Brentwood, such as "Southwood Riviera Royale," the Torrance tract that would be the site of CORE pickets and mass arrests for the next year and a half. Given his regional prominence and scale of operation, Wilson was an obvious target; but he also recommended himself as a symbol of discrimination because he was building a colored-only subdivision—Centerview in Compton—to exploit the desperate demand from Black homebuyers while keeping his other tracts totally segregated.[16] Although lionized regularly in the real estate section of the *Times* as one of the West's most visionary developers, Wilson, as CORE saw him, was a builder and major shareholder in the "Hate Wall" that kept Blacks penned within a super-ghetto.[17]

Demonstrations at Wilson's housing developments in Torrance (white only), Compton ("the Jim Crow tract") and Dominguez Hills (whites, Mexican-Americans and Asians, but no Blacks) began simultaneously at the end of July, but the confrontations were immediately most tense at the Dominguez site near 190th Street and Avalon Boulevard. The white residents as well as the Glendale–based American Nazi Party (a frequent presence at demonstrations throughout the

1960s) harassed picket lines and even attacked CORE chairman Earl Walter. Walter's wife Mildred, later a celebrated writer of Black children's books, recalled one incident: "About four cars drove up, full of white men dressed like Nazis. They had on Nazi uniforms, including the swastika … and their placards read, 'Ovens too good for niggers,' 'Niggers, go back to the trees,' 'You monkeys, go back to the trees.'" After one of her fellow protestors, a Jewish survivor of the Nazi death camps, left because his anger was overcoming his commitment to nonviolence, Walter asked herself: "'Why am I doing this? Why do I want people thinking that I want to live beside white people? Why am I here?' And somebody start[ed] singing, 'Oh, Freedom' … And I thought, 'Well, I'm not here because I want to live beside white people. I'm here because I want us to be able to decide where it is we want to live, and we can have the freedom to do that.'"[18]

When CORE members staged a sit-in at the Dominguez project office, two of them were kicked and beaten by one of Wilson's part-time salesmen, a Torrance police sergeant. In Compton, by contrast, community members applauded a fifty-mile march to the picket line by twenty CORE members from the San Fernando Valley, and some became regular members of the protest.[19] That fall both James Farmer and Mississippi NAACP leader Medgar Evers came to L.A. with stirring stories of the South to bolster local CORE fighters, and after a half year of demonstrations, California Attorney General Stanley Mosk sued Wilson under the Unruh Civil Rights Act of 1959 for six separate instances where Black homebuyers were turned away from Dominguez. Gitelson was again the judge and quickly indicated that he had little sympathy with the argument made by Wilson's lawyers that the state's highest law officer didn't have jurisdiction in such cases. He issued a temporary restraining order against any further discrimination. While Wilson appealed the Dominguez decision, CORE concentrated all its efforts on his Southwood project, advertised as located in "the country club section of the southwest area."[20]

Torrance was no country club, but it was an excellent theater for confrontation. As its mayor unblinkingly put it: "Torrance has no Negro problem. We only have three Negroes in the city." It was also a throne of sorts for Wilson, known as "Mr. Torrance," since he had

built more than one-third of the homes in the city.[21] Indeed, it was one
of the most dynamic local housing markets on the West Coast—with
an astonishing 21,500 new units added in 1962 alone. [22] Founded as
a union-free haven for Llewellyn Steel and the repair shops of the
Pacific Electric Railroad in 1912, Torrance had grown in little more
than a decade from a population of 20,000 to over 115,000.[23] Awarded
the National Civic League's "All-American City" designation in
1956, it was famed for its city-sponsored "Decency Crusade" and
annual "Stamp Out Smut Month."[24] This municipal inquisition, which
targeted the *Weekly People* (the ancient paper of the Socialist Labor
Party sold in news racks across the country) as well as Nabokov's
Lolita, disguised only thinly the city's notorious vice industries. As
Hal Keating of the *Times* recalled in 1965 after city hall scandals had
rocked Torrance to its foundations, "A few years ago it wasn't difficult
to find a narcotics pusher, a high stakes crap game or a bookmaker in
this city." Its politicians, Keating might have added, were the recipients
of lavish gifts from contractors and developers—a swimming pool in
the case of the city manager. At the center of corruption was a police
force that not only kept Blacks out of the subdivisions, but also broke
strikes, protected gamblers, harassed surfers, spied on dissident city
council members, chauffeured the chronic drunk who was mayor, and
moonlighted not only as salesmen for Don Wilson, but on occasion
as armed robbers and burglars.[25]

United Civil Rights Committee

The next phase of CORE's direct action in Torrance was subsumed,
however, in a broader campaign of protest that tracked events in both
California and Alabama. On April 2, after a vicious campaign heavily
financed by the California Real Estate Association, a majority of
Berkeley's white residents voted to repeal the city's new fair housing
ordinance, which had been adopted after a long crusade by CORE,
the NAACP and local Democratic Clubs.[26] But the initiative, as law
scholars warned, went beyond repeal, effectively establishing "that
housing segregation and housing discrimination should be legal in
Berkeley."[27] The Berkeley vote—a forewarning of the coming deluge

a year later of Proposition 14, the statewide initiative to repeal the fair housing law—greatly stiffened the resistance of segregating builders like Wilson and segregated cities such as Torrance, while it forced the civil rights movement to place all of its chips on the fair housing bill that Assemblyman Byron Rumford, with strong support from Attorney General Mosk and Governor Brown, was trying to force through the legislature.[28] CORE chapters throughout California prepared to send demonstrators—and soon, campers—to Sacramento.

April 3, meanwhile, was "Project C Day" (C for "confrontation") in Birmingham. The SCLC leadership had kept the planning for the campaign as secretive as possible in order to prevent a preemptive strike by Bull Connor (now an angry lame duck after passage of a new city charter that abolished his position); but Governor Wallace and his lieutenants in Montgomery, with rich intelligence sources that might or might not have included the FBI, had already rehearsed tactics that they hoped would defeat Martin Luther King for good, including injunctions and a special law, only applicable in Birmingham, that would hike misdemeanor bails and hopefully break the almost-depleted SCLC treasury. In the event, the marches on city hall and sit-ins in downtown restaurants failed to generate the community momentum that King had expected, and he was soon jailed and out of contact with the day-to-day planning of the struggle. (Isolation, however, did prompt him to begin writing his famed "Letter from Birmingham Jail," attacking white "moderates," especially churchmen, who refused to support the civil rights movement.)[29]

Reverend James Bevel, who had originally come to the campaign from SNCC, assumed a larger role in the leadership and implored the older ministers to let him reinforce the protests with high school, even primary school, students—an idea they initially rejected. In the meantime, a white CORE member from Baltimore, a postman and ex-marine named William Moore, had been murdered outside Gadsden while on a solo march from Chattanooga to Jackson wearing a sandwich-board sign that said "End Segregation Now!" With national attention again briefly focused on Alabama, Bevel once more pleaded with his colleagues to allow the students to defy the injunction against demonstrations. "Any child old enough to belong to a church," he argued, "should be eligible to march to jail." King, torn and reluctant but without any viable alternative, finally "committed his cause to the witness of schoolchildren."[30]

Newsweek called it "the Children's Crusade." On Thursday, May 2, wave after wave of Black kids poured exuberantly but peacefully into the streets of downtown Birmingham. Bull Connor's startled cops managed to arrest 600 of the nearly 1,000 kids who had signed up to be arrested on the first day, but the commissioner of public safety's stupefaction soon turned into fury. The next day, in full view of the press corps, he used fire hoses and police dogs on the student marchers, some of whom were only first graders. The photographs and films of these disturbing scenes and those that followed over the next few days focused the attention of the entire world on Alabama, making King (but, unfairly, neither Shuttlesworth nor Bevel) a universal hero. Birmingham's business elite, known locally as the "Big Mules," who for decades had pulled the strings of vigilantism to fight unionization as well as civil rights, were finally shaken out of their intransigence, and they quickly agreed to a phased integration of downtown lunch counters and sales jobs (schools would follow in the fall). When their former henchmen, the Ku Klux Klan, fought back with bombs, the Kennedys were forced to send federal troops to the city. The president, who had devoted a meager two sentences to civil rights in his earlier State of the Union address, asked Congress in mid June for a comprehensive ban on discrimination in public accommodation.[31]

The unexpected breakthrough in Birmingham galvanized Black communities across the country to follow its example. "The police dogs and fire hoses," the *Eagle's* Grace Simons pointed out, "did more in a day to advance the movement of revolt than had a thousand sermons."[32] Indeed, if mass activism is measured by the sheer number of protests and arrests, the summer of 1963 was unquestionably the high point of the civil rights struggle. From June to September, the Department of Justice "catalogued a total of 1,412 separate civil rights demonstrations around the country."[33] The national NAACP—faced with demands from its own youth for more militancy and fearing that CORE might seize civil rights leadership in key cities—uncharacteristically moved into a direct action mode in May.

In Los Angeles, nonetheless, CORE was first to act, organizing a four-mile march on May 10 from Vernon and Central Avenues in South Central (the location of the legendary "Dolphin's of Hollywood" record store) to city hall, where James Baldwin, then on a grueling CORE-sponsored speaking tour, told the crowd of 2,000 that "discrimination against the Negro is the central fact of American life." With other speakers, he condemned the Justice Department for watching from the sidelines while Bull Connor's storm troopers terrorized and jailed children. In a telegram sent from L.A., he reminded the attorney general that "those who bear the greatest responsibility for the chaos in Birmingham are not in Birmingham. Among those responsible are J. Edgar Hoover, Senator Eastland, the power structure which has given Bull Connor such license, and President Kennedy who has not used the great prestige of his office as the moral forum which it can be."[34] (Two weeks later he aggressively confronted the younger Kennedy during a meeting at Harry Belafonte's apartment in Manhattan. Bobby was so unsettled by the exchange that he ordered J. Edgar Hoover to tap Baldwin's phone.)[35]

CORE suddenly found itself with scores of new members. "Birmingham," one LA organizer wrote to the national office, "has done the recruiting for us."[36] It also attracted unexpected new allies. The Cal Tech YMCA, for example, voted to participate in CORE's campaign against housing segregation in Torrance and Dominguez Hills, while a group of young women teachers organized the "Friendship Guild" to organize dances and other fundraisers for CORE.[37]

L.A.'s NAACP chapter, for its part, began planning a massive Freedom Rally for Birmingham on May 26 at Wrigley Field. Dr. Christopher Taylor, the dentist who had succeeded Reverend Maurice Dawkins as the president of the local NAACP, sent a telegram to Bull Connor asking him to relay a speaking invitation ("send reply collect") to the jailed comedian and movement stalwart Dick Gregory. Gregory promptly made bail and flew to L.A. Martin Luther King and Ralph Abernathy changed tour schedules to attend the LA rally, and Governor Pat Brown acted as honorary chair, as he had when King spoke at the Sports Arena in 1961. Sammy Davis Jr. agreed to wrangle celebrities (Paul Newman and Joanne Woodward, Rita

Moreno, Dorothy Dandridge, Tony Franciosa and Mel Ferrer, among others), while Burt Lancaster volunteered to organize an after-rally party in Beverly Hills to squeeze money out of them. That Sunday's turnout of 35,000 to 40,000 was phenomenal, dwarfing the legendary King rallies of November 1960 and June 1961.

In King's "The Time Is Now" speech, he called upon President Kennedy to personally escort onto campus the two Black students that the courts had ordered admitted to the University of Alabama but Governor Wallace had blocked from entering. He received his most rapturous applause, however, when he urged the crowd to emulate Birmingham and unite to fight every form of segregation and discrimination in Los Angeles: "Birmingham or Los Angeles, the cry is always the same: We want to be free."[38] In making the equation between the two cities, King only echoed what Malcolm X had said the year before, and Baldwin a few weeks earlier. (Baldwin: "There is not one step, one inch ... no distance between Birmingham and Los Angeles."[39])

The interracial committee that organized the rally was soon nominated to lead such a struggle when Reverend Dawkins warned the *Times* that if immediate steps were not taken to desegregate L.A., the NAACP and its allies would launch a "Birmingham-type drive." "We are not just asking for a small specific adjustment," he declared, "but a total community integration." Whether Dawkins, who constantly sought the limelight of the media, actually spoke with the full permission of the coalition is unclear, but his statement was catalytic.[40] The official founding of the UCRC took place at a closed meeting of numerous groups under NAACP auspices on June 4. Predictably, Dr. Taylor was elected chairperson, although he would often be upstaged by the coalition's president: the dynamic young African Methodist Episcopal minister H. H. Brookins, who, through his close alliance with newly elected council member Tom Bradley and his success in building a superchurch with an estimated 19,500 members, eventually became one of the city's most important power brokers.[41]

Although the united front was originally called the NAACP-UCRC, the ACLU was an equally important player. Indeed, ACLU director Eason Monroe claimed in his 1974 oral history that

[we] played a dominant role in organizing [it], and a dominant role
in holding [it] together for a period of a year and a half or two years,
when other groupings in the community had more limited resources
than the ACLU had by that time, and when, as a matter of fact, the
fate of that organization [UCRC] rested, in a very important sense,
upon ACLU involvement.

He also emphasized the failure of the UCRC to bring to the fore
any leader of real stature apart from Reverend Brookins, clearly
implying the incompetence of Dr. Taylor.[42] Monroe, however, did
not clarify in these interviews whether this critique was one he had
directly expressed in executive meetings of the UCRC or simply
the wisdom of hindsight. CORE, in contrast, was openly skeptical
of the NAACP from the beginning. Irked by the NAACP's sudden
assertion of seniority, spokesman Danny Grey pointedly reminded a
Times reporter that CORE was already waging a "Birmingham-type"
campaign. But he could hardly demur when Taylor, acknowledging the "tremendous pressures from the Negro community 'to do
something right now,'" promised that the UCRC was "determined
to mount an all-out offensive in the areas of racial discrimination in
job opportunities and housing, de facto school segregation and the
abuse of police."[43]

Supervisor Kenneth Hahn, the elder of what would become Los
Angeles's most important political dynasty, represented a large portion
of the Black community and was the first to react to the UCRC's
emergence. He urged the County Human Relations Commission to
set up an emergency meeting between the organizers and the Los
Angeles "power structure" (the CHRC's term). With city government
almost paralyzed by relentless warfare between Yorty and a majority
of the council, the county Board of Supervisors became the sponsors
of a summit at the Statler Hilton on June 7 in order "to avert a spread
of racial tension": a euphemism for the large-scale urban disorder or
violence that they feared might be imminent.[44] About half of the 150
civic and business leaders invited to the Hilton conference actually
attended, mostly to sit in uncomfortable silence as Wendell Green,
editor of the *Sentinel*, "asserted there is more racial segregation in

Los Angeles than in any city in the South and more than in any large
Northern city except Chicago and Cleveland."

Dr. Taylor, in turn, outlined proposals for a citizens review board
for the LAPD, revision of school district boundaries to achieve integration, and a nondiscrimination clause in all government contracting.
The attendees were urged to support the Rumford fair housing bill
in the legislature, and if it failed to pass, to adopt muscular city and
county fair housing ordinances. "Birmingham-style demonstrations,"
Taylor explained, would be postponed for ten days to allow business
and government leaders to respond with concrete proposals for ending
discrimination in their respective areas of education, law enforcement,
housing and employment. Task forces in each area, coordinated by
CHRC, were set up.[45] But the newly born UCRC was making demands
from the cradle without proof that it could actually organize civil disobedience on a Birmingham scale, or, conversely, keep control over
spontaneous protest in the community. Certainly a new Black middle
class was flexing its muscles in electoral and activist politics, but, as
Loren Miller had sagely warned at a statewide Black leadership conference in 1960, the elite should "not confuse their own middle-class
attitudes with the needs of the people they purported to represent."[46]

During the ten-day UCRC "grace period," the national civil rights
crisis deepened with the murder in Jackson, Mississippi, of Medgar
Evers, the NAACP's field secretary for that state. In L.A. a week
later, 1,500 people sang "The Battle Hymn of the Republic" as they
marched from Wrigley Field through South Central in a memorial
procession for Evers organized by the UCRC; that same day in the
east, NAACP director Roy Wilkins lashed out with startling vitriol
against CORE, SNCC, and the SCLC for receiving "the publicity
while the NAACP furnishes the manpower and pays the bills."[47] It
was an unjust and selfish rant that immediately jeopardized the civil
rights united fronts emerging across the country. From the point of
view of other groups, local and even state NAACPs (as in Mississippi)
might occasionally take the lead in direct action, but the national
organization's commitment to mass protest and civil disobedience
remained equivocal at best. In Sacramento, meanwhile, it was CORE,
not the NAACP, that mobilized the volunteers—including, for one

day, Paul Newman and Marlon Brando—who occupied the rotunda while the Rumford Bill, even after being watered down by its author, remained bottled up in a Senate committee dominated by conservative Democrats. In order to break the deadlock, Mari Goldman of L.A. CORE led a "lie-in" in front of the Senate chamber until demonstrators were carried away "like lengths of cordwood" by the state police.[48] New convoys of activists headed toward the capitol, but an ominous rebellion broke out among white working-class Democrats in LA County, who opposed Rumford.

Negotiation Fails

Then came a stunning electoral upset—one that was universally interpreted as a backlash against the anti-discrimination policies of Pat Brown in Sacramento and Kennedy in Washington. A special election had been called to fill the congressional seat left vacant by the death, in March, of Representative Clyde Doyle, a Democrat in the midst of his seventh term. The district, where registered Democrats outnumbered Republicans almost two to one, encompassed L.A.'s industrial heartland, including the blue-collar suburbs of Compton, Lynwood, South Gate, Huntington Park, Bell, Bell Gardens, Bellflower, Paramount, Maywood and Downey. Both the president and the governor had endorsed Carley Porter, a veteran assembly member, but the winner, endorsed by the *Times*, was Del Clawson, the Goldwaterite mayor of Compton and a leader in efforts to slow integration in the formerly all-white city just south of Watts.[49] It was, as Becky Nicolaides emphasizes in her history of one of the cities in the district, the beginning of a major realignment in the political landscape of California—and later, thanks to Reagan, of the United States.

Meanwhile, the UCRC "waiting period" expired. The results were meager, to say the least. Sheriff Peter Pitchess expressed sympathy for the coalition's demands in a confidential meeting with attorney Tom Neusom and other members of the coalition's police practices committee, and as a result they showered him with praise for "his good posture in the community" and gave his department a free pass on civilian review—a unilateral action that infuriated CORE and anyone who had had encounters with racist sheriffs. Chief Parker, meanwhile, was predictably offended that the UCRC would even allege a "race problem." Nevertheless, he reassured the *Times* that should disorder break out, there would be no need to use police dogs since his officers were so expert in mob control that the State Department had conscripted them as instructors to help the Dominican military junta deal with Communist street protests.[50] (The San Bernardino County Sheriff, on the other hand, boasted that he would not hesitate to turn dogs on unruly crowds.)

Although Mary Tinglof, president of the LA Board of Education, was a vigorous advocate of integration, the majority of the board, even the two other "liberals," adopted the same attitude as Parker: "What problem?"[51] As Marnesba Tackett, NAACP stalwart and UCRC education committee chair, reported back to the coalition, the board majority refused even to discuss the demands for teacher and student transfers. She deplored as "unthinkable" that "an enlightened city like Los Angeles" would continue to "concentrate Negro, Mexican-American and other minorities into overcrowded and segregated schools" while there were numerous "under-enrolled schools in 'white areas.'" In housing, meanwhile, a coordinated backlash against integration was rapidly gaining power among realtors, white home-owners and developers. Leading the charge was the Los Angeles Realty Board, which, with its counterparts in the rest of the state, campaigned vigorously against the Rumford Bill while advocating a "Property Owners' Bill of Rights" (a California initiative adopted in early June by the National Association of Real Estate Boards) that would give realtors the constitutional right to discriminate. It would be repackaged in the fall as Proposition 14.[52]

On the employment front, Mayor Yorty, still trying to retain some Black support, applauded the UCRC's commitment to nonviolence and bragged about some of his minor appointments, but he other-wise ignored widespread complaints about discrimination in the city agencies and departments. The UAW under District Director Paul Shrade was an active participant in the coalition, but the Teamsters, who obviously wanted to forestall their own minority members from using the leverage of the UCRC, refused to discuss the various color bars in its beverages, liquor and construction operations as long as any teamster participated on the coalition side. The major employer organizations—the Chamber of Commerce, the Downtown Business Men's Association, and the Merchants and Manufacturers Association —had responded to the UCRC, but none were willing to go beyond hypocritical glad-handing and informal conversation about future Black job opportunities.

"We do not feel," Dr. Taylor told reporters at a press conference at the Biltmore Hotel, "that those who call the shots in the fields of employment, housing, education and law enforcement really believe that we mean it when we say that we want integration now ... We did not expect miracles, but we did expect some concrete progress as a result of negotiations." Paul Weeks, the white *Times* reporter (later PR director for RAND) assigned to the civil rights beat, published a story about discord between CORE ("it will want to precipitate direct action") and the NAACP ("willing to negotiate and conciliate longer") with the shadow of Malcolm X looming over all the non-violent groups. (As Woodrow Coleman, one of the more militant members of CORE in 1963, later told the *LA Weekly*: "If you stopped ten cats on the street and asked them where the NAACP office is, none of them would know, but four of five would know where the mosque is.")[53] Brookins, echoing King's recent "Letter from Birmingham Jail," leaned toward the CORE viewpoint. At a local conference of the California Democratic Clubs on June 22, he lamented that "to our great dismay, many informed, enlightened people appeared naive about segregation in Los Angeles." The only alternative, he argued, was to embrace the example of the labor movement and take the struggle to the streets. "There is no road back," he insisted. "There is nowhere else to go."[54]

6

Jericho Stands: The Beginning of the
Backlash (Summer and Fall 1963)

As summer 1963 approached, police across the country, from Baton Rouge to Philadelphia, went on a buying spree. Pennsylvania-based Federal Enterprises, the leading supplier of tear gas, was overwhelmed with new orders, as were makers of nightsticks and breeders of police dogs. Meanwhile law enforcement agencies were hastily training special "commando units" (Detroit PD), "riot companies" (Alabama state police), and "subversive squads" (Shreveport PD) to quell the expected Negro unrest. A United Press survey confirmed that police almost everywhere were girding themselves for riots—a tribute, in a perverse way, to the nationalization of the civil rights struggle. Meanwhile, the *Chicago Defender*, the nation's largest-circulation Black paper, worried about polarization within the movement as CORE and SNCC pressed ahead with protests while the NAACP, always worried about disorder, balked. Even the SCLC's charismatic leaders were put on the defensive during visits to Northern ghettoes. ("Rev. Martin Luther King," reported the *Defender*, "watched incredulously as militant hecklers pelted his car with eggs and shouted 'Uncle Tom' at him when he arrived for a rally at a church in New York's Harlem.")[1] The organizers of the planned August March on Washington increasingly conceived of it as not only a means of putting pressure on the Kennedy administration, but also as a safety valve to vent some of the huge frustration that might otherwise spill into the streets. "Freedom Now," to be blunt, was stalled by repression in the South and fiercely resisted in the North.

In Los Angeles the failed negotiations with the "power structure" forced the United Civil Rights Committee (UCRC) and the NAACP to announce a plan for a vigorous campaign that targeted the Los Angeles Board of Education and subdivision builder Don Wilson's Southwood tract in Torrance. Parallel civil rights united fronts, with the same focus as UCRC on police, education, housing and jobs, were emerging in Pasadena and Long Beach.[2] Of course, the UCRC's two major campaigns—education and housing—overlapped and drew resources from each other, but their stories are best told separately, starting with Torrance.

At the end of June the UCRC organized a caravan of more than 200 cars to Torrance, where they were greeted by the city's ready-to-rumble police department. As 700 to 900 people peacefully marched in front of Wilson's Southwood sales office, they were taunted by members of the American Nazi Party and gangs of racist surfers who later joined counterdemonstrators from something called the "Committee against Integration and Intermarriage."[3] Still, the size of the protest and the participation of the NAACP made an impression. When county officials pressured Torrance to set up a human relations group, the mayor and police chief skirmished over the available pool of Black citizens. According to the *Press Telegram*, "Told that Torrance Mayor Albert Isen had been quoted as saying Torrance has two Negro residents, Chief Bennett questioned the figure. 'I don't know where he gets that. I know of only one.'"[4] Instead, the city council, with hundreds of residents cheering them on, enacted an ordinance that made it illegal for "strangers" to be on the streets of Southwood on weekends or overnight. The ACLU immediately went to the superior court on CORE's behalf.

But there was an unexpected breakthrough. Dr. Taylor announced on July 12 that he had reached a truce with Wilson, implying that CORE's campaign had been too militant to allow negotiations. In exchange for a suspension of sit-ins and mass demonstrations, the developer promised to accept a deposit on one of the remaining unsold Southwood homes from any Black family that had adequate financial resources. Odis Jackson, a young lawyer who had previously been turned away, immediately renewed his offer and Wilson accepted his deposit. A week went by, and Jackson and the coalition heard nothing. Then Wilson suddenly announced that Jackson's financial bona fides were unacceptable, and that the deal was off. Taylor had been played for a fool, and UCRC immediately asked Governor Brown to revoke Wilson's builder's license. CORE, many of its members irritated over what they regarded as yet another example of the NAACP's foolish preference for negotiating with racists, resumed demonstrations despite the new curfew.[5] They were joined on July 27 by Marlon Brando and TV star Pernell Roberts (*Bonanza*'s "Adam Cartwright"), who found few fans in Southwood. Quite the contrary, they were jeered by residents, and someone thrust a placard in front of Brando that read: "Marlon Brando is a Nigger-Loving Creep."[6] Brando retained his famous cool. Forty-seven CORE supporters, sitting on the sales-office driveway, meanwhile were carried away to police buses limp and singing.

At the end of the month, following the arrest of sixty-nine more protestors, a superior court judge, arguing that Southwood home-owners "had civil rights too," upheld the anti-CORE curfew. The city immediately moved to clamp down on daytime demonstrations as well, filing a lawsuit against CORE and one hundred named individuals, including Brando and Roberts, and 1,000 "John Does."[7] For their part, Southwood residents tried to convince the press that they were the true victims, rather than the Black families kept out of suburban housing. One mother complained to the *LA Times* that her children were playing a new game: "picketing." "The children ask, 'Mommy, when are they coming again?' Then they run outside, grab signs and walk up and down the street until their stunned parents order them away."[8] Meanwhile a new force emerged from the shadows. Scores of screaming John Birch Society members, claiming to be local residents, broke up a human relations meeting at Torrance High School.[9]

Undeterred by ordinances or Birchers, new and mostly younger recruits continued to reinforce the ranks of the CORE protest, including the Civil Rights Improvement Coordinating Committee, a cross-city student group organized by Jimmy Garrett, just twenty years old but a veteran of the Freedom Rides and Southern jails. CRICC members were arrested after they blocked the entrance to the Torrance police headquarters, while CORE started new picket lines at the downtown and Beverly Hills offices of Home Savings & Loan, the lender to Southwood purchasers and in CORE's eyes the chief enabler of Wilson.[10] But, despite the willingness of its supporters to fight on, CORE, $100,000 in hock for bail bonds, was financially at the end of its rope, and enthusiasm for the campaign inside the UCRC, and CORE itself, was waning.[11] Many argued that it was better to concentrate scarce resources on efforts at the board of education. In any event, the superior court offered a face-saving way out: all 243 criminal charges against CORE members would be dropped; Wilson would post notices promising to abide by the Unruh Civil Rights Act; and CORE would end mass demonstrations. A nugatory number of pickets were allowed to remain.[12]

This second truce, in effect, conceded victory to Wilson since no one in CORE actually believed that he would comply with the law or ever actually sell a home to a Black family. After more than a year of protest, moreover, only a single Torrance resident, a brave Southwood housewife, had joined the picket line.[13] But CORE members who had endured rough arrests and beatings could at least find a morsel of pleasure in the scandal that was engulfing the All-American City. On July 6, two local cops robbed clerks carrying a money bag in front of an LA bank and were arrested after a dramatic chase and gun battle. A few weeks later another of Torrance's finest, this one a twelve-year veteran, was arrested for burglarizing a medical building. Agents from the DA's office began prowling through the city's underworld of drug dealers, prostitutes and gamblers; and, without notifying the Torrance police, the county sheriffs raided the city's flourishing bookmaking parlors. California Attorney General Stanley Mosk opened a separate investigation of corruption in the issuance of building permits, zoning changes, and city contracts. Eventually all these probes would lead to the suicide of the city manager, the resignation of the mayor, and the filing of perjury charges against police brass. But Torrance remained white.[14]

The Alameda Wall

The full measure of CORE and UCRC's defeat in Torrance would not be understood until the end of the year. In August there was exultation as some of Hollywood's biggest stars joined the fight. *West Side Story*'s Rita Moreno, wearing spike heels and carrying a sign that read "Stop De Facto Segregation Now," was at the front of the UCRC's August 8 march on the board of education. (When after two blocks Morena was forced to take off her heels, SNCC leader James Forman gallantly carried them the rest of the way.)[15] Nat King Cole performed a benefit concert at the Shrine for SCLC, SNCC, CORE and NAACP that brought out Edward G. Robinson, Gene Kelly, Natalie Wood, Edie Adams, Kirk Douglas, Cesar Romero (a longtime supporter of the NAACP) and even Jack Benny. A larger delegation, organized by Charlton Heston, left for the Washington March for Jobs and Freedom, scheduled for the twenty-eighth. It included Sammy Davis Jr. and Dean Martin of the Rat Pack (who, with Sinatra, would later organize their own benefit concert for civil rights), Judy Garland, Debbie Reynolds, Gregory Peck, Robert Goulet, Burt Lancaster, and, of course, militant Lena Horne.[16] Jazz musicians, some of whom had been active in local civil rights struggles since the late 1940s, organized a "Freedom Jazz Festival" for CORE in September that featured Stan Kenton, Buddy Collette, Hampton Hawes, Shelly Manne, Chico Hamilton, Gerald Wilson, and others.[17]

The day after the March on Washington, 5,000 civil rights supporters in L.A. marched down Broadway to city hall, again with an endorsement from vote-wrangling Sam Yorty. The speaker list—two of the six were Chicanos—brought back memories of the multiethnic civil rights coalition that had elected Edward R. Roybal to the city council fifteen years earlier. "On behalf of the Mexican-American community," proclaimed attorney-activist Frank Muñoz, leader of the Mexican American Political Association (MAPA), "we extend the hand of friendship and solidarity." "We must join hands like brothers," added Manuel Lopez, editor of the *East Los Angeles Almanac*.[18] This was a victory for Reverend H. H. Brookins of the UCRC, an advocate of "a stronger alliance between Negro and Mexican communities," but unity was precarious at best.[19]

Chicano organizations refused to participate in the sweeping integration lawsuit that the ACLU and the NAACP had assembled (*Crawford v. Board of Education*), even though it was a class action on behalf of "all Negro and Mexican-American pupils." With the sole exception of MAPA, Eastside organizations opposed the UCRC's four-part integration campaign. A month earlier, Ray Nora of the California Democratic Central Committee had testified to the LA County Commission on Human Relations that "the pressures Negroes are applying on employers has had this effect: When Negroes apply for jobs, employers are afraid not to hire them for fear of retaliation, and, so, in some cases they fire the Mexican-Americans to make room for the Negro."[20] Although veterans of the 1947 Roybal campaign might retain the vision of a united front that advanced the interests of both communities, Nora was expressing an attitude widely shared by Mexican-American business and political leaders, one that kept many tightly bound to the Yorty machine. One can only speculate about how LA history might have played out if the Southside and the Eastside had been able to unite around a common agenda in 1963.

The school integration campaign, relaunched by the big UCRC demonstration on August 8, followed the script from fall 1962, when the NAACP had attempted to enroll Black students at two almost all-white high schools, part of the LA Unified School District (LAUSD) system but located in the industrial suburbs of South Gate and Huntington Park, east of Alameda Boulevard, the principal freight route from downtown to the harbor. Underenrolled South Gate High, in particular, was only a mile from all-Black and grotesquely overcrowded Jordan High in Watts, on the other side of what civil rights activists had begun to call the "Alameda Wall." The NAACP and the ACLU argued that the board of education should redraw attendance boundaries to allow the Jordan overflow to register at South Gate.[21]

But the backlash was beginning. This feeble attempt at integration fueled the white backlash that cost the Democrats the Twenty-Third Congressional District in the Alameda corridor.[22] A month later the board of education majority voted down a modest proposal to allow the experimental transfer of 400 students from Fremont to Huntington Park; Jordan to South Gate; and Manual Arts to Westchester high schools. Marnesba Tackett of the UCRC countered by citing examples where the board had in fact transferred students *to maintain* de facto segregation. But even the UCRC was beginning to back away from the Alameda Wall and the angry white hordes behind it. Mary Tinglof, the pro-integration school board leader, warned her civil rights allies that if they kept pressing for integration at South Gate High, the community and its neighbors might secede from LAUSD and form their own strictly white ("San Antonio") school district. A more realistic short-term alternative, she suggested, was to shift the focus to the more liberal Westside, where underenrolled white high schools like Westchester and Hamilton had room to accommodate transfers from majority Black schools on half-day sessions. Her board colleagues, however, rejected this modest scheme.[23] An already-existing transfer program for individual students, which had no programmatic intent whatsoever, did allow a handful of Black students to attend white high schools, but its larger effect was to increase segregation by making it easy for white students to flee schools with increasing minority enrollments.

Nevertheless, a time bomb had been planted under the foundations of school segregation by the ACLU and the NAACP in the form of a lawsuit filed on the behalf of Watts high school students Mary Ellen Crawford and Inita Watson. *Crawford*, as the case was known, challenged a board plan to renovate and enlarge Jordan High while preserving segregated attendance boundaries. As Tackett later explained, "We noticed that the school board kept expanding Jordan's boundary as more black children moved into it instead of sending them to South Gate. On that basis we felt Jordan was the strategic school to target."[24] *Crawford*, variously modified over time, would not be heard by the superior court until October 1967, but the resultant finding by Judge Alfred Gitelson (of Torrance fame) was an integration order that would draw battle lines that lasted more than a decade.

As the board hearings dragged on, Tackett and Tinglof expressed their growing frustration, not only with the two right-wing members, but also with moderate and liberal ones. One area of contention was the refusal of the board to allow a racial census of the district in order to establish the extent of segregation. The absence of statistics allowed the two conservative board members to deny racial imbalance existed. It was a maddening situation. "We've talked long enough," Tackett said, which "clearly indicates that the Los Angeles board, like Birmingham, will have to be forced to provide integrated class rooms." She warned that the coalition was ready to oppose all school bond issues and the reelection bids of all members of the board, aside from Tinglof.

A long-awaited report on integration from an ad hoc committee of the board was released on September 14 and greeted with a hailstorm of criticism from the NAACP and CORE. "The recommendations," complained Tackett, "don't go far enough and the findings are absolutely nil ... There were no constructive suggestions about boundary changes. Nothing specific—just further study—and no urgency."[25] The board had discovered that studying and restudying the problem of segregation could postpone for years the imperative to do anything about it.

Meanwhile eight CORE members, led by Anthony Quinn's brother-in-law, the screenwriter Martin Goldsmith, began an eleven-day hunger strike at the board offices.[26] Their dedication to the fast was redoubled when news arrived of the Klan bombing of the Sixteenth Street Baptist Church in Birmingham, which killed four young girls. On September 19, 400 to 500 supporters of the hunger strike trekked five miles to the board offices from a rally at Wrigley Field. It was a school day, and Jordan High School was placed on lockdown to prevent its increasingly militant students from participating in the march. But many did anyway, along with hundreds of other determined truants from high schools across the city. Plainclothes police photographers carefully documented members of the demonstration as part of a plan by Chief Parker, announced two days later, to charge older demonstrators with "contributing to the delinquency of minors."[27]

The struggle against the board was, to a large extent, becoming a youth crusade led by CORE. College students and some faculty participated, including 28-year Jerry Farber, a lecturer at Cal State LA who headed CORE's education action committee; in 1967 he wrote "The Student as Nigger," first published in the *LA Free Press*, which became one of the defining texts of the era. But what was most striking was the high school contingent, which included seven students from Birmingham High School in Van Nuys. One of them told the *Times* that "members of her group felt they particularly could show sympathy for the bomb victims of Birmingham."[28] In the weeks that followed, L.A.'s high school activists were encouraged by the examples of similar but much larger protests in other cities, especially Chicago, where a quarter of a million kids, half of the total enrollment, boycotted their public schools on October 22 to attend "freedom schools" and demonstrate in the downtown Loop.[29]

One novel tactic adopted by LA students was a "study-in" at the board offices on Fort Moore Hill at the beginning of October. Wearing black CORE armbands, 300 high school and college students marched up from the Old Plaza, finding the entrance barred by a fire captain who warned them they were about to violate the law. The group, led by Farber, ignored him and entered the building where they sat in the corridors silently doing their homework, while board members in their chamber continued their usual bickering and fruitless discussion.[30] Three other study-ins were held in October, the last followed by an all-night vigil with over one hundred participants. "We have to keep finding dramatic ways to keep the board's eyes on the problem of segregation," Farber told reporters. "I'm sure that if we didn't they would forget the entire issue as soon as possible."[31] The next "drama" was the arrest of Farber and two other CORE members for supposedly injuring two security guards as they attempted to open a locked door to allow more demonstrators to join the all-night vigil.[32] But the movement was running out of steam. As fair housing advocate John Caughey summed up the situation: the board "would not take a racial census, it would not release what information it had on minority enrollment or employment, and, except for most nominal steps, it would not implement its so-called integration policy. The school year 1963–64 ran its course with school segregation still intact."[33]

Los Angeles CORE meanwhile was breaking up as its members disagreed over whether to carry the board struggle to the next level with mass arrests. CORE had made huge investments during the past year in the campaigns for fair housing and school integration, but so far it had achieved little except publicity about its goals. Meanwhile other CORE members worried that the student influx was reinforcing a perception in the community that the organization was becoming more nationalist. (Some chapters across the country were in fact already purging white members or assigning them to secondary roles.) In Los Angeles there was no simple coincidence between advocates of greater militancy and those who wanted a more nationalist orientation. What emerged was a direct action faction of about forty members, led by veteran CORE leaders Woodrow Coleman and Danny Gray, but also including Farber and Housing Action Chair Mari Goldman, who proposed to set up a separate chapter on Central Avenue, in the heart of the ghetto. When they proceeded to do so, the new chapter was not recognized by the national CORE, and the insurgents were forced to organize independently as the Non-Violent Action Committee. Like the official CORE, N-VAC was primarily focused for the next year on employment issues and defeating the anti-Rumford backlash; both groups had some small successes on the former front.[34]

For all the millennial hopes aroused by Birmingham, 1963 ended dismally. It was Jericho in reverse: more walls went up than were torn down. August Meier and Elliot Rudwick, in their masterful history of CORE, offer a bleak national balance sheet:

> Aside from gains in employment projects, the northern CORE chapters seldom experienced substantial progress. School segregation and police brutality seemed almost immune to attack; rent strikes and urban renewal demonstrations produced at best only temporary relief; drives for suburban fair-housing, where successful, brought merely token victories for the middle class; and even in the case of jobs. The highly publicized construction-trade campaigns led only to broken promises.

Even in places with significant activism, "repressive actions effectively crushed even the most militant demonstrations, not only in southern communities like Gadsden, Tallahassee, Plaquemine, and Chapel Hill, but also in a number of northern cities." Activists and others were realizing that "even where social change had occurred, CORE's demonstrations had not significantly affected the life chances of the black poor."[35]

In California, moreover, all the previous campaigns were overshadowed by what looked like an approaching civil rights Armageddon. In September, thanks to CORE's long siege of the legislature, the Rumford Fair Housing Act was at last passed into law, although it was missing half of its teeth after an exemption was made for single-family homes. But before its proponents had time to celebrate, those guard dogs of residential segregation, the California Real Estate Association, announced a massive initiative campaign to repeal Rumford with Proposition 14 on the ballot for November 1964. Despite warnings from UCRC leaders that in the event of a repeal, "racial strife such as California has never seen before will erupt," all the enemies of fair housing, from the American Nazi Party to the *Los Angeles Times*, rallied around the realtors' banner. The white riot had begun.

7

Equality Scorned:
The Repeal of Fair Housing (1964)

N ew Year's 1964 was a Sisyphean moment for Los Angeles civil rights activists.

"We're right back where we started from," fumed Dr. Christopher Taylor. The leader of the United Civil Rights Committee and NAACP was responding to the release, on January 6, of a long-awaited report on the LAPD, prepared by a blue-ribbon committee appointed the previous June by the County Commission on Human Relations. Although the Special Citizens' Law Enforcement Committee included two UCRC members (Reverend John Doggett of the Hamilton Methodist Church and Norman Houston, a wealthy insurance executive), its report, applauded in a *Times* editorial, rejected any need for a civilian review board—a chief demand of civil rights groups since the late 1940s. The improved procedures promised by the department, it contended, would be sufficient to ensure a fair hearing in the future for police brutality complaints. Instead, the committee urged the UCRC and its member groups to cooperate with the LAPD in recruiting minorities and improving the community image of the police and sheriffs. Taylor, normally mild-mannered, was outraged: "They have ignored all complaints of the community, and now they can keep on doing the same thing. They can keep right on whipping Negroes, shooting them—and then when a policeman is found guilty, they suspend him for two weeks without pay."[1]

Similarly, "square one" aptly described the status of the UCRC campaign for integration to relieve overcrowding in ghetto schools. An "open permit" individual-transfer policy adopted by the board as an alternative to redrawing segregated attendance boundaries had, as activists predicted, actually increased segregation by letting white students bolt from minority-majority schools. Almost all of the remaining white students at Fremont High, for example, immediately transferred to South Gate.[2] A plan to "de-ghettoize" the assignment of Black and Chicano teachers by allowing them to transfer within the district was blocked by the board in March, as was Mary Tinglof's attempt in May to put the board on record opposing repeal of the Rumford Fair Housing Act. Finally, in late summer, after several stormy meetings, the board canceled a pilot program that bused a small number of elementary students from two overcrowded South Central schools to underenrolled campuses in Westchester.[3] Over the course of fourteen months, every attempt by Tinglof, in coordination with Tackett of the UCRC, to garner a majority for some small step toward integration had been sabotaged by the defection of a self-proclaimed "liberal" or "moderate" board member to the other side. Until the composition of the board radically changed, or the *Crawford* case was adjudicated, there was little hope of progress.

Meanwhile, on the employment front, CORE, cutting its losses in Torrance and with the board of education, launched a statewide campaign to increase minority employment at the Bank of America and two major utilities. Its splinter group, N-VAC (Non-Violent Action Committee), targeted the Van de Kamp's restaurant and bakery chain, while the UCRC picketed several supermarket chains. But these protests were overshadowed by the immense and unlikely task of organizing voter resistance to Proposition 14, the constitutional amendment on the November ballot that would not only repeal the Rumford Act but also prevent the legislature from taking any further action on behalf of fair housing.

April Riots

The real temper of the community, especially the outlook of Black youth, could not be measured by the state of mind of middle-class civil rights groups and their stalled campaign. Even CORE, which had produced some outstanding young Black leaders, remained three-quarters white, and despite the efforts of its Central Avenue splinter, N-VAC, it could hardly claim to have much influence on grassroots opinion.[4] Moreover, the chasm between the ghetto and the rest of the city was deepening. At a time when realtors were talking about "super-prosperity"[5] and economists were predicting miracle levels of employment growth, joblessness was growing in South Central neighborhoods on a scale that could not be ameliorated by a few hundred white-collar jobs at the Bank of America.

In May, 1,500 unemployed people gathered at Wrigley Field to sign a desperate petition to President Johnson: "We need some jobs!"[6] One solution, offered by the LA County Board of Supervisors, was to turn the ghetto unemployed into replacement braceros. With the discontinuation of the program, which had brought contract labor from Mexico since 1942, California growers were eager to find new sources of farm labor, so Supervisor Kenneth Hahn, bemoaning the "tragedy that the small homeowner has to pay a large portion of his taxes to support able-bodied men," proposed that male welfare recipients be forced to work on farms.[7] The proposal was adopted by the board but quickly failed. The idea that people who had moved to Los Angeles to escape cotton peonage in Texas and Louisiana would meekly return to the fields of the Central Valley was patently absurd, especially when the urban industrial economy was booming.

Whatever hopes the Birmingham movement had kindled the previous year had been curdled into anger by the intransigence of white-dominated institutions, the pervasive sense of losing ground amid prosperity, and, above all, the ruthless iron heel of the LAPD. The real question was whether that anger would be displaced into intra-community violence or unleashed as a unifying wrath. The danger of the former was illustrated by the upward trend in gang warfare. In January, outside a basketball match between Dorsey and

Manual Arts Highs, a former star athlete from Dorsey was stabbed to death in a fight with members of the Gladiators gang. A month later, after several weekends of confrontations between the Parks and Businessmen gangs, a member of the latter (famous for their flashy suits and homburg hats) was shot outside the gym at Jefferson High School.[8]

Before spring 1963, a veteran unit of the probation department known as Group Guidance (GG), would have immediately stepped in and attempted to negotiate a truce between the warring gangs. But Chief Parker, loudly supported by Sheriff Peter Pitchess, had convinced the board of supervisors to disband the unit. Indeed, he had blamed increased gang conflict on the "dangerous activities" of the nine men and three women of GG. The gangs with whom they worked, Parker had claimed, committed three to four times the crimes of non-supervised gangs: proof, in the LAPD's eyes, that peace talks and other GG interventions were somehow incentives to violence. Raymond Herbert, the director of the probation department's delinquency prevention services, had scoffed at Parker's logic, pointing out that GG's mission was precisely to target the most violent or criminally involved gangs. "You see a lot of firemen at the worst fires but no one blames the fire department for starting the fires."[9] But Parker's use of sham statistics had little to do with the specifics of GG's work; his real aim was to evict the unit from LAPD turf and reinforce the dogma that Black youth were "junior criminals" warranting incarceration. Ironically, by removing GG from the streets and ratcheting up police pressure on youth, he inadvertently sowed the seeds (as did Daryl Gates a quarter century later) for the cessation of gang warfare. That came in August 1964, not as a result of Parker's autocratic policing, but rather as the fruit of a massive uprising against the LAPD.

The revolt was portended by a series of neighborhood riots in April that displayed a new fighting mood in the community. The first fray followed a track meet at Jefferson High School on Friday, April 10, when four plainclothes LAPD officers, moonlighting as event security, roughly arrested a spectator for drinking and placed him in a patrol car. Hundreds of students and other youth surrounded the car and began throwing rocks and sticks. One of the cops was knocked unconscious by a brick and two others injured. An ambulance rushed to the scene only to collide with a speeding police car, resulting in three more injuries. "More than 100 officers were summoned," the *Times* reported, "before the crowd, estimated at 600 persons, was dispersed." Early the next morning a Greyhound bus smashed into a car at Forty-Sixth and Avalon in South Central, killing the driver. Enraged by the delay in the arrival of an ambulance, an estimated 250 onlookers jeered the police, then started stoning them. The battle resumed that evening when police arrested a man near Sixty-Eighth and Central, during or just before (the accounts vary) a massive vice raid by sheriffs. A crowd of approximately one hundred attempted to rescue him and fought the police.[10]

The weekend's spontaneous disorder mocked the confident reassurances of the blue-ribbon committee on community-police relations and led to a new confrontation between civil rights groups and Parker's institutional supporters. South Central's council member Billy Mills told the press that he had been stopped by the LAPD seventeen times in the previous year "because they saw me at night driving a car provided by the city"; he demanded the police immediately undergo more training in community relations. On the other hand, the *Times* praised the LAPD, "whose record in recent years has been remarkably free of prejudicial conduct," warning that "the current soft attitude on the part of the public to crime and civil rights demonstrations could lead to anarchy." At his weekly press conference, Mayor Yorty declared that "if anything, the police have been too lenient."[11] How the police actually conducted themselves was revealed two weeks later when a traffic stop for a defective taillight escalated into a riot involving eighty to one hundred residents of the Pacoima area, the Black ghetto of the San Fernando Valley. As the *Eagle* summarized its interviews with witnesses: "They placed full blame on the two officers involved in the original arrest attempt, accused them of using vile racial epithets, knocking a young mother to the ground, grabbing a teenager by the hair, punching her and bashing her head against a car," the *Eagle* reported. "They claimed further that one of the officers drew his pistol and threatened to kill the man accused of a traffic violation."[12] The same weekend the LAPD arrested ten people on "riot" charges in the aftermath of a serious traffic accident at Fiftieth Street and Ascot in South Central. Following heckling and scuffles with police at the scene, a group of residents followed the ambulances to the Central Receiving Hospital, just west of downtown, where the "unruly, cursing mob" (*Times*) knocked down a cop.[13]

James Farmer was in town that week and, with local CORE chair Art Silvers, immediately called for the resignation of Chief Parker (who was rumored to be sick and considering retirement). He also joined a picket line outside the Newton Street Station protesting the surprise arrest of the N-VAC leadership—Mari Goldman, Robert Hall, Woodrow Coleman and Danny Gray—for a protest at a Van de Kamp's bakery earlier in the month.[14] In an interview with the *Sentinel*, Silvers, while reiterating CORE's commitment to nonviolence, warned that the patience of the community "is nearing an end. The forces of hate and love are lining up."[15] Calling for Chief Parker to step down immediately made CORE the target of vilification from all sides. First the city council voted thirteen to two to express its full support for Parker (with Bradley in favor, and Mills and Gilbert Lindsay, the city's first Black council member, in opposition), as did the police commission (including Elbert Hudson, the sole Black member).[16] This coincided with a column by nationally syndicated journalists Rowland Evans and Bob Novak charging that CORE protests, both in California and at the opening of the World's Fair in New York, had become the movement's own worst enemy: "If militant demonstrations persist," they wrote, "the vote in November promises to be a debacle for civil rights not only here but in the whole nation."[17] Then, Maurice Dawkins, the former NAACP head and UCRC founder, now moving rapidly toward the right, convinced three other religious leaders to join him in denouncing CORE for its peaceful sit-in at the Southwest Realty Board, a nerve center of the campaign to repeal the Rumford Act. "We oppose that type of demonstration in Los Angeles which violates law and order in our community."[18]

Two weeks elapsed before the UCRC's Dr. Taylor finally endorsed CORE's call for Parker's resignation.[19] But Taylor, besieged by critics of his administrative competence as well as of his tolerance for CORE's direct action methods, was soon forced to step aside for the more dynamic and politically astute Reverend H. H. Brookins.[20] The UCRC's new chairman, tacitly acknowledging the failure of protest, outlined a more elitist vision of the coalition's future—particularly, the need to refocus on educating and winning support from L.A.'s corporate powers. "The white community," he told the *Times*'s Paul Weeks in a lengthy interview, "must be made to understand that the vast majority of Negroes does not want to demonstrate, agitate and put on a show to feed the needs of pseudo-liberals, white or black. I want to bring more specialized, professional personnel into our work, lessening the influence of some of the more radical activists on whom we have had to depend." Although Brookins did not repudiate CORE per se, he made it clear that UCRC would only selectively endorse those of the group's actions that were congruent with its new strategy.[21] (Yes, for instance, to a demonstration against the formation of a local white citizens council; but no to CORE's Bank of America campaign and its sit-ins at realtors' offices.)

Meanwhile, all the real thunder was on the right. As California stumbled toward the June presidential primary, the confluence of the Goldwater and Proposition 14 campaigns, each supercharging the other, brought armies of conservative activists into the field. The John Birch Society, headquartered in the millionaire suburb of San Marino and generaled by John Rousselot, a former congressman from Orange County, shocked old guard Republicans by running candidates not only in every primary (where they emphasized support for Proposition 14) but also in every election for district and county Republican committees in Southern California. One of the society's chief constituencies was the LAPD, where under the benign eye of Chief Parker, officers openly wore Goldwater badges and distributed anti-communist tracts such as *None Dare Call It Treason*, a favorite among Birchers, from station houses. It was widely believed that the Fire and Police Research Association (Fi-Po), formally a subsidiary of the LA Fire and Police Preventive League, was a front for the Birch Society. During the 1964 elections, Fi-Po leaders circulated forged documents claiming that Senator Thomas Kuchel, California's last remaining liberal Republican and a foe of Proposition 14, had been arrested in 1950 for sodomy and drunk driving. (The principal author

of the forgery was indicted by a grand jury, but the charge was ultimately reduced to a misdemeanor.)[22]

As white supremacism seemed to emerge from under every suburban rock, so did the White Citizens' Councils movement, the
principal organizer of "massive resistance" to integration in the
South. Louis Hollis, the national director of the Mississippi-based
councils, announced that Kent Steffgen, a former Birch staffer, had
been appointed to lead a Los Angeles–area organizing campaign.
"Irresponsible and lawless activities by the racial agitators and Negro
pressure groups," he declared, "have awakened thousands of Californians to the dangers of permitting these groups to control their
state."[23] Journalists and civil rights groups, however, found it difficult
to believe that the proposed council was not simply another franchise
of the Birch Society—created, in this instance, to exploit the racial
polarization generated by Proposition 14. In addition to Steffgen,
Hollis was a well-known Bircher, as was the national administrator,
W. Simmons.[24] The continuity of personnel between all the anti-
integrationist camps became even more evident in January, when
the California Real Estate Association hired William K. Shearer, a
frequent contributor to the councils' magazine, for its Proposition 14
campaign. When CREA was later challenged to repudiate support
from the Greater LA Citizens' Council, its president, Art Leitch,
characterized the demand as "ridiculous."[25]

The inaugural meeting of the Greater LA White Citizens' Council
was held on June 30 in Pasadena's Civic Auditorium, a week after the
local school board had rejected an integration plan. Council leader W.
Simmons of Jackson, Mississippi, brought the audience to its feet with
his declaration that "integration is not inevitable. It is impossible."[26]
But the 500 enthusiastic attendees were considerably outnumbered
by the 800 chanting CORE and UCRC supporters picketing outside.
Simmons reassured the press that "such a demonstration wouldn't
happen in Jackson. We have an anti-picketing law." The LA Council
announced that its next activity would be to bring George Wallace to
the Sports Arena.[27] Meanwhile back in Mississippi, searchers were still
dredging the swamps for the bodies of three missing Freedom Summer
volunteers—James Chaney, Andrew Goodman, and Mickey Schwerner.

A toxic rumor arrived in Los Angeles around the same time as the Mississippi segregationists did, although it will always be unclear who actually released it: the Birchers, the council people, the camp followers of Goldwater, or perhaps all three. By the eve of the November election, it had spread virally across the entire country and infected political debate everywhere. The story, variously set in South Gate or Culver City, was that a group of adult Black males had castrated a three-year-old white child in a public bathroom. "Everyone" (white, that is) knew someone who knew someone else who verified the story (supposedly being covered up by liberals).[28] But columnist Paul Coates of the *Times* stumbled upon what he believed was the true genealogy of the evil fable. According to a letter he received from a reader who had been in secondary school in Germany in the 1930s, the "same story" had been used by Nazi leaders to enrage Hitler Youth before pogroms. "Only then, the 'little white boy' was a German boy, and the 'colored hoodlums' were Jews."[29]

A Meddlesome Priest[30]

The organizational core of the Proposition 14 campaign was the CREA and its 45,000 local realtors, all of whom were expected to canvas the vote in their sales areas. Flying the banner of the so-called Committee for Home Protection—a name first used in a 1948 initiative campaign against public housing—the realtors were joined by the California Apartment House Owners Association, the Homebuilders' Association, taxpayer groups, the *Times*, the California Committee for Equal Rights for the White Race, and the entire sprawling conservative wing of the Republican Party, including the co-chair of the statewide Goldwater campaign, Ronald Reagan.[31] But the realtors' greatest ally, according to historian Darren Dochuk, was the large population of Southern evangelicals in Southern California, roused in revivals and mobilized in their churches by leading Christian anti-communists and civil rights opponents such as Billy James Hargis, Fred Schwarz, Carl McIntire, and Senator Strom Thurmond (a frequent visitor to California in 1964). "Blending fears of communism and racial integration with biblical exegesis, conservative clerics in the Committee for Home Protection camp argued that the Rumford [Fair Housing] Act was a rejection of both New Testament teachings and Old Testament laws," Dochuk writes. "Pro-Rumford people were not only on a slippery slope to communism but also in violation of the Ten Commandments: 'Thou shalt not covet thy neighbor's housing.'"[32] Or as Dr. Nolan Frizzelle, president of the California Republican Assembly and a leader of the Christian Anti-Communist Crusade, put it: "The Rumford Act violates the right of the people to discriminate. Proposition 14 returns this right back to the people."[33]

In opposition to Proposition 14 were hundreds of progressive Protestant clergy (Episcopalian and Presbyterian especially), most rabbis, and all but one of California's Catholic bishops. That sole exception was Cardinal James McIntyre of Los Angeles, the single most powerful churchman in the state. McIntyre, consigliere to supreme Cold Warrior Cardinal Spellman in New York before moving to Los Angeles, was better known for his passion for real estate than his concern for human rights. He was also the chief supporter of L.A.'s most well-known Catholic layman, Chief Parker, and shared most of the latter's views on creeping socialism, moral degeneracy, and minority criminality. He was also an utter autocrat who stalled the Second Vatican Council reforms and outlawed any discussion of civil rights issues by priests and seminarians, despite the large number of Black Catholics, mainly ex-Louisianans, in the archdiocese.[34] When sixty theological students at the archdiocese's seminary in Camarillo held an informal discussion with John Howard Griffin, a Catholic civil rights advocate and author of *Black Like Me*, they were disciplined by McIntyre and several were forced to leave the seminary.

In May, a group of parishioners opposed to Proposition 14, Catholics United for Racial Equality (CURE), marched on McIntyre's Fremont Place mansion, only to be turned away by security guards. A few weeks later, *Ramparts* magazine (then a Catholic lay journal) published an article by an unnamed Los Angeles priest who condemned the "aura of fear of reprisal" in the archdiocese. "The feeling among the priests was that if they preached on racial justice they would be moved, as the doctrine is unwelcome and they are afraid." "Cardinal McIntyre," the cleric went on, "can continue to say that there is no racial problem in his archdiocese, an incredible statement. No one who is in touch, who reads, who knows what is going on could make it with a straight face."[35]

Twenty-nine-year-old Father William DuBay, an assistant pastor at the largely Black St. Albert the Great parish in Compton, became "the first priest since Luther to challenge his Cardinal in public."[36] Earlier, DuBay had been transferred out of his original parish in the ultra-segregated San Fernando Valley after publishing excerpts from Catholic writings on racial justice in the church bulletin. He later told the *Times* about a meeting he had with McIntyre: "He denied that there was a racial issue here and said it was not a moral issue. He said there were many other reasons for discrimination besides race. 'After all, white parents have a right to protect their daughters.'"[37] Now in a long telegram to Pope Paul VI, DuBay charged that McIntyre had "conducted a vicious program of intimidation and repression against priests, seminarians, and laity who have tried to reach the consciences of white Catholics in his archdiocese." The young priest, backed by his parishioners, asked the pope to remove the cardinal for his "inexcusable abuses" of church doctrine and his failure to redress "the insult and injury suffered by the several hundred thousand Los Angeles Negroes at the hands of white Catholics whom the local church refuses to instruct on their specific moral obligation." "I regret," he continued, "that I as a priest must accuse my bishop publicly, but all other means have failed. Letters, petitions, phone calls, and even sit-ins and pickets at his office and residence have not moved the Cardinal."[38]

DuBay was immediately relieved of his duties in Compton, but his audacious telegram drew public support from McIntyre's bête noire, the Jesuits, as well as from some of the Holy Cross priests and a few progressive bishops. Members of the "Cardinal's Carpet Club," as previously reprimanded priests in the archdiocese informally called themselves, while not necessarily supporting DuBay's tactic, confirmed the truth of his allegations, and rosary-carrying members of the Albert the Great congregation, Black and Chicano, conducted daily pickets at the chancery. "All we want," they said, "is for the cardinal to commit himself on Pope John's Encyclical, *Pacem in Terris*, which outlines justice for all."[39]

Unsurprisingly, the foes of integration within the archdiocese quickly lashed back at the "unChristian" conduct of DuBay and CURE, citing a declaration of Pope Leo XIII's from the 1890s—much loved by Proposition 14 forces—that "the first and most fundamental principle ... must be the inviolability of private property." McIntyre, for his part, kept a disdainful silence, although "someone close to the cardinal" warned DuBay that if he did not shut up, "the next step was that he would [be] defrocked and excommunicated."[40] Finally, in July, an intransigent McIntyre told the press that his mind was unchanged and that he would not take a stand on Proposition 14.[41]

He would, however, continue to enforce strict discipline within his ecclesiastical kingdom. In DuBay's case, it involved the humiliation of signing a statement that reaffirmed his loyalty and obedience to the cardinal. The silenced priest was also ordered to avoid contact with his picketing parishioners and members of CURE.[42] Meanwhile, a much-loved Eastside priest, Father John Coffield of the Ascension parish, whom McIntyre suspected of supporting DuBay because he too had taken a strong stand on civil rights, chose voluntarily exile as an urban missionary in Chicago over obsequious submission. "A Buddhist monk," he said, "could use self-cremation as the strongest form of protest. It isn't open to me."[43]

Equality Scorned

The Brown administration marshaled the opposition under the umbrella of "Californians against Proposition 14" (CAP 14), but as Daniel HoSang emphasizes in an astute analysis, its focus on white Democratic voters marginalized civil groups like UCRC and MAPA. "Why would CAP 14 leaders," he asks, "so committed to defeating Proposition 14, distance the campaign from the communities, organizations and leadership that bore the brunt of segregated and inferior housing?" The distancing, he argues, was largely intentional. "Early in the campaign, CAP 14 leaders made a strategic decision to attack the abstract ideas and extremist actors animating Proposition 14 rather than to defend the Rumford Act or assert the widespread prevalence of housing discrimination and segregation." CAP 14 leaders soon became

LAPD Chief William H. Parker, "warden of the ghetto," and Mayor Sam Yorty at the Police Academy graduation ceremony, 1961. During Parker's seventeen-year tenure (1950–66), he replaced boss rule with cop rule and was politically invulnerable—thanks to lifetime tenure, a Hollywood publicity machine, and a blackmail bureau that rivaled J. Edgar Hoover's.

Members of CORE raise funds in Pacoima for jailed Freedom Riders, July 24, 1961. LA CORE sent five integrated groups of Freedom Riders to challenge segregation in Southern train and bus terminals. Most of them were jailed at Mississippi's Parchman Farm, perhaps the scariest prison in North America.

Gordon Parks, *Malcolm X Holding up Black Muslim Newspaper*, 1963. © The Gordon Parks Foundation.

In April 1962, after an altercation where a cop was shot, LAPD officers attacked the Black Muslim temple, a block away, where unarmed members were leaving after evening prayers. The final tally: one Muslim man dead, seven others seriously wounded, fourteen arraigned on felonies, and the temple ransacked. Malcolm, at the funeral, praised LA Black organizations for protesting the attack: "Our unity shocked them and we should continue to shock the white man by working together."

Demonstrators protesting the refusal of developer Don C. Wilson to sell homes in the Dominguez Hills tract in Gardena to African Americans. They were harassed by white residents as well as by the Glendale-based American Nazi Party, a frequent presence at demonstrations throughout the 1960s.

Women Strike for Peace members marching at Old Plaza in Los Angeles, 1966, calling for an end to the Vietnam War. The previous year the group sent a delegation to meet in Jakarta with women of the Vietnamese National Liberation Front, which strengthened their standing to speak on war and peace, usually the preserve of men and "experts."

Dorothy Healey, December 1, 1961. The unorthodox leader of the Communist Party in Los Angeles in the Fifties and Sixties, Dorothy was a key link between white and Black radicals—she mentored Angela Davis—and between the old and new lefts. She resigned from the Party in 1973 after the Soviet invasion of Czechoslovakia.

LOS ANGELES

FREE

PRESS

NEWSPAPER

"THE DEPUTY" REVIEWED

WILCOCK IN GREECE (AGAIN)

LIPTON: A MORALITY PLAY

136 PLACES TO GO THIS WEEK - PAGE 12

10¢

Vol. 2, #34 (Issue #57)   COPYRIGHT 1965 THE LOS ANGELES FREE PRESS   Friday, August 20, 1965   10¢ (15¢ OUTSIDE OF LOS ANGELES)

The Negroes Have Voted!

L.A. TIMES, YORTY & PARKER DO NOT UNDERSTAND EVENTS

Art Kunkin

The demonstrations in the streets have completely ended the myth that the Negroes of Los Angeles are the happiest in the whole country.

It has been an election without ballot boxes and the Negroes have cast their votes. Whether or not the white majority likes this vote, it is time for the analysis which follows every election. It is time to listen to the Negro.

Attempts to simply establish "law and order," to simply establish the pre-demonstration status quo, are doomed to failure. Anyone who thinks in these terms is fundamentally anti-Negro and will be understood as such by the vast majority of Negroes.

"Law and Order"

The great tragedy is that the government officials and the major news media have not understood what has happened. They have simply seen the breakdown of "law and order" and have been showing by their statements and actions during and after the events that they did not hear the message that the Negroes were broadcasting for all with ears to hear.

Indeed the stage is now being set by the so-called responsible leaders of our community for reprisals against the Negro community, not for any positive confrontation of the problems which led thousands in Los Angeles, the "Safe City," to face death at the hands of police and soldiers because they had given up hope that ordinary democratic methods would really do anything for them and their children.

The climate locally is such that anyone who criticizes Chief Parker or the city administration for their role in the disturbances is called a Communist or a supporter of criminal elements. It is actually very dangerous in Los Angeles today to enter reasonable objections to the sensationalistic reporting and ridiculous charges of conspiracies.

Danger

Yet the voice of reason, of compassion, of immediate positive action must be heard, and it must be heard from the white community, or else the next Negro protest will be still more severe. Not only the Negro ghetto but every neighborhood in the city will become an armed camp. Not only white businesses in the ghetto will go up in flames but the very mountains and oil fields ringing Los Angeles.

And who will really be to blame then—the Negroes who act and explode out of sheer frustration, or the white community which has the power to act decisively but which did not listen before the explosion, and is not listening now?

The Los Angeles Times editorial of Tuesday, August 17, the very day the curfew ended, is a classic example of how not to listen and how to best provoke future disturbances. The Times states as one of certain "basic truths" that "What happened here was not the doing of the Negro majority in Los Angeles. Far from it, innocent Negroes were among the saddest victims of the turning and looting." Another so-called "truth" is that "even by inference, none should condone the criminal lawlessness, or dismiss it as the inevitable result of economic and sociological pressures." Then the Times makes its proposals—a Governor's Commission to inquire into the causes and circumstances of the riot and, above all, why the National Guard did not come to the scene sooner. "The Commission should be cautious of irresponsible criticism of the Los Angeles Police Department and its chief, William H. Parker. . . . Nonetheless, the Commission should concern itself with the possible [sic] need of better communications between law enforcement and the Negro community . . ." Furthermore, the Times calls for "an increase in the size of the Police Department." The third Times proposal is that aid be given for the rebuilding of destroyed businesses in South Los Angeles and guarantees given them against future disorders.

No Action Proposed

The astonishing thing is that in two editorials nothing concrete and specific is said about doing anything immediately about the conditions that led to the riots.

Nothing is said about education, jobs, or housing except in terms of advice to "proceed to ordinary fashion to secure still other advantages so long denied them." How long are people to wait, Times Editor Nick Williams and Times Publisher Chandler? It has been a super-disaster situation in the Negro ghetto for years. The people are fed up with unemployment, with subsistence on government handouts and Bureau of Public Assistance checks. The War On Poverty has done little and most of the loci publicity relating to it has emphasized the haggling among politicians.

As Police Chief Parker has pointed out with some perception, "You can not keep telling them that they are being abused and mistreated without expecting them to react." But, Chief Parker, do you really think that "they" need to be told about mistreatment? Don't you recognize that "they" are being mistreated? What would you have Washington do, Chief, not even promise to do, (Continued on Page 3)

"It is always a great crime to deprive a people of its liberty on the pretext that it is using it wrongly."
DE TOQUEVILLE

CORE LEADER OBSERVES GHETTO FIGHTING

Bob Freeman

On Wednesday night about 11 p.m. I arrived in Watts, a Negro ghetto in the heart of Los Angeles. Amid a hail of bottles, rocks, and stones, as an angry mob of residents, seething with resentment, was surging forth toward a group of policemen, I could hear shouting: "We will kill you, you beat and kicked that woman." "You've beat and we've been running. Who's beating who and who's running now?"

I would estimate the number taking part in this action at that time at about 1500 persons.

As I drove south on Avalon Boulevard south of Imperial Highway, I saw four police officers crouched over one man as two other officers sat on him. The four were beating him about the head, arms and shoulders with billy clubs. To my left approached a crowd, shouting "Don't kill that man!"

The crowd began to attack the officers as the officers responded with "Shut up, dirty niggers" and "You better get out of here and go home, niggers." Just then the crowd came closer and began to attack the officers. The officers first attempted to fight back but then ran away.

As I drove south another block I saw four officers approach one Negro who was walking along the sidewalk empty-handed. One officer said, "Come here, nigger." As the man turned, the officers jumped him and began to beat him.

He fell on the ground, but instantaneously the crowd was there running the officers off.

I felt then it was wise to park my car and inquire of some of the people on the street what had happened to start this. I approached two men who had just discharged their last stones and bottles and asked my question.

They replied that the cops had stopped some man about a traffic violation. Two women had approached the scene and during the ensuing events the officers had knocked one of the women to the ground and hit and kicked her. They said this had enraged the crowd which had been looking on.

While enroute to Watts I had

(Continued on page 2)

Watts Rebellion issue, LA Free Press, August 20, 1965. The nation's first and most successful underground paper of the Sixties, the Freep published forty-eight pages every week at its peak in 1970 and boasted a "faithful readership" of a quarter of a million. The LA Times headlines for its Watts Uprising front page were "'Get Whitey,' Scream Blood-Hungry Mobs," and an "expert" analysis, "Racial Unrest Laid to Negro Family Failure."

The Black Cat tavern protest against police raids on gay bars, February 11, 1967, two years before Stonewall. Los Angeles also had the first gay magazine, *The Advocate*, and, in 1970, the first official gay pride parade.

convinced that "specific references to the existence or prevalence of racism would only hurt the campaign's fortunes among the white voters who dominated the electorate." Thus, their strategy focused almost entirely on the dangers of Proposition 14, and they declined to "defend the original purpose of the Rumford Act in any meaningful way." Liberal activists campaigning against Prop 14 "rarely mentioned the housing crisis that had driven civil rights organizations to demand the passage of the legislation in the first place; nor did they reference the overwhelming levels of discrimination many home buyers and renters still faced." HoSang quotes from CAP 14 pamphlets reassuring white homeowners that, since only 1 to 2 percent of Blacks could actually afford to buy into newer subdivisions, they posed little threat to home values or neighborhood composition.[44]

CAP 14 failed disastrously. On November 3, with almost 90 percent of registered voters turning out at the polls, Proposition 14 won by a two-to-one margin—a 2 million vote majority—with white support ranging upward of 70 percent in much of Southern California. At the same time, Goldwater was crushed by LBJ, albeit by a smaller majority, as many Northern California Republicans defected from his extremist campaign. The composition of the legislature and congressional delegations remained almost the same, although a Bircher, John Schmitz, won a senate seat from Orange County. The election, in other words, neither registered a statewide swing to the right, nor did it evince any tendency toward a fundamental realignment. Various attempts were made to explain the overwhelming vote for Proposition 14 as a result of ballot error or confusion over its meaning, but detailed analyses of polling and vote data by two well-known political scientists dispelled these hypotheses. Voters clearly understood what they were voting for, and the result was a decisive affirmation of the right to discriminate by a majority of white Democrats and Republicans alike. Only in San Francisco and a few neighboring counties was the vote even close.[45]

The victory of Prop 14 (which was ultimately ruled unconstitutional by the Supreme Court in 1967) brought the curtain down on the civil rights era in Los Angeles, at least as represented by nonviolent protest and broad coalition building. The shock and demoralization experienced by activists was not unlike what their grandchildren would

confront in November 2016. Although judicial struggles would continue (the long simmering *Crawford* case, for instance), and renewed
energy would eventually be poured into the mayoral campaign of Tom
Bradley in 1969, the hope of winning ghetto youth to the strategies
of any of the major civil rights groups—whatever those strategies
now were—was defunct. White liberals on the Westside, of course,
could find joy in the huge Johnson victory and the promises of the
Great Society he claimed to be building, but this was little solace for
the minorities who were in the direct path of the juggernaut of white
supremacy unleashed by Proposition 14.

Meanwhile, L.A. CORE, heroic on so many occasions, was collaps-
ing internally. Early in 1965, one member wrote: "This chapter is no
longer able and/or willing to engage in meaningful direct action. We
straggle up Broadway to the Federal Building every now and then; we
call off membership meetings so we can picket the Citizens Council,
thus avoiding an occasion for serious discussion of just what the hell
we're doing."[46] UCRC continued in existence for another year, but its
"moderate" leadership became increasingly entangled in the quarrels of
competing factions of Black Democrats that mirrored the Sacramento
schism between governor Pat Brown and Jess Unruh, speaker of the
state assembly (the feud continued later, between Brown and the California Democratic Clubs). Councilman Billy Mills, for instance, was
an Unruh ally and would soon be ostracized by other Black politicos
for supporting a liberal Chicano candidate for the board of education.
Meanwhile, Eason Monroe of the ACLU quarreled with the NAACP,
which in turn was grappling with its own internal factions.

Even the great finale of the Southern struggle in Selma in spring
1965 would fail to elicit more than a tepid demonstration or two from
L.A.'s dying movement. In Northern California, by contrast, CORE
veterans and Freedom Summer returnees at Berkeley unexpectedly
found themselves leading the biggest student uprising since the 1930s.
There was no counterpart, however, at UCLA or other Southern
California campuses. Los Angeles at the end of 1964 seemed strangely
pacified. For white youth, unaware of how Vietnam would soon change
their lives, it was still the endless summer of beach parties, shining

new UC campuses, and the promise of brilliant careers, or at least an abundance of unionized blue-collar jobs. For their generational counterparts in the ghettos, however, L.A. had proven once again that it was the Deep South.

Part II

Alternative Culture

8

From "Ban the Bomb" to "Stop the War": Women Strike for Peace (1961–67)

White youth may have been politically disengaged at the beginning of the Sixties, but others saw storm clouds gathering—radioactive ones. In downtown Los Angeles, on November 1, 1961, 2,000 women gathered outside the State Building, carrying signs that read "Ban All Atomic Weapons." After speeches, they marched silently to city hall and then to the Federal Building to present officials with petitions. Their leaflet posed the question, "Who are we?" It answered, "We are housewives and working women." It said they were part of an organization called "Women Strike for Peace" (WSP).[1]

Sister demonstrations took place that day in dozens of cities, but L.A.'s was by far the largest. A first-person report describing how the event had been organized appeared in London's *Guardian*: "An old friend rang me up," Sophia Wyatt wrote. "She said she was sending me some literature which was the most exciting thing she had ever heard." The friend asked her to "pass it on to the neighbors, talk to my friends, and be a darling and give her a lift on November 1st. When I started to ask who and what, she cut me short. There were no names; it was not an organization; would I just read it and come."

So she did—but first, she said, "I changed into a respectable dress, hauled my one and only hat out of mothballs and put on gloves." The demonstration was big; when they marched from the State Building to city hall, Wyatt wrote, they were "eight deep in a line stretching for blocks and blocks." Along the march route, "a blossoming of faces appeared at every window to the uppermost storeys of the surrounding buildings, as the police halted all traffic." She asked a woman on the march, "What organization do you belong to?" The woman laughed and said, "I don't belong to any organization. I've got a child of ten."[2]

The women's march was a response to the discovery of deadly radioactive iodine and strontium isotopes in milk from dairies in western states. At the time it was believed that this was the consequence of a huge Soviet hydrogen bomb test and the resulting radioactive cloud that drifted eastward across the Northern Hemisphere—and that cows had grazed on pastures where radioactive rain had fallen. (New studies, decades later, found that American detonations from 1951 to 1961 were the major source of the radioactive plague, which produced thousands of cases of cancer in communities "downwind" of the Nevada test site.) Thus the marcher's banners read "End the Arms Race—Not the Human Race."

Their leaflets denounced both sides: "We appeal not only to our own government, but especially the Soviet Union." One sign declared, "The Soviet 50 Megaton Bomb Is an Outrage against Humanity." Of the new Kennedy administration (secretly racing toward the invasion of Cuba and the edge of nuclear Armageddon), the demonstrators made three major demands: an immediate cessation of nuclear tests, "concrete steps to be taken at once toward worldwide disarmament," and "immediate allocation of as much of the national budget to preparation for peace as was being spent in preparation for war."[3] As for the women's "strike," it was essentially Aristophanes' *Lysistrata* for the nuclear age. Women were urged to "suspend" their traditional roles as housewives and mothers in order to advocate for a test ban and "appeal for the future of mankind."[4]

At the rally following the march, a succession of women speakers emphasized the urgency of the moment. "Mrs. Wallace Thompson" chilled the crowd as she described the effects of a ten-megaton bomb targeted at the spot where they stood. "It would level every building in a circle 14 miles across ... More horrible than the blast would be the firestorm ... All those in fallout shelters would be suffocated ... 100 miles in any direction from where we now stand, everyone who did not find shelter would be dead within five days ... Fallout comes later." So, she concluded, "we are done with mere lip service to disarmament and co-existence. We are prepared to back up our demands with our votes. Though, goodness knows, unless we hurry we may not all be around for the next election."[5]

State Attorney General Stanley Mosk—the liberal Democrat whose career was later derailed by LAPD Chief Bill Parker—also spoke at the rally, trying to defend the Kennedy administration. He read a message from Governor Pat Brown: "Your demonstration today serves as an expression of public support for our President's determination to achieve a just peace through early and purposeful negotiations."[6] Actually, what they were expressing was the more like the opposite: a criticism of Kennedy for failing to move faster toward banning atmospheric testing and indeed all nuclear weapons.

The front page of the *Times*'s "Metro" section the next day was emblazoned with a photo of the 2,000 women demonstrators—but the accompanying article was mainly a soapbox for Mayor Yorty to fulminate against Communist deceptions: "Let us not be duped by Communist-inspired groups who try to make us feel a sense of guilt and shame just because we insist on the nation's interest." Chief Parker also criticized the marchers: "There undoubtedly were many fine people duped into thinking they were doing something constructive, but this type of revolution against constitutional authority serves the Soviets well."[7]

But who were these revolutionaries? That "Who Are We?" leaflet, signed by twenty women, said: "We are just ordinary people—teachers, writers, social workers, artists, secretaries, executives, saleswomen. Most of us are also wives and mothers." WSP, moreover, had "no board, no officers, no real committees." They were inspired, they explained, by the heroic civil rights activists in the South: "The sit-in strikers have reminded us, as the suffragettes did long ago, of the tremendous power for good in each single person. We hope you will add your individual strength to ours." The organizers added that "most of us belong to half a dozen of the usual organizations: the PTA, Hadassah or the church action committee, or SANE, or the United Nations Association, or the WIL."[8]

SANE and the WIL—those were clues. SANE, the National Committee for a Sane Nuclear Policy, was the first mass liberal organization
opposed to the arms race and working for an international ban on
nuclear testing. Founded in 1957, by 1960 it boasted more than one
hundred chapters, including one in Hollywood (led by Steve Allen and
Robert Ryan), and counted among its national spokespeople Eleanor
Roosevelt, Walter Reuther of United Auto Workers, and Socialist Party
leader Norman Thomas. However, after the group was red-baited by
members of Congress later that year, most of the leadership capitulated
to the Cold War ideology they had been founded to fight. The group
never really recovered. And there was one more thing: SANE was
now run by men. The lessons of SANE were not lost on the women
who left its ranks—not least the importance of noncompliance with
the anti-communist requirements of mainstream American politics.

In reality, the Women's International League for Peace and Freedom
(WIL), founded by Jane Addams in 1915 to protest the First World
War, was hardly one of "the usual organizations." Indeed, it had
opposed US participation in the Second World War, and it was one of
the few organizations on the left to have protested the internment of
Japanese-Americans. But, despite its female leadership and principled
politics, the WIL also seemed part of an older pacifist tradition that
was dwindling in significance. In her history of WSP, Amy Swerdlow,
who was also an early member, explains that women left the WIL to
join WSP because the new organization gave them "the space to initiate and engage in spontaneous direct actions ... without interference
from a national office." And, she writes, "we saw ourselves as new,
bold, and potentially successful. We believed we would accomplish
what the WIL women had failed to do." WSP appealed to WIL and
SANE veterans for many reasons: it was "simple, pragmatic, noni-
deological, moralistic and emotional."[9] Moreover, she explains, the
WSP expressed a deep moral outrage about the Cold War, which it
combined with a playful rejection of male leaders' claims to wisdom
and knowledge. It was serious about doing politics in Washington,
while also genuinely internationalist.

At that first demonstration in downtown L.A., the marchers were
responding to a call from an anonymous small group of women in

Washington, DC, led by children's book illustrator Dagmar Wilson—
herself a wife and mother. She had never been an activist, but she "had
long been worried about nuclear fallout" and its effect on children's
health.[10]

If the Los Angeles chapter was a leader in recruitment and activism,
it owed much to its remarkable and talented organizer, Mary Clarke.
The FBI called her "the guiding force behind the Southern California
WSP group," and they were right about that.[11] By the mid Sixties
she had traveled to Hanoi, Moscow, Beijing, and Havana as a WSP
leader. According to her younger sister, June Solnit Sale, she had not
been a political organizer prior to WSP, but was a wife and mother in
1961, just like the leaflet said, with two small children. But "it is not
accidental that Mary was destined to be a peace activist," Sale said.
"It comes from our mother and father." They were poor Jews in the
LA ghetto of Boyle Heights; when Mary went to kindergarten, she
spoke Yiddish but no English. But their father prospered, moving the
family to Sierra Madre, next to Pasadena. "Our father was always
active," Sale recalled. "He was always very pro-union. In the mid-
thirties I remember going to him with meetings of the Joint Anti
Fascist Refugee Committee. He voted for Socialists. Mary didn't go,
but it was always there. It was in her bones."[12]

Vigils and Picket Lines

The stunning debut of L.A. WSP in November 1961 was followed by
its steady expansion throughout Southern California in winter and
spring 1962. This was recorded in the group's news bulletin—*La
Wisp*, four mimeographed legal-size pages—edited by Mary Clarke,
who also typed and mailed it. That first issue included reports from
all over the region: the South Bay chapter was holding a fund-raiser
with Black folksinger Odetta; San Fernando Valley had organized
a symposium on disarmament at Valley State; Santa Monica was
running a "post card a day" campaign to President Kennedy; in the
San Gabriel Valley, members were staffing "peace tables" in Monterey
Park with literature on the futility of fallout shelters; Whittier had a
bake sale; Santa Barbara had opened a Peace Information Center and

was planning a demonstration "to coincide with those scheduled in New York and London"; and in San Diego, sixty-five people from WSP had demonstrated downtown for two hours—of which they reported, "public response cool, but interested."[13]

The first newsletter also reported that the LA group had sent fourteen women to the state capitol in Sacramento, where they had joined 250 other WSP members from Northern California to protest the state budget allocation for fallout shelters. Plans were underway for a Mother's Day demonstration with the slogan "Give Me the Gift of Peace." And the organization was running a "Peace Education Lecture Series," with weekly sessions: topics included "Communism, Capitalism, Socialism" with economist Stanley Sheinbaum, "Economics of Peace and War," and "Bias in Mass Media."[14] Clearly the WSP was doing its homework—far beyond what the public expected of "wives and mothers."

What followed the dramatic debut of WSP in L.A. was a long series of vivid public actions, many of which received coverage in the *LA Times*. January 1962: "Women Sail Balloons for 'Peace Race'"—700 women released 4,000 balloons in Hancock Park, each carrying a call to the superpowers to end the arms race. March 1962: "700 Women Stage A-Test Protest"—a silent march from MacArthur Park to the Atomic Energy Commission offices on Wilshire near Vermont Avenue.[15] April 1962: the day after Kennedy ordered the resumption of atmospheric nuclear testing, L.A. WSP conducted an all-day vigil at the Federal Building in downtown L.A., part of the organization's nationwide "Milk Strike," "to guard our children against the ingestion of thyroid-cancer-causing Iodine 131 released by nuclear explosions." The "strike" was to terminate after the eighth day, "when the half-life of Iodine 131 is spent."[16]

Then came July 1962: "Women in Bomb Protest at Las Vegas." L.A. WSP had sent a bus full of demonstrators to picket the Nevada Test Site. They started, the newsletter reported, at "two of the flossiest, busiest blocks" of casinos in Las Vegas, where they pushed empty baby carriages with signs saying "Empty because of Stillbirth" and "Empty because of Cancer." The response, according to the *Times*, was "rather negative," but "three local women joined in the march." The next morning they picketed at the gate of the test site for two hours, leafleting people on their way to work—many of whom accepted the leaflet.[17] The group then held a vigil at the Nevada Test Site—a national WSP mobilization coordinated by Mary Clarke.

Then came the Cuban Missile Crisis. While the LA schools distributed pamphlets for parents about "Procedures to be Followed in Event of Attack," WSP quickly mobilized 300 women and children for a march and silent vigil in Pershing Square downtown, carrying signs that read "Peace not Panic" and "We Don't Want War." And their focus extended well beyond L.A.; the organization announced that "several WSP members were leaving immediately for Washington by plane to seek an audience with President Kennedy."[18]

At the height of the missile crisis, WSP broke out of the prevailing Cold War framework and appealed directly to Soviet women, with a telegram to three they had met two months earlier: "At this moment of peril, [we] ask in friendship that you plead with your government, as we are pleading with ours, to pull back from the brink of war and to seek just and peaceful solutions to the conflicts that divide our two great countries." They got prompt replies, which were published in the next issue of La Wisp, including one from the president of the Soviet Women's Committee: "Share your anxiety at dangerous situation, convinced our government will do its utmost to prevent war. Ready, together with you, to work for peaceful solution to the conflict."

After the crisis, WSP held a "symposium" where members reported on peace conferences abroad they had attended over the summer. Indeed, WSP was internationalist from the beginning, framing its argument around the notion that women of all nations shared an interest in a peaceful world in which their children could grow up. The LA organization sent a delegation to Japan in August, where a Mothers' Congress had brought 20,000 Japanese women to Osaka to discuss the links among "the problems of civil liberties, civil rights, equality for women, and peace," and then march through the center of the city "with banners flying." Of the congress, Clarke told her LA colleagues, "to think that such a magnificent movement of women existed in Japan and that we were not aware that it had been in existence for 8 years, made me realize that ... we must never allow ourselves to be isolated and to experience the feeling of being alone in our common cause." Another member reported on the Voice of Women Meeting in September in Montreal, and another on the "World without the Bomb" assembly in Accra, called by President Kwame Nkrumah of Ghana.[19]

WSP in L.A. had also sent representatives to Moscow in July for the World Congress for General Disarmament and Peace, with 2,400 attendees from 121 countries. The organizers' call had a stellar list of signers: Anwar Sadat, Jomo Kenyatta and Che Guevara; Linus Pauling and Albert Schweitzer; Sartre and Neruda, Shostakovich and Picasso.[20] But the congress was also hugely controversial among peace movement activists in the United States and elsewhere. Because the Soviets were hosting, WSP ended up being the only American peace group to send an official delegation; SANE and the rest had declined. At the conference, moreover, WSP declined to join the delegates from eleven countries who signed a minority report that called the Soviet Union "obstructive" for rejecting proposals for inspection of nuclear facilities. Nor did WSP delegates join the twenty-five visitors who defied the Soviet hosts by distributing 10,000 leaflets in Moscow opposing testing by both sides, then marching to Red Square, where they unfurled a banner reading "No Tests East or West."[21] In a report that marked the organization's first anniversary, the L.A. WSP delegates concluded that the congress showed "people from both major camps *could* work together toward securing the peace."[22]

The Subpoenas

As WSP began its second year, subpoenas from the House Un-American Activities Committee (HUAC) arrived. Ten of the organization's leaders in New York were served with charges that the group had been infiltrated, led or controlled by Communists. Despite cracks of light in the Hollywood blacklist in 1960 and '61, a HUAC subpoena remained a frightening document—unless recipients wanted to inform on friends and colleagues; that is, to be "rats," "stoolies" or "finks."

No one from L.A. WSP received a subpoena, even though the FBI had reported that "eight security index subjects were observed marching" at the first WSP demonstration in L.A.[23] (The "security index" was the FBI's list of high-level radicals, mostly Communists, to be rounded up and detained in case of a "national emergency.") But the LA group took the lead in the organization's public response to the subpoenas. A full-page ad appeared in the *New York Times* West Coast edition on December 4, 1962, ten days before the scheduled hearing, bearing the title "Gentlemen: What Are You Afraid of?" "The women's peace movement has struck fear into the hearts of the House Committee on Un-American Activities," the ad declared. "We have been criticized for objecting to the contamination of the milk our children drink!"

To show how fearless they were, WSP members wrote the committee volunteering to testify publicly about their goals and policies —an unprecedented tactic in a world where leftists for more than a decade had done everything they could to avoid appearing before HUAC. During the hearings, seven L.A. WSP activists were interviewed on local and national radio and TV. "The response ... was terrific," *La Wisp* reported. Donations arrived in the mail "from San Diego to Portland." One LA woman wrote: "Please add my name to your mailing list. I would be delighted to receive anything with the exception of subpoenas. I can never remember the Fifth Amendment, and the House committee on Un-American Activities evidently cannot remember the First!"[24]

Meanwhile in Washington, Dagmar Wilson and other national leaders had gained the upper hand over the committee. The group packed the hearing room with noisy supporters; as leaders were called to testify, members presented them with roses. Wilson testified that in Women Strike for Peace, "nobody is controlled by anybody." She said there was "absolutely no way" of eliminating Communists from the membership, and that she would not expel them even if she could—this at a time when Reds had been kicked out of other peace groups like SANE, as well as the ACLU. She concluded by remarking that WSP was run by volunteers: "This is something I find very hard to explain to the masculine mind." The three HUAC members who conducted the hearing, according to *New York Times* columnist Russell Baker, "spent most of the week looking lonely, badgered and miserable."[25]

The state's version of HUAC, the state senate's Burns Committee, tried to get into the act six months later, when they issued a report declaring that "subversives" and "Reds" had "infiltrated" WSP in Los Angeles. They conceded that the group was not a "Communist front," but claimed that "the infiltration is clear and speaks for itself." (Apparently the committee did not find out that Clarke had been a member of the CP until 1955.)[26] The committee report submitted as evidence one item: the lecture series the group had sponsored in L.A. the previous year. The problem? "Four of the lectures were devoted to a study of Russian communism as compared to ... our own system of government."[27] As evidence of Communist infiltration, that was pathetic. Still, it made page two of the *LA Times*.

The same page of that day's paper reported on the WSP response. A member of the group's local coordinating council, "Mrs. Kay Hardman," reiterated Dagmar Wilson's statement before HUAC, had "absolutely no way of eliminating Communists from WSP and would not if she could." As for that lecture series, it featured "some of our finest scholars—from the Center for the Study of Democratic Institutions in Santa Barbara."[28] That was the end of Sacramento's red-baiting campaign against WSP in Los Angeles.

To Jakarta and Hanoi

On the larger issue of nuclear weapons, Khrushchev and Kennedy had been so shaken by the Cuban Missile Crisis that they went to work on a treaty banning atmospheric testing. On August 5, 1963, they signed the Partial Nuclear Test Ban Treaty, which meant WSP's first goal had been achieved—less than two years after the group came into existence. On September 24, WSP members traveled from L.A. to Washington to witness the Senate ratification vote. L.A. WSP in particular had made the treaty a top priority, organizing a summer "campaign for 100,000 letters on the Test-Ban." And the group understood the need to claim victory: the day after the treaty was ratified, WSP organized a celebration at the Federal Building in downtown L.A.

Kennedy himself gave credit to women for pressing for the Test Ban Treaty. When asked about women's protest actions in an interview with editors of the top seven US women's magazines—*Cosmopolitan*, *Family Circle*, *Good Housekeeping*, *McCall's*, *Parents Magazine*, *Redbook*, and *Women's Day*—he replied, "I would urge women to get into whatever groups they feel reflect their judgment as to how things ought to be done … it is very helpful to have a significant group of women working for peace in their communities." Dagmar Wilson commented, "He has not exactly told them to join WSP, but he has told them to join something."[29]

The WSP newsletter's report on the Test Ban Treaty celebration in L.A. was headlined "Don't Get Too Comfortable." The reality was that the treaty permitted underground tests, and Kennedy had begun underground testing in Nevada shortly after the treaty went into effect. At this juncture, the group announced a change in strategic focus: fighting fallout shelters and drop drills in schools.

Then came a banal-sounding sentence that turned out to be prescient: "A committee was set up to study the Viet Nam situation." That was September 1963, when 16,000 US troops were in Vietnam and Kennedy had not yet been assassinated. It was more than a year and a half before the first national anti-war demonstration, called by Students for a Democratic Society (SDS) in Washington in April 1965.

The Vietnam War transformed Women Strike for Peace, as was evident by the time of the organization's second anniversary in November 1963. That month, the LA chapter joined a demonstration at the Ambassador Hotel against Madame Nhu, the notorious wife of the head of the Saigon government; the march had the slogan "Stop Organized Slaughter in South Viet Nam." L.A. WSP also promoted a speech on Vietnam at the Music Box Theater by I. F. Stone, the radical journalist with the famous newsletter.[30]

In March 1965, 200 WSP members, wearing black dresses and veils and carrying yellow roses, marched to the Western Union office downtown, where they sent a wire to Lady Bird Johnson: "We have appealed to your husband, our president, but he has not listened." They asked her to intercede with him to "have Vietnam taken from the field of battle to the conference table." They also wired the first lady a bouquet of yellow roses, which they said signified "life which we feel is being trampled on in Vietnam." A month later L.A. WSP

sent a delegation to the SDS-sponsored March on Washington to End
the War in Vietnam, while members at home joined a vigil sponsored
by the SDS chapter at USC. (The first chapter in the state, it had been
organized by the remarkable Margaret Thorpe, a graduating senior
and the daughter of a railroad worker from Arcadia. Over the next
year she would become a familiar face on Channel Nine, robustly
debating future Republican congressman Dana Rohrabacher, as well
as other members of Young Americans for Freedom.)

That spring, as Johnson unleashed B-52s against North Vietnam's
cities ("Operation Rolling Thunder"), Clarke, together with Lorraine Gordon, a leader of New York City WSP and coproprietor
of the famed Village Vanguard jazz club, became the first members
of the American peace movement to visit Hanoi. They had traveled
to Moscow in May for the twentieth-anniversary celebration of the
end of the war in Europe and took the opportunity to meet delegates
from the Women's Union of North Vietnam and from the National
Liberation Front (NLF) in the South. The Vietnamese women already
knew of WSP through the sacrifice of Detroit member Alice Hertz,
who had set fire to herself in March to protest the carpet-bombing of
the North.[31] They urged the LA women to come see for themselves
the destruction being wrought by the US Air Force. The two left
immediately, flying from Moscow to Hanoi via Beijing. Historian
Jon Coburn later called the trip "one of the most significant acts
undertaken by WSPers during its history ... [and] Clarke and Gordon
demonstrated unique daring and courage in their expedition."[32]

In Hanoi, as Clarke recalled in a 1995 interview, they were "startled"
by the massive program to build air raid shelters for the population,
and deeply moved by meeting children in a Hanoi hospital who had
been napalmed by American planes.[33] Their visit was unofficial, indeed
secret, but they discussed with their hosts the possibility of a formal
meeting between American and Vietnamese women in the near future.
Pham Van Dong, the North's Prime Minister, responded that it was
too dangerous to bring delegates to Hanoi, suggesting Jakarta as a
more suitable site.

Plans for the Jakarta meeting were publicized by L.A. WSP with
appropriate fanfare. The announcement posed the question, "Why

will American women go thousands of miles to meet Vietnamese women face to face?" The answer: "They go to give and receive hope and courage." Mary Clarke headed the ten-woman delegation, which included Nanci Hollander of SDS, arriving in July for five days of talks with their nine Vietnamese counterparts, who were led by Nguyen Thi Binh—the stunning NLF leader who later became its chief negotiator. In the three months since the initial visit to Hanoi, 40,000 or so additional American troops had landed in the South, while the death toll from the bombing of the North had soared. The Vietnamese women not only described their experiences, but also gave WSPers a primer on how Washington and Saigon had caused the new war by abandoning the national elections promised by the 1954 Geneva Accords. Both sides considered the meeting an overwhelming success and arranged to maintain contact with one another—a relationship that eventually produced the joint Committee of Liaison, which organized contacts between American prisoners of war and their families back home.

The unprecedented meeting received much international applause. Stopping over in Tokyo on the way out, they were praised by peace groups and mainstream media for their audacity, while in Jakarta President Sukarno told them that Indonesia was honored to be the venue for "such a historic meeting." In London on the way back, dissident Labour MPs brought them to the House of Commons for a discussion. However, when they got off the plane in Washington, they encountered a firestorm of criticism from both the press and the White House. The *New York Times* headline, true to form, read "10 Americans Join Vietnam Reds." The article quoted the group's official statement in Jakarta, which said the US was committing "military aggression" in Vietnam and "waging a cruel war against the Vietnamese people," while using Vietnam as a "testing ground for new and more horrible weapons." All of that was true, but the *Times* nevertheless reported that it "echoed Hanoi's propaganda line."[34]

In Washington the returning delegation asked to meet with the president, but the White House declined—with a written note. They did meet with members of Congress, which had recently passed the Gulf of Tonkin Resolution, giving LBJ open-ended authority to make war. The group was struck by the fact that members of Congress "appeared to know so little about Vietnam."[35] They also met with White House officials, sharing with them the Vietnamese perspective on the war as a continuation of the struggle against French colonialism, and explaining that the Saigon government spoke only for the Catholic minority in the primarily Buddhist country. An aide to McGeorge Bundy (LBJ's national security advisor) responded dismissively, telling them the only relevant issue was the Communist threat to Vietnam.[36]

After their return to L.A., Clarke and the other WSP leaders were "inundated with requests" to speak and received "fantastic, never before, coverage from the mass media"—including appearances on four TV shows and a dozen radio programs. They talked about their meeting with Vietnamese women at "churches, women's clubs, colleges and universities, civil rights meetings, trade union meetings, teach-ins, and local demonstrations against the war," including "many groups previously unreached by WSP." The list included the first teach-in at UC San Diego, a talk at UC Santa Barbara and a debate at Long Beach State; appearances at many local Democratic Clubs as well as the state central committee of the Democratic Party; union groups, among them the American Federation of Teachers and the Garment Workers; and many Unitarian churches and Jewish groups.[37]

Clarke reported that the NLF women had "traveled on foot for two weeks through unsafe territory and across borders at night to catch a plane to Djakarta." "Many" of the Vietnamese women "spoke or understood" English. "We listened to many personal stories of tragedy and death," she reported. "The leader of the South Vietnamese delegation had spent 3 years in jail at the age of 18 under the French, and 1 year when Diem came to power." They described what Americans called the "strategic hamlet" program of moving Vietnamese peasants out of their ancestral villages into what "they described as 'concentration camps.'" As for the American argument that South Vietnam was a "victim" of "aggression from the North," the American women were told that their South Vietnamese counterparts "came back to defend their country." As for the American claims that bombing aimed at military targets, "the North Vietnamese women brought considerable evidence of repeated bombing and strafing of hospitals, schools, churches, markets, bus stations, fishing-boats and villages."[38]

While they were winning national and international attention, WSP was also reasserting their distinctive twist on their status as women. The WSP version of "End the War Now" was "Bring the Boys Home for Dinner"—accompanied by a cookbook published by the LA chapter that same year, under the title *Peace de Resistance*. "Conceived by Mary Clarke, written by Esther Lewin," and dedicated to Dagmar Wilson, "Chief Cook and Bottle Washer," the book contained more than 150 recipes submitted by members. The introduction declared:

> We women of WSP working for peace have walked thousands of miles, written plane-loads of letters to our president, our congressmen and the heads of our states. We've vigil-ed at the Federal Building; we've attended conferences of women like ourselves around the world. And at the same time, we've made hundreds of thousands of beds, changed a million diapers and cooked two million meals—not to mention the mountains of dishes we've washed.[39]

The first recipe was for "Russian Borscht"; the second, "Rushin' Borscht" ("make in 10 minutes in the morning before rushing off to your WSP meeting"). Others included "Albondigas Soup" ("Mexico's contribution to the peace movement—all in one dish"), "Chicken Kiev" ("If this is Russian propaganda, we're all for it!"), and Lime pie ("Neglected your family lately? All will be forgiven with this divine pie"). (It included a pint of whipped cream.)

The meeting with Vietnamese women in Jakarta in mid 1965 had come at a time when no one in Congress was calling for an immediate end to the Vietnam war, and when much of the peace movement was demanding "Negotiations Now" rather than "Out Now." In this respect the trip constituted a huge step, with reverberations that extended far beyond the near-term media attention received by WSP. For one, it strengthened women's standing to speak on foreign policy issues, usually the preserve of men and "experts." They spoke first of all on the familiar ground, as women defending children—but now they added to this a knowledge of history that was lacking in government leaders. Indeed, the firsthand authority they gained from speaking to Vietnamese women enabled them to directly challenge the dominant US narrative of the Cold War, which portrayed Vietnam as a front of a worldwide battle between "freedom" and "Communist tyranny." The WSP women could now counter that they had seen firsthand how the cruelty and destruction of this particular war was based on ignorance of its local origins and meaning.

They had a decade more of activism ahead of them, including draft resistance work, an official trip to Hanoi in 1967, a demonstration against Lyndon Johnson that brought a massive turnout to Century City that same year, and Gene McCarthy's 1968 campaign for the Democratic nomination for president. Through it all, they remained an all-female organization that openly rejected male political culture. They challenged the age-old claim that wars are waged by men to protect women and children, and instead proclaimed their ties with women around the world, including women in "enemy" countries.[40] Moreover, they remained an anti-hierarchical organization with impressive local autonomy. Their meeting with Vietnamese women in 1965 had made WSP, in L.A. and nationally, some of the most effective leaders of the anti-war movement.

9

From Bach to "Tanya": KPFK Radio (1959–74)

On June 24, 1960, L.A.'s listener-supported FM station, KPFK, aired a "Special Report" on the protests against the HUAC hearing in San Francisco the previous month, which had "investigated" the Communist Party in California. KPFK had begun broadcasting a year earlier as Southern California's first non-commercial FM station, part of the Pacifica Radio Network of three stations, which had started in Berkeley and now included New York. For the first time people had taken to the streets in a tumultuous protest against the committee. While 4,000 demonstrators marched and shouted and chanted outside San Francisco city hall, inside the hearing room thirty-six out of thirty-eight witnesses refused to cooperate with the committee, and the audience jeered committee members and the witnesses who were friendly to them. The program on KPFK, produced by the Berkeley Pacifica station, KPFA, had been recorded on site, and listeners heard the whole thing: the chanting crowd outside; a friendly witness telling committee members that he had been a "one-time hard-core member" of the party and that he had concluded that "the Communist Party lowers man to the level of a beast in the field"; and the audience's laughter when committee counsel Richard Ahrens asked the witness, "You have found your way back to God and patriotism, is that correct?"[1]

Nothing like that had ever happened at a HUAC hearing before. History was being made that day, and KPFK told the full story, including the part—described by demonstrators—where "officers of the San Francisco motorcycle squad, in helmets and leather jackets, appeared behind the barricade on the steps of city hall," and turned fire hoses on the demonstrators, but "we just stood our ground ... so they shut off the hoses and without any warning at all the cops just charged ... the cops were picking up the students bodily" and throwing them down the stairs. Listeners heard the crowd singing and cheering, and the students chanting; the crowd roar became more intense; above the roar, you could hear screams of a girl; and then, clearly, the singing: "We shall not, we shall not be moved."[2]

The documentary went on with the testimony inside the hearing room—including that of Bill Mandel, a Marxist with a show on KPFK, who opened his statement as follows:

Honorable beaters of children, and sadists, uniformed and in plain clothes, distinguished Dixiecrat wearing the clothing of a gentleman, eminent Republican who opposes an accommodation with the one country with whom we must live in peace in order for us all and our children to survive ... If you think that I am going to cooperate with this collection of Judases, of men who sit there in violation of the United States Constitution—if you think I'll cooperate with you in any way, you are insane!"[3]

It was great radio, and all of it was on KPFK in June 1960.

Of course, the HUAC documentary wasn't the only piece about the Left aired on the station. It also ran programs on the Highlander Folk School in Tennessee, which trained civil rights workers; on proposals for a police review board in L.A. (a cause for the next several decades); and a documentary about opposition to the death penalty. Also featured were physicist Hans Bethe and the Lobby for Peace, discussing nuclear disarmament; a series on "Californians of Mexican Descent"; and a program on "America's involvement in Africa."

KPFK in its first year—1959—also took another step that would shape its history for the next decade, and contribute to the history of L.A.: it invited Dorothy Healey, chairman of the Communist Party in Los Angeles, to produce a regular fifteen-minute public affairs show with the bold name "Communist Commentary." In the wake of Krushchev's "Crimes of Stalin" speech and the Soviet invasion of Hungary in 1956, the party was at a low point by 1959, with fewer than 500 members in L.A.—they had had more than 3,000 a decade earlier.[4] The national office tried to get rid of Dorothy because she led a group of reformers seeking a more democratic and less secretive party, but she held on to her position because the LA people recognized what Bettina Aptheker, activist and daughter of a prominent party leader, called her "energy and charisma." In subsequent decades, Dorothy would mentor the younger generation of LA activists.

Giving Dorothy Healey a show on KPFK aroused the red-hunters, and in 1962 the Federal Communications Commission withheld the license renewal of KPFK (and the other two Pacifica stations) pending its investigation into "Communist affiliations." In January 1963, the Senate Internal Security Subcommittee (SISS) subpoenaed KPFK and the other two Pacifica stations—because, the *San Francisco News Call Bulletin* reported, "the Los Angeles station has permitted a woman Communist to comment on current affairs."[5] When the SISS announced that its hearings would be held in secret, Pacifica leaders demanded that they be open to the public and requested permission to broadcast the proceedings. The request was denied.[6]

James O. Eastland, Mississippi Democrat and champion of segregation, chaired the subcommittee, with Thomas Dodd of Connecticut as vice chairman. Also in attendance at the KPFK hearing: Senators Hugh Scott of Pennsylvania, Kenneth Keating of New York and Roman Hruska—a Republican windbag from Nebraska best known for his 1970 speech in support of Nixon's nomination of G. Harrold Carswell to the Supreme Court. Carswell's critics had called him a "mediocrity." Hruska replied: "Even if he were mediocre, there are a lot of mediocre judges and people and lawyers. They are entitled to a little representation, aren't they? ... We can't have all Brandeises, Frankfurters and Cardozos."[7] (The Senate rejected Carswell's nomination.) Most of the questioning of KPFK witnesses was conducted by the subcommittee counsel, a Nevada hack with the wonderful name Jay Sourwine.

The day started with Trevor Thomas, acting president of the Pacifica Foundation, telling the committee in a prepared statement that "avowed members of the Communist Party have been heard" on KPFK and the other stations, but that was "in keeping with the foundation's policy affording a public platform for all." He emphasized that "seventy to eighty percent of our broadcast day is music, drama, literature, poetry, and children's programs." KPFK, he said, was not a left-wing station; instead (as the first *Folio*, the station's official publication, had declared), "All shades of the political spectrum are represented." Dorothy Healey was one of the ten commentators who had "different perspectives"; the list also included William F. Buckley and Russell Kirk. Thomas emphasized that Healey was on the air for only fifteen minutes twice a month with her "political views."[8]

Senator Hruska interrupted. "I do not believe the Communist Party has any political views," he said. "They have views that are calculated to overthrow this country. That is not political views."[9]

Sourwine then said he was concerned about Dorothy Healey getting airtime because "the Communists always seek to infiltrate mass communications as early as they can in every country" which is "a prelude to the Communist takeover in country after country." First Dorothy, then ... revolution! He asked whether KPFK or the other Pacifica stations "broadcast any programs from Radio Moscow." (The answer was "no.")[10]

Next came Peter Odegard, a director of the Pacifica Foundation and a professor in the UC Berkeley political science department. When he was asked about Healey and other Communists, he told the committee: "I do not like to be associated with these people. I loathe them." You might call that "pandering," or "opportunism"; but it's also possible he was sincere. He continued: "But I believe that our listeners have a right to hear this, just as they have a right to hear people like Gerald L. K. Smith, who we also interviewed." Gerald L. K. Smith was a neo-Nazi and white supremacist so far to the right he was shunned by segregationists like Strom Thurmond—you might say he was not exactly "balance" for Dorothy Healey. But Odegard concluded that KPFK put both Gerald L. K. Smith and Healey on the air "so that the people may judge what these, what I call 'enemies of freedom' are saying."

Hruska protested: "You created them."

Odegard: "No, we did not create them ... They exist. These are facts of life."[11]

He was right about that.

Next the subcommittee called Pauline Schindler, widow of the LA architect Rudolph Schindler. She was seventy years old; in the 1930s she had run a salon of left-wing intellectuals and artists at the famous Schindler House on Kings Road in Los Angeles.

Sourwine asked the inevitable question, "Are you now or have you ever been a member of the Communist Party?"

She answered "Not the party, but I was once a member of the Communist Political Association—ages and ages ago, briefly. In 1946 ... they threw me out. They did not approve of me."

That was the end of her testimony. The hearing was reaching its climax: Dorothy was next. They started by asking her, "What is your business or profession?"

She declined to answer, responding: "I believe the greatest danger that this country faces today is the possibility of concentration camps of the mind, the dictatorship of big business, of control exercised and expressed through agencies of government determining what people can or cannot think. It is my opinion that all areas of expression are protected by the First Amendment." She also pled the Fifth.

Sourwine then asked: "You are a fairly well-known commentator on radio. Do you want to decline to admit this?"

"The question of what or who is well known is, of course, a matter of opinion, but as I have already stated, I do not believe that this committee has any right to inquire into any questions regarding ... press or radio." And she again pled the Fifth.

"You have a program on radio station KPFK regularly, do you not?"

"The same answer ... for the same reasons."

Sourwine then showed her a document that had the fascinating title *Robert F. Kennedy, Attorney General of the United States, v. Dorothy Healey*. It said Bobby Kennedy had petitioned the Subversive Activities Control Board in 1962 to require that Dorothy register with the attorney general—himself—as "a member of a Communist-action organization." It then cited evidence from five witnesses that she was a Communist—two former party members turned snitches, and three reporters who had interviewed her and to whom she had said she was a Communist. One of the snitches said she had given the keynote address to the Southern California district convention of the CP in 1960, and that she had said, "Now is the ideal time to set about popularizing socialism in American terms: its rational productive relations, its elimination of material want ... its devotion to humanism and faith in the perfectibility of man," and "its respect for and encouragement of true culture as against mere amusement." That sounded suspiciously like KPFK.[12]

Sourwine continued, "Will you admit that you are the Dorothy Healey referred to as the respondent in this case?"

Dorothy's reply: "I am struck by the fact that the only dissenting opinions which the subcommittee wishes to defend are opinions which defend entrenched wealth." She was referring to a previous witness at a previous hearing—she mentioned "Katanga mining interests"—but it's hard to tell from this transcript exactly what had transpired. Whatever it was, her remark made Senator Hruska mad: "I move, Mr. Chairman," he submitted, "that all these comments of this witness ... be stricken from the record as ... self-serving statements and very unbecoming in the premises, and, besides referring unjustly and improperly to a member of this committee."

Senator Dodd, apparently the target of Dorothy's remark, stayed cool. "I am not offended," he told Sourwine. "I do not mind."

Sourwine then read a list of names of people who had testified in the Smith Act trial in 1952, a decade earlier, that Dorothy was a Communist. Dorothy replied, "After a six-month trial and after a decision of the Supreme Court, the Department of Justice came into the trial court in 1957 to admit that there was no evidence against me adequate for a conviction that I had at any time conspired to advocate the overthrow of the government by force and violence." She once again pled the Fifth.

"Mrs. Healey," Sourwine said, "You cannot have it both ways. If you are trying to tell the committee these people testified falsely, you cannot do it in the same breath in which you refuse to answer the question as to whether you know that they testified against you." He did have a point. "I am willing to leave the record there," he concluded. "I have no more questions, Mr. Chairman." Dorothy was dismissed. They never brought up any of the twelve transcripts of her KPFK shows produced by the FBI for the Senate subcommittee.[13] Apparently they weren't interested in what Dorothy actually said on KPFK—or maybe what she said wasn't criminal.

The next attack on KPFK came ten months later, in October 1963. This time it was the FCC, conducting its license renewal hearings, which asked all Pacifica board members, officers of the foundation, and the general manager of KPFK and the other two stations whether they were or had been members of the party. Like many other liberal-left groups, Pacifica had two factions with opposing strategies for responding to McCarthyism. One group of directors proposed a policy declaring that Pacifica would refuse to hire anyone "who is a member of the Communist Party." Members of the opposing group pointed out that that meant Pacifica would create its own internal McCarthyism—an endorsement of the repression of the Left that was being proposed "at a time when the political climate seems to be shifting away from such practices." The battle focused on Jerry Shore, executive vice president of the foundation and a former CIO organizer, who had been expected to become Pacifica's president, but apparently was, or had been, a party member. The left faction won the vote, but Shore resigned anyway. At that point the board voted to appoint Shore the general manager of KPFK, and the three board members who had led the right-wing faction resigned.[14] When the FCC renewed the licenses of KPFK and the other two Pacifica stations in 1964, the station and the network could claim a historic victory over McCarthyism—one that transformed forever the political identity of the station and the network.

Despite all of this political conflict, KPFK had not started out as a left-wing station. It was part of America's first listener-supported radio network, run by the nonprofit Pacifica Foundation, which had started with a station in Berkeley in 1949, founded by Lewis Hill and a group of pacifists who had refused to fight in the Second World War. The original Pacifica charter declared their goal was resolving conflicts "between nations and individuals" through "understanding" and "dialogue"—not exactly the Marxist position.[15]

In 1959, when KPFK got started, listener-supported noncommercial FM broadcasting was a radically new idea. L.A. had no public radio stations—KCRW wouldn't start broadcasting for another ten years, when it would become the region's first NPR station (and ten years after that, KCRW hired KPFK's general manager, Ruth Hirschman). Regular programming began on KPFK at 9 a.m. on July 26, 1959, with Pablo Casals performance of Beethoven's Cello Sonata No. 1—recorded the previous year at the Casals Festival in San Juan. (Casals refused to play in the United States because of the government's support for the Franco regime in Spain.) After an hour and a half of Casals came a half hour of poet Kenneth Rexroth, "Recorded in Aix-en-Provence, for KPFK." Rexroth was one of the elders of the San Francisco scene. Like the Pacifica founders, he had been a conscientious objector in World War II. In his youth he had been active in anarchist politics—the Communist Party had rejected his application for membership in 1930 because of his anarchist leanings. In the Fifties he had sold anarchist newspapers at City Lights Bookstore in San Francisco, and he was among the first American poets to explore haiku and other traditional Japanese poetic forms.[16] After Rexroth came a folk music show hosted by Ed Cray—for decades afterward a professor at USC's Annenberg School.[17] That was it for day one.[18]

Day two began with two and a half hours of classical music, followed by Harvard theologian Paul Tillich with a one-hour lecture on "Basic Religious Questions of Our Time." After that came more classical music and a short story. Later in the week, jazz shows featured Charlie Parker, Dizzy Gillespie and Miles Davis, as well as Django Reinhardt and earlier players including Jelly Roll Morton and Sidney Bechet. There was a book show, a Jewish folklore show, children's programs, and live drama—a reading of George Bernard Shaw's *Man of Destiny* in KPFK's own studio.

The public affairs programming in the first month included several of the big thinkers of the day: left-wing sociologist C. Wright Mills lecturing on "The Decline of the Left"; social critic and Harvard professor David Reisman on "The American Future"; Aldous Huxley, British expatriate novelist and author of the dystopian *Brave New World*, on "The Human Situation"; and UCLA chemist Willard F. Libby on "nuclear energy" (he would soon win the Nobel Prize for discovering radiocarbon dating).

The first KPFK *Folio*, the publication for subscribers that included the program guide as well as editorial comment, made its political stance clear: "All shades of the political spectrum are represented," the *Folio* declared; "ten commentators view the news from a different perspective." KPFK was committed to no political position. "Our aims are humanistic," it concluded. "We want to be a concert hall, a lecture room and a part of your living room." Notably missing: any promise to focus on civil rights or nuclear disarmament or the Cuban Revolution—big issues for the Left in 1959.

But KPFK's original management, unlike the Pacifica Foundation, did not come from World War II–era pacifists. The first general manager, who built the station, was Terry Drinkwater, later an award-winning reporter for *CBS News*. Far from refusing to serve in the military, Drinkwater had been an ROTC company commander as an undergrad at Pomona College, and after graduating in 1958, he served as a lieutenant in the US Army infantry. As a Pomona student his passion for radio had already been evident: he founded the Pomona College student-run radio station, KSPC, his roommate Spencer Olin recalled, "and spent countless hours there acquiring equipment, raising funds, and building it up. He was totally committed to that project." But politically Drinkwater was "not especially ideological," Olin recalled. "His father, Terrell Drinkwater Sr., was a very conservative Republican and president of Western Airlines. But Terry was not outspokenly Democrat or Republican."[19]

Between leaving Pomona and KSPC and coming to L.A. to start KPFK, Drinkwater went to Berkeley to work at KPFA. His Berkeley roommate, John M. Anderson, recalled that, at KPFA, "he promoted the idea of a Pacifica station in Los Angeles, the Pacifica board agreed,

and sometime in mid-1959 he moved to L.A. to help start KPFK."
Anderson agreed that Drinkwater "had no strong attachment to either
major party"; he "saw the world with a reporter's skepticism."[20]

The original KPFK news department "was anything but left wing,"
recalled Ed Cray, the first assistant director of public affairs and one
of three people who produced the news with journalist Gene Marine,
who had come down from KPFA along with Drinkwater. (After
helping set up the KPFK news department, Marine would return to
work in the Bay Area, later writing for the *Nation* and then *Ramparts*,
as well as publishing one of the first books about the Black Panthers.)
The news was "straight down the middle," Ed Cray recalled. "Gene
and I had plenty of opinions, especially on local politics, but we were
trained in the old school: your opinion doesn't count."[21]

The first week of programming also included Alan Watts's "Way
Beyond the West." Watts had started broadcasting a weekly show in
1953 for KPFA in Berkeley, and by 1959 he was well known not only
in the Bay Area but nationwide for his book *The Way of Zen*. He
became the most listened-to programmer in the history of the station.
Part of his strength was that his programs were not taped public
lectures like those of Aldous Huxley, David Reisman and C. Wright
Mills; Watts talked alone in a studio with a microphone, speaking with
remarkable clarity, calm and flawless diction, and seemingly one to
one. Then there was his message: the self is an illusion; the goal was
for "cosmic consciousness" to replace "self-consciousness," to live
in the here and now, in the "eternal moment," rather than thinking
about the past and the future—in particular, worrying about death.

Watts was "the perfect middle-class Zen master," historian Matthew
Lasar argues. According to Watts, you didn't need to engage in the
rigorous discipline of meditation and study with an approved teacher
to achieve a Zen-like state. He called that "square Zen." He rejected,
as well, a second false path, "Beat Zen"—dropping out, rejecting the
world. In fact, Watts was promoting what we now call "Orientalism,"
what Lasar calls the "well-worn imperial stereotypes" of an earlier
era. But in the Cold War context, telling Americans they had a lot
to learn from the Chinese was a bold and subversive message.[22] And
it was clearly "un-American" to embrace Zen Buddhism in a deeply

Christian country that had recently added "under God" to its pledge of allegiance (in 1954) and made "In God we trust" its official motto (in 1956).

KPFK's first week was greeted by the print media with enthusiasm. The *Times* headline read "KPFK 'Cultural Bomb' Will Explode Today." Calling it "the non-commercial, educational station," the paper declared that "listeners will be glad to hear that editorializing is reserved for the commentators and will not be contained in regular news shows." It added that "commentators range from liberal to conservative, so that all shades of opinion will be presented." A *Times* columnist called KPFK "the ultimate in FM broadcasting." And the *LA Examiner* declared that the station "will have the support of influential and creative people." "Thirty commercial FM stations are currently beaming their daily programs to the 52 percent of Southern Californians who own FM receivers," said *Westways*, the widely read magazine of the Automobile Club of Southern California; "Now we shall be fortunate enough to receive the first non-commercial, listener-sponsored FM station in the area ... our Southern California brain stimulator." *Time* magazine was equally enthusiastic: "Don't subscribe yourself unless you're prepared to be caught up in something: A radio station operated for adult minds really does get to be a religion, after you've had a chance to hear it for a while." *Frontier* magazine reported that "KPFK will be powerful enough—75,000 watts—to blanket the Southland in a sophisticated cloud that will reach its estimated 2,000,000 FM listeners."[23]

KPFK's first fund drive illustrated the station's early emphasis on "balance" and "quality" over left-wing programming. A one-day event, it came two days after the broadcast of the documentary on the HUAC protest in San Francisco. The problem, the *Folio* declared, was that "a scant 7,000 homes have subscribed ... not enough." The fund drive featured actors James Mason with Jack Lemmon and Rod Serling; an interview with Aldous Huxley; Vincent Price reading from *Henry V*, and Ray Bradbury reading one of his stories; a performance by Pete Seeger; Stan Freberg talking about advertising; humor from Mort Sahl; and a special jazz program for KPFK with Buddy Collette, Terry Gibbs, Shelly Manne and others. Fund-raisers pointed to the other distinguished programming of the previous month, including the Beckett play *Embers*, recorded by BBC; Faulkner reading from *As I Lay Dying*; and film director Jean Renoir talking about Albert Camus in the wake of his untimely death that January.[24]

After just one year on the air, KPFK in 1960 won broadcasting's highest honor, the Peabody Award. The citation—for locally produced programs—praised the station for covering "a wide range of subjects," naming the programs "Arming to Parley," on which Cold War liberal theologian Reinhold Niebuhr discussed "American military and political problems"; "Conversations on Freedom," with Brandeis University faculty talking about civil liberties; and "Not Merely a Business," a documentary on "Freedom and control of radio and television in a democratic society."[25] The station won a second Peabody the following year.

In 1963, the station launched the Renaissance Pleasure Faire, billed as "a benefit for the support and preservation of KPFK," to be held in May. KPFK subscriber Phyllis Patterson had the idea—she taught history and English in LA public schools and had assigned a class project of setting up a "Renaissance fair" in her backyard in the Hollywood Hills. More than 300 people showed up at an organizing party for her idea of a station fundraiser. Eventually 600 people "contributed materials, time and talent" in putting together the structures, booths and activities, with grounds—in North Hollywood—designed to suggest a spring market fair in England around 1580. Or, as the *Folio* put it: "Up the dusty lane procede the motley bande of revelers. Jesters leap high, the bright be-decked oxen pull commedia players on their cart ... bells of Morris dancers jingle loudly and they raise the Maypole." Also "canopied tradesmen's stalls ... recorder grounds, dancers and jugglers ... candles, jewelry, leather goods, paintings, pottery ... trestled tables laden with piping hot beef, leg of fowl and rich, dark breads; pastries, tartes and cakes"; and for the kids, "Punch and Judy, puppet making, fortune telling and donkey carts."[26] The first one was a complete success, with over 3,000 people buying tickets. The Faire became a huge event in subsequent years, a countercultural celebration of precapitalist village life that spread across the United States. Later, in the Nineties, it was taken over by a profit-making corporation.

In 1963, after fighting off HUAC, the FCC, and SISS, KPFK stopped trying to be a neutral forum. "The struggle for dialogue," Matthew Lasar explains, "seemed pointless in a society that swiftly punished those Americans who spoke their minds."[27] And the concept of "balance" was now radically redefined: instead of the station balancing Left and Right in its own programming, its public affairs shows would provide balance to the mainstream media and their unquestioning adherence to Cold War anti-communism in both domestic and foreign policy. At the same time, several of the station's leading commentators on the right had refused to appear on a station that broadcast programs featuring Communists—so the notion of "balance" in programming was undermined by the right as well as being redefined by the Left.

The political transformation became clear pretty quickly. Later that year, KPFK and Pacifica began airing I. F. Stone and Bertrand Russell opposing the US war in Vietnam, two years before the anti-war movement developed. In June 1964 the station broadcast an interview with Che Guevara by Betty Petty Pilkington, a freelance journalist.[28] Then, in 1965, KPFK broadcast WBAI reporter Chris Koch's reports from North Vietnam, making Pacifica Radio the first American news organization to send reporters to the North. In 1966 KPFK broadcast discussions of the future of the civil rights movement with leaders of SNCC, CORE, SDS and the SCLC.

The folk music, classical and jazz shows continued, and the children's programming continued, as did Alan Watts. In fact, even at the end of the Sixties, classical music still filled more hours at KPFK than anything else: on a typical broadcast day in January 1969, which ran from 6 a.m. until midnight, KPFK ran three one-hour programs of classical music. Though they did run a one-hour special about the Beatles that month, it was preceded by a Mozart piano concerto, and followed by Prokofiev's opera *War and Peace*.[29]

KPFK had become a key institution of the Left in L.A. In 1969, the station opened the "KPFK Watts Bureau," a project to train a dozen Blacks in South Central about radio production, writing, and reporting. Their work, broadcast on KPFK, included a thirty-minute documentary, *The Black Man 1970*.[30]

Then, on June 7, 1974, KPFK broadcast a tape that began, "This is Tanya." She said, "I want to talk about the way I knew our six murdered comrades." Tanya was Patty Hearst, heiress of the right-wing newspaper family; she'd been kidnapped in Berkeley three months earlier, when she was nineteen, by the Symbionese Liberation Army, which aspired to be an urban guerilla organization. A month after the kidnapping she had released a tape saying she was joining the SLA. Two weeks after that she was photographed robbing a bank; a month later, 400 LAPD officers surrounded a house in South L.A. where several SLA members were hiding. A furious gun battle broke out, broadcast live on TV, which ended with the house catching fire. Six SLA members were killed by the LAPD that day. Two weeks after the shootout, on June 7, 1974, the tape from "Tanya" was dropped off outside the KPFK studio in North Hollywood, and the station put it on the air. After paying tribute to each of her six dead comrades, "Tanya" concluded with the SLA motto: "Death to the fascist insect that preys upon the life of the people!"[31]

A federal grand jury investigating the SLA subpoenaed the tape, but KPFK general manger Will Lewis refused to hand it over, arguing that the subpoena violated the First Amendment guarantee of freedom of the press. Officials said the subpoena had been "personally approved" by Attorney General William Saxbe—who had been appointed by Nixon during the "Saturday Night Massacre" at the climax of the Watergate crisis, after Elliot Richardson opted to resign from the post rather than follow orders to fire the Watergate special prosecutor. Lewis pointed out that he had given authorities a copy of the tape, but not the original, which might have contained fingerprints or other identifying information about its source, and that journalistic ethics required the protection of sources. The federal judge presiding over the case, A. Andrew Hauk, found Lewis guilty of contempt and ordered him jailed for the duration of the grand jury term—three months.[32] (He was released—after sixteen days at the federal prison on Terminal Island in L.A.—on an order from Supreme Court Justice William O. Douglas, who declared that the case raised "substantial First Amendment claims."[33])

The jailing of KPFK's general manager marked the political climax of the fifteen-year history of the radio station that had become a key institution of the Los Angeles Left. At that point, the station, whose budget came from listener contributions, had 15,000 subscribers (donors), according to the *Times*, and a listening audience of 300,000.[34] That's why, in 1974, it was KPFK rather than any other station in Southern California that would broadcast the tape that began, "This is Tanya."

10

A Quarter of a Million Readers: The *LA Free Press* (1964–70)

T he underground press of the Sixties is often described as self-indulgent; critics said it "trampled the tenets of accuracy and fairness," while the mainstream media of the era is often portrayed as bland and cautious, and as practicing a phony objectivity.[1] That was not true of the newspaper landscape in Los Angeles. The *LA Times* was firmly and loudly right-wing, while the *LA Free Press* (the "*Freep*"), the first underground paper of the era, and the most successful, was often a voice of reason, albeit a passionate one. A simple comparison of the coverage of the 1965 Watts uprising reveals a great deal. The first day of the riots, the *Times* front-page headline read "'Get Whitey,' Scream Blood-Hungry Mobs" (an "eyewitness account"), accompanied by an "expert" analysis ("Racial Unrest Laid to Negro Family Failure") and the editorial "Anarchy Must End."[2]

The headline in the *Freep* read "The Negroes Have Voted!"

Freep editor Art Kunkin declared on page one, "It is time to listen to the Negro." The problem in Watts, he said, wasn't the breakdown of "law and order," but rather the old order itself, which in any case was "doomed." On the front page, a map of Watts was captioned with a quote from Alexis de Tocqueville: "It is always a great crime to deprive a people of its liberty on the pretext that it is using it wrongly."[3]

Meanwhile at the *Times*, the editorial declared that the "criminal terrorism" in the streets of Watts should not be "dismissed ... as the inevitable result of economic and sociological pressures." The *Freep* instead pointed to root causes: jobs, education, housing, "a super-disaster situation in the Negro ghetto for years," Kunkin wrote. "The people are fed up with unemployment, with subsistence on government handouts and Bureau of Public Assistance checks."

The *Times* called for a governor's commission to investigate, but said the number one question they should take up was why the National Guard wasn't called sooner. And, the editors warned, "the commission should be cautious of irresponsible critics of the Los Angeles Police Department and its chief, William H. Parker."[4]

It wasn't just the editorials in the *Times*; their reporters in Watts—all white, of course—emphasized the threat from "screaming" mobs of Black "wild men," who were reported to be shouting, "It's too late, white man. You had your chance. Now it's our turn"; "Next time you see us we'll be carrying guns"; and, "We have nothing to lose." The reporter concluded that the mood of Black people in the streets was "sickening."[5]

The *Freep*, for its part, published reports of the uprising written by Blacks—its most significant contribution. One, on the front page, described a corner where four cops were beating a Black man with billy clubs, as a Black crowd gathered, shouting, "Don't kill that man!" Then, "the crowd began to attack the officers." The cops told them, "Go home, niggers." The crowd grew; "The officers first attempted to fight but then ran away."[6] In the *Freep's* reporting, the Blacks' target was not "whitey" in general; instead they were retaliating against particular LAPD officers who were acting particularly brutally. Kunkin was able to recruit Black writers, he said, because "I did a lot of work with CORE. I built up personal capital in the Black community, so as soon as Watts happened there were people there writing for the paper."[7]

The nation's first and most successful underground paper of the Sixties, the *Freep* at its peak in 1970 published forty-eight pages every week, had a guaranteed paid circulation of 85,000, and boasted a "faithful readership" estimated at a quarter of a million. At the time, among alternative weeklies, only the *Village Voice*, started a decade earlier, had more readers. The *Freep's* founder, Kunkin, was not a naïve hippie or flower child, but rather an experienced Old Left journalist. When he published the first issue in 1964, he was thirty-five and already a movement elder. A New Yorker who had gone to Bronx High School of Science, he had become a tool and die maker, and—by then a Marxist—joined the Trotskyite Socialist Workers Party (SWP), working at GM and Ford in the Fifties and becoming business manager of the SWP newspaper, the *Militant*. In the early 1960s he moved to L.A. and, he says, "went back to school to become a history professor." A faculty member asked whether he wanted to work on a new Mexican-American newspaper, the *East LA Almanac*. It published eight pages, once a month, 5,000 copies, and was associated with MAPA, the new Mexican American Political Association, headed by Edward Roybal—the first Latino on the LA City Council, and later the first Latino member of Congress from California. "I was the political editor," Kunkin said, "listed on the masthead as Arturo, and I'm writing about garbage collections in East Los Angeles." By that time he had left the SWP, joined the less radical Socialist Party, and become its Southern California chairman: "I was working closely with Norman Thomas and with Erich Fromm, the famous psychologist," he said. "I wrote some resolutions with Erich Fromm against the Democratic Party drift of the Socialist Party."[8]

He started planning the *Freep* in January 1963, after a visit from the FBI. They had read his criticisms of LBJ in the *East LA Almanac*, and asked whether he was a Communist and whether he could identify names on a list of suspected Communists. He told them he was a socialist and an anti-communist, and that he refused to talk about other people. Two days later, after the FBI visited the *East LA Almanac*, he was fired. He had long been complaining to friends hanging out at the Sunset Strip coffee shop Xanadu about the *Village Voice*: while it excelled at covering the hip scene and ran some strong writing, politically it always supported liberal Democrats. People told Kunkin he couldn't publish a *Voice*-type independent paper in L.A. because the city had no Greenwich Village; it was too spread out and fragmented, and besides, it would require at least $10,000 to get started. But Kunkin went ahead anyway, looking for financial backers.[9]

Meanwhile, he became a commentator at KPFK, producing a show called "What I Would Like to Do with a Newspaper in Los Angeles." That was two weeks before the station's annual fundraiser, the Renaissance Pleasure Faire. The volunteer in charge of the fair, Phyllis Patterson, told him "I was going to do a paper for the fair, but I didn't have time to get it together. Maybe you'd like to do a paper for the fair." So he sold $200 in advertising, printed 5,000 copies of an eight-page paper, and put together a clever front page, reporting on contemporary issues as if they were medieval news: students holding ban-the-crossbow demonstrations, Shakespeare getting arrested for obscenity, a review of an exhibit of the *Mona Lisa*.

Inside the "Faire" issue, the distinctive logo appeared for the first time: "*Los Angeles Free Press*," and real news: a report on a police bust of a theater manager for showing the soon-to-be-legendary Kenneth Anger short *Scorpio Rising* (gay bikers apparently offended the DA); a story about Joan Baez's refusal to pay her taxes in protest of the military budget; and some music reviews—along with a statement that the editors wanted to start a paper like the *Village Voice* and a subscription coupon. They had a couple of thousand copies left when the Faire ended. So, Kunkin says, "I refolded the paper and put the *Free Press* pages on the outside." Those were sold mainly at coffee houses on Sunset Strip, and one of them, the Fifth Estate, run by Al Mitchell, let Kunkin use the basement as an office. "I spent the next month writing a business plan and trying to raise $10,000"—but got only $600. "I started the paper with that," he said. John Bryan, a one-time mainstream journalist who became managing editor of the *Free Press* before he quit in protest to start his own weekly, *Open City*, called Kunkin "a disappointed Trotskyist factory organizer."[10] Indeed, it turned out that Kunkin was much better at running a radical weekly in L.A. than at organizing auto workers in Detroit: he published the *Freep* every week for the next ten years without missing a single issue.[11]

The first standalone issue of the *Freep* was dated July 30, 1964. "A New Weekly," it proclaimed in a front-page statement, "Why We Appear." Kunkin opened by declaring that while the paper represented no party or group, "we class ourselves … among the liberals." Of course, Kunkin himself was not a liberal; he had been a member of the SWP and at the time was a leader of the Socialist Party in L.A., which made it a point to criticize liberals. Apparently he thought that L.A. in 1964 was not ready for a paper that criticized liberals from the left. Kunkin *did* promise that the *Freep* would be "free enough to print material disagreeing with liberal organizations," and indeed the paper would start doing that pretty quickly. But at the beginning, Kunkin declared his goal was "to link together the various sections of our far flung liberal community." He also said "we do not plan to deal with national and international events"—instead, the paper would focus on Los Angeles.[12]

The top story in that first stand-alone issue, however, was not about L.A., but San Francisco: headlined "Bank of America vs. CORE," it reported on protests against discrimination in hiring at the bank headquarters, where hundreds marched and eleven had been arrested. The cover also included a photo of a sculpture by a local LA artist charged with obscenity—an issue the *Freep* would cover often.[13] Inside the issue readers found a critique of L.A.'s mainstream newspapers; a column by the grand old man of the Beat era, Lawrence Lipton; a "calendar of hip events"; and reviews of Brecht, Baldwin and Nabokov.

The paper was sold on the street by hippies—mostly on Sunset Strip—and from street-corner vending boxes. After a year, circulation was only 5,000, a far cry from Kunkin's goal: to match the *Village Voice*'s paid circulation of 27,600. However, his outstanding coverage of Watts brought a dramatic jump in paid circulation—to 25,000—and by the end of summer 1965, Kunkin considered the *Freep* a success.[14] Another measure of success came in 1966, when the *Times* ran a big feature on the paper. The reporter opened the piece not with an analysis of the paper's contents or agenda, but rather with a description of "the little girl of 14" reading the paper on Sunset Strip. She had, he said, "the blondest of golden surfer-girl hair"; bare feet, "tight-tight red bellbottoms, and on top she wears a French, frilly-lace, crop-top halter that shows only about 12 inches of bronzed midriff." And amazingly, she was "holding a newspaper. Not a copy of *Tiger Beat*, or *Teen*, or *True Romance*." The *Times* article went on to describe Kunkin, in his "dismally brown sports jacket—no one could accuse *him* of being a beatnik"—and yet his receptionist was a girl who wore "fashionable sandals."[15]

Over the next decade the *Freep* covered the full range of Sixties issues: anti-war protest, civil rights action, draft resistance, the farmworkers' struggle, environmental politics. It published Herbert Marcuse, Jean-Paul Sartre, Allen Ginsberg and Susan Sontag.[16] It supported the gay rights movement in L.A. enthusiastically. Despite Kunkin's first-issue declaration that the paper was "liberal," the *Freep* consistently opposed the Democrats. "He Who Votes for Lesser of 2 Evils Forgets That He Is Voting for Evil," a front-page article declared just before midterm election of 1966. The piece challenged the argument made in an essay titled "Young Democrat Answers New Left," written by Henry Waxman, president of the California Young Democrats (and future hero of liberals for his thirty years in the House). Waxman said the real enemy of progress was "Birchites, Southern rednecks, and old-fashioned conservatives," but the New Left had "adopted an extreme hostility toward 'liberals' and a so-called 'establishment.'" The *Freep* replied that LBJ had been elected after promising not to send American boys to fight in Southeast Asia, while liberals had called Goldwater a warmonger—but once in office, LBJ sent 300,000 US troops to "wage war on the legitimate aspirations of the Vietnamese people."[17] In 1968 the paper covered the rise of the Peace and Freedom Party. But the paper's readers remained divided: in a 1968 "Man of the Year" poll, anti-war Democratic Eugene McCarthy beat Black Panther Eldridge Cleaver—by one vote.[18]

To his credit, Kunkin rejected attempts to paper over movement problems in print. Once, a reporter submitted an article about a memorial observance of Martin Luther King's assassination that failed to mention that a Black nationalist had shot at one of the scheduled speakers, or that a guard had accidentally fired into the ceiling of the room. "Why not?" Kunkin asked. "We didn't want to criticize the black movement," the writer replied. Kunkin responded with incredulity; in his eyes, the incident evinced "the divisions of the black movement, and the inadequate preparations of the guards. This story ought to be written before somebody gets killed."[19] Not long after, two LA Black Panthers were killed at UCLA by Black nationalists.

Of course, the *Freep* covered popular culture as well. For instance, it ran an outstanding column of TV criticism by legendary fantasy and science fiction writer Harlan Ellison. He described his "credentials" at the outset: "I am not a Communist, a drunkard, a doper, a lunatic, a straight, a hippie, a Democrat, a Republican, an astrology freak, a macrobiotic nut, a subscriber to *The National Review*, or even a member of the staff of the *Freep*. I am all alone out here, setting down what I've seen and what it means to me." But "make no mistake," he declared: "I am *not* really talking about tv here, I am talking about dissidence, repression, censorship, the brutality and stupidity of much of our culture … the dangers of being passive in a time when the individual is merely cannon-fodder, the lying and cheating and killing … in the sweet name of the American Way."[20]

One of the most distinctive elements of the underground press was the cartoons, which were crucial in defining the Sixties sensibility. Kunkin found the right cartoonist for the new era: Ron Cobb, whose work for the *Freep* was syndicated widely and became emblematic of the underground press, second only to that of Robert Crumb. A former Disney cartoonist and Vietnam vet, Cobb's unmistakable style featured grim black humor: in one cartoon, a confused man wanders through a postnuclear landscape carrying a broken portable TV, looking for a place to plug it in; in another, on the moon, two Black men in space suits clean up the junk left by previous missions.

The *Free Press* covered the music scene and reviewed movies, and, like the rest of the underground press, ran the "Dr. Hip Pocrates" syndicated column of drug and sex advice from a Berkeley psychiatrist. But compared to the rest of the underground press, the *Freep*'s focus was less on the counterculture and more on radical politics. One key example: criticism of Eastern and New Age religion. A few months after the Beatles met the Maharishi Mahesh Yogi, the founder of Transcendental Meditation, Kunkin published the piece "Maharishi's Take on Vietnam: Obey your Leaders."[21] The *Freep* was a New Left paper rather than a hippie paper.[22]

But despite its anti-capitalist politics, the paper was not collectively owned or managed. "I wasn't really concerned with making the paper a representative of the new society," Kunkin later explained. "What

I was concerned with was making it into as strong an influence as possible. My own attitude was that there was nobody else's name on the line. From one year to the next, there were entirely different people involved."[23] So Kunkin remained the owner as well as publisher and editor.

What about women's liberation? That topic, and movement, were blind spots for much of the rest of the underground press, where male editors were wedded to the notion that they were in charge, and that freedom meant publishing photos or drawings of naked women and ads for sex. At the *San Francisco Express Times*, editor Marvin Garson said "'Women's Liberation Front' sounded like a joke, then like a lesbian conspiracy ... and finally like a Trotskyist splinter group." At the *Berkeley Barb*, editor Max Scherr published a dismissive article on the new Berkeley women's movement headlined "The Women are Revolting."[24] Those were not Kunkin's responses. When he invited critics to a public meeting in March 1970, a lot of people (sixty) showed up. "Those representing women's liberation" were "the most visible, the most numerous, and the most vocal," he wrote in the following week's issue. They complained first about the sex ads—which, they said, "depict women in demeaning and offensive ways"—and also about the position, and pay, of women on the staff. Responding in print, Kunkin pledged to help a group planning to launch a "women's lib paper in LA"—a very good idea. He also promised to publish an agreement with the staff that would include a minimum wage and a fully prepaid medical and dental plan—which sounds amazing today—along with an equally amazing grievance procedure, providing for "an arbitration panel of movement leaders to intervene with full decision-making powers." As for the sex ads, he said he "would be willing to listen to anyone who had a serious plan to finance the *Free Press* without resorting to advertising, but doubted that such a plan would materialize."[25]

The *Free Press* did cover some aspects of the nascent women's liberation movement, especially abortion. "Is Mexican Abortion Dangerous?" a front-page headline asked in 1967—well before abortion rights became a national issue.[26] (The answer was "yes.") Starting in 1969 it regularly ran stories criticizing the conventional notions of feminine beauty, attacking the institution of marriage, and supporting lesbian rights. And, true to Kunkin's word, the *Free Press* celebrated the publication of the local feminist underground paper *Everywoman* when it appeared in 1970.[27]

The *Freep* didn't just report on events—it helped organize them. A month after Watts the *Freep* held a two-hour forum onstage at a movie theater in the Black neighborhood on West Adams Boulevard near La Brea. The six panelists included Black Assemblyman Mervyn Dymally, who served as moderator, and leaders of the local chaptersof CORE, N-VAC, United Citizens of Watts, and the Afro-American Cultural Association. Their main theme: the underlying cause of the riots was "the fact that over 30% of the people in Watts don't have jobs ... and do not control their community."[28]

The *Freep* also sponsored free music festivals. The 1968 "Bastille Day Bash" on Venice Pier featured Frank Zappa and the Mothers of Invention and other bands, including the Paul Butterfield Blues Band and Ramblin' Jack Elliot. "Wear costumes and masks," the *Free Press* poster said. "Do your thing on the beach: swimming, body painting, sculpture, sand castles, listening, loafing, dancing, playing, freaking ... Be kind, be pure, avoid busts." 25,000 people showed up.[29]

And the *Freep* ran bookstores—in Westwood, Pasadena and Fairfax. Its Fairfax store, "The Kazoo," was located right across the street from Canter's legendary late-night deli. The *New Yorker*'s Renata Adler visited, reporting that the Kazoo was open until two in the morning, and that along with books, it carried "innumerable little magazines and obscure works," including "works on drugs and hallucinogens, and some works on religions of the East." The store also sold posters, cigarette papers, roach clips, and buttons, including "Be Creative, Invent a Sexual Perversion."[30]

The *Freep* had all kind of enemies. Its offices were firebombed on May 1, 1968;[31] sheriff's deputies seized eighty street-corner vending boxes in January 1968;[32] and in September 1968, the FBI decided to mail copies of the *Freep* to the paper's landlord in the hope of getting them evicted. (It didn't work.)[33] The FBI investigated the paper in 1970 for "ITOM"—Interstate Transportation of Obscene Matter

—and the FBI file on the *Freep* includes carefully cut and pasted items from the paper's classified ads: "Male Nude 'Action' Photos," "Pornography from Denmark," "Color Climax Magazines."[34] The FBI closed its investigation after being told that the US Postal Service was considering prosecution of the *Freep* for mailing obscene matter, while the US Attorney concluded that the *Freep*'s advertising policy "appeared similar to other newspapers including legitimate Santa Monica and San Francisco newspapers." The US Attorney also noted that "The FREE PRESS is milder in content than many currently in distribution."[35]

It was an official national "problem"; Congress established a national Commission on Obscenity and Pornography, which held hearings in L.A., at which Kunkin testified. "The young American today knows more about sex and its place in human relationships than perhaps any other comparable group in human history," he told the commissioners, and "they do not see anything at all obscene about the human body." What was "obscene," he said, was "to kill people in Southeast Asia ... while mouthing words about democracy." The real function of obscenity prosecution, he said, was "to attempt a censorship of unpopular political and literary expression" with criminal trials that bankrupted small radical publications that relied on sex ads to pay the bills.[36]

The underground paper that the *Freep* gave birth to, *Open City*, began publishing in May 1967. Editor John Bryan, before working as Kunkin's managing editor, had been a reporter and editor for the *LA Herald-Examiner*, the *LA Mirror* and the *San Francisco Chronicle*. He was from the older generation—like Kunkin, in his mid thirties in the mid Sixties—and he quit the *Freep* when Kunkin refused to run a horrifying photo of a napalm-seared Vietnamese baby on the front page.[37] *Open City*'s circulation peaked at 30,000 before it stopped publication early in 1969.[38] Bryan started *Open City* with his own money, and in the first issue he promised that the paper would highlight "the angry and determined minorities who continue to challenge the worst contemporary madness and injustice"—which "the town's sell-out daily press so nervously ignores." And, he said, the paper would cover "the perpetuation of police state terrorism which singles out socially harmless psychic voyagers whose experiences with hallucinogenic drugs make them less likely to join in the current militarist-materialist rat race." He also published a column, "Notes of a Dirty Old Man," by LA beat poet Charles Bukowski; even *Time* called Bukowski "a laureate of American low life."[39]

Open City's greatest coup was reporting that mainstream media photos of LBJ bidding farewell to Vietnam-bound marines at Camp Pendleton had been staged; all the marines scheduled to leave for Vietnam, *Open City* discovered, had left a week earlier. When the brass at Camp Pendleton were told the president was on his way to give a speech to departing troops, they "rounded up all available Marines—many from local bars," put them in full battle dress, turned them out to hear the president, and then "marched them into waiting transport planes." The president, according to *Open City*, never knew the truth.[40]

It was obscenity charges that brought down *Open City*. The paper published a half-page ad for best-selling rocker Leon Russell that featured a photo of a naked woman with Russell and his partner, who was holding her knees apart. Defenders said it was a parody of the use of sex to sell products, and columnist Art Seidenbaum argued in the *LA Times*, "I'd rather see prosecutors restrain themselves instead of the press." Still, Kunkin himself had turned the ad down, calling it "exploitative."[41] Bryan was put on trial and fined $1,000, and *Open City* was shut down shortly thereafter, in March 1968. Kunkin paid tribute in an editorial: "The establishment didn't like *Open City*. It saw too much and said too much ... It let voices be heard which too often were smothered ... Where *Open City* died another must spring up. There's room in this town and this society for more than one alternate voice paper."[42]

At its peak in 1969, the *Free Press* sold a hundred thousand copies a week. The company, including the three bookstores, employed 150 people and made $2 million a year. Although Kunkin was publisher and editor, "the staff collectively decided what articles ran in the papers." The only clearly defined jobs were ad sales and bookkeeping. "Money was pooled," historian Abe Peck reports. Kunkin welcomed a union, and *Free Press* staffers "could be nearly as well paid as mainstream ad reps and editors."[43]

Then the trouble began. On August 8, 1969, the *Freep* front-page headline read "Narcotics Agents Listed: There Should be no Secret Police." Inside was a list of eighty undercover agents of the state bureau of narcotics, along with their home phone numbers and addresses. The paper called it "a public service announcement." Kunkin and reporter Jerry Applebaum were charged with receiving stolen property—the list—and the state attorney general filed a $10 million obstruction-of-justice suit against Kunkin, his corporation, and the staff. The agents also filed a separate civil suit for invasion of privacy, seeking $15 million.

You might say Kunkin had been foolish to risk everything on this one story, but his lawyers had told him there was no law against publishing the names—which was true at the time. (In response to the *Free Press* case, Governor Reagan quickly signed a bill making unauthorized publication of names of "peace officers" a misdemeanor.) The list, provided by a mail clerk in the state attorney general's office, had not been stolen; it was xeroxed and then returned. Nothing on the document indicated that it was classified or secret. In fact, it was the Bureau's Christmas card mailing list.[44]

Kunkin's front-page editorial made the case for publishing the names: "History demonstrates that the secret policeman invariably uses his anonymity to become unaccountable to the people over whom power is exercised." And the goal of the undercover narcs, the *Freep* declared, was to "enforce laws as unwise and unenforceable as the now-banished prohibition of liquor." Fifty years later, that assessment of the law became the basis for decriminalizing marijuana possession in many states, including California.

At the trial, the prosecutor (Ronald George, who later went on to become chief justice of the state supreme court) had to prove the list had been stolen, and that Kunkin and Applebaum had known it was stolen. Kunkin told the judge he was acting as a journalist and that the First Amendment guarantee of freedom of the press entitled him to examine any public document not classified or marked confidential. The prosecutor replied that it was not a freedom of the press case, but rather a stolen property case. In July 1970, the jury convicted the two of receiving stolen property, a felony, and the judge sentenced them to three years' probation plus fines of $1,000 for Kunkin and $500 for Applebaum.[45] By the end of the year, the *Freep* settled the obstruction of justice case by agreeing to a payment of $10,000; according to Peck, "a larger deal was made with the agents." Kunkin and Applebaum appealed their criminal convictions, winning their cases in April 1973 when the state supreme court ruled unanimously that the prosecution had not established that the defendants had received property knowing it was stolen.[46] And, according to Peck, "the narcs never received the money."[47]

The paper began a downhill editorial slide with its enthusiastic defense of Charles Manson, arrested in October 1969. Starting in January 1970, the *Freep* featured Manson on its front page for three weeks in a row: "Manson Can Go Free!" "M. D. On Manson's Sex Life!" "Manson Interview! Exclusive Exclusive!" Then the paper began a weekly column by Manson written from jail.[48] Several dozen "news" stories followed. *Rolling Stone* tried to explain: The *Freep* was "undoubtedly hypersensitive to the relentless gloating of the cops who, after a five-year search, finally found a longhaired devil you could love to hate."[49] To others it looked like Kunkin was choosing sensationalism over New Left politics.

In the meantime, in 1969, the company that printed the *Freep* had refused to continue—Kunkin said the prosecutors in the narcs case had told the owner he too would be sued unless he quit printing the paper. No other Southern California printer would take the job, and Kunkin was forced to print the paper in the Bay Area and put the new issues on the train to L.A. To end his reliance on fearful printing companies, Kunkin bought his own printing plant and a new state-of-the-art press—a monster twenty feet high, printing sixteen tabloid pages at a time (most presses at that point did eight). It cost a quarter of a million dollars but promised independence and freedom—and he could make money printing for other newspapers. But, he said, "the press didn't work!"

The expense bankrupted Kunkin. The staff quit and started their own paper, the *Staff*, which didn't last long. Kunkin was forced to sell the *Free Press* and its crippled printing operation to two pornographers, remaining as editor while becoming an employee. In July 1973, he was fired from the paper he had founded ten years earlier.[50] For the rest of the Seventies, it published mostly sex ads.

11

Before Stonewall: Gay L.A. (1964–70)

The crime: kissing at midnight on New Year's Eve, 1967; fourteen men arrested by the LAPD vice squad. The place: the Black Cat, a gay bar on Sunset Boulevard in Echo Park. The charge: "lewd conduct."

Police raids on bars had been a familiar part of gay life for decades, but this one had a sequel that made history. Five weeks later, several hundred people—perhaps 500 or more—gathered in the bar's parking lot to protest the raid. Marchers on Sunset Boulevard carried signs reading "No More Abuse of Our Rights and Dignity," "Abolish Arbitrary Arrests," "Stop Illegal Search and Seizure," "End Illegal Entrapment," and "Blue Fascism Must Go!" It was February 11, 1967, more than two years before the Stonewall Uprising in New York (June 28, 1969): the first gay rally against police violence in America, the earliest gay street demonstration, and the historic beginning of the gay liberation movement.[1]

The demonstration had been called by PRIDE, a group founded in L.A. in 1966—the name was originally an acronym for "Personal Rights in Defense and Education." They called their meetings "Pride Night" and the bar where they met "Pride Hall." According to historians Lillian Faderman and Stuart Timmons, it was "probably the first application of the word to gay politics"—another "before Stonewall" moment.[2]

The LAPD actions that provoked the first gay street protest in America were described in a leaflet circulated by *Tangents*, an LA gay magazine founded in 1966. That New Year's Eve,

12 vice-squad officers—plainclothesmen—started beating patrons to the floor about 5 minutes after midnight. They did not identify themselves except by their weapons. After beating the patrons, the 14 to be arrested were laid face down on the sidewalk outside the bar. 5 patrol cars, containing 2 uniformed officers each, were brought from a near-by side street where they had been parked for some time and the individuals arrested were taken to the newly opened Rampart St. Police Station. Three bartenders were among those arrested.[3]

The *LA Free Press* immediately saw that the Black Cat Tavern protest was a transformative moment for gay people. "All over the city, homosexuals are determined that they will no longer 'cop out' to the lesser charge if they are arrested. And when someone else is arrested, they will come forward as witnesses, even though police may bring pressure on their employers."[4]

One more thing: the same night as the Black Cat protest—February 11—the Sunset Strip protests a few miles to the west were reaching a climax—80,000 leaflets had been distributed calling for a demonstration that night, which "saturated the clubs and made their way clandestinely through every high school in the county." "One of the most interesting and pace-setting" developments in the Sunset Strip protests, the *Freep* noted, "came from homosexual organizations who are currently up in arms about New Year's Eve police raids on a number of Silver Lake area gay bars." PRIDE, while organizing its own protest for that night, also endorsed the February 11 Sunset Strip demonstration. The kids there carried one of the same signs as the gay demonstrators outside the Black Cat: "Stop Blue Fascism."

PRIDE founder Steve Ginsberg explained PRIDE's attitude in the *Freep*: PRIDE wanted to "take to the streets," unlike the "prissy little old ladies of some of the older groups."[5] The "older groups" against which the new libertarians were rebelling started with the Mattachine Society, an L.A. LGBT organization founded by Harry Hay in 1950. Given the temper of the times, the Mattachine founders had had as their goal the quiet integration of gays and lesbians into the mainstream, not loud street protests confronting the cops. Hay himself was a member of the Communist Party and a talented organizer; he organized the Mattachine Society, named after the medieval French secret societies of masked men, into cells that did not know each other's membership or leadership—a system he had learned from the Communist Party's experience with fascism in Europe and now with the rise of McCarthyism in the United States. The Mattachine Society organized the first national movement of what they called "homophiles." Starting out small and fearful, in the basement of L.A.'s First Unitarian Church, they took their first great leap forward in 1952 when the group challenged a vice squad arrest of Dale Jennings, a core member. They raised money for an attorney, who won an acquittal by arguing that Jennings had been entrapped—the first acquittal of an admitted homosexual charged with morals violations.[6]

But as the group blossomed, the red-baiters went after Harry Hay. The *LA Daily Mirror* published a column in 1953 charging that Mattachine had Communist ties, and at the group's convention that summer, Harry Hay and other founders, including his partner Rudi Gernreich (later a famous fashion designer), resigned when the convention denounced them as Communists "who would disgrace us all."[7] The irony was deep: Harry Hay had been expelled from L.A.'s Communist Party in 1948 because leaders feared gay party members could be blackmailed into informing for the FBI. As Dorothy Healey recalled: "I personally met with Harry Hay to tell him we were going to have to drop him from the Party rolls. I made it clear to him that this was not a moralistic judgment by the Party, and he could see the logic of the argument." Nevertheless, she wrote in her 1990 memoir, expelling Harry Hay and other gays was "a self-inflicted wound" on the party in L.A.[8]

Mattachine "never recovered from the loss of its founders," Faderman and Timmons report. The same convention that expelled Harry Hay also declared, "We do not advocate a homosexual culture or community, and we believe that none exists."[9] Meanwhile, the Mattachine group in West Hollywood took the opposite tack: in 1952 they launched the first national homosexual magazine in America. They called it *ONE Magazine* (the name came from a line of Thomas Carlyle, "a mystic bond of brotherhood makes all men one"), and their fourth issue, published in 1953, featured on the cover the terrific mock-HUAC headline, "Are You Now or Have You Ever Been a Homosexual?" In November they added the line "The Homosexual Magazine" to their cover, and soon they were selling 5,000 copies a month, featuring cover stories on "Homosexual Marriage" and "Homosexual Servicemen." Thus, Faderman and Timmons report, "*ONE* set a community agenda that would last for the next fifty years."[10]

But in August 1953, just seven months after publishing their first issue, *ONE*'s office in L.A. was raided and the magazine seized by postal officials as obscene. The ACLU, to its shame, refused to take the case, so it was left to a single attorney, Eric Julber, two years out of Loyola Law School, to appeal the initial conviction. He was in court for four years, and took the case all the way to the Supreme Court. On January 13, 1958, the court declared that a magazine could not be declared obscene only because it was about homosexuality, and ruled that *ONE* could be sent through the US mail. "*ONE Magazine* has made not only history but law as well," Don Slater wrote in the next issue. It "has changed the future for all US homosexuals. Never before have homosexuals claimed their rights as citizens."[11]

Two and a half years before the Black Cat Tavern protest, journalists were already reporting that something new and big was starting to happen in gay L.A., and that LAPD repression was a key to understanding the changes. In 1964, *Life* magazine ran a two-part feature, "Homosexuality in America: A Secret World Grows Open and Bolder." It reported on gay life in Manhattan, San Francisco, and L.A., and the report from L.A. focused on the LAPD. They had arrested 3,069 men for homosexual offenses in 1963, but, *Life* reported, "the LAPD could not help but notice that a mini-revolt was already occurring on the streets." LAPD inspector James Fisk explained: "The pervert is no longer as secretive as he was. He's aggressive, and his aggressiveness is getting worse."[12]

"Homosexuals everywhere fear arrest," *Life* reported. But "in Los Angeles, where homosexuals are particularly apparent on city streets, police drives are regular and relentless ... Leaders of homophile societies in Los Angeles and San Francisco have accused the police of 'harassment, entrapment and brutality' toward homosexuals." However, "there is no law in California—or in any other state—against being a homosexual. The laws which police enforce are directed at specific sexual acts." The magazine also noted that it was a crime in California "to solicit anyone in a public place to engage in a lewd act. Under these laws, the police are able to make arrests. In many cases, a conviction results in a homosexual being registered as a 'sex offender,' along with rapists, in the state of California." In L.A., the *Life* article conceded, there was a "running battle between police and homosexuals" that had "produced bitter feeling on both sides."

Two years after the Black Cat Tavern protest, the Stonewall Uprising got a lot of attention, and it has since been part of the historical canon; in contrast, the Black Cat Tavern protest was little known at the time and remains little known today. Some say the greater prominence of Stonewall explains why the gay liberation movement took off in New York City instead of L.A. But in fact, the Black Cat Tavern protest broke the ground for many historic developments in L.A. The first was the founding of the *Advocate*, today the oldest and biggest gay magazine in the nation, devoting regular coverage to the fight with the LAPD—again, before Stonewall. Second was the establishment, following another protest against the LAPD, of the Metropolitan Community Church in L.A.—eventually the largest gay church in the world. And finally, the demonstration presaged the first officially recognized gay pride parade in America—the result of a legal battle with the LAPD that ended in triumph for gay L.A.[13]

Issue number one of the *Advocate* was dated September 1967. It had begun publication as the newsletter of PRIDE; the editors, Richard Mitch (using the pseudonym "Dick Michaels") and Bill Rau (under the name "Bill Rand"), then turned it into a newspaper.[14] The first issue led with the sequel to Black Cat—a meeting between vice squad head Charles W. Crumly and gays at the home of Jerry Joachim, one of the founders of the *Advocate*. But meeting with the cops was a two-way street: "PRIDE is asking you to think about something," Joachim wrote, addressing gay men: "your conduct.

It must be above reproach in public places ... We are going to ask you *not to cruise* in public parks [his emphasis]. That represents an intolerable situation to the LAPD, and rightly so ... Every effort will be made to persuade the homosexual in LA to confine his sexual activities to private places. We are asking you particularly to boycott Griffith Park. Show the LAPD that we can keep our word—obey the law ... If we do our part, perhaps the LA police will grasp this opportunity to stop police harassment.

Joachim concluded asking readers to "remember there are arrests that are justified. Our skirts are not 100% clean, and you know it."[15]

Asking gay men to stay out of Griffith Park was huge. Jerry Joachim wasn't talking only about furtive one-on-one sex in the bushes late at night; Griffith Park was widely known as a place where "wild orgies involving scores of men were common ... even in daylight." John Rechy told historian Lillian Faderman that "he knew of no other city in the 1960s that had a daytime scene as thriving as Los Angeles did in Griffith Park." The LAPD, Faderman and Timmons report, "could not keep up" with "the exuberant gay male eroticism there."[16] It seems clear from Rechy's account that the request in the *Advocate* had no effect on sex in the park.

But the next page of the *Advocate*'s first issue took a different tack in dealing with the LAPD. In a column with the byline "Mariposa de la Noche," the paper noted that "summer is beach time," and said that "cruising the beach studying the regional 'wildlife'" was part of gay life—including "such little sea-beasties as crabs—a markedly unpopular subject; chicken-of-the-sea—constantly in great demand; and fish—popular mainly among biologists and dikes. Always a favorite study is anatomy. In fact many a bronzed body has been inspected and dissected on location, then picked up for further homework." The paper recommended a "noteworthy Pacific playground catering to our royal society ... Santa Monica State Beach, affectionately known as 'Fag Beach.' Whatever that means. Located cruisingly close to Chautauqua Blvd., State Beach offers much to the gay sea set ... the attire is rather unrestricted." But those cruising the beach had to be on alert for the LAPD: "The adjacent bathhouse is a definite no-no," the column reported. "The Vice Squad has a fetish for tearooms, especially the one at State Beach."[17]

Instead of boycotting Griffith Park, as Jerry Joachim and PRIDE requested in the first issue of the *Advocate*, a different group of activists—the Gay Liberation Front—declared the park the site for the first "Gay-In," on May 30, 1968. The park had already been the site of a "Be-In" in February of the previous year, a public celebration of the counterculture—including a performance by the Doors. Now, instead of keeping the park the secret site of gay sex, it would become the public site of gay celebration. "Come and Cavort!" the leaflet said, "at the Gala Los Angeles Gay-In." It identified the sponsors as the *Los Angeles Advocate*, One Incorporated (the publisher of *ONE Magazine*), *Tangents*, and a couple of lesser-known groups. And it called the event a "historic first, a gay day in the park."[18]

Griffith Park is huge—4,000 acres—so the question for organizers was where to hold the Gay-In. They chose what one called the "stunningly liberationist" merry-go-round.[19] The organizers intended the Gay-In as a "challenge to the police policy that effectively banned any public gathering of gays and lesbians." Thus the Gay-In featured speeches and music and dancing, as well as booths where "professionals and activists offered free legal advice and other services designed to help gays and lesbians come out at work and home and fight ... firing, eviction, or improper treatment by doctors and psychiatrists."

The *Advocate* reported that "more than 1,000 Gays, and a number of startled straights, paid a visit to the event." The group was "as diverse as gay life itself ... There were the long-haired love children, leather queens, a huge blue jean brigade, baskets at attention, everyday businessmen, college kids, streetwalkers, transvestites, lesbians in Levis, and bare chests were everywhere in abundance." A guerilla theater group presented "a modern day fairy tale" that involved "good fairies and an evil, old, closet queen who saw the light and learned to live outside of her closet." The *Advocate* reporter was particularly enthusiastic about the "Kiss a homosexual" booth, and by the fact that five couples were married at the Gay-In—three female and two male. The LAPD arrested only one person at the Gay-In, and not for sex-related activity: a fifteen-year-old boy with an American flag painted on his face was charged with "desecrating the flag," and they "hauled him off in handcuffs. A large crowd followed, jeering and demanding his release."[20]

Morris Kight had been born in 1919 in Comanche County, Texas, and had arrived in Los Angeles in 1958. He had been working in the civil rights movement since the early 1940s, a friend recalled, but "suddenly he found himself, like many other gays and lesbians in L.A., dealing with the brutal ways of the Los Angeles Police Department."[21] Kight himself recalled in a 1994 interview: "I was doing street organizing, street work, street counseling, one-to-one curbside counseling" with gay men. "My major goal was for gay people to be proud of themselves … Next I wanted them to live lives of usefulness and creativity … I wanted them to stay out of trouble." And last of all, "I wanted to get ready for the revolution."[22]

Kight was also an organizer against the Vietnam War, which he called "the worst of wars." Among other things he founded the Dow Action Committee in 1967, which protested the use in Vietnam of napalm, manufactured by Dow Chemical. "As the war rose, I gave more and more time and energy into protesting," he later recalled, "and less and less time to serving lesbian and gay people, and I felt horrible about that," he recalled. Also, "I was red-baited by gay people constantly," Kight said, but the Dow group also served as a training ground for gay and lesbian members, who were "seeing how to leaflet, how to organize, how to manipulate the press, how to deal with the police, how to do a sit-in, how to do civil disobedience, how to do a demonstration."[23]

Kight described his move from the anti-war movement to the gay liberation movement in that 1994 interview: In October, 1969, the national Moratorium to End the Vietnam War held demonstrations across the country, and Kight was invited to speak at the San Francisco event, where he was introduced as a gay person. Of speaking before tens of thousands of people, he said, "I felt euphoria, I felt dizziness, I felt almost like falling, I felt 'good grief, I should go home.'" He suddenly remembered seeing his father in 1926 in rural Texas plowing a field with a horse and singing a Protestant song, "I'm Going Home."

On the platform in San Francisco, he said, "I thought I would leave here and leave the antiwar movement, I'll remain a pacifist. I'll go home to Los Angeles and home to my people." He left the platform, went straight to the airport, flew back to L.A., and resigned from anti-war organizations, including the Peace Action Council. "The following day I announced the founding meeting of what was to become the Gay Liberation Front in LA."[24]

The GLF had already been organized in New York and Berkeley —L.A.'s group was third. Within a year there were almost 400 members. Kight later recalled that for the next few years, he spent a quarter of his time on GLF street demonstrations, and half of his time on the GLF's social services—its "Gay Survival Committee," which in 1971 became the LA Gay and Lesbian Community Service Center (later LGBT Center), the first and biggest in the world. The other quarter of his time he devoted to the anti-war movement, he said, "because the war in Indochina was still going on."[25]

Most of what the GLF did was organize street protests about discrimination against gays—at restaurants (Barney's Beanery, which had a "no faggots" sign), stores (Tower Records, which fired a gay clerk), and newspapers (the *LA Times*, which refused to run news about homosexual organizations and activities). But the GLF also did anti-war organizing and draft counseling. Support for the anti-war work wasn't unanimous; in May 1970, after the invasion of Cambodia and the Kent State killings, GLF leader Jim Kepner wrote in the *Freep* that "a few members feel Gay Lib should not be involved in other 'movement' issue," but that "the group overwhelmingly voted to wire Nixon an angry protest against the illegal invasion of Cambodia and the vicious shooting of students." The same article reported that "seventeen GLFers joined the thousands who demonstrated in Oceanside in support of anti-war Marines. We kept our own propaganda level low for the occasion, feeling it sufficient to let it be known that gays were supporting the main cause, and not seizing the occasion, as so many did, for side trips."[26]

The GLF organized for an anti-war demonstration in April 1969 in San Francisco. The leaflet had two slogans: "Out Now!" and "Come Out!" Another anti-war demonstration, this one in L.A. in October

1970, was endorsed by the GLF. And in November 1970, the GLF endorsed and collected signatures for the "People's Peace Treaty," where individuals signed a statement declaring that "the American people and the Vietnamese people are not enemies."[27]

And the GLF produced a key publication: *A Guide to Revolutionary Homosexual Draft Resistance*, a leaflet that declared, "The US government oppresses homosexuals in employment, military duty, tax laws, and criminal prosecutions" and asked, "Is this a system you want to die for?" The leaflet, organized as a Q and A, followed: "What is there about being gay that makes me unfit for military service?" The answer provided by the GLF was eloquent: "Nothing. All branches of the military have homosexuals, both men and women, who are serving capably and honorably." But the US "has laws against homosexuals being inducted," and "every year, in every branch of the service, men are dishonorably discharged and imprisoned because their homosexuality has been revealed." Therefore, the GLF recommended that at preinduction physicals, young draftees should check the "yes" box on the question about "homosexual tendencies." They should refuse to answer any questions about their experiences because "48 out of 50 states have criminal statutes against homosexual acts," and the Constitution protects Americans from self-incrimination. The leaflet recommended that "if there is a better way to avoid the draft, such as a student deferment or a medical disqualification, use it"—but instructed young men to "stand your ground," and in all cases "refuse induction."

But the GLF position on the draft was not anti-war, nor was it anti-imperialist: "No homosexual shall be drafted against his will," the GLF list of demands stated in 1970, "nor shall the military deny entrance or demand release of any person because of homosexuality."[28] The next year, when Congress had to decide whether to extend the draft, the GLF in L.A. took a stronger stand: "Our Gay brothers have been harassed and intimidated by this system. Now we have a chance to do away with it."[29]

Finally, the GLF also engaged in electoral politics, campaigning for Robert Scheer for Senate that year and other Peace and Freedom candidates for statewide office. The Peace and Freedom platform included a plank crafted by the GLF, which declared "the necessity to work to abolish all laws" that discriminated against gays and lesbians, as well as "all forms of economic and social exploitation." It called for the freeing of everybody who had been jailed on homosexual charges, and for sex education programs that would give "the same validity to homosexual forms of expression as to heterosexual forms." (Scheer got 57,000 votes, about 1 percent of the total.)[30]

The GLF, of course, became part of a national gay liberation movement, and one of its key strategists and spokespeople was Carl Wittman, whose "Gay Manifesto" was published in the *LA Free Press* Gay Liberation Supplement in 1970. Wittman had been a national leader of SDS but left the organization to devote himself to organizing the gay movement. "How it began we don't know," he said in his "Manifesto." "Maybe we were inspired by black people and their freedom movement; we learned how to stop pretending from the hip movement. Amerika in all its ugliness has surfaced with the war." But gay people were doing something new: "We are full of love for each other and are showing it; we are full of anger at what has been done to us. And as we recall all the self-censorship and repression for so many years, a reservoir of tears pours out of our eyes. And we are euphoric, high, with the initial flourish of a movement."[31]

Wittman's "Manifesto" also declared that "our first job is to free ourselves." That meant allying with the new women's liberation movement, and "junking male chauvinism." It meant recognizing that "marriage is a rotten, oppressive institution." It meant resisting the "'movement' types [who] come on with a line of shit about homosexuals not being oppressed as much as blacks or Vietnamese or workers or women." But it also meant forming coalitions, recognizing that "not every straight is our enemy. And face it: we can't change Amerika alone ... it's not a question of getting our share of the pie. The pie is rotten." As for the anti-war movement, he wrote, "we can look forward" to working with them "if they are able to transcend their anti-gay and male chauvinist patterns. We support [anti-war protestors], but only as a group." Wittman's "Manifesto" concluded that the "imperatives for gay liberation" started with "free[ing] ourselves: come out everywhere; initiate self defense and political activity, initiate counter community institutions." That's exactly what the gay movement in L.A. was doing.

A year and a half after the Black Cat Tavern protest, in August 1968—but still a year before Stonewall—gays in L.A. organized another, bolder, protest against the LAPD: a flower power march on the police station where men arrested in another bar raid were being held. The Patch was a gay bar in Wilmington, run by Lee Glaze, a comedian known as "The Blond Darling." The police had told Glaze he had to prohibit "not only drag but also groping, male-male dancing, and more than one person at a time in the restrooms." Glaze would play "God Save the Queen" on the jukebox to warn customers whenever the cops showed up. But one weekend night, when the bar was "packed with 500 patrons and the dancing was wild," the vice squad "burst in with half a dozen uniformed policemen behind them." They stopped the music, demanded IDs, and started arresting men they said had been dancing together. Glaze jumped up on the stage and shouted, "It's not against the law to be homosexual, and it's not a crime to be in a gay bar!" The raid, the *Advocate* reported, had become a political rally, mostly because of "the solid display of defiance ... by Lee Glaze," whose speech was "a minor masterpiece" that "infected the audience with some of his own courage." Glaze announced the bar would pay bail and provide a lawyer for the two men who had been arrested, and a dozen marchers set out for the jail.[32]

The marchers stopped along the way at a flower shop run by one of the bar patrons, and, Faderman and Timmons report, they left with "all the gladioli, mums, carnations, roses, and daisies." They arrived at the LAPD Harbor Division station bearing huge bouquets and posed for pictures under the "Los Angeles Police Department" sign. One of the marchers later recalled: "When we arrived at the police station, Lee told the officer at the desk, 'We're here to get our sisters out.' The officer asked, 'What are your sisters' names?' When Lee said, 'Tony Valdez and Bill Hasting,' the officer had this surprised look on his face—and called for backup."[33]

There was another fruit of the protests against the LAPD raid on the Glade: two months later, Troy Perry, one of the participants, who had been a Southern Pentecostal minister, started the world's first openly gay religious congregation—the Metropolitan Community Church (MCC). "Lee showed me you don't have to be afraid of the police," Perry said. "Once that happened, it encouraged me to become a gay activist." And it started when a friend of Troy Perry named Tony got arrested by the LAPD at the Patch. The two had been dancing to "La Bamba," when the police arrived and handcuffed Tony and another man. Both were charged with lewd conduct and hauled off to jail. Perry recalled his feeling at the time: "It was so unjust."[34]

"It took me until 5:30 AM to get Tony released," Perry recalled. "It was all due to delaying tactics by the police. The booking procedure, the mug shots, the fingerprinting, just took hours. It was part of the harassment that took place far too often against the gay community in those days." When Tony got out, he told Perry, "I've never been arrested before for anything in my life. Never! And I'm 26 years old now. The police kept telling me they are going to call my employer and tell him I'm gay. I'll probably lose my job. You know, Troy, I've learned one thing from this experience: People don't really care. Nobody likes a queer."

"I tried to be helpful," Perry recalled, telling Tony, "Even if people don't, I'm still convinced that God cares about you." But Tony "just laughed bitterly. 'Come on, Troy,' he said. 'God doesn't care about me.'" Troy Perry went home alone, and prayed: "Lord, we need a special church … if you want such a church started, just let me know when." Then, "a still, small voice in my mind's ear spoke, and the voice said, 'Now.'"[35]

Thus the MCC was founded to respond to the deeper emotional damage done by the LAPD. Starting with a group of twelve in Los Angeles in October 1968, by 2011 it had 172 churches throughout the world, including parishes in forty-six of the fifty states. It owns $100 million worth of property, and "is probably the world's largest employer of gays and lesbians."[36]

Perry announced its foundation in an ad in the *Advocate*, and the first gay worship service was held in his living room in Huntington

Park in October, 1968. At that first service he told the gathering what MCC "was going to be": a "three-pronged Gospel" consisting of "Salvation," "Community," and "Christian Social Action." "We would stand up for all our rights, secular and religious, and we would start fighting the many forms of tyranny that oppressed us." Thus from the first the MCC was committed to action. A parishioner later recalled, "Someone would call a protest, against … the Hollywood police for discriminatory policies—and then our telephone trees would be buzzing, and 80 per cent of the people who showed up at the demonstration would be from the Metropolitan Community Church."[37]

Another fruit of gay organizing that was spurred by the Black Cat Tavern raid: in May 1969, Paul Lamport, the LA City councilman said to have been behind the New Year's Eve raid, was voted out of office, in the nation's first openly gay electoral campaign.[38] Lamport had been endorsed by the new LAPD chief, Tom Reddin, and had campaigned against gays in a district that included not only Hollywood but also Silver Lake and Echo Park, which together "contained perhaps the greatest concentration of gay population and gay businesses in the nation."[39] Lamport blamed the *Advocate*, in part, for his defeat, and said the paper produced "a steady stream of filth and perversion"— indeed, the newspaper had vowed "to really swing an election" and defeat him.[40] (The *Freep* also campaigned against Lamport, who had condemned city officials for what he said was a "secret" program to "welcome an invasion of 100,000 hippies" to Los Angeles in summer 1967.)[41] Bob Stevenson, the man who defeated him on the basis of gay support, died in office and was replaced by his widow Peggy, who also won the election after campaigning for gay votes. Lamport tried to return to the city council in the next election, in 1973, this time seeking gay votes, but was defeated. The district has had a gay rights supporter as its councilperson ever since.

The LAPD confronted the third Gay-In on April 5, 1970, with a massive force, but the conclusion of the confrontation marked the beginning of a change. "The police really came to that one, really seriously," Morris Kight remembered, showing up in riot gear, forming a line and brandishing batons, preparing to clear the park. He recalled speaking to the commander on the scene, telling him:

If you want to cause a riot and hurt a lot of people including your-
selves, that's exactly what you are going to get … The crowd is
having fun, nobody is violent, nobody is armed, nobody wishes to
do any physical harm, they want to have fun, and your presence is
offensive. Why don't we agree that you will leave. I will go away
and go back down and associate with the people, and you will
quietly withdraw. Because if you don't, you will have a violent
riot here today.

"They withdrew within twenty minutes," Kight reported.[42]

The climax of the battle between gay L.A. and the LAPD came in
June, on the first anniversary of the Stonewall rebellion, when L.A.
became the site of the nation's first officially recognized gay pride
parade. (New York had a march, but L.A. got a police permit for a
parade, and the city closed Hollywood Boulevard to traffic for the
event.) Morris Kight recalled that their first idea to commemorate
Stonewall was to hold twenty-five simultaneous demonstrations
located at key "symbols of oppression, repression and exploitation,"
including churches, synagogues, schools, military recruiting stations,
and of course police stations. Troy Perry had a different idea. At a
meeting with Kight and Reverend Bob Humphries, he said, "This is
Hollywood. Why don't we just hold a parade?" Kight later recalled
that he agreed with Perry's idea to organize a single march down
Hollywood Boulevard: "It's a world-famous street and we wanted
to be where the people were, where the media were, where the
action was."[43]

They went to the police commission to apply for a parade permit
—which required a sponsoring organization. "We didn't have an
organization yet that was incorporated other than our church," Perry
recalled. Morris proposed they call it "Christopher Street West"—in
honor of the Stonewall uprising a year earlier. Before the meeting with
the police commission, Perry remembers, "we had agreed at first that
we wouldn't use the word homosexual until we had to." Chief Ed Davis
kept asking who they represented. "After about an hour, [the police
were] getting nasty a little bit," so Perry finally said, "We represent

the homosexual community of Los Angeles"—a simple statement, but a historic one. "And with that, oh, my god, all hell broke loose ... Chief Davis said, 'Did you know that homosexuality was illegal in the state of California?' I said, 'No, sir, it's not.'" The chief then told the commission that, as long as felony laws against oral copulation and sodomy were on the books, they "would be ill-advised to discommode the people to have a burglars' or robbers' parade—or a homosexuals' parade."[44]

At the end of the meeting, however, the police commission agreed to issue a permit—*if* the applicants could post two bonds, one for $1 million, the other for $500,000. The bonds, they were told, were "to pay the merchants whose windows are going to be broken out when people start throwing rocks at you all in the street." "My God," Perry recalled, "it was the Jews in Germany all over again. If a Jew ducked a rock and it broke out a window, the Jew had to pay for it. So they were doing the same thing with the queer community: the queers are gonna pay for it." In addition, the commission said "you will post in cash the amount of $1,500 to pay for the policemen that it will take to protect you." "We thanked them profusely," Perry recalled, "and said we'd be back."[45]

They went to attorney Herbert E. Selwyn, a longtime defender of gays in the courts and a lawyer with the ACLU of Southern California. He met with the commission and persuaded them to drop the bond requirements—but they insisted on the requirement of a $1,500 payment for police protection. Selwyn and the ACLU took that issue to the California Superior Court, where the judge, Richard Schauer, declared: "These people are taxpayers like anybody else. They don't have to put up any money to hold a parade. You don't require it of other groups, you're not going to require it of them." He ordered the commission to issue the parade permit and ordered the police to protect the marchers as they would any other group, without charging them for protection.[46]

The first officially recognized gay pride parade in US history stepped off on Sunday afternoon, June 28, 1970, at the corner of Hollywood Boulevard and McCadden Place, just east of Highland Avenue. Two thousand people showed up, Perry said, to "march, drive their floats, and walk their pets. I've never felt so empowered in my life." And along the parade route, he recalled, "50,000 people showed up to watch us march. I'd never seen more hats and dark shades in my life!" (Meanwhile, back in New York, gay leaders had failed to get a parade permit "and had to march on the sidewalks, without any formation," Perry recalled.)

"The parade was incredible for its time," Perry reflected. "We didn't get the bands that we wanted, so my roommate, Willie Smith, drove the parade route in his VW minibus, playing World War II German marches from an amplification system he'd hooked up. Willie's thinking? Since the Los Angeles police department treated us like the oppressed of WWII, they might actually enjoy the music and leave us alone."[47]

The parade down Hollywood Boulevard "had a little bit of everything," he said. The Society of Anubis took the lead with its float—they had 800 members, divided equally between gays and lesbians, plus a state charter stating their official purpose was to overturn unjust sex laws and "present to the public a true picture of the homosexual as a worthwhile member of society." Another group carried a sign that said "Heterosexuals for Homosexual Freedom." The parade included a guy with an Alaskan husky and a sign that read "We Don't All Walk Poodles" (he led what Perry called "the pet-walking section"). A photograph of the guy and the dog was later published in a *Time* magazine article about "the new gay militancy." The GLF of Los Angeles came down Hollywood Boulevard carrying banners and shouting, "Two, four, six, eight, gay is just as good as straight." Perry recalled that a gay group from Orange County brought a large sign that read "Homosexuals for Ronald Reagan." "I heard a woman on the sidewalk say, 'I can forgive them for being homosexual, but I will never forgive them for supporting Reagan.'"

And just in case people watching missed the point about fighting LAPD harassment, a float featured a man on a cross with a sign that read "In Memory of Those Killed by the Pigs." Another group made a similar point with a different approach: a "flock of shrieking drag queens" appeared, "running every which way to escape club-wielding guys dressed as cops."[48]

Troy Perry was asked, forty-three years later, what he remembered most about that day. He replied:

> The thing that stood out in my mind was that there was no one picketing against us. When we came around the corner [onto Hollywood Boulevard] we didn't know what to expect. I didn't know how many people were there—and to see that crowd. At first, I started tearing up, and then I said, No, you're not, this is a happy day, a good day, you're going to wave to the crowd. And people just cheered as we went down the boulevard.[49]

Morris Kight, a week after the parade, described it as "joyful, folksy, funky, and happy," noting that the parade "received more public notice than all the homosexual activities in the past combined. Sidewalks crammed with people came to watch." The "friendliness" of onlookers was wonderful, he said, but the thing that "counts for most, is that Gays are a lot taller, a lot stronger, a lot freer, a lot more honest with themselves."[50]

That first gay pride march opened the door to the flowering of gay L.A. The next year, 1971, the LA Gay and Lesbian Community Service Center opened, the nation's first and largest of its kind. Of course, there were plenty of attacks and setbacks—in 1973 the MCC at Twenty-Second and Union was burned down—and of course the AIDS crisis lay ahead. But defeating the LAPD and stepping out in the sunlight on Hollywood Boulevard that June day of 1970 marked a turning point for gay L.A. Kight, for one, called it the happiest moment of his life.[51]

What about the women? The story up to this point is almost all about men. However, photos of the Black Cat Tavern protest show several young women among the demonstrators. Women attended the first meetings of the Metropolitan Community Church; they celebrated at the first Gay-In in Griffith Park; they marched in the first gay pride parade down Hollywood Boulevard. And of course, women had been arrested by the LAPD in raids on lesbian bars. The crime for which gay women were arrested in the Fifties and Sixties was "masquerading" or "impersonation"—wearing masculine clothing. At the beginning of the Second World War—the era of Rosie the Riveter, who wore men's work clothes—LA Mayor Fletcher Bowron asked the city council to ban the wearing of pants by women who worked at city hall; he said that it was worse to see "masculine women much more than feminine traits in men," and that the city should not allow the war to "undermine those things we like to consider feminine and ladylike."[52] The courts had declared in 1950 that laws prohibiting women from wearing men's clothes were unconstitutional, but police raids on lesbian bars continued in the 1960s, Faderman and Timmons report, with the LAPD vice squad arresting women on charges of drunkenness or prostitution. But the leadership and organization of the gay movement in L.A. up to 1970, and the editors and writers for the gay magazines, were virtually all male. It was not until 1971, Faderman and Timmons conclude, that "both 'gay women' and 'lesbian feminists' came to the conclusion that "women had to do it for themselves."[53] That's a different story, a story about the Seventies. The story of the gay movement up to 1970 is thus a story about men as leaders and organizers.

Historians of gay L.A. always emphasize that the movement started in L.A. "before Stonewall"; it was host to the first protest march, the first publication of the *Advocate*, the first gay church, the first invocation of "pride," the first official gay parade. But why? Why would gays organize first in L.A. rather than New York? In part, the answer requires understanding the difference between the LAPD and the NYPD. The LAPD treatment of gays was worse—more systematic, more thorough, and more relentless—because the LA police were not corrupt. It seems paradoxical, or ironic, at first, but it makes sense: in New York City, the gay bars were run by the Mafia, and the Mafia paid off the police to leave them alone most of the time and provide advance warning of raids. The advance warning was to permit the bartenders to remove most of the liquor so it wouldn't be confiscated, but it also meant that regulars could be warned and only a few random patrons would be arrested. According to Martin Duberman, "a patrolman would stop by Stonewall once a week to pick up the envelopes filled with cash—including those for the captains and desk sergeants, who never collected their payoffs in person. The total cash dispensed to the police each week came to about two thousand dollars."[54]

The LAPD in the Thirties and Forties had been a notoriously corrupt institution, but it was famously cleaned up by Chief Parker after he took charge in 1950. He instituted military-type discipline, made the LAPD a "professional" force, and relied on his Organized Crime Intelligence Division (OCID) to keep the East Coast Mafia and organized crime elements out of Los Angeles. It was Parker who built up the vice squad that harassed gay people—one that, unlike in New York, couldn't be bought off by bar owners, because OCID was also charged with pursuing corrupt cops who took payoffs. As Faderman and Timmons report, the LAPD "prided itself on being one of the most determined enemies of homosexuality in the nation."[55]

One other factor: L.A. had many more gay bars than New York City. When the Black Cat Tavern was named a historic landmark in 2008, the *LA Times* reported there had been eighty gay bars in the city in the 1960s.[56] The combination of a large gay population, a big gay bar scene, and a particularly repressive police force created the pressures that finally exploded, and the organizing that flourished—starting with 500 people on the picket line at Black Cat protest in February 1967, and reaching a glorious climax with 2,000 marching down Hollywood Boulevard in June 1970 in the nation's first official Gay Pride Parade. "Out of the closet and into the streets"—in just three amazing years.

12

Sister Corita and the Cardinal:
Catholic Power and Protest (1964–73)

L.A.'s most famous artist in the 1960s was Sister Corita Kent. A member of the Sisters of the Immaculate Heart of Mary (IHM), her work was exhibited in hundreds of galleries and museums. She popularized what was then an uncommon medium, "serigraphs"— silk-screen prints. Her earlier work featured bright colors and playful text drawn from advertising. In the late Sixties, however, her prints became increasingly political, engaged with the civil rights and anti-war movements. At the same time, the faculty and students at Immaculate Heart College, where she was chair of the art department, began to involve themselves in the anti-war movement. All of this raised the ire of L.A.'s fabled right-wing cardinal, Francis McIntyre, whose campaign against Sister Corita landed her on the cover of *Newsweek* at the end of 1967. He issued a notorious my-way-or-the-highway ultimatum to her and her sisters: they should either confine themselves to traditional religious duties or renounce their vows. Sister Corita left in 1968, soon followed by most of the rest of the sisters at the college. "The cardinal won his battle," the liberal Catholic writer Andrew Greeley said. "It's a crime that calls to heaven for vengeance."[1]

The attack on Sister Corita was a small part of a much larger story: the reform of Catholic practice initiated by Pope John XXIII and the Second Vatican Council, which called for conducting mass in the local language rather than Latin, encouraging friendly relations with Protestants, Jews and Muslims, and pursuing social justice. Resistance to the Second Vatican reforms in the United States was led by Cardinal McIntyre, and resistance to Cardinal McIntyre was led by Immaculate Heart, personified by Sister Corita—not because she set out to challenge the cardinal, but because he focused on her as the exemplar of everything he abhorred in the reforms.[2]

The Juiciest Tomato

Frances Kent, the future Sister Corita, arrived in Los Angeles from Iowa in 1936 with the twin goals of entering the Immaculate Heart Order and becoming an artist. She studied at both Otis and Chouinard, at a time when the two art schools were electrified by surrealism, Mexican muralism, and the political Left. A few local artists at that time were experimenting with silk-screening, a commercial art technology that was not usually considered part of the fine arts tool kit. But for Corita it was ideal. She didn't want to make unique paintings to be sold at high prices to art collectors; she wanted to make art that would be available to everyone. So she became the master of silk-screening, preceding Andy Warhol in both the ironic use of hot colors and brand iconography. She was especially famous for *wonderbread* (1962), featuring the twelve colored spots from the package for Wonder Bread—which "builds strong bodies twelve ways." For her the spots represented the twelve apostles, and the bread represented the host, the symbolic body of Christ—that was the real "wonder."[3] Another well-known work, *for eleanor* (1964), featured a capital "G" in large script—the logo of General Mills—and next to it the company's advertising slogan, "The Big G Stands for Goodness." But, of course, for Sister Corita the "Big G" was not General Mills, it was God—a God who was indeed good.

By 1964, the Second Vatican Council under Pope John XXIII was in full swing, and church reactionaries were horrified by its reform proposals. Many saw it as the most unsettling event since the Reformation. But the Sisters of the Immaculate Heart embraced the spirit of the reforms, and that made them enemies of McIntyre and his ultraconservative supporters. Moreover, Corita did two things that year that especially angered the cardinal.[4]

First was Mary's Day at Immaculate Heart College. It had been a solemn day of "prayer and procession dedicated to Mary as Mother of God," college president Anita Caspary explained, but was transformed by Sister Corita into "a celebration of the real woman of Nazareth," with students in colorful dress, crepe paper flowers, streamers and banners (made by students in the art department), and "modern songs ... accompanied by guitars played by the students." It seemed very Sixties; the media called it a "happening," and it was featured in the CBS Sunday-morning nondenominational religious show for young people, "Look Up and Live."[5] Of course McIntyre didn't like it.

The artwork that got Corita into the most trouble with the cardinal (that is, until her later political work) was her 1964 piece *the juiciest tomato of all*. The word "tomato," divided onto two lines, was white on a red field with a yellowish stripe, and the last three letters, in the bottom half of the poster, were completely filled with tiny text. Like her other recent work, this piece took off from an ad—for Del Monte canned tomatoes—and bent it into a Christian message: the juiciest tomato, the piece declared, was Mary. McIntyre considered the piece a desecration, and prohibited it from being displayed. But other Catholics felt differently: the *National Catholic Reporter* ran a version of it in their Christmas issue.[6]

Corita's decision to move toward more topical political themes had a dramatic beginning: in April 1965, she met Father Daniel Berrigan, who had been invited to lead a Holy Week retreat for IHM. The year before, he had helped draft a "Declaration of Conscience" urging young men to resist the draft, because the war in Vietnam was based on "inhuman torture and senseless killing," and because it "suppresses the aspirations of the people for political independence and economic freedom."[7] That was a radical view in 1965, when the great majority of Americans accepted the official argument that America was fighting in Vietnam to defend a democracy facing invasion by a totalitarian state. And for Catholics to oppose the Vietnam war was a very big deal. The American church supported the war as a war to defend Vietnamese Catholics, who had fled North Vietnam after the Communist-led victory over the French in 1954. The first president of South Vietnam had been the Catholic Ngo Dinh Diem, installed by the Americans in 1955 and backed by America's most powerful Catholic, Cardinal Francis Spellman of New York City—the patron of L.A.'s Cardinal McIntyre.

"Dan Berrigan ... really brought us to political consciousness," said Liz Bugenthal, another of the IHM sisters at the retreat. "For Corita and others, he made political and social action natural, necessary. We spent most of our time pondering what to do and how. And Corita started immediately, with political statements in her work."[8]

Four months after the retreat came the Watts Rebellion. Sister Corita made a powerful Watts piece she called *my people*, which recalled the line from Matthew 25, "Whatsoever you do to the least of my people, you do unto me." (McIntyre at the time was denouncing the people taking to the streets in Watts as "inhuman, almost bestial."[9]) Corita's silk screen reproduced a black and white *LA Times* front page with the giant headline, "EXTRA: Eight Men Slain; Guard Moves In." (Other stories on that same front page included "'Get Whitey,' Scream Blood-Hungry Mobs" and "Anarchy Must End.") Below the image was a block of text, written in Corita's handwriting in white on a red field: "Those who live in the well organized, well ordered, nourished, clean, calm and comfortable middle-class part of Christ's body can easily forget that the body of Christ, as it now exists, is ... hungry, dirty, not motivated by reason, fermenting in agonizing uncertainty and certainly most uncomfortable." It concluded: "Rather than squelch the rebellion, we might better enlist the rebels to join that greatest rebel of his time—Christ himself."

The text was an excerpt from a sermon given earlier that year in Selma by Maurice Ouellet—a fearless white priest and civil rights advocate—after Alabama state troopers attacked civil rights marchers on the Edmund Pettis bridge during what would come to be known as "Bloody Sunday."[10] In response, the archbishop in Alabama had declared, "I won't stand for any priest of the Diocese going in parades or sit-ins ... there will be no picketing by priests or nuns, and no marching." Ouellet and his colleagues complied and did not march with King, but they did provide housing and food for the hundreds of marchers who came from out of town in response to King's call following Bloody Sunday. This led the archbishop to declare: "I want

Ouellet out of Selma … I have put up with as much as I am going to."[11] Ouellet was unknown to most Americans, but not to the Catholic Left—and not to Cardinal McIntyre.

Later in 1965, Corita made her first piece quoting Dan Berrigan: *power up*. It was also her biggest: four different panels, hung side by side, each with two giant letters in bright, contrasting colors that together spelled out "power up." As in her earlier work, that phrase came from advertising—an ad for a gasoline brand. Each panel featured a long block of text at the bottom. The first began: "God has chosen his mother to put an end to all distance." The last ended: "Come, beloved of my Father." The huge blocks of text, written in her own handwriting, were difficult and frustrating to read; mostly they testified to the new inspiration in her life. The piece didn't mention the war—that would come in another year—but it did quote the leading Catholic activist against the war. Moreover, that activist had just been reprimanded by Cardinal McIntyre for "conducting illegitimate services during the retreat" for the IHM sisters.[12]

Meanwhile the sisters had taken to heart the call from John XXIII and the Second Vatican Council and set out to be, in the words of their mother superior, Anita Caspary, "more open to the world … more part of the world, and more responsive and involved in it." The sisters had worked for decades as teachers; now they asked to be allowed to choose other kinds of work. They sought "options" for their dress, and for a return to their given names. It was, according to Jesuit historian Mark Massa, "exactly what Vatican II mandated." Some Catholic leaders applauded their proposals: thirteen Jesuit seminary professors called the IHM reforms "a splendid response to the call for renewal and adaptation of religious life." They were, however, in the vanguard—Caspary recognized that the reforms proposed by the IHMers were "more profound than any thus far announced by any American religious society of Catholic women."[13] In the lead of the vanguard was Sister Corita.

McIntyre objected—to Sister Corita, to her art, to her Mary's Day, and to everything about the new roles the IHM sisters were proposing. In November 1965 he sent three priests to IHM for an official investigation. Mother Caspary later called it "persecution," writing about "the humiliating interrogations by the visiting priests." The questions included: "'Do you have any books by non-Catholics in your library?' 'Do you want to look like a floozie on Hollywood Boulevard?' 'Do you have hootenany masses?' 'Do you read and approve of the diocesan newspaper?'" (That was where McIntyre's attacks were published.) On December 27, 1965, Cardinal McIntyre charged the IHM mother superior with "disobedience."[14] Obedience was one of their vows; the implications were ominous.

Nevertheless, in 1966 and 1967 it all came together for Sister Corita; her work engaged the Sixties in new and thrilling ways. Harvey Cox, a liberal Protestant theologian from Harvard, explained it well:

> The current split in the youth generation [was] between the people who are deeply involved in building a just society and those who are in quest of some kind of immediacy. On the one hand, you have a whole new political group, working for a new society. On the other hand, you have young people who are caught up with their bells, their feathers, their mantras, their music, and, at one extreme, their drugs. They seek immediacy, experience, instant love ... Since I want to keep these two poles—responsibility and celebration—together, Corita's work has an immense appeal to me. For her work speaks of justice, but uses an unabashed celebration of bright colors, of vivid imagery.

Corita, he concluded, "stands for a kind of festive involvement with the world."[15]

1966 also marked Dan Berrigan's return to the IHM annual retreat, and Corita's turn toward anti-war art. Berrigan later recalled that he taught the IHMers that "we couldn't just lose oneself in the harsh realities of war and survival, but we had to say 'Yes' that was a little louder than 'No.'" The celebration and rejoicing in Corita's art, he said, was part of that "yes."[16] Berrigan told his biographers that he and Corita were profoundly "simpatico"—"That doesn't happen twice," he said. "Their intimacy," his biographers wrote, "was based mainly on letters, as well as Dan's yearly visits to Los Angeles" for the IHM retreat.[17]

"I admire people who march," Corita said in 1967. "I admire people who go to jail. I don't have the guts to do that. So I do what I can."[18] That year she produced forty-four pieces, with colors and designs wilder than ever before, and text more engaging and varied. Her key work of 1967 was *stop the bombing*. The piece's title was in blue, rippling, flag-like, over a white and red field, with a text below that begins, "I am in Vietnam—who will console me? I am terrified of bombs, of cold wet leaves and bamboo splinters in my feet, of a bullet cracking through the trees, across the world, killing me." It came from poet Gerald Huckaby.[19] At that point, a majority of Americans did *not* believe it was a "mistake" to send troops to Vietnam—a Gallup poll showed about 50 percent for the war, and 35 percent against.[20]

Another key work that year was *different drummer*: the image was a waving flag, and the text was from Thoreau: "If a man does not keep pace with his companions perhaps it is because he hears a different drummer. Let him step to the music which he hears, however measured or far away." She also made pieces quoting Lennon and McCartney ("How does it feel to be one of the beautiful people?"), Philip Roth ("Life is a complicated business fraught with mystery and some sunshine"), Lorraine Hansberry ("I care. I care about it all"), and, of course, Daniel Berrigan—three in his case. In all these pieces the colors were vivid and the work exhilarating.

Corita was now hugely successful: she had 150 solo exhibitions in 1966 in galleries, museums, and universities, including the Met and MOMA in New York City, LACMA in L.A., and the Bibliothèque Nationale in Paris; she had received more than fifty awards in national and international print competitions; and she had been selected by the Vatican to do a forty-foot mural for their pavilion at the New York World's Fair. And the media spotlight shone on her. The White House invited her to join a presidential Committee on Education, and, in the last week of 1966, the *LA Times* named her one of their "Women of the Year"—along with Ella Fitzgerald and Billie Jean King.[21]

Meanwhile, Cardinal McIntyre was mobilizing to silence Corita. After her 1966 Mary's Day event, he wrote to the head of the order: "We hereby request again that the activities of Sister Carita [*sic*] in religious art be confined to her classroom work … Any other project that sister Carita [*sic*] may indulge in will have to be submitted to the Committee on Art"—that is, the one he had appointed. As for Mary's Day, "It is our suggestion that in the bulletin of the college that you send to the alumnae, a formal apology be inserted" for "the fiesta last week."[22]

The Second Vatican reforms reached a climax in summer 1967, and Sister Corita was again in the vanguard. John XXIII had died, and his successor, Paul VI, issued a call to all religious communities to undertake "renewal and adaptation"—to give up obsolete practices and find new ways to engage with the world. The IHM sisters convened a meeting to rewrite their rules, and Sister Corita was elected to serve on the committee. Key issues included their work as teachers—they didn't want to teach classes for which they were unqualified, and they protested the very large class size in many Catholic schools.

These were the grounds on which Cardinal McIntyre attacked. In mid October 1967, he responded to their statement on teaching: "You dare to threaten me?" He then declared he was firing all of them as teachers as of the end of the school year.[23]

Two months later, for Christmas 1967, *Newsweek* put Corita on its cover. Their story was titled "The Nun: Going Modern." The piece described the "blue-eyed, petite nun" as an "artist, teacher and woman" who "incarnates all the ebullience of the nuns' joyous revolution." They quoted a writer who described her as "the most extraordinary person I know." And "to clergymen who know her, Corita is herself a sign of hope for the church," because she "joyfully subverts the church's neat divisions between secular and sacred." Case in point: her Mary's Day at Immaculate Heart, they said, "became a prototype for the hippies' 1967 be-in in San Francisco."[24]

Then there were IHM's proposed reforms of Catholic practice: each convent of the order, *Newsweek* reported, would choose its own form of governance to achieve "broad participation in decision-making"—that sounded more like SDS's "participatory democracy" than the "obedience" of the traditional nuns' vows. And, *Newsweek* reported, IHM proposed "a shift of energies to the 'social, economic, intellectual and spiritual needs of the family of man'"—rather than the religious needs of Catholics. As for their teaching in Catholic schools, they "insisted" on "radical" changes: "classes must contain no more than 35 students"; nuns who lacked qualifications "must be allowed to return to college to obtain teaching credentials"; and finally, "all teaching nuns must be permitted to negotiate annual contracts" with church officials.

The *Newsweek* article also reported Cardinal McIntyre's response: he "exploded." He said they had presented him with "an unacceptable ultimatum." He "warned his pastors to tighten control of parish convents." And when the IHM sisters "did not back down," he took the case to the Vatican. Both sides were awaiting its ruling.[25]

"Serious Error"

1968 was the year things fell apart for Corita—as they did for the student anti-war movement, and for much of the rest of America. After the assassination of Martin Luther King on April 4, she made *You Shoot at Yourself, America*, with an image different from anything she'd ever done before: a sculpted head of a "Santo," a painted wooden sculpture from eighteenth-century colonial Mexico, most likely the head from a Christ at the Column, after the flagellation—but, in a shocking move, she has torn a bullet hole between his eyes. The text is by the Soviet poet Yevgeny Yevtushenko: "You are shooting not at King, but at your own conscience. You are bombing Vietnam and with this your own honor. When a nation is going dangerously insane … perhaps the only help is shame."

Just a week after King's assassination, the Vatican's apostolic delegate issued a statement: the IHM sisters' argument that Cardinal McIntyre was blocking their efforts to follow the Second Vatican Council was "groundless," and the reforms sought by the IHM sisters constituted "serious error."[26] The letter was sent to every religious order in the United States. However, many Catholic leaders supported IHM, and a pontifical commission arrived in May to conduct another inquiry. They proposed splitting the order in two. The reform-minded were to "reflect" on their future, while the traditionalists were to be given separate living quarters. The sisters were polled: 455 chose the reform group, while 51 stuck with the old rules. What would happen to the reformers remained to be seen.[27]

May '68 was a month of unprecedented action for the New Left worldwide, and also for Sister Corita. Dan Berrigan burned draft records in Catonsville, Maryland, in an act of civil disobedience—he and his comrades called themselves the "Catonsville Nine." At their trial, in October, they challenged the "safe American Catholic past," Massa writes: "the past of fitting in, of being a dutiful citizen, of displaying the American flag with a statue of the Virgin Mary on the front lawn."[28] Throughout 1968 Cardinal McIntyre increased the pressure. In June, the end of the school year, McIntyre forced all the reform-minded IHM nuns to quit their jobs as teachers in parochial schools. Corita's fellow sisters said goodbye to their students and the parents—nuns who had "served in Catholic schools for twenty, thirty, forty years."[29]

On November 22, 1968, Corita announced she was leaving the order of the Immaculate Heart of Mary, after thirty-two years as a nun. The news made headlines from L.A. to New York.[30] "She was crying all night" after she made the decision, said Helen Kelley, president of Immaculate Heart. She was fifty; she had never rented an apartment, learned to drive a car, or cooked a meal.[31] Leaving the order meant leaving the school where she had developed her art, leaving the students who had helped transform Mary's Day, and leaving the sisters beside whom she had struggled for reform. To make the break complete she left L.A. and moved to Boston, where she declined an offer from Harvard to teach.

Leaving the community of her fellow nuns and her students led to what critic Julie Ault calls "a dramatic shift ... in her work." The changes were "sudden, even shocking."[32] Now, she turned away from the bright colors and the joyous themes to feature grim documentary images from *Life*, *Time* and *Newsweek*, with text about the war and racism. Of course she had to do something about the Catonsville Nine: her 1969 work *phil and dan* shows the famous black-and-white news photo of the Berrigans burning draft records at that selective service office in Catonsville, Maryland, in May '68—she completed the piece after the conclusion of the trial.

In 1969 she also made *the cry that will be heard*, featuring a *Life* cover on "the Negro and the cities" with the face of a young Black boy crying, accompanied by the text "why not give a damn about your fellow man." *manflowers* had a photo of blinded US soldiers in Vietnam, with the text "where have all the flowers gone?." *news of the week* consisted of a *Newsweek* cover, "Profile of the Viet Cong," with a photo of a nearly naked Viet Cong prisoner, bound and tied, next to the plan for a slave ship. *if i* showed Coretta Scott King at her husband's funeral.

On April 9, 1970, the appeals of the Catonsville Nine were all denied. Dan and Phil Berrigan went underground; Phil was caught ten days later; Dan eluded the authorities for four months before they caught up with him in August 1970.[33]

Meanwhile back in L.A., on January 18, 1970, McIntyre won his victory over the IHM sisters. The Vatican had refused to support them; now they were ordered to choose between accepting McIntyre's authority or renouncing their vows. The procedure required each to apply to leave the order, and the application form said the decision was made "freely." Anita Caspary wrote in her book, "Virtually every sister, without consultation with the others, took one, final, important step: she crossed out the word 'freely.'"[34] Through this process, 150 of the IHM nuns, 90 percent of the order in L.A., were expelled—the largest group of religious women in the history of the American Catholic Church to be kicked out.[35] They stayed together, forming the "Immaculate Heart Community," and continued to run Immaculate Heart College and High School—but Corita was no longer with them.

McIntyre, however, couldn't celebrate his victory over Immaculate Heart—he resigned three days later. The official reason was his "advanced age"—he was eighty-four. "The more sophisticated view," Caspary wrote, "was that the cardinal's departure was a bargain struck by the Vatican because His Eminence had not found a diplomatic solution to the problem of the IHM community."[36]

Corita's art that year took an even more drastic turn. She abandoned the grim news photos of 1969 and instead made work with simple color splashes and text that consisted of platitudes: "this is the first day of the rest of your life." Her post-1970 work seems to have been done by a different artist. Corita tried to explain the change: "The time for physically tearing things down is over," she told an interviewer.[37] Julie Ault concluded she was experiencing "activism exhaustion."[38]

In March 1971 Corita came back to L.A. to speak at a rally with Sister Elizabeth McAlister, one of the "Harrisburg Six" indicted along with Phil Berrigan on federal charges of conspiring to kidnap Henry Kissinger. Sponsors of the L.A. event included Catholic, Protestant and Jewish groups, as well as Women Strike for Peace and the Peace and Freedom Party.[39] Corita read from Dan Berrigan's poetry. But now her great work lay behind her. In 1974 her gallerist told her "in no uncertain terms that her work wasn't what it used to be."[40] In 1985 the US Postal Service issued her "Love" stamp, which became the most popular in history—700 million stamps were sold. But they held the release ceremony on the set of the *Love Boat* TV show in Burbank, which outraged Corita—she considered that a trivialization of the idea of "love" and an insult to her—and she refused to attend.[41]

Thirty years after Cardinal McIntyre forced out Corita and most of the other IHM sisters, in 2000, his successor Roger Mahony publicly apologized to the Immaculate Heart Community.[42] Of course, that was much too late; the college had closed twenty years earlier, in 1980, and Corita herself had died sixteen years earlier, in 1984.

Part III

The Explosion

13

The Midnight Hour:
The Watts Uprising (August 1965)

1965 will be the longest and hottest and bloodiest year of them all. It has to be, not because you want it to be, or I want it to be, or we want it to be, but because the conditions that created these explosions in 1963 are still here; the conditions that created explosions in '64 are still here ... Brothers and sisters, let me tell you, I spend my time out there in the street with people, all kind of people, listening to what they have to say. And they're dissatisfied, they're disillusioned, they're fed up, they're getting to the point of frustration where they are beginning to feel: What do they have to lose?[1]

Malcolm X gave this speech in Detroit on February 14, 1965, two weeks after a high-speed escape from would-be Nation of Islam assassins in Los Angeles, and a week before he was murdered in Harlem.[2] He was often prescient, but what he was hearing on the streets could have been heard by almost anyone who bothered to listen anywhere in Black America—including on the streets of the South L.A. district of Watts.

Previous chapters have sketched the chain of events—the LAPD attack on the NOI in 1962, the defeat of the 1963 united civil rights campaign, the social ecology of overcrowded schools and homes, and the white backlash embodied in 1964's Proposition 14—that pointed inexorably toward Malcolm X's predicted explosion in 1965. But one

factor, to use a fancy but appropriate verb, "overdetermined" all
the others: the economic flytrap that snared the lives and hopes of
Black youth, particularly in the older, poorer half of the ghetto, east
of the Harbor Freeway. (West of Vermont, where the percentage of
intact, home-owning Black families with employed bread earners
was significantly higher, there were many fewer incidents during the
August upheaval.) This area, including Watts, was a principal focus
of an unprecedented study of hard-core unemployment and poverty
published in December 1965 by two veteran researchers at UCLA's
Institute of Industrial Relations, Paul Bullock and Fred Schmidt,
with former Freedom Rider Robert Singleton as their chief research
assistant.[3]

The institute, staffed by visionary faculty such as Ben Aaron, Art
Carstens, Irving Bernstein, and Fred Meyers, acted as a think tank for
the Los Angeles labor movement, working closely with figures like
Paul Schrade of the UAW and John T. Williams of the Teamsters.[4]
Its famed labor education program trained hundreds of shop stewards
and lower-rank union officials. Bullock, a labor economist, was the
institute's point man in South Central L.A. and a much respected
figure—especially in Watts, where he spent more than a decade conducting interviews with youth in the projects and eventually published
a unique book, *Watts: The Aftermath—An Inside View of the Ghetto by
the People of Watts*, in which he acted as amanuensis for community
voices.[5] His commitment to the community was profound and, after
the 1965 rebellion, particularly irksome to politicians and poverty
bureaucrats making false claims about the success of job-training
schemes in the Watts area.

The *Hard-Core Unemployment* report studied a spectrum of affected
groups in an area that included the Eastside, South Central, Skid Row,
and the concentration of elderly white poor, displaced by Bunker
Hill renewal, around MacArthur Park. Some of the findings were
predictable, for instance the overcrowding of male job-seekers, Black
and brown, in a few available niches, particularly construction labor.
Others were more surprising and counterintuitive, such as the fact
that long-established ghetto residents with relatively high educational
achievement (eleventh grade, versus ninth grade for the whole study

area) were more likely to suffer joblessness than newer, less-educated arrivals from the South. Or the discovery that the Black poor got at least as much income support from extended families, fellow church-goers, and neighbors as they did from county welfare and federal aid. The most striking finding, however, was the 60 percent unemployment rate among Black women needing to work outside the home: "The burden of long-term unemployment falls heavily upon Negro women, who suffer from a lack of available jobs and a necessity, in many cases, to support excessively large households." The survey found that two-thirds of all long-term unemployed women were younger than forty, but that the age barrier was "particularly formidable for Negro women who have lived in the state for ten years or more." Three-quarters of these older women were heads of households.[6]

In other studies Bullock used a "thick" ethnographic approach to analyze the situation of young, jobless males in Watts and elsewhere in the ghetto. His work highlighted the destructive roles of segregated education and the LAPD's "stop and frisk" policies. Black arrivals from the South (Texas, Louisiana, Mississippi, Arkansas and Alabama, in order of numbers) bore all the scars of a wretched Jim Crow education, and some were completely unlettered. There was no public program to address their need for remedial instruction and vocational education. Neighborhood youth who had grown up in the LA school system, by contrast, were generally literate but dropped out of their underfunded high schools at rates ranging from 40 to 70 percent. In one paper, Bullock argued that many dropouts were actually "kick outs," the victims of administrative policies that compelled students to transfer or leave school for offenses no more serious than learning problems, or, in one case, a single truancy.[7]

Meanwhile, the LAPD operated the nation's most successful negative employment scheme. While giving low priority to white collar crimes, whatever their impact on society, the department fastened a relentless dragnet on poor Black and Chicano neighborhoods. Without the slightest pretense of probable cause, the cops stopped and searched people, particularly young men, in the hope of finding some weed or a stolen item. Those who verbally defended themselves, however innocent, would usually be offered a ride to jail. The result was an extraordinary accumulation of petty arrests (but not necessarily convictions) that made a majority of young men unemployable. Thus stigmatized, youth entered the street economy, where they sold drugs, practiced petty theft, and inevitably earned further, more serious arrest records. Even in a booming economy (in June 1965 manufacturing employment and wages broke all peacetime records), there was no route to employment for a large minority of young Black men, except through minimum-wage job schemes that paid far less than selling pot or fencing goods from the trunk of a car.

Paul Jacobs, a reporter-activist who went on to help found *Mother Jones* magazine, brilliantly illustrated Bullock's vicious circle in an exchange with a staff member of the McCone Commission investigating the rebellion. He was asked, "What do you think is the most important bar to minority employment that could be eliminated quickly?" "The handicap that would be the easiest to wipe out is the arrest record," Jacobs answered. "If arrest records weren't held against people, you could probably change the employment situation overnight and put a hell of a lot of people to work." The staffer, a former prosecutor, glared at Jacobs: "I don't think a man who's got an arrest record should be employed in most businesses. I wouldn't hire anybody who had an arrest record for my family's business." The problem in a nutshell.[8]

Meanwhile, progress on the fair employment front was slight, to say the least. In July, *Times* labor reporter Harry Bernstein applauded gains by Blacks in the aerospace industry but acknowledged that smaller companies (those with 400 or fewer workers) "seem to have made no significant effort to end their 'whites only' hiring policies." Moreover, "the top-level managerial attitudes which now seem to oppose racial discrimination are often not reflected at the lower management level—which is where workers are actually hired." Don Smith, the new head of CORE, scorned the pervasive game among employers of paying lip service to fair employment while continuing their old discriminatory hiring practices. "Five years ago, we would go to an employer who was discriminating and either he would agree to try and correct the situation, or he would chase us out. Today, almost nobody chases us out. But they make promises of reform which are never kept. I prefer open discrimination to this kind of hypocrisy."[9]

Another major obstacle to addressing the unemployment problem was Mayor Yorty's stubborn refusal to accept federal guidelines that would have released millions of dollars of anti-poverty funds for youth jobs. In April 1964, backed by the Unruh camp and the downtown establishment he once scorned, Yorty was reelected in a landslide over Congressman Jimmy Roosevelt, FDR's war hero son and the candidate of Governor Brown and the California Democratic Clubs. It was a double victory since Roz Wyman, his bête noire on the city council, was also defeated.[10] But perhaps the most profound consequence of the election was that it freed Yorty from dependence on Black voters and their concerns. His inner racist was now given full scope. The election effectively created a ruling triumvirate of white power in Los Angeles: Chief Parker, Mayor Yorty and Cardinal McIntrye.

The War on Poverty's new Office of Economic Opportunity (OEO), headed by Sargent Shriver, had allocated millions for job programs in L.A., but it came with the stipulation (Title II) that the poor themselves, through open elections or town meetings, had to be represented on the required umbrella agency. Yorty, refusing to yield any power to Washington or local civil rights leaders, was unmovable in his insistence that he alone should have the power to appoint the members of such a board. Los Angeles thus became "the only major city in the United States," Shriver declared in August 1965, that "has failed to organize effective local antipoverty programs ... Everywhere else in America, almost without exception, elected officials have been extremely helpful."[11] As a result, a summer program that would have organized recreation for 20,000 LA teenagers was canceled, and several thousand youth jobs, the funding already budgeted by the OEO, were left in limbo.[12] Summer 1965, as Robert Conot later wrote in his account of the August uprising, was "the worst ever: one of chaos, disunity and suspicion ... As no jobs had materialized, [kids] lounged around getting high on cheap wine and marijuana, discussing among themselves which white motherfuckers and Uncle Toms were making a killing on the antipoverty program."[13]

"We've Come to Life"[14]

As spring turned toward summer, Tom Bradley became increasingly worried about the imminent possibility of an explosion on the streets of South Los Angeles, a concern shared by his council colleague Billy Mills, but not by the white members. Earlier the Johnson administration, recognizing the likelihood of summer disturbances, had offered Yorty and the mayors of nine other cities the services of federal conciliators to help expedite the expenditure of anti-poverty funds and to act as conduits for rapid information exchange between municipal officials, civil rights groups and Washington. To the consternation of Bradley and other Black leaders, Yorty was the lone mayor to refuse.[15]

Bradley believed that the likely epicenter of any explosion would be Watts, home to 80,000 of the poorest people in Los Angeles. The statistical profile of the area, publicized by John Buggs, executive director of the county human relations commission, was deeply disturbing. "Between 1960 and 1964, in a time of unequaled prosperity, the Negro unemployment rate in the poverty area rose from 12.6 to 19.7 percent," while in Watts the male unemployment rate stood at 30 percent.[16] Watts, moreover, had the greatest concentration of debilitating health problems, the most congested public housing, and police-community relations beyond the breaking point. Although the community was outside his multiracial Tenth District, Bradley decided to spend a day there fact-finding. "Taking the bus to emphasize his identification with the people he was serving," his biographers write, "he spent the day walking the streets and listening to members of the community." He was "surprised at the lack of even the most elementary reading and writing skills," and "moved by the depth of the hopelessness and the lack of self-esteem." He returned to his office "visibly shaken by the trip."[17] Meanwhile Sam Yorty sat on $22 million in OEO funds that represented thousands of youth jobs.

Chief Parker, for his part, made one small concession to ominous social reality. In June 1965, Alisa Kramer reports, Parker, seeking to "mollify black civic leaders and to attempt to discourage challenges to his authority," appointed a liaison to the Black community: Inspector James Fisk, commander of the bureau for stations in Black or mixed neighborhoods. Parker asked him to "do something about blacks in Watts and to gather all the intelligence he could about them." Parker told Fisk he had been selected because "he was the only one Parker knew who was interested in Blacks." Fisk later told a reporter that he "did not know whether to be flattered or appalled. At the time, Fisk said, having good relations with the black community was tantamount to treason."[18] The UCLA graduate and Presbyterian elder had only a few weeks to settle into his new, underfunded role when the volcano, as Black activists had warned, erupted.

The events of August, starting with a bungled drunk driving arrest on the evening of Wednesday, August 11, and ending with the lifting of curfew on Tuesday, August 17, became universally known as the "Watts Riot." This was something of a misnomer since the uprising, which claimed thirty-four lives and 1,034 major injuries, actually encompassed the entire 46.5 square miles of the LA ghetto as well as outlying Black communities in Venice, Pacoima, Long Beach, north Pasadena, Monrovia, Pomona and even San Diego. On the other hand, it started on the outskirts of Watts, reached its crescendo there, and was forever symbolized by images of the burning business district ("Charcoal Alley") along 103rd Street, so "Watts" was not an inappropriate metonym. Indeed, the international notoriety of Watts was widely embraced by its residents in what might be considered a pioneering instance of "community branding." The name became a universal talisman of Black power and pride.

Describing the uprising became a battle of hyperboles. After the first night, the *Los Angeles Times* editorially characterized the event as "a summer carnival of riot," but by the weekend it found "riot" too banal a description and instead ranted about "armed looters," "terrorists" and the "*guerrilla war* of south Los Angeles." One of its columnists Morrie Ryskind called it "an *anarchistic holocaust* of shooting and looting ominously reminiscent of the Mau eruption in British East Africa."[19] The *New York Times* was lazier and just characterized it as "blind, smashing madness," while London tabloids screamed "race war" and "insurrection."[20] But "riot" generally sufficed for the white media and its audience, although it had always been an ideological term freighted with connotations of mob violence, mindless destruction, and the absence of any moral restraint. "Rebellion," the gradually adopted moniker in the Black community, was a much better choice, although it needs to be modified by the absence of any central leadership (despite the conspiracy theories popular in the LAPD and on the extreme right) or platform of specific demands. But the uprising did have explicit grievances (police abuse, mercantile exploitation, unemployment, and so on); articulate voices (usually ignored by the media); clear, if informal codes of behavior (homes and Black-owned businesses, for instance were off limits to looting or arson); and an emotionally infused but *rational* strategy (the destruction of white-owned property as a means to force reforms and create a sense of urgency that nonviolent protest had been unable to achieve).

The sequence of events was accurately recounted in two mass-market paperbacks about the rebellion. Jeffrey Cohen and William Murphy's *Burn, Baby, Burn!* (1966) was the semiofficial *Times* account, containing poignant interviews with residents, albeit within a narrative that reflected all the prejudices and limitations of the mainstream media. Robert Conot's luridly titled *Rivers of Blood, Years of Darkness* (1967) took a different tack, relying more on residents' testimonies than those of the police and carefully reconstructing the circumstances surrounding each of the riot deaths—mostly unarmed looters or bystanders shot by police or national guardsmen. Together with Paul Bullock's previously mentioned *Watts: The Aftermath* (1969), Conot's remains the fairest and certainly the most vivid account of the rebellion. What follows, drawn from these and other sources (including personal recollections of MD, who was living in the curfew area at the time), is a précis that makes three fundamental assumptions:

First, both sides spontaneously adapted new tactics as the days progressed, with the initiative held by the community in the first three days, and then taken back by the police, reinforced by a division of the National Guard, during the last three. The "riot," in other words, metamorphosed from day to day, starting on the first night with groups of young people battling the police, not unlike the April riots of 1964; then changing on the second and third nights into widespread community retaliation against the police and exploitative local businesses; and then, over the weekend, turning into neighborhood resistance to military occupation; followed thereafter by what can only be characterized as a vengeful reign of terror by the LAPD.

Second, "mob" was almost as inaccurate as "riot" in characterizing the actual dynamics of the rebellion. Initially, groups of teenagers and young adults, often attracted simply by sheer curiosity or the sight of crowds, converged on hot spots and joined in stoning the police or looting. There was a "festival"-like atmosphere in the first few days, and attacks on whites were confined to the Watts area and the southern borders of the ghetto. (On the afternoon of day three, with police nowhere to be seen, I watched an interracial crowd happily looting furniture and appliance stores on Vermont just west of USC and north of Santa Barbara Avenue [renamed M. L. King for the 1984 Olympics]—then a mixed area with a substantial ethnic white presence, including La Tosca Filmbuehne, a German-language theater—MD.) But the rebellion quickly became more organized, albeit on a decentralized neighborhood basis, with familiar local personalities providing tactical initiative and flamboyant bravado.[21] There were informally organized cells of resistance, often gang cliques or bands of neighbors, but no evidence whatsoever of participation by "outside groups" as alleged by the police. The Black Muslims sold *Muhammad Speaks* on the street but played no part in the disorder. Those who painted the whole event as a result of primitive mob urges or irrational anger, the clichés preferred by much of the media, simply failed to visualize or understand the micro-structure of collective action.

Third, the August rebellion was not primarily a "race riot," since Mexican neighbors were for the most part left undisturbed, and the whites who were stoned or beaten were mostly a specific group: commuters crossing the ghetto on Imperial Highway to their homes on the white side of the Alameda Wall. Despite lurid stories in the press of rioters chanting "Kill! Kill!," there were few, if any attempts to actually murder whites, apart, perhaps, from attacks on police. White civilians, if pummeled by the gangs of youth, were usually rescued by older residents, or by activists such as Wendell Collins of CORE, and Woodrow Coleman and Robert Hall of N-VAC. And the prevalence of "snipers" and organized "guerrilla warfare" was more legend than fact. <u>The real mortal danger to the cops was friendly fire: the cause of the only police deaths—two officers.</u>

A Diary

Three Days Before (Sunday, August 8)

The Magnificent Montague, emperor of KGFJ soul radio in 1965, tells it best:

> I'm on stage, me and Wilson Pickett, on a broiling Sunday night inside the old 5-4 Ballroom [Fifty-Fourth and Broadway] in what's now called South-Central Los Angeles but was then known simply as the Negro area. We're one floor up a flight of wooden stairs, face to face with a crowd of screaming fans. Pickett wants to do "Midnight Hour," which had just come out, but he has this problem: the whole Stax Records revue has been hammering the audience for a solid hour   Rufus Thomas and Booker T and MGs and William Bell and Carla Thomas and the Mad Lads and the Mar-Keys, each of 'em pumping up the boys and girls with machine-gun-like one- and two-song sets. I'm promoting and emceeing the show ... keeping that frantic rhythm going, jacking up the pace, trading my line with the crowd: "Burn, baby! Burn!"—shouting it on the mike during the songs, on the right beat, so it sounds like part of the mix, and the echo from that feverish congregation comes back at me a thousand times as strong: "BURRRRNNN!"[22]

Day One (Wednesday, August 11)

"LSMFT": "Let's Shoot a Motherfucker Tonight!"
          —*Informal motto of the Seventy-Seventh Street LAPD.*[23]

"A catalyst is not a cause," a UCLA professor writing about the uprising in the *Saturday Review* later reminded readers. But by the same token, a catalyst is seldom a single incident, however universal the narrative custom of beginning with a unique event. In the case of L.A. in August 1965, the story always commences on a sweltering Wednesday evening with a motorcycle-mounted Highway Patrol officer pulling over the drunken Frye brothers: the shy, genial Ronald (the passenger), and the more combative Marquette (the driver), a short block from their home near 116th Street and Avalon Boulevard, just inside the LA city limits. Initially compliant, even joking with the officer, while onlookers laughed at his failure to pass the standard straight-line sobriety test, Marquette became obstreperous after his mother Rena arrived and bawled him out. He refused to be handcuffed, and the patrolman called for backup.

The response was an embarrassment of blue power. A seemingly endless stream of highway patrolmen and LAPD officers, twenty-six cars and motorcycles in all, started arriving with sirens screaming. The previously complacent crowd on the sidewalk, its numbers swelling as word of the confrontation spread through the neighborhood, turned angry at the menacing show of force. One of the early reinforcements initiated the violence by jabbing his nightstick into the solar plexus of Ronald Frye, doubling him up on the ground, then subdued Marquette with a baton blow to his forehead. His mother rushed to his aid, grappled with the cops, and was roughly pinned over the hood of a patrol car. Her younger son came to her rescue and was then arrested as well. Rena Frye was only five feet tall, and the spectacle of her arrest and the subsequent beating of Marquette as he attempted to escape the police car enraged onlookers like Vergie Nash. "Mrs. Nash," wrote Cohen and Murphy, "who had arrived with daughters Janet, twenty-four, and Justine, eleven, and grandson Lance, three, had remarked seconds before to a woman standing alongside her that she thought it 'a shame' Americans were fighting in Vietnam 'if this is the way they're going to treat people.' Then she shouted: 'Does it take all these people to arrest three people?'"[24]

Nash was soon joined by another daughter, Joan, twenty-two, and Joyce Ann Gaines, twenty, who cut hair, along with her two sisters, in her father's barbershop down the street. Her blue barber's smock over capris was easily confused with a maternity dress. As the patrolmen and cops began to depart on their motorcycles, one of them, an officer Gilbert, claimed that Gaines spat at him. She said later that she merely jeered him. In any event, he dashed furiously into the crowd and grabbed her. Nash rushed to her aid and ended up in a tug-of-war over Gaines with the cop and a fellow officer. Gilbert put Gaines in a stranglehold and dragged her backward into the street. "Goddam!" a woman called out. "Goddam! They'd never treat a white woman like that!" Another turned toward the men in the crowd. "What kind of men are you, anyways, to let them do that to our people?"[25] A third woman who had been standing next to Nash and Gaines later told Cohen and Murphy that "I could see the look on—especially the men's faces—when they saw the Highway Patrolman grab the girl around the neck. This is when the crowd became angry." She emphasized that the crowd, though upset, had gone along with the arrest of Marquette, but seeing Rena manhandled and then Gaines being choked was a different story. "But what really started it was, as I say, when the Highway Patrolman grabbed the girl." Battery charges against Gaines for spitting were soon dropped.[26]

The brutality escalated. Another witness told the *Times* that "my husband and I saw ten cops beating one man. My husband told the officers, 'You've got him handcuffed.' One of the officers answered, 'Get out of here, nigger. Get out of here, all you niggers.'" All the residents who talked to the newspaper were unanimous that the police and patrolmen had triggered the explosion.[27] As the remaining police finally attempted to leave, they were bombarded by bottles and cans (on such a hot night most bystanders had a drink of some kind in their hand), and someone, presumably a fan of Magnificent Montague, shouted "Burn, baby! Burn!" Hence began a five-hour-long melee involving about a thousand residents and scores of cops, many of them white Southerners, from the tough Seventy-Seventh Street Division.

But this standard account, variously retold by different authors, has always been incomplete because it ignored the presence of a ghost in the crowd, someone well known to every Black resident, even if whites had never—and would never—hear of her. Her name was Beverly Tate, twenty-two years old. Five weeks earlier, on the morning of July 1, she and her escort were pulled over by two LAPD officers. She was placed under arrest and driven away in the patrol car to a deserted street, and, while one cop waited outside, the other raped her. Her assailant, Officer W. D. McCloud, was fired the next day but never brought to trial. Her story immediately circulated in the Black community and soon was reported in the national Black press (twice in *Jet* magazine, for instance). The *Times*, without using Tate's name or her assailant's, printed a short column on July 31 on her prospective testimony to the grand jury, which was coming up in August. In October the paper again mentioned the case but only as one of the false "rumors" that had incited rioting two months earlier.[28] Two days after the article appeared, Tate, almost five months pregnant, died mysteriously, of "unknown causes."[29]

Since her name had never appeared in the *Times*, whites were totally oblivious of Tate. But in the ghetto it was a different story. On Wednesday night, at the beginning of the riots, Nelson Perry, a bricklayer who had been active in the Communist Party in Cleveland before moving to Watts, was passing a group of youngsters outside the Imperial Courts project when he heard this exchange:

"Hey, man! What the hell's going on up there?"

"I don't rightly know, but hell's fixing to bust loose. Looks like two cops raped some woman. [Tate] ..."

"I'm about sick of them stinkin' motherfuckers. Who the hell they think we are, some kinda dog?"

"You be less than a man letting' them white bastards beat your women and children and you don't do nothing about it. I ain't takin' no beatin's. I'm getting' my shit and going' back there."[30]

Day Two (Thursday, August 12)

Thursday started off as a normal day, with people going to work and conducting their ordinary routines. Schools and businesses were open as usual. The lightning of the previous night seemed to have discharged all the anger in the air, and the word in city hall was that the LAPD was in complete control of Watts. But at the "Parking Lot," a well-known open area in the Jordan Downs projects (103rd Street and Lou Dillon Avenue), scores of youth, gang members and not, met informally to discuss the resumption of the uprising against the police. Similar gatherings, spontaneous for the most part, were being held across South Central L.A. that morning and afternoon, but Jordan Downs became the "Pentagon."[31]

County human relations officials, headed by John Buggs, were simultaneously meeting with residents at Athens Park to talk about their grievances and how to end the disturbances, but the television coverage focused on a single teenager who made wild threats about invading white areas. The footage was replayed over and over again, each time sending out waves of alarm across the West Side and the Valleys.[32] Parker, meanwhile, told reporters that the riot began when "one person threw a rock and then like monkeys in a zoo, other started throwing rocks." He also repeated the charge that the riot was an outgrowth of earlier civil disobedience by CORE and N-VAC: an ironic accusation given that both groups were out on the streets that week rescuing trapped white people and attempting to cool down the temperature.[33] But long-pent-up anger was not so easily abated. By 6 p.m. several thousand people were back on the streets in the area around Avalon and Imperial Highway, and confrontations with the police quickly resumed. Once again LAPD tried to intimidate the crowds with a show of a force, but of the 103 patrol units dispatched to the scene, not one police car returned to the garage without significant damage caused by rock and bottle throwing. Supervisor Kenneth Hahn, who was observing the scene, suffered a serious cut on his neck when his car window was smashed.[34]

Day Three (Friday, August 13)

"Friday was 'Watts Day,'" wrote Paul Bullock. "For the first time, 103rd Street was struck en masse, and the building housing stores became infernos."[35] Billy Mills, whose city council district included a corner of Watts, wanted to hold an emergency council meeting to hear out "indigenous leaders," but some of his white colleagues feared that such a discussion would only bring the riot into city hall. "I can imagine the drapes being torn down and the furniture slashed," fretted council member John C. Holland, a conservative Republican. Mills replied that he wasn't afraid "they'll come in here and tear down the granite pillars ... I'm willing to run the risk of being told some embarrassing things."[36] But such testimony was never heard in a council meeting, although Mills did invite Watts residents to meet the press in his office. (Later, when the McCone Commission was investigating the events, open hearings were banned specifically to prevent such "things" from being publicized or the commission's procedures challenged.)

Meanwhile the Magnificent Montague—who had been playing a lot of Wilson Pickett while carefully refraining from his trademark interpellation—finished his morning program and then toured around the riot area with young men who would soon call themselves the "Sons of Watts." Montague, as usual, basked in his celebrity.

> I talked with my listeners. On approaching them, up came the fingers—riot code. One meant you were from Watts, two meant Compton, and three meant Willowbrook, an area next to Watts. I saw a lot of smiles and heard the greeting: "Burn, baby! Burn." Everybody was cool. Some were rummaging through stores, looking for items to take home. Some were dancing in the street. Some were still being chased by police. It was odd, watching people loot and jump with jubilance ... They didn't ask me if I thought they were wrong or right. We didn't have no political discussion. I was out there because I felt that I had to go and see for myself what my listeners were going through.[37]

"Looting," wrote Robert Conot, "had started along Avalon Blvd. again shortly before 11 o'clock and by noon mobs were roaming up and down the few blocks directly north of Imperial in numbers as least as large as the night before—with one difference. Everyone was participating, women and older people were not just standing and watching." Twenty past one and the first building in Watts went up in flames. By midnight the Los Angeles Fire Department (more segregated than the LAPD) had one hundred engine companies deployed, but they were overwhelmed by the 1,000 fire alarms received that night and next morning.[38] North of Watts, the gang called the Businessmen were hangin' at their regular haunt in South Park. When police attempted to arrest several of them, all hell broke loose. The Businessmen stormed a police command post at the edge of the park and rushed out to Avalon Boulevard to stone cars. Someone yelled, "The blood down in Watts need our help." By early evening a second front of the rebellion had been opened up in the South Park/Jefferson High School district.[39]

Paul Bullock later explained the looting and arson by analogy with the behavior of his infantry unit during the last phase of the war in Europe.

> In those days of rigid segregation, my battalion in the 102nd Infantry Division was lily white, and essentially, a pretty representative cross-section of the dominant racial and cultural groups in America. Yet, as we proceeded through Germany in the wartime years of 1944 and 1945, we looted and stole and, sometimes, raped. Even the most moral and moralistic among us felt no guilt about taking "souvenirs" from the closets and drawers of houses in which we were bivouacked, including items of some value. The High Command issued directives that the looting must stop, particularly in the light of criticism directed against the Russians for the same practice, but they had little effect in my outfit … All of us, at one time or another, "liberated" liquor, articles of clothing, guns, watches, silverware, radios, and anything else that we valued and could carry. We felt especially justified in these practices because we were taking from the Germans, who had systematically looted and pillaged throughout Europe and murdered millions of innocent people.

"I do not claim an ability," he continued, "to penetrate the mind of a black 'rioter' while in the act of 'rioting,'" but surely some of my own reasoning in our confrontations with the Germans must be identical to his. The conditions and circumstances are remarkably parallel." Ditto for the "moral economies" of the two situations. "The whites, especially the white merchants, are seen as exploiters and parasites, and the decades of brutality, discrimination and repression directed by whites against blacks become highly relevant. If stores are burned and goods are looted, this must be measured against the *systematic* exploitation of blacks by whites throughout a long and painful history."[40]

In their pursuit of looters, the police attacked women and children, as well as adult men. A resident of Watts, not a participant in the melee but what a later study would call "a close observer," told the story of one troubling incident:

This Friday night, I was standing in a phone booth watching. A little kid came by carrying a lamp he had taken out of a store. Maybe he was about twelve. He was with his mother. I remember him saying: "Don't run Mommy. They said we could take the stuff because they're going to burn the store anyway." Then, suddenly, about five police cars stopped. There were about 20 cops in them and they all got out. One came up to the booth I was standing in. The cop hit me on the leg with his club. "Get out of here, nigger," he yelled at me. I got out of the booth. Another cop ran up to the boy and hit him in the head with the butt of a shotgun. The kid dropped like a stone. The lamp crashed on the sidewalk. I ran out of the phone booth and grabbed the cop by the arm. I was trying to stop him from beating the boy. Two cops jumped on my back. Others struck the boy with their clubs. They beat that little kid's face to a bloody pulp. His mother and some others took him away. That's when I thought, white people are animals.[41]

Then came the National Guard. The Fortieth Armored Division's spearhead, a Glendale battalion with secret riot training, moved out of their armory around 8 p.m. Five hundred citizens had gathered to cheer them on. Glendale was Los Angeles County's most notorious "sundown town": no Blacks were allowed to live there, apart from a few servants, and any person of color on the streets after 7 p.m. was automatically arrested. No one could have selected a worse unit to send out into the streets of South Central L.A. They soon showed their mettle by killing two innocent people. One victim was simply standing in the doorway of his hotel, and the other was a Chicano resident in a car trying to evade a crude roadblock that he believed had been set as a trap by rioters. Meanwhile the unleashed LAPD was slaughtering unarmed looters and bystanders: ten shot dead Friday night and early Saturday morning. An unborn child died when its mother was shot in the head, and another looter was killed by store owners. A day or two later, firemen exhumed the charred bones of a mentally ill woman who had wandered into a burning store. A young, well-liked cop was accidentally shot by his partner, and a firefighter was crushed under a falling wall. As for the famous "snipers," one cop was nicked by a bullet, and another suffered a flesh wound from a ricochet that might as well have been a police bullet. Hundreds of looters were wounded or beaten, then jailed.[42]

Day Four (Saturday, August 14)

"More Americans died fighting in Watts Saturday night than in Vietnam that day."

—Nelson Perry, *Black Radical*[43]

On Saturday Mayor Yorty finally ventured into the riot zone (overhead in a Fire Department helicopter), an 8 p.m.-to-dawn curfew was declared, and all national guard units were ordered to load their M14s. Tanks were assigned to defend the USC campus. Looting resumed in the mid morning, with increasing numbers of looters simply looking for food and household items. Meanwhile new reports of snipers, this time in Hollywood and downtown, terrified whites who believed that rioters were about to invade their neighborhoods. As Conot reported,

> Television and radio faithfully transmitted each of these reports without evaluation, and the listener, who was in no position to make any judgment, and who never learned that the ominous snipers downtown were a couple of drunks, or that the location of the men seen loading shotguns was that of the Hollywood police station, assumed the worst and made it a banner weekend for gunshop owners.[44]

With thousands of guardsmen now available to support them, the LAPD began its campaign to retake the riot area block by block. Chief Parker observed, "This situation is very much like fighting the Viet Cong."[45] Two "VC" (looters), one of them desperately trying to climb a fence, were soon killed. The Vietnam allusion soon became rampant. Guardsmen were warned about dangerous groups of Blacks wearing red armbands: "A Guard officer indicated that according to intelligence reports available to him, it was the Viet Cong who were behind it."[46] Early in the evening a group of nervous, excited guardsmen, newly arrived from Northern California, killed a young

Chicano—the twenty-first fatality—who purportedly had refused to stop his car. The LAPD shotgunned a Japanese-American teenager, Eugene Shimatsu, as he purportedly was looting a liquor store. A toddler was killed in his front yard—the shooter unknown. The beat went on.

Later that night, Jimmy Garrett, the local SNCC organizer, was sitting on his parents' porch in the dark listening to a transistor radio and watching National Guard jeeps with mounted machine guns drive by, when he heard nearby bursts of gunfire.

> The radio newscast reported snipers being killed by police and National Guardsmen. I looked down the streets and seeing a police car driving toward me turned the radio low. As they approached and passed a cop yelled "Get your black ass back into your house!" I scooted back into the shadows and kicked my door open with my foot. They drove back. I saw the shot gun being lifted as I stood to enter the house. Three quick thunderous bursts as I scampered up the stairs slamming the door behind me ... I ran to my parents' empty bedroom and lay shaking on my back for the rest of the night.[47]

Garrett narrowly escaped the fate of Aubrey Griffith, who was executed by a firing squad of shotgun-toting cops twenty-four hours later. Cohen and Murphy recounted the inquest into Griffith's death. His widow was the first to testify.

> She said that she and her husband were in bed. They heard a noise. Aubrey got up, slipped into a pair of trousers and went to the front of the house to investigate. Their son Aubrey, Jr., [on leave from the Air Force] was in the living room watching television. Mrs. Griffith heard the front door slam. There was the sound of gunfire. She ran from the bedroom and found that her husband had fallen by the front door. He told her to call the police. Her son knocked her to the floor in the kitchen to protect her from shots crashing into the house. He testified: "I was sitting down watching TV. Mom and Pop had gone to bed. I heard shots. Some time elapsed.

There were more shots. One hit the house. The door closed. I went into the hallway. My father had been shot. I seen him walk outside, then return to the house. A volley of shots followed. They came through the door."

Aubrey, his body almost torn apart, had been hit by eleven shotgun blasts fired by *fifteen* cops outside his house. Their story at the inquest was that a national guardsman had pointed out the Griffith house as the possible hideout of a sniper. When they ordered the inhabitants to come out, they reported that a voice answered: "Fuck you. Come and get me." They then emptied their shotguns into the front door of the house. In a subsequent search of the home, investigators failed to find a recently fired weapon or any other relevant evidence. "The verdict of the coroner's jury, nonetheless, was justifiable homicide," wrote Cohen and Murphy.[48]

Day Five (Sunday, August 15)
By this time, according to Nelson Perry,

the military, Nazi-like occupation of Watts, the increasing brutality of the police, the shoot-to-kill orders issued to both soldiers and cops, the rounding up and detention of thousands, and the round-the clock struggle of the combatants was having its effect. Although fighting continued sporadically along 103rd on Sunday, August 15, the people were worn out and it was beginning to show. The police kept it going, pulling new forces into the fight by shooting randomly into crowds or homes they might suspect contained snipers.

After visiting his wife, who was hospitalized in Lynwood, Perry went to pick up his infant child from a neighbor. "You better hurry," she warned. "The Guard is shooting at anyone that's on the street." He almost made it to his yard, in sight of his older son on the porch, when he was accosted by three soldiers in a jeep, one of them pointing a .50-caliber machine gun. A young officer approached him with a drawn .45.

"Drop whatever you're carrying and put your hands in the air."

"I'm carrying my baby."

"I said drop it and raise your hands or I'll shoot."

Perry was a combat veteran of the war in the Pacific and not about "to beg this white Nazi son of a bitch for mercy." Besides, his older son was watching the confrontation.

"I'll tell you what, Captain. I was a damned sight better soldier than you are. I'm not going to drop my baby. You shoot."

The officer reluctantly holstered his 45. "Fucking Nigger."[49]

In another incident on Central Avenue, police, believing they had come under fire from the roof of an apartment building, stormed inside. Frightened residents were ordered "All of you niggers stay in bed!," as police tossed tear gas grenades into the attic and then left. No sooner had they exited than other cops outside thought they saw muzzle flashes from the top of the building. Guardsmen in a jeep, who were accompanying the cops, opened up with a .30-caliber machine gun. "As its sharp chatter resounded," Conot reported, "troopers all along the line took it as their cue to open fire on the apartment building. Every window collapsed. The entire front of the building was riddled, police and troops combined directing 200 rounds in its direction during a span of two or three minutes." As the residents were flushed out of the building, they were made to lie down in the street. "One of the women whimpered: 'Ain't nuthin' here but babies and one or two half-husbands. You shot right into a houseful of babies. Just because I'm a Negro doesn't mean I don't love my black babies just as much you love your white ones."[50] Two were arrested, but charges were later dropped, and the alleged sniper remained an unsolved mystery.

Day Six (Monday, August 16)

Billy Graham, en route to a bible conference at Disneyland, took a helicopter ride over the curfew zone. The previous day he had told an audience: "We are caught in a great racial revolution. We may have a blood bath. What we have seen in Los Angeles is only the beginning." Graham now warned that a "hard core is at work to destroy our country."[51] Many of his hard-core fans, meanwhile, were lined up at local gun shops. In a buying frenzy that would last for weeks, whites were arming themselves with shotguns and pistols and debating (so the *New York Times* reported) "what they'll do if the niggers attack." "One parent in the San Fernando Valley reported that his teen-age son had joined an adolescent vigilante band organized to fight marauding Negros."[52] Without arresting any of them, the LAPD turned away armed whites attempting to cross Alameda into the Watts area. Two carloads of whites from La Puente were stopped in South Central with caches of Molotov cocktails.[53] Levi Kingston, walking on West Twenty-Seventh Street near USC, was shot at by someone on a nearby fraternity house rooftop.[54] There were many other incidents like this, but white snipers and vigilantes did not fit into the master narrative of Black criminality.

The only major fire Monday night was at a drive-in restaurant on Avalon, but there were scores if not hundreds of accounts of snipers, although no casualties. A second policeman was killed, this time in Long Beach, but the culprit again was a fellow officer. Meanwhile nearly 4,000 arrestees, including 500 juveniles, were crammed together in the old Lincoln Heights jail and elsewhere in the county, under generally squalid conditions and mostly without access to lawyers. Looters of soft drinks, diapers and baby formula faced felony burglary counts with bail set at $5,000—unobtainable for most of them. Thirty-six adults were booked for homicide, but thirty-three of them had been arrested for merely being on the scene when police killed a looter or another suspect.[55]

Day Seven (Tuesday, August 17)

With the killing of a scavenger in a burnt-out furniture store, the riot was officially declared suppressed, and Governor Brown lifted the curfew. Chief Parker gloated, "We are on top and they are on the bottom." But his old friend Senator Robert Kennedy, deeply shaken by LA events, told reporters: "There is no point in telling Negroes to obey the law. To many Negroes the law is the enemy."[56]

Martin Luther King had wanted to fly out to L.A. earlier, but Governor Brown, Bayard Rustin, and local civil rights leaders had all discouraged him from coming, presumably because none of them wanted to see the Nobel laureate and apostle of nonviolence associating himself with "rioters." There was also justifiable concern that he would simply be repudiated and heckled by the militant younger members of the community. But King was insistent in a phone call to Reverend Thomas Kilgore, pastor of the historic Second Baptist Church and the SCLC's Los Angeles representative. "Tom," said King, "if Billy Graham can ride over in a helicopter, why can't I come out there and talk to those young people?" On Tuesday, with a reluctant Rustin in tow, King arrived at LAX. It was a difficult visit. At a community meeting in Watts, he was insulted and denounced before the audience was willing to hear him out. According to historian Taylor Branch, one man told him: "All we want is jobs. We get jobs, we don't bother nobody. We don't get no jobs, we'll tear up Los Angeles, period." King then held a press conference with Governor Brown that had little content beyond a vague promise of cooperation. The three hours he spent with Yorty and Parker, moreover, must have reminded him of trying to negotiate with George Wallace or Ross Barnett. "King emerged shaken after nearly three hours," reported Branch, and had to endure Yorty's rant to the press that King's visit was "a great disservice to the people of Los Angeles and the Nation" and that to call for a civilian review board, as King did, was simply to "justify lawlessness."[57]

Finally, King had a strange but emblematic encounter in Watts. In his own words,

> One young man said to me—and Andy Young, Bayard Rustin, and Bernard Lee, who were with me—"We won! We won!" I said "What do you mean, 'we won'? Thirty-some people are dead [and] all but two are Negroes. You've destroyed your own. What do you mean 'We won?'" And he said, 'We made them pay attention to us.'

Later King wrote that "there was joy among the rioters of Watts, not shame. They were completely oblivious to the destruction of property in their wake. They were destroying a physical and emotional jail; they had asserted themselves against a system which was quietly crushing them into oblivion[, and] now they were 'somebody.'"[58]

14

Whitewash: The McCone Commission and Its Critics (1965–66)

The coroners' inquest into the shooting deaths in the Watts uprising was a sham. When Hugh Manes, the lawyer representing the family of one of the victims, demanded the right to cross-examine police witnesses, he was ejected from the room. In every case involving death at the hands of the police or National Guard, the jury ruled "justifiable homicide."[1] Meanwhile, the nearly 4,000 arrestees, especially those crammed into moldy cells in the old Lincoln Heights Jail, stewed in the little judicial hell created by District Attorney Evelle Younger's opposition to setting bail until the background of each defendant was studied and evaluated, a process that could take weeks. A. L. Wirin, the ACLU's legendary counsel, got the courts to overrule Younger, only to have the judges throw out the state judicial council's bail guidelines by doubling the standard bail for misdemeanors and adding $3,000 to the prescribed bail for specific felonies—totally beyond the means of unemployed and indigent defendants. (The Compton courts, meanwhile, stubbornly refused to set any bail at all.) As prisoners were arraigned, Younger's prosecutors tacked on other petty charges such as disturbing the peace, unlawful assembly, participation in a riot and refusal to disperse.[2]

Chief Parker, in a dizzying succession of angry press conferences and statements, blamed the uprising on almost everyone but himself. First he accused the "pseudo-leaders of the Negro community"— whom he had refused to meet with during the previous week—for deliberately concealing the "high criminal element in Watts" and then preventing the police from quelling rioting by their appeals for the police to withdraw and let community leaders quiet the crowds. Then, two weeks later, he told NBC's *Meet the Press* that the California Highway Patrol was actually responsible for the riot because its officers at the scene during the arrest of the Frye family were untrained in crowd control. "He said he has concluded after study of reports on the incident that if city police, who have handled hundreds of arrests in that area, had made the arrests on August 11, the rioting would have been averted." (As for the community's supposed grievances, he produced another of his astounding statistics: "only 8 per cent of the Negroes interviewed felt any resentment against the city police.") In September, he claimed County Supervisor Kenneth Hahn had been a riot instigator because he attended a meeting with residents at Athens Park on August 12, during which one youth captured television attention with the wild claim that Black gangs were going to invade white neighborhoods. Then there were the "persons with bullhorns" who, Parker charged, were actually "directing the riot." (In fact a bullhorn had been borrowed from the police by a city employee in order to warn white motorists from driving into Watts.) Finally, in his testimony to the McCone Commission, Parker accused Sheriff Peter Pitchess of deflecting blame for any misconduct onto the LAPD: "He just sits there and keeps his mouth shut and doesn't get in trouble with anybody."[3]

But Parker's real wrath in 1965, as in 1962, fell upon his default scapegoats, the local members of the Nation of Islam. On Monday (day six), he had hinted ominously to the press that the Black Muslims had "moved in" on the riot, although he offered no evidence of their criminal purpose other than the fact that those arrested were quickly bailed out of jail.[4] So Parker moved in on the Muslims. At 2 a.m. Wednesday morning August 18, one hundred cops and sheriff's deputies, backed up by national guardsmen, launched a surprise military-style assault on Muhammad's Mosque No. 27 (5806 Broadway). The LAPD would later justify the berserk attack by saying that an anonymous informant had witnessed the Muslims moving a large cache of weapons and explosives into the mosque. Several cops also claimed that they had come under heavy fire from a gunman lurking on the roof of the two-story stucco mosque. In any event, the raiders laid down a wild fusillade of hundreds of pistol and rifle bullets and shotgun slugs, blowing away every window in the mosque and pockmarking every wall. Charging into the building, they found nineteen men on the bloodstained floor, four of them badly cut by flying glass, whom they handcuffed and dragged away.[5] They ransacked the interior in their search for firearms or any evidence that might link the Muslims to the previous week's riot, but found nothing—although they carted away all the mosque's files, business records and membership lists. On their way out, Billy Mills would later allege, the enraged cops set the building on fire.[6] Then, the *Times* reported, "as the Muslims were led away with shotguns at their heads, a sniper reportedly fired at officers two blocks away at 58th and Broadway. That set off another barrage of gunfire and heavily damaged the United Veterans of California Club and a barber shop at 5865 Broadway." The police stayed at the scene to arrest other Muslims who arrived after hearing reports that the Mosque was under attack. Bored national guardsmen, having missed all the shooting fun, dropped tear gas grenades into manholes in case armed Muslims were lurking in the sewers.[7]

In the end fifty-nine people were arraigned, the original nineteen for "assault with intent to commit murder," but all the cases were soon dismissed by Municipal Judge Armond Jewell for lack of evidence. "The only evidence of any shot having been fired from within the mosque," the judge observed, "are statements from some witnesses that they heard or saw flashes or reports or puffs of smoke. It wouldn't take much imagination to see reflections of lights on windows and to hear the sound of firing to believe they were fired upon." When Billy Mills subsequently asked Parker to appear and "explain the raid" to the city council, especially the logic of shooting up the entire neighborhood, he was predictably rebuffed, as was Assemblyman Dymally when he asked for a federal probe into the affair.[8]

Parker, meantime, was buttressing himself with commendations and statements of support from the Alabama State Police, both of L.A.'s daily newspapers, Robert Kennedy, William F. Buckley, all 239 Los Angeles County posts of the American Legion, the Downtown

Business Men's Association, a large delegation of conservative house-wives, and so on. He also enjoyed for the first time the fulsome and uncritical support of Yorty, who himself was basking in the love of his white voters. (In his history of the department, Joe Domanick describes the new Yorty "as the sixties equivalent of a cheerleading Laker Girl for the LAPD.")[9] And both of them knew that riding to their rescue was wealthy LA industrialist and ex–CIA director, John McCone.

The Commission

"In all of California," Paul Jacobs wrote of McCone, "it would be hard to find a man less qualified by training and attitude to investigate a social phenomenon like the one that shook Los Angeles in August 1965." Even before the lifting of the curfew, Governor Brown had can-vased the idea of an investigative commission with his special counsel Warren Christopher, a partner at O'Melveny and Myers, L.A.'s most prestigious and powerful law firm. Brown was looking ahead to the 1966 elections, when he would face formidable challenges from the right: Sam Yorty in the spring primary and probably Ronald Reagan in the fall. He and Christopher both felt that a riot study that read like a civil rights manifesto would be political death. They sought "a diagnosis of the city's sickness which would be acceptable to the very groups in the city which bore a heavy responsibility for creating the cancerous environment," Jacobs wrote. "Threatened by a real possi-bility of political defeat from the right, they gave the initiative to the right." In particular, Brown agreed with advice from Christopher and his senior staff that in order to bring the establishment along with the process, the chair of the commission had to be someone with unas-sailable conservative credentials and an "an impeccable reputation in the business community."[10]

McCone, who sat on the boards of many of California's largest corporations, fit the description to a tee. In the late 1930s he had cofounded the engineering firm Bechtel-McCone, which during the war operated a shipyard that employed many Black workers, thus giving him—rather ludicrously—standing as someone "who knew Negroes." Despite accusations of having been a war profiteer, he rapidly ascended the ladder of power in postwar Washington—appointed chair of the Atomic Energy Commission by Eisenhower in 1958, and then director of the CIA by Kennedy in 1961. As CIA director he oversaw early attempts to assassinate Castro and played a central role in the Cuban Missile Crisis. He resigned in 1965 in protest over LBJ's refusal to widen the air war against North Vietnam. (In the 1970s, as a director of manufacturing company ITT, he would be involved in plotting the overthrow of Allende in Chile.)

McCone reluctantly accepted the governor's invitation to chair the commission and agreed to his stipulation that the report must be ready within a hundred days. He quickly sat down with Christopher, and, as he later told Jacobs, they "drafted a memorandum, a sort of frame of references, and this memorandum was transmitted and became, with such modifications as the governor's staff added, the directive to the commission from the governor." To fill out the rest of the commission, they chose, in striking disregard for the authentic voices of the South Central community, two Black notables: a conservative Republican judge, Earl Broady, and a newly elected school board member, the Reverend James Jones. The latter's views were more aligned with moderate civil rights leaders like the Reverend H. H. Brookins of the United Civil Rights Committee, but he was not a forceful personality, and his dissent carried little weight. Of the four additional whites, the key selection, who immediately joined McCone and Christopher in the inner sanctum of the commission, was insurance executive Asa Call, the elderly kingpin of a Los Angeles power structure anchored by the Chandler dynasty at the *Times*. Call would arouse much mirth by traveling around South Central in a limousine with a white chauffeur.[11]

Justice Department officials, led by Ramsey Clark, had arrived in Los Angeles with an eye to conducting their own investigation, but McCone twisted arms at the White House and was reassured that no separate report would be issued. The triumvirate, moreover, quickly established their authority by vetoing the suggestion from other members to let witnesses testify in open hearings.

Preposterous deference was paid to city officials during the closed hearings. Chief Parker, for instance, began his testimony by whining to the commissioners that "when you talk about dislocated minorities, and I am not saying this for sympathy, because I don't have to, but the police of this country, in my opinion, are the most downtrodden, oppressed, dislocated minority in America."[12] Later, when the ACLU tried to introduce evidence about police abuse, McCone sharply cut them off. Charges of police brutality, he declared, were "a device ... [of] our adversaries, those who would like to destroy the freedom that this country stands for." It was obvious that the chairman had made up his mind about responsibility for the uprising even before the closed hearings had begun. The unusually concise commission report was made public on December 2, exactly as McCone had promised Brown.[13]

Violence in the City—an End or a Beginning began by denying that Watts or any part of South Central was a slum; indeed, quoting from an anonymous Black leader, Los Angeles was "the best city in the world" in terms of housing for Blacks. Residential conditions, in fact, were almost idyllic:

> Watts, for example, is a community consisting mostly of one and two-story houses, a third of which are owned by the occupants. In the riot area, most streets are wide and usually quite clean; there are trees, parks, and playgrounds. A Negro in Los Angeles has long been able to sit where he wants in a bus or a movie house, to shop where he wishes, to vote, and to use public facilities without discrimination. The opportunity to succeed is probably unequaled in any other major American city.[14]

Although unemployment was a problem, the commission blamed overgenerous welfare policies for discouraging Blacks from seeking work. In addition, the level of income support available in Los Angeles was a magnet attracting the Southern flotsam who played a key role in the riot.[15] As David Sears and John McConahay paraphrased this section of the report:

> Attracted to Los Angeles by dreams of welfare luxury, the southern blacks were filled with a 'special measure of frustration and

disillusionment' [McCone] ... Thus, not only were the rioters outsiders; even worse, they were ungrateful outsiders. In this form, the southern newcomer hypothesis suggested to the people of Los Angeles that the white community should avoid any feelings of guilt over its contribution to the conditions that produced the riot. Indeed, it had done too much, rather than too little, for the blacks. Hence, the appropriate response to the riots was indignation.[16]

In conclusion, the commission blamed the riot on two culprits. First was a tiny criminal minority of newcomers, who for reasons unrelated to substantive grievances were responsible for most of the arson, violence, and looting. Relying solely on the testimonies of Parker and Yorty, it estimated that "only about two per cent [of the Black population] were involved in the disorder. Nevertheless, this violent fraction, however minor, has given the face of community relations in Los Angeles a sinister cast." Later, in testimony to HUAC, which investigated the Watts uprising a year and a half later, District Attorney Younger characterized this "riot-prone group" as "young and psychotic ... Each is a potential killer."[17]

Secondly, the commission indicted the civil rights movement in general, and local activists in particular, for fueling outrage that had no legitimate justification in Los Angeles conditions:

To be sure, the civil rights controversy has never been the issue in our community that it has been in the South. However, the accusations of the leaders of the national movement have been picked up by many local voices and have been echoed throughout the Negro community here ... The angry exhortations and the resulting disobedience to law in many parts of our nation appear to have contributed importantly to the feeling of rage which made the Los Angeles riots possible. Although the Commission received much thoughtful and constructive testimony from Negro witnesses, we also heard statements of the most extreme and emotional nature. For the most part our study fails to support—and indeed the evidence disproves—most of the statements made by the extremists.[18]

"Put bluntly," wrote riot scholar Robert Fogelson, "*Violence in the City* claimed that the rioters were marginal people and the riots meaningless outbursts."[19] Although the report noted Black resentment against Parker, it found no substantive basis for such feelings and praised Chief Parker and his heroic department for their "efficiency."

The vindication of Parker along with the so-called "riffraff" thesis of the criminal 2 percent set off furious reactions in the Black community. Billy Mills called the report "pitiful"; Booker Griffin of the Westminster Neighborhood Association denounced it as "disgusting"; and the California Advisory Committee to the US Commission on Civil Rights condemned it as "elementary, superficial, unoriginal and unimaginative."[20]

But the decisive refutation of the commission findings came from UCLA's Western Data Processing Center and its IBM 7090 supercomputer (the same one used by NASA and the Strategic Air Command) that social scientists used to crunch a mountain of census data, arrest records, and interviews with residents. Even before the completion of *Violence in the City*, the county probation department had used this computer power to study 400 arrested juveniles. Far from being marginal criminals, most had "little or no previous contact with the police," and the majority had been born in California, not the South. Less than 10 percent had been arrested for arson, assault or possession of a weapon; most were booked for loitering, curfew violations or looting.[21]

A few months later Fogelson, working for the President's Crime Commission, and researchers at the UCLA's Institute of Government and Public Affairs, launched what became the "Los Angeles Riot Study." They published separate reports that "together," Fogelson summarized, "left little doubt that the McCone Commission completely misunderstood the character and implications of the Los Angeles riots." The rioters, as many as 50,000, were a "substantial and representative minority, sympathetically regarded by the black community," and the "violent acts were expressions of genuine grievances and as such meaningful protests."[22] Later studies by UCLA's David Sears and others confirmed that "up to 15 per cent of the adult population took part; another 35 to 40 per cent were active spectators; long-time

residents supported the rioting as much as newcomers; and support
for the riot was as great among those better off and better educated
as among those less fortunate."[23]

Watts's "Manifesto"

The most incisive critique of McCone, however, came from the pen of
Bayard Rustin in a celebrated March 1966 article where he contrasted
Violence in the City and the notorious Moynihan Report (March 1965)
on the Black family with the Watts "Manifesto" that had been enun-
ciated in the streets the previous August. According to him,

> Unfortunately, but inevitably, the emphasis on *Negro behavior* in
> both reports has stirred up an abstract debate over the interpreta-
> tion of data rather than suggesting programs for dealing with the
> existing and very concrete situation in which American Negroes
> find themselves. For example, neither report is concerned about
> segregation and both tacitly assume that the Civil Rights Acts
> of 1964 and 1965 are already destroying this system. In the case
> of the McCone Report, this leaves the writers free to discuss the
> problems of Negro housing, education, and unemployment in great
> detail without attacking the conditions of de facto segregation that
> underlie them.

Rustin went on to confront the widespread allegation, particularly
dear to Chief Parker and Mayor Yorty, that peaceful civil disobedience
was the catalyst to anarchy and violence:

> It would be hard to frame a more insidiously equivocal statement of
> the Negro grievance concerning law enforcement during a period
> that included the release of the suspects in the murder of the three
> civil-rights workers in Mississippi, the failure to obtain convictions
> against the suspected murderers of Medgar Evers and Mrs. Violet
> Liuzzo ... and the police violence in Selma, Alabama—to mention
> only a few of the more notorious cases ... And surely it would have
> been more to the point to mention that throughout the nation Negro

demonstrations have almost invariably been non-violent, and that the major influence on the Negro community of the civil-rights movement has been the strategy of discipline and dignity.

The McCone Commission, he concluded, had been "obsessed by the few prophets of violent resistance," and "ignores the fact that never before has an American group sent so many people to jail or been so severely punished for trying to uphold the law of the land."[24]

Jobs, he continued, were both the problem and the solution. The report's section on employment "not unexpectedly" was "the most ignorant, unimaginative, and conservative—despite its dramatic recommendation that 50,000 new jobs be created." On youth unemployment, the report suggested that "existing federal projects initiate a series of 'attitudinal training' programs to help young Negroes develop the necessary motivation to hold on to these new jobs which are to come from somewhere that the commission keeps secret." This, Rustin argued, was "just another example of the commission's continued reliance on public relations, and of its preoccupation with the 'dull, devastating spiral' of Negro failure." The truth of the matter, he said, was that "Negro youths cannot change their attitudes until they see that they can get jobs. When what they see is unemployment and their Economic Opportunity programs being manipulated in behalf of politicians, their attitudes will remain realistically cynical."

Rustin called Watts and neighborhoods like it elsewhere "ghettoes of despair." There were, of course,

the unemployable poor: the children, the aging, the permanently handicapped. No measure of employment or of economic growth will put an end to their misery, and only government programs can provide them with a decent way of life. The care of these people could be made a major area of job growth. Los Angeles officials could immediately train and put to work women and unemployed youths as school attendants, recreation counselors, practical nurses, and community workers. The federal government and the state of California could aid the people of Watts by beginning a massive public-works program to build needed housing, schools, hospitals, neighborhood centers, and transportation facilities: this, too, would create new jobs. In short, they could begin to develop the $100-billion freedom budget advocated by A. Philip Randolph.

In the aftermath of the rebellion, Reverend Brookins of the UCRC, Councilman Billy Mills, UCLA economist Paul Bullock, Paul Schrade of the United Auto Workers, and others were working hard to shift the debate to jobs. One of the most significant statistics to emerge from the probation department's study was that 44 percent of the jailed juveniles came from families where the principal breadwinner was unemployed. The UCRC proposed a crash WPA-type program—*à la* A. Philip Randolph's "Freedom Budget"—to put to work at a living wage "all the unskilled and semi-skilled workers who cannot be absorbed by private employment."[25] This emphasis on the causal centrality of joblessness in the August events received a surprise endorsement from the most unlikely of sources. Appearing on CBS in late August, Barry Goldwater said,

> The thing that happened in Los Angeles—and I think it will happen again in this country—was caused by people … just being fed up with not being able to get jobs, with not being able to live as well as other people live … I don't discount the agitation that took place, but I think we better get on with the job of providing training, providing incentive and providing integration wherever it doesn't exist for all people, whether they be Negro or white.[26]

Deadwyler

New Year 1966 arrived with few good tidings for the residents of Watts and its neighboring communities. While Mayor Yorty, Governor Brown and the Johnson administration continued to battle over the details of a federal response to conditions in Watts, the tension on the streets was still like a fallen high-power line, ready to kill the unwary. Most residents, moreover, had a family member or friend trapped in the gears of the judicial process or already on their way to a county road camp or state prison, and the LAPD, exonerated by the McCone Commission, remained ready to shoot at the slightest provocation.

So were some whites. On February 1 a carload of racists from Burbank, trawling South Central for random Blacks, murdered a young sailor, twenty-two-year-old Mickey Garron, who was waiting for a bus at the corner of Seventy-Second Street and Broadway. He was hit by no less than seventy shotgun pellets.[27] Opinion surveys had shown that many residents in South Central believed the rebellion would make whites more understanding and sympathetic to their plight; in fact, the reverse was the case. Nationally, 90 percent of whites believed that the police in L.A. and elsewhere had been too lenient on rioters, and a mere 5 percent believed that discrimination or white racism had anything to do with the uprisings.[28] Most white Angelenos were preoccupied by imaginary Black "savagery," not by the crisis of Black humanity.[29]

At the beginning of March the LAPD began complaining about the hostile attitudes of groups of young men "milling" around Watts. "It was just a question of time," one cop told the *Times* later. "It was building." But the anger was accumulating out of seemingly unrelated issues in diverse places. The shooting, for instance, of a Black Army captain in Louisiana while he talked on the phone with his brother in L.A. A bitter strike at a metal company on Alameda. A street fight on a downtown bus between Black and Chicano teenagers. The nonfatal drive-by shooting of two Black youth by three Chicano teenagers. Finally, the rough arrest of a Jordan High School student who had thrown a rock at a teacher's car coalesced and detonated all these tensions. High school students and young adults stoned passing cars near the Jordan Downs "Pentagon" at 103rd and Grape, followed by the burning of several stores and rock-throwing battles with police. Presumably retaliating for the earlier shootings, a Black teenager shot and killed Larry Gomez, thirty-five, a truck driver for a bottled water company who was known for being outspoken in support of Black civil rights. Meanwhile, police gunned down Joseph Campbell as he was walking on a sidewalk with other Black youth, then unsuccessfully tried to cover up their culpability. The press called these events the "Second Watts Riot" or "Watts II," but it would have been more accurate, in hindsight at least, to have seen this cluster of violence and anger as merely one episode in a continuing "slow riot."[30]

Indeed, in early May a police killing inflamed the Black community like nothing since the rape of Beverly Tate and the arrest of the Fryes. Barbara and Leonard Deadwyler, both twenty-five, had recently moved to Los Angeles from Forsyth County, Georgia, an area that had an infamous history. In 1912, following several lynchings, the county's *entire* Black population was violently expelled, and Forsyth remained almost totally white through the 1950s. The Deadwylers, presumably one of a small number of Black families in the county, left in 1964 around the time of a race riot in Gainesville, the county seat.[31] In Los Angeles, Leonard, like many new in-migrants, was able to find only occasional work, and on Saturday, May 7—the day of his death—he and Barbara were evicted from their home for nonpayment of rent. Barbara, eight months pregnant, felt labor pains, and Leonard asked a friend to drive them to County General hospital. The friend, however, was too drunk and nervous to drive, and passed the wheel to Leonard, who tied a white handkerchief on the car antenna—a common practice in the rural South—to alert police that it was an emergency.

He drove very fast, north along Avalon Boulevard, and was pulled over by police for speeding. Officer Jerold Bova, twenty-three, who had earlier been accused of abusing four boys for running a red light on their bikes, approached the Deadwyler vehicle from the passenger side with his gun drawn and its hammer cocked. (A witness would later testify that he had a furious look on his face.) According to Bova, while pointing the .38 at Leonard, he leaned into the car to shut off the ignition. The car lurched forward and the gun accidentally discharged, killing Deadwyler. Barbara Deadwyler, backed up by several witnesses, said Bova was flat out lying: he never leaned into the car, the car never moved (in fact it was blocked by another squad car in front), and the shooting was no accident. He simply murdered her husband.[32]

She soon retained a young lawyer to defend her account in the upcoming coroners' inquest: Johnnie Cochran. Only twenty-nine, he had just entered private practice after several years working criminal cases (the obscenity trial of Lenny Bruce, for one) for the city attorney. Years later, in his autobiography, he was to write:

> Many of the people who watched the Simpson trial believed they knew everything they needed to know about me by watching my work in his defense; it is impossible to know anything at all about me without knowing about this coroner's inquest. If one case could be said to have shaped my career, it was the investigation into the death of Leonard Deadwyler.[33]

His initial tactic was a press conference at County General with Barbara Deadwyler making a brief but dramatic appearance in a wheelchair. Tearfully she told reporters that when Bova approached their car, "my husband asked him to lead us to the hospital and then he didn't say anything and shot him." As she was wheeled back to her hospital room, Cochran schooled the press in some of the obvious contradictions in Bova's account. For one thing, the ignition was turned off, and besides, it would have been very "difficult to grab the ignition key from the passenger side of a 1957 Buick." Moreover Bova "never reached over [Barbara Deadwyler] in the passenger seat nor were his head and shoulders inside the car at any time." Smiling to reporters, Cochran hinted that this was only a foretaste of the case he would make at the inquest.

Deadwyler's funeral took place the following Monday, May 16. A silent cortege, several blocks long, walked behind his hearse to Praisers of Zion Missionary Baptist Church. The crowd of mourners was too large to fit inside the church, so hundreds stood quietly outside listening to the memorial service over a loudspeaker. After brief remarks by the local pastor, Reverend Brookins took the pulpit. "We're concerned about the truth and all the diabolical circumstances in the death of Leonard Deadwyler," he said. "Justice does not always remain on the scaffold. This is a blatant kind of situation. Why did the officer approach the car with a drawn gun? Why was it cocked?" The congregation echoed: "Why?"[34]

After the service, the Committee to End Legalized Murder by Cops, newly organized by the cadre of what would soon become the

Che-Lumumba Club of the Communist Party, circulated a sensational leaflet—*We Charge Murder!*—calling for protestors to gather the following evening at Will Rogers Park. Five hundred people showed up, including Southern California CP leader Dorothy Healey and her tiny but feisty mother, Barbara Nestor. After a brief rally, they were stirred by orators to march on the Seventy-Seventh Street police station. When they arrived they found it defended by police sharpshooters on the roof, and after some spirited picketing, a large contingent of protestors went to the UCRC office in the hope of continuing the debate about the direction of the campaign. The office was locked, and as people milled around outside, some broke off and went to a nearby liquor store where, in chaotic circumstances, they smashed bottles and fought with clerks. Police arrived and began skirmishing not only with the "looters" in the liquor store but also the peaceful crowd in front of the UCRC headquarters. At some point in the general melee, two *Newsweek* reporters, Karl Fleming and David Moberg, were attacked by youths wielding wooden four-by-fours. It was a tragic encounter since Fleming, who suffered a broken jaw and a concussion, was highly respected by Southern activists for his courageous reportage on the 1962 Meredith riots at Ole Miss and the 1964 murders of civil rights workers Chaney, Goodman and Schwerner. Moberg, future executive editor of *In These Times*, "escaped with a black eye and bruises."[35]

Mayor Yorty, looking for a wedge issue in the down-home stretch of his primary fight with Governor Brown, charged the next day that the Deadwyler campaign was simply a cover for a Communist conspiracy to discredit the LAPD. As proof, he evoked the name of Franklin Alexander, the national chair of the party-sponsored W. E. B. Du Bois Clubs, whom he claimed was the instigator of Tuesday night's disorder. "There are leftwing agitators," he declared, "who try to throw gasoline on any disturbance that breaks out." He also attacked Brookins for "very bad judgment" in his funeral oration and blamed the news media for "giving the Negro leader too much attention."[36] For the remaining weeks of the primary campaign, Yorty, who for decades had made anti-communism his bread and butter, hammered away on the conspiracy theme. For Alexander and his comrades, however, the notoriety generated by Yorty's fulminations was fungible as street credibility and helped them win a place in the leadership of the emergent Black united front.

To the consternation of the coroner and the county sheriffs, more than a thousand South Central residents showed up downtown at the old Hall of Records the morning of Thursday, May 19, for the beginning of the inquest. The assigned courtroom, however, could accommodate less than a third of the jostling, excited crowd, so a deputy announced a list of ministers to be seated as "community representatives." "We don't want no preachers in there," people screamed. "Let us in. We want in!" A platoon of baton-wielding sheriffs managed to secure the doors, but Younger realized that it would be almost impossible to move the jurors, and especially the witnesses, into the courtroom, so he shifted the venue to a larger room in the county courthouse. But the new courtroom was still too small to seat the entire multitude. So, amid much commotion, a loudspeaker was set up in the mall outside to allow the others to listen to the testimony.

The first witness was Mary Jones, who had observed the killing from a nearby parked car. When asked if she could point out Officer Bova, she delighted spectators by replying: "All of them look alike to me." But, she insisted seriously, "I think it was cold-blooded murder." The spectators cheered. The assistant DA who was leading the questioning asked for an immediate adjournment. The hearing had lasted only a half hour.

The day had been a fiasco for the DA's office, and in the evening the slow riot resumed, with 150 people stoning cars in Watts on 103rd Street, while a car caravan cruised around Watts attacking liquor stores and attempting to burn down a drive-in restaurant. The police responded with the wholesale arrest of teenage curfew violators, regardless of whether they had been involved in the incidents or not. Younger, who feared that all this signaled that the city was on the verge of a new uprising, quickly moved the next morning to have the inquest televised. KTLA, whose anchor George Putnam was the most reactionary on-air presence in Southern California, agreed to interrupt its daytime programming to broadcast the hearings.

The inquest was televised for eight days. It was a continuous back-and-forth of cops buttressing Bova's story while Black witnesses contradicted it. Bova himself was excused for "security reasons" after only an hour of testimony, while Barbara Deadwyler was subjected to a full day of hard grilling by Provenzano and ended up fainting and having to be revived with smelling salts. There was only one Black person on the coroners' jury, and the verdict of "accidental homicide" was preordained by the white proclivity to take a cop's word over that of a Black witness under almost any circumstance. Bova's acquittal was accepted with resignation by Brookins and other moderate leaders, but Billy Mills was furious, as were the kids on the streets of Watts that evening.

The white electorate, heavily pro-police in the Deadwyler matter, delivered a verdict of their own a week later: voting down a bond issue to build a hospital in Watts-Willowbrook—a key demand of the Black community and a major recommendation of the McCone report. For Black voters it was a direct slap in the face: Proposition 14 revisited. Meanwhile, Mayor Yorty, after losing the primary to Governor Brown, remained relentless in his quest to prove the red menace behind the Deadwyler campaign. Finally, in September, a grand jury indicted twenty-two-year-old John Harris for "criminal syndicalism," an archaic statute last used in 1934 to imprison eight Communist farmworker leaders. Harris, a Birmingham native and the former director of the SNCC project in Indianola, Mississippi, had recently joined the Progressive Labor Party, a small but active Maoist group. His offense, which carried a prison term of one to fifteen years, was the distribution of leaflets at the inquest that accused Parker and Bova of murder. Harris's fate hung in the balance for several years until the law was finally overturned, for good, by the California Supreme Court.

1966 was a grim year for social justice, but it had one bright spot. At a testimonial dinner in July and in front of hundreds of guests, Chief Parker keeled over dead. Across Los Angeles there were memorable celebrations of his departure, but also apprehension that he would live on through his protégés in the chief's office and in the militarized culture of the LAPD.

15

Cultural Revolution:
The Watts Renaissance (1965–67)

I n the weeks after curfew was lifted in 1965, strange wraith-like figures were seen sifting through the burnt debris left by the uprising. It was assumed by bemused residents and police alike that they were scavengers, but what value were the twisted pieces of metal, charred window frames, melted neon signs, broken glass, and smoke-stained mannequins they loaded into children's red wagons? In fact, these objects were ingredients of dreams and nightmares, and the scavengers were artists: Noah Purifoy (cofounder of the Watts Towers Arts Center), John Outterbridge, David Hammons, and others. Inspired by Marcel Duchamp, Simon Rodia (who built the Watts Towers out of colorful debris), and the folk artists of the Black South, they transformed three tons of riot detritus into fetishes, altars, images of mythic heroes, and visual manifestos in familiar but unknown languages. With the help of his musician comrade Judson Powell and other artist friends, Purifoy assembled sixty-six pieces (*66 Signs of Neon*), which were exhibited first at Markham Junior High School in spring 1966, and then traveled the university art gallery circuit for nearly two years, baffling most white viewers while delighting Blacks.

Mixed-media assemblage, or "junk art," according to critic Peter Plagens, was "the first home-grown California modern art." It was a trademark of seminal Ferus Gallery artists such as Ed Kienholz, whose noirish *Back Seat Dodge '38* led supervisors to threaten to cut funds to the LA County Museum of Art when it was exhibited the same week as the second Watts riot. But, as historian Dan Widener observes, "the form seemed particularly suited to the needs of Black artists." Assemblage, "a form given to juxtaposition ... allowed for the exposition of both irony and contradiction. That it did so relatively inexpensively was a bonus. That it blended a highly intellectual process of selection with an improvisational, even spontaneous, method made for a jazz-like sensibility." Like jazz, assemblage art "suggested the possibility of a non-essentialized form of black creativity whose racial codings might be deciphered by black audiences whether or not white artists or audiences sought to replicate, extend, or consume the end result."[1]

The artists were but one detachment of a broad movement of musicians, dancers, writers, actors, filmmakers, and poets who made Watts, as the Russian constructivists would say, into the "cultural condenser" of the immense energies unleashed by the rebellion. Indeed, by spring 1966, everyone was talking about a "Watts Renaissance"—although "cultural revolution," which Malcolm X had called for in 1964, might be a better term.[2] Like Purifoy and his magical riot debris, Black arts collectives scavenged space in the wrecked but recyclable shells of furniture stores and markets along "Charcoal Alley." Soon 103rd Street was home to some of the most vital cultural institutions on the West Coast: the Watts Writers Workshop, the Mafundi Institute, Studio Watts, Watts Happening Coffee House, and the Watts Towers Arts Center. The Westminster Neighborhood Association building, the only one on the block spared by rioters, acted as a headquarters for the Renaissance, while the annual Watts Festival, inaugurated in August 1966, showcased its achievements. At a time when the McCone Commission's warning about the "dull, devastating spiral of failure" in the Black community reflected elite white opinion, Watts was becoming, if only for a few seasons, Los Angeles's Left Bank. The seeds for the hothouse growth of Watts's cultural enterprises were provided by the unity, pride and community spirit generated by the rebellion, but the ground had been tilled much earlier.

Renaissance Man

The "Watts Renaissance" and the broader community arts movement have been the subjects of several groundbreaking studies, most notably Steve Isoardi's *The Dark Tree* (2006) and Dan Widener's *Black Arts West* (2010).[3] While both authors stress the important continuities with Central Avenue's florescence in the 1940s and the avant-garde jazz scene of the 1950s, they locate the principal aesthetic and political template for the Watts Renaissance in a picaresque band of free jazz musicians, led by pianist Horace Tapscott, called the Underground Musicians Association (UGMA). At the end of 1950s, after Ornette Coleman and Eric Dolphy had joined the exodus of LA jazz musicians to New York, Tapscott, who could have easily taken the same path and ended up on the cover of *Downbeat* magazine, decided instead to replant himself in the musical grass roots of South Central L.A.

Leaving Lionel Hampton's band at the beginning of 1961, he and pianist-singer Linda Hill organized what became a years-long jam session held in a succession of friends' garages and homes, starting with Hill's. It attracted outstanding but idiosyncratic musicians—Lester Robertson, Guido Sinclair, Arthur Blythe (from San Diego), Everett Brown Jr. and many others—all of them sharing Tapscott's interest in exploring newer, freer sounds, in ensembles of all sizes from quartets to UGMA's big band: the Pan Afrikan Peoples Arkestra. Although Sun Ra had, earlier in the 1950s, pioneered a jazz commune that transgressed musical (and planetary) boundaries, it was an autocracy in which Ra's creative authority was unassailable. UGMA, in contrast, was an anarchist participatory democracy, devoted to collective improvisation in the manner of early jazz and contemporary free jazz. Tapscott acted as gadfly, synthesizer, and pathfinder while pursuing his own compositional projects.

Amiri Baraka, speaking about what he and Larry Neal had christened the "Black Arts Movement," once said, "Coltrane is our flag." UGMA's own paradigm was Coltrane's *Ascension*, recorded at the end of June 1965, six weeks before the Watts Rebellion. This extraordinary forty-minute piece—the *Finnegan's Wake* of the so-called "new wave"—fissured the jazz world: most white critics, and some

Black, denounced it as "anti-jazz" and wrote obituaries for Coltrane's so recently brilliant career. But younger, more radical musicians— including Archie Shepp and Pharoah Sanders, who played in the session along with the Coltrane quartet and nine or ten others— acclaimed it as revolutionary, a utopic step to total freedom. "It broke the seal," writes *New York Times* music critic Ben Ratliff, "on full-bore, single-gesture, all-out, free-blowing sessions ... as well as the notion of the jazz band as community, a collective effort to make large-scale textural music rather than an exclusive, carefully structured machine moving through smaller and more defined parts." This, he concludes, "had obvious political implications in 1965."[4] It certainly did for Tapscott and the UGMA, for whom it was an anthem of Black liberation and so important to the group's self-conception that when the collective decided to rename itself, it chose "Union of God's Musicians and Artists Ascension" (UGMAA).

But UGMA's commitment to musical experimentation was insep-arable from their African-influenced conception of community arts. "From its inception," Isoardi emphasizes, "the movement initiated by Horace and his colleagues ... drew heavily from and was inspired by communal aspects of traditional West and West Central African cultures." The griots, in their civic roles as troubadours, collective historians, teachers, and master storytellers were potent models for the UGMA, as were their analogues in Southern Afro-American history. Like the griot guilds, the Arkestra was a school that included musicians at different skill levels: learners were not sent off to music teachers but invited onto the stage, where they served apprenticeships alongside musical masters. Meanwhile, African themes and motifs regularly recurred in Tapscott's compositions and in the poetry read during UGMA performances.

The free-form and eclectic aesthetic of UGMA could be discon-certing to first-time listeners. Walter Savage, a bass player who was responsible for organizing performances at Watts Happening Coffee House, told Isoardi about his first encounter with UGMA in late 1965:

I expected to have a jam session and did all I could to get people in there ... [UGMA] sort of straggled in, one or two or three at a time ... turned out to be about twenty-five of them. I never got to speak to anybody. They just started playing, and they weren't playing a song. I was kind of in shock. They just set up and started to going at it. I'm thinking, "Are they going to play a song or what?" ... But it was all free stuff. They never played a tune the whole time they were here."[5]

In fact, Tapscott, like Sun Ra, delighted in taking the least-traveled path and producing totally unexpected out-of-genre music. Thus the Arkestra in its innumerable facets could sound like a holiness church choir, a German brass band on psychedelics, a New Orleans funeral procession, an Afro-Latin drum carnival, or a wailing chorus of lost souls from the depths of hell.

UGMA was also a multimedia catalyst, bringing Black artists of all descriptions into collaboration. In Harlem, St. Louis, Chicago and elsewhere, the Black Arts Movement took much of its creative inspiration and programmatic ideas from the "new wave" jazz of Coleman and Coltrane, as well as from the Harlem Renaissance's fascination with poetry as jazz.[6] In Los Angeles UGMA went further and began to incorporate the spoken word together with theater and dance into its repertoire. The flexibly scaled and open performance structure of the Arkestra, together with the super-improvisational character of much of its music, constituted a natural environment for poetry, beginning with Jayne Cortez, Ornette Coleman's ex-wife and the founder of LA Friends of SNCC, whose skill with words was enhanced by her prodigious understanding of Black music. Soon Quincy Troupe, Ted Jones (Lena Horne's son), Kamau Daáood, Ojenke, and the Watts Prophets (the godfathers of rap) were also performing with UGMA. Ojenke, interviewed by Isoardi, recalled the excitement of these events: "I read with them in coffeehouses, parks, community centers, churches, schools. Horace liked to have poets there ... He would like to have all the artists represented, like a multimedia presentation before all that was happening. Everybody would be there—dancers, singers."[7]

Although the early UGMA was notoriously nomadic, moving between a succession of crash pads and jam session garages, after the rebellion it acquired rehearsal and performance space for several years in the former supermarket that had been converted into the Watts Happening Coffee House. A vital hub of the Renaissance, the Coffee House, funded by the Southern California Council of Churches and the Office of Economic Opportunity, was also the home of the Watts Writers Workshop and the Mafundi Institute, a theatrical workshop run by the acclaimed actor William Marshall. This fortuitous propinquity led to multimedia collaborations between members of the three collectives as well as with the poets who regularly read at the coffeehouse. What emerged, according to poet Aldon Nielsen, was an "omniverse of jazz and text."[8]

Tapscott and Marshall quickly formed a creative alliance. While the poly-talented Marshall regularly read poetry or sang spirituals during UGMA performances, Tapscott acted as the theater group's musical director. Some of their collaborations were legendary. When Marshall staged a production of *Oedipus Rex*, Isoardi writes, the play was "known to UGMAers as 'the original motherfucker' ... at the Coffee House, with the setting shifted to Theban Egypt, he organized an all-black, practically all-UGMA cast, with the band providing the music."[9] The Sophoclean "motherfucker" was followed by other coproductions, including Marshall's popular one-man performance *Enter Frederick Douglass* and the first English adaptation of Aimé Césaire's *La Tragédie du Roi Christophe*.

Tapscott also worked with Studio Watts, located just down 104th Street in a former furniture store. Organized in fall 1964 by the ubiquitous Jayne Cortez and James Woods ("an accountant who moonlighted as the doorman at Shelly's Manne-Hole" in Hollywood), the studio offered an omnibus selection of workshops in the visual arts, dance, theater, poetry and music. The theater component, however, soon spun off as the Watts Repertory Theater Company. At the studio, Tapscott and other UGMAers rubbed shoulders creatively with musicians John Carter and Bobby Bradford, who were rehearsing the unit that became the New Art Jazz Ensemble. Carter, a clarinet virtuoso and academic prodigy who had a music BA by age nineteen, had like Tapscott resisted the siren call of Manhattan and spent most of his career teaching in Los Angeles public schools.[10] Born in Fort Worth, he had played in an R&B band with fellow Texan Coleman before going off to college, while Bradford, a trumpeter and also a school teacher, was an alumni of Coleman's late-Fifties LA sessions and briefly preceded Don Cherry in Ornette's early Sixties quartet. In 1969 Tapscott, Carter and Bradford joined forces to record *West Coast Hot*, an album that featured "The Dark Tree," Tapscott's signature composition, with an astonishing interplay between piano and clarinet. Carter would continue to be a key musical ally of UGMA, although recognition as one of the finest clarinetists in jazz would only come late in life. Just before his death in 1991 he completed *Roots and Folklore*— an extraordinary five-album cycle of Afro-American history—that was in many ways the capstone to the Black Arts project of cultural recovery and communal memory.

Above all else, however, UGMA was the peoples' orchestra of South Central L.A., the movement's band. It performed at countless rallies, fundraising benefits, and celebrations for organizations and causes as diverse as the Black Muslims, SNCC, the Communist Party, the Black Student Alliance, and later the Free Angela Davis campaign. It also participated collectively in progressive coalitions such as the Black Congress and the Peace Action Committee, and touched bases with the New Left through the Ash Grove, the folk and blues club. However, as both Isoardi and Widener emphasize, it was the UGMA's increasingly close relationship (but not affiliation) with the Black Panther Party that became most striking from the summer of 1968 onward. Tapscott knew Elaine Brown, a singer and future chairwoman of the BPP, from Watts Happening, and he arranged and performed on her famed BPP album *Seize the Time*. Three Panthers, moreover, were members of the Arkestra, while John Huggins, the leader of the LA chapter who would be killed by US members at UCLA in 1969, sang in its choir. The band energized almost all Panther benefits, helping to raise much of the staggering amounts of bail imposed on Party members.

The Panther rank and file reciprocated this solidarity. Once, when the musicians' union usurped "the Ark"'s regular gig in South Park, sending a group of Black and white musicians, "two Black Panthers got on the stage with their guns and demanded to know, 'Where's the Ark?!' They shot some rounds in the air, and the band broke up."

"Monday morning," Tapscott remembered, "the president of the union called my house: 'Horace, your Arkestra has the job at South Park next week.'"[11] These ties, of course, made the UGMA a target of the FBI, who listed it as a "black nationalist hate group," and also a target of the LAPD, which repeatedly raided Watts Happening. Yet for Tapscott and his griots, such harassment was inadvertent tribute to the cultural revolution they helped launch and would keep alive for several more decades.[12]

103rd and Hollywood

He was the odd man out in Watts in fall 1965. A stocky 51-year-old Jewish guy whose résumé included sparring with Hemingway, arresting Nazi idol Leni Riefenstahl, and winning the 1954 Academy Award for screenwriting (for *On the Waterfront*). A month after the rebellion, he left Beverly Hills and drove south on an impulse, and put up a note on the bulletin board at the Westminster Neighborhood Association building: "Creative Writing Class—all interested sign below." "It would be pleasant to add," Budd Schulberg later recalled, "that a dozen aspiring young writers signed immediately and we were off and writing. The truth was, nobody signed up. Nobody came. Week after week I sat there like an idiot shepherd without a flock, shuffling my notes."[13] Gradually a writing group coalesced, a random cross section of Watts society: several young homeless men, a school dropout preyed upon by the LAPD, an unemployed warehouseman, a middle-class matron, a former chorus girl, an Army veteran who arrived in Watts clueless on the first night of rioting, and so on.[14]

There were eventually dozens, even scores, of workshops in Watts in 1966 and 1967, but none had the cache or resources that Schulberg was able to mobilize. After a few phone calls, checks arrived from James Baldwin, Elia Kazan, Ira Gershwin, Richard Burton, the Kennedys, and so on. When this proved insufficient, Schulberg had a word with his close friend John Steinbeck—and the Watts Writers Workshop (WWW) received a grant from the National Endowment for the Arts. The workshop soon became one of Hollywood's favorite feel-good philanthropies, although to call it "radical chic" in the Tom Wolfe fashion would ignore the fact that at least a large minority (perhaps even a majority) of actors, unlike studios and producers, acknowledged their creative debt to Black America and authentically wanted an open door to Black talent.

But as the workshop matured, an inevitable conflict broke out over what Widener characterizes as Schulberg's "cultural liberalism": his belief that racial injustice within Hollywood and in its depiction of American reality could be corrected in collaboration with the industry's elites. Later members of the WWW had a very different agenda. In the fall of 1968, Widener writes, "thirteen members of the group left, citing 'subtle censorship' and 'literary sharecropping.'" The thirteen secessionists published *Watts Poets* (1968), which Widener contrasts with *From the Ashes* (1966), Schulberg's anthology of work in progress from the first WWW cohort: "In place of positing literature as a vaccine against social upheaval, Milton McFarlane's introductory sentence in *Watts Poets* proclaimed, 'There can't be a successful adjustment of black people to the American economic system.'"[15] As WWW alumni like Kamau Daáood and the Watts Prophets (Father Amde Hamilton, Richard Dedeaux and Otis O'Solomon) turned toward Black power, repression soon followed. In 1973 the FBI superinformant Darthard Perry—who had already conducted surveillance on Mervyn Dymally, California's first Black lieutenant governor, and bugged the studios of KPFK-Pacifica—burned down the WWW headquarters and theater.

The other cultural project growing out of the rebellion that also brought community together with Hollywood was the Inner City Cultural Center (ICCC). Its lasting importance, moreover, was much greater than the WWW. It was the brainchild of Dr. Alfred Cannon, who, with his UCLA colleague Hiawatha Harris, was part of a group of Black psychiatrists studying the psychological ramifications of the civil rights movement and the long-term effects of racism on Black mental health. Before he moved to Zimbabwe in 1983 to help organize its postcolonial medical system, Cannon had helped set in motion an extraordinary number of vital community institutions, including the Mafundi Institute, the Frederick Douglass Child Care Center, the Inner City Mental Health Program and the ICCC. According to

Dymally, Cannon was also "the one who conceived the idea of the Drew School," the medical school in South L.A. that opened its doors in 1970 in association with county-administered Martin Luther King Hospital. He was the founding head of psychiatry.[16]

Cannon, like Dymally, had a cordial relationship with Ron Karenga of US, in part because of the shared belief that the psychological health of the Black community required an African cultural core. Cannon frequently compared the Black "diasporic" condition to that of American Jews, stressing the profound effect that the establishment of Israel had had upon Jewish self-perception. Blacks, he argued, needed to transcend the legacy of slavery through positive identification with newly independent Black states in Africa and the Caribbean.[17] They collaborated together in the establishment of the Mafundi Institute and in the design of the Black studies program at UCLA, which became a battleground between US and the Panthers. Because he and Dr. Harris supported Charles Thomas, Karenga's nominee for chair of the program, they were denounced by the Panthers as "government bootlickers" and "part of the vicious [US] plot" (the assassination of Bunch Carter and John Huggins at UCLA in 1969).[18] These recriminations, together with a series of other setbacks and disappointments at UCLA and Drew, led to his eventual departure to Africa, where he died in 1989.

Unlike 103rd Street's participatory and largely amateur scene, the ICCC was envisioned as a major professional repertory theater company, offering classical, modern, and avant-garde performances at low cost to the adult inner-city public and for free to high school students, as well as providing training programs in a variety of theater and media trades. Cannon's goal, he said, was "to establish a center of excellence so that there will be an opportunity for major performances to appear right in the heart of a minority community so that minorities can witness first-hand events of cultural excellence in an institution that is a part of the community."[19] To build such a stage required powerful alliances beyond the nominal reach of an untenured UCLA faculty member, as well as an expert knowledge of the different currents within contemporary theater. This role fell to Gregory Peck. Beyond playing Atticus Fitch, Peck was a progressive anti-war

Democrat who had undertaken significant fundraising for civil rights causes during UCRC days. He was an equally experienced builder of acting institutions, from a pioneering Irish film school to local theaters across the country. With a little arm twisting, he added Budd Schulberg, Robert Wise and Max Palevsky to the board, along with Arab American actress Marlo Thomas, hugely popular for her sitcom *That Girl*. With the support of Julian Nava, the first Chicano elected to the LA School Board (in 1967), the board negotiated a federally financed contract with the LA Unified School District to present live theater to 35,000 high school sophomores every year.[20]

The genius of the ICCC, however, was its understanding of the creative potential in an inner city that, while majority Black, had substantial communities of Chicanos, Japanese Americans and elderly whites, as well as groups of Native Americans, Samoans and Latin Americans. In a sense, Cannon and the ICCC invented multiculturalism long before the concept existed, aspiring, in Cannon's words, "to develop a Black, a Brown, a Yellow and a Red theater—but in an atmosphere of collaboration and cooperation."[21] To make this possible, the ICCC took over the old Boulevard Theater at Washington and Vermont, a mid-city crossroads of minority neighborhoods. The remodel started in summer 1966 when the city was on edge from the Deadwyler inquest. The alchemist who made multiculturalism work was C. Bernard Jackson, the second artistic director after the brief tenure of Andre Gregory (subject of the 1981 film *My Dinner with Andre*), who left after the school board censored his version of a Molière play.[22] Jackson had grown up in Brooklyn, moved to L.A. after military service and, while a graduate student in music at UCLA, scored an "agit-prop musical about the growing civil rights movement entitled *Fly Blackbird* that utilized a multiethnic cast." It won an Obie.[23]

Jackson and Cannon were both strikingly original in their conception of the ICCC and at the same time gave life back to an old ghost. A year after its opening, the *Times* theater critic Cecil Smith compared the ICCC to the Federal Theater Project of the Depression years. He fondly recalled "as a youngster seeing superb productions [in L.A.] of Hauptmann's 'The Weavers,' the Negro 'Macbeth,' 'Triple-A Plowed

Under' and the Duke Ellington–Hall Johnson [collaboration] 'Run Little Chillun.'" By 1939, he reported, "Federal Theater productions here had been seen by 2.5 million people." But this hugely successful peoples' theater was destroyed by HUAC in 1939 after allegations that it was a front for Communists and other subversives. One of the committee's interrogators, Smith relates, sternly asked the theater's founder, Hallie Flanagan: "Who is this Christopher Marlowe? Is he a Communist?"[24] Smith's comparison of the two theaters was apt, as was his implied warning that ICCC might face the same kind of witch hunt.

Historian Nathan Rosenberger, in "Art in the Ashes," a comparative study of the ICCC and other Black art centers, expanded on Smith, showing how closely Jackson's concept of the new theater resonated with the ideals of Popular Front public culture—described by Michael Denning as one that "sought to forge ethnic and racial alliances, mediating between Anglo-American culture, the culture of ethnic workers, and African-American culture, in part by reclaiming the figure of 'America' itself, imagining an Americanism that would provide a usable past for ethnic workers."[25] The multiculturalism of the ICCC, Rosenberger argued, was not framed by a "standard liberal ideology or a middle-class attempt at inclusion," but by radical commitments to social movements and insurgent cultural forces. The ICCC "created interracial coalitions [and] reached out across the cityscape to develop cross-class alliances." The fulcrum of the project, in many ways, was the alliance that Jackson created with East West Players, L.A.'s vanguard Asian theater group, and Luis Valdez's El Teatro Campesino. In particular, the plays of El Teatro "offered a beautiful balance to ICCC performances and rounded out a political social dialog that put the working class, regardless of race, at the center."[26]

Yet, while diverging from "standard Black Arts and Black Power narratives" in its embrace of multiethnic solidarity, the ICCC retained a vital connection to the renaissance on 103rd Street. The Watts Prophets, for example, first debuted before a mixed public at the center's highly popular Monday night "talent show."[27] Black actors, moreover, remained a majority of the regular ensemble and included such future stars as Denzel Washington, Paul Winfield, Adolph Caesar,

Lou Gossett Jr., and others. Yet most of the plays staged at the center, almost regardless of content, remained gloriously multicultural in their casting—Jackson's distinctive signature. For example, in ICCC's version of Thornton Wilder's *Our Town*, "Emily Webb, the girl, is being played by a Negro, her father by an Apache Indian, her mother by a Russian-American and her brother by a Mexican-American. George Gibbs, Emily's sweetheart and young husband, is being played by a blond Caucasian, his father by a Japanese-American, his mother by a Negro and his sister by a Chinese-American."[28]

As Smith had predicted, the ICCC, like the Federal Theater before it, came under repeated attack from the Far Right in Washington and Sacramento, but its Hollywood allies helped repel assaults on its budgets.[29] More difficult were the internal conflicts between Cannon and Jackson, on one side, and Peck and other elite board members over the repertoire and level of professionalism. Peck, although comfortable with some measure of experimental theater, generally saw the ICCC as a ladder that would allow underprivileged but gifted actors to climb into high-paying film and television jobs. Cannon and Jackson agreed this was an important goal, but they had a broader agenda that included educating inner-city audiences, sponsoring local playwriting, and allying with other "third world" theaters. Unlike other offspring of 1965, however, these tensions never produced a split or secession, and the ICCC retained both its vitality and integrity for several decades. Although Jackson is the more celebrated—in appropriate recognition of the enormous energy that he poured into hundreds of productions until his death in 2015—Cannon was remarkable for his ability to balance an essentially Afrocentric attitude about Black survival with an equal dedication to radical, grassroots multiculturalism.

Culture Warriors: Ron Karenga and US

In his 1935 essay "Racial Consciousness and Social Revolution," Aimé Césaire, the great poet and revolutionary from Martinique, wrote, "Before making the Revolution and in order to make the revolution—the true one—a devastating groundswell, not the mere shaking of surfaces, one condition is essential: to break up the mechanical identification of the races, tear up superficial values, apprehend in ourselves the immanent Negro, *plant our négritude* like a beautiful tree until it bears its most authentic fruits." "Should we not denounce," he continued, "the stultifying culture of identification and place every one of our racial values, like so many liberating bombs, under the prisons that white capitalism has built for us?"[30] Césaire's thesis—that a people's capacity to liberate themselves grows from the decolonization of their identity and the recovery of pre-European cultures—figured centrally in the ideology of Négritude, a concept he developed together with Léopold Senghor, future leader of Senegal, and Léon Damas, French Guiana's best-known poet. It also became the core principle of Black "cultural nationalism," whose most influential West Coast exponent was the US Organization, led by Ron Karenga (born Ronald Everett).

US shared some DNA with their future enemies, the Black Panthers, through their association with a seminal Bay Area nationalist group. Electrified by the Southern sit-in movement, Black students at Berkeley organized an ad hoc forum in the fall of 1960 to promote the study of Black history and to debate alternatives to integrationism. In 1962 the group formalized itself as the Afro-American Association (AAA) under the leadership of Donald Warden (soon, Khalid al-Mansour), a young lawyer recently graduated from Boalt Hall. Warden admired Harlem's old-line nationalists who agitated on street corners, and he introduced their soapbox methods to the Bay Area's Black communities. "Like a prophet calling for the millennium," recalled a comrade of Warden, "he walked through the streets of Oakland, Berkeley, and San Francisco, in and out of schools and colleges, office buildings and coffeehouses, telling black peoples where they were. 'The time has come to break with white America.'" Thanks to his charisma, the AAA attracted several hundred members and in its short existence became the seedbed for the formation of diverse Black radical and nationalist groups in California.

By the time Karenga came into contact with Warden, an impressive number of future revolutionaries, including Huey Newton, Bobby Seale, and Marvin X, were members of the AAA. Warden invited Karenga to organize an LA chapter of the association, and within a few weeks he had gathered a cadre of militants, some of whom—Ayuko

Babu and Tut Hayes, for example—would eventually lead their own groups. But AAA in the Bay Area was soon plunged into crisis as its more militant members began to reject Warden's emphasis on Black capitalism. Many left to join Seale and Newton's audacious new group in Oakland, the Black Panther Party. In Los Angeles, after winding down the chapter, Karenga took a different direction. He organized a small number of like-minded activists at the Afrocentric Aquarian Bookstore on West Adams Boulevard, the country's oldest continuously operated Black-owned bookstore, founded in 1941. He had been exploring the possibilities of cultural nationalism since his LACC days and was now ready to outline a new politics of Black identity. The February 1965 assassination of Malcolm X—the lodestar to all Black nationalists—and a few months later, the Watts Rebellion, accelerated the conversation, and that fall Karenga and his comrades—Hakim Jamal, James Doss-Tayari, Samuel Carr-Damu, Tommy Jacquette and a few others—announced the formation of the US Organization ("Us, not them, the whites").[31]

Karenga preached that Black liberation required a reconstitution of Black identity that purged white influences and reclaimed African roots: cultural revolution, in his view, must precede sociopolitical revolution. Although he admired the Négritude theorists as pioneers, their ideology, he argued, especially in the case of Césaire, retained too many associations with Communism, was confoundingly Francophone, and envisioned Black identity within a global humanist contest. It also defined Négritude, at least initially, by the shared experience of slavery rather than by membership in an African "civilization." Pan-Africanism, for its part, was perfectly coherent as a political project that united radicals in the diaspora with those on the continent, but it did not provide a cultural practice. Moreover, the term "African culture" was problematic. Like "Asian culture" or "European culture," it was a vaporous abstraction that upon close inspection reduced itself into components—West African, Bantu, Hamitic, and so on—that shared few genuinely common beliefs and practices. Earlier Black nationalist movements in the twentieth century, including Marcus Garvey's Universal Negro Improvement Association and the Nation of Islam, had found a way out of this dilemma by mythmaking and invented traditions.

Karenga applauded the "partial liberation" from white culture achieved by the NOI, but he felt the movement had become outdated and, without Malcolm X, lacked a realistic relationship to contemporary African experience. Widely read in anthropology, linguistics, and history, Karenga fabricated a systematic ideology, based on his studies of African cultures and liberation movements, that he called *Kawaida*. Its "Seven Principles" borrowed from diverse sources: Senghor's Marx-less version of Négritude; Julius Nyerere's African socialism (Ujamaa); Sukarno's "five pillars" of Indonesian nationalism (Pantja Sila); and Jomo Kenyatta's ethnographic study *Facing Mount Kenya*, where he discovered the term *kareng'a* (Kikuyi for "keeper of the culture"). His vision of a latter-day Black warrior culture was based on a careful study of Zulu history and social organization. As a "Pan-African language" he chose Kiswahili, in which he, of course, was fluent, despite the fact that it was really just the lingua franca of those parts of East Africa affected by the Arab slave trade.

Communal celebrations were one of the most attractive features of the movement, and five holidays were created, including Kwanzaa (now widely celebrated as an African alternative to Christmas) and Uhuru Day, a commemoration of the Watts Rebellion. To underscore US's claim to be the legitimate bearer of his ideas, there were two holidays devoted to "Saint Malcolm." Dhabihu (meaning "sacrifice") was first celebrated on the anniversary of his death in February 1966, in barbed defiance of the Nation of Islam. US also crusaded to make Kuzaliwa, Malcolm's birthday, a national Black holiday. According to historian Peniel Joseph,

> The novelty of Karenga's approach lay in its promise of a reclaimable African past through the adoption of creatively interpreted cultural, social, and political practices in an easily digestible and expertly marketed package. Possessing the agile mind of an intellectual and the flair of a natural-born showman, Karenga pushed his philosophy as an inevitable reclamation of an African identity stripped of slavery's brutal legacy of physical displacement, psychological anguish, and social stigma.[32]

Karenga reinforced the credibility of the US movement through a close alliance with Harlem's most well-known cultural nationalist, Amiri Baraka (LeRoi Jones). In his autobiography, Jones recalled their first meeting: "One early evening a short, stocky bald man dressed in a green olive-drab dashiki, accompanied by two brothers dressed very similarly, came up to the top floor of the Spirit House [in Newark] to see me." Karenga began "by telling me he knew my work. He said he liked *Blues People*, but that he thought the blues were reactionary. That blues were talking about slavery and submission. I blinked and politely disagreed. But Karenga is nothing if not aggressive." He "went on, elaborating his theories on culture and nationalism, talking at high speed nonstop, laughing at his own witticisms and having two members of a chorus, yea-saying, calling, 'Teach!' when Karenga made some point he considered salient." Despite his initial skepticism, however, Jones soon rallied to Karenga's side, particularly impressed by the cool discipline of US. "I felt undisciplined and relatively backward. Here was *organization*. The worst thing a person could be as far as Karenga was concerned was *Ovyo*, a Swahili word meaning 'random,' a person acting at random, disorganized and unpredictable. This was the problem with the 'basic blood,' as Karenga called blacks." The Black Power movement in Newark, of which Baraka was both architect and ideologue, drew heavily from Kawaida principles and rituals, and for several years the Committee for Unified Newark acted as US's eastern embassy.[33]

Later, after blood was spilled, the Panthers would caricature and deride Kawaida as reactionary make-believe disguising a dangerous personality cult. Certainly it was true that Karenga made up many things as he went along, including Kwanzaa, but most of his confections corresponded at least in spirit to some genuine African practice or principle. It was also true that Kawaida was expurgated of any trace of the ideas of that "European madman," Karl Marx. Yet at the same time it was a communitarian ideology heavily indebted to the "African socialism" of Julius Nyerere and Kwame Nkrumah (both of whom read Marx), not a gospel of Black capitalism, as sometimes portrayed. Moreover, US was not culturally nationalist to the exclusion of struggles against racism. On the contrary, it was in the forefront of organizing rallies, protests and political conferences. Until 1968 Karenga was a principal advocate of a Black united front ("operational unity" as he called it), an outspoken opponent of the war in Vietnam, and a prominent supporter of other Black militants under attack, including Huey Newton. Until the arrival of the Oakland Panthers in Los Angeles in 1968, US was unquestionably the most dynamic and popular Black Power group in Southern California.

But US from the beginning had an indisputable dark side: its despotic attitude toward women. Kawaida asserted that "each Black man is God of his own house." Accordingly, women's duty was submission to patriarchy and acceptance of polygamy as a sanctioned practice. In her autobiography, Elaine Brown, the future Panther leader, recalls an US house party that she attended with SNCC activist Bobbie Hodges. When the two women, after paying for a meal, were told that they would only be served after the US men had eaten, they complained. "Bobbie and I smirked and stood our ground," wrote Brown, "until a bald-headed dashiki came over to us, folded his arms across his chest, and explained the 'rules' to us in a way we could understand. Sisters, he explained, did not challenge Brothers. Sisters, he said, stood behind their Black men, supported their men, and respected them. In essence, he advised us that it was not only 'unsisterly' of us to want to eat with our Brothers, it was a sacrilege for which blood could be shed."[34]

The Watts Festival

One remarkable outcome of the Watts Rebellion surprised the LAPD and Black activists alike: gang warfare in South Central L.A. came to an end during the second week of August 1965 and did not reappear on any large scale until the early 1970s. Unlike the gang truce negotiated on the eve of the 1992 uprising, which was the culmination of years of arduous attempts at peacemaking by Black radicals and religious leaders, gang unity in 1965 grew spontaneously and naturally out of the act of rebellion. Virtually a social miracle, it generated much of the incredible energy manifested in both the Watts Renaissance and the proliferation of the Black Power groups that united in 1966 as the Black Congress. Its moment of creation was captured in an exhilarating black-and-white photograph that showed Ron Wilkins (Brother Crook), a well-known member of the Slauson gang, flashing signs with some Watts brothers behind an overturned police car. (At least one of the architects of the 1992 truce, Cle "Bone" Sloan, had this icon on his living room wall.)

The ending of gang violence, however, did not mean the end of neighborhood rivalries. These persisted, but in a new form that owed much to what might be called a "founder effect." For example, Karenga recruited a few key veterans of the Gladiators, a large gang located in the Manual Arts High School area, and others quickly followed. The Panthers, whose LA chapter was formed in the summer of 1968, relied heavily on the charismatic leadership of Bunchy Carter, a legendary Slauson, who attracted many others from the sprawling gang. Neither US nor the Panthers had any intention of becoming territorial tribes, but it was inevitable that street warriors would tend to recruit through their old networks. In Watts, however, neither US nor the Panthers could claim a historical mantle; that belonged, as we have seen, to the Sons of Watts, the transfigured "Parking Lot" gang. Their "ideology," moreover, was defiantly parochial and shrewdly utilitarian: helping the community by helping themselves. Although they incorporated as a nonprofit improvement association and variously operated as security guards for local businesses and counselors for parolees, their original raison d'être was the Watts Festival—a miracle of sorts in its own right.[35]

Officially sponsored in its early years by the Jordan High School Alumni Association, the festival was the brainchild of Stan Sanders and Bill Tidwell. Sanders was Watts's first Rhodes Scholar and in 1965 a second-year Yale Law student. He had returned home just a few weeks before the uprising and mobilized volunteers from local law schools to set up a Police Malpractice Complaint Center at the Westminister building, which, after the rebellion, was taken in hand by the ACLU. Sanders, however, was understandably wary of the LAPD becoming the main object of community protest. "Police brutality is an issue. It is not minor or unimportant. But if we solve the police brutality problem we are no further ahead."[36] Tidwell, Sanders's cochair and high school friend, was also Watts's informal chief of police because of his role in transforming the "Parking Lotters" into the Sons of Watts. Tommy Jacquette and his group SLANT, along with US and Karenga, became strong supporters of the festival. Sanders and Tidwell had wanted Martin Luther King to open the event, but he declined because of illness. (In fact, King was edging toward a nervous breakdown after white rioting defeated his open housing campaign in Chicago.) Instead, Sargent Shriver, head of the OEO, was chosen as parade marshal, and James Meredith, the outrageously brave Air Force veteran who integrated Ole Miss in 1962, accepted an invitation. The festival began on August 14, a mixture of Mardi Gras and avant-garde. Six blocks of 103rd were closed off so that 10,000 people could dance, browse booths and exhibitions, and listen to jazz. Purifoy showed his *66 Signs of Neon*, while Les McCann and Sonny Criss performed at Jordan High.

From the very beginning the proposed festival had been denounced by a few militants, including a tiny Maoist sect headquartered in Watts, as an exercise in "riot control" and community pacification. In the later years of the event, such criticism would gain unfortunate validity, but the first festival was a grassroots production that exuded the spirit of the rebellion. Budd Schulberg considered it a victory party. "Watts—August '66—was neither snarling nor trying to play 'good dog' and sit up and do tricks for the happy and relieved white man," he wrote. Instead,

> it was celebrating a new-found sense of power. There was dancing in the streets, dancing such as Los Angeles has not seen since its true Mexican fiesta days. And instead of fires along Charcoal Alley No. 1 there were great tents displaying jazz groups, exhibitions of sculpture, and painting. There were street plays and street entertainers that revived the flavor of commedia dell'arte. In the Coffee House, Jimmie Sherman presented his *Ballad from Watts*. Studio Watts performed its own interpretation of Genet's *The Blacks*. And our Writers Workshop, now grown to some twenty members, gave a nightly program of readings—a historic literary moment for Watts.[37]

16

Black Power: Stokely Carmichael and the Black Congress (1966)

I n fall 1966, with Malcolm X gone, white America's worst nightmare was Stokely Carmichael, the brilliant Trinidad-born organizer and SNCC leader who had launched a historic call the previous June at a rally in Greenwood, Mississippi. "Almost as soon as it was uttered," writes Peniel Joseph, "a new wave of black aspirations, dreams, and dissent became encapsulated within one powerful slogan—Black Power—that would become as hard to define as it would remain controversial."[1] Although Carmichael was actually arguing the case for an independent Black politics based on SNCC's experiences in Mississippi and Alabama, his electrifying phrase immediately became a Rorschach test for the white racial imagination. The media, singularly focused on goading Carmichael to make inflammatory statements, never paid any attention to what he was actually saying.[2] Thus "to most whites," Carmichael complained in a *New York Review of Books* article, "black power seems to mean that the Mau Mau are coming to the suburbs at night."[3] After a while, he gave up trying to sort out its meaning for the press and left them to their hysteria. But as Mississippi's James Eastland and other Southern senators called for Carmichael's arrest, and newspaper editorials denounced him for advocating "Black racism," his popularity soared among young Blacks and radical whites.[4]

At a Berkeley conference in October, standing tall and cool, he addressed a crowd of 10,000, thanking them for the invitation to "the white intellectual ghetto of the West." He garnered thunderous applause after a blistering attack on President Johnson and the war in Vietnam, capped by a declaration that he would refuse the draft. Then, quoting knowingly from G. B. Shaw, Camus and Sartre—Carmichael had a degree in philosophy—he carefully explained SNCC's attitude toward the New Left. White progressives should act with urgency to build strong anti-racist, anti-imperialist organizations within white working-class communities—in Appalachia for instance. To the extent that this was achieved, a foundation would be laid for an alliance with the Black Power movement to transform US society. If, on the other hand, the white Left wasn't ready to take up its historical responsibilities, then "we have no choice but to say very clearly, 'Move over, or we're going to move on over you.'"[5]

The mainstream media, predictably, latched onto this last line, ignoring the gist of Carmichael's talk, which was a sobering but not unfriendly ultimatum to the New Left to push harder against racism. Pat Brown, in the final days of a bitter electoral battle with Ronald Reagan, said he was "dismayed and disgusted" by the speech.[6] Carmichael's next stop was Los Angeles, where the *Times* warned against his "reckless perversion of the civil rights movement" and the county board of supervisors attempted to prevent his scheduled talk on November 26 at Will Rogers Park in Watts. Supervisor Kenneth Hahn, supposed champion of his South Central constituents, denounced the Black Power movement led by Carmichael as "nakedly designed to foment racial hatred, violence and civil disorder." Woodrow Coleman, representing the Black Congress, a new federation of civil rights and nationalist groups that was the official sponsor of the rally, rejected "this attack on free speech" and sought judicial relief, which was promptly granted by the superior court.[7]

Carmichael, vowing that he would not change a word of his planned speech, told the *Times* that the primary reason that Hahn and others were attempting to prevent his appearance was because "SNCC has the most militant stand on Vietnam." In the event, more than 6,500 people (the *Times*'s estimate) showed up at the park that Saturday for the rally. Before Stokely mounted the stage (actually the bed of a pickup truck), Robert Hall, the former N-VAC activist and current vice president of the Operation Bootstrap job program, told the crowd: "This is a black people's meeting. White people will not tell us what to do or say."[8] Carmichael's speech, much shorter than the one at Berkeley and without allusions to existentialism, focused on militant unity as the sole guarantee of Black survival:

> The only protection we have is each other. We have to begin to let this country know that if they shoot a black man walking down a Mississippi highway with a Bible in his hand, if they shoot a black man taking his wife to the hospital in South Los Angeles, they aren't dealing with one black man, they're dealing with twenty million black Americans ... Once we're together, ain't nobody going to mess with us. Now all those people running around talking about how the rebellion didn't do no good. The rebellions did one good thing for this country: it let white men know that if they think they are going to play Nazi, black people are not Jews.[9]

The Black Congress

Carmichael's speech in Watts, so redolent of Malcolm X's call for unity at the funeral for Ronald Stokes in 1962, raised a fundamental question: Was such solidarity best represented by a united front of existing organizations—or did it require the creation of a new Black Power party? Or, as SNCC seemed to suggest, was the first the precondition for the second? Carmichael's commission, having replaced John Lewis as SNCC's chair, was to educate the North about what had been achieved in Alabama with the Lowndes County Freedom Organization (LCFO) and in Louisiana and Mississippi with the Deacons for Defense and Justice—independent Black political movements defended by armed communities.[10] The refusal of the 1964 Democratic Convention to seat the Mississippi Freedom Democratic Party had embittered the entire civil rights movement and convinced a majority of SNCC's staff that the liberal civil rights coalition was dead, and that Black communities had to set a course independent of the Democrats. Even Bob Moses, around whom the interracial "beloved community" of Mississippi SNCC organizers had once coalesced, declared "that he was breaking off all relationships with whites."[11] Although Carmichael sometimes exceeded his mandate—SNCC had not been an organization that particularly appreciated celebrity or overwrought rhetoric—he was hugely successful in winning the attention of young urban Blacks, who otherwise knew little about the Southern civil rights experience.

By encouraging the formation of local "freedom parties" and providing them with a potent symbol—the LCFO's black panther—SNCC was confident these diverse currents would eventually merge into a national political movement or third party that could negotiate alliances from a position of power. "The creation of a national 'black panther party,'" Carmichael wrote in 1966, "must come about; it will take time to build, and it's much too early to predict its success." While asserting the right of self-defense, SNCC was primarily talking about the power of elected office that the 1965 Voting Rights Act made possible, not the power of the gun.[12] In the North, Carmichael argued in an interview, Black Power would obtain even as a minority if the Black electorate were organized en bloc. "If, for example," he told Friends of SNCC people in San Francisco, "you have 40 per cent black people in an independent force and 60 per cent whites fighting between the Republican and Democratic parties, you can just take over."[13]

Urban united fronts were necessary starting points for "one, two, three, many" Panther parties, but the collapse of Martin Luther King's "open city" campaign in Chicago after confrontations with homicidal white mobs during the summer of 1966 convinced young activists that unity had to be built from the bottom up—and not necessarily by nonviolence. By the late 1960s, in fact, urban Black Power coalitions had begun to coalesce into the "new convention movement" whose culmination was the historic 1972 National Black Political Convention in Gary, Indiana, that brought 10,000 Black activists and political aspirants together. Newspaper histrionics aside, SNCC's vision of Black Power was a rational, even compelling, alternative to the failure of integrated civil rights protest to win new victories after Selma.

Los Angeles, as much as Newark, Oakland or Detroit, became a major laboratory for the Black Power experiment. In the aftermath of the Deadwyler case, community anger had catalyzed the formation of the Temporary Alliance of Local Organizations (TALO) to continue the fight against police abuse without unleashing a new uprising. It included US, CORE, SNCC and leaders of two of the largest gangs, the Slausons and the Businessmen. The NAACP, represented by Norman Houston, one of the organization's more militant "Young Turks," also joined. But TALO was an unwieldy creature, lacking any serious platform and built out of half-hearted commitments. It collapsed when US withdrew its support. Karenga complained that "if they spent half the time fighting the white man that they do against brothers we wouldn't be in the shape we are in today." Moreover, TALO gave too much of a forum to Karenga's competitor, Hakim Jamal, only six months earlier a founder of US, who promoted his Malcolm X Foundation in Compton as the only authentic voice of Black nationalism.[14]

TALO's successor, the Black Congress, with radical groups in the majority and Jamal nowhere to be seen, was more congenial to Karenga, who became its vice chair and most commanding personality. "US identified completely with this alliance," says Scot Brown, moving its Hekalu (headquarters/temple) to the Black Congress building and transforming its own newspaper, *Harambee*, into the organ of the congress. Since US cohabited the coalition with nineteen other groups, however, it did not in any sense control the Congress or dictate policy. Frictions between groups and personalities still occurred, but the Congress's executive director, Walter Bremond (soon, the founder of the Brotherhood Crusade), usually smoothed things over. Moreover, the Congress was not just a coalition, it was a building, a Black city hall, that functioned much like an old-fashioned Labor Temple, providing office space for constituent organizations as well as a large hall for meetings and performances.

The US's important contribution in this period has been clouded over by its subsequent war with the Panthers, starting with the murders of John Huggins and Bunchy Carter at UCLA in 1969. The Panthers charged that Karenga was a reactionary cult leader acting as a mercenary for the FBI and police—an allegation that was uncritically accepted by most of the white Left. Contemporary historians who have studied the COINTELPRO files, however, have achieved a more complex understanding of how both organizations were set against one another by the FBI and its local police allies. In light of these revisions, it's fair to say that US played a generally nonsectarian and constructive role in the first year or year and a half of the Black Congress. In contrast to the UCRC of 1963, where the infighting between CORE and the NAACP reflected conflicts between their parent national organizations, the Congress was more parochial, conducted operations on a less ambitious scale, and tended to act as a clearinghouse more than a programmatic coalition. Although some were troubled by the latent threat of US's burgeoning, and often swaggering, military branch, younger activists of all denominations, buoyed by a spirit of unity, socialized and argued politics together, and for the most part found common ground in Carmichael's open-ended vision of independent Black politics and Karenga's espousal of "operational unity." This was the brief springtime of Black Power.

Two of the most interesting projects operating under the umbrella of the Congress were the Freedom Draft Movement (FDM) and the Community Alert Patrol (CAP). The first was the creation of Levi Kingston, the former LACC activist, who had applied for conscientious objector (CO) status back in 1960 and was now casting a critical eye on the anti-draft work being carried on by groups such as the AFSC and the SDS regional office. Although conceived as protest against the Vietnam War, draft counseling (not yet draft *resistance*) was largely targeted at middle-class whites, ignoring the young Blacks, Chicanos and working-class whites who bore the real burden of conscription. "Our community," Kingston later said, "doesn't know a goddamn thing about the draft laws. Poor people, and black people in particular, don't know what the alternatives are to the draft. To the average black cat in the street, when he gets that draft notice in the mail, it's just like getting busted." However, his initial attempts to involve social service agencies in educating youth about the conscientious objec-tion option ran into a wall of cynicism. "A lawyer at the Legal Aid Foundation told me he would advise youngsters to go to war because the only other alternative was to go to jail." But Kingston forged ahead with help from the Friends of SNCC and the Black Congress, buoyed by SNCC's national commitment to building an anti-draft movement.[15]

By 1967 the FDM had expanded throughout South Central Los Angeles, while nationally the CO movement was paralleled by outright draft resistance. After Muhammad Ali announced that he would refuse induction that spring, the emerging second-generation Black student movement sprang into action, especially on traditional Black campuses. In March, for example, the Black Power group at Howard University disrupted a talk by the selective service director, General Lewis Hershey. "Someone in the audience yelled, 'America is a black man's true battleground,' and about forty students rushed the stage."[16] An early LA example of draft defiance, supported by Kingston and the FDM, was the refusal, in early 1967, of Karl Von Key, twenty-one, and Norman Richmond, twenty, to report for induction on the grounds that they were "colonial subjects, not equal citizens," who should not be required to "fight a white man's war." In addition, both claimed that because of their Black nationalist beliefs their applications for deferment were transferred to an all-white draft board in Gardenia, where they were unfairly denied. Their trials illustrated what Black resisters making similar claims of discrimination could expect in white courts. The judge rejected their arguments about the illegality of the war as "asinine ... ridiculous ... bunk," threatened the defense lawyers and a key witness (Robert Brock, the former chair of TALO) with perjury indictments, and, when challenged about his own racial beliefs, replied that "I once had a clerk and a bailiff who were both Negroes and both were fine men."[17] In spite of hostile courts, however, opposition in the South Central to both the draft and the war soared in 1967–68, increasing numbers of youth went underground, and Black marines and sailors began to organize Black Power groups at Camp Pendleton, Air Station Tustin, and the San Diego and Long Beach naval bases.

CAP, incorporated as a nonprofit in December 1966, was an ingenious response to the Deadwyler case. In the absence of a civilian police review board and given the LAPD's propensity to fabricate evidence and lie in unison, how could the Black community ever hope to win abuse cases in court, much less deter brutality in process? The solution was a civilian patrol, armed with two-way radios and carefully obeying all laws, that would follow and monitor police activities in the ghetto. Initially funded by TALO, and supported by Congress-man Augustus Hawkins and City Council Member Billy Mills, CAP made its debut a week after the Deadwyler verdict (and a week before Carmichael's first Black Power speech): four cars, flying emblematic white handkerchiefs from their antennas, cruising in circles around the "Glass House" (the new LAPD headquarters). CAP's initial leaders were Brother Lennie (Lenier Eggleston) and Brother Crook (Ron Wilkins), while Karenga was the spokesman. He told the press that CAP would be on the streets until 2 a.m. every night of the week, ready "to channel to responsible citizens groups and social agencies accurate reports growing out of police misbehavior."[18]

Brother Lennie was later forced to resign after being photographed with Carmichael in Berkeley—an association that the TALO board feared would endanger its application for federal anti-poverty funds.[19] (The Department of Health, Education and Welfare approved the grant, but it was retracted after Mayor Yorty and Chief Tom Reddin, Parker's successor, made a huge uproar.) This left Brother Crook, a charismatic figure, as the commander. An alumnus of the Slausons, Crook was a well-known lowrider, whose wheels included a pimped-out 1931 DeSoto and a 1938 Plymouth. Widener notes how CAP managed to combine Southern California car culture with Black Power activism. "The members of CAP stenciled 'To Protect and Observe' on the sides of their rides," he writes (the LAPD slogan was, and remains, "To Protect and to Serve"), "turning Oldsmobiles and Buicks into customized symbols of alternative authority."[20] CAP became hugely popular among young people in South Central and was an inspiration to the Oakland group around Huey Newton that became the Black Panthers. It also became a moving target of the LAPD, which wrote sixty tickets for minor violations in the first week of CAP's existence. Frequently a CAP car following a patrol unit would look in the rearview mirror to find another black-and-white following it.

As the first Watts Summer Festival approached, CAP was asked to provide security for the event. One hundred members of the "Parking Lot Gang," soon to become the Sons of Watts, were drafted as a foot patrol, and motorcycles were added to CAP's auto patrol.

In the event, CAP, including many US members, smoothly handled the few minor disturbances at the festival and garnered fulsome praise from grand marshal Sargent Shriver (head of the OEO), the County Human Relations Commission, and even an LAPD commander. But behind the scenes there were bitter exchanges between the Parking Lot and CAP people over finances, and between CAP and TALO over the latter's decision to suspend the patrol as an "act of good faith" in the hope of opening negotiations with the LAPD. The patrol was eventually back on the streets, under the Black Congress's sponsorship and with continuing support from US, but the attempts to yoke it to federal funding and use it as a bargaining chip with the police had alarmed some activists. Brother Crook and his board chair, Louis Gothard, however, defended the integrity of CAP and kept the Black Power lowriders dogging the heels of the LAPD through 1967.[21]

Freedom or Neocolonialism?

"Freedom City" was the brainchild of Los Angeles SNCC and its director, Cliff Vaughs, originally sponsored by TALO. With the Lowndes County template in mind, Vaughs believed that an independent political movement could be built around the cause of greater Watts's secession from Los Angeles and its incorporation as "Freedom City."[22] Vaughs advertised it as the ultimate solution to the iron heel of the LAPD, and promised that "as a first order of government business," the new city would "establish a municipal commission to bond ex-convicts ... No resident of Freedom City who has been convicted of a crime and who has paid his debt to society will be denied work because of his past offense."[23] Moreover, secession would reverse a racist history: until 1926, Watts, in fact, had been a separate city, but it was annexed by Los Angeles, at a time of high in-migration from the South, to prevent possible Black majority rule. The concept, moreover, was not entirely different from the 1960 effort to incorporate East Los Angeles as a Chicano political base, and it was quickly endorsed by TALO and later the Black Congress. Karenga, as he had with CAP, became its public spokesperson, along with Vaughs.

The proposal garnered surprising support from politicians and the Black bourgeoisie. Yvonne Brathwaite, a state assembly candidate just beginning an ascent that would carry her to Congress and then to the LA County Board of Supervisors, argued that municipal independence would allow the area, with federal aid, to overcome some of the previously intractable obstacles to economic growth. As matters now stood, she said, Blacks "can't get insurance on business property and they can't get a home loan." Even more enthusiastic was local NAACP leader Norman Houston, a wealthy insurance executive and well-known "moderate." When asked if a separate Black city wasn't in direct contradiction with his organization's historical commitment to integration, he acknowledged that "the separate-but-equal aim was without question ironic." "[But] I have to agree with Stokely Carmichael, that in certain cases integration should not be the prime objective. Increasing the standard of living and the status and dignity of citizens would be the goal."[24]

But at the NAACP's convention in Los Angeles in early July, Houston's national leadership dropped a bomb on the project. Louis Stokes, the organization's leader in Cleveland who would soon become Ohio's first Black congressperson, called the idea "idiotic": "If I were a Los Angeles white supremacist, I'd do everything I could to help them succeed." Roy Wilkins, in high dudgeon, denounced all forms of "go it alone" and separatism as Black racism. Carmichael and others, he fulminated, were advocating "a reverse Mississippi, a reverse Hitler, a reverse Ku Klux Klan" whose inevitable result would be "Black death."[25]

Although Freedom City faced what were probably impossibly high hurdles on its path to the ballot, Vaughs, Karenga and the Black Congress saw the campaign as a goal in itself, a means to build community organization on a broad scale. Any hope of attracting national support and funding for the campaign, however, died with Wilkins's denunciations. By equating Black Power with reverse racism, moreover, the NAACP had recklessly given its imprimatur to efforts to discredit, defund and destroy initiatives such as Black studies, independent Black candidacies, defense campaigns backed by nationalist organizations, and so on. It was the movement's own version of McCarthyism.

But the demise of Freedom City did not end the dream of Black majority rule: what the *Times* patronizingly labeled "an experiment in Negro self-government" was taking shape in Compton, just south of Watts. Compton, until the 1940s, had been the capital of Los Angeles's dairy belt, exploiting rich deposits of artesian water for irrigation. After the war, it was subdivided at a frenzied pace and became the fastest-growing suburb in California (until Torrance stole its title). Religiously, it was distinguished by a large number of Mormon residents, perhaps the densest concentration in Southern California. Politically, however, it remained the plantation of Colonel Clifton Smith, a character out of a Tennessee Williams play who was the publisher of the *Compton Herald-American* and the city's unchallenged political boss. Under his leadership, the city and its homeowner groups fought every effort by middle-class and skilled working-class Blacks to move into the new subdivisions, but one developer in northwest Compton, finding the huge demand for open housing irresistible, began to sell to anyone who could afford a mortgage.

By 1959 Compton High School was one-quarter Black, and when white students divided their votes over homecoming queen, a Black girl won the vote. The result was an explosion of racist graffiti and attacks on Blacks. Local whites called in members of the notorious Spook Hunters gang from Lynwood and South Gate, while the Huns gang, who had taken the Black Westside under their protection, defended Black students. "Instead of dealing with the growing problem of racial hostility, the city council and the school district decided to further separate the races. In the aftermath of the riot at Compton High, they built a new high school, Dominguez Compton, on the far eastern edge of the city, where the population was still entirely white."[26] Despite these constant "conflicts with white Compton residents," Emily Straus writes, "the town ... provided one of the few opportunities for African Americans to gain access to the suburban American dream." By the early Sixties, segregation persisted, but now as an internal boundary: the western half of Compton was increasingly Black majority or integrated, while the eastern half remained exclusively white. The dividing line between the two Comptons, not surprisingly, was Alameda Boulevard.[27]

For once, however, the Wall was not impregnable. By 1965, the city was at a tilting point, almost equally white and Black, with smaller numbers of Chicanos and Samoans. The Watts Rebellion, although it did not directly affect Compton, became the signal for a veritable white Dunkirk. In headlong flight, whites abandoned almost 2,000 homes. By 1969, when Douglas Dollarhide was elected mayor—the first Black mayor in California—the city was at least 60 percent Black, and the new majority found itself left with scorched earth as a goodbye present from the fleeing whites. The exodus, for example, stripped the city of most of its retail capital: Compton Boulevard was left without a single restaurant, hardware store, movie house, or pharmacy. Then South Gate, Huntington Park, and the other east-of-Alameda white suburbs lobbied successfully to have the route of a proposed east-west freeway (eventually the Century Freeway) moved further south, where its construction would wreak years of devastation on the Willowbrook area, unincorporated but part of the Compton school system. Compton Superior Court, meanwhile, was transferred to South Gate, a move that the NAACP and others denounced as an outrageous attempt to preclude Black representation in the jury pool.[28]

Compton's fiscal survival, especially its ability to fund schools, depended on an aggressive campaign to annex industrial tracts within its large unincorporated periphery. But the all-white LA County Local Area Formation Commission, which dispensed permission for such annexations, systematically discriminated against Compton. Although surrounded by new industry and port-related warehousing, Compton had to watch as its potential tax base was stolen instead by white-majority cities like Torrance, Carson and Long Beach. At a municipal level this was a white embargo; Compton might have as well been Haiti or Cuba. The only sector that the old regime left intact—in fact, expanded—was the police department, and for many years the Black majority had to live with the mocking anomaly of a white racist police force. As late as 1968 there were only about five Black cops on a force of 130, and a group of brutal white cops, the "Dirty Dozen," armed with illegal weapons including saps and machine guns, ran rackets, took bribes, and routinely administered justice "Compton style."[29]

Without an expanded corporate tax base and with retail sales still in decline, Dollarhide and company had little choice but to relentlessly increase the fiscal pressure on its homeowners. At the same time, the major banks cut off most home and small business financing. Residents were unable to rehabilitate old and substandard housing, while new home construction virtually ground to a halt. High property taxes, redlining, dereliction of the central business district, and rising crime, in turn, propelled a slow exodus of Black middle-class families during the 1970s—many of them headed, ironically, a few miles further south to white, tax-rich Carson. Thus the racial transition of the 1960s was followed by a class recomposition in the 1970s. Home ownership declined, and median family incomes plummeted from 92 percent of the county average in 1970 to 62 percent in 1990, while poverty, overcrowding, welfare dependency, illiteracy and unemployment soared. Absentee landlordism spread over the city like a toxic fungus. Increasingly, Black public sector professionals, together with white cops and Latino store owners, commuted to work in Compton but lived elsewhere. White conservatives and liberals, including those most responsible for its fiscal asphyxiation, shook their heads and pointed to Compton as an example of the Black incapacity for self-rule, often making a comparison to failing or broken African states. Black activists, on their side, began to use the term "neocolonialism" as they recognized that occupancy of political office was no match for the ownership of economic power.[30]

17

The Cat Arrives:
The Panthers and US (1967–68)

I n early 1967 Don Wheeldin, a radical journalist who had been the pioneer of the postwar civil rights movement in Pasadena, attempted to sum up the "progress" made in Watts since the rebellion:

Burned-out buildings, vacant lots, boarded-up businesses still pockmark the main areas there. At the corner of 103rd Street and Compton Avenue, heart of its business section, is to be seen Mayor Sam Yorty's optimum contribution towards "an improved Watts community." It consists of a printed statement proclaiming free pony rides for the kids.

[Further east on 103rd Street, at Lou Dillon Avenue, there stood] an old abandoned gas station that now headquarters a new organization called the Sons of Watts Improvement Association. "Sons of Watts," ages 20–26, claim a membership of nearly 100, drawn from former neighborhood gangs. Their stated purpose is to rebuild Watts into a prosperous community by seeking a return of job-supplying businesses and industry. How have they been advised to do this? They've gotten a few traffic signs posted and been urged to distribute 100 containers bearing a legend "Keep Watts Clean" in which people are asked to drop their empty bottles and trash.[1]

Wheeldin concluded that, compared to conditions before August 1965, "the situation has grown alarmingly worse." (This downward trend would be confirmed a few years later when the US Department of Labor reported that "unemployment in the Watts area jumped 61 per cent in the four years following the 1965 riot.")[2] In the other riot epicenters, the Vernon-Central and Avalon districts, progress was equally bleak.

The Sons of Watts and a score of other community groups won economic footholds through OEO programs or benefited from third-party initiatives, most notably the Watts Labor Community Action Committee, sponsored by the UAW. But the War on Poverty was beginning to die the slow death of a thousand cutbacks. The expansive federal commitments made by Sargent Shriver to South Central L.A. in the aftermath of the rebellion proved to be a short-lived financial bubble. The astronomical costs of the war in Vietnam gave Congressional Republicans lethal ammunition with which to attack the OEO. In Sacramento, Reagan used the budget deficit as an excuse to close down programs initiated by the Brown administration after the Watts Rebellion. The first federally funded projects to be cut back were the neighborhood Teen Posts, which provided recreation and educational activities to poor youth, followed by the closure of state-funded community service centers that offered "one stop" access to employment, mental health and other vital services.[3] Both were highly popular initiatives that had been portrayed as models of community empowerment. The cuts continued through the winter of 1967–68. In February, the Westminster Neighborhood Association, the primary conduit for OEO expenditure in Watts, lost most of its funding amid accusations of corruption and mismanagement. Its staff was reduced from 188 to less than 30, and a reporter described "the two-story green center ... once bustling with students of prevocational training classes, counselors and job finders" as "almost deserted."[4]

As such programs contracted, competition over a shrinking pie exacerbated existing rivalries between client groups as well as between Black and Chicano communities. The private sector suddenly became a possible savior, and many activists trimmed their once-radical sails to become acceptable supplicants to local corporations and philanthropists. For example, Operation Bootstrap, started by Lou Smith of CORE and Robert Hall of N-VAC, evolved over time from a job-training scheme to an encounter center, where streetwise residents of the Avalon neighborhood mingled with wealthy white donors from the Valley at a for-profit toy company.[5] Most of the organizers of these start-ups were simply chasing a mirage, but a handful became successful "community entrepreneurs" (derided on the street as "poverty pimps"), well connected to the white business establishment and wealthy political donors. Their organizations came to resemble classic patronage machines, whose control of scarce resources undermined more genuinely grassroots groups. This was the issue that split the Black Congress at the end of 1968, when its chair Walter Bremond and insurance executive Norman Houston founded the Brotherhood Crusade—supported by an alliance of white and Black business leaders. Accusing Bremond of "exploiting the concept of unity" to misappropriate funds and turn the congress toward Black capitalism, the United Parents Council, led by fiery Margaret Wright, along with the Black Student Alliance, SNCC, the Malcolm X Foundation, and the Afro-American Association left the congress to form the short-lived Black Alliance.[6]

Karenga's Rising Star

US occupied a curious position in this emergent web of corporate-community relationships (never partnerships). On the one hand, it was in the forefront of protest, projecting a fierce image of militancy; yet, on the other, Karenga had opened an important back channel to Republican elites. One of the earliest and most important of these connections was to the young publisher of the *Times*, Otis Chandler. It is unclear who approached whom first. Dennis McDougal, who interviewed Chandler extensively for his biography, quotes him as boasting, "I got to know Ron Karenga who was one of the leaders [who] picked me out to be spokesman/intermediary so I could bring the police chief in and be in the same room so we could get some peace."[7] In 1968 a story in the *Wall Street Journal* stunned many activists and sowed considerable paranoia about the real purpose of US. "A few weeks after the assassination of Martin Luther King"—April 4, 1968—Karenga "slipped into Sacramento for a private chat with

Governor Ronald Reagan, at the governor's request. The black nationalist also met clandestinely with Los Angeles Police Chief Thomas
Reddin after Mr. King was killed."[8] Reddin publicly commended a
special Black Congress committee, headed by Karenga, for helping
to keep the streets calm while more than one hundred other cities
experienced rioting leading to forty-three deaths and 15,000 arrests.

Unlike the Nation of Islam, which, as we have seen, was repeatedly
the target of violent police attacks despite having no proven role
whatsoever in any of the 1960s disturbances, or the Black Panther
Party, whose members would be hunted down and killed in 1969 by
the LAPD, US led a relatively charmed life in its early years, spared
the brunt of repression borne by others. Needless to say, Karenga's
movement enemies interpreted this as evidence that he was secretly
collaborating with city hall and the LAPD. If this was the case—and
the evidence is unclear—it doesn't necessarily follow that Karenga was
sabotaging the movement. More likely he was wrangling a degree of
protection and implicit legitimacy by convincing the "power structure"
that the US organization alone had the capacity to regulate disorder
in the ghetto.

Meanwhile, Karenga's star had continued to rise in the national Black
Power movement. In September 1966, Representative Adam Clayton
Powell had convened a closed leadership meeting to plan a National
Black Power Conference for the following summer, and Karenga was
appointed vice chair of the continuations committee. In January he
appeared with Stokely Carmichael at "Conference '67—The Survival
of Black People" in San Francisco. (White commentators, even New
Left sympathizers, typically failed to understand the centrality of
"survival"—and, conversely, of "genocide"—in the discourse of the
Black Power movement, but what they took as hyperbole was a real
existential possibility to activists who had faced Southern mobs only
to find equally virulent race hatred in the North.)

A month later, US hosted its second Malcolm X remembrance
(Dhabihu) at Prince Hall Masonic Temple, followed by a "Black
Leadership Conference" that brought together a miscellaneous group
of figures, ranging from Willard Murray (special assistant to Mayor
Yorty) and John Buggs (of the county human relations commission) to

Carmichael, actor Ivan Dixon, and Earl Anthony—a USC graduate who acted as an informal emissary of the Oakland Panthers (and later became a key FBI informer). Karenga spoke on "A Theory of Black Revolution: A Cultural Approach," the most detailed and coherent public presentation of US politics to date.

Three months later US was integrally involved in the organization of a Southern California follow-up to the January's Black survival conference. The three-day event in late May was held on the Jefferson High School campus and attracted 1,300 people. Officially sponsored by three Black state legislators—Senator Mervyn Dymally and Representatives Bill Greene and Willie Brown—it featured an all-star lineup of Black Power speakers, including Carmichael, Baraka, Huey Newton, Dick Gregory, the Kenyan ambassador to the UN, Floyd McKissick (CORE), Julian Bond (SNCC), John Shabazz (NOI), and, of course, Karenga. There was spirited discussion about Martin Luther King's recent declaration of opposition to the Vietnam War, Muhammad Ali's refusal of induction into the Army, and the Oakland Panthers' armed demonstration at the capitol in Sacramento.

Karenga reportedly drew the most applause for his speech, but the audience was also riveted by Huey Newton—his first formal appearance in L.A. The Oakland Panther leader made one of the subtly non sequitur statements that would become so characteristic of his thinking. He urged Blacks to arm themselves "and, in the process, [to] learn about political organization." (Most revolutionaries would reverse the order.) Several of the speeches challenged or derided the principles of early civil rights struggles. Dr. Herman Blake from the new UC campus at Santa Cruz, for example, inverted the premise of CORE's earlier open housing campaigns in the suburbs by arguing that Blacks should stay in the ghetto, where their political clout was potentially greatest. Dr. Joe White, an LA psychologist, parroted US's position on male supremacy by arguing that Black women needed to step aside to let men lead. "Negro women have to develop a hold pattern while their men are on the firing line so that male leadership can emerge."[9]

Summer 1967 saw the bloodiest urban insurrections since the New York Draft Riot of 1863. One after another, Newark (July 12), Detroit (July 23), Milwaukee (July 30), and Washington, DC (August 1) went up in flames. Eighty-three people died, almost all at the hands of police, guardsmen, or the regular army; several thousand were injured, and a vast amount of commercial real estate in the inner city was destroyed. Despite the still-smoldering streets and a military occupation, organizers (including Karenga) went ahead with the National Conference on Black Power in Newark on July 20. There was much bickering and division, but Karenga once again emerged as the tribune of unity. As conference chair Nathan Wright noted, "Those who attended the … conference … were impressed by Maulana Ron Karenga's emphasis upon the need to develop what he called 'operational' [unity]." As Wright understood the idea, "it did not require the creation of a new organization. All groups keep their own identity. A coalition of leaders is, however, created to conduct a dialogue and decisions for work in parallel and mutually supporting ways."[10]

US's Uhuru Day remembrance was held on August 14, just after the finale of the Watts Festival, with Huey Newton and H. Rap Brown—Carmichael's successor in SNCC—as guest speakers. US had arranged to hold the meeting in a large parking lot next to the Congress building, but the turnout was overwhelming, with 5,000 or more people overflowing the lot onto sidewalks and a nearby vacant lot. Although the festival had made a dramatic political statement by choosing Muhammad Ali as its grand marshal, Brown was not impressed. "Watts was not burned so black people could have a picnic and a festival," he declared. In the aftermath of the great riots, Brown was 200-proof Black anger without a semblance of a program.[11] The white press loved his doomsday rhetoric: "The civil rights movement is dead, thank goodness"; "Detroit is a lesson to the nation. It is not Detroit anymore—it's destroyed"; "There has been too much lootin' during the rebellions and not enough shootin.'" (The next day he was indicted in Maryland for inciting riot and arson earlier in the year.) Karenga had to scramble awkwardly for clichés equal to Brown's supermilitancy, vowing that if violence ensued, "let it be 'even Steven' because you cannot be nonviolent with a red neck, straw-chewing, overall-wearing, racist honkie."[12]

Although the idyll would not last, Karenga had consistently been a generous force for Black unity throughout a turbulent and very bitter year. On every occasion, he had extolled SNCC, heaped praise on Baraka and his Newark movement, and defended the Oakland Panthers. Early in 1968 there would be one last spectacular display of unity.

Red and Black

At the November 1967 Black Youth Conference, James Forman of SNCC shocked the audience, especially the supporters of US, with an impassioned critique of "reactionary Black Power," which he characterized as a politics "that says we are exploited solely because of our skin color." In some instances that had led its exponents to denounce the anti-war movement as a "white thing," and in general it encouraged posturing and theatrics rather than the grassroots organizing that had been the soul of SNCC. In contrast, "revolutionary Black Power" asserted that "our exploitation results from both class positions and race" and advocated a united front of the "dispossessed" that included "people of African descent, the Puerto Ricans, the Mexican Americans, and many poor whites." He extolled the Viet Cong as selfless exemplars of revolutionary dedication and described their struggle as the cutting edge of the global anti-imperialist revolt. He also cited the ideas of Walter Rodney, the young Guyanese revolutionary and historian, whose synthesis of Pan-Africanism and Marxism would become increasingly influential within SNCC and other groups.[13]

"Revolutionary Black Power," with its emphases on international solidarity, inter-ethnic united fronts, and the centrality of community organizing, was obviously a nod to the Black Panther Party with whom SNCC was then in alliance, but Forman's definition applied equally to the recently organized Che-Lumumba Club of the Communist Party in Southern California. The Communists were the only interracial organization in the Los Angeles area with significant young Black leadership, and their influence within the wider Black Power movement was largely due to three individuals: the chair of the CP's Southern California district (CPSCD), Dorothy Healey; and the founders of Che-Lumumba, Franklin and Kendra Alexander. Healey was fond of quoting from Lenin's 1916 review of the *Youth International* journal:

The middle-aged and the aged often *do not know how* to approach the youth, for the youth must of necessity advance to socialism *in a different way, by other paths, in other forms, in other circumstances* than their fathers. Incidentally, that is why we must decidedly *favour organisational independence* of the Youth League, *not only* because the opportunists fear such independence, but because of the very nature of the case. For unless they have complete independence, the youth *will be unable* either to train good socialists from their midst or prepare themselves to lead socialism *forward*.[14]

In this case, Lenin and Healey were strictly at odds with the national committee of the CPUSA, which was scaldingly critical of New Left formations like SDS, with their shifting ideologies and distrust of the USSR, as well as of Black Power groups that excluded whites. The Southern California district, by contrast, advocated entering or working closely with such movements to open dialogue with their activists. When the CP launched the W. E. B. Du Bois Clubs in 1964, the Los Angeles clubs, instead of competing with SDS, allied with the SDS regional office, shared memberships, and opened a New Left School to debate ideas with college students and others.

But it was over questions of Black liberation that the CPSCD departed most radically from national policy. According to Healey, the Southern California district had 400 to 500 Black members in the late 1940s, and it retained an important core of that membership, the "Moranda Smith Section," through the 1960s. One of its oldest members, and certainly among its most extraordinary, was Cyril Briggs, a major figure in the histories of Black nationalism and the Harlem Renaissance. Born on Nevis, in the Leeward Islands, he emigrated to New York in 1905 and in 1917 founded the African Blood Brotherhood, which was both anti-capitalist and separatist. Recruited to the underground Communist Party USA in 1921, he later became the secretary of the National Negro Congress and helped shape the Comintern's advocacy of a Negro nation in the American South. Kicked out of the party in the Popular Front period because of his nationalism, he was readmitted in the late Forties and moved to Southern California. He convinced Healey in the early Sixties that Malcolm X was moving in a revolutionary direction and should not be stereotyped or condemned by the party. But James Jackson, the editor of the *Daily Worker* and the Black leader with the most clout in the CP, "developed an absolute hatred of Malcolm X," and Healey was rebuffed when she took Briggs's position to the National Committee.

Franklin Delano Alexander, meanwhile, was the son of a Communist railroad laborer from Chicago. He followed in the footsteps of his older sister Charlene Mitchell, who had joined the party as a teenager and become a member of the National Committee in the late 1950s. (In 1968, as the candidate of the CPUSA, she became the first Black woman to run for president.) Alexander had been the president of the Independent Student Union at LACC, later becoming the target of Yorty's red-baiting for his role in the 1966 Deadwyler protests. In April 1967, as national chair of the Du Bois Clubs, he spoke at Texas Southern University, a historic Black school in Houston where Friends of SNCC had recently been kicked off campus and its faculty advisor fired. He was arrested along with other speakers and ended up in the same jail where LA Freedom Riders had been so viciously beaten in 1961. A few weeks later, after a student allegedly threw a rock at a police car, hundreds of Houston cops pumped 3,000 rounds of carbine and pistol fire into one of the men's dorms and then arrested 488 students. A ricochet killed one cop, but five students were charged nonetheless with his murder.

Kendra Harris from Compton was a freshman at Cal State LA when she became active in CORE and was one of the protestors arrested at the Federal Building during the Selma demonstrations in March 1965. She spent that summer in Louisiana working on civil rights projects, missing the rebellion in Los Angeles. When she returned she began to attend SCDCP meetings and in 1966 married Franklin and joined the party. She initially worked as a community organizer in the Nickerson Gardens housing project in Watts. Together with Charlene Mitchell, and influenced by the legacy of Briggs, who had just passed away, Franklin and Kendra argued for the creation of an all-Black club that could become a pole of attraction to Black Power activists and street youth.

Healey supported the formation of what became Che-Lumumba, later explaining:

> It was perfectly possible to have an all-Black group committed to a politics that transcended a narrow nationalism. The presence or absence of a white face wasn't going to make much difference in terms of the politics represented. But it might make a huge difference in terms of our ability to recruit and hold on to Black Communists ... The formation of the C L Club allowed Black Communists to play a role within the Black community and among Black students on campuses in Los Angeles that they never could gave pulled off as a mixed group during that period of intense pressure from Black nationalism.[15]

But James Jackson was apoplectic. He had recently denounced the Lowndes County Freedom Organization for nationalism—and now found "separatism" growing in the party's own backyard. He convinced a majority of the National Committee to pass a resolution against Che-Lumumba, but SCDCP ignored it. The first chair of the new club was Charlene Mitchell, but she soon moved to New York to become more active in the national leadership, turning over the reins to Franklin and Kendra. They were serious revolutionaries in every sense: fearless, forceful, and politically sophisticated.[16] They were also relatively uncommitted to CP dogma or the cult of the USSR; their models were Cuba, Vietnam and the anti-colonial struggles in Africa. Their most renowned recruit, of course, was Angela Davis, who in 1967 returned from study in Europe in order to participate in the Black liberation movement.

In looking for a group to work with, she was initially disappointed, later writing, "I decided that the organization I wanted to join did not really exist." Instead she organized a Black student union at UCSD, where she was a graduate student of the German Marxist philosopher Herbert Marcuse, and helped steer it into a coalition with Chicano and radical white students. The coalition, after many protests and arrests, was eventually successful in the establishment of a new college on campus, oriented to the needs of communities of color. (It was called Third College, although the movement had wanted the name "Lumumba-Zapata.")[17] But San Diego was a backwater of struggle, and she began commuting to Los Angeles, where she attended the November Black Youth Conference at the Second Baptist Church, where she was particularly impressed by the presentations of Forman and Franklin Alexander, as well as one by a small group of activists led by John Floyd, a school teacher, who had just formed the local Black Panther Political Party (BPPP). She joined the latter: "I saw them as an interim political base from which I could think over and decide upon the ultimate political direction I was going to take."[18]

"Ain't That Right, John Floyd?"

In his September 1966 "What We Want" article, Carmichael noted with satisfaction that groups were organizing under the Black Panther symbol in Los Angeles, New York City, Philadelphia and New Jersey. In several cities, the underground Revolutionary Action Movement (RAM) was the organizer of the first Black Panther parties. RAM was led by Max Stanford, a graduate of the extraordinary Detroit Marxist circle around James and Grace Boggs that also included the future leaders of the League of Revolutionary Black Workers. Stanford blended Malcolm X and Robert F. Williams (the refugee North Carolina NAACP leader who advocated armed defense against racists) with an eclectic sprinkling of C. L. R. James, Elijah Muhammad, and Marx. RAM promoted Malcolm X's conception of the Black liberation movement as part of a worldwide anti-imperialist struggle, spearheaded, in Stanford's version, by Cuba and China. It took the Deacons for Defense, the community self-defense movement in Louisiana, as an adaptable model for Northern ghettos, and tried, not very successfully, to imprint their own ideology onto the Southern original. RAM members, mostly students or ex-students, were generally required to become active within existing public groups, especially SNCC (Stanford was close to Carmichael), or to form front organizations—such as the Soul Students Advisory Council at Oakland's Merritt College, where Bobby Seale and Huey Newton were enrolled.

RAM and its revolutionary nationalist politics was Seale and Newton's next step up after leaving Warden's Afro-American Association.

The Black Panther Party for Self-Defense was cobbled together in
Oakland during the summer and early fall of 1966. "Revolutionary
nationalism" and "anti-imperialism" were taken directly from SNCC
and RAM; the panther symbol, of course, had no copyright; and the
ten-point program was assembled, according to legend, in about forty
minutes. Armed self-defense, of course, was the motto of the entire
Black Power movement, but the Oakland group, fatefully, put guns
together with another idea. "Newton," according to Joshua Bloom
and Waldo Martin's history, "soon experienced an epiphany sparked
by an article he read in the August 1966 edition of the West Coast
SNCC newspaper, the *Movement*, about the Community Alert Patrol in
Watts." The Panthers would also monitor the police—but with loaded
guns at hand. (Newton was pre-law and had crammed local and state
criminal codes to establish the legality, or rather the non-illegality, of
doing this.) At first the Oakland organization coexisted with the Black
Panther Party of Northern California formed by RAM members in San
Francisco, former comrades of Seale and Newton. But in the summer
of 1967 Newton issued an ultimatum: "They could merge with us or
change their name or be annihilated." They changed their name.[19]

Meanwhile, the Los Angeles Panthers, organized by John Floyd
and Ayuko Babu, belonged to the Black Congress and espoused a
politics similar to the James Forman wing of SNCC. At the February Black Leadership Conference organized by US, Floyd had
announced: "Today we are forming the Black Panther Party in Los
Angeles. Malcolm X is going to be our patron saint. Our political
philosophy is black nationalism." He received a standing ovation
from the overflow audience of 250.[20] The local Panthers were allied
with Che-Lumumba and worked without friction with US. Indeed,
Karenga had converted his paper, *Harambee*, into the Congress house
organ and given the editorship to Floyd, assisted by a volunteer named
Elaine Brown.

Born in Philadelphia, she had dropped out of Temple University to
move west, where she became caught up in a fast Hollywood crowd
of producers and entertainers. An accomplished pianist and singer,

she had her conscience piqued by a Black friend who suggested she teach piano to kids in Watts. At Jordan Downs, where she taught on Saturdays, she met Tommy Jacquette, who urged her to check out the scene at the Black Congress. Eventually she gravitated to the circle around Harry Truly, a Cal State LA sociologist who had founded the Black Student Alliance. Although Brown was not a student, Truly asked her to represent the BSA on the Congress executive committee.[21] She was an intelligent, striking figure who caused a stir wherever she went, but no one could have expected that she would someday rise to become the chairperson of the Black Panther Party.

Although Huey Newton, as we have seen, spoke in L.A. several times in 1967, the first regular Oakland Panther presence was Earl Anthony, a USC graduate who had moved north for law school and joined the BPP. Before he returned to Southern California, he was recruited or blackmailed into becoming an informant for the FBI. He arrived at the Black Congress in November 1967 as the representative of the Huey Newton Defense Fund. In late October Newton had been involved in a shoot-out with the Oakland police, which ended with the cop dead and Huey seriously wounded. "Free Huey!" would soon resound across the country on white college campuses as well as Black streets. Anthony became a regular observer at Congress meetings but made no effort to claim Congress membership for the defense fund or the Oakland BPP. In Oakland, however, the decision was made to create a Los Angeles chapter with an exclusive franchise to the Panther name.

In her autobiography, Angela Davis, who had become the San Diego representative of Floyd's group, recalled her first terrifying contact with Newton's organization. During a visit to the Black Congress headquarters she was ambushed by a drunken Oakland henchman, who pushed her into a corner and held a gun to her head. "'The Black Panther Party for Self Defense," he screamed, "demands that your motherfuckin' party get rid of the name the Black Panther Party. In fact, you better change it to the motherfuckin' Pink Pussycat Party. And if you haven't changed your name by next Friday, we are going to off you all.'" To underscore the ultimatum, "he told me that he had found that I lived in San Diego; that he had my address and that

I could expect someone to knock on my door if we didn't do what they were demanding."[22]

The builder of the new LA chapter was Bunchy Carter, the former leader of a Slauson set. He had been imprisoned in Soledad with Eldridge Cleaver and, like him, had converted to the Nation of Islam. Upon release, however, Cleaver, on the verge of becoming a best-selling author for his memoir *Soul on Ice*, joined the Newton group and convinced Carter to follow. Because of his imposing character, his street reputation in South Central, and his ties to his old set, Carter was the obvious choice to raise the Oakland flag down south. Brown vividly remembered the unexpected appearance of Carter at a community poetry reading sponsored by the BSA in January. Quincy Troupe had just finished a poem in tribute to John Coltrane when "the double doors to the large Black Congress hall where we were seated brusquely flung open," and Carter entered, followed by twenty of the "fiercest -looking Brothers I had ever seen … Some of them wore leather gloves, at least those with sawed-off shotguns pressed to the sides of their thighs. Some wore hats cocked over one eye and pistols in shoulder holsters." Carter announced that he had some poems to read. After a brief recitation, he thanked the audience but explained that he had actually come with a different purpose. "I came here to make an announcement: we have just officially formed the Southern California chapter of the Black Panther Party for Self-Defense." After a moment, he continued. "I came here also to make it crystal clear that *we* are the Black Panther Party, that there is but *one* Black Panther Party and that is the party headed by Minister of Defense Huey P. Newton—ain't that right, John Floyd?" Carter approached Floyd. "I said, ain't that right, John Floyd! There's only *one* Black Panther Party. And we don't want to hear about another soul trying to use our name again unless authorized by the Central Committee of the Black Panther Party. Is that *clear*, John Floyd!"[23]

Declaring War on Babylon

James Forman became the mediator of the dispute between Bunchy and the LA Panthers. "I knew that all of these groups were trying to build self-defense units in California and in tense situations it can become easy to point the gun at one another rather than at the oppressor," Forman explained. "After hours of discussion, with some of the individuals involved separately and then getting some of them to sit down 'face to face,' I succeeded in ironing out many of the difficulties."[24] The LA Panthers agreed to become SNCC, although with little formal connection to the national office, and to surrender their logo. Angela and others accepted Forman's argument that getting rid of the name issue would actually strengthen the group. "We would also acquire new national dimensions for own collective and overcome, thereby, some of the provincialism that plagued us," Angela later wrote. "From Forman's standpoint we would be assisting SNCC—which then was considered by many to be the leading force in the Black Liberation Movement—to build a base on the West Coast. Finally we would be able to cement the relationship between the BPP and SNCC. If a lasting coalition were to develop, it would be a tremendous advance."[25]

Meanwhile, with the franchise question resolved, the BPP formally joined the Black Congress, and its influence grew rapidly as Carter recruited Slauson alumni, including a brilliant self-educated Marxist, Ray "Masai" Hewitt, who eventually became the Party's minister of information.[26] Although the popularity of the Panthers soon began to challenge the hegemony of US over the local Black Power movement, Karenga kept to his principle of operational unity, and US helped advertise a "Free Huey" rally at the Sports Arena in February 1968. Estimates of the turnout ranged from 5,000 to 10,000, and the atmosphere, as described by Elaine Brown, was electric. "Women and men in black leather coats were marching military-style, back and forth outside the huge arena, backed up by the beat of several parade drums, chanting the battle cry … 'Free Huey! Or else! The sky-y-y's the limit!'"[27] (This was not just hyperbole. Forman had proposed a list of targets—"ten war factories, fifteen police stations … one Southern Governor, two mayors," and so on—to be destroyed or killed in the event of the assassination of Newton or any of the other radical Black leaders.[28])

"A new black leadership," Brown continued, "had gathered in Los Angeles that day ... as it had in Oakland the day before, to, as Eldridge Cleaver had defined it, declare war on 'Babylon.'" Seldom had so much rhetorical heavy artillery been gathered in one spot: Carmichael, Forman, and Rap Brown from SNCC; Cleaver, Seale, and Carter for the Panthers; Karenga; and Reies Lopez Tijerina, leader of the Alianza from New Mexico. Cleaver introduced Carmichael as "the new prime minister of the Black Panther Party." Brown was enthralled by his speech, which she described as a "charismatic delivery that turned the crowd wild. There was a long standing ovation." But others had a different opinion.[29]

For Angela Davis, "the importance of the rally was obvious. I was, therefore, especially disturbed by the content of some of the speeches. Stokely, for example, spoke of socialism as 'the white man's thing.'" Marx, he said, was a white man and therefore irrelevant to Black Liberation. "'As Black people,' Stokely shouted, "we have to forget about socialism!'" "Because he knew how to turn a phrase," Davis continued, "he had the audience applauding, not so much what he said as his way of saying it. I was glad he was no longer the chairman of SNCC, because after hearing such a speech, I would have left the organization on the spot." Although she was more enthusiastic about Rap Brown's speech, the whole evening struck her as devoid of a line of march:

> We were supposed to be calling for mass support for Huey Newton. However, no strategy followed, graced or even decorated this demand. There were no specific, concrete proposals placed before the people in attendance. In response to the appeal, the applause was ample enough, but where were we to go from there? The only answer to this question was the slogan "The sky is the limit."[30]

Dorothy Healey's reaction was even more critical. "Stokely is an enormously effective orator, with every flourish, every technique really incredibly well honed," she wrote, but the content of his speech she found "dreadful":

I sat and listened to it, and to me it was just a monstrous deception being played in that what he had to say—his analysis, his proposals—were totally devoid of any concreteness as far as the U.S. was concerned, totally devoid of a strategy that really would have provided a capacity for either uniting Blacks as Blacks or providing a bridge of Black-white unity in the country."

Healey noted that that meeting also marked the first Black effort to "bring in Chicanos." Reies Tijerina, from New Mexico, also gave a speech. "He, too, illustrated the same problem of the new militancy of the country, although he's not a young man; he's a middle-aged man, but newly radicalized. His speech, too, was rhetorical—slogans, bombasts, rhetoric—but again, nothing that lent itself to practical organization nor that pointed a way for a long-range perspective."[31]

The Sports Arena event was both the high point of Black unity and the proximate cause of its decline. Squabbles over the order of speakers and other such trivia had inflamed relations between some of the groups, but it was the disposition of the funds raised that became casus belli. US claimed, probably with justice, that it had not been reimbursed as previously agreed for its expenses, and when it found out that the Panthers were using part of the money not to defray Newton's legal expenses but to open a new office in L.A., the proverbial shit hit the fan. "Operational unity" had been based on the assumption that US, if not the dominant group, would be at least be an equal among equals. Now it confronted a competitor who aggressively, even violently, claimed to be the only legitimate representative of Black liberation. To make matters worse, Karenga had strenuously wooed SNCC, praising Carmichael to the heavens, only to now find a merger in process between it and the BPP. US girded itself for battle.

But first SNCC took center stage. On the afternoon of the February 18 rally, eighteen-year-old Gregory Clark and a friend were pulled over by the LAPD and accused of car theft and drunken driving. In fact, they had a valid registration card and were drinking pop. The arresting officer, Warren Carleson, became furious when Clark refused to be handcuffed. "According to those watching the encounter," writes Angela Davis, "he knocked Gregory Clark to the sidewalk and while he lay face down, his hands cuffed behind him, Carleson shot Gregory in the back of the head with a .38 revolver."[32] Franklin Alexander, who had earlier joined L.A. SNCC without any objection from the other members, became the public spokesman of the campaign to indict Carleson. The coroner's jury, meanwhile had split four to three over the shooting, with the minority refusing to accept a verdict of "justifiable homicide."[33]

Posters soon appeared on walls: "Wanted: LAPD Cop for the Murder of Brother Gregory Clark." SNCC organized a "Peoples' Tribunal," supported by both US and the Panthers, which staged a mock trial of Carleson in South Park on March 17 before hundreds of residents. SNCC hoped to use the trial to mobilize the community to demand a special council hearing on the murder, but many in the crowd wanted immediate revenge. As Davis wrote, "Death! Death! Screamed a group of people. Others voiced their agreement. 'Death to the pig!' brothers continued to shout. Appoint a commission to execute the sentence, as they said. They were volunteering."[34] After much commotion, Alexander managed to calm things down. What no one knew, until revealed by a Senate investigation in 1970, was that Army intelligence officers were in the crowd, presumably because of Franklin's participation, and were sending weekly reports on L.A. SNCC to "six Army commands around the world."[35] The Gregory Clark campaign continued through May. Billy Mills convinced a city council committee to schedule a special hearing on the Clark killing, but under pressure from the *Times* and the LAPD, the council reneged, leading to stormy scenes at city hall when 150 protestors led by Alexander showed up.

But all of this took place under the shadow of Martin Luther King's assassination on April 4 and the ensuing disturbances in over one hundred cities, with major riots in eleven. With the Eighty-Second Airborne on the streets of Baltimore, and Marine machine gunners on the steps of the National Capitol, L.A. seemed primed for another explosion. That it was averted was largely due to the Black Congress, especially US and SNCC. Everyone worked around the clock, with sound trucks and high school leafleters urging residents to attend a memorial for King at the Coliseum. A one-day strike of Black labor was also called. Police Chief Tom Reddin told the press that "particular tribute must be paid to members of the Black Operational Unity Committee. Without its leadership, and its mobilization of important community influences, peaceful, unified action would not have been possible." Behind the scenes, as noted earlier, Karenga had met secretly with both Governor Reagan and Reddin. SNCC's contribution, however, was rewarded with a police raid that trashed their office, destroyed their printing equipment, and put most of the members behind bars. In an infantile tantrum, the LAPD even put tacks in their food.[36]

Despite the attack, SNCC had suddenly acquired real momentum, attracting some of the most serious militants in the city, launching a youth group with fifty members, and setting up a Liberation School under Angela Davis. Since it had decent relations with both US and the BPP, SNCC was poised to broker the dangerous tensions building between the two militarized groups. But unexpected internal conflict—a revolt against "matriarchy"—disrupted and eventually destroyed SNCC. Some of the men in the group and others in the Congress began to attack Angela and two other sisters—Bobbie Hodges and Rene—for usurping leadership. "All the myths about Black women surfaced," wrote Davis in her autobiography:

> Bobbie, Rene and I were too domineering; we were trying to control everything, including the men—which meant by extension that we wanted to rob them of their manhood. By playing such a leading role in the organization, some of them insisted, we were aiding and abetting the enemy, who wanted to see Black men weak and unable to hold their own.

Although the two male full-timers, Franklin and "Frank," the head of security, sided with the three women, the situation spun out of control, and it was decided to ask the SNCC national office to arbitrate. The national representative sent to L.A., however, was less interested in mediating gender issues than in expunging the chapter of any taint of Marxism. Apparently the prominence of Franklin in the Clark protests had upset Carmichael's supporters, and he was summarily expelled, soon followed by Angela and by Franklin's younger brother Deacon. Local SNCC collapsed. Angela bitterly noted: "Whereas we had had over two hundred workers whom we could count on and hundreds more who could be mobilized, by the beginning of the summer there were no more than ten people left."[37]

Davis, after intensive discussions with Healey and the Alexanders, joined Che-Lumumba in July, and the young Black Communists turned their eyes toward possible collaboration with the Panthers as well as participation in the Black student revolts brewing on several campuses. Unfortunately, the six-month-long career of L.A. SNCC rehearsed the fate of larger Sixties movements: at the very moment when a group's popularity opened the door to becoming a genuine mass movement, it collapsed into internal conflict. This would shortly be the fate of SNCC nationally, then, in 1969, of both the Panthers and SDS. For years afterward, veterans of these groups would be haunted by the historical possibilities squandered in struggles that, in the last instance, hinged on personal ambitions and attendant vendettas.

Part IV

Vietnam Comes Home

18

"Unlawful Assembly": The Century City Police Riot (1967)

Lyndon Johnson, like all Texas gamblers, had a card up his sleeve when he opened his 1968 reelection campaign in Los Angeles. The city was home to some of the Democratic Party's wealthiest donors as well as its most glamorous celebrities—and of course it was also a city rich in Democratic votes. In 1964 L.A. had given him more votes than any other city in the country except New York.[1] A festive gala was scheduled for June 23, 1967, at the newest and most prestigious spot in town: the Century Plaza Hotel. It was the jewel in the crown of the massive Century City office and residential development under construction adjacent to Beverly Hills in what had only recently been the back lot of Twentieth Century Fox studios. Party donors and Hollywood stars would pay $1,000 a plate, legendary old-time comedian Jack Benny was to be the MC, and the Supremes would provide the entertainment.[2] And then LBJ would give a speech.

When Johnson arrived in L.A., he knew it was a gamble of sorts: the pundits said he would be playing against the anti-war forces inside the Democratic Party. "As the 1968 elections approach," a *Times* political reporter explained, "it is not the Republican opposition which worries the President so much as the threat of defection by Democratic liberals who have been a vital part of the successful Democratic coalition since the New Deal."[3] Indeed, the morning of the president's Century City fundraiser, three entire pages of the *Times* were filled with 8,000 names of "dissenting Democrats" who signed an "open letter" addressed to LBJ. The letter quoted George McGovern: "We seem bent on saving the Vietnamese people, even if we have to kill them and demolish their country to do so." The statement concluded: "Mr. President, we advise you ... that, from this day on, our campaign funds, our energies and our votes go to those and only those political figures who work for an end to the war in Vietnam."[4]

Johnson believed he had a wild card in the hole: he would make an announcement at the Century City dinner that would "give his political stock an enormous boost" with anti-war Democrats and take him "off the hook on the war issue."[5] He was flying into L.A. directly after a meeting with Soviet Premier Alexei Kosygin, where the two had discussed ending the war in Vietnam. He planned to announce that night that "President Kosygin and I agreed in our talks today that we both want a world of peace."[6] He was calling it "the Glassboro Summit"—after the town in New Jersey where they had met. He hoped playing that card in Century City would provide a kind of "peace is at hand" moment. In fact the Glassboro Summit was quickly forgotten, but what happened in Century City that night was not.

As Johnson headed for Century City, anti-war demonstrators gathered in a nearby park for a rally before their protest march past the hotel. The police expected one or two thousand, but ten or fifteen thousand turned up at Cheviot Hills Park, adjacent to the Rancho Park public golf course. They came not just from the liberal Westside, but from all over LA County, from groups with all kinds of names: the East LA Peace Committee, the Glendale Vietnam Project, Long Beach Citizens for Peace, the Malibu Discussion and Action Group, the Orange County Committee to End the War, the Emergency Councils of Pasadena and San Gabriel Valley, the Noho-Silverlake Committee on the Crisis in American Foreign Policy, the Pomona Valley Community Council for Opposition to the War in Vietnam, the South Bay Peace Council, and the Valley Peace Center. The Westside was, of course, prominent: the Westside Committee of Concern on Vietnam had eight chapters, representing different neighborhoods.[7] Women's groups were particularly conspicuous, and there were groups of gays, artists, teachers, trade unionists, doctors, veterans, and "Mental Health Professionals Acting for Peace."[8]

The Old Left was there: the Veterans of the Abraham Lincoln Brigade, the LA Committee for the Defense of the Bill of Rights, and the Du Bois Clubs, all in the orbit of the CP; others came with groups on the left opposed to the CP: the Socialist Party, the Trotskyist Socialist Workers Party and their Young Socialist Alliance, and the Maoists of Progressive Labor. They also came from the New Left, from SDS and the Vietnam Summer Project. Then there were the progressive religious groups—and the atheists—and even a couple of Democratic Party clubs. Not since Henry Wallace's 1948 crusade to stop the Cold War had such a large and diverse coalition come out on the streets of L.A.

The Official Story

There were two narratives about what happened when marchers arrived in front of the hotel that night. In the police version, echoed by Mayor Sam Yorty and to some extent by the daily press, the cops were the heroes of the hour, saving the president from a violent mob. In contrast, protestors, the *LA Free Press* and the ACLU told an entirely different story: an indiscriminate and sometimes berserk attack by cops on entirely peaceful demonstrators. The contrasting accounts agreed only on one fact: as Johnson's guests arrived, nearly 1,000 police, a gigantic mobilization, confronted 10,000 anti-war protestors, whom they forcibly dispersed. The official parade permit issued by the police allowed the demonstrators to march past the hotel, but they were supposed to keep moving; instead, they stopped across from the hotel entrance, and some sat down in the street. The police then broadcast an order, "Disperse or you will be arrested," and declared, "This is an unlawful assembly.'" But thousands of demonstrators "refused," chanting, "Hell, no, we won't go!"[9]

At that point, "platoons of officers stepped forward, shoulder to shoulder, holding batons before them with two hands." The objective, they said, was to force the crowd back, break it up, and move the thousands into an empty lot across from the hotel and down to adjoining streets. "Cries rang out: 'Gestapo. Heil Hitler. Sieg Heil. Bastards.'" Then, "when the officers met resistance, they used their nightsticks." The response, according to the official story: "Rocks and pieces of wood rained on police. Some of the spectators spat on the officers, ripped off their badges and stoned them." "A veteran press photographer" was quoted in the *Times* saying, "These people were like animals. All I can say is that the Los Angeles Police Department did one hell of a good job."[10] Mayor Yorty told reporters, "It was a superb job of security by our Los Angeles Police Department."[11]

In the next day's paper, the *Times* sounded even more like a press release from LAPD headquarters. "Four policemen were treated at Central Receiving Hospital and released"—one had a broken foot from being run over by a protest truck; another had chest injuries from a thrown brick.[12] Despite the violence of the marchers, "there were instances of police compassion," the *Times* reported. "Mothers with children were pulled to safety behind police lines." Finally, the *Times* reported, "Police say they suspect many persons who claim to have been seriously hurt by police were faking."[13]

Subsequent justifications for the "dispersal" emphasized the danger to the president. LBJ "ate his dinner at the Century Plaza expecting to be rushed from the hotel at any minute"—because the LAPD and the Secret Service "had received intelligence information that the demonstrators … planned to break through police lines and rush into the hotel." With "only" a thousand cops facing more than 10,000 marchers, Chief Tom Reddin said, "We could never have held the hotel against a rush."[14] That was why, when the front of the march halted outside the hotel, the Secret Service agent in the police command post on the tenth floor of the hotel "alerted the evacuation party to be ready to move the President … Johnson would have been in his helicopter and in the air within five minutes." And after the demonstrators were dispersed, the Secret Service agent "turned to a police officer and indicating an inch with his thumb and forefinger said, 'We came that close to jerking him out of there.'"[15]

The Other Side

The march had been "dispersed" on Friday night; on Monday the *LA Free Press* published a special eight-page issue documenting police violence. The marchers represented "a complete cross-section of America," the *Freep* reported—"all ages, all types. Many small children and toddlers." A reporter who had been a block or two back from the front of the march described what happened when it came to a halt. People heard

> rumors that the police were narrowing the march to two abreast ahead ... More and more cops, stationed every few feet ... someone said cops had ordered the march dispersed. No one was sure what was happening ... Suddenly the cops were massed waves deep, jackboots and helmets gleaming in the fitful glare of TV klieg lights. People found themselves packed tighter ... about 9pm, suddenly the cop in front of me swung his truncheon against the face of a man. Blood spurts. Other cops join in. The first cop started hitting a girl, about 20, with a baby in her arms. She fell down trying to protect the child, the same cop kicked her in the back. A doctor tried to go to her aid and was beaten down by several cops.[16]

The *Freep* ran more than a dozen eyewitness reports, including one from Sherwin Shayne, an attorney who served as a parade monitor and wore a suit and tie along with his armband. He heard "an officer" command, "Everyone move back."

> I then asked the crowd to move backward. A police officer ... knocked down two boys on my right and one of them fell in front of me and I fell over him with my back to the officer. He then hit me on the left side of my head with his club and as I arose gasping for breath he hit me with the tip of his Billy club in my abdomen. When I was able to catch my breath I asked him why he hit me and he motioned to the officer on his right and that officer hit me in the abdomen with the tip of his Billy club. [The first cop then said,] 'I want him.' I was bleeding profusely from the head ... I was taken very roughly and violently to a patrol wagon and all the way protesting that their force was unnecessary and that I would walk with them willingly. I was taken to three different locations and booked at each ... I was covered with blood from head to foot.[17]

But it wasn't just the *Freep*. The *Times* revisited the story a week later in a piece headlined "The Anti-War March—What DID Happen?," which drew on reports from nine staffers on the scene plus eyewitnesses and participants. "I saw a solid wall of white helmets and billy clubs descend on the demonstrators with clubs swinging, pushing and jabbing," one eyewitness said. The *Times* quoted a Hollywood attorney: "I heard the sickening cracking sound made by a club striking a man's head, and saw men, women and even children fall under the assault of policemen. I saw people injured, bleeding, frightened and crying."[18]

By far the most thorough investigation and report came from the ACLU, which spent a month investigating the incident, and had dozens of investigators taking statements. At the end of the month, they published a forty-six-page report, which remains today the most complete and thoughtful analysis of what happened that night.[19]

The section on "The Dispersal"—they used the police term—included the following first-person reports:

> At the right of me was a very old woman and she could not move fast enough to avoid the police. A policeman moved forward and smacked her across the face with a billy club. She immediately fell to the ground and lay still.

> There was an awful charge of policemen plunging into the crown to our right, swinging clubs viciously on the heads of men, women and children.

> 20 or so marchers heard the sounds of crack! Crack! Crack! Of two clubs against a man's bones and body, and of shouts, moans and shrieks ... we saw the great arcs of clubs as the officers swung them over their heads and then down full force ... upon the defenseless man's neck, left shoulder, and upper back. The blows, at least five, bent him double to the ground, chest to his knees.[20]

> My sister was struck on the forehead above the right eye. She fell to the ground on her back as she tried to turn and run. I attempted

to help her ... I was hit by a policeman with a club on the head and back and began to bleed profusely.

But the ACLU report went far beyond documenting police violence. It evaluated the organizers' preparation for the protest, as well as the preparations made by the FBI and the hotel; and it also retraced in detail all of the events that night, starting with the rally in the park and, outside the hotel, what police had called a "failure to disperse."

Protest Planning: The Organizers

While the ACLU was deeply critical of the LAPD, they also criticized the leadership of the protest, mostly for not providing enough monitors to deal with potential problems along the march route. (The FBI undercover agents reported that 125 had signed up as monitors, while organizers said seventy-five more were needed. In fact, only one hundred showed up at the park, and new volunteers were recruited on the spot.)[21] Perhaps the most amazing failure in the demonstration planning was that the organizers made no plans or preparations for problems with the police. The only potential problem addressed in the "Duties and Responsibilities of Monitors" was hecklers. The policy —of course—was "just ignore the provocations" and "don't heckle back."[22] Indeed, the American Nazi Party did show up and do some provocative yelling. The only other potential problem they considered was "an accident such as a person tripping, fainting, etc." People by the hundreds being clubbed to the ground by the cops was not considered a possibility.

The Peace Action Council, the official organizer of the march, prepared carefully for civil disobedience, for people sitting-in in front of the hotel. Like many such protests, then and now, some more-militant people wanted to engage in civil disobedience and get arrested. In 1967, the sit-in was the much-admired tactic of the recent lunch counter integration protests of 1960–61, which involved thousands of people in dozens of cities. The theory had been outlined in Martin Luther King's greatest work, "Letter from Birmingham Jail." King had called the sit-in an act intended to create "constructive, nonviolent tension" that would dramatize the depth of people's opposition to an unjust policy.[23] The groups considering sitting-in included the War Resisters League, Progressive Labor and SDS. After a lengthy debate at several meetings, the Council voted to "disassociate" their march from civil disobedience. (The Council gave one vote to each participating organization, regardless of its size.)[24] So in the planning for this march, as for many others, the organizers understood that some would commit civil disobedience and get arrested, separately and independently from the main march, which would abide by the terms of the parade permit. Meanwhile, SDS and Progressive Labor hoped their sit-in would inspire people from the march to join them.[25]

The debate over civil disobedience was no secret; Peace Action Council meetings were public events, and the *LA Times* ran an article about the debate a week before the march. The paper quoted one PAC member from the California Democratic Council as saying, "If anyone intends to indulge in civil disobedience I will disavow him ... and not participate." It also quoted Mary Clarke of Women Strike for Peace, who said the group had no plans to engage in civil disobedience at the upcoming march, but "we do not disavow civil disobedience," except for "acts of violence." She said she "saw nothing wrong with sit-ins, sit-downs, or standing in front" of the Century Plaza while the president was inside. Don Kalish, cochair of the march—and a philosophy professor at UCLA—said he was "in deep sympathy with Mary Clarke's statement."[26]

Protest Planning: The FBI

Two different undercover operations had infiltrated the march organization: the FBI, and a private security firm hired by the Century Plaza Hotel. They came to contradictory conclusions. The FBI reported that their undercover agents—three "reliable sources"—found no planning for civil disobedience. The day before the march an "urgent" coded teletype from Director J. Edgar Hoover to the White House and the Secret Service reported that "there is no civil disobedience scheduled during the demonstration, and the [Peace Action] council has strongly urged that no civil disobedience be conducted." "All sources unaware of any scheduled civil disobedience," the director was told that day by the Los Angeles FBI office.[27] These documents suggest just how ignorant and incompetent the FBI was—and they also contradict the *LA Times* reports published after the march that the Secret Service believed demonstrators were planning to "rush the hotel.")

The undercover agent working for the Century Plaza, Sharon Stewart, presented sworn testimony to a Santa Monica judge the morning of the march, when attorneys for the hotel sought an injunction against various forms of protest. The 27-year-old, "an employee of International Investigation Systems of Beverly Hills," testified that she had attended a meeting where people proposed "unleashing mice, cockroaches, and stink and/or smoke bombs in the hotel," and also "storming the lobby in force by breaking through police lines." As a result of her testimony, the judge issued an injunction barring demonstrators from "taking any noise-making device, or any device intended to frighten, harass, annoy or obstruct" anyone attending the LBJ event. The injunction also enjoined the demonstrators from "loosing any animal on the premises."[28] (The judge apparently wasn't worried about the cockroaches.)

Stewart also testified that she had enlisted in the protest organization five days before the march and had been "instructed to trigger a wave of civil disobedience outside the Century Plaza while President Johnson was inside." Peace Council leader Don Kalish, she said, had instructed her to "approach police lines and demand to see President Johnson." The plan, she said, was for her to be "hysterically trying to beat my way through the police line, and the police would arrest me." The demonstrators, she said, might then either sit down and chant, "Let her through," or "get up and fight with the policemen" to let her through. Then "there will be a riot," she concluded, and "everyone will say that the police were being brutal."[29]

When Stewart testified the morning of the march, no one from the demonstration planning committee showed up to challenge her claims. It turned out that neither the march leaders nor their attorney, A. L. Wirin, were told of the hearing. The Century City attorneys told the judge that they had called Wirin and the office of the Peace Action

Council that morning at 8 a.m. to inform them about the emergency hearing—but no one answered. That was because neither office opened until 9 a.m.

Of course, there were no plans to release mice or stink bombs in the hotel, much less cockroaches. Nothing like that happened, and nobody arrested by the police that night was found to be in possession of mice, stink bombs or cockroaches. Sharon Stewart had left one thing out of her testimony: those proposals made at the planning meeting for the march, which had been open to the public, came from members of the audience—perhaps provocateurs. None of those proposals were taken seriously by the organizers, the ACLU later reported; "all were turned down out of hand." And of course, nobody had to stage a phony scene in order to provoke the police "being brutal"—and Kalish later stated in sworn testimony, "We didn't plan any role for her at all."[30]

The Rally in the Park

The rally in the park before the march, almost everyone agreed, had had a "happy and festive" spirit—the *Freep* described an afternoon with "the sounds of music, bells and tambourines" and "the ritual exchange of flowers."[31] Dr. Spock was the headliner—a legendary father figure for America and for the peace movement. "We do not consider the Vietnamese people, North *or* South, to be the enemy," he said. "They wish no harm to the United States. The enemy, we believe in all sincerity, is Lyndon Johnson."[32] He concluded by asking for "no violence." H. Rap Brown, chairman of SNCC, was next; according to the ACLU, he "gave the wrong speech, criticizing Israel in the recently ended Israeli-Arab war." He got "scattered boos."[33]

Then came the big surprise: Muhammad Ali—"the hit of the rally," the ACLU reported, and a late addition to the program. He was a hero of the anti-war movement: two months earlier he had refused induction into the military, saying, "I ain't got no quarrel with them Vietcong." And three days before the Century City march, he had been convicted of draft evasion. The penalty was horrifying: five years in prison, a $10,000 fine, and the greatest boxer in the world

Reprinted with permission of the Corita Art Center, Immaculate Heart Community, Los Angeles.

Sister Mary Corita in studio at Immaculate Heart College, circa 1964. L.A.'s most famous artist in the 1960s, her prints became increasingly political, which led L.A.'s famously right-wing cardinal, Francis McIntyre, to order her either to confine herself to traditional religious duties or to renounce her vows. She left the order in 1968, followed by most of the rest of the sisters at the college.

Watts, August 12, 1965. The "riot" metamorphosed from day to day, starting on the first night with groups of young people battling the police, then changing on the second and third nights into widespread community retaliation against the police and exploitative local businesses, then turning into neighborhood resistance to military occupation, followed by a vengeful reign of terror by the LAPD.

Stokely Carmichael defines "black power" at the University of California's Greek Theater in Berkeley, October 29, 1966, jammed with 14,000 people. His next stop was L.A., where the County Board of Supervisors attempted to prevent his scheduled speech in Watts—but 6,500 people showed up to hear him say that militant unity was the sole guarantee of Black survival.

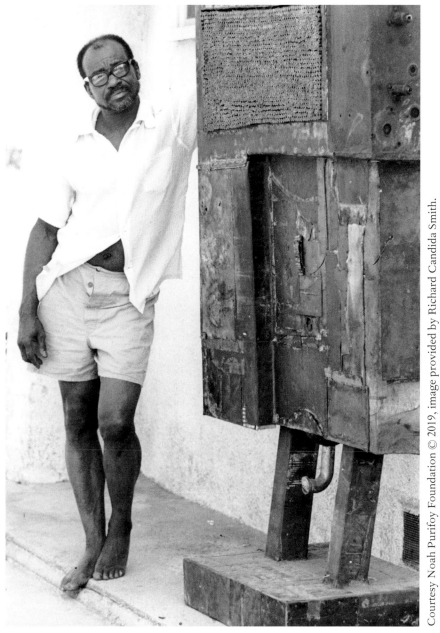

Noah Purifoy at Watts Towers Arts Center, circa 1965. Purifoy, a sculptor, was part of the "Watts Renaissance" that included the free jazz of Horace Tapscott, plus dancers, writers, actors, filmmakers, and poets, whose creative energies had been unleashed by the rebellion.

Photo by William S. Murphy. *Los Angeles Times* Photographic Archive, Department of Special Collections, Charles E. Young Research Library, UCLA.

Ron Karenga outside a courtroom in Los Angeles, May 29, 1971. Karenga, the head of US, was in the forefront of protest in 1967 in L.A., projecting a fierce image of Black Power militancy. The FBI's COINTELPRO provoked conflict between US and the Panthers, and most of the left blamed Karenga for the 1969 murder of two LA Panthers on the UCLA campus—but it's doubtful that he had foreknowledge of the killings.

Los Angeles Herald-Examiner Collection,
Los Angeles Public Library.

When LBJ announced in 1967 that he would open his reelection campaign with a gala fundraiser in Century City, 15,000 people joined an antiwar protest. Many marchers wore suits and ties and brought their children—while the LAPD brought 1,000 cops in riot gear.

Los Angeles Times Photographic Archive,
Library Special Collections, Charles E.
Young Research Library, UCLA.

At the Century City anti-war protest, a small group sat-in outside the hotel where LBJ was speaking, violating the permit which required the marchers to keep moving. They expected to be arrested for civil disobedience.

Los Angeles Times Photographic Archive, Library Special Collections, Charles E. Young Research Library, UCLA.

At the Century City protest, instead of arresting the people sitting-in, officials declared the entire march an "illegal assembly" and ordered its "dispersal." One thousand police then attacked 15,000 marchers, most of whom were white and middle class. The events marked a turning point in L.A. politics, forging an alliance between westside liberals and Black voters that culminated six years later in the election of L.A.'s first Black mayor, Tom Bradley.

CLEAVER FOR PRESIDENT

BLACK PANTHER PARTY PEACE & FREEDOM PARTY

PEACE AND FREEDOM PARTY

POWER TO THE PEOPLE
BLACK POWER TO BLACK PEOPLE

THE BINDWEED PRESS

Cleaver for President poster printed by The Bindweed Press, 1968.
Image courtesy Lincoln Cushing / Docs Populi.

The Peace and Freedom Party collected 37,000 signatures in L.A. County to get the Party on California's presidential ballot in 1968—a tremendous achievement. Although Dick Gregory, the greatly admired satirist-activist, was a candidate for the party's nomination, the Black Panther Party insisted that Peace and Freedom nominate Eldridge Cleaver despite the fact that he was under 35 and thus ineligible to run. Cleaver, the loose cannon in the Panther leadership, soon lost all interest in the campaign.

The Vietnam War era saw the largest movement against the draft since World War I. Draft resistance quickly became the leading edge of the anti-war movement; resisters served the same role in the anti-war movement that Freedom Riders and students sitting in at lunch counters had played in the civil rights movement.

was banned from the sport for three years. Ali spoke briefly: "We are not for violence," he said. "If anyone starts something, it won't be this group. The police will have to start it." The *Freep* called that "prophecy."[34]

As the rally ended and the marchers headed out of the park for the hotel, there was an incident that resulted in felony charges of "assaulting an officer with a deadly weapon." The "deadly weapon" in question was a Toyota pickup truck, which had been driven to the head of the parade as it set out from Cheviot Hills Park, even though the parade permit did not allow trucks. The driver, according to the police, was ordered to stop, but instead he drove the truck "into the path of Officer Frank L. Petrasich, who was attempting to remove a prone demonstrator." The truck ran over the officer's foot, after which other officers "smashed the windshield with their batons" and "removed" the driver—who turned out to be a sixteen-year-old named Stephen Daniel Lippman.[35]

Because of the significance the police gave to the incident, the ACLU investigated it thoroughly. The pickup truck carried a sound system, and it was intended by Progressive Labor and SDS to encourage marchers to join their sit-in in front of the hotel when the time came. The Peace Action Council was not aware of this plan, and when the truck approached the point where the march was beginning to form, monitors linked arms and surrounded the truck to prevent it from joining the parade. "Two PAC leaders attempted to persuade the driver" not to continue. The truck halted, the ACLU reported; but after one minute, "suddenly one of the police sprang forward toward the drivers' compartment, striking one person with his club. He then took his club in both hands and began beating on the windshield of the truck ... the driver was not asked to get out of the car. The police just attacked," but "another officer attempted to restrain him." At the same time, "a girl's voice amplified [over the truck's sound system] was shouting, 'Protect the truck with your bodies. Make a shield of bodies around the truck.' Leaders of the march, however, advised against this and asked the marchers to sit down."

More cops joined in beating on the truck's windows and began clubbing the girl and boy in the bed of the pickup. Monitors "begged" the marchers to "sit down" and "offer no resistance," arguing that "the peace march might be cancelled" before it ever started if this incident escalated into a major battle. Marchers did sit down, but the police took one of the monitors into custody, and while one held him with his arms pinned behind him, a second cop "kicked the monitor in the monitor's genitals."[36] The cops finally dragged the driver out of the truck, and four cops held him while a fifth clubbed him. Finally the police stopped, then they dragged away the four kids who had been in the truck, which was left behind as the parade departed for the Century Plaza Hotel: doctors and nurses wearing white coats, mothers pushing baby carriages, small children perched on their fathers' shoulders.[37] Afterward one officer was treated for a broken foot. The truck incident in the park made it clear that the police were ready to club and beat demonstrators long before the order to disperse was given outside the hotel an hour and a half later.

The "Failure to Disperse," Revisited

When the front of the march reached the hotel, the march stopped. That provided the rationale for the police attack—"failure to disperse." The media and the police said the marchers had sat in outside the hotel entrance, but the ACLU found the sit-in had "little tangible effect" because the march had already come to a halt before people began sitting down. The people sitting in the street had "less importance in stopping the march" than three other factors. First was "the attraction of the hotel itself, an attraction intensified through the denial by Century City's management of the use of an available parking lot [down the block] for a post-march rally and dispersal point." The march also stopped because "police had narrowed the line of march drastically at a critical point" just past the hotel. The third problem was that 500 spectators, who were not marchers, had shown up outside the hotel, many to cheer for what was to be the biggest anti-war protest in LA history. They "spilled off the sidewalk" and "clogged" the street where the demonstrators were supposed to be marching.[38]

What do you do when a march has stopped moving? Thousands of marchers were backed up for a mile, pressing forward and eager to proceed past the hotel. But, the ACLU noted, "the police did nothing to get it restarted." The marchers had a permit with an approved route; the police should have cleared the route ahead of the march, kept the spectators on the sidewalk, arrested the people sitting-in— that's what they expected—and worked with the march monitors to get the demonstrators moving again. That was made more difficult because the police had refused to give the organizers permission to use sound trucks. But instead of clearing the street to get the march restarted, the police issued an order to all the marchers to disperse. The ACLU argued that this was the fundamental problem—an order that was "arbitrary" and "served no lawful purpose."[39]

Before the dispersal order, the ACLU found, none of the marchers "engaged in acts hostile to the police on duty, the hotel, or the President." Most of the marchers never heard the dispersal order. The police waited half an hour after issuing the dispersal order before attacking the demonstrators. Most important, instead of arresting the several dozen demonstrators who were sitting in, the police "used excessive force to disperse the entire parade" of ten or fifteen thousand people. "Unresisting demonstrators were beaten—some in front of literally thousands of witnesses—without even the pretext of an attempt to make an arrest."[40]

One other remarkable feature of the police attack was that it continued for more than an hour after the initial order to disperse was given. During that hour, police chased demonstrators for more than a mile from the hotel, beating and clubbing them. One group of marchers was chased into Beverly Hills; others trying to get back to the park where their cars had been parked said they were pushed, jabbed and clubbed along streets by police several blocks from the Century Plaza. People waiting at bus stops several blocks away more than an hour later were attacked and beaten by police. The last reports of police harassment were at 11p.m., two hours after the dispersal began: so much for protecting the president from demonstrators rushing the hotel while he was speaking.[41]

A Communist Conspiracy?

One more thing: the Reds. "Legion Charges Red Directed L.A. Protest," a banner headline proclaimed on page one of the *Herald Examiner*. The statewide convention of the American Legion ended the same week as the protest by passing a resolution calling on HUAC to investigate the leadership of the march, pointing to Irving Sarnoff, a cochairman of the Peace Action Council. Their resolution was supported, conveniently, by "massive photographic and eyewitness documentation assembled by Los Angeles police in support of a request for felony riot-conspiracy indictments against top leaders of the demonstration"—which of course included Sarnoff—who, according to the Legion, had pled the Fifth in 1958 when appearing before HUAC. While it was a misdemeanor "to cause or urge" a riot, conspiracy to riot is a felony.[42] (No felony charges of conspiracy to riot were ever filed.) In response to the Legion, Sarnoff told the *LA Times*: "I am not a member of any political party, even though I am a registered Democrat."[43] Thirty years later, the *Times* revisited the 1967 events at the Century Plaza hotel, and reporter Kenneth Reich asked Sarnoff whether he had ever been a CP member. He "said he once was a Communist, but he left the party in 1951 at the age of 21"—sixteen years before the Century City demonstration.[44]

Dorothy Healey, in her memoir, wrote that

> the Party ... played a central role in the peace movement in southern California, particularly through the Peace Action Council. Irving Sarnoff, who initiated the group, was a very dedicated man who had been active in the Railway Brotherhood. In Los Angeles, the Peace Action Council was the primary source of education and mobilization during the war in Vietnam, and communists were an accepted part of the anti-war coalition.[45]

On the other hand, the FBI's informant inside the Southern California CP "advised" on the day before the march that "Communist Party in Los Angeles has issued instructions to its members to stay away from demonstration of six twenty three next in view of all the talk about possible trouble with LAPD and civil disobedience."[46]

Consequences: For LBJ and L.A.

The police attack on ten or fifteen thousand middle-class white people in one of the country's biggest Democratic strongholds, at the first event of LBJ's reelection campaign, marked a historic turning point in his political career. The official story had been that the demonstration had "failed in its major purpose" because "the demonstrators never got near the President to press their antiwar message."[47] But LBJ must have seen the headline in the *LA Times*, "Anti-War Protest Nearly Drove President Out of Los Angeles," and the report that "the president ate his dinner at the Century Plaza expecting to be rushed from the hotel at any minute ... to a waiting helicopter."[48] And now thousands, maybe millions, of people had read or heard that news— about the city with the biggest Democratic turnout anywhere west of Manhattan. He must have wondered how he could campaign at all in the coming months. And indeed, after Century City, Johnson didn't campaign in public, except for "appearance at safe places like military bases."[49]

Just eleven weeks after Century City, on September 8, LBJ discussed with his trusted Texas advisor John Connally whether he should abandon his reelection campaign. Connally told him he "didn't think he could get reelected," and they came to a "decision that he should not" run. This was almost six months before the New Hampshire primary. In December, he decided to announce his "retirement" at the end of his 1968 State of the Union message.[50] That part of the speech was drafted but kept secret, and when he appeared before Congress in January he didn't read it. He finally made that announcement on March 31, after nearly losing the New Hampshire Democratic primary to peace candidate Eugene McCarthy.

Century City marked a turning point in LA politics as well. Two years after Watts, white liberals on the Westside had suddenly experienced firsthand the brutality of the LAPD that Blacks had been protesting against for years. The Westside now turned against Mayor Sam Yorty, and also against the LAPD. When the city council voted to endorse the police action at Century City, the council member most critical of the LAPD was Tom Bradley, who represented Black L.A.[51] Two years later, Bradley ran for mayor, and the white Westside supported him. They lost that year, but the same coalition would eventually succeed in electing him, two years after that. Thus the Century City protest was a key moment in the seismic political shift that transformed LA politics in the next decade. It would take a lot longer to change the LAPD.

19

Eldridge Cleaver for President: The Peace and Freedom Party (1967–68)

B y 1967, with the War on Poverty dismantled to pay for the war in Vietnam, disllusionment with the Johnson administration had turned into the bitter conviction that stopping the war in Vietnam meant stopping LBJ's reelection in 1968. Anti-war activists in California believed they had two options: challenging him with a peace candidate in the state's Democratic primary or organizing a third party to run an anti-war candidate against him in the general election. Left-liberal Democrats had had their own statewide organization ever since the Fifties: the California Democratic Council (CDC). By 1967 it had 33,000 members, was passionately anti-war, and was eager to dump Johnson by getting a peace candidate to challenge him in the primary coming up on June 4, 1968. Of course, Bobby Kennedy was their first choice, but he said he wouldn't do it, so they turned to Gene McCarthy, the anti-war senator from Minnesota. He met with the head of the CDC, a San Francisco lawyer named Gerald Hill, and national anti-war organizer Al Lowenstein, on October 23, 1967, at the Ambassador Hotel in L.A. Hill told McCarthy that a peace candidate "would not only win California" in June "but run well nationally" in other primaries. They assured McCarthy that CDC had the money and volunteers to run a national campaign. After an hour of conversation, McCarthy told them he would do it. He announced on November 30 that he would enter the California primary, and three others.

The New Left wing of the anti-war movement, however, deemed this a hopeless and quixotic quest. They scoffed at the idea that the Democrats, under a leadership that still avidly supported the war, could become the vehicle for bringing the troops home. In addition, they accurately pointed out that most states did not have primaries, and that LBJ could win re-nomination at the convention even without winning any primaries. (This is exactly what happened in the summer of 1968, when Hubert Humphrey won the nomination without a single primary victory.) The better alternative was an anti-war third party with a platform that also supported Black liberation, the farmworkers' struggle, and other progressive movements. However, California' s election code placed a high hurdle in the path of a new party: 66,000 people had to declare in writing that they wanted to change their registration. The Progressive Party had surmounted this obstacle in 1948, although its presidential candidate, former vice president Henry Wallace, ended up with less than 5 percent of the state's vote. Since then, left-wing parties had all been limited to write-in candidates, who got a few thousand votes each. So supporters of the third-party strategy in Los Angeles—they called themselves the "Peace and Freedom Party" (PFP)—began collecting signatures in summer 1967. On June 23, at the rally before the Century City march, they got thirty signatures; the PFP dated this as its founding. The big question beyond registration, of course, was who their candidate would be.[1]

Similar efforts to come up with a third-party challenge to LBJ were underway in many states in 1967, and on Labor Day weekend, Los Angeles activists joined 3,000 others in Chicago for the National Conference for New Politics to try to organize a national effort. Planning for the September convention had gone on for more than a year; 327 political groups were represented. Maybe there could be a national Peace and Freedom campaign with a single candidate running in many states. Maybe Martin Luther King could be persuaded to run for president—he had come out against the war at Riverside Church four months earlier. Or maybe somebody had a better idea.

The convention opened on August 31 at the Chicago Coliseum with King's keynote address:

Many assembled here campaigned lasciviously for Lyndon Johnson in 1964 ... We were the hardcore activists ... We were the dreamers of a dream ... Now our hopes have been blasted and our dreams have been shattered. The promise of a Great Society was shipwrecked off the coast of Asia, on the dreadful peninsula of Vietnam ...

We've deluded ourselves into believing the myth that capitalism grew and prospered out of the Protestant ethic of hard work and sacrifice. The fact is that capitalism was built on the exploitation and suffering of black slaves, and continues to thrive on the exploitation of the poor—both black and white, both here and abroad ... The problems of racial injustice and economic injustice cannot be solved without a radical redistribution of political and economic power ... This is the meaning of New Politics.[2]

That was precisely the idea behind the Peace and Freedom Party. But King was heckled and interrupted by Black nationalists, and he left the Coliseum, according to his biographer, looking "afraid, worried, and tired."[3]

The next day everything fell apart. King and his lieutenants departed, and so did Julian Bond, former head of SNCC, even though he was the convention's national cochair. A Black caucus demanded that the convention adopt a thirteen-point resolution that included an agreement to form "white civilizing committees" to deal with "the beastlike character" of "all white communities ... as exemplified by George Lincoln Rockwells and Lyndon Baines Johnsons." (Rockwell was the founder of the American Nazi Party.) The nonnegotiable proposals also included a demand that "this conference ... make immediate reparation for the historic, physical, sexual, mental and economic exploitation of black people." Even though the Black caucus never had more than fifty delegates, and it didn't include the Black cochairs of the convention, they demanded that Blacks get 50 percent of the convention votes "to insure equality within New Politics." Finally, the Black caucus demanded that the convention adopt an anti-Zionist resolution.[4] The Black caucus didn't seem very interested in launching a third-party campaign to challenge LBJ; they didn't include anything about the Vietnam War in their thirteen-point resolution. The convention, which was at least 80 percent white, nevertheless voted to give Blacks 50 percent of the vote, and endorsed all of the nonnegotiable demands.

The LA delegates returned from the New Politics convention in a state of rage and dismay. The convention was "a political fiasco," one wrote in the *LA Free Press*, calling the Black caucus demands "stupid, racist, destructive, and most of all, opaque, impenetrable." She quoted a member of the Black caucus, who at the end told her: "If the white man let the black man do this to him, he no radical. He a baby with a guilty conscience trying to get somebody to help him feel better." The *Freep* put that in a box in big type.[5]

Why the white man did that was explained on page one of the *Freep* by Marvin Garson, founder of the *San Francisco Express Times*. The sense of the convention, he wrote, was that "it's going to be very embarrassing if we have nothing but white faces here. We don't know exactly who these blacks are or what they represent, but they've got black faces and that's what we need. Let them have their 13 points; we can ignore the resolution after it's passed. Anything to keep them from walking out."[6]

In mid September 1967, two weeks after the New Politics fiasco in Chicago, California activists met in San Luis Obispo to organize a campaign to get the Peace and Freedom Party on the statewide ballot in 1968. As in Chicago, a "Black caucus" demanded 50 percent of the votes. White radicals—led by Michael Hannon, the left-wing former cop who had run for Congress in 1966 on an anti-war platform, and Jack Weinberg, a hero of the Berkeley Free Speech Movement who had moved to L.A.—counter-proposed equality of white and Black voting blocs, giving each veto power, but the Black caucus rejected this formula. The California PFP leaders were not going to make the same mistake they had in Chicago, so the meeting ended without agreement. As for the whites who supported the Black demands, "The Black Caucus will find that an alliance with such supine servility is an alliance with nothing," Hannon wrote. "Such persons are incapable of building a power base of their own, hence their panic to become the white tail on the black panther."[7]

The PFP's signature-gathering campaign in LA County was one of the local Left's biggest organizing efforts of the decade. According to Santa Monica PFP activist Paul Rosenstein (later mayor of Santa Monica), "at least 75 Peace and Freedom clubs" were involved, and each had to have a minimum of twenty-five members—that's almost 2,000 members gathering signatures in LA County.[8] The PFP presented free outdoor concert-rallies in MacArthur Park and other places; thousands of people came, and, the PFP paper reported, as many as a thousand people would register for the party at each event. And of course, signature gatherers "systematically blanketed" Sunset Strip, Fairfax Avenue and Hollywood Boulevard, and installed themselves for fourteen to sixteen hours a day at places like the *Free Press* bookstore and Kazoo (a psychedelic shop). The climax came on December 18, when hundreds of college students on winter break began working on a "Christmas Blitz." The most spectacular was the "Venice Blitz," which broke all previous records and netted the party more than a thousand new members in a single day.[9] When the signatures were handed in on January 2, a spokesman told the *Freep*, it became clear that the campaign had succeeded "beyond our wildest dreams." Sixty-six thousand signatures were required to get PFP on the ballot in California; they ended up with 105,000. LA County signature gatherers had registered an incredible 37,000 of these.[10]

There was, however, a dark secret behind the Peace and Freedom registration campaign. The biggest challenge to signature gatherers was to convince Democrats to switch their registration to the new party. That meant they would not be eligible to vote in the Democratic primary coming up in June, when Gene McCarthy would be running against LBJ. Voting PFP rather than McCarthy was the correct position, according to the party leadership, because the PFP offered "a permanent, radical political party," rather than Gene McCarthy's "gesture" of opposition.[11] Nevertheless, to get reluctant Democrats to change their registration, signature gatherers often told Democrats they could register for Peace and Freedom before the January deadline, and then change their registration back in time to vote for McCarthy in the primary in June. The chickens would come home to roost on that one.

Meanwhile in Vietnam, the Tet Offensive began on January 30 with simultaneous surprise attacks on every city and provincial capital in South Vietnam. Most shocking to ordinary Americans, young National Liberation Front fighters penetrated the heart of the US Embassy compound in Saigon. For the next month, moreover, the NLF turned Huế, the country's ancient capital, into their version of Stalingrad, repelling wave after wave of American and South Vietnamese attacks. Whatever the final cost to the Viet Cong—and their sacrifice was immense—they had given the lie to the US command's insistence that they were winning the war and could already see the "light at the end of the tunnel." The war, in fact, looked increasingly unwinnable, exactly as the anti-war movement had warned. The case for PFP became stronger—and so did the case for Gene McCarthy.

On March 12 Gene McCarthy nearly won the New Hampshire primary—an astounding victory that exposed just how weak LBJ was in his own party.[12] Four days later Bobby Kennedy declared that he was running for president. Suddenly all the anti-war action seemed to be *inside* the Democratic Party. The tasks facing Peace and Freedom became much more daunting. But the PFP was huge in L.A. at that point: in March, the party had sixty functioning neighborhood groups, ranging in size from 20 to over 200, for a total participation of around 2,500.[13]

Two days after Kennedy declared, on March 18, California PFP held its first statewide convention. More than a thousand people showed up—547 delegates from local clubs, and 492 alternates. The convention, held in the working-class town of Richmond, near Berkeley, was meeting to draft a platform; it was not meeting to pick a presidential candidate—although, now that King had said he wouldn't do it, a lot of people wanted Dick Gregory, the movement's Black anti-war comedian. The most profound line from his act: "I sat in for six months at a Southern lunch counter. When they finally served me, they didn't have what I wanted." He really had sat in at lunch counters, and marched in Selma. And the year before he had run for mayor of Chicago against the hated party boss Richard Daley.[14]

At the convention, Paul Jacobs, a labor organizer and writer from San Francisco, gave a speech explaining why the party wasn't supporting Bobby Kennedy or Eugene McCarthy: Kennedy was part of the government that started "the policy we all deplore in Vietnam," and McCarthy's "position on withdrawal from Vietnam is not easily distinguishable from LBJ's"—which was sort of true; Johnson was now saying he too was seeking a negotiated end to the war in the Paris Peace Talks.[15]

Eldridge Cleaver, the ex-convict and author who had recently become minister of information of the Black Panther Party, also gave a speech to the convention: "The Black Panther Party looks upon the black members of the Peace and Freedom party as misguided political freaks who are trying to maintain in an incorrect manner a dual status," he declared. "They have one foot in the mother country and the other foot in the colony, and their political manhood gets strangled on the border separating the two nations."[16] This was the guy who would end up being Peace and Freedom's presidential candidate. In 1968 he was a heroic and controversial figure on the left. He had published essays in *Ramparts* magazine starting in 1965, when he was in prison in California for armed assault and attempted rape; the essays were remarkable works tracing his evolution from street criminal to radical thinker. In December 1966 he won probation after nine years in prison, when *Ramparts* promised to employ him as a reporter. He became the Panther minister of information in 1967, and in February 1968 *Ramparts* published a book of his essays under the title *Soul on Ice*. It became a bestseller, compared favorably with *Malcolm X Speaks*, and the *New York Times* named it one of the ten best books of the year.[17]

At the California PFP convention, a Black caucus demanded the convention urge that imprisoned Panther leader Huey Newton "be freed by any means necessary." Mario Savio of the Berkeley Free Speech Movement objected: "I don't think the revolt in America depends on burning down Oakland because one person is in jail," he said. That resolution was narrowly defeated, 227 against and 223 in favor. But then an amendment was passed that said Huey should be freed "by any means which will further the black liberation movement."[18] Next the Panthers demanded that Huey be the PFP candidate for Congress in the East Bay. Kathleen Cleaver declared that if the PFP didn't run Huey, the new party would "fall into the same pit of cynicism, hypocrisy, and decadence of the Democratic and Republican Parties," and the failure would be "an invitation to certain destruction."[19] Of course, the convention agreed to make Huey their candidate in the East Bay, and also to run Panther leader Bobby Seale for the state assembly seat in Oakland.

So the main result of the founding convention was an alliance between the PFP and the Panthers. Peace and Freedom had agreed to work to free Huey Newton and support Panther leaders running for office; would the Panthers now work to turn out the Black vote for PFP candidates? In the ensuing weeks, PFP statewide chair Jack Weinberg later recalled, "the Panthers did do voter registration in the African American neighborhoods of Oakland, so there was a period of time when they took it seriously." Of course, they were organizing for their own leaders, Newton and Seale. But, Weinberg said, there was no similar effort in the Black neighborhoods of L.A. Shermont Banks was a leader of the Panthers in L.A. When he was asked about the party, "he didn't seem to know very much about the PFP in Los Angeles and he didn't seem to have much interest in what the PFP was like," the SWP reported. "He never talked about any projects which the Panthers were working on in common with the PFP ... He was pleased that here was a group of white people who supported the Black Panther Party."[20]

On March 31, nineteen days after Gene McCarthy's near-victory in New Hampshire, and two days before LBJ would face McCarthy again in Wisconsin, Johnson announced he was withdrawing from the race. Never before had an incumbent president been forced out of his own reelection campaign by voters in his own party. Never before had an anti-war movement been so effective. Working inside the Democratic Party, rather than in a third party, suddenly seemed to be the way to change history, and Peace and Freedom's task became more difficult now that it might actually be possible to get a peace candidate at the head of the Democratic ticket.

Then, on April 4, King was assassinated. Suddenly electoral politics seemed to be no match for the violent undercurrents emanating from the Far Right in America. Two days later, Cleaver and seven other Panthers were involved in a shoot-out with the Oakland police. Bobby

Hutton, who was only seventeen, was killed; two cops were shot; and Cleaver was injured and arrested, jailed on charges of attempted murder. Thirty years later, he admitted—in a 1998 PBS *Frontline* interview with Henry Louis Gates Jr.—that he had initiated the shoot-out.[21] He said it was an attempt to spark an insurrection in Oakland.[22] Meanwhile, more than a hundred writers and intellectuals called for his release in a statement in the *New York Review of Books* in May 1968—they were led by James Baldwin, Ossie Davis, Amiri Baraka, Ron Karenga, and many others, including New York literary luminaries Norman Mailer, Jason Epstein of the *New York Review*, Gloria Steinem, Alfred Kazin and Susan Sontag. Their statement declared that Eldridge and the other Panthers "were victims of an attack by Oakland police ... whose leadership that force seems determined to exterminate." The statement also explained that "the Panthers have established a coalition with the Peace and Freedom Party ... for the basic purpose of freeing Huey Newton."[23] Significantly, they did not mention that other purpose of the Peace and Freedom Party: running candidates opposed to the war.

Bobby Kennedy and Gene McCarthy now fought an intense state-by-state battle that culminated in the California primary on June 4. Kennedy's base was in the Latino, Black, and white working-class neighborhoods of L.A., and his campaign did a lot of work registering voters there. Michael Harrington, a democratic socialist and author of *The Other America*, campaigned for Kennedy in California. In Hollywood, Paul Newman and Dustin Hoffman supported McCarthy, along with Simon and Garfunkel, but the other liberals joined "Hollywood for Kennedy," headed by singer Andy Williams, and including Warren Beatty, Henry Fonda, Kirk Douglas, Candice Bergen, Bobby Darin, and Jefferson Airplane, plus the big names of Black show business: Sidney Poitier, Bill Cosby, and Sammy Davis Jr. They held a gala at the Sports Arena featuring Sonny and Cher, Gene Kelly, Mahalia Jackson, the Byrds, and Jerry Lewis.[24] (Frank Sinatra supported Vice President Hubert Humphrey, who had replaced LBJ as the candidate of the party bosses; but Humphrey had announced his candidacy too late to enter the California primary—or any others.)

McCarthy was clearly to the left of Kennedy on many issues: he wanted to recognize Communist China and replace J. Edgar Hoover. On Vietnam, McCarthy emphasized the Cold War premises of the war, while Kennedy talked about the possible role of the UN. But on ending the war, both had pretty much the same vague position. Both said the United States should get out of Vietnam, but how and when were never specified. When they held a televised debate in California on May 31, McCarthy called for a coalition government in South Vietnam, and Kennedy replied that McCarthy wanted to impose "coalition with the Communists" on Saigon. McCarthy said he was in favor of building public housing in the suburbs; Kennedy replied, "You say you are going to take ten thousand black people and move them into Orange County." He was obviously playing to the Right, which was depressing to his supporters. Neither Gene McCarthy nor Bobby Kennedy advocated immediate withdrawal from Vietnam. That's why Peace and Freedom was on the ballot.

On June 4, Kennedy got 46 percent of the vote in California and McCarthy 42. In Los Angeles County, Kennedy won easily, with a margin of more than 125,000 votes. He took all the Black and Latino precincts by huge margins. It was Kennedy's showing in L.A., analysts concluded, that gave him the victory.[25] Then, that night, Kennedy was assassinated. That pretty much ended the fight for an anti-war candidate inside the Democratic Party; McCarthy, having lost the biggest primary, now had no way to the nomination. With both King and Kennedy killed in a two-month period, despair about American politics replaced whatever hope people had held. But for those who still were interested in voting against the war in November, the case for the PFP suddenly got a lot stronger.

The Nominee

Two months later, on August 3, 1,200 PFP members from L.A. gathered in Elysian Park on a sunny Saturday afternoon to vote on which presidential candidate their delegates would support at the upcoming national convention. The two leading candidates were Dick Gregory and Eldridge Cleaver, who—notwithstanding his mocking speech at the PFP's founding convention in Richmond—had made headlines when he announced that he would run for president, seeking the PFP nomination.[26] Eldridge had won release from prison on a habeas corpus petition on June 12—pretty amazing, since he had been charged with trying to kill cops, and was already on parole for assault.[27] Both Cleaver and Gregory came to the LA convention and gave speeches. Eldridge got 52 percent of the vote, barely a majority, while Dick Gregory got 41 percent and Gene McCarthy got 7 percent.[28]

Los Angeles PFP members joined 200 delegates from nineteen other states on August 17–18 at the PFP's first national convention. The delegates in Ann Arbor included only a dozen Panthers—Eldridge, Bobby Seale, and Panthers from L.A., San Diego, Omaha, and New York, as well as the Bay Area.[29] At last the party would select its candidates for president and vice president. Once again the two leading candidates were Dick Gregory and Eldridge Cleaver. Both gave speeches; Gregory "urged the building of a third party electoral alternative for 1972," and Eldridge declared that the way to support the Vietnamese was by opening "a second front right here in Babylon." That got a standing ovation. Paul Jacobs said he was endorsing Cleaver because "he has the capacity to make me feel utterly uncomfortable." Bruce Franklin, another California delegate, said "Cleaver has the unique ability to provide the analysis and the strategy for changing the society." Cleaver won, 161 to 54, despite the fact that he wasn't old enough to hold the office—the constitution specified that the president had to be thirty-five, and Cleaver was only thirty-three. (Gregory was thirty-six.)

Then it was time to pick the vice presidential candidate. Tom Hayden declined, as did Paul Jacobs and Jack Weinberg. Howard Zinn and Dave Dellinger had already said no. That was distinctly ominous. Eldridge was asked who he wanted, and instead of naming someone from PFP, he replied "Jerry Rubin." But Eldridge and everybody else knew that Jerry had other plans: in two weeks, outside the Democratic National Convention in Chicago, he would lead the Yippies in nominating a pig for president.[30]

Disaster hit the PFP in California a week after Cleaver was nominated as their presidential candidate: the secretary of state ruled him off the ballot, on the grounds that he was too young to hold the office. Of course, they knew that when they nominated him. Appeals to the state supreme court, and then the Supreme Court in Washington, both failed. The party considered organizing a write-in campaign, but the state declared it would not count write-ins for a party that had qualified for the ballot.[31] So the PFP would appear on the November ballot in California, but it would have no candidate for president.[32]

Why nominate as your presidential candidate someone who was ineligible to appear on the ballot? If Peace and Freedom was serious about the "Freedom" part of their agenda, they couldn't be an all-white party. But on the Black left, the Panthers were pretty much alone in seeking alliances with white groups. In the other Black radical groups of the era, Black nationalism dominated. Of course, Dick Gregory wanted to be the PFP presidential candidate—and in fact, he would have been a much better one; many PFP people (almost a majority at the California conventions) thought so at the time. But he didn't lead a group, and he didn't have an organization. So PFP made an alliance with the Panthers, and the Panthers wanted Eldridge Cleaver as the presidential candidate. Another puzzler: Why run someone who had been the leader of an attempt at armed insurrection? Insurrection is usually seen as the opposite of campaigning for political office. But Eldridge said he had been an innocent victim of an attack initiated by the Oakland Police, who were known for their racism and attacks on the Panthers; so the PFP and many other white radicals believed him.

Pussy Power

But after Eldridge got out of prison, he changed his thinking about politics. Jack Weinberg had been statewide chair of the PFP during the 1968 presidential campaign; he recalled that, by midsummer, "Eldridge had no interest in running for president. He had no interest in supporting the Peace and Freedom Party. He had no interest in the alliance that we had built with the Black Panther Party." During the campaign season he gave speeches not about ending the war in Vietnam, or supporting the other PFP candidates, but about "pussy power." In an October speech at Stanford, for example, he declared that "political power grows out of the lips of the pussy. Ladies constitute a strategic reserve for the revolution." He urged women to "cut off the sugar" from men who weren't part of the movement.[33] August 26–29 was the Democratic National convention in Chicago.

The National Mobilization Committee to End the War in Vietnam —"the Mobe"—together with the Yippies, planned a huge "Festival of Life" in Chicago to protest the war; they hoped 100,000 would come. The turnout was uninspiring—only 15,000—but it didn't matter; thousands of police and national guardsmen beat young demonstrators on live national TV, while the Kennedy and McCarthy delegates inside the convention hall were crushed by the party bosses. As a best-selling chronicler of elections put it, Hubert Humphrey "was nominated in a sea of blood."[34] In turn, the case for some kind of third-party vote again became stronger.

Meanwhile in L.A. the PFP stuck with its part of the alliance with the Panthers. When Huey Newton was found guilty of killing an Oakland police officer in early September 1968, PFP State Chairman Jack Weinberg wrote a long defense of him in the *Freep*, concluding, "The Peace and Freedom Party extends an invitation to all Huey supporters to join the Free Huey parade down Hollywood Boulevard," to be held the next week.[35] The march wasn't successful; only 200 people showed up.[36] But the PFP tried again—on Sunset Strip on a Saturday night—with much different results: 3,000 people came to confront the sheriffs, the historic enemy on the Strip, who had declared a tactical alert. The chant became "Free Huey—Free the Strip!" When they reached the end of the march route, Jack Weinberg shouted into a bullhorn, "Let's go home." But hundreds of people who had joined the march en route wanted to keep it going. Someone shouted, "Let's march to the Donovan concert—the people there will join us!" The concert was at the Hollywood Bowl—five miles away. Weinberg shouted, "Let's vote on it!" Someone else shouted back, "The revolution will not be won by a show of hands!" Then someone else shouted, "Let's march to the sheriff's station!" That was only a few blocks away, and the kids set off. When they arrived, someone in the crowd suggested that Weinberg "make a speech about the history of oppression." "All of it?" he said. "I'm tired. It's too long." But he started on the recent historic demonstrations in Berkeley and at the Pentagon. After that, everybody (except for seventy-five anarchists) went home.[37]

As election day approached, with the Democrats running Humphrey, the Republicans running Richard Nixon, and segregationist George Wallace running as an independent, the mainstream media treated the PFP's "Cleaver for President" campaign as a joke. A poll showed him getting 1 percent of the California vote.[38] A feature in *New York Times Magazine* bore the headline "If you don't like Hubert, Dick, or George, how about Lar, Yetta or Eldridge?"[39] "Yetta" was Mrs. Yetta Bronstein, running as a write-in candidate for president on the "Jewish Mother ticket," and "Lar" was Lar Daly, a perennial "America First" candidate who campaigned in an Uncle Sam suit. To the shock of many, the *Freep* ran an election preview that wasn't much different. The paper had been a passionate supporter of Peace and Freedom, and had devoted most of an issue to the party's founding convention. But now, the *Freep* merely listed Eldridge Cleaver among the "write-in candidates," including Pigasus, the pig candidate of the Yippies, Frank Zappa, and Alfred E. Neuman of *Mad* magazine.[40]

On election day the presidential ballot in California listed four parties: in addition to the Democrats and Republicans, voters found "American Independent" and "Peace and Freedom." The PFP line was blank for its presidential candidate, but they did have a vice presidential candidate you could vote for—a Chicago activist named Peggy Terry. There was also a space for a write-in candidate, and the state registrar of voters told the *Freep* they would count and report the votes for six of the write-ins.[41]

There was one other strategy for election day: "Vote with your feet—vote in the streets." Tom Hayden and Rennie Davis made the case, in the *Freep*, for the "election strike" called by SDS and the "Mobe"—which had organized the march on the Pentagon in 1967 and the demonstrations at the Democratic National Convention in Chicago in August 1968. Hayden and Davis were still thinking about the battle with the police outside the DNC three months earlier, where, they wrote, we hurt the people who rule this country. We damaged the machinery and discredited the authority of the Democratic Party ... We won respect for ourselves in the eyes of those oppressed people who have been wondering whether white youths are serious about social change ... The battle line is no longer drawn in the obscure paddies of Vietnam or the dim ghetto streets, but is coming closer to suburban sanctuaries and corporate boardrooms.

But what about the anti-war candidates who were on the ballot? "Join the election strike," the headline said. "We must show the world that our 'democratic process' is a contemptible mockery and that a political strike against the Presidential election has wide American support. Students should close down American universities to join the election strike." They called for "leafletting and picketing of polling booths ... not a passive 'stay-at-home' boycott of the meaningless Presidential race, but an active campaign to raise the relevant political issues."[42]

But on election day the "vote in the streets" protests were small, in L.A. and everywhere else—a sign of the despair and hopelessness that were sweeping the Left. Downtown, several hundred turned up to rally at Pershing Square and march to the Federal Building. At Claremont Men's College, 150 students, mostly from the Black Students' Union, staged a sit-down on Mills Avenue that lasted nearly an hour. Rallies were also held at Valley State, LA City College and Cal State LA, with a few hundred students in attendance at each. Additionally, two voters in Venice set fire to their ballot cards in protest against the "meaningless election."[43]

Nixon carried California, 48 to 45 percent, and shockingly, he carried LA County, 48 to 46 percent. Four years earlier LBJ had won 57 percent of the vote in LA County. Nixon got 1.3 million votes in LA County, 43,000 more than Humphrey (as compared to LBJ, who won by a margin of 400,000 over Goldwater in 1964). And most shocking of all, George Wallace got 151,000 votes in LA County. The other official LA County results: "Peace and Freedom Party, No Eligible Candidate Certified for President; Peggy Terry for Vice President, 9,564."[44] They had registered 37,000 in LA County in January.[45] That meant about three-quarters of the people who registered PFP before

January did not vote for the party's crippled presidential ticket in November.[46]

The outcome was tragedy concealed within a farce: Eldridge Cleaver gave a "concession" speech, throwing his support to Pigasus, the candidate of Jerry Rubin and the Yippies. "The pig is mightier than the Cleaver," he declared.[47] Three weeks after that, the PFP's former presidential candidate jumped bail and fled the United States, flying first to Cuba, then to Algiers, where he spent seven years in exile—before becoming a right-wing Christian, returning to the United States, and joining the Republican Party.[48]

1968 had been an overwhelming year for everybody. For the Left in L.A., it had started in January with a triumph of historic proportions: the thousands of people who worked to get PFP on the ballot in California and made it the first left party to qualify in twenty years. And they did it even before the Tet Offensive showed that the war couldn't be won. The success of the registration drive had been the first evidence anywhere in the country of LBJ's vulnerability to an electoral challenge.

But PFP's alliance with the Panthers, formed in March, had disastrous consequences. Fifty years later, Jack Weinberg, reflecting on his time as statewide head of Peace and Freedom Party during the 1968 presidential campaign, concludes, "We actually had an opportunity, for a moment, to create something of substance—if third parties are a valuable thing, which I now have questions about anyway. But from the perspective of building a third party, I reckon we did everything wrong."[49]

20

"Time to Stand Up": Draft Resistance and Sanctuary (1967–69)

wenty-seven million American men were eligible for the draft during the Vietnam War, and 25 million of them didn't go to Vietnam. The Selective Service System gave deferments to students in college, graduate school, and professional school, as well as to married men, and those who could demonstrate economic hardship. If you couldn't get one of those deferments, you could fail your physical, or tell them you were gay. Joining the National Guard or the Army Reserves kept you in the states. You could claim conscientious objector status if you were a pacifist, and perform alternate service. You could move to Canada and ask for "landed immigrant status." You didn't have to be an opponent of the war to want to avoid service; in fact, almost all the pro-war politicians of subsequent decades avoided going to Vietnam: George W. Bush joined the Texas Air National Guard; Dick Cheney got student and marriage deferments; Donald Trump was declared 4-F—medically unfit—because of bone spurs.[1]

There was one other way: you could refuse to take a deferment, and instead take a stand against the war that was, in the words of draft resister Bruce Dancis, "public, dramatic, and irrevocable."[2] The Vietnam era saw the largest movement against the draft since the Civil War. Draft resistance quickly became the leading edge of the anti-war movement; resisters served the same role in the anti-war movement that Freedom Riders and students sitting in at lunch counters had played in the civil rights movement.[3] Although the first draft-card burning had occurred in Berkeley in spring 1965,[4] a national strategy of resistance based on mass refusal of conscription emerged only in the winter of 1967, and then only after long debates within SDS and campus peace groups. Although the movement emerged simultaneously in Northern California and New England, it was the Boston Draft Resistance Group that became the national coordinating center for the thousands of potential draftees and their supporters who responded to the call to move "from protest to resistance." The local franchise—the LA Resistance—opened an office near UCLA in April 1967, staffed by Winter Dellenbach with help from Sherna Gluck (women would play a central role in the Resistance), while the rent and stipends were paid by UCLA professor Don Kalish, one of the co-chairs of the Century City protest. (He would hire Angela Davis to teach at UCLA in 1969 and become her foremost champion.) The opening coincided with a huge demonstration at Sheep Meadow in New York's Central Park, in which around 150 young men burned their draft cards. Two weeks later Muhammad Ali refused induction in his hometown of Louisville. "Why should they ask me," he asked, "another so-called Negro, to put on a uniform and go 10,000 miles from home and drop bombs and bullets on brown people in Vietnam while so-called Negro people in Louisville are treated like dogs and denied simple human rights?" Two months later he was sentenced to five years in prison, stripped of his title and banned from boxing.

The Resistance went out into the streets that October as part of the national "Stop the Draft" week. Six thousand demonstrators, including Joan Baez, were badly mauled by cops in a battle outside the doors of the Oakland Induction Center, while in L.A. the cops blocked an attempt by several hundred protestors to enter the federal courthouse downtown. Eight men burned their draft cards on the steps, and over a hundred turned in their draft cards. During the rally men in academic robes held up a banner reading: "We have encouraged, will and do honor these draft refusers. We are prepared to share any reprisals taken against them." They identified themselves as college teachers from the area. Karen Dellenbach, speaking for the Draft Resistance Union, explained that "more than a hundred women and men ineligible for the draft have signed statements of complicity." Then demonstrators again surged up the steps, chanting "Open the door" and "We built the building."[5] On the second day of Stop the Draft week in L.A., hundreds demonstrated downtown at the induction center, blocking the doors. Twenty-five LAPD cops in riot gear arrived at 7:30 in the morning. They formed a wedge and quickly pushed the demonstrators back, arresting nineteen who refused to move.[6]

The next national day of noncooperation and draft card turn-in was December 4, 1967. The LA Resistance observed the day with a "service of conscience" at the First Unitarian Church, attended by 400 people. Resisters dropped their draft cards in one of two chalices, one filled with human blood.[7] Twenty-two men deposited their draft cards, including Bob Zaugh. The church service was followed by a three-mile march carrying the chalices to the Federal Building. Staff there refused to accept them, so they were left for authorities. That same month the LA Resistance opened two additional offices, one near LA Community College and one in Pasadena.

January 1968 brought news of the government crackdown on the resistance movement, with federal indictments for conspiracy of Dr. Benjamin Spock, Reverend William Sloane Coffin Jr., Michael Ferber, Mitchell Goodman, and Marcus Raskin. (All except Raskin were convicted on June 14, 1968, and sentenced to two years in prison—but an appeals court overturned the convictions a year later, finding fault with the judge's jury instructions.)

The Trials

In March one LA resister made the headlines: "Sterling Hayden's Son Burns Draft Notice During Protest: Says Father Backs Stand." Nineteen-year-old Christian Hayden told 250 demonstrators outside the induction center, "I would rather go to jail than go to war and kill people." His father, Sterling Hayden, had been a Hollywood leading man in the 1950s and before that a World War II hero—a Marine captain who had been awarded the Silver Star for running guns to supply left-wing partisans in Yugoslavia. Now he told the *LA Times*, "This is the only thing the kid can do under these conditions ... It's that damn simple."[8]

Sterling had been hated by the Hollywood Left for having named names before HUAC—he was only the second witness to cooperate with the committee back in 1947, and he had named, among others, his former mistress. But he recanted in his 1963 memoir, where he denounced his HUAC testimony as "my one-shot stoolie show."[9] He went on to star in Stanley Kubrick's 1964 anti-war classic "Dr. Strange-love," where he played the nuke-crazy General Jack D. Ripper. And he appeared alongside Christian at UC Berkeley's official 1968 "Vietnam Commencement," where he told 6,000 students he was proud of his son's action in "refusing to join in this savage and excremental war."[10]

April 3, 1968, was the third national draft card turn-in. LA Resist-ance organizers held ceremonies at three college campuses, where fifty-three draft cards were turned in. A week later, Joe Maizlish was indicted for refusing induction. At his trial in June, Maizlish acted as his own attorney. The jury found him guilty—the first draft resister in L.A. to be convicted and jailed. When he began serving his three-year sentence at Safford Federal Prison in Arizona, he was featured in an *LA Times* column by Art Seidenbaum. Maizlish had received a student deferment, and at age twenty-five was almost old enough to avoid the draft forever, Seidenbaum reported. "But Joe had to protest." He had stood outside the induction center carrying a sign that read, "Wars will cease when men refuse to fight." Seidenbaum raised the question that was central to the movement debate over draft resistance: Isn't it better to stay out of jail, and organize people to stop the war? "My square conscience would rather Maizlish chose to make his argument among us," Seidenbaum concluded. "But those who would call this convict a creep should be reminded: he refused to run or beg or betray himself by violence."[11]

The next big trial was that of Bill Garaway—a full-time Resistance organizer and spokesman. "At my trial I admitted everything," he recalled in a 2015 interview.[12] "I had walked through the induction center, refused induction, and talked fourteen people into coming outside with me instead of going through with it. I told them the military doesn't own me and they don't own you—they can't order you around." He said in court that "because of my conscience, I was compelled to do what I was doing." But the judge ordered the jury to find him guilty. They did, and he was sentenced to five years. "I was ready to go to jail," he said.

At that point he was working as an actor in the Michelangelo Antonioni film *Zabriskie Point*. (The film featured nonprofessional actors.) He had never wanted to become an actor, Garaway said. But when Antonioni came to L.A. to start work on the film—the first he shot in the United States, with a story about anti-war activists—he was trying to understand what was going on in America, so he was interviewing radicals. His casting director came to a couple of Resistance meetings, and he invited Garaway to the MGM studio one night. "I watched the sunset and smoked a joint with my girlfriend," he recalled.

> Then, barefoot in a tee shirt, I went down to MGM. There were one hundred people standing in a line, dressed to the teeth in coats and ties. The casting director sees me at the end of the line and says, "Bill! Come with me!" She walks me past the one hundred people and into the office. Antonioni was on his way out, going to Chicago for the Democratic National Convention, with suitcases under his arms. She says, "this is the guy I was telling you about." He steps back, looks at me, barefoot in a tee shirt, and says "Ah, perfect!" I say, "What does he mean?" She says, "He means he wants you in the movie." I say, "But I can't act!"

Antonioni hired a law clerk to keep Garaway out of jail long enough to finish the movie. She had just graduated from law school. The appeal she came up with was based on the principle of jury nullification. She argued that the judge was wrong to order the jury to find him guilty. Amazingly, it worked—she got the conviction thrown out, and her argument has been used many times since. Indeed, the convictions in the Spock trial were overturned by an appeals court that ruled that a judge's instructions in a criminal trial should not deprive the jury of its ability to decide a case in "an independent and unfettered way," acting as "the conscience of the community."[13]

The government prosecutors wanted a new trial and gave Garaway two weeks to prepare. During those two weeks, he recalled, he went to see the judge—Jesse W. Curtis Jr. "I said, 'the first time I saw you, I was talking nonviolence, but I was angry. I want to apologize for being hostile in the courtroom.' He replied that he had two sons in Vietnam and had wanted to give me as much time in prison as they were serving in Vietnam." Then, Resistance organizers learned, one of the judge's sons had come back from Vietnam and told him that "the war was a sham and we shouldn't be in it."[14] That night, Garaway recalled, he got a call from the prosecutor's office and was told that Judge Curtis didn't want to prosecute him. He was told to go to the induction center, take a physical, and "get disqualified." (Garaway had Reiter's syndrome, an arthritic condition that qualified for 4-F.) "I told them I couldn't do that." So the next week, his second trial began. The courtroom was packed, he recalled, and on the way in, the prosecutor gave him a document. "I put it in my pocket without looking at it. When it was time for opening statements, the judge says, 'Do you have a motion for me?' I give him the thing. He calls a half-hour recess. When he comes back he says, 'Case dismissed.' Clicks the gavel. Stands there smiling. People are yelling, 'We love you.' Everyone is cheering." Garaway was never exactly sure what the basis of the dismissal was.

He went back and finished the movie. With the money Antonioni paid him for *Zabriskie Point*, Garaway helped found a commune in Arizona, not far from the Safford federal prison where his Resistance comrades were serving their sentences, so they could visit frequently.[15]

Greg Nelson's trial was scheduled to begin the next month, on October 1. Instead of going to court, he took sanctuary at Grace Episcopal Church. Several clergy, resisters and supporters chained themselves to Greg. US Marshals cut the chains and took Greg into custody. He was convicted on October 4 and sentenced to three years.

Next came the trial of Mike Schwartz. He was a complete noncooperator. Judge Harry Pregerson sentenced him to three years. Unlike the rest of the resisters, he was sent not to Safford but to the federal prison in Lompoc, California. Schwartz also refused to cooperate in Lompoc, Bob Zaugh recalled: "They sent him to the hole, solitary confinement. He didn't eat for thirty-seven days and he wouldn't wear clothes."

Decades later, Zaugh interviewed Judge Pregerson, and asked him how Schwartz got out of prison. Pregerson told him, "I visit everybody I sentence to prison ... I went to the prison to visit a bank robber or something, and I asked for the manifest, and I saw Mike Schwartz's name, and I said, 'What's this guy doing in here? I thought he was picking corn in Safford, Arizona.'" Zaugh explained:

> So he asked to see him, and he's in the hole. When Pregerson came back, unbeknownst to anybody at the time, he called the advisor in his trial and asked, "Can you do a writ of habeas corpus for me?" He brought Schwartz into court on a writ of habeas corpus. "All stand for the judge"—Mike wouldn't stand, wouldn't speak. So they lifted him up, then sat him down. Then Pregerson released him, and he stands up and goes, "Thank you judge!" Smiles, and then leaves. A few weeks later ... my trial came up, and I drew Judge Pregerson. Nine possible judges, and I got Pregerson. Wow.[16]

To be successful in court, Zaugh recalled, "I had to speak the truth. And I could not be afraid." He walked into court carrying the *Autobiography of a Yogi*, stepped into the stand, and the clerk announced the case: "The People of the United States versus Robert Zaugh." "I felt this huge wave of fear bolt through me—and then it was gone. I stood up at the podium and started to explain why I refused induction." The prosecutor objected. Legally, he was correct; it doesn't matter why you didn't show up. The only legal question is, did you or didn't you? With other judges, that's where the case would have ended. But Pregerson said, "I want to hear what he has to say."

So Zaugh told the judge,

> "I want you to understand that I'm not a draft dodger. I could take a physical deferment. I could take a CO deferment. But I can't participate in a draft in any way." I said, "This draft has a very negative effect on people. It makes them motivated by fear rather than any love for life." I said, "An example of that is, they declared that, on such and such date, you could no longer get married and have a deferment. So a bunch of people were lined up down the

block in Vegas to get married. Not because they wanted to get married, but because they were guided by fear. Then it changed: to get that deferment you have to have a kid, be married with a kid. So people are having children, not because of any love of children, but because of fear."

Pregerson, Zaugh recalled, "began to turn away. To my mind, it was because he couldn't face this thing. He was looking for a way to get me off. Because they had an agreement amongst the judges in Los Angeles that, if you're convicted of refusing induction, you get three years. And he kind of felt bound by that."

He convicted Zaugh of refusing to take a physical, a felony that carried up to five years and a $10,000 fine, but he acquitted him of refusing induction. Then, he said he was sentencing Zaugh not to prison but to alternative service, "work in the national interest." Zaugh replied, "'I am working at Peace Press. We print for the Communist Party. And for the Ellsberg trial, and the Black Panthers, and a few others. That's in the national interest. I am working in the national interest.' And they never did anything about it. That was my sentence from Judge Harry Pregersen."[17]

The Friends

In the days before Christmas 1968, Quakers opened their doors to deserters and draft resisters at the Orange Grove Friends Meeting House in Pasadena. The Quakers' Pacific Southwest regional office had decided on "total resistance to the draft and a fight for its abolition" —page one news in the *LA Times* in January 1969. The Quakers had been pacifist since their founder, George Fox, had told English King Charles II in 1660, "We utterly deny all outward wars and strife and fighting with outward weapons, for any end and under any circumstances." If a draftee was a Quaker, he was automatically granted CO status. But with draft resistance on the rise in 1968, "we now feel uncomfortable that we've been given this kind of exemption," said Bob Vogel, a Quaker and a leader of the American Friends Service Committee (AFSC) of Pasadena.[18] So on December 18, 1968, after the Orange Grove meeting house decided to "support any person who because of conscience is making a nonviolent witness against the military system and the draft," the group decided to offer sanctuary to three deserters: marines Neil Blanton (nineteen, of Washington) and Steve Davis (twenty, of Chicago), and Army private Timothy Springer (twenty, of Hacienda Heights).[19] They had decided to resign from the military and had written letters of resignation and sent them to the White House. Then they asked the Quakers in Pasadena for sanctuary.

The three had agreed to submit to arrest. The Quakers notified the shore patrol and the military police that the three were in the meeting house. The press showed up and interviewed them. "Everyone thought they would be arrested that night," the *LA Times* reported, "and that would be the end of it." After church leaders announced that a vigil would continue throughout the night, the sanctuary immediately became a rallying point for Quakers from all over L.A. as well as members of the Resistance. When two shore patrol officers arrived at the Orange Grove Meeting House later that night, they found one hundred people sitting in silence—a classic Quaker meeting. The Quakers invited the shore patrol to "join in the worship service, and meet the AWOLs at its conclusion." The officers went back to their car and radioed for instructions. Ten minutes later they left, never to be seen again.[20]

What started out as a symbolic sanctuary became a real one. The Resistance joined with the Quakers to establish what they called "a sanctuary support community." It was an unlikely alliance between what the *Times* called "unshaven" and "hippie-clad" young people who "talked, strummed guitars, and sang freedom songs," and the Quakers, whose religious practice was mostly silent. They were respectable and in many ways conventional citizens of Pasadena.[21] But, "beyond the bongos," Vogel said, "there emerged a strange and beautiful community." As the Meeting House became a Mecca for hundreds of young people, Vogel said, young people who had "rejected the Church and religion found a new dynamic in the silent worship." And the Quakers themselves "discovered in many of these young people a devotion and commitment reminiscent of early Friends, who actively resisted the authority of the state over lives and consciences."[22]

Times columnist Art Seidenbaum visited the Orange Grove sanctuary one day in January. No law prevented the MPs from entering the Meeting House, he said, "so it was a strange time of waiting, waiting to see whether the system would reclaim the men for courts martial ... waiting for possible imprisonment." But, he said, inside the Meeting House "there was a particular sort of joy"—thirty members of the Resistance who kept vigil with the three resisters "brought good books and rock music and laughter with them."[23] Seidenbaum described a typical day at the sanctuary, starting with the three deserters. Steve Davis "explained why he decided to stop running after successfully escaping the service for a few months: 'We got our heads together to figure out whether we just wanted to do something for ourselves, or whether we wanted to help change the system.'" And Neil Blanton "wonders when he'll hear from home. His father is a career military man and Neil enlisted to please his parents. Now he would like to explain why he must live by personal conscience, even if that means confinement."[24]

January gave way to February, and still the MPs didn't show up. Then a new issue arose. Some of the older Quakers began to object to what the *Times* politely called "the live-in situation in their meeting room." Some nights twenty-five or thirty people slept over. One Quaker woman told the paper, "Boys and girls were staying here together. It was a promiscuous atmosphere—and I just don't think the Quakers ought to be involved in that sort of thing." There were also people they took in who were having bad drug trips. And there were the late nights with music and dancing that brought complaints from the Lutheran retirement home next door—they said they had been "kept awake by the racket."[25] A split developed among the Quakers. Fifty-seven-year-old Beach Langston, former clerk of the meeting, said "some could swing with it, and some couldn't." Since their founding in 1909, never had there been such a split among the Orange Grove Quakers. On February 4 a monthly Orange Grove meeting decided to limit the number staying overnight in the meeting house to the four who'd received sanctuary, along with four others from the Resistance and the Meeting House. They restricted girls to daytime and early evening visiting hours, and established a curfew.

Moreover, they continued the schedule of anti-war films, pacifist speakers, discussions of resistance, and a workshop on nonviolence.[26] Basically, draft resistance and desertion were to be encouraged, but not the sex, not the drugs, and not the rock 'n' roll.

After almost three months, the Resistance support community decided it was time to move out of the Orange Grove Meeting House and set up their own place three blocks away. On March 6, with support and help from some of the Quakers, fifteen people from the Resistance moved into what they called "Peace House." With the departure of Davis (the last of the original three AWOL soldiers) for the Peace House commune on March 31, the 104-day-old sanctuary came to an end. The Quakers pledged to continue to show up to witness trials and sentencings, and to support Peace House with "love and service." The Resistance people, however, saw the end of the sanctuary as a loss. Resister Todd Friend wrote, "If we can't groove with the Quakers, who CAN we relate to?"[27]

A Bus Named Beulah

Part of resistance work was to visit the ten or fifteen Resisters serving time at Safford, Arizona. They traveled, Bill Garaway recalled, "in a bus named Beulah. It was beautifully painted in psychedelic colors. We called our trips 'the medicine show.'" They stopped in towns along the way, gathered a crowd of young people, played music and talked about the war and the draft. One particular outing involved thirty or forty people, Zaugh recalled. When we got into one town, "we went into a store, and the store owners threw one of our guys, who was on crutches, down the stairs." The police came. "They said, 'Please, you just need to leave.' They weren't against us; they just said, 'People here don't like you, move along.'"

Instead, they went to a school that some kids had invited them to, and started playing music. But "pretty soon these people show up in pickup trucks with gun racks. They get out and say, 'We don't like people like you in this town. We're giving you fifteen minutes to get out of town.'" Zaugh recalled:

I'm scared to death ... they've got guns. But Bill [Garaway] goes, "Okay, I'll take the fifteen minutes and talk to you about how your religion accounts for the way you're treating me, and the way you're treating the Black people who are here." And the Black people from town are going, "We're not part of this demonstration!" [Garaway keeps talking.] Finally, the cops come up and they go, "We'll tell you what, you can go over to the park."

So we went to the park, and the whole town came to the park. A thousand people. The police had never had a crowd like this before. We weren't demonstrating, we split up and our people started talking to people. Some people sang. We had this twelve-year-old kid, David Israel; he was like a wizard and poet, and he just looked and sounded like what you think Jesus might sound like. That defused the situation. People came to kick our ass, and now they no longer felt like that. Not only that—they invited everybody to stay overnight in their homes.[28]

The Deserters and the Commune

In Whittier, thirteen miles southeast of L.A., the town where Richard Nixon grew up, the Unitarian church decided on March 12, 1969, to offer sanctuary to Craig Murphy, a Marine Corps deserter. He had left Camp Pendleton, north of San Diego, saying, "I don't think they have the right to do this to any human being." The national board of the Unitarian Church had voted earlier that year to provide sanctuary to draft resisters and servicemen opposed to the war in Vietnam. Ten days later, at two in the morning, two young men in civilian clothes showed up at the church claiming to be AWOL marines needing help. They woke up several members of the congregation who were staying in the church with Murphy and said they wanted to see him alone. Murphy recognized the two as his former sergeant from Camp Pendleton, Winster Minton, and a Marine corporal, Roland E. Rawls. Murphy told the churchman supervising the sanctuary, 51-year-old Robert Kennedy, that he thought they might try to take him back to Pendleton—so he laid down on the floor and refused to leave. Minton kicked him in the face and dragged him, bleeding, down the stairs and out to a Volkswagen in the church parking lot.[29]

The car sped off with a bloodied Murphy lying in the back seat, but was stopped almost immediately by police because Minton was driving the wrong way on a one-way street. Minton told the police he was Murphy's sergeant and that Murphy was a deserter he was taking back to Camp Pendleton. The police sergeant on the scene said he took Murphy into "protective custody," and when Murphy said he did not want to file an assault complaint, the marine's abductors were released with a warning for driving the wrong way on a one-way street. The Whittier police knew who Murphy was—he had been big news in Whittier—but they had respected the Unitarian sanctuary as long as he was inside the church. But now that he was out, the police, at 5 a.m., turned him over to the shore patrol in Long Beach, and the shore patrol transported him back to Pendleton —and to the brig—to await court-martial.

The next day the abduction was a big story in the papers, which reported that the Marine sergeant "was not authorized to take Murphy into custody." Murphy had had "a spotless record" in the Marines when he went AWOL, they reported, and quoted him saying, "The military is a fascist organization. I don't like losing my individuality and I don't like being a professional killer."[30]

The Unitarians, meanwhile, were outraged by the attack on their church. "If ever I could think of an act which would underscore Craig's reasons for leaving the military," the Reverend Richard Weston told the *Times*, "this was the act." The church responded to the Marine Corps abduction by providing sanctuary to two more Marine deserters over the next two days. The first was twenty-year-old Bob Hamburger from Cincinnati—in fact the very medic who had treated Craig Murphy at Camp Pendleton for the injuries he had suffered in the abduction. That "triggered something in my mind," Hamburger told the *Times*, "and I knew that now was the time to stand up." He had been in the service for twenty-six months when he sought sanctuary in the Whittier church. The military, he declared, "cannot suppress Craig's views with brutality. There will always be someone to take his place."[31]

The second was Jack Lunsford, of Tulsa, who had gone AWOL from Camp Pendleton eight months earlier and taken refuge in Vancouver. After reading about Craig's abduction, he decided to replace him in the Whittier sanctuary, and flew down from Seattle.

Within a week a third Marine deserter joined them: Dave Jones of McCullough, Alabama. Jones had taken asylum with the Quakers in the San Fernando Valley at the Valley Friends Meeting in Sylmar, but he had been apprehended, court-martialed, convicted of being AWOL, and sentenced to three months at hard labor. But minutes after the court-martial concluded at the Marine Corps depot in San Diego, he escaped. He got away, the *LA Times* reported, "apparently by talking a guard into going AWOL with him."[32]

The news media were fascinated by the "anti-war commune" that joined the deserters at the church—a support group of young people, from eight to twenty at a time. They were described by the Associated Press as "boys and girls with long hair, bare feet and peace symbol pins." They included "girls like Linda Boone, 19, Los Angeles, who cook, type stencils for peace literature, organize rallies at their colleges and rap—talk—for peace." The AP seemed amazed that church members voted to allow twenty to live there.[33]

Then in mid May, two months after Hamburger and Lunsford sought sanctuary, church officials were served by US marshals with warrants for their arrest. The two were arrested in the church at 6 a.m. by agents of the Naval Criminal Investigative Service.[34] Reverend Richard Weston, minister of the church, told the media that the idea of sanctuary was "not to avoid arrest," but rather "to confront the government and make a public statement." Meanwhile, Jones, the third AWOL marine, had left the church sanctuary after a few days, and, newspapers reported a month later, had not been seen since.[35]

A Wedding at Fort Ord

Meanwhile, Tim Springer, who had left the Peace House in Pasadena, was court-martialed at Ford Ord on the Central California coast—the charge was desertion. Back in Pasadena he had asked to be married to his girlfriend Monica Case "under the care of the Meeting," but he'd been apprehended before the wedding could be held. The Orange Grove Quakers thus enlisted the Monterey Quakers in a request to the commandant at Fort Ord to allow the wedding to be held in the Fort Ord chapel during visiting hours for prisoners in the base stockade, but the commandant said no. So instead, the Quakers asked, and got permission, to hold a wedding ceremony during a recess in the court-martial, scheduled for June 3.

At the court-martial, the small courtroom outside Monterey was filled with Quaker supporters from the Orange Grove Meeting who had driven up from Pasadena, along with some of the Monterey Friends. When court adjourned for the day at 4:30, the Friends gathered in a circle around the bride and groom outside the barracks that served as the courtroom, on a grassy spot under a Monterey pine. All the military and civilian attorneys in the case came to the wedding, as well as Tim Springer's military guard. A member of the Orange Grove Meeting presided. Immediately after their exchange of vows, the base PA broadcast the loud blast of a bugle. One Friend said he "hoped that the bugle, like this marriage, was sounding the end of the old way of life and heralding the dawn of a new day." Then the Army prosecutor spoke. He said he had been married for ten years and knew the joys and responsibilities of married life. He wanted Tim and Monica to know that, regardless of how the case turned out, there was nothing personal in his role as prosecutor. He wished them happiness and gave his blessing to the marriage.

Then the Friends sang "We Shall Overcome."

The following day, Tim Springer was found guilty of desertion and given a dishonorable discharge. The judge gave him no prison sentence.[36]

Part V

The Great High School Rebellion

21

Riot Nights on Sunset Strip (1966–68)

A moment in rock-and-roll dreamtime: Saturday night on the Sunset Strip, a few weeks before Christmas in 1967. Along that famous twelve blocks of unincorporated Los Angeles County between Hollywood and Beverly Hills, new names blazed in the neon firmament—the Byrds, the Doors, Sonny and Cher, the Mamas and the Papas, and Buffalo Springfield. But the real spectacle was out on the street: several thousand demonstrators peacefully and exuberantly snaking their way west along Sunset, then circling back to their starting point at Pandora's Box coffeehouse (8180 Sunset), just inside the LA city limits. On one side of the boundary between the city of L.A. and the county territory, several hundred riot-helmeted sheriff's deputies massed; on the other side, an equal number of LAPD, fidgeting nervously with their nightsticks as if they were confronting angry strikers or an unruly mob, instead of friendly fifteen-year-olds with long hair and acne.

The demonstrators—relentlessly caricatured as "striplings," "teeny boppers," and even "hoodlums" by hostile cops and their allies in the daily press—were a cross section of white teenage Southern California. Movie brats from the gilded hills above the Strip mingled with autoworkers' daughters from Van Nuys and truck drivers' sons from Pomona. There were some college students and a few uncomfortable crew-cut servicemen, but most were high school age, fifteen to eighteen, and, thus, technically liable to arrest after 10 p.m., when dual county and city juvenile curfews took effect. Kids carried hand-lettered signs that read "Stop Blue Fascism," "Abolish the Curfew," and "Free the Strip."

The demonstration had been called—but scarcely organized—by RAMCOM (the Right of Assembly and Movement Committee), headquartered in the Fifth Estate coffeehouse (8226 Sunset). The coffeehouse's manager, Al Mitchell, acted as the adult spokesman for the high school students and teenage runaways who clustered around the Fifth Estate and Pandora's Box, a block away. This was the fifth in a series of weekend demonstrations—perhaps more accurately, "happenings"—that had protested a yearlong campaign by sheriffs and police to clear the Strip of "loitering" teenagers. In response to complaints from local restaurateurs and landowners, the cops trawled nightly, after the early curfew, for under-eighteens. They targeted primarily the longhaired kids in beads, granny glasses, and tie-dyed shirts.

It had become the cops' custom to humiliate curfew violators with insults and obscene jokes, pull their long hair, brace them against squad cars, and even choke them with billy clubs, before hauling them down to the West Hollywood Sheriff's or the Hollywood Police stations—where they would be held until their angry parents picked them up. This evening (December 10), however, had so far passed peacefully, with more smiles exchanged than insults or blows. The high point had been the appearance of Sonny and Cher, dressed like high-fashion Inuit in huge fleece parkas, waving support to adoring kids. (Later, after photographs appeared on front pages across the world, the city of Monterey Park reneged on a previous agreement and banned Sonny and Cher from their Rose Parade float for this gesture of solidarity with "rioting teenyboppers.")[1]

By midnight the demonstration had returned to Pandora's, and a happy Al Mitchell had officially declared the protest over. As the crowd began to disperse, LAPD officers entered Pandora's to check IDs. Eason Monroe, head of the Southern California chapter of the ACLU, complained that they were acting illegally: Pandora's didn't serve alcohol and the curfew ordinance exempted teenagers inside licensed businesses. The response of the cops was to handcuff and arrest Monroe. When Michael Vossi, a PR agent for the Beach Boys who was acting as a legal observer for an entertainment industry support group, spoke up in Monroe's defense, he was pummeled by another officer. The few hundred remaining demonstrators outside Pandora's shouted at the police to leave their adult supporters alone. Riot-equipped police reinforcements converged from all sides.

Paul Jay Robbins, another adult supporter—from the awkwardly titled Community Action for Facts and Freedom (CAFF), whose members were a veritable who's who of the liberal pop culture scene—a few days later described in the *Free Press* the unprovoked fury of the LAPD's attack on panic-stricken and fleeing protestors. After Robbins himself was hit by a police baton, he watched in horror as police flailed away at a helpless teenager.

> I saw a kid holding a sign in both hands jerk forward as though struck from behind. He fell into the path of the officers and four or five of them immediately began bludgeoning him with clubs held in one hand. I stood transfixed watching him as the officers continued beating him while he attempted to alternately protect himself and crawl forward. Finally he slumped against a wall as the officer continued to beat him. Before I was spun around and set reeling forward again, I saw him picked up, belly-down, by the officers and carried away. Later legal representatives of CAFF measured a trail of blood 75 yards long leading from this spot to the point where he was placed in a car. Where is he now?[2]

The night's peaceful demonstration had been wantonly turned into another of those police "massacres" for which Los Angeles was becoming justly notorious. (Six months earlier had been the now-infamous attack on thousands of peace demonstrators at Century City). The two daily newspapers—the *LA Times* and the Hearst-owned *Herald Examiner*—as usual characterized the unwarranted police aggression as a teenybopper-inspired "riot."[3] Gossip columnist Norma Lee Browning, writing in the far-away *Chicago Tribune*, predicted the end of Hollywood's "great white way" as "barefoot bearded boobs, who are more far out than ordinary beatniks" rioted and scared away upscale diners and club customers. She estimated that the "Playboy club's business is off 25 per cent from last year."[4] Mitchell and the other adult supporters, meanwhile, were so appalled by the police brutality that they called off the next weekend's planned demonstration out of fear that the police might yet kill or seriously injure one of the kids. After two months of political debate, litigation, and frustrating negotiations, the protests resumed, massively, in February 1967, and continued episodically through the autumn of 1968. Thousands of kids would be arrested for curfew violations, and American International Pictures would immortalize the "riots" in a camp film (*Riot on Sunset Strip* [1967]) with a haunting soundtrack.

From Mobsters to Hippies

This legendary "Battle of the Strip," from 1966 to 1968, was the most celebrated episode in the struggle of teenagers of all colors during the 1960s and 1970s to create their own realm of freedom and carnivalesque sociality within the Southern California night. There were other memorable contestations with business and police—over Griffith Park "love-ins," beach parties, interracial concerts, countercultural neighborhoods (like Venice Beach), "head" shopping districts ("L.A.'s Haight-Ashbury," on Fairfax), cruising strips (Whittier, Hollywood, and Van Nuys Boulevards), street-racing locales, and the myriad local hangouts where kids quietly or brazenly defied parents, police, and curfews.[5]

Of course, such battles were not a new story (Los Angeles had passed its first juvenile curfew in the 1880s), nor were they unique to Southern California. But postwar California motorized youth rebellion. A culture of cars, high-speed freeways, centrifugal sprawl, and featureless suburbs generated a vast ennui among bored but mobile teenagers. Any hint of excitement on a weekend evening might draw kids from anywhere in the hundred-odd-mile radius of local AM radio. Thus, when one rock station incautiously advertised a party at Malibu Beach in 1961, nearly 20,000 teenagers showed up—and then rioted when sheriffs ordered them to leave. Nor is it surprising, after the Strip "riots" were celebrated in song by Stephen Stills in 1966 ("There's something *happening* here / What it is ain't exactly clear"), as well as in *Time* and *Life*, that the 8000 and 9000 blocks of

Sunset Boulevard became an even more powerful magnet to alienated kids from the valleys and flatlands. Indeed, decades later, to claim that you had been busted on the Strip in '66 or '67 was the Southern California equivalent of boasting that you had been at Woodstock.

But why the Strip? The parents of many Southern California teenagers in 1966 had their own lustrous memories of a night—returning from the Pacific War in 1943 or after college graduation in 1951—when they had dined, danced, and rubbed shoulders with celebrity in one of the famed Sunset Boulevard nightclubs such as Ciro's, Mocambo or the Trocadero. The Strip, one of those strange "county holes" in the Los Angeles urban fabric, was for a generation the major center of movie colony nightlife, and thus the epicenter of tabloid scandal and romance. It was also a city-state run by famed gamblers and their gangster allies in league with a corrupt sheriff's department. During its most glamorous years, from 1939 to 1954, the Strip's informal mayor was the indestructible Mickey Cohen, prince of gamblers and king of survivors. Operating from a haberdashery on the 8800 block of Sunset, Cohen defied all odds by emerging unscathed from an incredible series of Mob ambushes and bombings that took the lives of half a dozen of his bodyguards.

By the late 1950s, however, Cohen was cooling his heels in the pen, and the Strip was in steep decline. Las Vegas, thanks to Bugsy Siegel, had usurped the lucrative symbiosis of movie stars and mobsters that the Strip had pioneered, and hijacked its star chefs and famous entertainers. Yet precisely as urban decay was taking a huge bite out of its golden mile, the popular television show 77 *Sunset Strip* generated a new mythology. Ed "Cookie" Byrnes—the program's Elvis-like co-star, who played a parking-lot jockey who was also a part-time sleuth—briefly became the biggest youth celebrity in the country. The Strip was portrayed as a dazzling nocturnal crossroads for a handsome Corvette-and-surfboard set.

In fact, the Strip, like the larger Hollywood community, was in transition between its golden age and two competing strategies for reusing vacant nightclub and restaurant space. The "Times Square" option was to reopen clubs with topless or, later, nude dancers. The Body Shop, a burlesque house in the 1940s, was revived and soon became the flagship of the new XXX-rated exhibitionism. The other option, more unconventional, was to cater to juvenile audiences with rock music. Centralizing the youth club scene was doubly useful to rock producers, allowing them to talent-scout new bands while developing those already under contract. The success of *77 Sunset Strip*, moreover, established a national cachet and name recognition for groups weaned on the Strip. In 1965 the county reluctantly acceded to club owners' and record companies' pleas and created a tiered licensing system that allowed 18-to-21-year-olds inside clubs where alcohol was served, while creating special liquor-less music venues for younger 15-to-18-year-olds. The youth club scene promptly exploded.

For older teenagers and young adults, the premier clubs were the Whiskey a Go Go, Gazzarri's, and the Galaxy. The newly baptized teenyboppers favored It's Boss (formerly the renowned Ciros), The Trip (formerly Crescendo), and Sea Witch, as well as cheap, atmospheric coffeehouses like Pandora's (owned by former tennis star Bill Tilden) and the Fifth Estate (bankrolled by teen magazine mogul Robert Peterson). As the clubs inexorably hiked their cover charges, younger and poorer kids preferred simply to be part of the colorful street scene, wandering in groups down Sunset or hovering near club entrances for a glimpse of Jim Morrison or Neil Young. As the nightly teen crowds grew larger, however, the Strip's upscale restaurant owners and their wealthy adult clientele began to protest about the lack of parking and the increasing sidewalk congestion. Beverly Hills matrons and Century City lawyers recoiled from contact with the beatified throngs.

"Moreover, at this point," wrote Edgar Friedenberg and Anthony Bernhard in an account of the riots, "the good behavior of the 'teeny boppers' had become a problem." Because the kids were generally "not hostile, aggressive nor disorderly," there was no obvious pretext for driving them off the Strip. Eventually, the Sunset Strip Chamber of Commerce and the Sunset Plaza Association, representing landlords and restaurant owners, cajoled the sheriff's department to stringently enforce a youth curfew. During the 1940s, when teenage "B-girls" were a national scandal, both the city and county had adopted parallel curfew regulations that forbade anyone under eighteen from loitering in public after 10 p.m.[6] "Loitering," Friedenberg and Bernhard noted, "is defined as 'to idle, to lag, to stand idly by or to walk, drive, or ride about aimlessly and without purpose'—a definition that may well make the entire solar system illegal."[7]

The Crackdown Begins

The West Hollywood Sheriff's Station, responding to the complaints of businesses and landowners, began its crackdown on Strip kids in September 1965. By the following summer the sheriffs, joined by the LAPD in the adjacent Hollywood and Fairfax districts, were mounting weekend sweeps with hundreds of officers—an effort that far exceeded the attention given to mobsters in the Mickey Cohen era. (The sheriffs, in fact, were reputed allies of Cohen.) Curfew arrests soared into the thousands, with 300 hauled away from the sidewalks outside Canter's Restaurant on Fairfax on a single July evening. "It was just like shooing ducks in a duck pond," boasted one deputy. When the city's largest newspaper needed a dramatic image for a story about the teenage hordes, the deputies obligingly arrested ten kids and stood them handcuffed in a line "for the direct accommodation of the *Los Angeles Times*."[8] "Throughout the spring and summer," Renata Adler reported in a later *New Yorker* article, "licenses permitting minors to be served anything at all were revoked at one place after another: several of these places reluctantly went adult and topless—a change that seemed to cause the authorities no distress." Indeed, it was widely rumored that the kids were being cleared off the Strip to make way for the return of Mob-connected sex entertainment and "for more serious, less conspicuous forms of vice than lingering after curfew."[9]

Shortly after Halloween, a couple of angry teenagers decided it was time to organize a formal protest against the arbitrary arrests and police abuse of kids on the Strip. They printed a flyer—"Protest Police Mistreatment of Youth on Sunset Blvd. No More Shackling of 14 and 15 year olds"—calling for a demonstration the night of Saturday, November 12. It was at this point that Al Mitchell, the leftist ex-merchant sailor and filmmaker who managed the Fifth Estate for Robert Peterson, became their informal sponsor. Cans were soon being circulated around the coffee house to raise money for additional leaflets. Rock stations began to luridly warn that a "major riot" was brewing, and cautioned kids away from the Strip on the twelfth. This was irresistible publicity for a demonstration whose urgency was underlined by the arrest of eighty kids for curfew violations on Friday night.

The next evening by 9 p.m., according to the *Freep*, more than 3,000 teenagers, flanked by adult curiosity-seekers and hostile servicemen, gathered in front of Pandora's. Aside from a handful of placards hastily painted at the Fifth Estate a few hours before the demonstration, there was no apparent organization or leadership. In the spirit of the times, the protest had been conceived as a spontaneous "happening" (or "flash mob" avant la lettre), and the overwhelming majority of the crowd complied with its peaceful purpose. At one point the police called a fire company to the scene, and some of the kids nervously asked the firefighters whether they were going to hose them. A bemused fire captain replied: "Have a good time and let me go home." The engine left.

The overflow of protestors onto Sunset and Crescent Heights Boulevards created a traffic jam; several bus drivers angrily honked and screamed at the kids. In response, demonstrators climbed up and danced on the roofs of the buses. One youth scrawled "Free the 15 Year Olds!" on a windshield; another broke a window with a fire extinguisher. On the fringe of the crowd, there was a brief scuffle between longhaired protestors and some young sailors and marines. Shortly after 10 p.m., a hundred cops used their nightsticks to roughly clear the sidewalks. Police with drawn revolvers chased kids into Pandora's. Panicky protestors who tried to retreat westward down Sunset collided with a wall of riot-ready sheriffs, and about fifty were arrested.[10]

The LAPD declared a "tactical alert" the next evening, closing Sunset from Fairfax to Crescent Heights. State highway patrol officers and private Pinkerton guards reinforced the sheriffs' side of the line. Thanks to wildly escalating rumors in the station houses, the atmosphere was irrationally tense, and the *Freep* reported that "many of the officers seemed to be in a state of panic." While Al Mitchell shot footage for his documentary *Blue Fascism*, 300 or so protestors jeered, "Gestapo, Gestapo!" at the police line and then dispersed after they were declared an "unlawful assembly." They vowed to return the following weekend.[11]

On Monday morning, it was the turn of the Establishment to riot. Although a handful of protestors had been involved in the bus incident (total estimated damage: $158), the *Herald Examiner*'s headline screamed: "Long Hair Nightmare: Juvenile Violence on Sunset Strip." A *Times* editorial likewise warned of "Anarchy on Sunset Strip," and blamed the teenagers and their "senseless, destructive riot" for a "sorry ending for the boulevard that was once Hollywood's most dazzling area." The *Times* also gave much space to the melodramatic claims of Captain Charlie Crumly, commander of the LAPD's Hollywood Division, that "left wing groups and outside agitators" had organized the protest. Crumly also asserted that "there are over a thousand hoodlums living like bums in Hollywood, advocating such things as free love, legalized marijuana and abortion."[12]

Los Angeles, in the eyes of its Establishment, suddenly seemed like a besieged patriarchy. Hollywood Councilman Paul Lamport demanded a full-scale investigation into Crumly's charges of a subversive plot, while his county counterpart, Supervisor Ernest Debs, ranted that "whatever it takes is going to be done. We're going to be tough. We're not going to surrender that area or any area to beatniks or wild-eyed kids."[13] The Sunset Plaza Association, representing Strip restaurant owners, called for a city crackdown on such "kid hangouts" as Pandora's and the Fifth Estate that offered sanctuary to protesting teenagers across the county/city border.

Only the *Free Press* challenged the daily press's characterization of the previous weekend's police disturbance as a "teenybopper riot": "To the editorial writers of the *Times*, sitting in their bald majesty on First Street, entirely isolated from the events, unable to properly evaluate or analyze them, it is only possible to say: 'You are stupid old men who make reckless and irresponsible statements that can only make a bad situation worse.'"[14] The kids, the Weekly claimed, were actually caught in the middle of an economic conflict between the Sunset Strip Chamber of Commerce (with its ties to the adult-entertainment industry), on one hand, and the Sunset Strip Association (representing the youth venues), on the other. "The police, in effect, have been cooperating with one very wealthy group of property owners on the Strip against a less powerful group of businessmen."[15]

The lopsidedness of the battle was further demonstrated when the LA City Council unanimously acceded to the Sunset Plaza Association's request and voted to use eminent domain to demolish Pandora's Box. At the same time, Sheriff Peter Pitchess and Supervisor Debs lobbied the county public welfare commission to veto the renewal of the permits allowing music clubs on the Strip to admit under-twenty-ones. When the commission balked, the supervisors themselves rescinded the offending ordinance and effectively banned teenagers from the clubs. Suddenly, Los Angeles's celebrated rock renaissance itself was under threat, and this quickly galvanized the younger generation of music producers and agents into unexpected solidarity with the next wave of protests on the Strip.

Although the second weekend of protests (November 18–20, 1966) again pitted thousands of flower children against huge phalanxes of police and sheriffs, the still-leaderless protestors broadcast enough seductive warmth, as well as carnival-like mirth, to take the grim edge off the evening. As they marched down the Strip, they handed out flowers and blew bubbles and kisses. Art students passed out leaflets proposing a series of "happenings" based on the "implications of certain works by Allen Kaprow and Wolf Vostell": "A continuous environment Benediction service; a R.I.O.T. band playing in the streets, giving of a temperance lecture, couples kissing, passing out of old photographs, savage chanting of the word 'ART,' having tables of clay where passersby can model male and female genitals, and so on."[16]

The cops seemed disarmed by the happy mood, although at 10 p.m. a sheriffs' sound truck began warning under-eighteens to clear the street or be arrested. Hundreds of kids resolutely faced off a cordon of deputies, police, and Navy shore patrol around the Crescent Heights and Sunset intersection. Although several score of curfew violators were ultimately arrested, there were no baton charges, and the crowd, still in surprisingly good humor, dispersed by 2 a.m. There were widespread rumors, however, that the business interests were upset with the evening's outcome, and that the sheriffs were under pressure to use more aggressive tactics the next weekend.[17]

The Music Industry Responds

To forestall the expected violence against their fans, a group of concerned celebrities and music industry executives went into a huddle the following Friday. The meeting was called by Jim Dickson, manager of the Byrds, who took full-time leave to organize Community Action for Facts and Freedom. CAFF's initial membership included Dickson's partner Ed Ticker, the ubiquitous Al Mitchell, the Whiskey's co-owner Elmer Valentine, Sonny and Cher's manager Brian Stone, television star Bob Denver, millionaire sportsman and Woolworth heir Lance Reventlow (a member of the sheriffs' aero squadron), and Beach Boys Enterprises' Michael Vossi and David Anderle. The meager political clout of the club owners was now dramatically augmented by support from the top bands and music industry leaders. CAFF decided to mobilize its members and friends to attend the next evening's demonstration as legal observers in yellow armbands. A group of sympathetic Hollywood ministers and the local chapter of the ACLU promised to pitch in as well.[18]

In the event, sheriff's deputies ran amok, giving CAFF and some thirty clergy a shocking exhibition of the abuse that the kids had been complaining about all year. "People were viciously clubbed and beaten," wrote the *Freep*'s Brian Carr. "There was no plan or purpose evident in the beatings or the subsequent arrests. It seemed the handiest people, with no regard given to age, sex or social position were clubbed, punched and/or arrested."[19] The immensely popular Bob Denver—a one-time mailman and former teacher before becoming a star as Maynard G. Krebs on *The Many Loves of Dobie Gillis* (1959–1963), then as Gilligan on *Gilligan's Island* (1964–67)—was left almost speechless by the scene. "Unbelievable ... just unbelievable," he mumbled as deputies spat on a woman in his group, then charged down the street to baton some harmless teens. Peter Fonda, who was filming outside the Fifth Estate with actor Brandon deWilde, was arrested with twenty-seven others, mainly adults, as they watched the LAPD emulating the sheriffs. "Man, the kids have had it," Fonda later told reporters.[20]

Meanwhile inside the lobby of the West Hollywood Sheriff's Station, Brian Stone—who was already a legend for his creation of Sonny and Cher as well as Buffalo Springfield—was arrested for refusing a demand to produce identification. His business partner, Charlie Green, was in turn busted for protesting Stone's arrest. Before the night was over, the sheriffs and LAPD together had made enemies of one of the most powerful, if unconventional, industries in Los Angeles. As the Mamas and the Papas later explained to reporters, even millionaire rock stars could no longer "drive down the street with any feeling of safety from harassment."[21]

The even more promiscuous police violence at the December 10 protest (described at the beginning of this chapter) solidified CAFF's apprehension that "blue fascism" posed a direct threat to Los Angeles's billion-dollar rock culture. As the city council and board of supervisors forged ahead with their plans to bulldoze Pandora's and gut the Strip club scene, CAFF joined with the club owners and the ACLU in an ultimately successful legal defense of the status quo ante. If the *Times* red-baited the longhaired protestors as dupes of the "left-wing W. E. B. Du Bois Clubs," AM stations fought back with a dramatic recording of a defiant teenager saying, "It's our constitutional guarantee to walk unmolested on Sunset Strip" as he was being bundled into a sheriffs' car.[22] And within a few weeks, tens of millions of teenagers across the world were listening to the haunting words—"Stop, children, what's that sound?"—of the Buffalo Springfield battle anthem of the Strip, "For What It's Worth."

Meanwhile Al Mitchell and CAFF, supported by the *Freep's* Art Kunkin, suspended demonstrations over the Christmas holiday while they held "peace talks" with county officials. Verbal progress on that end, however, was undercut by what was widely seen as an escalation of police pressure on youth and adult countercultures throughout the Los Angeles area. In mid December, for example, Pasadena police raided the popular Catacombs art gallery and arrested one hundred young people on a variety of drug charges, many of them utterly bogus. Then, on New Year's Eve, the LAPD vice squad rampaged through the gay bars in the Silver Lake district, roughing up and arresting scores of patrons. The LAPD also increased its illegal harassment of the *Freep*'s sales force. Despite a city ordinance authorizing them to sell papers from the curb to passing cars, *Freep* vendors were systematically ticketed and frequently arrested, especially on the Strip and in front of Pandora's. Since local television and the two dailies had blacked out images of police brutality, the *Freep*, together with a few rock stations and the local Pacifica franchise, KPFK-FM, were truly the alternative media. Persecution, moreover, only made the *Freep* vendors into heroes and boosted the paid circulation of the paper above 65,000—a phenomenal figure for the "underground press."[23]

Back to the Street

The "phony war" on the Strip lasted until the end of February, when Al Mitchell announced that "we must go onto the streets again." "Police and sheriff's deputies have again and again violated the terms of a 'truce' RAMCOM and other concerned groups negotiated on 16 December with the Los Angeles Crime and Delinquency Commission." Indeed, Captain Victor Resau of the West Hollywood Sheriff's Department humiliated the commission when he publicly renounced the truce or any other constraint on the vigorous enforcement of the curfew law. The county's earlier attempt to outlaw teenagers from rock clubs by ordinance had been ruled unconstitutional, so sheriffs and police were once more under terrific pressure from property owners to use brute force to drive the kids off the Strip. Mitchell was particularly outraged at repeated raids on the Fifth Estate and other alcohol-free coffeehouses. Some 80,000 leaflets calling for a demonstration on Saturday night, February 11, 1967, saturated the clubs and circulated clandestinely through every high school in the county.[24]

For the first time, organizers undertook strategic planning to broaden the base of the protests to incorporate the grievances of gays and people of color. As the *Freep* noted, "one of the most interesting and pace-setting reactions to the call to demonstrate came early this week from homosexual organizations who are currently up in arms about New Years Eve's police raids on a number of Silver Lake area gay bars." Two leading gay groups, PRIDE and the Council on Religion and the Homosexual, endorsed the February demonstration and added plans for their own simultaneous march along Sunset in Silver Lake. Mitchell's loosely knit RAMCOM group also plotted actions in Watts, East L.A., and Pacoima in the hope that angry Black and Chicano youth would be drawn to participate. The self-concept of the Strip movement was shifting from an amorphous "happening" to an all-embracing coalition of outcast and police-persecuted street cultures.[25]

A crude attempt was made by the LAPD to frame the movement's principal adult leader. Ten days before the scheduled demonstrations, Al Mitchell—a veteran of harassment for such offenses as allowing singing in the Fifth Estate and obscene anti-police graffiti in its lavatories—was arrested (but not booked) on suspicion of 150 counts of statutory rape. The fortyish leftist, whom the *Times* had caricatured as the "muezzin of the teenyboppers," was now unmasked as a sinister sex criminal preying on his teenager followers—or so it was claimed on radio and television news. In fact, Mitchell's seventeen-year-old accuser quickly confessed that her allegations were lies told in anger after she had been thrown out of the Fifth Estate for drug use. The *Freep* pondered why Mitchell had been so brazenly arrested and demonized in the media before the LAPD had even checked out the teenager's story.[26]

In any event, the hubbub around Mitchell did not deter more than 3,000 teenagers, along with unprecedented numbers of college students and adults, from once again assembling in front of Pandora's on Saturday night. For the first time, there was an organized rally—with speeches by Mitchell, civil liberties lawyer Marvin Chan, and ACLU counsel Phil Croner—as well as an ingenious tactical plan. Every hour new contingents of protestors were sent west on the county Strip, where sheriff's deputies, impassive for the most part, allowed them to march without harassment. The demonstrators, carrying signs that read "Stop Beating the Flower Children" and "Stop Blue Fascism," were both exuberant and disciplined: vivid refutation of the hoary myth of "wild-eyed, drug crazed rioters."[27]

Meanwhile 500 protestors in front of the Black Cat gay bar at the corner of Sunset and Hyperion were making history as speakers urged gays to make "a unified community stand in Silver Lake against brutality." But unfortunately, the other protest venues were flops. Only a desultory crowd turned out in Venice, where most residents had preferred to join the main action on the Strip, and in Pacoima a small group of hapless RAMCOM kids with good intentions but poor communication skills were set upon and beaten by local gang members. The *Freep* could find no evidence of any protests in either Watts or East L.A.[28]

This did not mean, however, that the Strip protests had no impact upon the ghettos and barrios. Black and Chicano flower children were beginning to integrate the Strip in small numbers, despite frequent racist treatment from club bouncers and, of course, cops; and some Black leaders, both moderate and radical, were rallying to the idea, pushed by Mitchell and New Left groups, that there really was new ground for a broad, anti-police-abuse coalition. In March, after another large protest on the Strip, Georgia legislator and civil rights hero Julian Bond spoke to admiring youth at the Fifth Estate while cops loomed threateningly on the periphery in riot gear.[29] From February onward, every protest on the Strip self-consciously identified itself with the victims of far more deadly police brutality in South Central L.A. Radical groups, especially SDS and the International Socialists, began to play more prominent roles in the protests and actively recruited high school–age memberships.

But many Angelenos had no inkling that mass protests, larger than ever, were continuing on the Strip. In April, the latest addition to the local alternative media, *Los Angeles Underground*, bannered the huge headline: "STRIP WAR: News Blackout Conceals Struggle, Police Sabotage Truce Agreement." The paper excoriated the *Herald Examiner*, but even more the *Times*, for their refusal to print a word about the huge, but now disciplined, demonstrations on the Strip.[30] The *Times*, however, did continue its vilification of youth culture ("teenyboppers" had now metamorphosed into "hippies") with constant stories and editorials of the ilk, "Hippies Blamed for Decline of the Sunset Strip." Furthermore, the *Times* warned, the bell-bottomed hordes were now poised to "invade" and presumably destroy Hollywood as well. Much attention was given to a speech that a local real estate appraiser, Robert

Steel, had made on May 17, charging that longhaired teens had done more damage than the Watts rioters two years earlier. Steel claimed that the under-eighteen youth had reduced property values along the Strip by 30 percent and scared away potential major investors, including a large savings and loan company.[31]

The *Times*, at least, was accurate in pointing out new hot spots in Hollywood where property owners were squaring off against new youth venues—notably, Hullabaloo, a vast rock emporium that sometimes featured a dozen popular bands in all-night marathons. On July 28, 1967, the LAPD, using elaborate decoys and commando tactics, had swept down upon the ticket lines at Hullabaloo and arrested 200 fans for curfew violations, although their IDs were only checked at the station. As usual the incident went unreported in the *Times*, but it sent shock waves through the music world and revived CAFF-type interest in defending the industry's local fandom.

Nineteen sixty-eight was year three of the struggle, and the baby sisters and brothers of the original protestors were now on the front line. No one could much recall what a "beatnik" was, but hippie phobia was reaching a crescendo, with the *Times*, as usual, providing a rich diet of innuendo and stereotype. Yet the immense engines of the culture industry were slowly turning the great ship of mainstream taste around. Straight young adults, from secretaries to longshoremen, were quietly letting their hair grow and putting on bell bottoms. The young sailors and Marines who a few years before had waylaid unwary teenyboppers in the Strip's back alleys were now happily trading drugs with their hippie connections. Store owners and restaurateurs who once had apoplexy at the sight of a madras-clothed teenybopper now considered them as familiar as the palm trees.

As the mainstream went countercultural, much of the counterculture, including its music, moved, however temporarily, to the political left. The LAPD and the sheriffs had to shift deployments to deal with the new specters of the Black Panther Party in South Central and high school unrest on the Eastside. Curfew enforcement on the Strip became a less urgent law enforcement priority. Although police harassment would continue for another decade or more, the Strip war came to a climax on September 28, 1968, the day after Huey Newton had been sentenced to prison. This time the protest was organized by the new Peace and Freedom Party, which gave equal billing to three demands: "Free the Strip. End Police Brutality. Free Huey Newton." "Flower Power" had become "All Power to the People," and kids boldly shoved "Fuck the Sheriffs" and "No More Murder of Black People" placards into the faces of their old tormentors. For the first time the shoe was on the other foot. For an hour or more protestors besieged the West Hollywood Sheriff's Station, whose denizens locked inside or on the roof toting shotguns were clueless as to how the lambs had suddenly turned into little lions.[32]

22

The Blowouts (1966–68)

In 1915 the city of Los Angeles annexed a hilly area on its northeastern periphery where sheep ranches and strawberry fields were starting to give way to cheap tract homes. It was known as Bairdstown, but developers and realtors, busy branding the landscape with romantic evocations of a mythic "Spanish California," renamed it El Sereno. Many of its early residents were Italian-Americans from neighboring Lincoln Heights, but Mexicans were excluded by the restrictive covenants that whitewalled new subdivisions. When the US Supreme Court overruled the California Supreme Court in a landmark 1948 case (*Shelley v. Kraemer*) and prohibited racial covenants, Mexican families began to trickle in. By the 1960s, Spanish-surname kids were the majority at Wilson High School on Eastern Avenue, which, in addition to El Sereno, served the City Terrace and Ramona Gardens neighborhoods.[1]

Unlike the older Eastside high schools (Lincoln, Roosevelt and Garfield) that until the 1950s had long histories of integrated and diverse student bodies—Jews, Mexicans, Japanese, Russians, Filipinos, Okies and Blacks—Wilson (opened in 1937) had experienced a difficult transition from its original Anglo enrollment. Although it was sometimes considered the "middle-class" Mexican-American[2] high school, its students confronted the same barriers to graduation and college admission as kids in the three older high schools: the banning of Spanish on campus, a curriculum that excluded Mexican history and customs, impossibly overcrowded classes, low reading scores, culturally biased testing, wanton use of corporal punishment, and the tracking of Mexican students, whatever their potential, into vocational classes to make them replacements for their fathers and mothers in low-wage jobs. White teachers, the overwhelming majority at Wilson, had little understanding or even sympathy with the students, and some, resentful of the change in the school's ethnic composition, were blatantly racist. The tiny group of Mexican-American teachers and white progressives who saw the need for reform faced the rock wall of an authoritarian school administration.[3]

Revolts are often detonated by events that initially seem to be small, or even trivial: a tax on tea, rumors of aristocratic plots, maggots in sailors' food, or refusal to sit in the back of a bus. In the case of the Chicano revolution it was a Neil Simon play. In the winter of 1968, Wilson theater students had poured heart and soul into a production of the hugely popular *Barefoot in the Park*. At the final dress rehearsal, the school's much-disliked principal ("so conservative," remembered Lincoln High School teacher Sal Castro, "that he wore suspenders and a belt to hold his pants up"), hearing a line that he considered "risqué," raged at the students and forbade the play's performance. The next day the cast and several hundred other kids, including twelve- and thirteen-year-olds whose junior high shared the same campus, walked out of their first-period classes. The principal immediately locked the gates and called the police; the supposed ringleaders were suspended.[4]

The walkout, although sparked by an unexpected provocation, was not entirely spontaneous. For weeks small groups of students in all four of the Eastside high schools, counseled by Sal Castro and a cadre of college students, had been laying the groundwork for a mass walkout at the beginning of spring. Castro, long active in liberal and Mexican-American causes, had carefully choreographed the protests to minimize harm to students while maximizing the political impact. He wanted school authorities to know about the walkout planning in the hope that the board of education might feel forced to negotiate with the community, making the actual protests unnecessary. In the event, Wilson had set the ball rolling, and the following week the other high schools would give it a hard kick.[5] To understand why the "Blowouts," as they were soon called, were genesis events in the emergence of a new, militant "Chicano" identity, it's necessary to recall the immense frustrations that the world east of the LA River had experienced in its quests for political voice, equal employment and successful education.[6]

Locked Out

The first half of the 1960s were wilderness years for Los Angeles County's largest minority. Mexican-Americans—a community that included descendants of native Californians and *californios*, as well as three generations of immigrants from northern Mexico and the Southwest (especially Texas)—had been marginalized in the period's big debates over reapportionment, fair housing, school integration, and police abuse. Without a seat on the city council since Gilbert Lindsay replaced Congress-bound Edward Roybal in 1962, they had no champion for the next twenty-three years to advocate for their interests in city hall. Although Roybal had come within a few hundred votes of winning a seat on the county board of supervisors in 1958, thirty-three years would pass before Gloria Molina finally walked through the doors at the Hall of Administration. They were also locked out of the board of education, the hierarchy of the Archdiocese of Los Angeles, the command structure of the LAPD, and the boards of major area universities and colleges. The Mexican-American situation in L.A., at least in its political aspects, more closely resembled that of the disenfranchised Black populations of Southern cities than that of the Black community a few miles away that had dramatically increased the number of its own elected officials since 1962.

Three factors conspired to deny Mexican-Americans representation proportional to their population. *First*, as we saw in the first chapter's discussion of the unsuccessful campaign to incorporate the "county island" of East Los Angeles in 1960, political boundaries, sometimes drawn as deliberate gerrymanders, fragmented and diffused their voting power. Despite the fact, for instance, that the majority of Spanish-speaking people lived in contiguous districts east of the LA River, the community was divided into three parts and allocated to different assembly districts with Anglo majorities.

Second, political unity was far more elusive on the Eastside than on the Southside. Although Black elected officials and their principal backers were divided by allegiances to the two warring camps within the state Democratic Party—Brown and Unruh—they shared a common civil rights program around which they easily combined forces. The Eastside, in contrast, had a more significant Republican contingent, and, of course, a large share of noncitizens. Its religious culture was controlled by L.A.'s reactionary Cardinal McIntyre, who, as we saw earlier, formed a triumvirate with Chief Parker and Mayor Yorty. On the whole, the Mexican-American middle class was more conservative and less activist than L.A.'s "Black bourgeoisie." Moreover, Sam Yorty enjoyed authentic popularity on the Eastside, a constituency that he cultivated intensely after his final break with Black supporters in 1965.[7]

Third, liberal Democrats in city hall and Sacramento were the worst sort of false friends, rhetorically championing brown empowerment but tolerating rampant discrimination in government hiring, supporting urban renewal in Eastside neighborhoods,[8] and refusing to invest in Mexican-American election campaigns. When community-backed candidates ran against incumbent Anglo or Black Democrats, the party was consistently the defender of the status quo. This was the case, for instance, in a 1963 effort to reclaim Roybal's old council seat from Gilbert Lindsay, and also in a campaign to elect a Mexican-American to the school board in 1965. Likewise in 1965, when the California Senate was reapportioned on a population basis, giving Los Angeles County eleven new seats, Democratic leaders ignored pleas to ensure that the boundaries of one of the new districts encompassed a majority of Eastside voters.[9]

Statewide the situation was little different. For instance, when the legendary Delano-to-Sacramento march of the United Farm Workers reached its destination in March 1966, Cesar Chavez requested a meeting with Governor Brown. Brown refused and left town for a golfing vacation in Palm Springs. *El Malcriado*, the voice of the union, warned in response: "If you want to keep your job, Pat, you better not take us for granted. You better prove to us that you care about our problems. Because if we're going to have another four years with one enemy in Sacramento, we would rather have an honest enemy like Reagan. At least we would know where we stand."[10] When aides urged Brown to make amends to Chavez and embrace greater representation for Mexican-Americans, Brown ignored them. In November he lost to Ronald Reagan. Also voted out of office was the sole Mexican-American member of the assembly, leaving California, on the eve of the Reagan era, as the only state in the Southwest without a Spanish surname in its legislature. (In contrast, Texas had ten; Arizona, four; Colorado, one; and New Mexico, thirty-three.)[11]

Voter registration efforts, especially in Lindsay's Ninth Council District, had faltered after the high point of the "Viva Kennedy!" movement during the 1960 elections. The Community Service Organization (CSO), which had registered 15,000 new voters to help elect Roybal in 1948, abandoned such expensive efforts in 1960 to refocus on "community self-improvement."[12] By 1966, defunded by its adoptive parent—Saul Alinsky's Industrial Areas Foundation—it was shedding membership and struggling to survive on the dole of the Office of Economic Opportunity. It was also drifting rightward. Meanwhile, local chapters of the League of United Latin American Citizens (LULAC), the oldest (1929) and most middle-class of national Mexican-American organizations, were still great at hosting banquets, conducting award ceremonies and raising scholarship monies—but not at generating mass activism. The same was true of the GI Forum, the veterans' organization that had been such an important force in the desegregation of Texas and California schools in the early postwar period.

The statewide Mexican American Political Association, newly founded in 1960, had the goal of unifying voters around a common program, but it soon polarized internally between a camp led by veteran labor organizer Bert Corona that wanted to combine electoral mobilization with community organizing, and another camp, led by Eduardo Quevedo (a Brown appointee), that envisioned MAPA primarily as a caucus within the party. In L.A., MAPA became a significant force, but it would never be as dynamic or unifying as CSO had in its earlier days. Statewide, despite boasting many large and active chapters, it failed to leverage enough clout in Sacramento to make Brown act on its agenda.[13] The only well-known Democrat to enthusiastically embrace *la causa* both in the fields and the cities was Bobby Kennedy during the 1968 California primary, but he, of course, was murdered in the Ambassador Hotel just minutes after delivering his victory speech.

Whose War on Poverty?

In July 1965, a month before the Watts uprising, a new federal agency, the Equal Employment Opportunity Commission (EEOC), was established by Section VII of the Civil Rights Act of 1964. The commission was universally seen as a concession to the civil rights movement with a secondary mandate that vaguely addressed job discrimination against other minorities (sex discrimination cases, however, went unheard for years). Symptomatic of their invisibility in the national debate, Mexican-Americans, the second-largest minority, were not represented on the commission. When a coalition of major Mexican-American organizations protested this lack of voice, the new commission reluctantly agreed to hold a hearing on employment issues in the Southwestern states, including California. But the March 1966 conference in Albuquerque barely lasted an hour. To add insult to injury, only one of the EEOC's five commissioners, a Wisconsin Republican, had bothered to show up, and he opened the conference with a warning that "the commission would not be dictated to" and that it would only focus on individual cases, not purported patterns of economic discrimination against Mexican-Americans as a group.[14] Incensed, all fifty Mexican-American delegates walked out. In a telegram to President Johnson, the group complained that "our employment problems are severe and complex, yet we have no one on the commission with any insight into them." Dr. Miguel Montes, representing San Fernando's Latin American Civic Association, pointedly added: "I find it difficult to see how the commission can go out and enforce laws on fair employment when it practices discrimination itself against the Mexican-Americans."[15]

A few months earlier, the Department of Commerce had released a report that underscored the economic crisis in Mexican-American communities. Spurred by the Black economist Andrew Brimmer, a member of a task force that the White House had assembled to explore the causes of the Watts explosion, the department had conducted a "special census" of riot areas and minority neighborhoods in L.A. It confirmed the earlier warnings from Paul Bullock and his fellow UCLA researchers that while the city's white labor force was thriving in a boom economy, working families in Black neighborhoods had lost ground in the first half of the Sixties. Median family incomes on the Southside, for instance, had fallen from $5,100 in 1959 to $4,700 to 1965—a statistic widely cited in the national press.[16] Less publicized, however, was the report's finding that family incomes in three predominantly Mexican-American study areas—Boyle Heights, City Terrace, and East Los Angeles—had experienced a parallel erosion, from $5,513 to $5,106. Moreover, poverty and unemployment rates were similar in both communities, if slightly higher in Southcentral.[17]

In the abstract, the similarity of their economic plights should have predisposed the two communities to unite under a banner of jobs and equality, as they had at times in the 1940s, but local circumstances led instead to an embittered competition for War on Poverty funds. The fires of August, of course, had made youth unemployment in Southcentral an urgent national issue, and the Black community, with its enhanced clout on the city council and in the legislature buttressed by its growing alliance with liberal Westside whites, was incomparably better positioned to press the priority of its claims to federal aid. Moreover, there were few bridges between the communities. The Communist Party, once an important builder of interethnic unity, was still a presence in the Black community but had long lost an active membership on the Eastside. Of existing Mexican-American organizations, only MAPA, which had participated in the 1963 United Civil Rights Committee campaign, advocated joining the emerging Black-Westside alliance that would ultimately run Tom Bradley for mayor.[18] Other sections of adult Mexican-American leadership, especially the influential group of Eastside businessmen and politicos close to Yorty, were as unsympathetic to "Black Power" as white Republicans in the Valley. Although union activists sometimes worked together, especially in sectors like meatpacking that were organized by progressive unions, there were also serious frictions, most persistently in Local 300 of the Laborers, a key construction union where Mexican-Americans warily guarded their majority against any increase in Black membership. With most of the Eastside workforce crowded into a handful of niches in construction, garment, furniture, brickmaking, and low-skill assembly work, it was feared that the easiest way for white politicians to create more employment for Blacks was through displacing Mexican-Americans.

Outside forces, meanwhile, were working blatantly to inflame conflicts and sabotage potential Black-brown unity. Mayor Yorty, unsurprisingly, was the prime culprit. As we saw earlier, he had sabotaged the War on Poverty in Los Angeles by refusing to give elected community representatives a role in the administration of programs as required by the "maximum feasible participation" clause of the 1964 Civil Rights Act. The major contested ground was the newly consolidated city/county Economic Youth Opportunity Agency (EYOA), where Yorty's intransigence had tied up millions of dollars of federal funding allocated for job training, youth employment, and summer schools in the crucial months before the August uprising. The mayor feared that power sharing with the community would enable the Black ministers and politicians—organized as the Community Anti-Poverty Committee and led by Reverend Brookins and Tom Bradley—to build a competing patronage machine under the protection of the Johnson administration.[19] Although eventually forced to give way on community representation, Yorty counterattacked the CAPC camp with appeals to the Eastside's sense of grievance over perceived Black control of local poverty programs.[20]

Tensions reached a climax in spring 1966 when Yorty attempted to purge Opal Jones, the dynamic welfare rights activist who directed one of the EYOA's major programs, the Neighborhood Adult Participation Project. NAPP, which operated thirteen neighborhood outposts, was originally funded by the OEO as an employment program, but under Jones's leadership it refocused on movement-style community organizing, including voter registration—activities that Yorty perceived, accurately, as threats to his power. The executive director of the EYOA, Joe Maldonado, was a Yorty appointee, and he fired

Jones after she refused to stop sending "change agents" (her term for locally recruited NAPP workers) into the neighborhoods to listen to popular grievances and organize protests. The firing quickly back-fired as hundreds of Jones's supporters rallied in front of the NAPP headquarters at Wrigley Field and the city's Black elite bombarded the OEO's Washington headquarters with angry telegrams. The head of the OEO, Sargant Shriver, who had come to despise Yorty, resolved the problem in a straightforward matter by separating NAPP from the EYOA, making it an autonomous agency under the restored leadership of Jones. On the Southside this was savored as a victory, but many on the Eastside interpreted it as a further power-grab by Black leaders.[21]

There was no question that NAPP's resources were skewed in a one-sided manner: despite comparable populations and needs, only three of the thirteen outposts were in Mexican-American majority districts. Jones, exulting in her new powers, unwisely provoked a confrontation in September when she fired Gabriel Yanez, the NAPP director in Boyle Heights who had become increasingly outspoken about his community's minority role in the poverty program. In solidarity with Yanez, Irene Tovar, his counterpart in Pacoima and a future leader of the Chicano Moratorium, resigned her post. Tovar—collaborating with Rodolfo "Rudy" Acuña, a young professor at Pierce College in the Valley who would soon become the pioneer of Chicano studies at Valley State—campaigned for greater parity in NAPP hiring and leadership.[22] Although both were progressives and took pains to acknowledge the justice of Black demands, other forces in the community, cheered on by Yorty, saw the conflict with Jones in strictly zero-sum terms. So did the media: one contemporary *Times* article was headlined "Mexican-Americans in L.A. Called Anti-Negro."[23]

Such rhetoric was damaging to both communities, especially at a time when Congress, faced with the rocketing costs of the war in Southeast Asia, was whittling away OEO funding. (All the Teen Posts, for example, began closing at the end of 1966, and a dozen other programs were scheduled for extinction.)[24] Eventually Ed Roybal, whose career had been launched by a coalition of Blacks, Jews and

Mexican-Americans, intervened. He set up a summit of sorts with Opal Jones that was also attended by Gus Hawkins, George Brown (a liberal congressman who represented a piece of the Eastside), and Bert Corona, now the president of MAPA. They agreed to work together to increase funding for projects and staff in Mexican-American areas while fighting to keep the whole anti-poverty enterprise afloat. But amity at the top translated badly at the neighborhood level, where hiring parity was never achieved.[25] Thus, for the next five years interethnic tensions within the poverty programs remained at a boil, with episodic firings, walkouts, and unsuccessful attempts at peacemaking. Only "Amigo Sam" Yorty clearly benefitted from Black-versus-brown conflict, defeating Tom Bradley (who had been endorsed by Cesar Chavez) in 1969 by a margin that has often been attributed to angry Eastside voters.[26]

Failed Schools

Schools were the eternal grievance for Mexican-Americans.[27] California, whose education code explicitly segregated Asian and Native American students, allowed local districts to categorize Spanish-speaking students with darker complexions as "Indians" and then force them to attend separate ramshackle schools. A 1928 *Saturday Evening Post* piece by best-selling novelist Kenneth Roberts exemplified the blithe bigotry that justified Mexican exclusion from white schools: "In Los Angeles ... one can see endless streets crowded with the shacks of illiterate, diseased, pauperized Mexicans ... bringing countless numbers of American citizens into the world with the reckless prodigality of rabbits."[28] When, after heroic campaigns by Mexican-American communities, courts finally prohibited local school districts from explicitly segregating their children, the result was seldom different from what followed the outlawing of racially restrictive residential covenants in 1948.[29] Very little actually changed. If realtors and their political allies were the principal force maintaining a de facto color wall around the new suburbs, conservative school boards supported by white parents played a comparable role in the schools. Even where Mexican kids were allowed on campus, they were still segregated for the most part in vocational tracks and were rarely encouraged to go to college.

Encompassing most of the largest urban Mexican-American community in the country, LA Unified School District (which included some satellite suburbs as well as the City of Los Angeles) was naturally the main battlefield. Ethno-racial isolation in schools had increased during the 1950s as the other traditional ethnic communities on the Eastside, such as Jews and Japanese, moved to newer neighborhoods on the Westside. The all-white LA County Board of Education, meanwhile, focused most of its energies and resources on opening new schools in the Valley, rather than maintaining or upgrading older campuses in poor neighborhoods. The separate Catholic school system under Cardinal McIntyre was not an alternative for working-class families unable to afford the tuition, and its reputation for advancing Mexican-Americans to college was little better than that of the public schools.[30]

One statistic, above all, summarized the school crisis: half of Mexican-American kids, *especially* those who were native born, routinely failed to graduate from Los Angeles high schools. A 1965–66 survey found that Roosevelt and Garfield were the most extreme cases: at the latter, a 96 percent Mexican school, the dropout rate was almost two-thirds.[31] Board members and their spokespeople usually blamed parents for encouraging their kids to leave school to work, but, as Ruben Salazar reported in the *Times* in 1962, "the number of pupils asked or required to drop out exceeds the number voluntarily quitting despite the fact that the school records themselves list only half of the total drop-outs as being 'uneducable.'" This finding was confirmed by UCLA's Paul Bullock: "The simple fact is that the Board of Education either does not know or does not publicize the real factors underlying the high drop-out rates in many of the schools, particularly in minority-group areas. Local school administrators unhesitatingly confirm that a significant proportion of the so-called drop-outs are either encouraged or invited to leave school." As a result, the median educational level on the Eastside was a mere nine years, as contrasted with eleven in the Black community.[32]

In the decade before the Blowouts, several major studies highlighted other structural causes of this educational catastrophe in Los Angeles and the rest of the Southwest. In addition to the attitude of principals and counselors with their sinister category of "uneducable," the National Educational Association emphasized the refusal of the schools to provide bilingual classes or even allow Spanish to be used on playgrounds for 1.75 million Mexican-American children. The NEA called Spanish-speaking children "an 'alienated' group totally forgotten in the civil rights drive."[33] Since Mexican migration to Los Angeles was rapidly increasing during the 1960s, the county board of education's prejudice against Spanish was taking an ever-greater toll on Eastside children. In the same vein, a report by the state advisory committee to the US Commission on Civil Rights, based on 1967 research and hearings, expressed shock at the frequency with which Mexican-American students were "put in classes for mentally retarded [individuals] simply because they cannot speak English." It also spotlighted the lack of Mexican-American teachers, as well as the large number of Anglo teachers and administrators who "were rejected by other schools" and dumped on the Eastside.[34] Additionally, UCLA's Mexican American Study Project found that kids had weak incentives to graduate, since a high school diploma did not correlate with increased income: graduates tended to end up in the same low-wage jobs as friends and siblings who dropped out. Clearly, "discrimination in labor markets" was part of the problem.[35]

Since the Korean War a succession of groups had tried to address the schools crisis, most notably the education committee of the Council of Mexican-American Affairs (CMEA). In the mid Sixties it had been rejuvenated to some extent by a leadership of younger Mexican-American educators and professionals. The *Times* styled them "as a corps of Pancho Villas to lead the Mexican-American out of his inferior role in California education." In fact they were anything but revolutionaries. Indeed, Ralph Guzmán, the assistant director of UCLA's Mexican American Study Project, contrasted them to the "old firebrands" of the 1940s and 1950s. "Many of the young people coming up have bypassed the old militant phase. You hear a different language being spoke now ... less angry. They're talking politics now.

They want to participate."[36] Their mainstream ambitions, moreover, did not connect in any urgent or passionate way with the kids sitting in overcrowded classrooms listening to indifferent teachers droning on about the Pilgrims. The real Pancho Villas were teenagers, and their "cradle," as Sal Castro called it, was a Jewish retreat on the Malibu coast. Camp Hess Kramer, opened in 1952, was the first Jewish summer camp west of the Mississippi. Its prime mover, Rabbi Alfred Wolf of the Wilshire Boulevard Temple, had been a Zionist youth leader in Germany and brought to Los Angeles the *wandervogel* ethos and love of nature that inspired German youth before the dark age of Hitler. In the 1960s, moreover, Wolf was the city's leading ecumenical figure and the chair of the short-lived blue-ribbon commission established to address the demands of the United Civil Rights Committee in 1963. Working with the LA County Commission on Human Relations, of which he became chair in 1965, Wolf made Camp Hess Kramer available for weekend conferences and retreats, the most notable of which was the annual Mexican American Youth Leadership Conference.[37] Sal Castro, who had long experience as a playground supervisor, volunteered to be one of the counselors at the first session in 1963. For most of the 150 or so students, nominated by teachers and principals as "potential leaders," the conference was a unique experience. "There were wall-to-wall Mexicans," Castro later recalled. "Mexicans ran it and Mexicans attended."[38] Although the first conferences didn't stray far from usual boilerplate emphases on good citizenship and school achievement, Castro encouraged his students to voice complaints about school conditions and explore the history and meaning of their ethnicity. Gradually the annual conversations became more radical, reflecting the impact of the Watts uprising, the fight in the fields, and the rebellions on college campuses. Soon some of the alumni, now in college, were returning as Camp Kramer counselors, while others were founding activist groups at East LA College, UCLA, Cal State LA, and elsewhere. Moreover, the kids getting off the buses after the long drive from the Eastside were a different breed as well: more defiant and ready to rebel. They also had started using an old slang term, not only as a synonym, but also as an alternative, to "Mexican-American." They were beginning to call themselves Chicanas and Chicanos.[39]

In 1967 a many-faceted movement began to crystallize out of the Camp Kramer conferences, the trips to Delano, and the skirmishes with school administrators and cops. A striking innovation was the rise of an Eastside underground press that included *La Raza* (edited by Eliezer Risco) and *Inside Eastside* (edited by Raul Ruiz and Victor Franco); the latter was specifically aimed at high school kids, with reporters on different campuses. *La Raza* was published at the historic Church of the Epiphany in Lincoln Heights, which had become and would remain for years the key movement center for the Eastside. Its young Episcopalian pastor, John Luce, a veteran of civil rights struggles in East Harlem, kept its doors open to anyone who wanted to make change in the community, no matter how "militant" or radical.[40] As Sal Castro recalled,

> Father Luce was a very valuable ally to us, especially since I found it difficult to get Catholic clergy to support our efforts. Because I wanted Mexican parents to think that the Church was supportive, I once asked Father Luce if he didn't mind wearing his priestly collar at our meetings and demonstrations. "I need you to look like a Catholic priest," I told him. Father Luce took this well and complied.[41]

Luce also provided funds for a second movement center—La Piranya, at Olympic and Atlantic in unincorporated East L.A. The organizers were a spin-off of the 1967 Camp Kramer conference, calling themselves Young Citizens for Community Action. Like other Eastside groups, young and old, they canvassed votes for Julian Nava, a graduate both of Roosevelt High and Harvard, who won a seat on the board of education in November—a victory finally made possible by a united front of community organizations. But it was their involvement in protesting several shocking cases of violence by the sheriff's department, including the killing of a fifteen-year-old boy and the beating of an entire family, that led the group to transform themselves into the Brown Berets, with Kramer alumni and former Yorty intern David Sanchez as "prime minister."

Inspired by both the Panthers and the iconography of the Mexican Revolution, the Berets cut a striking, audacious figure in the community, one that appealed to tough youth otherwise alienated from vote-gathering and demonstrations. In contrast to the Panthers, however, whose Oakland leadership shared a substantial political education in Black nationalism and Third World socialism, the embryonic Chicano movement, including the Berets, did not yet have a clear political identity. As Raul Ruiz remembers:

> At our meetings at the Church of the Epiphany or at La Piranya there was no discussion of history, of ideology, or of political theories. We talked about community issues, period. In time the movement developed an ideology that came to be known as chicanismo, or cultural nationalism, but not in the beginning.
>
> We were issue-oriented, and if anything was influencing us, it was a sense of pragmatism. Consciousness and ideology would be built on action rather than ideology creating action.[42]

Likewise on local college campuses, Chicanos were forming groups and debating their identity and purpose. In the beginning, their major concerns were winning representation in student government, expanding recruitment of high school graduates, increasing financial aid for low-income students, ending white fraternities' common practice of racist caricatures, and including Mexican and Mexican-American history in the curriculum. The latter demand soon became a call for full-fledged Chicano studies departments, similar to what Black students were fighting for at San Francisco State and elsewhere. In May 1967 the Los Angeles City Human Relations Commission sponsored a "Mexican-American Collegiate Conference" at Loyola University that brought together almost 200 students from fourteen campuses. The participants, including Roybal's daughters, Lillian and Lucille, voted to create the United Mexican American Students (UMAS) as a regional (soon statewide) federation of campus chapters, with a coordinating *centro* chaired by Alberto Juarez, a former Kramer counselor and Teen Post director who had recently returned to East LA College.[43] Over the next eight months active chapters were consolidated at Cal State LA, LA City College, and UCLA, with seedlings at Valley State, Occidental, Loyola, Long Beach State and elsewhere. East LA College, which had the largest Mexican-American enrollment, already had a group called MASA (Mexican American Student Association), but its leadership resisted becoming UMAS and then, in 1968, refused to support the Blowouts. (Juarez, Brown Beret Carlos Montes, and others punctually left and formed a more radical group that published the alternative campus paper *La Vida Nueva*.) UMAS's campus organizers in this period were a galaxy of future community leaders and intellectuals: Vickie Castro, Carlos Muñoz, Susan Racho, Carlos Vasquez, Moctezuma Esparza, Juan Gómez-Quiñones, Ramses Noriega, Phil Castruita, Maria Diaz, Gil Cardenez, Hank Lopez, and others.

But in its early months, even as it was studying the examples of SDS and BSU, UMAS was still mostly moderate in its orientation and demands. This began to change at a statewide UMAS conference held at USC in mid December, which included an electrifyingly radical contingent from the Bay Area dressed in paramilitary garb and quoting Malcolm X and Che.[44] The Northerners emphasized the importance of forming alliances with Blacks and working to aid struggles back in the barrios. Two months later, the elders of the *movimiento*—Corky Gonzales, Bert Corona, and Reies Tijerina along with Teatro Campesino's Luis Valdez—turned the heat up another notch at UCLA with an event organized by student council member Rosalio Muñoz and UMAS. Buses brought kids from the Eastside high schools, and the auditorium was packed.

"The speaker I remember the most," Muñoz later told Mario García, "and the one who had the most impact on me, was Reies Lopez Tijerina," the militant and fiery leader of the land grant movement in New Mexico. "I was particularly impressed because he spoke in Spanish. But it wasn't just his use of Spanish; it was his evangelical style of speaking. I learned later that he had been a Pentecostal preacher, and his speech showed that. It was incredible!"[45]

No one welcomed this turn toward direct action more than Sal Castro. In the movement centers, underground papers, the Berets, UMAS, and the recent Camp Kramer graduates busy organizing on their high school campuses, he saw a full-scale orchestra ready to play an overture that would shake the walls at the board of education. With his confidential student planning group, Castro outlined a sophisticated plan. Each UMAS chapter would adopt a high school to support. The walkouts would be peaceful, but in the event of attacks by the LAPD or sheriff's department, the college students and Berets would shield the kids, taking whatever blows were rained down. But, "in planning the walkouts," writes Castro, "I kept to myself a deep, dark secret."

> Yes, I felt that something like the walkouts was needed to shake things up, and I was prepared to go through with it. But what I really wanted was to bluff the school board and school officials. I wanted to use the threat of a mass student civil disobedience as a way of forcing them to listen to the kids and to change their attitudes and practices about our students. I thought that a bluff would be sufficient to achieve our objectives, but I also did fear that if we carried out this protest what might happen to the kids and their safety. In the back of my mind was the Watts Riots and how the police and the military came down on blacks with unneeded force that killed and wounded a large number.[46]

The "bluff" was an understandable but unrealistic hope. In any event, the Wilson kids preempted the plan and unleashed a revolution.

Walk Out! 1968

The first week of the walkouts (March 4–8) was clouded by the fear that Cesar Chavez was dying.[47] The farmworkers' leader, invoking the example of Gandhi, had started a hunger strike three weeks earlier, on February 13. Despite two and a half years of demonstrations and boycotts, the union had failed to bring the grape growers to the bargaining table, and continuous attacks on the picket lines by sheriffs and private guards had sapped morale. Many of the younger workers, disgruntled with nonviolence, wanted to fight back tit for tat. The hunger strike was thus aimed not at the growers, but at the union base—with the aim of reasserting Chavez's control over the union's direction and strike tactics. By the beginning of the third week, he was unable to walk unaided, and his doctors, who had warned against a water-only fast, began to fear for his life. Bobby Kennedy flew to

Delano to give his support. (Chavez would end the hunger strike on the twenty-fifth day—breaking Gandhi's record.)

In this generally tense atmosphere, Castro and his UMAS "kitchen cabinet," as he called them, went into a frantic huddle on the weekend following Friday's protest at Wilson.[48] The new plan called for a mass walkout on Wednesday, March 6, with staggered starting times in order to maximize news coverage at each school. But Garfield in East Los Angeles jumped the gun—possibly at the instigation of the Berets— and an estimated 2,700 kids bolted classes on Tuesday afternoon. They gathered outside the school, where some of them were roughed up and several arrested by sheriffs.[49] The big surprise, however, was a simultaneous noon walkout at almost all-Black Jefferson High School just south of downtown, a campus known for its musical alumni, including a dozen of the country's most celebrated jazz musicians. The Jeff students, angry at the indifference of white administrators and teachers, the wretched quality of cafeteria food, and a bizarre dress code that banned Afros, wanted immediate reforms, including a Black history curriculum and the replacement of the principal by a Black educator.[50] Their boycott of classes, with considerable parental support, continued for a full week alongside the Eastside high schools and illustrated the dual nature of the "Blowouts": on one hand, the "official" Chicano walkouts, involving an estimated 10,000 kids, coordinated by Castro's student organizers; and on the other, a series of spontaneous and parallel protests on Black and even majority-white campuses that mobilized another 3,000 or so students.

On Wednesday the protests (and news coverage) finally conformed to plan, and thousands of students walked off all four Eastside campuses. (Chicano students at Belmont High, just west of downtown, were also supposed to participate, but their protest had to be postponed because its guardian angels, UMAS members at LA City College, were delayed in mobilizing.) At Roosevelt, cops from nearby Hollenbeck Station declared a tactical alert and then aggressively cleared kids from the sidewalks with prods from their batons. A *Free Press* reporter observed one particular cop in action: "After slamming one young Chicano up against the school fence Badge #1191 politely told him, 'Listen fuck ass, when I say move, get your ass out of here.' The

250-plus-lb. officer began seizing prettily dressed Roosevelt girl students who weighed less than 100 lbs. and roughing them up." At Garfield, student protestors agreed to attend an assembly called by the principal but warned they would again walk out if their demands were not taken seriously. As students began to fill the school bleachers, four sheriff's cars roared into the stadium, discharging helmeted officers with their batons unlimbered. The rally descended into chaos.[51] Meanwhile Castro was leading most of the Lincoln student body out the school's front door along with a few sympathetic teachers.

He was surprised that "not only had senior high school students walked out, but also junior high school ones. I had targeted primarily the older kids for the demonstration and not very much the younger ones. I didn't want to put these *chavalitos* in any jeopardy, but here they were on the sidewalks." As Castro and the Lincoln kids marched to a school district office in Hazard Park, the cops from the Lincoln Heights precinct, in contrast to their thuggish brothers from Hollenbeck, let the orderly crowd pass without interference. With Moctezuma Esparza as their spokesperson, they explained the reasons for the walkout to a skeptical administrator and promised a continuing boycott until the board of education agreed to meet with students and parents and hear their grievances.[52]

That evening, Castro, who wanted a brief intermission to analyze the day's events and organize more community support, including contact with Black schools, convinced kids to postpone the next walkout until Friday. However, Belmont, where frustration was high from missing the Wednesday protests, was given a green light to do their thing on Thursday. Carlos Muñoz, then a graduate student and UMAS president at Cal State LA, was a Belmont alumni. In his oral history, he fondly recalled the cosmopolitan character of the campus:

> I was probably one of the very few [UMAS leaders], if not the only one, that had not had a bad experience in high school as a Chicano ... Belmont at that time was the only public high school that was integrated—almost completely—because it was the only school that was designated as being focused on foreign students.

In other words, students coming from all over the world would get automatically placed there.[53]

The lunchtime walkout was also well integrated, with many white kids joining their Chicano schoolmates. The principal, an authoritarian ex–Navy captain opposed to mutinies of any kind, immediately ordered a campus lockdown, which prevented many of them from leaving campus, so instead they roamed the halls chanting slogans until the LAPD appeared and started shoving and beating them with nightsticks. Raul Ruiz remembered the bold feat of one Anglo girl:

As the cops were trying to prevent the students from leaving the school she asked the police if she could borrow their bullhorn so that she could try to convince the kids to return to their classes. They agreed, but instead of doing what she said she would, she yelled into the bullhorn, 'Walkout! Walkout!' She then ran away carrying the horn, with the cops chasing her.[54]

The biggest and most surprising melee on Thursday, however, occurred at majority Black Carver Junior High, a campus that would be the epicenter of a second wave of student revolt the following year. According to one of the teachers interviewed by the *Times*,

students had arrived in class Thursday morning highly excited by reports of troubles the day before at nearby Jefferson High School and three East Side high schools. "They wanted to be involved, too," she said. When the noon hour came [they] dashed outdoors and immediately began ripping things up. Through the noon hour and afterward a carnival atmosphere prevailed. Students did not appear angry.

The principal, instead of calling in the riot squad as his counterparts had done at Belmont and Roosevelt, simply sent students home. Their frolic left a schoolyard full of debris: "broken windows, the top half of the school flagpole bent at a right angle from the bottom, garbage strewn about, and burned bushes."[55]

Rain showers on Friday (March 8) scarcely affected the enthusiasm of Eastside students or their willingness to climb fences, pull down gates, or do whatever was necessary to leave campus. The Lincoln students, however, once again walked out the front door and trekked down to Hazard Park. Stung by media criticism for their rough methods at Roosevelt and Belmont, the LAPD accommodated the marchers, stopping traffic and even letting Castro ride to the park on the hood of a squad car. "As the kids walked on the sidewalks, I passed by on the car with my dark glasses on, waving to the students, who were shouting and happy. I felt like I was the grand marshal of the Rose Parade." Waiting at the park were Nava and Roybal, as well as a nervous white board member. This was the first time that most of kids had seen their two elected representatives. Although they expressed sympathy for student grievances, even Roybal, who complimented the students for their discipline and nonviolence, was not yet ready to endorse the walkouts, although he promised to send a statement when he returned to Washington. (He never did.) Nava, for his part, promised he would try to prevent reprisals against walkout leaders, but he offered no encouragement that the board would accept the students' demand that it hold a meeting at Lincoln High to hear grievances. (Superintendent Jack Crowther meanwhile told reporters that if kids wanted to talk to the board they could come to its regular public meeting on Monday night.) In so many words, the Barrio's two ambassadors to the larger power structures had patted the students on the back and told them to go home.

This disillusioning response, however, was balanced by exciting news of spontaneous support actions throughout the city, including a sit-in at Jefferson, a second walkout at Carver, and another on the Westside at University High, where a New Left group was organizing. In addition at Belmont six girls were arrested, including sixteen-year-old Fran Spector, whose father—a local Communist leader—had in the 1930s been sentenced to San Quentin for the crime of organizing a farm strike in the Imperial Valley.[56] The pressure points on the board were rapidly multiplying, and no one could predict what would happen the following week.

Although Castro was elated by the massive turnouts and the soaring spirits of the protestors, he was shocked by the lack of support from fellow teachers and the Catholic clergy. In preparing for the Wednesday blowout, he had met with representatives from the American Federation of Teachers to seek a pledge not to cross the student picket lines. But most union teachers on the Eastside did, and some of them, including several outspoken Mexican-Americans, became bitter public enemies of the emergent movement. At Belmont and Roosevelt, when the police entered school grounds to beat students, white teachers watched without protest. The situation was even worse at Jefferson, where teachers staged their own three-day walkout, demanding a crackdown on student organizers and restoration of the status quo ante—that is to say, the restoration of what kids had long referred to as the "plantation."[57] At stake was nothing less than white control of minority schools, classrooms and even kids' self-image. The racism of many white teachers was vividly documented in a letter to *La Raza* that spring from a white teacher who had supported the walkouts:

> I stopped using the cafeteria and teachers' lounge a long time ago.
> I don't want to listen to teachers discuss your children—"I give
> up on these dumb Mexicans." "Felipe is so dirty I can't stand him."
> "These damn parents should go back to Mexico." "These parents
> are as dumb as their kids." "I went to Juan's house; what a smell!"
> "I've never seen such lazy children."[58]

The unsupportive, even hostile, attitude of parish priests was more surprising since everyone expected that at least a handful would rally to the side of the youth they knew so well. But that didn't happen. "I had already attempted to get some of the Catholic pastors in East L.A. involved, but they avoided me," Castro recalled. "I even told the students to see if the priests in their churches might support them, but they got nowhere." One kid, "perhaps in frustration," went to his church and "took the banner of Our Lady of Guadalupe from the church and used it in the march to Hazard Park. It was a great image to have and gave the kids a sense that Guadalupe was looking after them. However, when the student returned the banner, the priest had him arrested."[59] (The following year, Cardinal McIntyre's paternalistic attitude toward the Eastside would be dramatically challenged by a new group called Católicos por la Raza.)

The churchman who did show up to support the movement was a physically imposing Armenian Baptist who had grown up in Tijuana—Reverend Vahac Mardirosian. He would soon be elected chair of the Educational Issues Coordinating Committee (EICC), a parent-community support group organized in the second week of the walkouts as an interlocutor to the board and city hall. Mardirosian was a powerful orator in the evangelical mode—and, he had another ability that most of the organizers lacked. "We began to realize that to communicate with parents, we needed Vahac," Ruiz said. "He spoke Spanish better than any of us could ... I couldn't speak worth a damn in those days and especially in Spanish."[60] Another ally, whose wholehearted public support was all the more dramatic given the silence of most liberal Democrats, was Bobby Kennedy. Flying out of LAX after attending a ceremony in Delano to mark the end of Chavez's hunger strike, he warmly welcomed a delegation of high school walkout leaders. "He shook each of our hands," Paula Crisostomo from Lincoln remembers. "He raised his fist and said 'Chicano Power.'" After an hour-long conversation, Kennedy posed for a photograph with the protestors, which La Raza published with the caption "Outside Agitator?"[61]

The second week added parents to the ranks of protest. Several hundred of them showed up at a board of education meeting on Monday (March 11). The most right-wing member of the board, Robert Chambers, was so unnerved by the boisterous crowd that he reportedly pulled a pistol out of his briefcase. ("Nothing happened," recalled Castro, "and I guess Chambers put the gun away. But it showed me how much we had scared the shit out of the board.") After three hours of listening to and arguing with the Eastsiders, the board majority gave ground on two demands: they agreed to meet students and community at Lincoln High sometime later in the month; and they agreed to amnesty for the thousands of ordinary protestors. But they rejected parents' pleas to remove police and sheriffs from campuses and release the students who had been arrested. This infuriated the students in the audience, and a Beret took over the microphone, while other students, in an eloquent gesture, burned their student ID cards. The meeting broke up in confusion. Nonetheless, Castro felt that the two concessions were enough to declare victory and end the boycott. He wanted the UMAS and the high school organizers to start working out formal demands to present to the board at the Lincoln High meeting. EICC, meanwhile, would take the lead in unifying the community around the program.[62]

So the Eastside kids returned to school, taking with them a proud understanding of their collective power. On Tuesday, moreover, the Jefferson boycott ended in an almost complete victory with the removal of the white principal and the appointment of a Black replacement.[63] But the energy released by the Blowouts continued to roil other campuses. Kids at Edison, another Southside junior high, emulated Carver and walked out for a day, after breaking windows and setting some fires. At Venice High on the Westside, a mixed group of activists, long skirmishing with the administration of free speech issues, led half of the mostly white student body out for three days, despite a crackdown by a helmeted, baton-swinging phalanx of cops. The principal suspended forty students on March 14 for "defying authority," although he himself was seemingly defying the board's promise of amnesty.[64]

Venice was the last blowout. According to Castro's scorecard, 20,000 students at fifteen campuses had participated in protests during the ten days that shook the LA County Board of Education. Together with the following year's wave of strikes on Black high school and junior high school campuses, echoed by solidarity demonstrations at several Westside schools, L.A. became the uncontested national capital of the 1960s high school rebellion.[65]

Sixty-Six Years in Prison

The historical importance of the Blowouts was immediately acknowledged. Shortly after the walkouts ended, Julian Nava told Superintendent Jack Crowther: "Jack, this BC and AD. The schools will not be the same hereafter." Crowther replied, "Yes, I know." A

Times headline asked if the events weren't the "Start of a Revolution?"[66] However, with the revolutionaries back in school, leadership of the campaign was passed to the EICC, the parent-community support group that was now endorsed by MAPA and the East LA Democratic Club. As Vahac Mardirosian told the press: "Now it is up to the adults to take over ... We are not going to let young people below the age of eighteen to do the work that belongs to us." But the reality was somewhat different. "In fact," Castro explains, "the college kids proved to be the driving force behind the EICC, although they wisely allowed the others to assume more public leadership. Mardirosian, for example, became the nominal leader of the group and its principal spokesperson. Still, the college students, such as Juan Gomez-Quinones, Carlos Vasquez, Jesus Trevino, and others, guided the EICC, since they attended all the meetings and had more critical perspective on the schools, in addition to being more politicized."[67]

Working with the high school walkout leaders, their immediate task was to formulate demands to present to the board at the Lincoln High meeting on March 26. At the top of the eventual list were reduction in class size, bilingual/bicultural education, Latino administrators in Mexican-majority schools, Spanish-language training for English monoglot teachers, more counselors, a new high school on the Eastside to relieve overcrowding, the abolition of corporal punishment, an end to ethnically biased testing, and a curriculum that included Mexican-American history and folklore. But, unlike parents and students in Southcentral, the EICC did not demand integration or busing to better schools. They wanted reforms in situ, under community control, with bilingual classes as the bottom line. Although the ACLU's integration lawsuit (which, it will be recalled, arose out of an unsuccessful attempt by Black students to attend South Gate High School, across the tracks from Watts, in 1963) had been revivified and now included Chicanos, it had little support on the east bank of the LA River.[68]

The thousand-seat auditorium at Lincoln High could barely accommodate the huge community turnout on the twenty-sixth. Castro was elated by the size and solidarity of the crowd, as well as by the forceful presentations by Mardirosian, Gómez-Quiñones, and other EICC spokespeople. But the board, with its peerless record of stalling reform in minority schools, had not come to make a deal. Although its newly elected Black and Mexican-American members, James Jones and Julian Nava, were genuinely sympathetic, they still sang along with the rest of the board, whose familiar refrain was: "We agree with most of your demands, but we don't have the money to implement them." It was true that school districts all over California were being hit hard by Reagan's drastic budget cuts. He had beaten Pat Brown two years before on the promise "to clean up the mess at Berkeley" and was now fulfilling his promise of reducing middle-class taxes by targeting schools of all kinds. But students knew that this excuse was disingenuous; many of the demands, including ending corporal punishment, appointing more Chicano administrators, and transferring openly bigoted teachers, required only political will, not bigger budgets. Several hundred students, disgusted with the board's evasions, stood up and left the meeting. "We walked out because we were getting nowhere," one Garfield student leader told reporters. "We wanted to discuss issues and they were not being discussed." He raised the threat of a new walkout.[69]

The EICC, however, was willing to test the board's promise of a negotiating process that included regular meetings with its urban affairs committee and future community hearings. Castro, meanwhile, decided to step back from the limelight and let the community take charge of negotiations, through the EICC and the newly formed parents' councils. His recusal was admirable; others would have capitalized on the celebrity to run for office or seek a higher position. But his leadership was sorely missed, since extracting reforms from the board was a grindingly slow effort, especially without representation on the city council and with only one, very moderate, voice on the board. Moreover the assassination of Martin Luther King in April, followed a month later by that of Bobby Kennedy, diverted the media's attention from Eastside concerns as schools raced toward the summer break.

On the other hand, it was an election year, and the Blowouts became grist for the propaganda grindstone of the Far Right. Earlier in February, groups had spread a rumor that the board had secretly prepared a massive busing program, and that white children would soon be forced to go to ghetto schools and vice versa. The near-hysteria among white parents, especially in Hollywood and the Valley, was cultivated by gun-toting board member Chambers, who introduced a resolution to "immediately and completely discontinue consideration of busing children for integration."[70] After the Blowouts, other reactionary figures stepped in. California's ultraconservative superintendent of education, Max Rafferty, who later moved to Alabama and became a leading campaigner for George Wallace, chastised the LAUSD leaders for their failure to punctually punish the thousands of students who had boycotted classes. "Under no circumstances is it ever justified for students to leave classes for any reason except illness," he declared. "This is the state law and you must uphold it."[71] And, most ominously, a grand jury went to work, secretly investigating the Blowouts.

The 1968 grand jury was an instrument of the outsized political ambitions of Evelle Younger, L.A.'s district attorney. Elected in 1964 and now setting his sights on the 1970 race for state attorney general, Younger was guaranteed a place in constitutional history by his attempts to carpet-bomb campus protest and radical speech with felony indictments. During the protests following the killing of Leonard Deadwyler in 1966, for instance, he ordered the arrest of John Harris, the young Black organizer for the local Progressive Labor Party, and charged him with violating California's notorious Criminal Syndicalism Act on the basis of some wording in a mimeographed flyer. The case went all the way to the Supreme Court. The year after the Eastside walkouts, when BSU members were arrested at Valley State during an occupation of the administration building, he hit them with more than a thousand felony counts of kidnapping and false imprisonment.[72] The case that he brought against Castro and twelve other blowout leaders in late May, following an undercover investigation led by three agencies, was the most Kafkaesque of all. The "East LA 13," as they were soon called, were charged with having conspired to commit misdemeanors ("disturbing the peace" and "disturbing a school") that usually did not involve jail time, but since conspiracy was a felony, their maximum sentence compounded on multiple counts added up to a nightmarish sixty-six years in prison.[73]

In the "civil disobedience" section of its final report, the grand jury revealed the kind of fervid mindset exploited by grand inquisitors like Younger in pursuit of legal precedents that would felonize any campus protest. "The concept of peaceful protest," wrote the jurors, "has been discarded as an obsolete tool to be replaced by overt criminal behavior indiscriminately directed against both property and person. Within a relatively short span of time, acts of violence have increased both in frequency and magnitude as a result of concerted efforts which seek to effectively utilize the lever of mob action to attain desired goals." But what evidence of planned violence, other than that by the police and sheriffs, was attributable to the organizers of the walkouts? Younger's team later revealed that they had presented the jurors with two crucial examples of conspiracy: a cop's claim that he was threatened by a protestor and an anonymous bomb threat phoned into one high school. That was about it.[74]

Nava, at a reception for Cesar Chavez, had warned Castro of the impending arrests, but Castro had discounted the likelihood. He was arrested as he was preparing for Lincoln's senior prom. His fellow "conspirators"—several of whom were dragged out of their beds—included Eliezer Risco of *La Raza*, Carlos Muñoz, Moctezuma Esparza, and David Sanchez of the Berets. (Muñoz was writing a paper for a graduate seminar on Marxism and had left a pile of books on the subject on his desk. The delighted officers thought they found unassailable proof of a Communist conspiracy. Muñoz was mortified.) Several of the indictees were in Washington for the Poor People's March at the Capitol and had to be arrested by DC police.[75] Younger, taking advantage of inflamed accounts in the media that equated the Berets with the Panthers (an exaggeration that the Berets themselves played up), had a subordinate tell the press that all the defendants, except possibly Castro and Risco, were Beret leaders.[76] Later news accounts, however, hinted that Castro was a secret member, even the "godfather," of the Berets. Younger, of course, knew from his several undercover informants as well as from police surveillance that only four of the thirteen were Berets, but he didn't let that fact stand in the way of the invaluable electoral propaganda manufactured from the case. He further bolstered the image of defendants as dangerous agitators by imposing a higher bail than normally would be applied to robbery or burglary cases. (A judge quickly ruled the bail excessive and reduced it.)

Thanks in some measure to the publicity generated by these indictments, as well as two other mass felony cases in 1969 involving the BSU at Valley State and Brown Berets accused of disrupting a Reagan speech at the Biltmore Hotel, Younger took office as the state's hard-as-nails attorney general in 1970; the governorship was his next ambition.[77] All thirteen defendants, meanwhile, had to live under the shadow of a prison sentence for the next two years until the indictments were finally thrown out by an appeals court.

Castro's ordeal was unique. His was the Dreyfus case of the Eastside. After his arrest, the board removed him from his classroom and eventually charged him with forty-six counts of "unprofessional conduct," mostly arising from his persistent "insubordination." After several mass demonstrations and a week-long sit-in by parents, he was returned to Lincoln High, where forty of his colleagues immediately protested his reinstatement by demanding transfers. Chambers, likewise, mobilized his right-wing base against Castro's return—and, in a surreal episode, an elegantly dressed group of white women from the upscale suburb of Marina del Rey sat in at the board offices to demand a policy outlawing such sit-ins.[78] Six months later, Castro was again evicted from Lincoln and rotated through a series of white schools and nonteaching assignments. Community support remained strong; there were more picket lines, civil disobedience leading to the arrests of supporters like Father Luce, a walkout at one high school, and the resignation-in-protest by the board's Mexican-American Education Committee.[79] At the beginning of the 1973–74 school year, he was finally reassigned to a majority-Chicano high school, but Belmont rather than Lincoln. During his years in exile, Castro had received numerous job offers, especially from colleges searching for Latino administrators, but he never wavered from his original commitment to teach and inspire the next generation of *la raza*.

23

The Children of Malcolm X:
Black High School Activists (1968–69)

The March 1968 Eastside Blowouts, as we have seen, were both preceded and accompanied by similar protests in South Central schools. From the fall of 1968 through the winter of 1969–1970, newly formed Black Student Unions took the lead in a rolling series of protests that included the first and only student-led general strike in a major urban school district in the United States. Simultaneously, Chicano teenagers, now organizing in chapters of United Mexican American Students, continued their own actions but increasingly sought to synchronize their campaign with the more powerful and broadly supported BSU movement. In March 1969, operational unity, never formalized but effective nonetheless, emerged between eighteen predominantly Black junior and senior high schools, four or five majority-Chicano schools, and a half dozen white or ethnically mixed high schools, as well as three junior colleges with significant minority enrollment. State college and university chapters of the BSU, UMAS, and SDS also provided significant support, as did the Black Congress, the Panthers, the Che-Lumumba Club, the Brown Berets and other radical groups. At the height of protest, 12,000 LAUSD students, and perhaps 3,000 more junior college students, were on strike against what they regarded as a racist, failed education system—a system, moreover, that answered community demands for change by calling the LAPD onto campuses to beat and arrest kids as young as twelve.

The resulting turmoil became the backdrop to the most racially charged mayoral election in LA history.

The centrality of the BSUs in these events begs a brief examination of the larger national picture of student Black Power. The "first wave" of Black student activism, of course, arose in traditional Black colleges in Border and Deep South states in the early 1960s and provided the cadre for the organizing campaigns of SNCC and CORE. The "second wave," embracing different iterations of Black consciousness, was national in scope and led to protests on some 200 campuses in 1968 and 1969. Its chief institutional expressions were the BSUs or, on some eastern campuses, Student Afro-American Societies. Martha Biondi, in her history of the movement, writes:

> These students constituted the first critical mass of African Americans to attend historically white universities. Deeply inspired by the *Autobiography of Malcolm X* and the charismatic leadership of Stokely Carmichael, yet shaken by the murder of Martin Luther King, Jr., they were engaged in a redefinition of the civil rights struggle at a time when cities were in flames, hundreds of thousands of young Americans were at war in southeast Asia, and political assassination was commonplace. where?

In this context, she concludes, "student leaders were turning the slogan 'Black Power' into a grassroots social movement."[1]

Unlike the first wave that recruited from campuses to launch and sustain struggles in Southern communities, the second wave was for the most part focused on the campus itself, where BSUs and similar groups fought for Black studies programs, more Black faculty, scholarships and special programs to raise Black enrollment to levels proportional to population, and (especially on campuses with authoritarian administrations) for free speech and the democratization of campus life. The resistance to these demands, especially in the South, was often brutal, leading to the police murder of students at South Carolina State in Orangeburg; North Carolina A&T in Greensboro; Jackson State in Mississippi, and Southern University in New Orleans, with dozens of others wounded by police gunfire at Texas Southern in Houston.[2]

Outside the South, second-wave struggles grew to epic dimensions, especially in California, where the battle for Black studies at San Francisco State, led in its early stages by 24-year-old former L.A. SNCC organizer Jimmy Garrett, produced the longest student strike of the era in the winter of 1968–69. Before it ended, another, more violent, strike broke out on the UC Berkeley campus in January 1969 after the BSU joined with Chicano and Asian students to form a Third World Liberation Front to demand the establishment of an ethnic studies college on campus. (Similar demands had been raised earlier at UC San Diego.) Black enrollment in California's university and state college system was shockingly small. At San Jose State, for example, there were only 200 Blacks out of a student population of 22,000, while Valley State in Northridge in 1967 had exactly twenty-three Blacks and seven Chicanos enrolled.[3] In Los Angeles the Black Student Alliance / BSU at Cal State LA was organized in 1967. BSA was envisioned by its founder, sociology professor Harry Truly, as the first step in building a regional alliance of BSUs. Active BSU chapters subsequently emerged at LA City College, UCLA, LA Southwest College (a new community college where the Che-Lumumba Club played a leading role), Long Beach State and especially at Valley State (later Cal State, Northridge), where mass felony arrests produced a crisis.

What made Los Angeles unique, however, was the commanding role of students in grades seven to twelve, usually organized in their own BSUs, in a sustained struggle for local control over education. Although the movement recalled to a certain extent the 1963 protests against the LA County Board of Education, it was much more massive, and it sought community control rather than integration. (The ACLU's Crawford case had been reactivated but would be delayed for years by the board's stalling tactics and stunning duplicity.) The LA protests, while sharing most of the same complaints, unfolded in a dramatically different fashion than the famous New York school battles of the same period. In the latter metropolis, white teachers struck in 1968 *against* a newly elected community school board in a Black and Puerto Rican section of Brooklyn, while in Los Angeles, Black and brown students walked out in 1968 and 1969 to force concessions from conservative white teachers and administrators. In Ocean Hill–Brownsville, the community side was led by adult organizations, but in L.A., students initiated and led the struggle with the support of parents and adult civil rights groups (reversing also the pattern of leadership in the earlier UCRC campaign).[4]

Political scientist Jeanne Theoharis, in an important article on the March 1968 Blowouts, has criticized the literature on community control movements for leaving out "the ways young people also spearheaded these efforts." Moreover, in the specific LA case, "while the walkouts are considered seminal in Chicano history as a founding moment of Chicano Power, they have been all but ignored by scholars of African American history, even by those studying L.A.'s black community."[5] In fact, the seventh-to-twelfth-grade and junior college protests were arguably the most original and populist social movement of the entire decade in Southern California, especially when considered in their full multiethnic spectrum. The March 1968 Blowouts, the mass arrests of BSU members and white supporters at Valley State, and the murder of Panther leaders at a UCLA BSU meeting all receive intensive treatment elsewhere in this book, so this chapter will focus on three important but forgotten protests: Manual Arts High School in fall 1967, Fremont High School in fall 1968, and the police invasion of Carver Jr. High School in March 1969 that led to the general walkout in Black schools.

"Toilers" Arise

The city's third-oldest high school, Manual Arts High (MAHS) at Forty-First and Vermont, was opened in 1910 as part of a campaign to industrialize Los Angeles. Focused on vocational training, particularly in the metal trades, its tough working-class student body—like the cast in some proletarian novel—were officially called "the Toilers." One of its early graduates was a deeply estranged Sicilian immigrant named Frank Capra, whose idol and friend was a daredevil brawler, Jimmy Doolittle. The former would become Hollywood's chief mythologist of small-town America, while the latter would bomb Tokyo and then command the Eighth Army Air Force in Europe. Later, MAHS would earn a footnote in the history of modern art for expelling

Jackson Pollock and Philip Guston, the foremost pioneers of abstract expressionism, after they circulated a vaguely communistic broadsheet urging students to "Awake and Use Your Strength!"[6] MAHS began to slowly integrate in the 1930s, and after the war there was rioting between Black and white teenagers in the neighborhood around the school. When bigoted director Frank Capra went back to his alma mater for the 1950 commencement, "he felt 'scared to death' to look into the faces of so many black people."[7]

By 1967, the now almost-entirely Black school had seen years of underfunding, neglect and squalor. Parents were alarmed by the poor quality of instruction, draconian school discipline, overcrowding (3,700 students), filthy corridors and classrooms, and a shocking dropout rate. Like L.A.'s other predominantly Black and Chicano high schools, its teaching staff was full of deadwood: alienated and incompetent whites serving out their time with little affinity for students or their families. The tipping point came in June 1967 when a white English teacher flunked, and therefore prevented from graduating, a girl with an otherwise good academic record. NAACP leader Celes King III attempted to negotiate with white principal Robert Dehany, explaining that the student's family had been the victims of a cross burning. His plea was summarily rebuked. The next group of visitors included US cofounder Tommy Jacquette and three brawny members of the Community Alert Patrol. "Making their way past security guards, they stormed into Principal Dehany's office and warned him that Angela Bates would graduate 'no matter what. We don't give a damn what you or the school board say. If you want trouble, you can have it.'" For King, Jacquette, many other community leaders, and most of the Black parents, the Bates's case condensed years of grievances against the school's administration and its majority-white teachers. Eventually the school board, unnerved by rumors of a possible riot, gave in and allowed her to graduate with her class. Far from reducing tensions, however, this initial victory for the community merely set the stage for a much-larger confrontation over Dehany.[8]

Transferred a year earlier from the Valley, Dehany began the new school term in September by taking disciplinary action against students without notifying their parents. To the outrage of the student body, moreover, he locked bathrooms because he claimed they were being used for smoking marijuana. He also inexplicably refused to allow Manual Arts's PTA to meet in the evening or hold fundraisers. When students attempted to organize an Afro-American study group, he kicked it off campus; likewise he "permitted an English instructor to accept a book report on Hitler's *Mein Kampf* while refusing to allow one on Malcolm X's "Report [*sic*] to the Grassroots.""[9] The girls' vice principal, also white, was equally resented for her authoritarianism and aloofness, as well as her opposition to holding school dances. Both parents and students were primed to revolt.[10] One group protested that Dehany was "insensitive, inhuman, incompetent and hates children."[11] The coalition demanding Dehany's removal was remarkably broad, including the NAACP, the Black Congress organizations (US, CORE, the Panthers, Operation Bootstrap, CAP, and so on), and the United Parents Council, led by the fiery Margaret Wright. In addition, the campaign was endorsed by Congressman Gus Hawkins, Assemblyman Bill Greene, school board member James Jones, and normally conservative Police Commissioner Elbert Hudson. Boycotts and pickets were organized, and Margaret Wright, who would be involved in educational activism for decades, was arrested for the first time.

Many of MAHS's white teachers, like their counterparts in New York City and elsewhere, were shocked that Black Power groups or Black community groups per se were now claiming a right to intervene in school governance. If the community succeeded in getting rid of Dehany, they reasoned, then some of them might be the next target. Many teachers were particularly outraged when Walter Bremond argued for the inclusion of Black history in the curriculum. "You want us to invent a mythology for you?" asked one irate teacher. Another demanded to know: "What about other minorities? Do we teach Chinese and Japanese history too?" And a white male teacher sighed: "When this thing is over, we'll have to put more emphasis on achievements by Negroes, like Nancy Wilson, who, I think, is some kind of actress."[12]

According to the editor of the 1968 MAHS yearbook, *The Artisan*,

The faculty took matters into its own hands, and instead of reporting to school on Monday, October 21, went to the school board to
demand the immediate attention of the board to Manual's problems,
and an injunction against those who disrupted school procedure.
Both were promised by the board, so the faculty returned to school.
The injunction was granted by the Los Angeles Superior Court,
and a task force was sent to Manual by the board to investigate the
problems, of which all complained."[13]

The vice principal was removed, and eventually so was Dehany, only
to be replaced by another white principal. As always, the board continued its "studies" of conditions with little actual remediation.

Tensions were still high at Manual Arts when the Western Regional
Black Youth Conference, welcomed by Ron Karenga and the Black
Congress, opened at the historic Second Baptist Church on Thanksgiv-
ing Day. The conference call announced: "We must begin to institute
programs that speak to the needs of AfroAmericans and not programs
that are a reaction to white definitions." The event was memorable for
two reasons. First, it was an initial opportunity for BSU organizers
and potential members from Northern and Southern California to
compare experiences and strike up friendships. Second, it inaugurated
a movement to boycott the 1968 Mexico City Olympics unless three
demands were met: (1) the restoration of Muhammad Ali's boxing
title, taken away after his refusal to fight in Vietnam; (2) the exclusion
of South Africa and Rhodesia from the Games; and (3) the firing of
Avery Brundage, the notoriously racist president of the International
Olympic Committee. The Olympic Project for Human Rights was the
brainchild of one of the most compelling figures in the Black Power
movement: Dr. Harry Edwards, a sociologist from San Jose State
who had been a national champion discus thrower. Edwards told an
audience that included a half dozen world-class athletes (Tommie
Smith and Lew Alcindor, among others): "It's time for black people
to stand up as men and women and refuse to be utilized as performing
animals for a little extra dog food ... We want to show the world that
the United States is just as racist as South Africa ever hoped to be."

As a result of this electrifying meeting, the Black student movement met the new year with tremendous self-confidence.[14]

The Puddle at Fremont

Fremont High School at Seventy-Sixth Street and San Pedro was built in 1924 and remained predominantly white until the mid 1950s, when Black families began to move into surrounding neighborhoods in large numbers. After the school board liberalized its transfer policies in 1964, ostensibly for the purpose of racial balance, the final contingent of white students bolted to South Gate High, and by 1968 Fremont was 95 percent Black. Like the other South L.A. schools abandoned by the white working class, its once-stately red-brick campus suffered physical and educational neglect. Fred Hoffman, the *Freep* reporter who covered the December 1968 protests, was astounded by the difficulty of simply entering the campus. "On rainy days the sidewalks around the school vanish under an enormous lake." The administration, he wrote, had found "enough money to build a fence around the faculty parking lot, but no money could be found to deal with the drainage problem in front of the school."[15] For students and parents, the giant puddle was a seasonal reminder that they did not live on the Westside.

As at Manual Arts, the school's troubles coalesced around the figure of its white principal, Robert Malcolm, and an aging crew of white teachers, some of whom disdained even to go through the motions of teaching their oversized classes. As dropout rates soared and parental demands for reform increased, Malcolm sought to bridge the racial gap by sending a half dozen Fremont students to attend Chatsworth High School for a week, staying over with local families. The stunt was designed to "help improve relations between Negroes and Caucasians without the cost and controversy of busing." Chatsworth's principal, Gjertrud Smith, an outspoken opponent of busing, called it "a darn good plan where Negro youngsters who live in the ghetto area can find out that white kids are really decent kids and not full of hate."[16] Regaling a handful of kids with the splendor of a modern white suburban high school and then sending them back to their disheveled and overcrowded classrooms was a cruel joke that only rubbed salt into the wounds of the Fremont community.

The uprising began over the simple right to be heard. Unlike at Manual Arts, where adult leadership defined the issues, Fremont's newly formed BSU chapter was Principal Malcolm's primary interlocutor, and then opponent. On the night of Monday, December 9, students unsuccessfully attempted to discuss their grievances with the teaching staff at an after-school meeting of the school's human relations council. The next afternoon they made a second attempt. With 200 students waiting outside, four BSU leaders entered a faculty meeting called by Malcolm. Most of the teachers refused to hear them out and left. Several dozen, however, stayed to talk with the BSU. As the president of the faculty association, Gail Van Meter, later told reporters: the kids "just wanted to attend the faculty meeting. They wanted to have the faculty listen to them." Their chief complaint, she said, was the number of bad and racist teachers—"and it is true, we do have some. They do not arrive for class on time, they allow students to go early and they do not teach during class."[17]

Malcolm, refusing to concede any legitimacy to the BSU, immediately suspended the four leaders and gave a lurid account of the event to the *Herald Examiner*, whose headline read "High School Invasion," as if the students were outsiders or aliens. The next morning, a thousand students boycotted classes and gathered in front of the school to debate what to do about the suspensions. While the rally was taking place, a small group lowered and burnt the US and California flags and raised a makeshift "BSU" standard. A few stones were thrown. The administration panicked and called in the LAPD, which declared a tactical alert around the school. Hundreds more students left their classrooms, and the crowd moved to the athletic field. As the emotional temperature soared dangerously, a vice principal announced that Malcolm had lifted the suspensions. The crowd broke up, and most students returned to their last class. However, the next morning students discovered that the suspensions had been lifted "only conditionally." The BSU decided to rally students for a strike. Fred Hoffman described in the *Freep* what happened next:

Most of the students were in the auditorium when police and security guards came in, guns drawn, and arrested three students. The kids went wild ... and a crowd rushed to the principal's office in protest. Charles Hawkins, a Board of Education Security Agent who had taken part in the auditorium arrest, tried to push students away from the door of the principal's office. Someone threw a pop bottle and it smashed on the wall near his head, the shattered glass gashing Hawkins across the face. The guard was given first aid treatment in the principal's office while police, again on tactical alert, moved in on the students. Shouting "the pigs are coming!" the students fled.[18]

The following morning the BSU boycotted classes and announced a noon rally to discuss "How to get rid of Mr. Malcolm." The principal had invited concerned members of the community to his office to discuss a resolution to the crisis. When a college BSU member showed up, he was promptly arrested, and as students flooded into the streets in protest, Malcolm closed the school. Meanwhile, BSU students at Jordan High attempted to hold their own rally, both to support the Fremont students and to address their own identical issues of poor instruction and a catastrophic dropout rate. But Jordan was sealed off by its Black principal Lionel Joubert, who mobilized varsity athletes to eject BSU members. He refused to negotiate with the group and expelled its officers. At Crenshaw High, meanwhile, 300 students rallied, taking down the American flag and burning it. Margaret Wright, of the newly formed Community Black Board of Education, told a Saturday meeting of students and parents from Fremont and Jordan that

to burn a flag is a disgrace to most Americans, but they do not think it a disgrace to burn people. There are many Black youth who will not pledge allegiance to the flag—they do not feel they have an allegiance to the flag and, after all, the pledge is a lie. If it said: "One nation, divisible, with liberty and justice for some" maybe they would say the pledge.[19]

On Monday the LA County Board of Education, fearful of a chain reaction on inner-city campuses and knowing that many teachers were afraid to come to campus, closed Fremont and transferred Malcolm. That evening, at a board meeting called to discuss the urgent need for more school revenue to address the problems of minority campuses, a contingent of parents from the Eastside made sure that the members understood there would be more trouble if renovation of Lincoln High School wasn't at the top of the list. When the board agenda turned toward the crisis at Fremont, the school's BSU president, Rickie Ivie, demanded that "the next principal be picked through a governing board made up of parents, students and faculty." The students and parents were sponsoring the candidacy of a popular Black vice principal, but the board had already decided to replace Malcolm with Donald Bolton, a respected Black administrator. They thus refused to concede a governing board or anything remotely resembling community control.[20]

Although no one had particular objections to Bolton, the BSU, acting with considerable political sophistication, refused to back down from their stand on joint governance. Ivie told board officials that the selection of a popular Black principal wasn't enough: "It doesn't make any difference; You picked him." He also reiterated the students' central demand for a review of teachers popularly held to be racist or incompetent. The group's faculty advisor, Coach Virgil Grant, warned the board: "We want control of our schools. Until this happens Fremont will continue to be in turmoil." When the vast majority of the student body followed the BSU's lead and boycotted a school assembly to introduce Bolton, he responded patiently that he understood their point of view and agreed that the board was evading the question of consultation. He also reassured the BSU and concerned parents that he, on the other hand, was completely sympathetic to the larger movement for community control of schools. Having made their point, the BSU soon accepted that Bolton's appointment was at least a partial victory.[21]

The *Times*, beginning to show signs of a "liberal" turn in editorial policy, also got the big picture. "The eruption of student unrest at predominantly Negro Fremont High School three weeks ago," it reported, "signaled the arrival of 'local control' of schools as a live issue in Los Angeles," which it called "the first step in Black people determining the way their children are educated in the city school boards or councils. They want power sharing with community boards or councils." The paper described "the common feeling": "The schools couldn't get any worse than they are now. The high dropout rate, the lack of skills in basic subjects like reading and the low level of self-image and personal aspirations are facets of school life." Indeed, the paper concluded, "failure of schools in minority areas is no longer challenged by most members of the Board of Education and top school administrators."[22]

BSU on Strike!

The return to school in January opened a new period of turmoil. Two hundred eighty-six Valley State students were arrested on January 9 during a peaceful rally to support BSU members previously charged with felonies for the occupation of the administration building. A week later Panther leaders Bunchy Carter and John Huggins were murdered on the UCLA campus by US members, in a struggle over control of a proposed Black studies program. Sheriffs, meanwhile, occupied East LA College for several days after a confrontation with the BSU chapter led by Melvin X. Yet the BSU agenda was making real gains: a Black principal at Fremont, Black studies at UCLA and grudgingly at East LA College, and most spectacularly, the agreement of the Valley State administration in mid January to the creation of full-fledged Black and Chicano studies departments. (BSU members and their supporters there, however, still faced trial and possible imprisonment.) These precedents made it more difficult for hard-line administrators in LAUSD and the junior colleges to deny legitimacy to BSU and Chicano demands, even when students raised the most subversive of issues: funding for new programs, campus renovation, and the hiring of superior teachers. The battle over the quality of inner-city schools, moreover, directly challenged the policy of fiscal retrenchment in education that was a hallmark of the Reagan administration in Sacramento and its conservative supporters in local school districts.

The pivot of the struggle in Los Angeles shifted in early 1969 to the unique alliance that had been formed the previous fall between the BSUs at Southwest College and Carver Junior High School. Southwest was the fruit of a generation-long battle, led by Odessa Cox and her South Central Junior College Committee, to open a college in and for the Black community. Carless students in Watts and Willowbrook had been forced for years to spend two hours each way riding trolleys or buses to reach LACC: a negative inducement to higher education. A site for the new school was purchased in 1950 at the intersection of Western Avenue and Imperial Highway, but seventeen years passed before the benignly neglectful board of education allocated any funds for construction. Thanks to the Watts Rebellion, 2 million dollars was finally appropriated, and the college opened in a dozen temporary bungalows in fall of 1967.

Over the next two years the student body expanded from 600 to more than 2,000, but Southwest remained more of a campsite than a proper campus, with the board of education claiming that it lacked funds for the next stage of construction.[23] When West LA College opened a year and half later, however, Southwest students were able to contrast their overcrowded conditions with the idyllic new—almost entirely white—campus. General dissatisfaction was quickly turned into active discontent with the formation of a large BSU chapter, whose most dynamic components were members of the Che-Lumumba Club led by Kendra Alexander. Other Black Power groups were also represented, but the young Communists had the strategic clarity to understand how Southwest could become a cadre engine for struggles at all levels of LAUSD.[24]

Carver High School—the first school in L.A. to be named, or rather renamed, after a major Black historical figure—was more than seventy blocks north of Southwest, in the Central Avenue community that had been the central business district of Black Los Angeles from the late 1930s until the early 1960s, but many Southwest students lived in the area and had younger siblings or cousins enrolled there. Joseph Jones, a skilled organizer and effective speaker, became Southwest's emissary to Carver, assisting with the organization of its BSU and sometimes acting as an interlocutor with the principal. "The Southwest-Carver coalition," he later told the press, "is interesting because it is the first time schools at different levels have moved together on demands." Jones was particularly impressed with fifteen-year-old Rickie Ivie, the mature and charismatic president of the Fremont BSU, whom administrators would soon grow to dread. In a suprising reversal of seniority, the college students would call first upon Ivie and his kids to support their strike at Southwest.[25]

In January, after talks over a Black studies department broke down, Southwest's president, John Grasham, had student negotiators arrested. The BSU organized a strike, and the campus soon became a war zone, with several bomb explosions, widespread vandalism, and more arrests. (Later, at the trial of sixteen BSU and student government leaders, the prosecutor would begin his case by saying: "Here is Southwest College, a school that is really nothing but bungalows ... It was put there for lower class people who can't go anywhere else. Most of the students ... don't know what they're doing. Most of the students are Negro or black.") As the Carver BSU members got caught up in the excitement of the Southwest strike and the never-ending round of meetings and events organized by other BSUs, they decided to become more confrontational in their own demands for Black studies and school improvements. At the end of February, their white principal cracked: "bawling like a baby," he fled the campus.[26] The next day the acting principal suspended the BSU and students walked out. A new principal, Andrew W. Anderson, was parachuted into Carver from the Valley purely on the basis of his seniority, without any effort to find a Black candidate of the caliber of Bolton at Fremont. Although Anderson rescinded the BSU suspension, that did little to relieve the suspicion that tough disciplinary action was coming.[27]

At the beginning of March the Carver students asked Jones to mediate with Anderson. The two argued for an hour and a half without any result. The LAPD began spreading a rumor that Carver was high on the "militant target list" for changing from white to Black principals. On Thursday, March 8, 500 Carver students walked out of class to attend a BSU rally in support of the Southwest strike. There was an informal rally the next morning as well, and Anderson suspended a BSU leader named Teddy Gibson. The kids immediately phoned

Jones and asked him to again intercede with the principal. He arrived at the school at 9 a.m., where he was arrested and handcuffed by campus security, and held in Anderson's office for the LAPD. Some 200 kids, many wearing the fatigue jackets favored by BSUs, crowded into the administration building. Anderson told them they could sit in the hall if they refrained from disruption. A little later, without any warning, more than a dozen Metro Squad cops burst through a door, panicking the students, who fell over one another trying to escape. Gwen Scott, a field director for the teachers' organization, later said, "Many fell down and I did too. Policemen had their clubs up and were saying 'Move! Move!'" Many were jabbed with riot batons and some were hit over the head. Five students were hospitalized, including a twelve-year-old girl, and a half dozen were arrested. A rumor spread like wildfire through the city that one girl had been killed.[28]

The following Sunday afternoon, 500 or more students, parents and college BSU members gathered in South Park to discuss what to do. Dedani, chairman of the BSU at Southwest said, "Schools must close Monday because we must move to give power to the students and to the black people so they can control their own community." A large group of parents endorsed the strike and volunteered to accompany students to meet with principals. "The quality of education," one father pointed out, "is so low that students are not being educated, anyway."[29] A delegation then went off to South Park, where Tom Bradley was holding an election rally. With the stridently racist campaign of Yorty chipping away at his white support, Bradley angered BSU members by refusing to endorse the demand to keep cops—particularly Metro Squad—off campus. In the weeks ahead he would be unable to surmount the increasing polarization between middle-of-the-road white voters and insurgent Black and brown youth.

The school week started with a police tactical alert. "From Watts to the Crenshaw District," reported the *Times*, "junior and senior high schools were hit Monday with fires, vandalism, walkouts, picketing, rock throwing and wind breaking. 'In sympathy,' and obviously close coordination, demonstrations also burst forth at junior colleges as far away as Santa Monica."[30] All eighteen Black junior and senior high schools were on strike, and the board of education closed Carver and Manual Arts for two days. "At Fremont High School, gasoline was poured in the auditorium and set afire." At Crenshaw, creative strikers soldered the locks of classroom doors. Almost all of the student bodies at Washington and Jefferson were out on the sidewalks picketing and chanting. Meanwhile at battle-scared Southwest, most of the faculty threw in the towel: forty-seven out of sixty requested immediate transfers.[31]

On Tuesday the strike spread across the city, and white and Chicano students became involved. At East LA College, UMAS organized a rally calling for the creation of a "black-brown-white coalition against the use of police force on school campuses." At LA City College, the BSU/BSA, assisted by UMAS, SDS, and a contingent of anti-war veterans, began building barricades in anticipation of a total shutdown on Wednesday. The college's student council, meanwhile, voted to divert all of its remaining budget to a bail fund. The LAPD was quickly called in, as they were at Manual Arts, Crenshaw, Dorsey, Locke and San Fernando High Schools. Fires were reported at Berendo Junior High, Los Angeles High and Taft High in the Valley, while at Maclay Junior High in Pacoima there was a melee between white and Black students. Scores of BSU/BSA members moved between campuses, offering support and advising younger students. Parents also mobilized and that evening at Carver, 700 of them crowded into the auditorium to denounce Friday's police attack and unanimously vote in support of the strike.[32]

Wednesday saw a nine-division LAPD tactical alert—the largest since August 1965. The LAFD was almost as busy, with sixty-five reported campus fires. Forshay and Washington Irving Junior Highs went out, and there was a disturbance at Grape Street Elementary in Watts. At the new campus of Cal State Dominguez Hills, the faculty—in marked contrast to their colleagues at Southwest—voted to support the strike and assist the development of a Black studies program on campus. But Wednesday's storm center was the strike at LA City College, where a confrontation occurred between BSU supporters and a "student group" known as the Victory in Vietnam Association. VIVA had originated at UCLA, cheered on by the *National Review*'s Russell Kirk and local right-wing television commentators George

Putnam and Robert Dornan. Historian Bruce Franklin, in his book on the MIA movement, describes the group's sponsorship:

> On March 9, 1967, the Victory in Vietnam Association received a state charter from California as an educational institution, and less than two months later the IRS granted it tax-exempt status as a "charitable and educational" organization. VIVA was now able to hold the first of its lucrative annual Salute to the Armed Forces formal dinner dances, organized by its Ladies Auxiliary (made up of wives of wealthy business, military, political leaders), which allowed the guests—including Barry Goldwater, Alexander Haig, H. Ross Perot, Bob Hope, Los Angeles Mayor Sam Yorty, and California Governor Ronald Reagan—to receive tax deductions for their contributions. With brimming coffers, VIVA expanded rapidly and planned ever more ambitious campaigns to thwart the anti-war movement.[33]

VIVA thought it could provoke a violent reaction from the BSU by removing some of the barricades in front of the college while thirty cops waited across the street to intervene. But the strikers ignored the bait. "The VIVA men, all white, many of them big and husky, and most of them shorthaired, advanced on a strikers' barricade at the cafeteria." One of the strikers turned to a reporter and said, "If these freaks want to appease their egos, let them go ahead." The VIVA members then "furiously dismantled the cafeteria barricade, then moved to the main entrance where the [barricading] tables lay. The antistrike group grabbed the tables and started hurling the barricade apart with violent force, bending umbrellas, hurling chairs into Vermont Avenue." For so heroically destroying college property—something that the strikers had carefully refrained from doing—Steve Frank, the leader of LACC VIVA, received a letter of commendation from President Nixon and briefly became a right-wing media star. (The BSU later presented its own award to Frank when a member punched him in the jaw.)[34]

On Wednesday evening a striking student was murdered. The setting was ordinary: a group of Washington High students went to

Pepperdine College to play basketball in the college gym, as they had many times before. Pepperdine, whose founder had made a fortune in the auto parts business, was a conservative Christian school whose campus at Seventy-Ninth and Vermont was originally surrounded by neighborhoods full of fundamentalist whites from Southwestern states. After the 1965 rebellion, Pepperdine's board decided to relocate the college far away from the inner city—Malibu was the ultimate choice— and in the interim they added security to protect its majority-white student body. Fifteen-year-old Larry Kimmons, noted for his mild manner, was one of the kids from Washington, and he and his friends, finding the gym locked, were leaving campus when a security guard stopped them. He tried to handcuff Kimmons, but the agile youngster broke free. The guard, inexplicably it seemed to the others, blasted him with a shotgun. Many were convinced the school would burn, but behind-the-doors negotiations between Pepperdine's president and community leaders lowered the temperature. In November, after a travesty of a manslaughter trial, the guard was sentenced to probation without jail time and ordered to pay a $500 fine. Such was the value set on Kimmons's life.[35]

By the end of the week, though the walkout remained almost total at Carver and Jefferson, elsewhere students were trickling back to classes. The BSU/BSA leadership began to debate an exit strategy. According to Lil Joe Johnson, a Compton-based activist whose erudition impressed everyone who met him, the most compelling argument was made by Franklin Alexander. "Che-Lumumba's organizers at Southwest were experienced, disciplined and smart strategists," Johnson later said. As the student strike approached its climax, "Franklin recognized that the strikes were nearing a transitional stage where they would either peter out with a whimper or set up for a bang by the police. In either case it would be designated a failure by the media." So Alexander argued at a community/student meeting that "the protestors must take the moment in their own hands by culminating the strike of their own accord."[36] There was also a desire to declare victory before US and the Panthers renewed open warfare. Outside a BSU meeting at Victory Baptist Church on Friday night, four US members shot 24-year-old Ronald Freeman, a leading Panther. He was badly wounded but survived, thanks, he claimed, to the Little Red Book in his pocket that stopped one of the bullets. (According to Lil Joe, this hugely increased the popularity of Mao's volume of aphorisms.)

At the same time, the Right was furious over school administrators' inability to repress the BSUs and restore order to their campuses. A combined LAPD/DA taskforce was set up to marshal evidence that the strike was a carefully planned criminal conspiracy. Addressing the city council on Friday, March 14, Chief Reddin made the bizarre charge that "funds are being channeled into the disruptive elements in Los Angeles through the Chinese Communists, the National Council of Churches sources and others."[37] He also revealed that Dorothy Healey, the red nemesis, had been seen at a BSU meeting the previous Tuesday agitating for a march on city hall. Interviewed by the press, Healey just chuckled. "That's good news. I happened to be at home watching TV last night. Obviously Chief Reddin doesn't know any more about what I'm doing than what the students are doing." She went on to reassure reporters, however, that Communist youth were just where they were supposed to be, in the thick of the struggle.[38]

In the event, the BSUs took Alexander's advice and declared victory on Friday, March 21. At Carver, however, students and parents, led by Reverend Arthur Peters of Victory Baptist, continued to picket for several more days.[39] (Peters, renowned in the gospel music community, had made his church, just two blocks from Carver, the staging area for the struggle and continued afterward to sponsor events for the Black Panthers and other Black Power groups. In 1975 he was found tortured to death, a victim of a serial killer in a case never solved.)

Aftershocks

The impressive demonstrations of student power on Los Angeles campuses inspired similar protests in nearby cities with Black minorities. A week after the conclusion of the LAUSD strike, an attempt to organize a BSU chapter at Duarte High School led to two days of clashes between Black and white students in the San Gabriel Valley suburb. In the meantime, administrators in Pasadena, site of an endless battle over school integration, had primed campuses for trouble. Black students at local high schools had been incensed by the exclusion of any girls of color from the song-leader selections; after brief sit-ins at five schools, the administration included one Black teenager. She was suddenly disqualified in April. Simultaneously, a racist pamphlet was circulated on the Pasadena High School campus: "We must do something about the continual movement of Negroes toward becoming the dominant race at PHS." (In fact Blacks were barely 10 percent of the student body.) An altercation between Black girls and their white PE instructors on April 30 led to arrests and the expulsion of seventeen Black students. Blacks immediately went on strike at Pasadena, Muir and Blair High Schools, as well as at Washington Junior High.[40]

In Long Beach a few weeks later, a similar racist pamphlet at Poly High incited attacks on Blacks, who responded with a boycott. Two days later, with Black students rumored to be returning to campus, a large crowd of white teenagers assembled at a nearby park and marched to the school. "More than 200 white students," reported the *Times*, "shouting 'Get the niggers!' charged onto campus en masse Thursday morning."[41] But Black parents, warned of the ambush, had diverted their kids to the Martin Luther King Recreation Center, six blocks away. Chicano students showed up to express their solidarity, and the subsequent alliance between the two minorities quelled further mob attacks. But in San Bernardino that fall, white violence on campus led to a student strike followed by four days of rioting on the Black Westside. The trouble started in the second week of October when Black students arriving at San Bernardino High School were stoned by a large group of white students. In the resultant melee, which involved hundreds of kids, there were a number of injuries, and the campus was shut down. Although whites had been the instigators, Blacks were targeted for arrest and expulsion. A month later, after weeks of further skirmishes on campus, the police made a controversial arrest on the city's westside that brought hundreds of youth onto the streets. Mayor Al Ballard, a politician with a disturbing Mafia connection, ordered a dusk-to-dawn curfew, armed firefighters with shotguns, and authorized the use of tear gas.[42] Similar confrontations would recur in the city throughout the 1970s.

The major backlash to the BSU strikes, however, was electoral. In addition to the defeat of Tom Bradley that fall, the Far Right seized control of the new seven-member LA Junior College Board in late May. Joseph Orozco, Reagan's former chief political representative in Southern California, led a victorious slate that included Mike Antonovich, a 29-year-old reserve cop who would eventually spend decades on the board of supervisors. They won on a platform that stressed three policies: kicking BSU and similar groups off campus; deploying police at the first sign of struggle; and, most importantly, no tax increase to hire more faculty or expand facilities at campuses like Southwest. At their inauguration, a chief supporter, Mrs. Floyd Wakefield, declared that "the image of higher ed has been damaged by a few militants who are hell-bent on revolution ... and it's time to make clear to all that higher education is a privilege."[43] As a result of their fiscal stance in face of a growing budget deficit, 6,000 students were turned away at the beginning of the fall semester, and conditions continued to deteriorate at overcrowded campuses such as LACC. The victory of Yorty and the right-of-Reagan Republicans ended, at least for several years, any hope of liberal reform in city and school politics. With the doors slammed in their faces, young people of color and their white allies looked toward the revolution advocated by the Black Panther Party.

Part VI

There Is Only the Gun

24

A "Movement Crusade": Bradley
for Mayor (1969)

One weekend in May 1969, a parade of convertibles filled with Black people drove down Ventura Boulevard, the main drag of the all-white and politically conservative San Fernando Valley. They gave the Black Power salute—the clenched fist—to passersby, and their cars carried banners reading "Black is Beautiful" and "Bradley for Mayor." It was three days before election day, the day L.A.—including the Valley—would choose between the incumbent mayor, Sam Yorty, and the first Black challenger, city council member and former cop Tom Bradley. Don Rothenberg, in charge of field operations for the Bradley campaign, reported that a couple of days earlier, he had gotten a call from "an individual in the Black community" who said that Yorty's campaign had offered him $5,000 to organize a Black Power car caravan through the Valley, "and he would consider turning down the offer if we could come up with some more money." The Bradley campaign declined the offer. In the election that next week, Yorty won, 53 to 47 percent. The Yorty vote in the Valley was overwhelming.[1]

Four years later, Bradley would be elected with 54 percent of the vote—a historic event in a city where Blacks made up only 18 percent of the population. But while Bradley's 1973 victory marked a turning point in LA history, his 1969 campaign was remarkable and in many ways unique: the leading historian of that era, Raphael Sonenshein, concluded it was closer to "a movement and crusade" than it was to a traditional political campaign. The primary, in particular, was marked by a powerful spirit of unity and purpose, and the director of field operations estimated that the campaign had 15,000 volunteers.[2] The effort resulted in a stunning success: In April, Bradley had beaten Yorty in a four-way primary involving Democrats and Republicans, 42 to 26 percent, leading to their head-to-head runoff in May. L.A. had never seen anything like it—and never would again. (Bradley's 1973 campaign was run in a more traditional and professional way with big money and big media.)

L.A. in 1969 was, like much of the rest of the country, recovering from the political traumas of the previous year: the April murder of Martin Luther King; the June assassination of Robert Kennedy; the police riot in August at the Democratic National Convention in Chicago; and of course, Nixon's victory in November. Los Angeles County seemed to mirror a national shift rightward: in 1964 LBJ had easily carried the County with 57 percent of the vote, but after the Watts Rebellion, the defeated Goldwater forces regrouped around Governor Reagan, who won with the same percentage of the vote in 1966 that LBJ had gotten just two years earlier. Nixon, who had been resoundingly defeated by Pat Brown in the statewide election in 1962, turned the tables in 1968, winning the county by 46 percent—two points ahead of Hubert Humphrey. Peace and Freedom, as we saw earlier, won less than 1 percent. George Wallace, on the other hand, got 6 percent—and in some white working-class communities his percentage was in double digits. Thus, when Tom Bradley decided to run in 1969, the odds—and recent history—were against him.

Bradley, as we have seen, was a complete contrast to his histrionic opponent. He was dignified, smart, and always stayed calm and cool—a persona that worked well in debates and with the news media. Although proud of his career in the LAPD, Bradley was strongly liberal. He had supported Bobby Kennedy in '68—opposing LBJ and the war in Vietnam—and had been a Kennedy delegate to the Democratic convention in Chicago. After the LAPD attacks on anti-war marchers at Century City in '67, when the city council took up a resolution to support the police action, Bradley had been one of the few to vote "no." He was also in command of a coalition of Black,

Japanese-American and liberal white (mainly Jewish) activists that had made his Tenth District a laboratory for progressive multiracial politics. Exceptional levels of volunteer activism sustained the Bradley camp, but few city hall veterans believed that this model could be repeated on a citywide scale.

But the campaign, drawing on its support among Black churches and California Democratic Clubs (CDCs), ultimately mobilized that army of 15,000 volunteers. An unprecedented effort, it enabled the campaign to mount a door-to-door canvasing blitz in every part of the city. To coordinate canvasing and recruitment, nearly forty campaign offices were opened: ten in South L.A.; ten more in the white neighborhoods of West L.A., Venice, Westwood, and the Jewish neighborhoods of Fairfax and Beverlywood; seven in Latino East L.A.; four in Hollywood; and a surprising eight in the San Fernando Valley, Yorty's base of support.

The campaign infrastructure, meanwhile, was reinforced by support from Californians for Liberal Representation. Founded in 1962, the CLR regrouped local veterans of Henry Wallace's third-party movement in 1948 and the Stevenson campaigns of the 1950s; in several aspects it was a revival of the L.A.'s old Popular Front alliance of liberal New Dealers and leftists, including some Communist Party people. Its leadership included Art Carstens, a visionary UCLA professor and industrial relations expert; Jack Berman and Eleanor Wagner, former organizers for the Independent Progressive Party (the California sequel to the Wallace campaign); and Maury Weiner, a brilliant political tactician who became the brain of the Bradley camp. Steve Allen, the comedian and TV star, was its emissary to the Hollywood Left, while the chief fundraiser was Gifford Phillips, a McLaughlin Steel heir and art collector who had been Gene McCarthy's campaign treasurer in California in 1968. Both the CDC and CLR played key roles in bringing Kennedy and McCarthy Democrats together behind Bradley.

The campaign had an ambitious but straightforward strategy that combined grassroots energy with endorsements from a stellar list of celebrities, ministers and popular politicians. The campaign assumed that Bradley would get every Black vote, so their effort in Black precincts focused on turnout. The biggest effort, after Black turnout, was to win the Jewish vote, centered on the Westside—especially in the Beverly and Fairfax neighborhoods, which the campaign saw as a counter to the expected white backlash in the Valley. The Jewish support group's events included a Sunday rally outside Canter's Deli on Fairfax. The invitation came from a rabbi, and was cosigned by James Roosevelt, eldest son of FDR, who had been elected to the House from L.A. and then had run against Yorty, and lost, in 1965 (he later joined Democrats for Nixon, opposing McGovern in 1972). The invitation was also signed by Victor Carter, who had founded the home improvement chain Builder's Emporium and then devoted himself to the United Jewish Welfare Fund, the State of Israel Bond Organization, and the American Friends of Tel Aviv University. Jewish Committee activists included Henry Waxman, at the time an Assembly member in Sacramento, who would go on to spend forty years as a leading liberal in Congress. The statement from Jewish leaders declared that they supported Bradley as "a member of a minority group who understands the dangers of discrimination," and emphasized "his outspoken defense and deep sympathy for Israel's valiant struggle"—which, they said, had led the previous year to an invitation from the Israeli government.[3]

The Fairfax field office distributed a leaflet, "Jewish Leaders Respond to The Ugly Smear!," in which several dozen prominent figures, including six rabbis, declared that Bradley "is not a militant of any sort"—which was certainly true. They also distributed a *Times* article, "Black Anti-Semitism Assailed by Bradley," and an article from the *B'nai B'rith Record* by an official of the Anti-Defamation League declaring that "'Black anti-Semitism'"—in quotes—was "a galloping myth" whose "hardest riders are, regrettably, Jews who ought to know better." He quoted Bradley as saying, "The black anti-Semite does not represent the views of the overwhelming majority of American black people."[4]

The campaign also worked hard to win white votes in the Valley, where Bradley took every speaking opportunity he could. TV Comedian Carl Reiner hosted "dessert and coffee" at a Q and A with Bradley at a restaurant in Sherman Oaks. A Saturday "Valley Rally ... exceeded all expectations" when 500 people came to a sidewalk event outside the Studio City campaign office, where Bradley was introduced by

Times columnist Art Seidenbaum, Republican Congressman Alphonzo Bell, and the cast of Star Trek.[5]

The volunteer canvassers did the bulk of the work of the election, but the campaign had many other parts. They had Women for Bradley and Young Professionals for Bradley organizations, and a Youth for Bradley group (headed by 28-year-old Howard Berman, who would go on to serve thirty years in the House, representing the San Fernando Valley). There was an Insurance Agents for Bradley organization— whose fundraising gala, at the Black Fox Supper Club in South L.A., featured Billy Eckstein and Hugh Masekela.[6] More unexpected was the group Street Racers for Bradley—an integrated group of drag racers, men and women, headed by "Big Willy," who were "working long hours in headquarters" in their blue embroidered logo jackets. "Street racing is their thing," according to the *Bradley Beat*, the campaign newsletter, "but they want to show the world that there can be a 'new breed of brotherhood.'" Their duties included arranging Bradley's motorcades, "recruiting students, working security and walking precincts." One campaign worker later recalled that, "since we couldn't get reliable police protection, we had Big Willie and the Street Racers on the inside to protect us." The Street Racers had one demand: a raceway in the Sepulveda Basin, which would include "a dance pavilion, a car show arena, a restaurant and a place where young people can just 'get together.'" Most important: at the raceway, "there will be no LAPD needed to enforce law and order. The Street Racers will provide their own security and will maintain the entire operation themselves."[7]

The Bradley campaign was also supported by a who's who of show business liberals. The "Hollywood for Bradley" organization was headed by Robert Wise—who had recently won Academy Awards for directing *West Side Story* and *The Sound of Music*. The cochairmen were Burt Lancaster, Olympic track medalist Rafer Johnson, and Gene Barry, star of *War of the Worlds*—an appropriate metaphor for the battle between the Bradley forces and the Yorty supporters. The steering committee included Black celebrities Diahann Carroll and Bill Cosby, plus movie stars Peter Lawford, Shirley MacLaine and Shelley Winters. The rest of the group included comedians Milton Berle and Sid Caesar; musicians Herb Alpert, Burt Bacharach, Eddie

Fisher, and all ten of the New Christy Minstrels—a white-bread folk group whose recording of "This Land Is Your Land" had made the pop charts in 1962. The white stars supporting Bradley in 1969 included Tony Curtis, Angie Dickinson, Janet Leigh, Jack Lemmon, Gregory Peck, Debbie Reynolds, and Dinah Shore. Of course, the Black elite was there: Sidney Poitier, Sammy Davis Jr., Richard Pryor, Lou Rawls, Dionne Warwick, Roosevelt Grier, the Fifth Dimension (known for "Stoned Soul Picnic"), and James Brown—who had just released his first album, *Please, Please, Please*, with the hit single that could have been Bradley's campaign theme: "Try Me." (It wasn't.) Other members of Hollywood for Bradley included Cass Elliot and John Phillips from the Mamas and the Papas, and also Hugh Hefner, Barbra Streisand, and Frank Sinatra. Hollywood for Bradley's big event was a Sunday night "Gala All-Star Rally" at the Hollywood Palladium on Sunset Boulevard, featuring music by Quincy Jones and Henry Mancini. Tickets: $1.50.[8]

Yorty hoped to pit Latinos against Blacks and argued that Bradley, if elected, would ignore Latino needs. It's true that La Raza for Bradley was not an impressive group—headed by Ramón Ponce, a film industry exec who failed to leave a mark on Latino politics in L.A. in subsequent years. In addition to precinct canvasing in East L.A., the campaign ran events like a Cinco de Mayo celebration sponsored by "Viva Bradley." It featured Bradley with "Mrs. Cesar Chavez"—along with *Mad* magazine cartoonist Sergio Aragonés (not exactly a high-profile political figure), and, from *Star Trek*, Leonard Nimoy (who was Jewish) and George Takei (who was Japanese-American). It also included two stars of TV's all-white *Peyton Place* (one of whom, Joyce Jillson, said in 1988 that she was the astrologer to Nancy Reagan; the Reagans denied it). That lineup suggests a certain weakness in the Latino campaign—not to mention that the event was held in Marina del Ray, a far cry from East L.A.[9]

Red-Baiting Bradley

The smear campaign went into gear shortly after Bradley's stunning surprise victory in the primary, when the Hearst-owned *Herald*

Examiner ran a screaming headline: "Top Communist Backs Bradley."[10] A local TV news show also played a tape of a meeting where the CPUSA's Gus Hall said the party in L.A. should have a "total focus" on electing Bradley—to which Bradley replied that he was "opposed to Communism." Then, the Yorty campaign revealed that Don Rothenberg had once been a member of the Communist Party. Bradley replied that Rothenberg had left the party in 1956, after the Soviet repression of the Hungarian uprising. That wasn't enough for Yorty, who asked, "How did he quit? Did he go to the FBI and help us ferret out those subversives? Oh, no ... his record is getting longer and longer in the left-wing causes."[11] All that, of course, was true—Rothenberg had recently worked in the victorious campaign that made Carl Stokes the first Black mayor of Cleveland.

Unlike the Gus Hall story, the report on Rothenberg was "devastating" for many campaign workers, according to Sonenshein, and "stunned the organization." It created a big problem for Bradley: whether to fire Rothenberg, as many in his campaign suggested. To his credit, Bradley steadfastly refused. Years later, asked about the effect of the Rothenberg revelation on his defeat, Bradley replied, "I don't think that many people were persuaded to change their votes or their position just because of Don Rothenberg." The report, he said, merely gave opponents another reason for doing what they would have done anyway.[12]

The Yorty campaign, apparently, felt differently; they kept up the red-baiting. Yorty brought up Hall's support for Bradley at a speech to the Sherman Oaks Highlands Association, a neighborhood group in the Valley, but young people in the audience of 250 laughed. "Yeah, see, see, see who laughs," he said. "I feel sorry for 'em. Little kids. I went through this in '39 and '40 when I tried to tell 'em that Hitler was a menace."[13] At another event, LA Police Chief Tom Reddin warned that Bradley was supported by the "New Left," which was "out to destroy the government of the United States." For his part, Bradley "denied any attempt to destroy the government," the *Times* reported, and called the charge "absolutely the most idiotic, insane statement I have ever heard."[14] The Yorty campaign tried again two days later when a city council member, Art

Snyder, in the words of the headline, "Link[ed] 2 in Bradley Camp to Reds." The story described a pro-Bradley flyer distributed in East L.A. by a group called the Committee of 100, which included two people who in the mid Fifties had been named as CP members in testimony before HUAC. Again, Bradley shrugged off the allegations: "There are thousands and thousands of volunteers in my campaign. I do not intend to check the backgrounds of each and every one of them."[15]

Bradley was almost certainly right that the red-baiting didn't turn many potential supporters against him—after all, this was 1969, not the mid Fifties. Be that as it may, the Yorty campaign's efforts to link him to Black Power radicals almost certainly played a decisive role in his defeat.[16] Yorty pounded away at the Black radical imagery. He declared that Bradley's election would bring to power a coalition of "Black Power advocates and left-wing militants"—an alliance that could somehow gain the support of more than half of the LA electorate. The Yorty forces also produced a bumper sticker with the Black Power fist and the message "Bradley Power"—it was attached overnight to cars parked in the San Fernando Valley. But what about the fact that the streets of L.A. were quiet and peaceful and free of rioters? That was just more evidence, Yorty said, that the Black militants "don't want to jeopardize Mr. Bradley's chances."[17]

Endorsements—and "Invasions"

As the general election approached, the Bradley campaign gained a key source of support—and a surprising one: the *Los Angeles Times*. The paper had supported one of Bradley's rivals in the primary, but late in the campaign the editorial page expressed outrage over Yorty's turn to "the ugliest lines possible in this troubled day and age: racism, guilt by twisted association, and stark fear," arguments that were "absurd," "dangerous," and "vicious nonsense."[18] Two days before the general election, the *Times* endorsed Bradley.

And there was another surprise source of support for Bradley as the general election approached: seventeen "leading industrialists and business figures," many of them well-known supporters of Nixon and

Reagan, who repudiated Yorty and endorsed Bradley. They called themselves "Businessmen for Bradley."[19]

Another impressive Bradley initiative came as the general election approached: the formation of the "Law Enforcement Committee for Bradley," which included 117 retired LA cops, DAs and US attorneys. They tried to counter Yorty's charge that Bradley was "anti-police." A leaflet on "Bradley's Work for the Police" pointed out that he favored a pay raise for cops (which Yorty had vetoed), agreed with Chief Tom Reddin on creating a "crime task force," and supported the creation of new police divisions and stations in the Valley and West L.A.

In the closing weeks of the campaign, Bradley concentrated most of his efforts in the Valley. Instead of giving speeches at campaign events, he invited questions, which, the *Times* reported, "inevitably led him into a denunciation of protest violence and into a pledge to use force, where necessary, to put down lawlessness." In particular, he invited questions about "the race issue," which he answered by talking about his rise through the Depression era, then college, then up through the ranks of the police force, and into public life—which, he would say, set an example for others to follow: "if it can happen to a Tom Bradley," he would say—implicitly referring to young Black men—"there's hope for them too." The message his campaign tried to convey to white voters was that Bradley was calm and dignified; a former cop who could reassure the law-and-order types; a liberal and a Robert F. Kennedy supporter who, they said, could win support from conservative backers of Reagan. Ten days before the general election, two polls showed Bradley ahead.[20]

The weekend before the election the Yorty campaign turned the volume of its racist campaign all the way up. In addition to the Black Power car caravan through the Valley, they ran full-page newspaper ads with the headline "Will Your Family Be SAFE?" Next to it was a picture of a very Black-looking Tom Bradley. "Bradley's Record: Anti-Police," the ad continued. It said Bradley had voted against an ordinance that was designed to "help the police control mob violence."[21] Another full-page ad, in the *Times*, declared, "Women Civic Leaders are Supporting Sam Yorty for Mayor"—and gave their reasons: "Because Mayor Sam Yorty is not beholden to those who advocate militancy. He represents all the people." The ad displayed the names of eighty women, including Mrs. Henry Salvatori, whose oilman husband was a Republican kingmaker and ran Yorty's campaign; three members of the Doheny oil family; and Mrs. Walt Disney.[22] The message was an old one: white women should be afraid of the Black man.

In the last days before the runoff, the papers were full of news about disruptions of white church services by Black militants, demanding reparations of $500 million to be paid by "the Christian churches and the Jewish synagogues." Their manifesto had been issued by the National Black Economic Development Council, headed by James Forman.[23] The church disruptions came the two Sundays before election day, as militants demanded that they be allowed to read their manifesto from the pulpit. L.A.'s First Methodist Church was one of the targets for what it termed an "invasion." At one Episcopal church Sunday service, militants demanded a list of all the parish's assets and donation of 60 percent of the parish's endowment funds to the reparations campaign. The Episcopal bishop said his church would continue to "support the poor," but he warned that the disruptions "can only hamper or even destroy commitments made by the diocese."[24] The head of the Lutheran Church in Southern California protested that "we must insist on the right of assembly and religious worship without disruption and harassment." The Yorty campaign publicized those stories widely.

Two days before the general election, the *Hollywood Citizen-News* ran a six-column headline: "Siege of the City: Yorty Emphasizes Danger." L.A. was "under siege," Yorty said, threatened by "the Black Panthers and Third World Liberation" (along with SDS) who "are not fooling when they say they intend to destroy the social order." They quoted the Black reparations manifesto demanding $500 million from "the Christian churches and the Jewish synagogues." What did any of this have to do with Bradley? "He has surrounded himself with people openly sympathetic to the movements and organizations which disrupt our campuses and make our streets unsafe," the Yorty campaign said. Next to this "news" story, the paper recommended a vote for Yorty.[25]

Bradley got 96,000 more votes than he did in the primary, but in the end, he still lost the general election. "They did an effective job of scaring the hell out of people," Bradley later said.[26] Yorty got 263,000 more votes in the general than he had in the primary.[27] The turnout was unprecedented, the highest in the history of the city. Bradley lost not just because of white opposition in the Valley, but also because he didn't do well with Latino voters; in fact, Yorty won two-thirds of the Latino vote. Bradley's only real non-Black base, Sonenshein concluded, was among Jews. Jews were twenty points more pro-Bradley than either white Gentiles or Latinos.[28] But Bradley didn't win among all Jews: he carried 80 to 90 percent of those with college educations and higher incomes, but only 50 to 60 percent of the rest. Yorty got 68 percent of white Gentiles' votes. Nevertheless, Bradley had won by far the highest percentage of the white vote of any first-time big-city Black mayoral candidate in the country. In large cities, it remained a record for decades.[29]

Later, Bradley recalled feeling a sense of conviction after the returns showed he had lost: "I decided that night that I was going to run again four years later. I would work twelve hours a day in every section of the city, so that people were unlikely to become victims of that kind of campaign strategy again."[30] Four years later, with more money, more establishment support from downtown business leaders, and with white Gentiles tiring of Sam Yorty's antics, he did win—and served for twenty years, longer than any mayor before or since.

25

Living in the Lion's Mouth: The UCLA Murders (1968–69)

As the third anniversary of the Watts Rebellion approached in August 1968, the newly formed Panther chapter in Los Angeles and its mother organization in Oakland faced multiple crises. Huey Newton was on trial in Oakland for the murder of Officer John Frey, leaving Eldridge Cleaver, minister of information and best-selling author, to define both the rhetoric and political direction of the Party. Cleaver's bombastic eloquence made him a favorite on campuses and among reporters looking for sound bites—Newton was a poor speaker—but his incessant advocacy of the "power of the gun" and calls to "off the pigs" was a gift to the FBI and local police departments, who used such hyperbole to justify their harassment, arrest and sometimes murder of rank-and-file Panthers. Bobby Seale, who later emerged as a voice of sanity, was largely immobilized in 1968–69 by high-profile trials (in Chicago and New Haven), so it was David Hilliard, the chief of staff, who became the main rival to Cleaver. But Hilliard's authoritarian style was widely disliked by the Panther rank and file, and he seldom electrified a crowd.[1] Meanwhile, the Party's major initiative to create Black unity, an alliance with SNCC, had floundered, thanks in part to the FBI's counterintelligence program (COINTELPRO), which had poisoned relations by releasing forged documents, anonymous accusations, and a storm of scurrilous rumors. (Among other dirty tricks, the FBI had terrified Stokely Carmichael's mother with a phone warning that the Panthers were going to kill her.)[2]

Locally, the Southern California chapter was robustly recruiting under the leadership of Bunchy Carter—the former prison comrade of Cleaver—but even the veteran gang leader had trouble maintaining discipline over a membership that included many tough street people with previous vocations in the criminal arts.[3] Veterans of the LA chapter have testified in their memoirs to the drastic lack of political education in this period, as well as the conundrum that the local party faced from Oakland's decision to create a parallel underground organization whose membership and purpose were only known to the leadership. In L.A., the underground members, the so-called "Wolves," according to Elaine Brown, were largely ex-Slausons fiercely loyal to Carter. "Few people knew their real names or their complete names, and none of us knew where they lived," she later wrote. "Everybody above-ground had heard of them. Only Bunch knew all of them."[4] The lack of a real firewall between the chapter's open and clandestine activities, between "serving the people" and carrying out robberies and shootings, bedeviled it with problems throughout its brief history. Moreover, the rivalry with US—exacerbated, as we saw earlier, by the dispute over funds raised from the February "Free Huey" rally at the Sports Arena—had become more dangerous.

Both US and the Panthers were now competing for influence within the BSA and individual campus BSUs. In any showdown, Carter recognized, his armed membership, both public and clandestine, was no real match for US's more numerous and better trained Simbas (whom the Panthers liked to deride as "Karangatangs"). He regularly lectured his members (sometimes threateningly) on the need to avoid conflict with other Black groups, and he met with Karenga several times to discuss how to keep the peace—which was not easy, with so many younger and wilder members in both groups nursing nonpolitical grudges against each other.[5] Each organization had its particular advantages. For the Panthers that was a national notoriety easily convertible into street celebrity. US, on the other hand, enjoyed relative immunity from police persecution, and Karenga had recently burnished his connections with the white establishment by taking credit for preventing rioting in April after King's assassination. The Panthers, however, were squarely in the crosshairs of massive campaigns by both the FBI and the LAPD to literally annihilate them.

The Black Ford

Chief Tom Reddin's racist cops needed little encouragement to carry out a comprehensive campaign of harassment against Huey Newton's people in L.A. Individual members could expect to be pulled over, searched and questioned, and arrested or beaten, almost by whim. Party notables, particularly if traveling together, faced possible police ambush. Thus, shortly before the third Watts Festival, Panther Captain "Franco" Diggs lent his black 1955 Ford to four younger Panthers. Diggs, an ex-con who had served twelve years in Sing Sing for murder, was Carter's enforcer as well as head of the chapter's clandestine activities. Party members frequently used his car to transport arms and carry out assignments.[6] The squad, whatever its errand, consisted of Robert Lawrence (twenty-two), Stephen Bartholomew (twenty-one), his younger brother Anthony (twenty), and Tommy Lewis (eighteen). Later Reddin would portray the quartet as "either in charge of or in great degree responsible" for the organization of the local Party.[7] This was more or less true. Steve Bartholomew, who had been one of Carter's first young recruits, was the second-ranking captain in local hierarchy and was carrying an attaché case that contained names, addresses and organizational details of the chapter. Lawrence, a lieutenant, was a Vietnam combat veteran, one of the first of a number of recently discharged or active-duty Black marines who gravitated to the Party and gave it an entrée to an underground Black Power movement at Camp Pendleton. Lewis ("Monkey Man"), a former Baby Slauson who never learned to read but nonetheless diligently attended political education meetings, was a rising star and chapter favorite. Anthony ("Ozzie") Bartholomew, according to his father, simply "worshipped the ground that [his brother] Steve walked on."[8]

  The black Ford was headed west along Adams when a squad car began to follow it. The two officers later testified that occupants were "acting suspiciously," meaning that they appeared nervous. (The LAPD would also allege that the Ford resembled a "car used in a robbery," but everyone on the street knew this was just a cop euphemism for Black men in a ride.) As the Panthers approached Crenshaw they pulled into a gas station and parked next to a pump. Steve Bartholomew got out and lifted the hood. There were multiple accounts of what happened next, vexing reporters and, later, jurors in the trial of the surviving Panther, Anthony Bartholomew. The LAPD initially claimed that the Panthers came out shooting—then revised the story, saying the four had obeyed instructions to leave the car and place their hands palms down on the trunk of the police cruiser, while officers standing on each side questioned them. In this version, one of the Panthers whirled around shooting and gravely wounded both officers before they returned fire, with deadly results. In either case, the police insisted that "both officers were wounded before they could return fire."[9]

But journalists and Black leaders found it difficult to believe that with seven life-threatening wounds among them, the cops were able to unholster their guns and kill three of their assailants. It made more sense to assume that the cops had fired first. Earl Anthony, the Panthers' deputy minister of information, had rushed to the scene with some other members after hearing that three Black youth had been shot by the police—not knowing if they were Panthers or not. At the gas station a reporter gave him the bad news, while a youth who had been across the street at Johnny's Pastrami Stand reported what he had seen.[10] In an interview with the *Freep*, Anthony recounted what the witness had told him:

> After killing the first brother who was out checking up under the hood, the pig with the shotgun turned and fired on the other brothers getting out of the car, leaving the two other brothers no alternative but to attempt to defend themselves. Tommy Lewis, a young brother 18 years old, was able to get from the car and return the fire. He was apparently shot from the other side of the pig dept. car. He was wounded and not killed. The eye witness said the pig approached the brother Steve Bartholomew and said a few words to him to the effect of you dirty nigger, you should be dead and then fired four rounds from his service revolver into the head of

the man already laying on the ground. The 18 year old Tommy Lewis was wounded, they handcuffed his hands behind his back and began to stomp and kick him ... These reports came directly from eye witnesses that were there on the scene.[11]

Anthony, who in fact was the FBI's most highly placed informant inside the Party, did not clarify how two seriously wounded cops, one of whom was shot in the groin and the other in each thigh, were able to stomp Lewis. Like the competing testimonies being given in Huey Newton's trial up north, there was hopeless confusion not only between but within the proffered scenarios. The only person who might straighten all this out was Ozzie, who at that moment was the most hunted fugitive in California. His mother told the press that the LAPD had threatened that if he didn't immediately turn himself in, he would be tracked down and killed. The NAACP implored Bartholomew to surrender himself and promised to arrange a safe procedure, but Panther Chairman Bobby Seale scoffed at the offer: "They are bootlicking niggers ... the Black Panthers will never give up one of its own to the murdering racist pigs."[12]

Governor Reagan, meanwhile, was at the Republican National Convention in Miami Beach, garnering favorite-son votes for the presidential nomination and flirting with the national press, when word reached him of the deadly gun battle in L.A. Fearing it might spark another riot, he immediately sent Lieutenant Governor Robert Finch to investigate the situation. Yorty was apoplectic at the unwonted interference and accused Reagan of arousing "false rumors and fears. Such rumors and fears are just the things that spark trouble." DA Evelle Younger added that "there is absolutely no reason to antici-pate a major disturbance or any organized violence in Los Angeles at the present time." Celes King of the NAACP, in contrast, warned reporters, "I have never seen this community any tenser. If anyone thinks this is a placid community that can't blow up, they're watching cowboy movies at night."[13]

Five days later, at the end of the Watts Festival, the LAPD attacked the crowd in Will Rogers Park in South Central, provoking the "third Watts riot" and three deaths. Many people believed that the police rage was driven by the earlier shooting of the two officers. Bartholomew, meanwhile, had surrendered and was put on trial. The jurors, unable to resolve the disparities in the police version, and finding no evidence that Ozzie was armed or participated in the shooting, freed him after brief deliberations.

In a separate incident before the August shootings, Bunchy Carter's brother Glen, who acted as his bodyguard and advisor, had been ambushed and killed in Compton. He was the first Panther to die, and nothing in the published literature illuminates the reason for his murder or the identity of his assassins. According to Earl Anthony, the new chapter was deeply shaken, and Bunchy was left without a reliable right hand.[14] That slot, however, was soon filled with the recruitment of Elmer "Geronimo" Pratt, a highly decorated veteran of two tours in Vietnam who was studying political science at UCLA. He brought to the chapter the kind of military expertise and understanding of discipline that had made Ngao Damu, another former Army sergeant, such an effective trainer of Karenga's Simbas. Geronimo (or "G" as he was known inside the Party) was a Louisianan, like Carter, and soon became his inseparable companion and leading pupil. Decades later he recalled one of their early conversations: "The hair stood up on my neck when Bunchy read me a line from *Invisible Man* by Ralph Ellison: 'Live with your head in the lion's mouth,' Bunchy said. 'Even better, *be* the fucking lion!'"[15] Lions indeed were needed as the Party geared up to launch ambitious community programs, while at the same time preparing to defend itself against lethal attacks from all sides.

True Conspiracies

The president's National Advisory Committee on Civil Disorders, best known as the Kerner Commission (after its chairman, Governor Otto Kerner of Illinois), was established during the 1967 Detroit Rebellion to probe the causes of urban uprisings and make recommendations about their prevention or containment. The commission's *Report*, released in February 1968, shared the rare distinction with the *Warren Commission Report* of becoming a popular bestseller, selling 2 million copies. Even fifty years later its famous judgment that "our nation is moving toward two societies, one black, one white—separate and unequal" and its pinpointing of blame on white racism are still widely quoted as a rare moment of truth in American racial discourse. But the commission's major work, its recommendations in different policy areas, have largely been forgotten.

One of the most significant task forces, on which LA Police Chief Tom Reddin was a major participant, addressed the control of civil disorder and emphasized the importance of comprehensive riot-response plans. Thus at the same time that the *Report* was released from the Government Printing Office, a "secret" 150-page *Model Civil Control Plan*, written by LAPD inspector (and future chief) Daryl Gates, was circulating. It was formally presented by Reddin to forty-five other police chiefs, including those of Washington, Baltimore and Miami, at a secret meeting on the Cal Poly Pomona campus at the end of September.[16] But the secrecy around the *Report* was quickly breached by the media, and Reddin ended up on the cover of *Time* magazine, lauded as the country's most innovative cop.[17] His LAPD had become the flagship for a national experiment in the militarization of law enforcement.

Although *Time* had focused on the new priority that the LAPD supposedly assigned to community relations, what riveted the attention of other cops and the public in general was its deployment of fifteen four-man Special Weapons Attack Teams (SWAT).[18] The prototype had been unveiled in 1967, the brainchild of an ex-marine turned patrol officer named John Nelson who, according to an account in *Police Magazine*, had been inspired by a visit to the Delano Police Department in the San Joaquin Valley. These guard dogs for the big growers had created a special tactical unit to control farmworker protests and strikes. Inspector Gates, the former driver for Chief Parker, then championed the proposal to the top brass. SWAT made its debut during the "Century City Massacre" in November 1967 and was subsequently retailed by Reddin to other big city PDs.[19] In the 1968 *Civil Control Plan*, each SWAT unit was basically a sniper team: "a rifleman whose weapon has telescopic sights, a spotter and two officers with shotguns and handguns to provide cover fire." In a riot— or rather, "urban battlefield"—situation, SWAT would operate under the instructions of a field commander and his military-style staff, housed in a mobile command post, with a separate communications trailer containing state-of-the-art radio equipment. Shotguns, walkie-talkies and tear gas grenades were stocked as standard issue to the troops, while, "to protect themselves from flying bottles and rocks, officers will use fiber shields similar in appearance to those carried by the Crusaders." (Reddin reassured the *Times*, however, that "mass destruction weapons" such as machine guns and tanks would never be used against rioters.) The plan's budget also provided for two armored cars and two additional helicopters—the LAPD's cavalry and air force.[20] But the cornerstone of the *Plan* remained the LAPD's largely illegal intelligence system of undercover cops, informers, tapped phones, and the notorious archive of files on persons of all kinds that Reddin inherited from Parker and regularly updated.[21]

Although built around a riot scenario, the LAPD's plan was soon amended to include a showdown with the Black Panthers. Well aware that the Party was recruiting skilled veterans such as Geronimo and had found access to military weapons through its marine sympathizers, the department began thinking about how it could use its SWAT teams and new technology to concentrate overwhelming firepower against the Panthers in an ultimate battle. At the beginning of 1969 Reddin created a Criminal Conspiracy Section to coordinate the department's intelligence efforts against the Panthers and related radical groups.

As the LAPD plotted the destruction of the Party from the outside, the FBI had begun efforts to destroy the Panthers from the inside.[22] Thanks to an intrepid group of anti-war activists in Media, Pennsylvania, who in 1971 stole the records of a local FBI office and then shared them with the world, a special Senate committee headed by Frank Church and including Barry Goldwater launched a three-year investigation of the FBI covert action campaign against domestic dissent—COINTELPRO. While ordinary FBI agents routinely spied on protest movements and radical organizations, COINTELPRO, in the words of the Church Committee, "went beyond the collection of intelligence to secret action designed to 'disrupt' and 'neutralize' target groups and individuals. The techniques were adopted wholesale from wartime counterintelligence ... In essence, the Bureau took the law into its own hands, conducting a sophisticated vigilante operation against domestic enemies." William Sullivan, the head of the domestic intelligence division and number three in the FBI's hierarchy, confirmed that COINTELPRO was indeed the Cold War brought home. "No holds were barred," he told the committee. "We have used [these methods] against Soviet agents. They have used [them] against us." The same techniques were "brought home against any organization against which we were targeted. We did not differentiate. This is a rough, tough business."[23]

Set up in 1956, COINTELPRO originally targeted the Communist Party and anyone who could be remotely connected to it. In the Sixties, it focused intense effort on undermining the reputation and personal life of Martin Luther King and enflaming the Nation of Islam against Malcolm X, before turning attention to undermining SDS, the SWP (because of its important role in the anti-war movement), and SNCC. For two years Stokely Carmichael was the presumptive "Black messiah" whom Hoover believed had to be stopped at all costs. Only with the formation of the Los Angeles chapter did the Black Panther Party really register itself as a COINTELPRO target under the jurisdiction of the "Black Nationalist Program" supervised by the Racial Intelligence Section. In September 1968 Hoover labeled the Party as the "greatest threat to the internal security of the country" coming from any Black group. According to the Church Committee,

> a letter to certain field offices with BPP activity dated November 25, 1968, ordered recipient offices to submit "imaginative and hard-hitting counterintelligence measures aimed at crippling the BPP." Proposals were to be received every two weeks. Particular attention was to be given to capitalizing upon the differences between the BPP and US, Inc. (Ron Karenga's group), which had reached such proportions that "it is taking on the aura of gang warfare with attendant threats of murder and reprisals."[24]

Equally important was letting the Party know that it was being infiltrated by government and then focusing internal suspicion upon individual members. According to committee investigators, the "snitch jacket" is a particularly nasty technique even when used in peaceful groups. It gains an added dimension of danger when it is used—as, indeed, it was—in groups known to have murdered informers. For instance, a Black Panther leader was arrested by the local police with four other members of the BPP. The others were released, but the leader remained in custody. Headquarters authorized the field office to circulate the rumor that the leader "is the last to be released" because "he is cooperating with and has made a deal with the Los Angeles Police Department to furnish them information concerning the BPP."[25]

Who was this Panther leader? One of the most mysterious events in the LA chapter history was the murder of "Captain Franco" (Frank Diggs), on New Year's Day 1969. He had been shot three times in the head and his body dumped in the harbor area. Wayne Pharr, one of the Party's most courageous and idealistic activists, would explain years later how Diggs had come under suspicion of being an FBI plant:

> Shortly before his death, Captain Franco had been arrested for armed robbery after leading the police on a high-speed chase. Shortly after the arrest, he was mysteriously released without charges being filed, which led some Panthers to say that he had snitched. How else could he have just walked away from that kind of situation with no consequences? It was hard for comrades to accept.[26]

The LAPD, following a tip that Franco was executed by the Party, arrested Geronimo and other Panthers but released them for lack of evidence. Later, after a raid on the Panther headquarters at Forty-First and Central, an automatic was recovered that the police said matched with the bullets that killed Franco. Pharr was not surprised.

> Some of the comrades were stunned, while others believed that the police had planted the bullets or just lied. But for me it wasn't a head-twister at all. I had already concluded that the police had not killed Captain Franco. It was an inside job, and I felt it was a dirty deed. I wasn't sure who had given the order, nor did I know

how high up the chain of command the matter had gone. Was it a directive from the leadership of the Southern California chapter, or was the Central Committee in Oakland involved?[27]

The congruence between the FBI memo quoted in the Church Committee report and Pharr's memo is more than striking. Frank Diggs was almost certainly the first of at least a dozen Panthers who would die because of FBI "snitch-jacketing" or the Bureau's incitement of the Party's enemies. Diggs was barely in the ground before the Los Angeles COINTELPRO operation chalked up the rest of the trio that had constituted the chapter's top leadership: Bunchy Carter and John Huggins.

The UCLA Murders

Although the high school and junior college BSUs were the soul of the Black Power movement in Los Angeles, they had little influence over the kind of power resources that adult groups craved. At the outside, the high school protests opened up some opportunities for Black administrators and teachers, while BSUs in the junior colleges won a few student elections and were able to dispense small budgets, perhaps even sway a few hiring decisions, but little more. At state college and university campuses, however, the stakes were much higher. At San Francisco and Valley State Colleges, for example, Black and Chicano students were fighting for the creation of new departments with substantial budgets, autonomy in hiring, special student recruitment programs, and the ability to generate research and policy for their oppressed communities. In the context of the times, there was little apprehension that the "long march into the institutions" might lead to the absorption and dilution of militancy; on the contrary, there was enormous confidence that if such battles could be won, then campuses might become "permanent bases of resistances," training movement professionals who would return to the grassroots.[28]

The big prize in Southern California was, of course, UCLA ("Berkeley with mothers" according to disgruntled radicals), which was in the midst of an extraordinary faculty expansion and building boom. Great things were happening in its laboratories and classrooms, including in 1969 the invention of the Internet.[29] But the campus enrolled a ludicrously small number of Black students—a scandalous situation that many feared would ultimately produce a San Francisco State–like explosion. UCLA's 36-year-old chancellor, Charles Young, who one day would be regarded by his peers as the ablest campus administrator of the Sixties, sought to defuse the inevitable unrest in 1969 by setting up a special admissions program to recruit talented minority students.[30] Through this High Potential (HP) program gateway, which waived many of the traditional prerequisites, the Panther leadership went back to school. Carter enrolled first, meeting and recruiting Pratt, who was already studying political science on the GI Bill; later, Huggins, Brown and others joined them. Their interest in academic content (all accounts testify to the thirst for knowledge among young Panthers) was authentic but at the same time secondary to the strategic consideration of influencing program resources on such an affluent public campus.

US had the same idea, perhaps earlier, and a number of its leading members, such as Larry and George Stiner, former Gladiators and now Simbas, also entered the university through HP. A BSU quickly formed on campus out of an existing Black student group, although its membership was regarded by Elaine Brown as at best half-hearted. "Even the poorer black students, the others in the High Potential Program, wanted to break their bonds with the ghetto. All of them wanted to avoid issues and relax in the sunshine of Westwood."[31] In this regard UCLA was different from other campuses where the BSUs had produced their own strong leadership, or where third parties, like Che-Lumumba or the regional BSA, enforced coalitional peace. At UCLA it was just US and Panther cadre glaring across the table at one another, an enmity that quickly poisoned the atmosphere at Campbell Hall, the headquarters of High Potential.

The proximate cause was a Black studies program that Young had endorsed as one of his preemptive reforms. A Community Advisory Committee had been created that allied Karenga, a UCLA alumnus, and Walter Bremond of the Black Congress with psychiatrists Alfred Cannon and Hiawatha Harris, who were sympathetic to US's cultural nationalism. Karenga, of course, was the most outspoken, and Young freely accepted his leadership in the project, possibly because of a favorable recommendation from Karenga's powerful friend Otis Chandler. (Young's predecessor, Franklin Murphy, had left UCLA to become the *Times*'s CEO.) In any event, Charles Thomas, a psychologist who worked out of the Watts Health Center, was nominated as the program's director. Although he would later be denounced as a "Karenga lackey" by the Panthers, Dr. Thomas was in fact a veteran civil rights activist and a pioneer in community medicine, sometimes honored as the "father of Black psychology." His credentials were genuinely impressive, but many of the students still felt that they were being steamrolled by the Community Advisory Committee and that they should be the ones to vote on a director. They complained to Huggins that they had been intimidated from speaking out by armed Simbas who attended every meeting, and they asked the campus Panthers to provide security as they attempted to take control of the program.

The clutch meeting on January 15 was predictably tempestuous as nonaligned BSU members, opposed to the appointment of Thomas, clashed with Karenga and, according to Brown, eventually expelled him from the meeting. If the Panther presence reassured the dissenting students, it also brazenly threw down a gauntlet on territory that Karenga believed rightly belonged to him. At a Black studies rally the next evening, Geronimo Pratt recalled, "fistfights broke out. You couldn't hear the speakers over the boos."[32] The follow-up meeting the next day in the cafeteria of Campbell Hall was equally rancorous. Karenga was out of town, but the usual group of armed US supporters was present, along with a similar contingent of Panthers with concealed weapons. (Huggins reputedly packed a huge .44 Magnum.) The discussion ended in a tense stalemate. As it broke up, Elaine Brown was accosted by Harold "Tuwala" Jones, a Simba whom she knew well from earlier days at the Black Congress: "You need to watch what you say, Sister."[33]

She immediately complained to Bunchy and Huggins and then left to go upstairs.[34] According to J. Daniel Johnson, the chair of the meeting and the founder of the BSU chapter, there were "13 or 15 people" left in the room when Huggins confronted Jones, who hurled obscenities back at him. Huggins then pulled out his gun. Another Simba, 21-year-old Claude "Chuchessa" Hubert, immediately shot Huggins in the back. The hollow point bullet did catastrophic damage, but before Huggins collapsed he got off a few wild rounds, one of which hit Larry Stiner in the shoulder. "Then," says Johnson who was standing only a few feet away, "Bunchy tried to take cover behind a chair and Chuchessa shot through the chair and killed him instantly."[35] There was panic in Campbell Hall, and fleeing students trampled the bodies of the two Panthers. In the melee, all the Simbas managed to escape. Hubert, the shooter, and Jones disappeared forever, reputedly to the Caribbean. (Years later there was an unsuccessful attempt to extradite Hubert from Guyana.)

Distorted accounts of the shootings, depicting the event as a carefully planned assassination carried out by an elite team of Simbas, have been so widely reproduced over the years that they constitute the standard version. Yet these descriptions often err in the simplest details. Ward Churchill, for example, has written in different places that Carter and Huggins "were duly shot to death by a team of five ostensible US members," or that the murderers were the "brothers George and Joseph Stiner and a man named Claude Hubert." Floyd Hayes and Francis Kiene, two well-known Black studies professors, repeat the charge that the trio killed them and add that Hubert was convicted with the Stiners at a subsequent murder trial. Joshua Bloom and Waldo Martin, in their otherwise excellent history of the Party, claim that "ranking members of the US organization fired guns at Los Angeles Black Panther leaders."[36] Even Angela Davis, in her *Autobiography*, charges that "two members of Ron Karenga's US-Organization were the ones who actually pulled the trigger."[37] In fact, only Hubert and Huggins fired weapons, and the former, while indicted, never came to trial because he was never apprehended. Moreover, the Simbas who eventually went on trial—the Stiners, along with eighteen-year-old Donald Hawkins—were never accused by the Panthers or the DA of being shooters; they were tried instead as conspirators and accessories.

Media and police accounts undoubtedly abetted confusion about who shot whom and in what order. The *Black Panther Paper*, while typically hyperbolic, was not wrong to observe: "As always, when our people are the victims of rape, robbery, or murder, a cloud of mystery and racist-press misinformation descends on the Black ghetto like a hoard of starving locusts."[38] Wayne Pharr, the president of BSU at Harbor College and a new Party member, first heard about the murders on CBS: "Three members of US, after a BSU meeting, around 2:40 this afternoon, shot Alprentice Carter and John Huggins." Later, Long John Washington, one of Bunchy's chief lieutenants, confidentially explained to Pharr and others that Huggins had in fact pulled out his gun first and had been shot, along with Carter, by Hubert.[39] (The LAPD were still claiming that Carter and Huggins were unarmed.)[40] Whether or not the killings were spontaneous or resulted from a conspiracy was not self-evident from these bare facts.

What did appear to be preplanned was the reaction of the LAPD. In the chaotic hours that followed the shootings, several hundred LAPD officers hit the Panthers like a tornado, vacuuming up every individual and as much Panther property as could be found, while daring members to resist. As Jack Olsen put it in his book on Geronimo Pratt,

> Across Central Avenue from Panther headquarters, police emerged from behind a building facade and arrested every African American in sight. They confiscated ammunition, medical supplies, Panther literature and propaganda, gas masks, address books and marijuana. By midnight nearly a hundred Panthers had been herded into paddy wagons, driven to Los Angeles County Jail, booked, finger printed, run through showers, sprayed for bugs and locked into seven-by-eight-foot maximum-security cells. Police confiscated party files and pored over boxes of information—drivers' licenses and license plate numbers, unlisted phone numbers, names and addresses of financial supporters like the actresses Jane Fonda and Jean Seberg (who used the code name "Aretha" on her checks) and prominent Hollywood citizens.[41]

US was spared such raids and mass arrests. Since Hubert and Jones had rather miraculously (and suspiciously in the eyes of most) fled the country, the LAPD's haul consisted of the Stiners, who surrendered themselves in late January, and then, arrested at his UCLA dormitory in February, eighteen-year-old US member Donald Hawkins. The brothers were easy targets since they were out on bail at the time of the shootings, charged with robbing and shooting up a bar in Santa Ana. Before their trial in August for conspiracy to murder and second-degree murder, they were convicted by an all-white Orange County jury of the robbery and sentenced to fifteen years in prison, making them less-than-sympathetic figures to the UCLA jury. (According to one defense attorney, their huge Afros didn't help either.)[42] Instead of going through a preliminary hearing, which would have slowed down the proceedings, the three were indicted by the grand jury after it heard graphic testimony from Elaine Brown and other Panthers.[43] (That the Party eagerly collaborated with the DA's office against three other Black activists is a topic usually avoided in memoirs and accounts of the shootings.)

Deputy DA Stephen Trott's case for conspiracy to murder, a death-penalty offense, was entirely circumstantial. The judge facilitated this by an unusual decision to allow "hearsay" evidence to be presented to the jury.[44] The defense team contended "that the shooting was spon-taneous, that there was no conspiracy to kill or intimidate anyone and that their clients were only innocent bystanders. They also charged that Huggins started the gun battle by pulling a weapon on Jones."[45] Trott counterattacked not by presenting any actual evidence of a conspiracy—reports from informers, wiretaps, incriminating notes, and the like—but by mesmerizing the jury with the Panther claims of a diabolical US plot.[46] Despite vigorous efforts by the defense to debunk the unsupported conspiracy theory, the Stiners were convicted and received life in prison on top of their previous fifteen-year sen-tences. Hawkins, almost an afterthought in the trial, was committed to the Youth Authority, where he served seven years. US did not lift a finger in their defense.

Was there actually a US conspiracy? At the time, it was easy to discern a plot involving US and the FBI and/or the LAPD. The Panthers, confronted with attacks from every side, were realistic to be paranoid. Immediately after the shootings, Shermont Banks, Carter's de facto replacement as leader of the chapter, told a news conference with great certainty that Karenga was "personally responsible" for the deaths of his comrades. The *Wall Street Journal*, the year before, had already revealed the US leader's history of secret meetings with Reagan, Reddin, and Yorty. And in 1971–72, the FBI files "liberated" by the Media, Pennsylvania, burglary that helped spur the Church Committee's massive investigation of COINTELPRO, in turn, revealed the bureau's program to foment conflict between US and the Panthers. Although the FBI documents reviewed by Church did not explicitly discuss collusion with US leadership, a seeming smoking gun was produced in later years by ex–FBI agent Wesley Swearengin when he claimed knowledge that the bureau's LA office arranged for US members to kill Carter and Huggins. For most friends of the Panthers and later students of the events, the case for conspiracy has always seemed overwhelming.

But there are good reasons to be skeptical. To begin with, it's doubtful that Karenga had foreknowledge of any assassination. He was in Harlem on the seventeenth, waiting to speak at an event organized by Amiri Baraka's Committee for a United Newark, when he received a call from the West Coast. According to Baraka,

> Karenga was frozen by what he had heard on the phone. He was scheduled to speak very shortly and it was obvious he could not. His eyes seemed to dart around in his head, glassy with fear. He said he wouldn't speak, but I began to try to convince him that he must speak, that all the people sitting out front were waiting for him. But he was extremely paranoid, thinking that perhaps the word had already reached East about what had happened. He thought maybe Panther sharpshooters were sitting in the audience. Finally, he did go out to speak, surrounded on all sides by the security, the L.A. brothers, and our own people.[47]

If he wasn't personally involved, might not FBI plants have instigated Simbas to go rogue? Certainly, but one cannot rely on Agent Swearingen's 1995 book. An expert in "black bag" break-ins, he was assigned to the Los Angeles bureau in May 1970 to pursue local links to the Weather Underground (see below).[48] At some point he heard a rumor that "[agent] Nick Galt had arranged for Galt's informers in the United Slaves to assassinate Alprentice Carter, the Panthers' Los Angeles minister of defense, and John Huggins, the deputy minister of information. Following Galt's instruction, informants George Stiner and Larry Stiner shot them to death on the UCLA campus." Such ignorance of the facts of the case makes one skeptical of Swearingen's claim to have later found files proving that the Stiners were FBI informers. For the most part he draws his account, as did Huey Newton in his 1980 PhD thesis on the repression of the Panthers, from the lurid revelations of Darthard Perry—alias Ed Riggs, code name "Othello."[49]

Perry's illustrious career as an FBI asset included sabotaging the Watts Writers Workshop after he was hired there. He systematically stole or damaged its equipment and ultimately burned down its new theater, bankrupting the collective. As for the UCLA killings, he claimed that his handlers, "agents Cleary and Heaton," had ordered him to attend the January 17 meeting at UCLA. For some reason, he took a break and went out to a parking lot, where he heard shots from Campbell Hall. (Those familiar with the campus know that five-story-high Rolfe Hall stands between Campbell Hall and Parking Lot Five. Would Perry really have been able to hear the gunfire?) Rather than rushing toward the scene, he remained in the parking lot, where he fortuitously saw "George Stiner, Larry Stiner, and Claude Hubert also known as Chuchessa, jump into a 1967 or 1968 light tan or white, four-door Chevrolet driven by Brandon Cleary of the FBI." He immediately took a bus to the FBI headquarters.

> I went to the building and met with my supervising agent, Will Heaton. While in his company, I observed George Stiner, Larry Stiner and Claude Hubert in the company of Brandon Cleary ... I asked Cleary what was happening and was told that there had been a "fuck up—no one was to be killed by 'our' people" ... I also learned that that it was Claude Hubert who fired the shot that killed John Jerome Huggins and the same Claude Hubert who fired the shot that killed Alprentice "Bunchy" Carter and not George or Larry Stiner.[50]

This is a perplexing account in several respects, including the fact that Stiner had been shot in the shoulder at Campbell Hall yet was wandering around the FBI building an hour later. But it is also fascinating that Perry labels the Stiners as informers while simultaneously rebutting the idea of a murder conspiracy. If it was a "fuck up," then the deaths of Carter and Huggins may not have been an FBI "assassination" in any literal sense. Nevertheless, the bureau was fully responsible for spreading the rumors and anonymous denunciations that led to the confrontation. It is curious, however, that the Stiners, if they were informers, were so casually thrown to the wolves by the bureau and ended up with life sentences. Why in their defense did they not expose their FBI roles? What did they have to lose? In any case, it is hard not to agree with their attorneys (including Loren Miller Jr., later a distinguished judge) that they were railroaded to San Quentin by an outrageous verdict based on hearsay and influenced by a biased judge.[51]

Killer Cartoons

The UCLA killings inflicted wounds on the entire Black Power movement. The first casualty was the Black Congress, which was now branded by the Panthers as a front for US conspiracies. (The Panthers had earlier split from the Congress in opposition to its peacekeeping role after the assassination of Martin Luther King.) Walter Bremond, who had allowed US to borrow a Congress car to take the Simbas to the campus, resigned two weeks after the deaths of Carter and Huggins. He had already been accused of financial malfeasance by Margaret Wright and a handful of activists who wanted to replace the Congress with something called the Black Alternative. That never got off the ground, but Wright's calumnies, along with the perception that he had conspired with Karenga at UCLA, put him under threat from the pro-Panther forces in the community. On the other hand, disputes over poverty funding (Bremond was the head of the Brotherhood Crusade) aggravated relations with US. In October his home was firebombed and the *Sentinel* reported widespread speculation that it had been ordered by Karenga.[52] Meanwhile, the memory rapidly faded of what the Congress had achieved in the days when "operational unity" was a dynamic reality, Karenga was the chief unifier, and members of US, the Panthers, and SNCC easily socialized together.

For Karenga, Campbell Hall was simply a catastrophe. If he was shielded in some way from entanglement in the UCLA trial, his organization had become radioactive to the downtown establishment and mainstream civil rights groups as well as the entire white Left. Living under the permanent threat of Panther retaliation, moreover, his fear became delusional. "This period," writes Scot Brown in his history, "came to be known in US lexicon as 'The Crisis' ... Most striking was US's rapid militarization. Every facet of US ... had to shift its main activities to ones relating to protecting the organization's leader from the immediate threat of an attack from the Black Panther Party or the police."[53] US's formerly prominent role in the community dramatically contracted, and the group began to bleed members as street-level opinion turned against them. The Panthers, in contrast, launched their popular Free Breakfast for Children and Free Health Clinic programs in April and expanded their role in the Black campus movement. An energetic, largely white Friends of the Panthers group was organized to support the programs and raise money for the Party's defense fund. With Carter and Huggins now enshrined as heroic martyrs, recruitment surged.[54]

In the meantime US was plunged into another crisis, this time involving its vice chairman, James Doss-Tayari. When Panther Ronald Freeman was wounded by US members outside a meeting of Carver parents and students in March, Party gunmen using automatic weapons punctually shot up Tayari's family apartment. Tayari didn't hesitate to strike back and was arrested a few days later on attempted murder charges, following a ferocious gun battle that left one Panther seriously wounded.[55] What really rocked the organization, however, was his subsequent indictment, along with his wife Carmelita, for the robbery of a Bank of America branch near Exposition Park the previous January. Carmelita was accused of driving the getaway car while Tayari, wielding a shotgun and shouting orders, held up the bank with three other men. (In February the police killed two masked robbers at the same branch, whom they identified as suspects in the first job.) The trial was easy work for the DA's office. Tayari was identified in a lineup by witnesses, while his wife's alibi, that at the time of the robbery she was at a doctor's office with her baby, was refuted by a sitter or friend who had actually been with the child. They were convicted in July, lost an appeal, and Tayari was sent to prison for twenty-five years.[56]

All of this ratified the perception that US was an out-of-control criminal conspiracy and ended whatever elite tolerance or protection Karenga had previously enjoyed. The following January, after an incident where the LAPD brazenly opened fire on the US headquarters, Karenga tried to arrange a meeting with Reddin's successor as chief, Ed Davis. He was rudely rebuffed. Referring to the UCLA killings and the Tayaris' conviction, Davis told a press conference: "I won't dignify him by meeting with him till his group stops being involved in murder and robbery."[57]

The FBI, meanwhile, had been busy greasing the skids for US's rapid decline. The UCLA killings, even if an unplanned "fuck up," as Perry alleged, were seized upon by local COINTELPRO agents as a golden opportunity to inflict incalculable damage on both groups. The damage was greatest in San Diego, where US and the Panthers were competing for hegemony over the city's relatively small Black community. According to investigators for the Church Committee,

> In early March local agents began mailing cartoons to the homes of Panther activists and the offices of two underground newspapers. These mailings included flyers that had US members gloating over the corpses of Huggins and Carter, and Panthers calling US a collection of "pork chop niggers." Bureau agents and informants tacked up additional copies of the cartoon flyers on walls and telephone poles ... While this was going on, the San Diego office placed anonymous calls to Panther leaders naming other Panthers as police informants.[58]

When the San Diego Panther leadership arranged a peace conference with US, the local FBI immediately escalated its cartoon war. This puerile tactic, which delighted the agents involved, was surprisingly effective, and by April the two groups were raiding one another's events and attacking each other on the streets. The committee noted, "The FBI's Special Agent in Charge in San Diego boasted that the cartoons had caused these incidents." Guns were soon drawn. On May 23 two US members jumped out of a car and killed a 21-year-old Panther named John Savage. A week later the Panthers shot up the US headquarters, wounding two people inside. In June a US member was wounded while walking down the street with his girlfriend; in revenge, local Panther leader Sylvester Bell was assassinated while selling the Black Panther paper in a shopping center. According to the Church Committee, the COINTERLPRO agents were jubilent:

> The San Diego office pointed with pride to the continued violence between black groups: "Shootings, beatings, and a high degree of unrest continues to prevail in the ghetto area of southeast San Diego. Although no specific counterintelligence action can be credited with contributing to this overall situation, it is felt that a substantial amount of the unrest is directly attributable to this program."

Two weeks later, when the Panthers blew up the local US headquarters,

> The San Diego office of the FBI viewed this carnage as a positive development and informed headquarters: "Efforts are being made to determine how this situation can be capitalized upon for the benefit of the Counterintelligence Program." The field office further noted: "In view of the recent killing of BPP member Sylvester Bell, a new cartoon is being considered in the hopes that it will assist in the continuance of the rift between BPP and US."[59]

The FBI kept fueling the war through all of 1970.

There was rage at these events in LA and Oakland, but it was exceeded by the confusion and fear inside Karenga's Inglewood compound. While bodies were falling in San Diego that summer, there was a "mass exodus" of US cadre, including an entire collective that moved to Newark to work with Baraka's Congress of African People.[60] Later Karenga's wife Brenda would testify that a change came over Karenga after the summer of 1969 when he began believing that everyone … were trying to poison him. She said he surrounded himself 24 hours a day with from three to seven bodyguards and from time to time would order that all of their food, including that was in unopened cans, be taken from the house because he thought it was poisoned.[61]

His descent into Macbeth-like paranoia and madness culminated in early May 1970 when he accused two of the young US women living in the compound of "trying to kill him by placing 'crystals' in his food and water, on his clothing and in various areas of the house." According to subsequent trial testimony, Deborah Jones and Gail Davis were stripped naked by several followers, whipped with an electrical cord and beaten with a nunchuck to force their confession. When they refused, Karenga, boasting that "Vietnamese torture is nothing compared to what I know," ordered a hot soldering iron put into Davis's screaming mouth. When Jones proved more stoic, her toe was put into a vise. Karenga's companion and presumed mistress, Luz Tamayo, then put a caustic detergent in their mouths while one of his bodyguards used a water hose to make them swallow it. His wife and children, meanwhile, were huddled in another room listening to the commotion and screams.[62]

Karenga was arrested, convicted on the testimony of his wife and one of the victims (the other was in hiding), and, after a sixty-day psychiatric evaluation, sentenced to one to ten years in prison.[63] All the important cultural institutions which he had helped to create or supported were now put under threat. The Mafundi Institute, one of the pillars of the Watts Renaissance, was particularly vulnerable because Karenga was on the board of directors. When it succeeded in winning an important federal grant to train Watts residents as film and television technicians, Governor Reagan vetoed it. Karenga was taken off the board, but Reagan wasn't swayed.[64] While nationally the Black convention movement was becoming stronger and Black politicians, with nationalist support, were beginning to win important political offices, Los Angeles was becoming Black Power's graveyard, just as COINTELPRO had intended.

26

Killing the Panthers (1969–70)

I n the chaos that followed the UCLA killings and the mass roundup of Panthers by the LAPD, the question of who would become Bunchy Carter's successor threatened to divide the embattled Southern California chapter. Deputy Chairman Shermont Banks took the public reins of the chapter after Campbell Hall, but within a few months he removed himself from competition when he turned to full-time study at Cal State LA and married a local CBS reporter. Although respected for being articulate and well-organized, Banks was considered a cold fish by many Party members, lacking the warrior spirit and personal charisma that had made Bunchy so inspiring.[1] Meanwhile Julius "Julio" Butler, a 36-year-old hairdresser and former LA County sheriff who was a Westside section leader, made an aggressive bid to claim the mantle. But Oakland, shocked by the scale of repression in L.A. and disturbed by rumors that Butler was a snitch, selected Geronimo Pratt to reorganize and defend the chapter, with Elaine Brown as his deputy. Ray "Masai" Hewitt, well-grounded in revolutionary history and theory, was charged with political education and, together with Brown, named liaison with the local Party's Hollywood supporters. One of the first acts of the new leadership was to purge Butler, who would return a few years later as Geronimo's nemesis, allegedly under the aegis of the FBI.[2]

Other purges from the ranks were aimed at members accused of being ill-disciplined (being late for meetings and other petty acts were now punished with beatings) or linked too closely to other revolutionary groups. With Carter's permission, Deacon Alexander, the younger brother of Franklin, had joined the Westside section of the Party the previous fall, along with Angela Davis, at that point a graduate student at UC San Diego. Angela immediately took charge of political education, while Deacon organized a campaign against a shop owner who had killed a Black youth for kicking over his garbage can. The Westside office began to attract as many as 200 people to meetings, and it also attracted increased harassment from the LAPD as the Panther boycott of the killer's store gained community support. Then the expulsions began. "Deacon," writes Davis, "was called up on the question of his membership in the Communist Party—in very much the same way he might have been called before the Subversive Activities Control Board. Obviously, there was something more behind this than simply the fact that he was a Communist ... Sure enough, around this time, a leading member of the BPP—one who had helped a great deal with the building of the West Side section—was found one morning in an alley with a bullet through his brain." The victim was "Captain Franco" Diggs, and the paranoia around his suspected but unproven betrayal "practically decimated" the Westside office. Although the leadership knew better than to confront Angela in the same abrupt manner as Deacon, she withdrew from the Party to focus on the struggle being waged by her sister Fania for a "third college" at UCSD.[3]

As winter turned to spring, the chapter faced relentless pressure from Parker's reincarnation, Chief Ed Davis, as well as from COINTEL-PRO's dirty tricks campaign. In 1968 the LAPD's old riot and vice squad, the Metropolitan Division, had been enlarged from 70 to 200 officers and set loose on the Panthers.[4] Metro now had the resources to dog individual Panthers on a daily basis, and Pharr and other Party veterans have vividly recalled the grim routine of being pulled over by a team of cops, beaten with saps or choked into unconsciousness, then charged with assault or resisting arrest.[5] An even better charge from Chief Davis's point of view was "conspiracy to murder," the same vaguely defined capital offense that had been used to railroad the Stiners to prison for life. Thus in April, when "Long John" Washington and a comrade made an illegal U-turn and parked in front of the Watts office, an officer followed them inside and was confronted with a drawn pistol. As a result, the five Panthers in the room, including Washington, were booked on suspicion of conspiracy to commit murder.[6] The same charge was leveled against eight other Panthers in July, who were arrested after police saw them in an alley "pointing at them objects they said appeared to be guns." There was no evidence, and all were released in August, but the murder allegations, headlined in newsprint and on television, were remembered by the public, reinforcing the idea that it was the Panthers who were stalking the police, rather than vice versa.[7]

This high-intensity harassment and the consequent need to raise large amounts of bail sapped morale and diverted resources from survival programs. It also immobilized the leadership. The *Black Panther* would later report that Geronimo, between his assumption of chapter leadership in early 1969 and his decision to go underground in September 1970, had been jailed no less than *thirty-seven* times on bogus charges.[8] (The repression, of course, was national in scope. Panther lawyer Charles Garry, based in San Francisco, told the *Times* in July 1969 that he already had 200 separate cases to defend "from this spring alone.")[9] Some members of the Southern California chapter itched to retaliate, but Oakland, via Geronimo, had imposed a strict rule that only the Panthers' underground members were authorized to carry out "offensive" operations, such as the counterattacks against US in San Diego.

Pharr remembers the frustration of a group of young, very tough ex-cons led by Walter "Toure" Pope who joined the Party at end of spring:

> I felt bad for the new crew in Watts. They had only been in the Party a few months, and already most of them had suffered three or more arrests: they'd experienced the wrath of billy clubs, saps, chokeholds, and guns shoved in their faces. The billy clubs hurt like hell and could do a lot of damage, but those saps were the real bitch. Those suckers could exact a lot of damage on flesh and bones. With all their government-backed weapons and resources, Metro was inflicting serious harm on the Party collectively and on most all of us individually.[10]

One evening Pharr was kicking back with the crew when Pope became very grave. "You know," he reflected somberly, "we'll never be able to focus on education and liberation until we stop these pigs. We're spending all our time on fighting them and defending ourselves against those bastards." A few months later, Pharr was in a Seventy-Seventh Division holding cell when a Metro cop eyed him with surprise. "'I thought we got you tonight,' he said cryptically. 'But I guess it was the other [wanted Panther] … Yeah, we got him on the ground and shot your boy in the head.'" It was Toure. Toure and another comrade, Bruce Richards, had attacked an unmarked police car that was on a burglary stakeout at a Jack in the Box drive-in when their ambush was itself ambushed by Metro. Toure died on the spot, while Richards, who escaped but was critically wounded, was reluctantly taken by Party members to the hospital where he was arrested. According to Pharr this was a completely unauthorized action, and the death of Toure was "devastating to the Party." It was also a warning to Geronimo and other leaders that the grassroots of the Party would no longer passively submit to Metro's abuse.[11]

Since every Panther chapter in the country faced similar pressure, and the three top leaders—Newton, Seale and Cleaver—were in jail or exile, the Party desperately needed its own "survival program." Both locally and nationally, the Panthers poured new energy into building alliances: with the white Left, with other oppressed communities (Chicanos, Puerto Ricans, Asians and, in Chicago, poor Appalachian whites), and with a small group of left-wing celebrities, including Leonard Bernstein and Jane Fonda, who were brave enough to weather public opprobrium. A few prominent Blacks—above all, James Baldwin (who attended Carter's funeral), Ossie Davis and a handful of others who had previously defended Malcolm X—publicly put themselves on the line, but mainstream civil rights groups in the post-King era kept their distance or denounced the Party. Stokely Carmichael had resigned and was now attacking the Party precisely for its friendship with the white Left. In addition, the Black press, the left-leaning *Amsterdam News* aside, was generally hostile, including the *LA Sentinel*. The Party desperately needed more allies.

In late July, Bobby Seale, briefly free on bail, presided over the Party's major initiative to create a supportive national coalition: the United Front against Fascism conference in Oakland, attended by almost 5,000 people. The three-day-long event was organized to address the escalating, often murderous repression directed not only against the Panthers, but also against BSUs, radical Chicano and Puerto Rican groups, the emergent Native American movement, and anti-war protesters. The Panthers also hoped to secure official recognition as the "vanguard" of the anti-imperialist movement from the broadest possible spectrum of Third World groups and the white Left. In many aspects, however, it was a strange meeting, with Seale summarily reversing many of the positions espoused by Cleaver (now in Algeria). In contrast to the latter's apocalyptic rhetoric, he urged petition drives on behalf of a campaign to put police decentralization on the ballot in local elections. (While the white Left in attendance enthusiastically applauded community control of law enforcement in communities of color, they were aghast that Seale would apply the same principle to racist white neighborhoods and suburbs.) Where Cleaver had sometimes alluded to the necessity of a separate Black nation-state, Seale made the eventual creation of a multiethnic workers' party the strategic goal. Cleaver liked hippies and had promised that they would be protected by Panthers, whereas Seale denounced their "anarchistic" counterculture.

The conference, as a result, disoriented many of the delegates who had expected a more revolutionary stance. Moreover, it failed to come up with a concrete national campaign to address the increasingly destructive police and FBI attacks on the Party. While it did resolve to establish multiracial National Committees to Combat Fascism around the country, besieged Panther chapters lacked the resources to effectively coordinate these groups, and only in a few locales did they have any success—and then only briefly. As for petitions and participation in local politics, Seale was soon in jail in Chicago, then in New Haven, and the essentially rudderless Party returned to the confusing, bellicose rhetoric that promoted community service programs on one hand, and fantasies of imminent revolution and guerilla warfare on the other. One particularly off-the-wall quote from Huey was helping cops across the country gird themselves for Armageddon: "When the masses hear that a Gestapo policeman has been executed while sipping coffee at a counter, and the revolutionary executioners fled without being traced, the masses will see validity of this type of approach to resistance."[12]

Friends of the Panthers

In the end, the Panthers relied on local alliances, such as the dynamic "Rainbow Coalition" of Blacks, Puerto Ricans and poor whites organized by Fred Hampton in Chicago, or the broadly inclusive community coalition that arose to support Panthers on trial in New Haven. In the LA area, the Party retained impressive support among Black youth, especially those leading the high school revolts, and was beginning to recruit Black workers—most of them young Vietnam veterans, including an informal section in Terminal Annex, the oddly named central post office. (In the Bay Area the Party cultivated an impressive membership at GM's Fremont assembly division.) But faced with a recharged enemy in city hall after Bradley's defeat, the branch needed an active, public periphery, including some big names as well as new sources of funding. Brown and Masai were thus assigned to celebrity fundraising as well as helping out with the Friends of the Panthers, a group founded in March whose spokesperson was the playwright and conspiracy sleuth Donald Freed. But a diversity of other groups rallied to support the Party, including active-duty Black marines, the Che-Lumumba Club, members of the BSA, a small collective led by veteran socialists Edith and Milt Zaslow, the reliable Brown Berets, the local chapter of the National Lawyers Guild, and some young white anti-war activists from Orange County who in the Algerian War would have been called *les porteurs de valises*, for their willingness to take risks on behalf of the underground resistance.[13] Other allies were more or less AWOL by the summer of 1969. SDS, then splintering between Maoist factions and the Weathermen, was of little help locally, while some of the college BSUs were moving away from serious activism.

Elaine Brown offers a sympathetic portrait of the local "A-list" of Panther supporters, the group that Tom Wolfe viciously caricatured in his famous essay in *New York Magazine* about how giving money to or simply rubbing shoulders with Panthers had become the essence of "radical chic."

> People like Don and Shirley Sutherland, and the writer Don Freed, and actors like Jon Voigt and Susan St James and Jane Fonda, and, most consistent of all, producer Bert Schneider had begun lending us their homes for fund-raising soirees that produced thousands of dollars in hard cash ... They sent monthly checks for our breakfast program, and paid our incessant bails. As most black artists, along with other black professionals, steered around and away from us, we clutched Hollywood, and did not analyze it. We thanked our stars. That was what made me so resentful of author Tom Wolfe's wholesale appraisal of such white supporters with the epithet "radical chic" ... There were surely those titillated by the danger and daring seemingly involved in being near real black "militants." There were surely those who imagined themselves vicariously linked to some dramatic revolutionary act ... None of that was the point. We were dying, and all of them, the strongest and the most frivolous, were helping us survive another day.[14]

The FBI, which a generation earlier had terrorized and blacklisted the Left in Hollywood with the help of the Hearst press and the *LA Times*, was determined to repeat the process with the Panthers' celebrity supporters. In addition to Schneider, the cocreator of the Monkees and producer of *Easy Rider*, who would later arrange Huey Newton's bail-jumping escape to Cuba, the most important Hollywood supporter was Jean Seberg, unforgettable as Preminger's *Saint Joan* (1957) and Godard's *américaine* selling the *New York Herald Tribune* on the streets of Paris in *Breathless* (1960). Actually "supporter" is a misnomer; Seberg, who contributed money anonymously under the name "Aretha," became part of an extended family around Brown and Masai. Both she and Brown were pregnant at the same time; Seberg from an affair with a young actor while on location in Mexico (her marriage with French director Romain Gary was already de facto dissolved), and Brown from a relationship with Masai. Of COINTELPRO's many targets, Seberg, an idealistic woman from Marshalltown, Iowa, must have been most tempting because of her perceived vulnerability to the FBI's increasingly sophisticated canards. The secret campaign the Bureau mounted against her from 1969 to 1972 was a staggeringly oversized operation that included the CIA, military intelligence, and the Secret Service, as well as John Ehrlichman, Nixon's consiglieri, whom Hoover kept regularly updated. The FBI monitored her bank account, wiretapped her conversations and tracked her daily movements. The Secret Service was told that she was "dangerous," and in 1970 she was put on the "Det-Com" register for detention in national emergency. The FBI's zeal had a sick sexual aspect, as Seberg was repeatedly described in their internal documents as a "promiscuous and sex-perverted white actress"—meaning that she had love affairs with Black radicals. In April 1970 the Los Angeles FBI office proposed to Washington that she be "neutralized" through spreading a false story that she was carrying the baby of a prominent Black Panther. Hoover readily approved.[15]

COINTELPRO enlisted the assistance, witting or unwitting, of the *Times*'s Metro editor, Bill Thomas, who was informed that the information came from a wiretap. He immediately tipped off Joyce Haber, Hedda Hopper's successor as the paper's gossip columnist and "Hollywood's No. 1. Voyeur." His memo read: "Informant sez actress Jean Seberg is four months pregnant by Ray Hewitt, known as 'Masai,' and identified as present Black Panther minister of information. Informant adds that she has sed she plans to have the baby."[16] Haber obligingly put the claim, "Miss A Rates as Expectant Mother," at the top of her syndicated column and provided all the necessary clues ("she is beautiful and she is blonde" and "came to Hollywood some years ago with the tantalizing flavor of a basket of fresh-picked berries") so that anyone who didn't live in a hilltop monastery would immediately know her identity. The result was a cascade of disaster for Seberg that has been chronicled over the years in several books, documentaries and a 2019 feature film. In rapid order, her Hollywood career was wrecked, she became severely depressed, had a stillbirth (she reportedly insisted on an open casket to prove the infant was not Black), and began a series of attempted suicides that ended when her decomposed body was found in her car parked on a Parisian street in 1979.

The LAPD was less successful in its efforts to frame two leaders of the Friends of the Panthers. The actress Shirley Sutherland (née Douglas) could claim to be the daughter of the leader of the first socialist government in North America. Tommy Douglas—champion boxer, Baptist minister and fervent socialist—led the Co-operative Commonwealth Federation to victory in Saskatchewan in 1944 and remained premier until 1961. Canada's universal healthcare system was largely his achievement. Shirley, after a role in Kubrick's *Lolita* (1962), met and married fellow Canadian Donald Sutherland. They moved to Hollywood in 1967, and she quickly became a prominent supporter of civil rights and the Panthers. (Years later she would recall: "I didn't think they were a violent group. Their 10-point program was very close to the CCF, except the Panthers wanted the right to bear arms to defend their homes.") Her involvement soon became front-page news when the FBI raided the Sutherland estate and arrested Arthur League, a fugitive Panther accused of murdering a Santa Ana cop. She claimed no knowledge of the crime and was not arrested, although she was now an obvious target of COINTELPRO and the LAPD.[17]

The other mover and shaker of the Friends of the Panthers was Donald Freed, a talented playwright whose fascination with conspiracy theories eventually led him into unsavory relationships with both Jim Jones (Peoples' Temple) and the O. J. Simpson defense. After members of the Friends had been regularly followed, harassed and assaulted by right-wing Cuban exiles—probably from the same group that later burnt down the Ash Grove nightclub and the Haymarket coffeehouse—Freed accepted an offer from an ex–Green Beret named James Jarrett, who knew Geronimo in Vietnam, to train members of the group in self-defense techniques as well as first aid. As often happens with left-wing groups, newcomers who walk the walk (even if they quack like undercover cops) are absolved of suspicion by the assumption that real finks would be heavily disguised and not obvious in demeanor. As Freed would later acknowledge, "Jarrett talked freely about atrocities he had committed in Vietnam and his current life as a cat burglar and gun-runner." Jarrett, in fact, was a veteran of the CIA's Phoenix Program in Vietnam that had carried out the systematic murder of thousands of students, village leaders and trade unionists suspected of being Viet Cong sympathizers. The LAPD had recruited him to help train SWAT teams, but because of his unusual skill set he was soon assigned to the elite Criminal Conspiracy Section and parachuted—perhaps with Geronimo's unwitting aid—into the Friends.

In September, after the rape of one of the young women in the group—again, by supposed *gusanos*—Jarrett urged members of the group to carry Mace to ward off future attackers. Sutherland wrote a check for $100, and on October 2 Jarrett dropped off a cardboard box at Freed's home. Instead of Mace, the box contained hand grenades. The Metro squad soon arrived, guns drawn, at both the Freed and Sutherland residences. Shirley, with her husband out of the country, was alone with their three children, including two-year-old Kiefer, when she was arrested. Freed, too, was arrested, and both were booked for "unlawful possession of a destructive device"—a charge that carried a potential ten-year prison sentence.[18]

But Chief Davis and his investigators then stupidly overreached. First they set up warrantless wiretaps of conversations between the defendants and their attorneys; then they arranged in December for an informer to burglarize the apartment of the chief investigator for the defense. He stole documents and hours of confidential tapes that revealed every detail of the defense strategy. The prosecutor, US Attorney Matt Byrne, however, quickly worked out that notes shared with his office by the LAPD contained information that had been obtained illegally, and he was forced to make a full written disclosure to the US District Court. He also had to inform the judge that the key witness, Jarrett, was being sent out of the country by a federal agency. According to *Times* reporter Roy Haynes, "Jarrett told others the CIA was sending him to Israel to train commandos." In any event, the judge soon ruled that the federal statute under which Freed and Sutherland had been arrested was unconstitutional since it required "registration" of illegal devices—a clear case of compulsory self-incrimination.[19]

The Alamo on Central Avenue

As fall approached, the skirmishes between the police and the Panthers grew more deadly. "Our worst fears," writes Pharr, "were beginning to turn into reality." At the beginning of September, forty cops, looking for LA Panthers Ronald Freeman and "Blue" Lewis, stormed the Party's San Diego office with guns blazing, igniting a small riot after neighbors gathered to jeer the raiders.[20] A few days later, two highway patrolmen pulled over Panthers Luxey "Lux" Irving, Robert "Caveman" Williams, and Romaine "Chip" Fitzgerald, supposedly for "inadequate lighting of a rear license." The encounter rapidly escalated into a gun battle that would leave one of the officers permanently paralyzed. The three Panthers, one of them also wounded, then hijacked a pickup truck and, in a confused chain of events, ended up in Gardena, where they took a mother and her five-year-old daughter hostage, commandeering their family car. The police, however, quickly caught up with them in an alley, blocking both exits. A dozen more units of Gardena and Torrance police soon arrived, and in the ensuing gunfight, a ricocheting bullet wounded one cop, while Lux was shot in the leg. He and Lewis surrendered, but Fitzgerald, with a head wound from the earlier encounter, somehow escaped to a Panther safe house—where he was given first aid by, of all people, James Jarrett. (This was a month before he delivered the hand grenades to Freed.) Fitzgerald, despite his suppurating wound, stayed at large until early October, when he was finally arrested. Lux and Williams later received consecutive ten- to fifteen-year sentences for attempted murder, robbery, and kidnapping, while Fitzgerald, who was accused of killing a security guard in a separate incident, was sent to death row at San Quentin. (In 1972 the California Supreme Court ruled against the death penalty, and Fitzgerald was resentenced to life. As of 2019, he remains incarcerated, the longest-held of all Panther prisoners.)[21]

Early on the morning of December 4 in Chicago, fourteen members of a specially trained police unit, armed with shotguns and at least one Thompson submachine gun, broke into the apartment of Panther leader Fred Hampton and murdered him in bed. A downstate Panther leader, Mark Clark, was also killed in the same apartment, and four others wounded. The next day more heavily armed cops raided the apartment of Bobby Rush, the chapter's cofounder, but he had the good fortune to have spent the night elsewhere. Stupidly the cops failed to seal off Hampton's apartment, and Rush was soon giving press tours of the bloody scene. There was no evidence of a gun battle—just of a massacre of sleeping people.

The shock of the Chicago police killing Fred Hampton was nowhere greater than in L.A., where Geronimo immediately ordered an all-out effort to fortify the chapter's Central Avenue headquarters with sandbags and boxes full of telephone books (a bullet-stopping defense suggested by Gene Warren, a former stuntman active in the Friends). The Panthers also sped up work on the excavation of an escape tunnel from the building to the city's underground storm drain system. A month earlier the LAPD had encircled the headquarters with seventy-five cops and SWAP snipers, but their timing was poor. The raid was scheduled at 5:30 p.m., and the Panthers were able to quickly mobilize reporters and local residents to the scene. The police retreated, without explanation to the media. Hampton's killing convinced the group that another raid—this time better planned and not conducted during rush hour—was imminent.

Indeed, the police were already in court seeking warrants for a second assault. The pretense for the raid was the claim that the Panthers had possession of machine guns and M14 rifles stolen from Camp Pendleton, but in obtaining arrest warrants for Geronimo and others, the Criminal Conspiracy Section deceived a municipal judge by claiming that the weapons disappeared at the same time that George Young, a Panther member, went AWOL from Pendleton. In fact Young was in the stockade at the time of the theft. In a preliminary hearing after the raid, lead defense attorney Leo Branton confronted Sergeant Raymond Callahan, who had signed the affidavit for the warrants: "You know he could not have stolen the weapons ... you were attempting to willfully mislead the court into thinking he had those rifles." Callahan had no answer. Branton was also able to establish that the FBI was involved in planning the assault, which also had the help of an LAPD informant inside the Panthers who provided details about the layout of the building at Forty-First and

Central, as well as the arsenal it presumably contained.[22] (Although the Panthers would soon be staggered by the revelation in court that Melvin "Cotton" Smith, the chapter's chief of security who led the defense of the building, was giving evidence to the prosecution, it is unlikely, indeed implausible, that he was an informant prior to his arrest. Most likely the mole was the havoc-maker Darthard Perry.)

In the first hours of December 8, an army of cops under the command of Acting Police Chief Daryl Gates gathered at the old Navy armory in Elysian Park, a few blocks from the police academy. Forty SWAT members in black overalls and bulletproof vests, some armed with sniper rifles, comprised the assault team, with an equal number of officers as their backup. One of the lead party was James Jarrett, his long hair now replaced by a crew cut. (Later, at the Panther trial, the court was told by the LAPD that Jarrett—a major figure in all this—was unavailable for cross-examination, having been sent on an overseas mission for the CIA soon after the raid.) After a final briefing, the long convoy of police vehicles left the park and headed to Forty-First and Central. There were thirteen Panthers, mostly teenagers, asleep or standing guard in the two-story headquarters when SWAT attacked at 5 a.m. Wayne Pharr (nineteen years old) was awakened by Cotton Smith, who wielded a Thompson submachine gun. As he vividly recalled,

> I was standing a couple of feet from the front door when suddenly *boom!*—it blew open. I immediately jumped into a bunker we had built on the right side of the room as a uniformed blur of police stormed past me. Just then Cotton opened with the machine gun, moving forward in the direction of the front door. *Bam! Bam! Bam!* I heard in rapid succession ... The cops were stopped in their tracks; then they bunched up in the hallway trying to get back to the front door. As they moved back past my position, I let loose with the shotgun, catching the police in the side and front. Good thing for them they had on bulletproof vests. But now they had no choice but to withdraw. "They're shooting back!" a couple of officers yelled as they retreated, running and limping out the front door.[23]

Three of the cops were seriously wounded, and as one reporter later pointed out: "If the Panthers had held their fire for a few moments more, the entire SWAT would have made it into the alcove—and been shot to pieces."[24] Round one thus went to the defenders, who were now in their firing positions armed with M14s, M1 carbines and shotguns, as well as pipe bombs.

What SWAT-Metro had so carefully planned to be a precision, surprise assault turned into a chaotic, four-and-a-half-hour-long battle, with the young Panthers fighting back like veteran soldiers. Massive amounts of tear gas were lobbed into the building, but when SWAT members on the roof used dynamite to blow several holes through to the second floor, they created a vent that allowed most of the gas to escape. Meanwhile the defenders stuffed their noses with cigarette filters, a surprisingly effective substitute for gas masks. Thanks to the bunker they'd constructed in the front room of the building, they were able to counter fire from police snipers on rooftops across the street. Two female Panthers in the building had made contact with the media, which began to arrive in droves. As one tactic after another failed to turn the tide of battle, LAPD commanders—relying on the constant arrival of reinforcements—attempted to overcome the resistance with sheer volume of gunfire: about 5,000 rounds. "Gunfire echoed up and down Central Ave. Bullets smashed against buildings in which police were positioned across the avenue from the headquarters. Window shades in the sandbagged embrasures of the Panther building disappeared, shot to pieces." With justification, the *Times* would later call it "one of the biggest shootouts in American history," and the building was so badly damaged that it was eventually torn down by the owners.[25]

After several hours of this intense fusillade, the Panthers were forced to abandon the second floor and regroup on ground level, where police fire and ricochets began to take a toll. Six were wounded, including Pharr (shot in the chest, arm and wrist), Roland Freeman (both arms) and Tommy Williams (both thighs). The others had run out of ammunition for their shotguns and carbines. A National Guard armored personnel carrier had arrived at the front of the building, and the defenders feared that the police would soon begin to use more powerful weapons such as bazookas or grenade launchers. Finally at 9:45 a.m., after a brief debate, they agreed to surrender and were led out the front door by a defiant Renee "Peaches" Moore (nineteen) in a torn yellow dress, waving a white flag. Amazingly no one had been killed.

While bullets were flying on Central Avenue, more than sixty cops raided another Panther office on Exposition Boulevard, pumping in tear gas as they encountered unexpected difficulty in battering down the front door. Without resistance, they arrested four Party members, who were charged with conspiracy to possess illegal explosives. Geronimo and Sandra (Lee) Pratt were asleep in bed in another neighborhood when two dozen police broke into their home. (A few months later a superior court judge would rule that both of these "no-knock" raids were illegal.)[26] Altogether, twenty-one Panthers were arrested, eighteen of whom would eventually stand trial with eight of the Central Avenue defenders charged with "conspiracy to commit murder"—a death-penalty offense.

But even after the Panthers had been taken away to hospitals or jail, the police remained in a blue rage—which they took out on a large crowd of local residents and Panther supporters (including the cadre of the Che-Lumumba Club) gathered near the Central Avenue battleground. The "white niggers" of SDS and Friends of the Panthers—as one cop called them—were especially singled out for random attacks.[27] Charles Baireuther, a reporter for the *Sentinel*, described one incident:

The reporter overheard a lieutenant tell his men "watch this" then ... pointed his finger in the direction of the Jack-in-the-Box lot and said something like "that's the one." The squad circled around a group of persons there and suddenly some 10 or more officers began rushing at one [long-haired Caucasian] ... The charged youth's first reaction was shock and horror. His second reaction was to try to duck down an alleyway. Within five seconds officers had him on the ground with repeated clubbing, even after the handcuffs were on his wrists. One policeman tried to shield the scene from a *Sentinel* photographer.[28]

Barbara Brittain, a member of the Friends well known to LAPD intelligence, was so savagely beaten that she had to be hospitalized.[29] These grim scenes were repeated the next day when several hundred volunteers, including Angela Davis, answered a call to help clear out the rubble from the Panther headquarters—a difficult task given all the tear gas that still saturated the interior. Some of the volunteers were overcome and fled outside, in some cases stepping into the street. This provided an excuse for the LAPD commander to call a tactical alert when the volunteers refused to leave. A phalanx of cops were sent in, all too eager to break more heads. Scores were injured, including Davis, and when Mervyn Dymally, now a state senator, attempted to calm things down, he was punched in the mouth by a cop.[30]

The two days of wild police violence, five months after Yorty's racist victory and shortly after the murder of Fred Hampton, produced a tremendous outpouring of solidarity with the Panthers. Booker Griffin, a Motown Records publicist who wrote a column in the *Sentinel*, expressed the viewpoint of Black moderates and radicals alike: "I think that [the police] entered Central Avenue confrontation ready to massacre every living soul."[31] There was a pervasive feeling that the Black community itself, not just a few revolutionaries, was under attack. For the first time since the summer of 1963 and the United Civil Rights Coalition, almost the entire spectrum of civil rights and liberation organizations, from the NAACP to Che-Lumumba, as well as major church leaders like Reverend Brookins, coalesced in an ad hoc united front, with Dymally as its stormy tribune. (Months later Herb Carter, the executive director of the county human relations commission, would tell the *Times* that community anger at the attacks on the Panthers "have done much to accomplish what we've tried to do for a long time without success.")[32]

Meanwhile Elaine Brown, who had been in Oakland on the morning of the fourth, unveiled her skills as a super-organizer. In one day she mobilized several hundred of the BSU high school kids to canvass the Southside for a demonstration at city hall. Five thousand showed up to hear Angela Davis declare that the Panther raids had been organized on a national scale by Attorney General John Mitchell and the FBI, following the orders of President Nixon. Brookins chaired the rally, and Dymally provided rhetoric that was almost as red-hot as Angela's. After the speeches, the crowd, overwhelmingly young Black people, marched downtown to the Hall of Justice where they believed the Panthers were jailed (in fact, they had been moved as a precaution back to Central Jail) and briefly took over the building.[33]

It was clear that the teenage Panthers who had defended their headquarters had won two victories. First, they had survived an over-whelming police attack; second, they had inspired several thousand ghetto youth to lay siege to the center of power downtown, for a few hours at least. This wave of support from both moderate groups and street youth was not unique to L.A.: parallel movements were occurring in Chicago and New Haven. Despite its casualties, the Black Panther Party was offered an exceptional opportunity to become a truly mass movement with a social base that included high school kids and factory workers. But the prerequisite was a leadership able to adapt itself to the moment and lay out an action program that could attract support from militant politicos like Dymally and shrewd churchmen like Brookins. (There would be a time when Oakland Central would attempt to implement a municipal strategy like this, but by then the Party had suffered too much damage from internal conflict and crim-inal behavior by Newton.) Another obvious precondition was the democratization of decision making, freeing the rank and file from the leadership's expectations of robotic followers.

But the last thing that David Hilliard, acting leader of the Party, wanted was an influx of new members. Quoting Lenin's "Better Fewer, But Better," he had told an interviewer back in April 1969 that "the purging is very good ... the very fact that your purge strengthens the party ... You will become stronger, more of a fortress ... Our doors are not open to anyone that decides that they want to join the party."[34] As for a change in line, Cleaver was already signaling that the Party, far from expanding breakfast programs and experiments in electoral politics, needed to burrow underground and become a true guerrilla army. Whether or not he followed orders from Algiers, Geronimo Pratt, a key Cleaver ally, skipped bail in August and returned to the South to train the Black Liberation Army that he and Bunchy had fantasized about two years earlier. He and several others, including

"Cotton" Smith (now a full-fledged informant), were arrested in Houston in December.

Meanwhile the FBI had been working overtime since the beginning of September or even earlier on a new poison letter campaign inciting Newton followers against Cleaver and vice versa. This probably contributed to the decision of Hilliard in consultation with Newton to excommunicate Pratt. The LA leader was labeled a "counterrevolutionary" and government informant, and accused of threatening the assassination of both Newton and Hilliard. Anyone associating with Pratt, the *Black Panther Paper* later warned, would be considered an enemy of the Party, and by implication, fair game. This was a stark declaration of war against Panther members—especially the "New York 21"—who supported Cleaver, embraced the strategy of guerrilla warfare and had publicly praised the Weather Underground for their bombing campaign. Soon, writes activist-historian Akinyele Umoja, "the East Coast Black Panther Party became the aboveground apparatus of BPP members who joined the BLA." They launched a newspaper, *Right On!*, which extolled prison breaks, airline hijackings, ambushes of police, and virtually anything that could be construed as striking a blow against the "Pig Power Structure."[35]

Eventually Cleaver and Hilliard realized that the letters and rumors circulated by the FBI were fake, but the damage had already been done. As Ward Churchill observes,

efforts were made to reconstitute a viable working relationship. Prospects for success in this regard were, however, severely impaired by a combination of Cleaver's distance from day-to-day events [he was in exile in Algiers] and the fact that Hilliard had been thrust by circumstance into a position of responsibility well beyond his capabilities: "David Hilliard [Churchill is quoting from the *Cointelpro Papers*] had implemented a harshly authoritarian policy that engendered intense resentment." Purges of rebellious Panthers were disrupting entire chapters, and the rank and file across the country were furious at the heavy-handed treatment meted out from Oakland. Transfers of Panthers from chapter to chapter and cultivation of loyalty to the central staff kept decision making tightly centralized.

Faced with mushrooming trials and arrests, Hilliard had attempted to keep order at the expense of continuing revolutionary activity.

The expulsion of Geronimo was not rescinded, and not long afterward, Sandra (Lee) Pratt's body, hideously tortured, was found wrapped in a sleeping bag in the LA River. Hopes that the release of Newton would lead to reconciliation were cruelly disappointed. As another movement historian, Errol Henderson, put it, the Panther leader emerged from prison and long terms of solitary confinement as "a Jekyll and Hyde individual at best"—often drug addled and subject to mood swings from charming modesty to homicidal rage.[36] Whiplashed by these events, the LA chapter began to disintegrate, a process that was accelerated by the indictment and conviction in 1972 of Geronimo for the 1968 robbery and murder of a woman on a Santa Monica tennis court. Half a lifetime would unroll, most of it in San Quentin, before Geronimo, who was out of town on the day of the slaying, would finally be exonerated in 1997. The key witness who discredited his alibi and fatally damaged his defense was none other than Julio Butler, whom Pratt, as we have seen, had earlier expelled from the Party. In this sinister fashion, with police frame-ups and internecine murders incited by the FBI, the time of the Panthers ended.

27

Free Angela! (1969–72)

B y any measure, the most famous American radical of the Sixties
generation was and is Angela Davis. Growing up in Birmingham, Alabama, at a time when the tough industrial city was
becoming the national capital of white terrorism and police violence,
she had militant family role models, especially her mother, Sallye,
who had been one of the leaders of the leftish Southern Negro Youth
Congress in the 1930s. Angela left Alabama to study at Brandeis,
where Herbert Marcuse became her faculty mentor and close friend.
He arranged for her to study at the University of Frankfurt with
the regnant pope of critical theory, Theodor Adorno. Then, after
Marcuse moved to UCSD in La Jolla, she followed to work with
him on a PhD thesis on Kant's theory of violence. Her exceptional
academic training marked her for a stellar scholarly career, at a time
when the work of Marcuse and the Frankfurt School was stirring
huge interest on campuses across the country. Princeton quickly
made her a job offer, but she instead accepted a position at UCLA
that enabled her to continue her activities with the Che-Lumumba
Club. Later, much would be made of the fact that the chair of the
philosophy department was Donald Kalish, a prominent figure in
the local anti-war movement, but he would protest with justice that
Angela, already scouted by the Ivy League, simply had the best credentials of any applicant for the job. Others on the hiring committee
agreed that it was a coup to bring such a talented young philosopher
on board.

UCLA philosophy, moreover, had a long-established reputation for controversy. In 1947 Hearst's *LA Examiner* charged that the department was a seedbed of atheism, sponsoring a letter-writing campaign that forced the withdrawal of the distinguished philosopher Max Otto, coauthor of *Is There a God?*, from a visiting appointment at UCLA. When the University of California two years later joined the national anti-communist witch hunt and imposed a loyalty oath on faculty, Kalish was one of the five philosophers who refused to sign it. Another tribune of free speech was Hans Meyerhoff, one of the department's first PhDs, who had served as Bertrand Russell's teaching assistant during the great British philosopher's visiting year at UCLA in 1939–40. Immediately after graduation in 1942, Meyerhoff, a German Jewish refugee, joined the Office of Strategic Services (the forerunner of the CIA) and participated in the Battle of the Bulge and the liberation of Dachau. Hired by his old department in 1948, he taught wildly popular classes in "continental philosophy," a euphemism for the family of theories—existentialism, phenomenology, and Hegelianism—that were excluded from the curricula of most US philosophy departments both for dogmatic reasons (the British analytic tradition ruled almost everywhere) and because of the widespread reputation of the continentals, particularly the existentialists, for pro-Communist sympathies.[1] In 1965 Meyerhoff was a prime mover, together with Kalish, in the founding of the University Committee on Vietnam, which organized a hugely successful twelve-hour-long teach-in on the war on November 12. Meyerhoff's indictment of the Johnson administration was one of the highlights. Then, just eight days later, he died in an automobile accident, and Angela was hired, essentially to fill Meyerhoff's continentalist shoes and maintain the department's reputation for intellectual fearlessness.[2]

The summer before her teaching appointment was to begin in October 1969, while she was traveling in Cuba, the FBI had one of its informants, a former Du Bois Club member named Bill Divale, send a letter to the *Daily Bruin* warning that the philosophy department had just a hired an unnamed member of the Communist Party. The *San Francisco Examiner*, the Hearst flagship, promptly revealed that Angela was the red in UCLA's bed. Enraged, Governor Reagan immediately began to turn the screws on the UC Board of Regents to get rid of her, and they obliged with a letter demanding that she reveal her affiliations. So, as Dorothy Healey relates in her memoir,

> Angela arrived home to find herself a cause celebre. She came to my house to decide what to do. She was understandably unhappy with being forced into this martyr's role just as she was beginning her first teaching job. Her comrades in the Che-Lumumba Club were pushing her to defy Reagan and the Regents by openly avowing her Party membership and daring them to do their worst. I had seen too many people pressured into doing something that they really didn't want to who later felt that they'd been betrayed. I didn't want Angela to go through the same experience, so I just stated her alternatives as clearly as I could and told her to make her own decision.[3]

Healey arranged a meeting with the CP's longtime lawyer and civil liberties expert, John McTernan, who explained that if Angela took the Fifth Amendment she would have a good chance of saving her job. Instead, she chose defiance, and proudly acknowledged her membership. The regents punctually fired her, putting UCLA's liberal chancellor and advocate of academic free speech, Charles Young, in the hot seat. The philosophy department, meanwhile, refused to back down and insisted that Angela would teach her assigned class, "Recurring Philosophical Themes in Black Literature," in which 169 students had enrolled. The regents, a stacked deck of Reagan appointees, were used to fighting rebellious students but not a rebel department, particularly one that had the apparent sympathy of a chancellor. One regent told the *Times* that the board would "use police or whatever force is necessary to prevent it." Another remarked, "That gets down to the fundamental question of who decides what is done with the property of the university." Thirty-four members of the state legislature promptly endorsed the use of police to demonstrate the university was "under the control of the Regents."[4]

The regents' almost-hysterical reaction escalated the affair into the most important free speech fight since the Berkeley uprising in

the fall of 1964. Indeed, UCLA officials warned that they were provoking another Berkeley since the case might "lead to a coalition of
black students and white radical students," an alliance that, at least
according to the *Times*, "has not formed on the Westwood campus in
the past."[5] Reagan, of course, dismissed such concerns: Angela was
simply grist to his mill, another campus outrage to mobilize his voter
base. The hiring of Angela, he said, was "deliberately contrived as a
provocation to bring about a confrontation."[6] The *Times*'s editorial
page went a bit further, declaring that her hiring "smells unmistakably
like a carefully contrived plot" by "revolutionaries who are stage-
managing the Davis case," whose "real purpose is the disruption of
the university and, as the New Leftists put it, the 'radicalization of
the masses.'" On the other hand, the *Times* worried, it might be a bad
idea to use police to block Angela from entering a classroom to teach.
The regents, of course, had the right to use the police to enforce their
will, but "in the existing emotional climate at UCLA that would be
the worst thing that could happen, for it would surely bring chaos
to the campus" and only "serve the purposes of the revolutionaries
involved in the Davis affair."[7] The regents apparently came to the
same conclusion, and announced what for them was a compromise:
the police would not block Angela from the lecture hall, but the school
would not give academic credit to students for taking her course.[8] The
Daily Bruin responded with an editorial headlined, "Don't riot—Yet."[9]

For the radicals on campus, especially the Black Student Union
(reorganized following the Panther assassinations in January), the
inaugural lecture was an immense opportunity. On the first day of
classes the BSU plastered the campus with leaflets urging students to
support Angela by coming to her lecture. On the first day, an astounding number showed up: 2,000 students. The lecture was quickly moved
to the largest auditorium on campus, Royce Hall, for what was probably
the single biggest philosophy class in the history of the school. The
BSU was prepared for that, too, and handed out buttons reading "On
Campus, For Credit, As Planned."[10] When Angela took the stage to
deliver her opening lecture—on "freedom and its relation to the Black
slave," focusing on the work of Frederick Douglass—she received a
standing ovation that lasted almost a full minute.[11]

As the class ended, a BSU leader, Sonya Walker, invited everyone in the hall to remain there for a student assembly to discuss what to do next to keep Angela on the faculty and to get course credit for the students who had enrolled. The group—seven hundred strong—decided by voice vote to call on UCLA faculty to refuse to teach until Angela's course was offered for credit. Thus, Angela's supporters were already numerous, and, by the end of the first class, already hugely successful; the student government passed the same resolution the next day.[12] But the uproar surrounding her first class was only the first sign that the Angela Davis "case" would be a big one.

Two days later, before her second lecture, she gave a political speech on campus, at the invitation of the Associated Students. Over twelve hundred students showed up to hear her at Pauley Pavilion, the basketball arena, where she said the Communist Party didn't tell her what to say in her lectures. "I can't and I won't keep my political opinions out of the classroom," she declared, insisting that students should "be free to criticize and discuss" her views. But, she added, it "might be overestimating the intelligence of the regents" to expect them to understand the distinction she was trying to draw.[13]

The courts had no problem overruling the regents. A couple of weeks into the term, LA Superior Court Judge Jerry Pacht said they couldn't fire a faculty member for belonging to the Communist Party.[14] After that, the chancellor said students would get credit for taking her class.[15] Angela's defenders had won—for the 1969–70 academic year, at least.

Meanwhile supporters were mobilizing all over Southern California. At UC Irvine, the new campus fifty miles south of L.A., an overflow crowd of 1,600 students came to hear her say, "Of course I'm going to talk about my political beliefs in the classroom."[16] (When the UCI chancellor was asked at a Kiwanis Club meeting in Santa Ana whether he would hire Angela, he said, emphatically, "Lord, yes.")[17] And when 2,000 anti-war demonstrators marched in December in Oceanside, the site of the immense Camp Pendleton Marine base south of L.A.—at a profoundly radical protest that included active duty marines demonstrating against the war—the marchers chanted, among other things, "We Love Angela Davis."[18]

A Movement Icon

For Angela and her comrades, the question was what to do with the massive energy and numbers behind her defense at UCLA. The faculty's Angela Davis Defense Committee didn't have that problem. For them, restoring her job and ensuring her ability to teach was the sole objective. But for the Left, it had to be bigger than that, and the opportunity was clear. Here Angela's membership in the Che-Lumumba Club became important: the CP spent a lot of time thinking about strategy and the relationship between short-term and long-term goals. They understood that the problem at UCLA was how to connect her "case" to larger issues.

One approach came from Robert Singleton, director of the new Center for Afro-American Studies at UCLA, who made headlines when he declared that firing Angela was "a racist act." That was easily refuted by defenders of the regents: no other Black faculty were fired—indeed, the university had a policy of seeking out and recruiting Black faculty. The university did, however, have a long-standing policy of firing Communists. Angela herself had a better way of connecting race with her firing. In her Pauley Pavilion speech after her first class, she said the regents were part of a racist system, pointing out that the board had been all-white for decades. She called it "the kind of racism that is not immediately visible."[19]

But what was the best way to connect the fight for racial justice with the fight for Angela's job? In her memoir Angela says "it became clear" to her that "the assault on my job was only a tiny part of a systematic plan to disarm and destroy the Black Liberation struggle and the entire radical movement."[20] She describes the intense political work that took place that year in Black L.A., including that of the CP's Che-Lumumba Club and Panthers against police violence, culminating, of course, with the five-hour attack launched at dawn on December 8 on the Panther headquarters on Central Avenue.[21]

Angela and the rest of the Che-Lumumba Club worked feverishly over the next day to organize a protest rally at city hall with the Panthers and the BSA—high school students, mostly from nearby Jefferson High. The NAACP and the Urban League joined in sponsoring the rally, and on December 11, eight or ten thousand people showed up.[22]

In her speech at the rally, Angela called the attack on the Panthers' headquarters "genocide," and "an attempt to exterminate the people."[23]

At the end of the rally, thousands marched on the jail where they thought the Panthers were being held—in the nearby county Hall of Justice. As detailed earlier, the city had already moved the Panthers back to Central Jail, but the crowd briefly took control of the building, in an impressive show of force. Still, Angela and her Che-Lumumba comrades feared that "if the police decided to attack, it would be a bloodbath." She tried to speak, but her voice didn't carry; instead Franklin Alexander, the Southern California CP leader, "with his voice blasting forth like a trumpet ... explained our immediate tactical disadvantages." After that, thousands left the lobby and marched around the jailhouse changing "slogans of resistance."[24]

Meanwhile back at UCLA, Angela's classes continued, with less fanfare—she taught two courses in the winter quarter, "Dialectical Materialism" and "Kant and Idealism."[25] Her teaching evaluations made headlines in the spring, when the *Times* reported that 87 percent of her students rated her "excellent," and faculty members who had observed her teaching praised her openness: the *Times* quoted history professor Temma Kaplan, who said Angela "seemed to be more impartial than most other teachers I have known." The reporter added that Angela wore "a brown leather miniskirt" and "blue denim jacket" to a recent class—typical of the media coverage, which seldom failed to mention her appearance and clothing.[26]

But the quarrel over her appointment once again returned to the headlines at the end of that academic year, in May: "Campus Turmoil Feared if Regents Reject UCLA's Controversial Communist: Young Expected to Ask Rehiring of Angela Davis." That would be her second "probationary year"—at a time when "tensions have never been higher, at UCLA and other UC campuses as well." All the appropriate faculty and administrative bodies had agreed that there were no grounds for firing her. Some "observers" thought Governor Reagan would not only get rid of Angela but also fire UCLA Chancellor Charles Young if he tried to reappoint her, even though the firing "might trigger a major blowup on the tense UCLA campus." But Reagan seemed determined to get rid of Angela, no matter what the cost.[27]

And indeed, at the end of June, after students had left the campus, the regents announced they were rejecting UCLA's recommendation to rehire Angela. They said they accepted the reports that she "had not used propaganda on her students and that her political activities had not interfered with her teaching duties." But they came up with a new reason to get rid of her: outside of her teaching she had made "public statements"—in four talks—that were "obviously deliberately false" and thus constituted "unprofessional conduct." "We deem particularly offensive," the report said, "such utterances as her statement that the regents 'killed, brutalized (and) murdered' the People's Park demonstrators [in Berkeley], and her repeated characterizations of the police as 'pigs.'"[28] After that, the UCLA faculty voted to defy the regents, schedule Angela's courses, and pay her salary "out of their own pockets"—bold moves.[29]

The Soledad Brothers

The *Times*'s front-page report about the regents' refusal to rehire Angela was accompanied by a photo of her picketing the State Building downtown, carrying a sign that read "Save the Soledad Brothers from Legal Lynching." The Soledad Brothers were three inmates at Soledad state prison charged with killing a guard. Behind her in the photo a young Black man carried another sign reading "End Political Repression in Prisons."[30] He was Jonathan Jackson, a high school student who would play a fateful role in the rest of Angela's life.

The case against the Soledad Brothers had always been weak—indeed, they were acquitted when they finally came to trial in 1972. One of the three, George Jackson, the older brother of Jonathan, published a volume of prison letters in 1970, *Soledad Brother*—he had been in prison for more than a decade, since he was eighteen, when he was convicted of taking part in an armed robbery of a gas station. The book was, among other things, a revolutionary call to arms. In the *New York Times Book Review*, *Soledad Brother* was called "the most important single volume from a Black since *The Autobiography of Malcolm X*."[31] When George Jackson, along with Fleeta Drumgo and John Clutchette, was charged in mid February 1969 for the murder of the guard, Angela wrote in her memoir that she was immediately drawn to their "three beautiful virile faces."[32]

A few weeks later the Che-Lumumba Club decided to organize a "Free the Soledad Brothers" defense committee, and Angela volunteered to make it her project, despite her full-time job at UCLA. This was their answer to the question of how best to build on Angela's authority and celebrity: the UCLA philosophy instructor would organize support for these Black prisoners falsely accused of major crimes. By mid June 1970, Angela says, she had become the leader of the movement. The decision to set up the Soledad Brothers Defense Committee would transform Angela's life. Little did the committee realize that the Black prisoner charged with murder whom they would be defending would soon be Angela herself.

The Soledad Brothers defense got a lot of support from prominent leftists, including Marlon Brando, Jane Fonda, Noam Chomsky, Lawrence Ferlinghetti, Allen Ginsberg, Tom Hayden, William Kunstler, Jessica Mitford, Linus Pauling, Pete Seeger, and Dr. Benjamin Spock. But despite its rallies and protests, "the Soledad Brothers campaign," Dorothy Healey reports, "never succeeded in drawing much support outside radical circles."[33] Along the way, however, something else happened: Angela and George Jackson developed an intense relationship through letters; some said they were in love. George knew of the stream of threats to Angela, and asked his younger brother Jonathan to serve as one of her bodyguards.

On August 7, 1970, Jonathan Jackson entered a courtroom in San Rafael where a Black prisoner from San Quentin named James McClain was on trial for a prison disturbance unrelated to the Soledad Brothers. Two other prisoners were in the courtroom waiting to testify for the defense—Ruchell Magee and William Christmas. Jonathan pulled out a shotgun and two other guns, armed the prisoners, and took the judge, the DA and several jurors hostage, shouting, "Free the Soledad Brothers!" They then tried to escape in a van he had parked outside. Guards opened fire on the van, killing the judge, McClain, Christmas—and Jonathan. He had just turned seventeen.

Angela was in San Francisco when she heard the news, and she immediately went underground. Four days after the shootout, the DA announced that Angela had purchased and licensed the guns. The FBI put her on their "Ten Most Wanted" list, and Nixon called her a "dangerous terrorist." She became the most famous fugitive of the decade. For two months she eluded capture—months full of anxiety and exhilaration for her supporters, as posters declared, "Angela, Sister, you are welcome in our house."[34] *Life* magazine featured her on its cover with the headline "The Making of a Fugitive."[35] But the FBI finally caught her in New York on October 13, eventually bringing her back to California, charged with murder, kidnapping and conspiracy. The DA argued that she had provided the guns, knowing Jonathan's plan—which made her an accomplice, equally responsible, under California law, for the killings.

The morning after Angela's arrest in New York City, Franklin Alexander spoke at a press conference in L.A.: "The hounds have captured her physically and made her a political prisoner. With the people, we will set her free again." A few days later the National United Committee to Free Angela Davis and All Political Prisoners was founded in L.A., with Franklin Alexander and Angela's sister Fania as leaders.[36]

Already a pop icon, she now became the most famous Black political prisoner in American history. Among Blacks the support for her was overwhelming, including Black Democratic congressmen John Conyers and Ron Dellums, who issued statements of support. The Black press virtually unanimously urged her release on bail, and a fair trial; several demanded that the charges be dropped. Aretha Franklin declared she would post Angela's bail: "I've been locked up for disturbing the peace," she said, "and I know you've got to disturb the peace when you can't get no peace."[37]

Black writers and artists made headlines in New York with a statement of support. The signers included Maya Angelou, Nikki Giovanni, Sonia Sanchez, and Toni Cade.[38] After *Newsweek* ran a cover photo of Angela in chains, leaving a courtroom, James Baldwin wrote an "Open Letter to My Sister Angela," which was published in the *New York Review of Books*:

Dear Sister,

One might have hoped that, by this hour, the very sight of chains on black flesh, or the very sight of chains, would be so intolerable a sight for the American people, and so unbearable a memory, that they would themselves spontaneously rise up and strike off the manacles. But, no, they appear to glory in their chains; now, more than ever, they appear to measure their safety in chains and corpses. And so, *Newsweek*, civilized defender of the indefensible, attempts to drown you in a sea of crocodile tears ("it remained to be seen what sort of personal liberation she had achieved") and puts you on its cover, chained. You look exceedingly alone—as alone, say, as the Jewish housewife in the boxcar headed for Dachau, or as any one of our ancestors, chained together in the name of Jesus, headed for a Christian land.[39]

It took the CP a while to get the defense organizations going. The LA Committee to Free Angela held its first meeting on November 7; 200 people came. The National United Committee published their first *Free Angela* newsletter on November 13, 1970, a month after she was captured. (That issue included the text of her first two lectures at UCLA on Frederick Douglass, accompanied by a statement signed by thirty UCLA faculty members: "We take pride in presenting these lectures of a distinguished colleague and friend. May they everywhere contribute to the defeat of oppression."[40]) The Peace Press mailed 1,500 copies. CP organizers set up Free Angela committees in big cities across the country, opening forty-seven offices over the next two months—including some in unlikely places such as Toledo.[41] And there was music: Bob Dylan wrote a song in 1971 about George Jackson; John Lennon and Yoko Ono sang a song about Angela (released in 1972 on *Some Time in New York City*); and the Rolling Stones released their own, "Sweet Black Angel" (recorded in 1970, released in 1972 on *Exile on Main Street*.)

Communist parties around the world organized Free Angela campaigns, including huge demonstrations in the Soviet Union, in Poland and East Germany, and in Western Europe. Thousands of letters of support for Angela poured in from organizations in Eastern Europe and schoolchildren in East Germany.[42] "Ironically," Dorothy Healey noted, "the Free Angela campaign in the US was probably the most poorly organized of all of them." The work of the foreign groups was indeed awesome. The *New York Times* provided a sampling of events: "In Ceylon, a three-day vigil by 2,500 women in front of the American embassy; in Sydney, Australia, a march by 700 women; from Greece, a telegram demanding Angela's freedom signed by the entire cast and crew of the film 'Z,' including Yves Montand, Simone Signoret, director Costa Gavras and composer Mikis Theodorakis."[43] Still, everyone in the United States knew who Angela was. "The problem," Dorothy Healey later wrote, "was to turn that awareness into meaningful support, to get people to become actively involved in her defense"[44]—helping to organize meetings and rallies, raising money, spreading the word.

A Revolutionary Lesson?

The biggest problem facing the defense committees was what to say about Jonathan Jackson's actions: Should they be condemned, or honored as part of the Black freedom struggle? Some potential allies and supporters hesitated because they feared supporting Angela meant agreeing that Jonathan Jackson's suicidal hostage-taking was, as Huey Newton put it in his eulogy at Jonathan's funeral, part of the Black "quest for freedom." Jonathan, he told 3,000 people at the funeral, "taught us a revolutionary lesson": he had "intensified the struggle and placed it on a higher level."[45]

The Panthers were united in endorsing Jonathan's action, but the Communist Party itself was not. The *Daily World* repeatedly called the San Rafael Courthouse hostage-taking "adventurist" (one of the worst things a leftist could be), and many members of the party's 120-member National Committee believed that any defense of Angela required a "repudiation" of Jonathan's "individual acts of terrorism."[46] When Angela found out about that, she thought they were "betraying the memory" of Jonathan, and, according to Dorothy Healey and Bettina Aptheker, talked about resigning from the party. Dorothy visited Angela in jail and told her that quitting "would certainly guarantee the Party's withdrawal from her defense campaign"[47]—which seems to have changed her mind. And the defense committee defended Jonathan: The *Free Angela* newsletter called his courthouse action "a revolt," and "a dramatic attempt to unveil the excesses of oppression and stark inhumanity" in the prisons, which "exposed the deeply motivated aspirations of thousands of captives who want to make concrete and active contributions to the Black liberation struggle." It quoted Frederick Douglass: "Those who would be free, themselves must strike the first blow."[48] George Jackson had a different view of his younger brother's action. "If I'd known ahead of time, I would have stopped him," he said in mid August. "I know the guards here. I knew they'd shoot. I knew they'd kill Jonathan."[49]

The defense committees also had to explain Angela's purchase of the guns. That was pretty simple: although it was unusual for a member of the philosophy department at UCLA to own guns, it was not unusual for prominent activists to have armed bodyguards; even Martin Luther King's bodyguards were armed. Angela, it was explained, bought the guns for the Che-Lumumba Club; she bought the shotgun for the Soledad Brothers Defense Committee, and did it all perfectly legally. Most important, the defense committees argued, she had no idea Jonathan had taken the guns and knew nothing of his plans.

And the defense had a terrific argument: purchasing a gun two days before the shooting was "evidence not of guilt but of innocence." At a defense committee rally at the First Unitarian Church in L.A., attorney John Abt argued that "no rational person who would engage in a hazardous venture of this nature would purchase a weapon and register it in her own name." The November 1970 event, cosponsored by the Unitarian Church Fellowship for Social Justice, was attended by 1,000 people. The defense attorney was also asked at the event whether Angela's going underground, fleeing arrest, wasn't evidence of guilt. "The courts have said that flight is a very low grade of evidence," Abt replied. "An innocent person is as likely to flee, because of the fear of being framed, as a guilty person."[50] Black people didn't have to be convinced—an *LA Times* opinion survey found that 80 percent of African Americans in Los Angeles believed she was innocent and that she couldn't get a fair trial, and thus had been "justified in being a fugitive." A Central Avenue liquor store owner told the pollsters, "They are after Angela because she has been giving them hell."[51]

The defense committee programs in L.A. started with the old-time CP heroic victims: Albert Maltz of the Hollywood Ten, who had served six months in prison in 1950–51 for refusing to name names for HUAC, spoke on "Angela and the Jewish community"; Morton Sobell, who served almost eighteen years after being convicted in the Rosenberg "atom spy" case, spoke on "exposing the prisons." But the range and depth of the programs in L.A. were impressive. Carmen MacRae headlined a jazz benefit in an Altadena backyard. Jazzmen Buddy Collette and Hampton Hawes headlined an "Angela Davis Happening" in the Fairfax district. The Ash Grove held a benefit headlined by Chicago bluesman Jimmy Rogers. An "Art for Angela" auction featured work by Sam Francis, Larry Bell, Leonard Baskin, and Judy Chicago; the auctioneers included Maurice Tuchman of LACMA. (The New York Artists for the Defense of Angela, for its part, included Jacob Lawrence, Alice Neel, and Raphael Soyer.) And the most surprising Angela event in L.A. featured James Baldwin. He had been living in southern France in Saint-Paul de Vence but "thought it important enough to return to the US to assist Angela"— arriving for the opening of the defense in her trial. His LA event was an exclusive one—a private meet and greet in a Mandeville Canyon home in Brentwood.

But of course, not everything was so upscale: an "Open Forum on Bail for Angela" was held at the Ralph's Grocery Community Room at 103rd and Avalon, in the heart of Watts; an International Women's Day "Gala Affair" was held at Thirty-Sixth and Vermont, in South Central; and the Needle Trades Workers Committee had a guest speaker on Angela at the Hungarian Hall on St. Andrews Place in South Central.

And there was a big theater piece: *Angela is Happening!*, at the Inner City Cultural Center, had "a cast of hundreds," featuring William Marshall (star of the Blacksploitation hit *Blackula*) as Frederick Douglass. The music was directed by jazzman Horace Tapscott. The *Times* reported that the show was standing room only. As the trial began, a "Southern California Conference for Angela" was held at Holman United Methodist Church on West Adams, one of the biggest Black churches in L.A.; the sponsors included Mary Clarke of Women Strike for Peace, Latino labor leader Bert Corona, State Senator Mervyn Dymally, Jane Fonda, and several UCLA faculty members. [52]

Support for Angela went far beyond left-wing and Black circles. The general assembly of the Presbyterian Church, representing 3 million members, voted to contribute $10,000 to her defense committee. Conservative congregations in Southern California immediately protested: churches in Santa Ana, Bellflower, Arcadia, Monterey Park, Hollywood, Ventura, and Los Gatos, along with the ultra-elite 2,500-member San Marino Presbyterian Church, all declared that their ruling elders deplored the decision. And when elders at Hollywood First Presbyterian—with 7,500 members, the largest Presbyterian church in the country—unanimously declared that legal aid to Angela was "completely alien" to the purposes of the church, officials of the national organization replied that "the defense of Miss Davis's views is not our cause; the strong defense of her right to justice and a just trial is involved with the basic beliefs of the Christian faith itself." [53]

The biggest LA fundraising event was at the Shrine Auditorium in March 1972, where 6,500 people saw Sammy Davis Jr., Aretha Franklin, Quincy Jones and Donald Sutherland "In Concert for Angela." Sammy Davis Jr. said that although he wasn't a Communist, "I share something more than her political beliefs. I share her blackness." [54]

The trial started a year and a half after the shootout. The prosecution presented ninety-five witnesses over eight weeks. The defense presented only eleven, in less than three days. In June 1972, an all-white jury acquitted Angela on all counts. It was a stunning victory.

Four days after the verdict, Angela launched a thank-you tour, starting with a victory rally at the Embassy Auditorium in downtown L.A. Fifteen hundred attended, the *LA Times* reported, including "a large number of whites." [55] At the rally she called on supporters to "keep the movement alive" to aid political prisoners still behind bars. [56] The next stops on the tour were Chicago, Memphis, Birmingham and New York.

Over the following six weeks, she took her thank-you tour to the USSR, East Germany, Bulgaria, Czechoslovakia and Cuba. She explained that in her view, she had won acquittal because "the international campaign"—led by Communist parties abroad—had "exerted serious pressure on the [American] government."[57] As she headed for Moscow, the *Times of London* published an appeal to her by Jiří Pelikán, one of the heroes of the 1968 Prague Spring, crushed by Soviet tanks, who asked her to call for the release of political prisoners in Eastern Europe as well as in capitalist countries. A spokesperson for Angela replied, telling the *Guardian* that, because Pelikán was living in exile in Britain, he was "acting in opposition to the socialist system, objectively speaking."[58]

Angela won acquittal, she said in her *Autobiography*, because "millions of people from throughout the world rescued" her from "persecution and death."[59] Dorothy Healey had a different view of the "not guilty" verdicts: the defense team, headed by Leo Branton, deserved most of the credit. "Through the pioneering use of jury selection techniques," Dorothy wrote, "the defense managed to seat a sympathetic jury." The "foreperson" of the jury—a woman who refused to call herself the "foreman"—had a son who was a conscientious objector, and "she came to court some days wearing a peace button."[60] And of course there was one other reason why the "Free Angela!" campaign succeeded so completely: you didn't have to be a Communist to see that the charges against her had been outrageous from the beginning.

Part VII

Reigns of Repression

28

The Ash Grove and the Gusanos (1968–73)

Beginning in 1968 a group of anti-Castro Cubans, embittered survivors of Kennedy's Bay of Pigs fiasco, declared war on anyone and anything in Los Angeles that they deemed friendly to the regime in Havana. Apart from the violent labor war that led to the blowing up of the Times Building in 1910, their three-year campaign of bombings and arson retains its title a half century later as the greatest wave of terrorism in California history. The *gusanos* ("worms," in pro-Castro terminology) launched their attacks in spectacular fashion. More than a dozen sites in L.A. were bombed, including five during a single three-hour period on July 19, 1968. At first the targets were mainstream corporations with ties to tourist travel to Cuba: Air France, Japan Airlines, the offices of the Mexican National Tourist Council, and—for some reason—the Shell Data Processing Center.[1] Less than two weeks later, they bombed the British consulate—and left their name, "Unete Poder Cubano" (United Cuban Power). The explosives used in the attacks, the FBI told a grand jury, originally came from the CIA. Two bombers were later convicted and sentenced to prison terms; one said he had been trained by the CIA to use those explosives when he was part of a group preparing for the Bay of Pigs invasion.[2]

In the fall the right-wing terrorists turned their attention to the Left, bombing the offices of the *Free Press* and the Socialist Workers Party —later returning to bomb the SWP headquarters in Boyle Heights a second time. As during the summer attacks, "bombers of the SWP left a calling card above the rubble," the *Berkeley Barb* reported: "a sticker bearing the words 'United Cuban Power.'" There were also dozens of bombings in New York and Miami claimed by the same group, events that propelled the FBI into action. Soon they had arrested and charged a score of suspects, including the two implicated in the nine LA bombings, and it appeared that the case was closed.[3]

But then, on April 14 and 15, 1970, the Cubans launched a second wave of attacks. The first target was the Haymarket, a nonsectarian movement center near MacArthur Park that housed a bookstore and coffee shop, a large meeting room, a printshop, and living quarters for three staff, plus offices of the National Lawyers Guild and the Committee on Latin American Solidarity. Marilyn Katz, newly arrived in L.A. from Chicago, remembers it as "a center of activity for all. Here Bob Duggan and I taught martial arts, others taught dance, while it served as a center for political meetings, cultural events and more. Here I found a welcoming ready-made family—an extended left that had built a real counter-culture in the middle of America's dream world film culture."[4]

The Haymarket had scheduled a showing of the pro-Castro documentary *Fidel*. Fully aware that it might invite some sort of attack, some of the staff had armed themselves and took turns on a night watch. Fortunately, when nine armed men stormed into the building, the volunteer on the roof laid down his shotgun and surrendered. The attackers ordered the twenty people inside to lie facedown on the floor, sprayed a caustic substance (most likely oven cleaner) in the faces of those who hesitated, and then set the building on fire. All of the Haymarket people escaped, and although many required first aid, no one appeared to have any serious injury. Weeks later, however, a LACC student who had inhaled the full blast of the spray developed pneumonia and eventually died. The LAPD made no attempt to pursue this as a manslaughter case. Meanwhile, insurance adjusters told the landlord that the building was a total loss. The staff issued a defiant statement: "This attack was meant to teach us a 'lesson,' but the only lesson we have learned is that we must work even harder to defeat racism and repression."[5] Within months, their ranks bolstered by new supporters, they opened an even larger center—the Long March—near the old location, in an old union headquarters.

Meanwhile, the gusanos repeated the same assault tactics at their favorite site, the SWP headquarters. (The SWP later said its offices in L.A. were attacked at least six times between 1968 and 1970.) A dozen or so heavily armed men invaded the building and forced four campaign workers to lie on the floor while they set the offices aflame. The SWP people narrowly escaped.[6]

Having destroyed the Haymarket, and apprehensive of the heavy security now mobilized around the SWP headquarters, they shifted to a softer and more improbable target: the renowned folk and blues venue, the Ash Grove, in West Hollywood. There were a total of three fires at the Ash Grove: 1969, 1970 and 1973. The founder and owner, Ed Pearl, has said ever since that all three were the work of violent and fanatical Cuban exiles.[7]

But why would a folk music club be targeted? And why two or three times—more than any other place in L.A., except for the actively pro-Fidel SWP? The Ash Grove had opened on Melrose Avenue on July 1, 1958; Ed Pearl was twenty-two at the time and had no experience running clubs, but he had learned to love "authentic" American folk music from his guitar teacher, Bess Lomax Hawes, daughter of musicologist John Lomax. As a student at UCLA in 1957, when he learned that Pete Seeger had been banned from performing at the university, Pearl helped move the performance to a church just off campus. Then, with $10,000 raised from family and friends, he bought an old furniture factory on Melrose Avenue and converted it to a 250-seat auditorium.

Mostly, the Ash Grove was the place to hear Black and white roots music. Brownie McGhee and Sonny Terry sang "Easy rider—see what you done done," "The things that I used to do / I ain't gonna do no more," and "Trouble in mind, I'm blue / but I won't be blue always."[8] McGhee, who walked with a polio-related limp, sang and played the guitar; Terry, who was blind, played the harmonica, with whoops and hollers. They always started their show the same way— instead of the curtain going up with them on stage, they entered from the back, Brownie limping, Sonny holding his arm—the lame leading the blind. They were the most frequent and most beloved performers at the Ash Grove, returning almost every year.

At the club, you could hear Muddy Waters, Howlin' Wolf, and Lightnin' Hopkins,[9] and in its early days, it was also the starting point for a local group, the Chambers Brothers. Their first album was recorded live at the Ash Grove in 1964, featuring as its title song Curtis Mayfield's "People Get Ready."[10]

When Linda Ronstadt arrived in L.A. from Tucson in 1964, she later recalled, the first place she went was the Ash Grove: "That's where I met Kenny Edwards. Kenny liked Mexican music and we started the Stone Poneys."[11] Roger McGuinn met David Crosby at the Ash Grove in 1960; they formed the Byrds in 1964.[12] At the Ash Grove in 1965 they sang "Hey Mr. Tambourine Man" and "Turn! Turn! Turn!"—the defining songs of folk rock. Dave Alvin, later a cofounder of the 1980s roots rock band the Blasters, started coming to the Ash Grove when he was fourteen. In a 2007 interview, he still remembered that first show in 1969: "T-Bone Walker and Big Joe Turner backed by Johnny Otis. That was it for me. My path was set in life after that."[13]

Ry Cooder first played guitar onstage at the Ash Grove when he was sixteen, in September 1963, backing up nineteen-year-old Jackie deShannon; the next year she opened for the Beatles on their first US tour, and the following, she had a huge hit with "What the World Needs Now Is Love."[14] June 1965 brought the debut of a new band featuring Cooder, still a teenager, and Taj Mahal, who was twenty-three—"The Rising Sons," one of the first interracial bands of the Sixties.[15] And Bob Dylan, recalling his youth in *Chronicles*, wrote, "There was a folk club in Los Angeles called the Ash Grove ... I used to dream about playing there."[16]

The Ash Grove also featured other kinds of music: Miriam Makeba performed there in 1963, and Jose Feliciano in 1964.[17] And some nights, there were musical surprises; manager Gordy Alexandre recalled one show when Mother Maybelle Carter, an autoharp player and singer, canceled at the last moment and sent a replacement: Johnny Cash. (Four years later he would marry her daughter June.) When he arrived, Alexandre recalled, he'd just come from playing some big stadium shows—but at the Ash Grove, "he just put the autoharp on a little chair, hunched over, and sang like Maybelle."[18]

It wasn't only the city's counterculture who played audience to all this. On country music nights, older people who had grown up in Oklahoma would show up to see and hear their heroes; for a while in 1967 and 1968, a dozen local Hells' Angels would come to the club, especially when the white electric blues band Canned Heat was playing, or Mississippi bluesman John Lee Hooker. Pearl remembered their leader telling him: "I love the Ash Grove. The thing is, I get excited, and when I get excited I like to break chairs. So listen. I'll pay you for the chairs." Ed replied, "Thank you, that's very nice. But, you see, the thing is, these are Bentwood chairs and you can't replace them." "He was really crestfallen," Pearl recalled in a 2009 interview.[19]

Which Side Are You On?

If the Ash Grove was mostly a music club, it also was part of the movement. In August 1963, the CORE Freedom Singers came to sing "Ain't Gonna Let Nobody Turn Me Around," "Which Side Are You On?" and "Get Your Rights, Jack"—to the tune of Ray Charles's "Hit the Road, Jack" ("Don't turn back—and don't be a Tom no more, no more"). Their run at the Ash Grove began during the most intense period of civil rights action—the day after the March on Washington. Indeed, that year had seen the monumental Birmingham campaign, as well as the Medgar Evers assassination in June; and while the Freedom Singers' performances were going at the Ash Grove, four Black girls were killed in the bombing at Birmingham's Sixteenth Street Baptist Church in Birmingham. The Freedom Singers did two shows per night, at two dollars a ticket—a run that turned out to be the longest engagement in Ash Grove's fifteen-year history.[20] And when Berkeley's Free Speech Movement transformed campus politics in 1964, the Ash Grove supported it by hosting a weeklong FSM benefit, held in December.[21]

In 1965–66 the club started a film series on Mondays and Tuesdays, when they didn't feature live music. They screened *The Exiles*, Kent MacKenzie's 1961 film about the American Indian community on Bunker Hill in Los Angeles, with a print provided by the LA Public Library's film department (the film didn't find a distributor until 2008). And of course, they screened *Salt of the Earth*, a dramatization of an

Arizona mining strike produced in 1954 by blacklisted Hollywood people and Arizona locals.[22]

By the mid Sixties, the Ash Grove was engaging with all kinds of cultural politics. June 1967 brought the Watts Repertory Theater Company with *The Super Spook Show*, written by Stanley Crouch and Jayne Cortez. It was "a bizarre, chilling, and humorous anti-minstrel show," the *Times* drama critic wrote, that opened with Super Spook explaining that "a nigger's mouth is like a garbage can," but that his colloquial speech sought only to "tell it like it is."[23] Cortez, who had founded the Watts Repertory Theater in 1964, would eventually publish twelve books of poems, translated into twenty-eight languages, and release nine albums performing her poetry with music.[24] The 1965 Watts riots led Crouch to join Studio Watts, and to start writing poetry as well as plays. In 1967, when *The Super Spook Show* ran at the Ash Grove, he was twenty-two; later he would become a columnist at the *Village Voice* and then the *Daily News*, and was awarded MacArthur Foundation "genius" grant.

Significantly, politics at the Ash Grove included programs about Cuba—the only thing that mattered to the gusanos. In 1969, Ed Pearl says, "we were scheduled to have a debate between somebody from the Socialist Workers Party that supported everything in Cuba completely, and another progressive group, it might have been the International Socialists, that didn't like the repression of dissent and censorship and top-down leadership" in Fidel's Cuba. However, the event didn't take place.

The First Fire

Two days before the scheduled debate, the Ash Grove burned down, and the club was left a smoking ruin. Arson was never proven, though Ed Pearl would later say that a gusano group "called somebody at KPFK to claim credit for it."[25]

The club promptly organized a series of benefits to rebuild. The first was at Santa Monica Civic Auditorium, home of many legendary rock concerts over the following decade. This one featured Canned Heat, Albert Collins and Lightnin' Hopkins. A second benefit was held in

June at the Pilgrimage Theater in Hollywood. It was headlined by the Byrds, John Hammond, and the Firesign Theatre comedy troupe.[26] The bill also included a couple of local groups, including one with their own version of James Brown's "Say it Loud: I'm Black and I'm Proud"—theirs was "Say It Loud: I'm White and I'm Hippy."[27] The Ash Grove reopened three months after the first fire, in August 1969.[28]

The Second Fire

Club manager Gordy Alexandre had come to the Ash Grove as a UCLA student in 1968, not for the music, but because the club had become the Southern California center for voter registration for the Peace and Freedom party. "My entry was politics," he said in an interview. "That's how I met Ed. He hired me in 1969 to do publicity for the concerts. I was 22 years old. I knew bubkis about music."[29]

On the evening of Sunday, June 7, 1970, Alexandre went to work as usual. Around 6 p.m., three men with automatic rifles walked into the concert room and told him to lie facedown on the floor. "They pointed these automatic weapons at my head and asked me if I was Ed Pearl. Fortunately I wasn't. I said, 'No, I just work here.'"[30] They poured kerosene around the room, set it on fire, and ran out the front door. Meanwhile another club employee, Berta Slote, had seen them; she ran outside, found a phone across the street, and called the police and fire departments.

Ed Pearl was away at a political meeting that night. He later described what happened next: two of the club waitresses, Patty Swenson and Anita Frey, were being driven to work by Patty's father, who happened to be a former captain in the LA Fire Department. "He dropped them off and then saw them screaming as three guys ran out of the club with drawn guns. The guys jumped in a car, so he chased them." He quickly caught up with them and pulled his car in front of the suspects and slowed them down. The LAPD then arrived and "apprehended the suspects"—still within walking distance of the club. The three men had been carrying a loaded .38 automatic, a loaded M1 semi-automatic carbine, and a bull whip—perhaps intended for Ed Pearl.[31]

The apprehended attackers were Rinaldo Castro, twenty-five; Mario Peláez, thirty-two; and Rinaldo Gonzalez, eighteen.[32] The Los Angeles DA filed seven felony counts against each of them, charging the four with attacks not only on the Ash Grove but also on the Socialist Workers Party offices and the Haymarket. "All three attacks were part of a larger anti-communist campaign," the DA told the judge.[33]

The three didn't deny their guilt; instead they "boasted of the raid, seeing themselves as 'anti-communist patriots.'" They found passionate defenders in the exile publication La Actualidad Política, which called itself "a Cuban anti-communist magazine." Peláez, Castro and Gonzales were pictured on the front page, and an article on their "commando actions" described the attacks on the Ash Grove and the Haymarket as "the Los Angeles successes." The magazine included a fascinating report on the campaign to raise bail for the three attackers. Representatives of several groups met at the headquarters of RECE (Cuban Representation of Exiles), the largest of the violent exile groups, headed by Jorge Mas Canosa. (Canosa went on, in 1981, to lead the largest anti-Castro lobby, the Cuban American National Foundation. RECE, according to declassified FBI documents, had bombed the Soviet library in Mexico City in 1965 and planned to bomb Soviet and Cuban ships and other targets.)[34] Those attending the meeting included representatives of Alpha 66, another violent terrorist organization; Plan Torrente, which at the time was raising hundreds of thousands of dollars to invade Cuba; Círculo Güinero, a nonprofit exile group whose website featured a "traitors' gallery" of "envious, resentful, subservient and boot-licking lackeys" who "enforce the desires of Fidel Castro"; and the Los Angeles president of Brigade 2506—veterans of the failed Bay of Pigs invasion. One person at the meeting declared he was "not in favor of acts which violated the laws of this country," but "he was refuted by our editor," the article said, "who said they were acts to combat communism."[35]

The key decision at the meeting: five members of each organization would raise the bail money by going "from store to store" in Cuban neighborhoods. The fundraising succeeded, and the three were released on bail five days after their arrests.[36] The three were due in court for a hearing on September 17, but they failed to appear. Trial was set for November 12, "with all-points bulletins out for the arrest" of the three. They didn't appear for the trial, either.[37]

The June 1970 fire at the Ash Grove had not been serious, and this time the club reopened after just three days. In April 1971, the Ash Grove launched an ambitious monthlong series on "Miners, Mines and Music." It featured not only performances of the songs of the workers' struggles, but also films, photographs, and early recordings of songs sung during the organizing campaigns.[38] September 1971 saw a weeklong arts festival, "El Mundo Chicano," featuring poets, speakers, films, music and an art exhibit, with proceeds going to the Mechicano Art Center, the organization that started the mural program at the Ramona Gardens housing project.[39]

The Ash Grove held a two-week Women's Multimedia Festival in October 1971: more than seventy performers making music, films, theater, dance, poetry, photography, and arts and crafts for exhibits. One of them was Wanda Coleman, who read her poetry—"Poems to Beat Your Black Head against the Wall With."[40]

The San Francisco Mime Troupe brought their agitprop street theater to the Ash Grove stage in April 1972, performing "The Dragon Lady's Revenge," a spoof of a 1940s spy movie, with a message about American involvement in the drug trade in Southeast Asia.[41] In June, eight students from South Vietnam came to the Ash Grove with a program of song and poetry about "the deep tradition of struggle that has made their people so resilient."[42] Then, in December, the Ash Grove screened *FTA*—a documentary on Jane Fonda and Donald Sutherland's controversial anti-war live show "Fuck the Army"— as a benefit for the Long March, the radical movement center near MacArthur Park.[43]

And the club also featured comedy and political satire—especially the Credibility Gap, a group featuring Harry Shearer, Michael McKean, and others. Shearer later recalled,

> We played there a lot. We always wrote our material, memorized in a big hurry, and got it up onstage while the news was still news. In the summer of '73, Ed loved the idea of us doing a whole Watergate summer project.[44]

Then on November 11, 1973, yet another fire broke out at the Ash Grove.

The Third Fire

At the *Freep* in fall 1973, the reporter who covered the Ash Grove was Dennis Levitt. As he recalled decades later, he and his wife Jane Gordon—a Peace and Freedom Party activist—were "hanging out with Ed Pearl at our home in Topanga Canyon when Ed got the phone call that the Ash Grove had been attacked again. The three of us raced down there. Ed was a wreck."[45]

The latest fire had caused extensive damage, leading the club to close permanently. Ed Pearl was sure it was arson, but as Gordy Alexandre remembered, "the common wisdom is that it was an electrical fire." Shearer recalled that when the Credibility Gap was playing the club, "one day our sound man bade me come back behind the stage. He was troubleshooting some tech problem, and what he found, quite simply, was that everything in the club—lights, sound, cash registers, appeared to be plugged in via one octopus plug way in back. It's possible that setup may have been responsible for the last fire."[46] Unlike previous waves of gusano terrorism, no other targets had fires in November 1973. There had been no pro-Castro events at the Ash Grove that season. And nobody claimed credit for the third fire at the Ash Grove—all of which adds credence to the "common wisdom."

Nevertheless, the second fire, in 1970, was certainly the work of anti-Castro Cubans. Why were they focused on the Ash Grove? They explained it in *La Actualidad Política*. The magazine said the Ash Grove appeared to be a music club, but in fact,

> this was the communist den of the "Social Worker Party" … the center of activities of the "Young Socialist Alliance," the faction of young radical communists in the SWP who are fanatics of the theories of Trotsky, and who advocate violent means of the destruction of the democratic system in this country … Their activities consist of showing films of Fidel and of Che, and of carrying out proselytizing campaigns for the Bearded Tyrant, while mocking the pain of 60,000 exiles in the city.

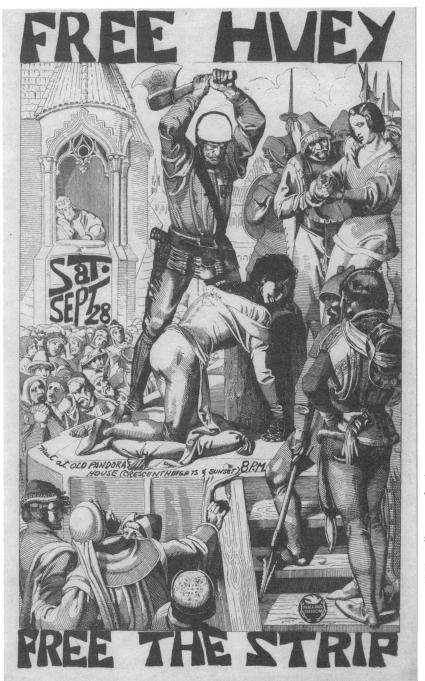

The Battle of Sunset Strip, from 1966 to 1968, was the most celebrated episode in the struggle of teenagers of all colors during the 1960s and 1970s to create their own realm of freedom and carnivalesque sociality within the Southern California night. Here the Peace and Freedom Party connected the kids' protests with the Black Panthers.

Los Angeles Times Photographic Archive, Department of Special Collections, Charles E. Young Research Library, UCLA.

Sal Castro with walkout students at Lincoln High School, March 1968. Castro, a high school teacher long active in liberal and Mexican-American causes, was a key force in organizing student walkouts to protest school conditions in East L.A. The "Blowouts," as they were soon called, were genesis events in the emergence of a new, militant "Chicano" identity.

Boys outside Roosevelt High School in East L.A. in 1970, encouraging other students to come out and join the picket line to protest conditions at the school. Unlike the movement in South Central, the East L.A. Blowouts did not demand integration or busing to better schools. They wanted reforms in situ, under community control, with bilingual classes as the bottom line.

Eldridge Cleaver Photography Collection, The Bancroft Library, University of California Berkeley; courtesy of Roger Williams University and Kathleen Cleaver.

Alprentice "Bunchy" Carter (right) with Eldridge Cleaver (in dark glasses). Carter had been imprisoned in Soledad with Cleaver and afterwards followed him into the Panthers. He became a peacemaker who attempted to cool tensions with Ron Karenga's US Organization. Carter, together with fellow chapter leader John Huggins, was murdered in UCLA's Campbell Hall in 1969 by a US gunman who subsequently fled the country.

"By lifting their hands against John,
they lifted their hands against the best that humanity possesses."

John Huggins - Born Feb. 11, 1945   *Assassinated by US organization Jan. 17, 1969*

John Huggins was one of three key leaders of the LA Panthers in 1969 when he and Bunchy Carter were shot and killed at UCLA. What was widely perceived as their heroic martyrdom spurred membership in the Panthers and brought crisis to Karenga and US.

Charles Brittin photo. Courtesy Getty Research Institute, Los Angeles.

Black Panther funeral, Los Angeles 1971. The LAPD in 1968–69 enlarged its Metropolitan Division from 70 to 200 officers and, with help from the FBI COINTELPRO's dirty tricks campaign, went after the Panthers with high-intensity harassment and wild police violence. Police frame-ups and internecine violence incited by the FBI precipitated a rapid decline in the Party's membership and influence.

Photo by George Louis via Wikimedia Commons.

In 1969 the UCLA philosophy department hired Angela Davis, a stellar graduate student mentored by Herbert Marcuse, the most popular Marxist thinker of the era. An undercover agent exposed her membership in the Communist Party, and the Regents fired her, but the courts promptly reinstated her. Here she enters Royce Hall at UCLA for her first lecture in October 1969—2,000 students showed up. At her right, Che-Lumumba Club leader Kendra Alexander.

Photo by Rolland J. Curtis. Rolland J. Curtis Collection, Los Angeles Public Library.

After the four-hour LAPD attack on the Black Panther headquarters in South Central in December 1969—the LA Times called it "one of the biggest shootouts in American history"—Angela Davis led a protest march to LA City Hall and spoke from the steps.

FREE ANGELA DAVIS

"I think that if we look around us we see that somehow or another a very small minority of people in this country have all of the wealth in their hands and to top that, we don't even see them out working. We do not see them in the factories. We don't see them in the fields. We don't see them using their labor to produce the products which they then present. That tells me that something is wrong. Why is it that the masses of the people in this country have to work eight hours a day every day and somehow or another what they produce goes to some people who are sitting out at a country club, on a golf course, and not doing a damn thing?

That tells me that something is wrong and it tells me that the real criminals in this society are not all of the people who populate the prisons across the state, but those people who have stolen the wealth of the world from the people. Those are the criminals. And that means the Rockefellers, the Kennedys, and that means the state that is designed to protect their property, because that's what Nixon's doing, that's what Reagan's doing, that's what they're all doing. And so every time a black child in this city dies, we should indict them for murder, because they're the ones who killed that black child."

—Angela Davis, June 27, 1970

printed by Peace Press ⚫ a people's printing collective

"Free Angela Davis" poster, 1970; Peace Press, Los Angeles. Courtesy of the Center for the Study of Political Graphics.

Angela Davis was charged with murder after guns she purchased were used in a courtroom shoot-out in northern California. Her imprisonment and trial made her the most famous Black political prisoner in American history. The international "Free Angela" campaign was the biggest and most successful defense effort of the era. In the end, the jury acquitted her of all charges.

That's a lot to credit the Ash Grove for. *La Actualidad Política* concluded that the SWP, before establishing their headquarters on Melrose
"disguised" as the Ash Grove, "formerly had their headquarters at
507 N. Hoover, and at 1704 E. 46th Street," both of which had been
"destroyed by commando forces for democracy." The location at North
Hoover was indeed attacked by anti-Castro arsonists in 1970—but
that was the Haymarket movement center, not the SWP office. Moreover, the SWP office was at 1702 (not 1704) East *Fourth* Street—and
had been for twenty years; it was indeed attacked by anti-Castro
arsonists, but not destroyed. But here's the strangest thing: the *LA
Times* report on the arson identified the Ash Grove building at 8162
Melrose Avenue as "the West Hollywood headquarters of the Socialist Workers Party." The headline called it a "Leftists' Office" rather
than a "Folk Music Club."[47] They must have gotten that from the
arsonists.

But the Ash Grove was not the headquarters of the SWP. The
arson at the Ash Grove—if *La Actualidad Política* was correct—was
a mistake, based on a misunderstanding. It's not hard to see the cause
of the misunderstanding, Alexandre says. The first fire came two
days before a debate in which Castro's revolution was to be defended
by the SWP. The fact that they were to be challenged in a debate by
members of another group seems to have been overlooked by the
gusanos. "Ed was a socialist," Alexandre says, and "always identified
with the Trotskyite part of the socialist movement"—but he was never
associated with the SWP; instead "he was a member of IS [Interna-
tional Socialists] for a while." He was also the Southern California
coordinator of the Peace and Freedom Party voter registration drive,
and the Ash Grove was the field office of Peace and Freedom from late
1967 through spring 1968. In fact, Alexandre says, many on the left in
L.A. regarded the Ash Grove as "a front for Peace and Freedom." But
"the Ash Grove was nonsectarian. It tried to help Peace and Freedom
while being open to SWP and Panthers and others who wanted to use
the space." But these finer points were apparently missed by people
who were focused on the SWP as their main target.[48]

But finding the true cause of the third fire doesn't really answer
the more important question: Why didn't the Ash Grove recover, as

it had done twice before? Gordy Alexandre has been thinking about that for forty years. In his view,

> The Ash Grove had been a product of the Sixties, and its flame glowed as the Sixties glowed. But as the counterculture evolved into a more nihilistic phase, the support needed to sustain the Ash Grove dried up. We had Altamont in 1969, then the breakup of SDS, and then here in L.A. we had the Manson Family murders in 1971. The Ash Grove could not sustain itself without a Left, without young people seeking creative alternatives, some kind of culture they could identify with. Even without the third fire, the Ash Grove would not have survived past the mid Seventies.

Ed Pearl, in 2009, said pretty much the same thing: "The Ash Grove was really floundering at the end of 1973," he explained. "People … were exhausted."[49] It was the end of the Sixties that brought the end of the Ash Grove.

End of the '60s.

29

"The Last Place That Sort of Thing Would Happen": Valley State (1968–70)

I n 1958, someone looking down on the San Fernando Valley from the top of Mullholland Drive would have seen an ocean of building sites, new subdivisions and burgeoning traffic congestion. Only a few years earlier all this had been citrus groves, beet fields and pasture with scattered small towns such as Reseda, Northridge and Woodland Hills. Now tens of thousands of Ozzies and Harriets were moving into their dream homes with expectations that government would provide new schools and nearby college campuses for their kids. Valley State College, which opened that year, was the intended crown jewel: the first completely suburban four-year campus in the state.[1] Given the Valley's ultra-segregation, it was almost entirely white, as well. The campus was designed for a student body of 5,000, but its planners underestimated the baby boom, and within two years the administration was begging for funds to accommodate an enrollment of 12,500. This overcrowded white commuter school with vast parking lots but no adjacent student district was an unlikely environment for student politics in any form. Located, moreover, on a former ranch in the northwest Valley 30 miles from downtown, Valley State—although just within the LA city limits—served a world apart. "If it hadn't been for the orange groves nearby," Marc Cooper, a campus activist, later said, "it could have been somewhere in West Texas."[2]

Nevertheless, by the late 1960s Valley State was the scene of epic confrontations between a small enrollment of Black and Chicano students and their white supporters on one hand, and an authoritarian administration on the other. The escalating factor was District Attorney Evelle Younger, the ambitious conservative and former protégé of J. Edgar Hoover who was also a local TV celebrity, as well as a general in the Air Force Reserve. His policy-cum-campaign strategy was to crush campus unrest with dramatic mass felony prosecutions and conspiracy indictments. Valley State became the test bed for Younger's iron heel. When the campus's newly formed Black Student Union, fighting for a Black studies program, occupied the administration's offices on November 4, 1969, he charged twenty-eight of them with a total of 1,730 felonies, most of them arising from "criminal conspiracy"—a charge that transformed misdemeanors into prison sentences. Despite the protracted conflicts at San Francisco State, Berkeley, Columbia, and a hundred other campuses, the Valley State crackdown, according to the *LA Times*, led to "the first mass prosecution in this country of campus activists on felony charges."[3] Younger was in fact going beyond the kind of repression that had been used repeatedly against students on historical Black campuses below the Mason-Dixon Line. (The so-called "riot" at Texas Southern in Houston in 1967 and the resulting conspiracy trial of campus activists was one of several earlier examples.)[4] When several thousand students and sympathetic Valley State faculty, most of them white, organized a peaceful support rally two months later under the protection of student government sponsorship, the administration called in the LAPD, who hauled 286 of them off to West Valley Jail—the largest mass arrest at any campus in Southern California in the Sixties.[5] ~~January 1970~~

Then, at the end of the year, came the verdicts in the felony cases: of the twenty-eight indicted, twenty-four were tried; three were acquitted, but the rest were found guilty, with eight sentenced to three months to one year in the county jail, and three leaders receiving California's notorious indefinite sentence of one to twenty-five years.[6] Faculty, parents, community leaders, and even hard-core radicals were equally stunned. As one local Black activist said, everyone assumed "the Valley was the last place that sort of thing would happen."[7]

Election Day 1968

How *did* it happen? Before the Black movement emerged at Valley State, a white anti-war movement took shape. At the beginning of the 1965–66 academic year, a campus SDS chapter was organized by a small group including Mike Klonsky (who went on to be elected national secretary of SDS in summer 1968, and after that became a leading American Maoist). Valley State SDS became "one of the most active and imaginative chapters in the area," according to historian Kirkpatrick Sale, notable for being among the first chapters to try GI organizing—in November 1966, when students were arrested after speaking to national guardsmen at the Van Nuys Air National Guard Base.[8] A few days later, more students were detained; the charge: "handing out unauthorized anti-war fliers" on campus. They organized one of the first campus demonstrations against recruiters for Dow Chemical, manufacturer of napalm.[9] Valley State SDS also organized against the draft, calling for a walkout from classes to attend an anti-draft forum; the student newspaper reported that 200 attended. The next month, SDS launched a protest against a scheduled campus visit by a recruiter for the CIA; in mid November the visit was canceled, and anti-war radicals had another victory.[10] By the end of the 1966–67 school year, campus radicals could mobilize 500 students to confront the dean after he suspended nine students for "manning an anti-draft table" in violation of school regulations prohibiting "distribution of literature inside campus buildings."[11] In fall 1967, the faculty senate urged campus administrators to stop bringing in the LAPD during campus disputes and protests.[12] The campus at that point had twenty-three Black students in the freshman class—out of a total student body of 15,000.

Election Day 1968 marked a turning point not only for the nation but also for Valley State. Facing the choice between Humphrey and Nixon, the white radicals on campus held an Election Day rally, part of the national protest organized by SDS: "Vote with Your Feet, Vote in the Streets." The message was simple: as the special pre-election issue of the SDS publication *New Left Notes* declared in giant type on a page suitable for use as a wall poster, "The Elections don't mean shit. Our power is in the street."[13]

Mike Lee was one of the SDS leaders at Valley State. He had started out as a Goldwater supporter in 1964, while he was in high school, but had been radicalized by the sight of LA cops beating "little old ladies" at the Century City anti-war demonstration in 1967. He later recalled that 350 or 400 students showed up for the Election Day rally on campus.[14] During the rally, word came down that the BSU had taken over the administration building. "Vote with your Feet" suddenly took on urgent new meaning, and a hundred people from the SDS rally marched up to the building.

The issue that had mobilized Black students wasn't the election, or the war in Vietnam; it was racism on campus, especially in the athletic program. Their protest had been sparked by an incident two weeks earlier, at a school football game. On October 18, a scuffle had broken out on the field, and a Black player on the bench, freshman George Boswell, ran onto the field to help his teammates. A volunteer coach ordered him back to the bench. When Boswell walked back instead of running, the coach, Boswell later testified in court, "grabbed me around the neck, turned me around, and kicked me in the groin."[15] The coach was white—and an off-duty LAPD cop.

In the stands were twenty members of the BSU—the group had been chartered as an official campus student organization the previous year. They had been campaigning since the spring of that year for the recruitment of more minority students and for courses on Black studies. They had met with faculty members, administrators, and eventually with the school's acting president, Paul Blomgren. The response from the administration to their various proposals had been painfully slow. The BSU had also complained about racism in the athletic department—they said people in the department had used racial slurs and discriminated against Blacks in athletic assignments and financial support. Now they demanded a meeting with the athletic director to complain about the treatment of George Boswell and to call for the firing of the football coach. The meeting was set for November 4, which also happened to be Election Day.

At the meeting, the athletic director told three BSU leaders that only the college president could fire the coach. Thirty BSU members then marched over to the administration building, bringing the athletic director with them, to present their demands to the president. They occupied the fifth floor, where the president's office was located. Dozens of people were at work on that floor, ranging from high-level administrators to clerks and secretaries. The students held thirty-four of them hostage while they presented their demands to the president. Very quickly they decided to expand their list of demands beyond changes in the athletic department. They presented a list of twelve, headed by the creation of a Black studies department. After four hours, the president announced he had agreed to all twelve demands, and also agreed to granting amnesty to all the students who participated in the takeover. The students declared victory and released their hostages, and everybody went home.

But the next day the president announced that he had agreed to the demands only under duress, only to end the hostage situation. He said agreements made under duress were void, and called for the arrest of the students. He added that he nevertheless wanted to "build a solid program for minority students," but didn't say anything about what he meant.

The next day the *Times* ran a banner headline across all six columns, "Sit-In Aftermath: Attacks on Faculty Members Told." "Faculty members were kicked, hit, called 'pigs' and had their lives threatened during four hours as prisoners of Negro militants," the page-one story began. But in spite of such allegations, the *Times* reported, former hostages said they were "not harmed, but were 'subjected to lectures' on 'how the white people are responsible for the Negro condition.'"[16] At a closed meeting of 500 faculty members, the athletic director said that at the "meeting" at his office the day before, he was told, "Stand on your feet, you pig, when I'm talking to you!" and his chair was kicked out from under him. The associate dean of fine arts said that after he refused a student's order to leave his office in the administration building, he was grabbed by two students while a third "twisted his right arm to escort him out of his office." All the hostages were taken to a conference room where they said they had been "forbidden to leave their seats or speak" for four hours.[17] If all of that was true, it didn't seem like a good way to launch a Black studies program.

The next day the LAPD arrested twenty-eight participants in the hostage-taking, and, although all the students had been unarmed and had caused no injuries or damage, on December 20 the grand jury charged each of them with seventy-two felonies: kidnapping, false imprisonment, assault, and the big one—conspiracy.[18] That made for a total of more than 1,700 felonies, "surely some sort of record in cases of this kind," according to the NAACP magazine the *Crisis*.[19] None of the accused felons were white—one was Latino, and one identified as "Hawaiian" or "Asian." The conspiracy charge was particularly outrageous, since the event had clearly been spontaneous—they went to the president's office because they were told, at the meeting with the athletic director, that only the president could fire the football coach. The *Times* ran a photo on page one of Black students in chains outside the courthouse being loaded onto a sheriffs' bus.[20]

The same day, after President Blomgren's announcement, Governor Reagan said in a speech in Pacific Palisades that the Valley State BSU members should have been "taken out by the scruffs of their necks," and that the whole thing left him with a "feeling of disgust."[21] Of course, Mayor Yorty issued a statement supporting the arrests. On campus, the faculty voted to support the president, and the Associated Students Senate revoked the BSU's charter.[22] The SDS chapter was pretty much the only organization to support the BSU action.

The white students from the SDS Election Day rally had joined in the occupation of the administration building, occupying the second floor—"a very un-militant demonstration," Mike Lee recalled; "we just sort of sat around." He decided to go up on the roof and speak to the crowd that had gathered outside the building, a thousand students who were trying to find out what was going on inside. He recalled leaving the building to go to the campus audio-visual office and check out a loudspeaker; then, he and SDS organizer Cliff Fried went back up on the roof and explained the BSU demand for a Black studies department. Right-wing students also checked out a PA system, and debated the issues with the SDSers on the roof. The whole time, Mike Lee later recalled, "we never knew they had any administrators" held hostage. The police assumed the white radicals from SDS were coordinating with the BSU, but "I couldn't figure out why the police kept telling us, 'If you let the people go, we'll let you go.'" Lee replied, "What do you mean, if we let the people go? Who are the people?" Two days later police arrested eight of the SDSers, including Cliff Fried and Mike Lee, and charged them with trespassing and disturbing the peace—misdemeanors.[23]

"We must have spent a hundred thousand dollars on bail" for the BSU students, Lee later recalled. Raising bail money was a big undertaking, with rallies and smaller private events; "I know we raised like five hundred dollars one night in Malibu at some rich peoples' house." A lot of people, he recalled, were bailed out by the LA Committee for the Defense of the Bill of Rights, an Old Left group organized in 1950 to defend immigrant radicals from deportation.[24]

Now, the SDS leaders were working full time—swept up in "the 'romanticism of combat,'" as Mike Lee later recalled, "when you know the enemy's stronger than you, and you know you can beat him."

> We were fanatics. We'd have a rally at noon and we'd go from two till twelve at night, going to neighborhood groups and speaking … From twelve till five in the morning, we'd print leaflets, then we'd get up at seven to hit the first 8:00 class. And this would go on, day after day after day … Sometimes we'd sleep on the floor of the Jericho House, the religious center where we'd print. When you're 19, 20, 21 years old, you can do that.[25]

Two weeks after the arrests, the BSU and SDS led 300 students in a march on the administration building demanding amnesty. That was front-page news in the *Times*: "Valley State Students March to Back Negroes."[26] Three weeks after the arrests, the BSU and SDS held another rally demanding amnesty. Eight hundred students heard speeches by Archie Chapman and Bill Burwell of the BSU and Cliff Fried of SDS, after which about half held a silent march on the administration building, led by the arrested students, who were symbolically chained together.[27]

Then on December 8, a Sunday, a fire gutted the office of the president. It looked like arson, but no one was charged. Right-wing students held their own rally two days later: the *Times* headline conveyed their message: "Students Warn of Militancy at Valley State; Continued Activity Could Destroy School, Bring Loss of Life, Speakers Declare." Larry Labovitz was identified as "head of a newly formed group opposing campus disruption," and was quoted saying, "We are sick and tired of being pushed around by a bunch of little militants on this campus. We want to get this element off the campus."[28]

The grand jury announced the unprecedented felony charges while students were off campus for Christmas break. Then President Blomgren was hospitalized, and replaced on January 7 by the vice president for academic affairs, Delmar Oviatt. The day after he took over as president, when students returned to campus after Christmas break, 500 students marched on the administration building, demanding to meet with him. The LAPD declared a tactical alert, massing their forces at the edge of the campus but not entering. The *Times* ran a big photo of "two bearded Negro students" knocking down a white student who "had tried to go to the aid of Larry Labovitz," the leader of the right-wingers.[29] The next day, January 8, there was another rally and march on the administration building, demanding amnesty. It had the support of Martin Luther King's SCLC; the group's LA representative, Reverend James Hargett, led the march. Outside the administration building, fifty cops beat back a crowd of a thousand student demonstrators trying to get in. Somebody broke a window, and the police arrested fourteen students, badly injuring one of them.[30]

The next morning the campus saw one of the most amazing demonstrations in LA history. At 7:00 a.m., Oviatt, who'd been acting president for all of two days, declared a "state of emergency" on campus and banned "all demonstrations, assemblies, rallies, and meetings."[31] Within two hours SDS and the BSU organized a rally to protest the ban, and between 2,000 and 3,000 students (figures from the *Times*) gathered in the campus free speech area. The police arrived, declared it an "illegal assembly," and ordered the students to disperse. When they didn't, the police began arresting students. Marc Cooper was one of them. He recalled that "the illegal assembly was completely peaceful. The students sat down. It's not like they were throwing rocks. So many people—it literally took hours to make all the arrests."[32] A total of 286 students and faculty were arrested that morning—the largest mass arrest in the history of campus protest in Southern California—for a completely peaceful act of civil disobedience. Those arrested included faculty members, among them English professor Richard Abcarian, and Warren Furumoto, a biologist. (MD was another one of those arrested; "What I remember most vividly about the arrests," he said forty-five years later, "was the ride to jail in a police bus. The girls started singing, 'Hey Jude, don't be afraid.' I fell in love with all of them.")[33]

While the 286 students and faculty were being charged at the courthouse with unlawful assembly or trespassing, the acting president met the press at noon to explain exactly what was wrong with students sitting peacefully in the free speech area. "He said he was told by police intelligence officers that militants had planned to have 1,500 persons from other schools converge on Valley State" that morning. The police told him the off-campus demonstrators "had been warned to wear heavy clothing and crash helmets," so that they could fight the police, and that "male demonstrators were urged to bring women and babies to the confrontation." "Questioned by newsmen," the *Times* reported, "Oviatt said he did not know the names of the individuals or the organizations that issued the call."[34]

The peaceful mass arrest was a triumph for SDS and the BSU, and a disaster for the school administration and the LAPD. "It was gigantic," Mike Lee recalled. "They'd lost control." Even Mayor Yorty said, "I wish the school had used its power of suspension instead of calling the police."[35]

The day after the mass arrests, the administration, desperate to recover from its self-inflicted wounds, revoked the ban on demonstrations and called in the head of the LA County Human Relations Coalition to lead negotiations over the BSU demands. The BSU and UMAS, the Mexican-American Student group, held a triumphant rally, second in size only to the one the day before. Twelve hundred students gathered to support the demands for African American studies and Chicano studies, many of whom had not participated before. One told the *Times*, "after I watched those arrests [the day before], I couldn't eat or sleep. I made up my mind that if there were any more demonstrations, I had to be in them." After speeches at the rally, the

BSU led a silent, single-file march to the administration building. The *Times* reporter was amazed at the discipline: "They were so quiet, the loudest noise was the sound of the campus police walkie-talkie radios." As they marched past the administration building, the students raised their fists and then quietly dispersed.[36]

Less than two weeks later, on January 23, the school announced the creation of a department of African American studies, and also a department of Mexican-American studies. A department rather than a program—that was crucial, because a department had its own budget and hired and promoted its own members, while a program consisted of faculty appointed by, and subject to, other departments. Moreover, the university pledged that the African American studies department would be "headed by a Negro," and that the Mexican-American studies department would be "headed by a Mexican-American."

Also announced was an increase in admission of 350 more Black students and 350 more Latinos "who cannot satisfy the usual academic or financial qualifications," who would get financial aid and academic tutoring. Finally, a faculty-student committee would be set up to "handle student complaints against faculty members." The *Times* called it "an agreement unique in American colleges and universities."[37] BSU leader Archie Chapman had a different view; asked by the *LA Times* if he was "satisfied" with the agreement, he replied, "Ask me in six months ... when I see those black and Chicano kids on this campus, I'll believe it."[38]

The faculty senate passed a resolution commending the leaders of the BSU and UMAS for their "seriousness, perseverance, and diligence." The president of the faculty senate declared that "the militancy of these students is the best thing that has happened to this campus."[39] Even now-president Oviatt, who had barred student assemblies, declared that he "never questioned their ability, their dedication, and the basic justice of their cause."[40] He resigned a few weeks later. As for the 1,730 felony charges against those serious and diligent students, the faculty senate voted down a resolution calling for amnesty but called on the DA to drop the kidnapping and conspiracy charges, on the grounds that they "seem unduly harsh in terms of the youth and level of awareness of the participants."[41]

The lesson was clear: to achieve a goal like the creation of a Black studies department, taking hostages was a bad idea. Nonviolent mass protest—several thousand people peacefully committing civil disobedience, facing arrest and jail to demonstrate the depth of their commitment—was an immensely powerful idea, even in a state where Reagan was governor, elected by campaigning against student activists and Black radicals; even in a city where Yorty was mayor and where the LAPD ruled; even in the whitest of white suburbs, where thirty-seven civic organizations, from the Kiwanis Clubs to the American Legion, had demanded harsh punishment for protest leaders.

The Trials

Then came the trials—weeks of trials for the 286 arrested sitting down in violation of the "state of emergency," and more weeks to adjudicate the hundreds of felony charges against the twenty-four BSU students involved in the occupation of the administration building. "The campus was in constant turmoil because of the trials," Marc Cooper recalled. Angela Davis spoke on campus, and 2,000 people showed up to hear her. Jane Fonda, Tom Hayden, Jerry Rubin, and William Kunstler spoke. SDS brought Mark Rudd, leader of the Columbia student movement.[42] The amnesty campaign won broad support among students: 3,000 signed a petition that read "All that they demanded has now been achieved through negotiation, yet their futures, their very lives, hang in senseless jeopardy."[43]

But outside the campus, right-wing politicians were in a fury. Mayor Yorty said the whole thing had been "masterminded, instigated and sponsored" by Communist front groups as a way to "promote urban violence and social turmoil." A week before the trials of the BSU students began, Reagan signed a bill that cut off financial aid for student demonstrators at the university and state colleges.[44]

The 286 students arrested in the mass protest in January were tried four at a time, and almost all of them either got the charges dismissed or won acquittals. The defense found an irrefutable technicality: the police order to disperse was prompted by the president declaring the student gathering "unlawful"—but the judges all ruled that the president "had no power in law to make such a declaration."[45]

The BSU trial began in September 1969. The NAACP took up the defense of the twenty-four students charged with seventy-two felonies each—one count of conspiracy, thirty-four of kidnapping, and thirty-seven of false imprisonment.[46] The defense emphasized that even in Mississippi and Alabama, Black students had never faced such massive legal penalties for campus activism. They sent some of their biggest legal guns to the courtroom in Van Nuys to face the prosecutor, Vincent Bugliosi (who would later gain fame for prosecuting the Manson Family and for writing the monster bestseller about the case, *Helter Skelter*). He told the court that the students had "gotten away with murder" and, if punished severely, "might think twice before doing it again." The NAACP attorneys persuaded the students to waive their right to a jury trial, over the objections of the more militant leaders. Their defense focused especially on rebutting the conspiracy charge. "If there was any conspiracy," NAACP attorney Morgan Moten told the judge, "it was a conspiracy of whites against blacks, to keep these kids from getting an equal education."[47] The trial made the national news, including in the *New York Times*, which informed readers that the "audience consisted mainly of … young Negroes with bushy Afro hairdos and defiant faces."[48]

The *LA Free Press* took a different tack, running a Monopoly-style board game on page one, "How to Play Valley State." Instead of Boardwalk and Park Place, you had "Open Forum," where "first 286 persons to land here go to jail," and "Student Protest in Progress," where "you have one turn to disperse." The big square in the corner, instead of "Jail," was "Selective Service." If you landed there, you rolled the dice again: "1—you receive a student deferment. 2—you go to basic training … 6—you are killed in action." Also, "females" who landed on "Selective Service" "must go to Wedding Day."[49]

The BSU trial lasted two months. In mid November, Judge Mark Brandler acquitted three students for lack of evidence, and found twenty of the remaining twenty-one guilty on at least some of the felony charges. Thirteen were found guilty of conspiracy and false imprisonment, and twelve of kidnapping.[50] The *LA Times* editorial page endorsed the verdicts.[51] Sentencing came in January 1970. Nine got probation, eight got jail terms of up to one year, and three leaders—Archie Chapman, Eddie Dancer and Robert Lewis ("Uwezo"), got one to twenty-five years. Protests against the verdicts came not only from the campus but also from the NAACP and the ACLU. More surprisingly, they also came from the Probation Officers Union, which criticized the judge for an "intemperate, one-sided and outrageous assault"—on the officers who had recommended probation for all defendants. The Probation Officers Union described the sentence as "harsh, politically motivated and a manifestation of the racism present in our society."[52]

The probation officers' protest turned out to be crucial. The NAACP appealed the sentences, and after the three BSU leaders had served three months of their twenty-five-year sentences, they were released by Superior Judge George M. Dell—who said he was acting on the original recommendations of the probation department. But in addition to five years' probation, each of the three were banned from returning to Valley State—a harsh punishment for people who had worked long and hard for a Black studies department, which was now about to become a reality.

There was one BSU leader who had not participated in the building occupation: Bill Burwell. He took a seat at the negotiating table after the mass arrest in January and was soon appointed associate chair of the new Pan-African studies department. He was only a junior at the time, but eventually pursued a doctorate and was appointed professor and chair of the department, which hired six other full-time faculty members.

"Some Call It Nationalism"

The most long-lasting result of the action at Valley State was also the most surprising: the campus developed the largest Chicano studies department in the nation. Fifty years later it was offering more than 166 sections per semester, taught by twenty-six full-time faculty members and forty-five part-time instructors.[53] (Black studies, which became Africana studies, had only ten faculty members fifty years later.) It's surprising because Northridge is not a center of Latino population in southern California—that would be East L.A., where, according to the 2010 census, 97 percent of the local population was Latino. (The Latino population of Northridge in 2010 was 14,000, 26 percent of the population.) It's also surprising because in 1968 and 1969, UMAS, the campus Latino group, played only a small role in the demonstrations, which were led by SDS and the BSU. They got a Chicano studies department without occupying any buildings, and without any felony charges or twenty-five-year jail sentences for their leaders.

Chicano studies at Valley State was the work of one person above all: Rudy Acuña. He was appointed in the spring of 1969 as the founding chair of the department. He had been born in L.A.'s Boyle Heights and had lived in the Valley for fourteen years; he had been active in community organizations there, first teaching at high schools and then developing a Mexican-American studies curriculum at Cal State Dominguez Hills in L.A.; and, most important, he had a PhD in Latin American studies from USC and a tenured position at Pierce, a community college not far from Valley State.[54]

His appointment was the result of organizing by UMAS, which participated in SDS's anti-war rallies, and, Acuña later wrote, had been radicalized by their involvement when the BSU occupied the administration building. UMAS, Acuña reports, was a group with thirty students, including a dozen "hard-core" leaders who "knew the limitations of the group and … did not get sucked into the craziness of the times."[55] Seven UMAS activists were part of the mass arrests of January 8, 1969, along with the UMAS faculty advisor, Warren Furumoto.

In the negotiations that followed the arrests, African American students moved to include UMAS, which was demanding the creation of a Chicano studies department parallel to the African American studies department. The demands included the appointment of a Chicano studies director that spring who could organize a department to begin teaching the following fall, and the admission of 500 Chicano students, with financial aid and academic support, that fall. UMAS was explicit in arguing that most of those students would not be "academically prepared," so the Mexican-American studies courses would have to teach them the basics of literacy and provide "the skills to survive in other courses."[56] That proposal immediately met opposition from the Spanish department, which placed an ad in the student newspaper opposing the recruitment of "unqualified" students—and everybody knew who they were talking about.[57] Professors in the Spanish department also "harassed the new department," arguing that the new department's courses were "reducing the quality of academic offerings" on campus, and challenging the nominations of candidates for faculty positions. Similar battles were going on across the state—at UCLA, Cal State LA, Cal State Fullerton and elsewhere—and Valley State students met their counterparts from other area campuses to compare notes and coordinate strategy. But the initial success of the program at Valley State, Acuña reports, came from the fact that the Black studies program took the lead, and administrators and faculty felt they couldn't reject similar proposals put forward by the Chicano studies department.[58]

When classes began in the fall of 1969, 252 new Chicano students had enrolled at Valley State, joining the forty-five who were already there.[59] This was the semester the felony trial of the BSU students was underway, and, according to Acuña, the BSU decided not to "expose its members to further attacks." That left the Chicano students in the lead among students of color, and they organized now as MEChA, "El Movimento Estudiantil Chicanos de Aztlán," more militant and more engaged, with new leadership consisting of two older activist students who had transferred from LA City College. MEChA now had a hundred students at meetings, ran an office, and joined faculty in interviewing candidates for the new faculty positions.[60]

Nixon's invasion of Cambodia and the Kent State killings on May 4 brought a crisis to campuses everywhere, including Valley State—and, it turned out, especially to the Chicano movement there. A national student strike was called, and once again SDS took the lead at Valley State. They organized a march on the administration building. Acuña says he "warned" the MEChA leaders to "be careful," and "to let the white student radicals be the shock troops."[61] He later recalled that some students moved to take down the American flag flying outside the administration building. But at the key moment, he reports, "the white students stepped back," and the Chicanos "rushed to the fore-front," took down the flag, and burned it. "I was furious," Acuña says. He knew what was coming: the police would arrest the leaders of the flag burning, right-wing politicians would have a field day, and then courtroom proceedings would dominate the campus for another semester. Acuña describes what happened next: "I warned students that the police investigators would be around and they should keep quiet. I had photos confiscated." When the police arrived with questions for him, he said, "No, MEChA was not involved!" They showed him photos of the flag burners, but he said he didn't know who they were. "They then proceeded to name the suspects. I chuckled. They were not even close. I realized that all Mexicans looked alike to them, and we should just deny, deny, deny. They never apprehended who did it."[62]

That day happened to be Cinco de Mayo, and after the police questioning ended, Acuña went to give a talk at a celebration on campus—which was interrupted by shocking news: "the Chicano House was on fire." Chicano House was a three-room building used by MEChA for meetings and events, and by the time Acuña and students arrived, it had been totally destroyed. Police arrested two Chicanas at the site, which further outraged students. The fire appeared to be arson, probably "the work of right-wing extremists" retaliating for the burning of the American flag earlier that day.[63] No one was ever charged with arson.

The next morning, SDS had called for another rally against the war and the Kent State killings, and in support of the national student strike. MEChA didn't join the anti-war rally; instead they organized their own silent march, protesting the burning of Chicano House. Forty-five years later Marc Cooper still remembered what happened that morning: "The rally was big. I was on the stage. Coming over the hill of the quad, I could see the entire Chicano studies department marching toward us—with a Zapata flag. They had been part of the strike. As they come toward the stage, everybody starts applauding. They keep going and they take over the stage." They announced they were withdrawing from the strike. The student newspaper quoted José Galván, president of MEChA, saying at the rally that "due to the destruction of our home, we must put all of our physical energies into this issue and not join any active strike."[64] Fifteen hundred students then marched on the administration building in support of the student strike[65]—but without the members of MEChA.

Rudy Acuña later explained MEChA's thinking: "There was a general uneasiness with the white leadership. The principal reason for Chicanos was that they did not believe enough attention was being given to the burning of the house." Thus, to protest the fire, "we called for the shutting down of the department [of Chicano Studies]. At the same time we went into the community to explain what was happening." The administration promptly gave them a different building for Chicano House, and they returned to focus exclusively on building the Chicano studies program. "One of our strengths," Acuña later said, "was that we were united—some call it nationalism."[66]

The Indefatigable Organizers

Why did it all happen at Valley State—the white school in the middle of conservative suburban nowhere? Politically, the western San Fernando Valley was not "nowhere"—it provided the voting base for conservative politics in LA County, politics that were becoming explicitly anti-Black. The same fall that Valley State BSU members were charged with hundreds of felonies, the first Black candidate for mayor was running—Tom Bradley—and, as we've seen, the right-wing incumbent Sam Yorty worked hard to mobilize his political base in the Valley. School desegregation was also being debated that year, and while the BSU students were on trial in 1970, Judge Alfred Gitelson was taking testimony that led to his ruling that L.A.'s board of education and school district had engaged in school segregation in violation of the state and federal constitutions. He ordered Los Angeles to desegregate its schools; the Valley became the political base of the opposition to the desegregation plan, as white politicians a few years later organized the anti-busing group BusStop Inc. The felony charges and guilty verdicts expressed the anti-Black political culture of the Valley.

And SDS at Valley State didn't come out of nowhere—a couple of experienced LA radicals organized the chapter and led its actions.[67]

Mike Klonsky, who helped start the chapter, was a red-diaper baby—his father had been not just a CP member but a member of the party's district committee in Southern California.[68] Cliff Fried was an active CP member and "an indefatigable organizer," according to Marc Cooper. "He was a little older than us," but was enrolled as a student. "Because he was in the Communist party," Cooper explained, "Cliff was our link to the whole rest of the world. That's how we all knew Dorothy Healey, who was very close to all of us. That's how we knew the Black Panthers. That's how Tom Hayden came to the campus. That's how Jane Fonda came to the campus. All of that in some way begins with Cliff, who was the liaison with the national movement."[69]

Another key to the strength of the white radicals in SDS, Mike Lee later argued, was that the Valley State chapter was nonsectarian and did not get torn apart by the faction fighting that crippled SDS chapters elsewhere—battles between the Progressive Labor faction of disciplined Maoists and New Left SDSers, fights about organizing workers versus students, between opponents of the counterculture and participants in it, and between defenders of "base building" and advocates of "revolution."[70] It also seemed like Valley State SDS "had more than its share of talented leadership-type people," Mike Lee argued—"forty people, who were very politically aware, had skills, could write, could speak, had connections." As a result, when Mike Lee and Cliff Fried were arrested after the election day building occupation, "it made no difference whatsoever" to the functioning of the group, "because Marc Cooper and other people just kept at it the next day."[71]

Nor did the BSU come out of nowhere. The San Fernando Valley had its own Black ghetto—Pacoima—where varieties of Sixties Black radical politics flourished.[72] Bill Burwell, one of four founders of the BSU in fall of 1967, was from Pacoima, and already "a seasoned activist" when he arrived on campus—he had led a Black nationalist organization called Afro-Pac (short for "Afro-Pacoima"), which rejected integration. Robert Lewis, a baseball player who would later be featured in *Life* magazine as the Black student leader "Uwezo," was another Pacoima kid who had been recruited by Ron Karenga's US Organization in 1965 while he was a high school student. "They came to Pacoima," he later recalled, and "I had never heard anybody talk like that against the white man, and the symbols of white culture—like Christianity—and get away with it." He split with Karenga in 1967 ("for reasons I don't want to go into") and formed his own group in Pacoima, which he called House of Umoja. Police harassment led him to shut down the group, he said, and he went to Valley State in 1968.[73]

Racism in college sports—the spark that set off the BSU building occupation and hostage taking—had become a big issue starting in 1967, especially in California, when Harry Edwards and student athletes at San Jose State forced the cancellation of the opening day football game. Protests spread to thirty-seven other schools in 1968, which Edwards called "the revolt of the Black athlete."[74] Of course, the protests culminated at the Mexico City Olympics that fall, when San Jose State students Tommie Smith and John Carlos gave the Black power salute on the medal podium. That was October 16, 1968—the BSU at Valley State occupied the administration building in a protest over racism in the Athletic department less than three weeks later. Archie Chapman, one of the four BSU founders at Valley State, was a student athlete who quit the football team and became "a vocal critic of the exploitation of black student-athletes."[75]

It also helped the movement at Valley State that two days after their occupation of the administration building, the San Francisco State student strike began, also in pursuit of a Black studies program—and that battle set new standards of militancy (and also of official repression). However remote and isolated Valley State might have been from the centers of activism, they knew they were part of the vanguard of something much bigger—a feeling that was confirmed when Governor Reagan denounced student radicals at both campuses. The connections were more than abstract—Valley State activists like Chapman visited San Francisco State.

The Black student activists at Valley State, and elsewhere, demanded a Black studies department not only for their own education but as a place to learn skills they could "bring back" to the Black community —in particular, Pacoima. The Black "ethos of community service and racial uplift," Martha Biondi points out, is "deeply rooted in the historical formation of the African American middle class," where "the responsibility to stay engaged in a struggle for social justice is a life-long commitment."[76] Their demand was not just for faculty members and classes but also for admission of many more Black students from Pacoima, including those lacking the required test scores and financial resources, with the school providing tutoring and financial aid.

While SDS continued its anti-war campus campaign, the BSU at Valley State took a radically different path, as Black activism on campus came to an abrupt end. Three of the top four leaders of the BSU were banned from the campus, and the fourth—Bill Burwell—went to work creating the African American studies department. Even the *Times* noticed, reporting ten years later, that on the one hand, the Black studies academic program became a success, the largest in the state university system in terms of student enrollment. But "the original goal" had "faded": "a collective effort in which students would gain academic training and then put it to use in a variety of social projects and movements in the black communities of Pacoima and Los Angeles," The reason, according to the *Times*, was that "so much effort went into surviving—into meeting the academic requirements of CSUN and making compromises to convince the university's academic estab-lishment of the department's legitimacy."[77]

Meanwhile Chapman, who had been banned from the campus for his role in the building occupation, had changed his name to Adewole Umoja. Along with Robert Lewis, *Life* magazine's "Uwezo," and another founder of the BSU, the three abandoned the organi-zation in the early 1970s and flew to Guyana, the English-speaking former colony in South America where socialist Cheddi Jagan led the opposition to a US-backed post-independence regime. The three returned after a few years, and in 1979 Umoja was working in L.A. on a campaign to get the United Nations to charge the United States with genocide against Black people.[78] The Chicano movement took a different course; the large and successful department established under the leadership of Rudy Acuña produced lots of community leaders and high school teachers, along with some professionals, elected officials, and journalists.[79]

The end of the Valley State uprising dramatized the differences between white radicals and the Black and Chicano movements there.

For a couple of years, the three groups fought side by side against the war, and for ethnic studies departments. But the utter incompetence of the school's administration in the face of radical protest, and the unprecedented and awesome mass civil disobedience on January 9, 1969—the 286 arrests—brought victory in unanticipated form. The school administration capitulated completely on the ethnic studies demands—and, for different reasons, both the BSU and MEChA withdrew from the anti-war struggle to focus exclusively on building new academic programs. For the Black students, that was at least partly because the BSUs' radical leadership had been traumatized and crippled by the felony trials and by being banned from campus as a condition of parole. For the Chicanos, it was the trauma of the fire at Chicano House on May 5 that led to the ill-conceived split from SDS.

The white radicals of SDS were shocked at what they regarded as the sellout by their former allies—most of whom, it turned out, didn't share the SDS goal of transforming the system; instead, they wanted a share of the benefits of the system, which they had never had—a college education that served the needs of their communities. SDS called this "co-optation"; liberals called it "inclusion." So Bill Burwell accepted a faculty position in the new Pan-African studies department, Rudy Acuña turned the Chicano studies department into a national model, and Marc Cooper went off to Chile—to work with Allende on the socialist transformation of South America's oldest democracy.

30

The Battle for the Last Poor Beach: Venice (1969)

July 4, 1969, was a day of festive parades and picnics across Southern California: Pacific Palisades had its annual "Americanism" parade, the West Covina parade had two Vietnam vets for its grand marshals, and Claremont had an "Old Tyme Parade." But not Venice: the LAPD rejected the application for a permit for a July 4 parade down the boardwalk (officially "Ocean Front Walk"), and when it seemed like people might parade there anyway, the city mobilized a massive force to block them. It was probably the largest LAPD deployment since the anti-war protest in Century City: hundreds of cops—maybe 500 or 600—occupied the entire parade route on the boardwalk. The police had run many sweeps in Venice over the previous few years, but this was an unprecedented operation, involving police boats, helicopters, a command post, and preparations to arrest and hold hundreds of people.

What the police wanted so badly to stop was an Independence Day parade led by the Free Venice Organizing Committee. Organized in opposition to the redevelopment of Venice, the parade was to end at the Venice Pavilion, on the beach, with the reading of a "Declaration of Free Venice" seeking the secession of Venice from the City of L.A.

Venice in the Sixties was legendary, known for its bohemian past, its countercultural present, its boardwalk lined with booths selling candles and sandals, its buskers and drum circles and nude swimming, its weight lifters at Muscle Beach, and, in the blocks behind the beach, its little old houses occupied by aging beatniks, aspiring artists, elderly Jews, left-wing activists, Black families who had been there since the twenties—and of course, those pot-smoking hippies. All of them were people with no money, and all were threatened by gentrification—Venice was, in the words of writer Carolyn See, "the last poor beach."[1]

The city and the developers wanted to move them out. The vision of redevelopment proposed by L.A.'s Department of City Planning was chilling: raze all of Venice Beach, and rebuild it along the lines of Miami Beach, or Waikiki, with luxury high-rise condos and resorts and upscale shopping.[2] Under the plan, the new beach would be connected to the rest of the city by two new freeways, ripping the heart out of Venice's old residential neighborhoods.

Redevelopment of Venice would complete the upscaling of the entire coast from Palos Verdes to Malibu. Just north of Venice, Santa Monica had bulldozed, in 1966, several blocks of what it called "deteriorated but charming" seashore houses, and put up two 17-story luxury apartment buildings, called "Santa Monica Shores," completely alien to their surroundings—with six tennis courts, a twenty-five-meter lap pool and a twenty-four-hour concierge. Immediately to the south of Venice was the massive new yacht harbor and real estate development the city dedicated in 1965 as Marina del Rey—radio comedians Bob and Ray called it "Marina del Diablo." There, the city turned wetlands along Ballona Creek into what was billed as "the world's largest man-made small craft harbor," home port to 6,500 boats and a population of almost 9,000 in new apartments next to the docks, along with hotels, office complexes, seafood restaurants, and the Fisherman's Village shopping center (where no fisherman lived or worked). The city also built the Marina Freeway to connect the development to the city's freeway system. LA planners and the department of highways had two additional freeways on the table. The "Venice Freeway," which had been on planning maps since the Fifties, connecting the San Diego Freeway with the beach, would run along Venice Boulevard; and a new "Coast Freeway," with a route to be determined.[3] In one proposal, it would start at the terminus of the Santa Monica Freeway, rip through the heart of Venice, and then run down Lincoln Boulevard, seven blocks in from the beach, to the marina. But there were bigger and wilder ideas: one was to build the Coast Freeway directly on top of the beach and the boardwalk in Venice, and then haul in tons of sand to build a new beach on the bay side of the new freeway. And the wildest of all plans called for putting the new Coast Freeway on an offshore causeway running across Santa Monica Bay.[4] If you could do it in the Florida Keys, why not in Venice?

De-Annexation and Dancing

The Free Venice Organizing Committee set out to stop all of that —the freeways, the high-rises, the luxury shopping, the bulldozers. They had two strategies for blocking the developers: first, stop the city planning commission from adopting the new master plan; then, secede from L.A. Venice had once been an independent city, a dream-scape of canals, gondolas, and amusements developed by the wealthy tobacco heir Abbot Kinney. But this "Coney Island of the Pacific," with a population that added 90,000 visitors to 10,000 residents every summer weekend, was plagued by poor civic management, unpaved streets, and insufficient water resources. In 1925, after a long campaign, residents voted to join the City of Los Angeles, and annexation was consummated the following year. Residents' desire for a middle-class city, however, was frustrated for almost half a century by the oil boom that began in 1927, polluting the canals and turning what is now called the "Marina District" into a forest of oil rigs. Free Venice's proposed "De-Annexation" would face powerful opposition, but it was legally possible if a majority of residents voted in favor. Organizers planned to kick off their campaign with the Independence Day Parade and the reading of their "Declaration of Free Venice."

Free Venice was the logical offspring of a vibrant neighborhood political culture. John Haag, publisher and editor of the *Free Venice Beachhead*, explained that their vision went beyond stopping the bulldozers:

Would you believe dancing in our Venice streets? Non-violent police? An art festival the length of Ocean Front Walk? A Venice radio station? Cooperative, low-cost housing? An art cinema and sidewalk coffee house? Experimental theater in the Pavilion? Schools that could teach what the kids wanted to learn? Venice planned and run by the people in it?

Haag then pointed to some of the problems:

> Venice poets don't read in the Pavilion since their poems must first be approved by the Los Angeles Board of Recreation and Paris. Venice teen-agers don't dance in the streets because their dances must be permitted in advance by the Los Angeles Police Department. We don't plan our own community because plans are made for us by the Los Angeles Department of City Planning. And we don't even get to vote on their plans![5]

Haag had been a Venice activist since the Fifties, when he ran the Venice West Café, the center of the beat poetry scene and a frequent target for police harassment. After working with CORE and the ACLU in Venice, he went on to found the *Beachhead* in 1968, and then the Venice Peace and Freedom Party.[6] "Three times this year," Haag reported in 1968, "the Los Angeles police have told me and a lot of my friends, 'If you want to stay out of jail, you better get out of Venice.'" But, he said, "I choose to stay in Venice. I will fight for my home. So will a lot of my friends ... They haven't convinced us to get out of Venice. Rather, they have convinced us to get Venice out of Los Angeles."[7]

At the hearing for the parade permit a few weeks earlier, Free Venice organizers explained that it would be a festive march, with "children, flags, and balloons." They said they expected around 700 people. The police commissioners then called on their own speakers, who said that they expected 30,000 people at the beach, because another group was promising free food, and that the parade would make it impossible to get emergency vehicles down to the beach. What if one of the old Jews had a heart attack on the Fourth of July? The parade organizers replied that they would comply with all traffic requirements. The head commissioner asked the Free Venice spokesperson Rick Davidson if it was true, as reported in the *Beachhead*, that a celebration would be held along the parade route even if the permit were not granted. He replied that "that was true." The police commission voted unanimously to reject the application.[8]

The "Declaration of Free Venice" that the police prohibited from being read began: "When one section of a city proposes to break off from the whole and assert its right to self-government, it is only reasonable that the causes be stated clearly." The list of grievances was, like the 1776 document, long and detailed: The department of building and safety had required "the demolition of usable buildings, the dislocation of hundreds of residents, and prevented the development of local enterprises." The assessor's office had "collaborated with absentee land speculators and profiteering realtors." The department of parks was "planning to limit assembly and speech in the only public areas available for such use." When they went to the city council to protest, a participant reported, "over 200 of us were locked out of the Council Chamber." And most of all, the declaration complained about the police: they had "terrorized our community, breaking into our homes, confiscating our property, harassing and arresting residents without justification, beating residents on the streets and in the jail, and denying us use of public places for peaceful assembly."[9] That was why 2,200 Venice residents had petitioned the planning commission to reject the proposed Master Plan for Venice, and to allow Venice residents to "create our own plan for our own community and to hold its hearings in Venice at hours convenient to working people."

After the parade permit was denied, and the plans for a major police mobilization at the beach became clear, Free Venice made a painful decision: the parade would be canceled, and instead a silent vigil would be held outside the Venice police headquarters, several blocks from the beach and the festivities. The decision was explained in a leaflet headlined, "Free Venice Warns of Violence July 4," distributed widely on July 3: "The police began predicting a riot on Venice Beach weeks ago. We know of no instance where the police have prepared for a riot without producing one." The silent vigil at the Venice City Hall "will express our sadness at intimidation against a community whose special character includes tolerance and non-violent customs." The leaflet concluded by reiterating the goal of "separating ourselves from the tyranny imposed on us by outsiders," and living in an independent city where "the savagery of the Los Angeles police is only a bitter memory."[10]

Hundreds of police nevertheless patrolled the beachfront on July 4 and arrested a total of sixty-one people, with most of the arrests coming after the TV cameras had left at 10 p.m. An eyewitness reported:

> 10:15 pm: A young couple is walking up Ocean Front Walk, seemingly engrossed in each other. A cop approaches from behind and shouts, "get moving!" The young man turns to question. The cop grabs him by the neck and shoves, yelling "Move!" The young man turns around again and is thrown to the ground and handcuffed. His girl runs at the officer screaming, "turn him loose! He hasn't done anything!" A police car backs up, an officer jumps out and grabs the girl in a painful wristlock. A second offer puts her other arm in a wristlock, even though she is making no effort to resist. Screaming in pain, she is led to the waiting [police] bus … An old lady of about 70 walks by, shaking her first at the police cars, shouting, "Gestapo! Gestapo! This time I fight!" The cops glower, but do not stop her.[11]

July 4 was hardly the biggest LAPD action at the beach. Sunday, April 20, 1969, was one of the big ones: the day of the *Free Press* birthday party and free concert. Fifteen thousand people showed up for what the *Freep* described as "six good rock groups playing free sets on a free public beach on an equally free and beautiful Sunday afternoon." In the *Beachhead*, Carol Fondiller described what she saw:

> An old man tells me to dance because young people should dance. "I can't dance any more now, but when I was young …" His old lips smile. Families go by with picnic baskets and children play with dogs.
>
> Four o'clock. Men with rifles appear on the roofs of apartment houses. The lazy sun-filled crowd is ordered to disperse by the police—who come in with their clubs. The crowd starts running up the Ocean Front Walk, followed by officers. Some of the crowd try to run up the alleyways. They are blocked off by police. "But we

were told to disperse ..." Hands are pulled into handcuffs. "What did I do?" Waiting paddy wagons are jammed ... Sirens, screams, curses, children crying.

Six o'clock. The beach is in suspended animation between sunset and dark. A chill wind curdles the hurriedly dropped objects on the beach. A lifeguard truck drives down the beach, its loudspeakers blaring: "the lifeguards love everyone! Free Venice!"[12]

One hundred seventeen people were arrested that Sunday. The police told the *Times* there had been a "rock and bottle throwing melee" in which three officers received "minor injuries."[13] The *Santa Monica Evening Outlook* headline was "Police Scatter 14,000, Thwart Venice 'Orgy.'"

The problem, apparently, started not around the bandstand, but down on the beach, 500 feet from the boardwalk. There, according to the *Freep*, a lifeguard got into an altercation with a young man, and a few police officers "ran down to the scene" and beat the guy "pretty badly." People who were nearby "didn't like what they saw and in one glorious moment of supreme idiocy, someone threw a bottle and hit one of the cops."

The next day community activists organized a bail fund, and the ACLU, the public defender's office, and Neighborhood Legal Services went to work defending those who had been arrested. When Rick Davidson of Free Venice drove through the beachfront area with a bullhorn announcing that people with complaints about police violence should go to Neighborhood Legal Services, he was arrested and then beaten at the Venice jail—but an immediate response by community activists resulted in Rick's release three hours after his arrest. The police didn't stop; for a week after that Sunday attack, the *Beachhead* reported, "16 'units' of the notorious Metro Squad occupied our community." They beat and arrested people daily.[14]

A petition was then circulated among the old people who lived at the beach to "get rid of the *Free Press* types and the hippies"—it wasn't clear who was behind it. There had been some friction over the years, especially when people at the Israel Levin Senior Adult Center complained about the noise from a nearby drum circle. The *Beachhead* published an "Open Letter to the People of Venice," signed by "Yitzak Gershman," about the petition: "I have seen this before," it began.

> The American police on the beach are not yet Nazis but the story is the same. They want to eliminate undesirables so that "better people" can live in their place ... Do you think these anti-Semite cops care about you? Don't sign their petition to get rid of the young people. Better you should sign a petition that the police behave like Americans and stop acting like the Nazi beasts of Europe.[15]

People over Property

The Free Venice campaign tried to focus not just on the police but on the big picture, which meant on the work of the LA Planning Commission. At the climactic hearing and vote on the Venice Master Plan, in May, Free Venice brought 200 people downtown to City Hall—"homeowners and renters, businessmen and clergy, Black, Mexican and white." Thirty-seven of them spoke in a four-hour meeting. The speakers included Reverend Oliver B. Garver Jr. of the Westside Episcopal Clergy Task Force, who said that "the plan doesn't give priority to the needs of the people over the needs of property." Abe Osheroff, a Spanish Civil War vet and lifelong activist, said the city plan "benefits mainly those who don't live in Venice—the real estate agents and absentee landlords." Don Wright, leader of the Venice Education Cadre, called the plan "another case of genocide against Black people." And Haag declared that the people would "stop your plan by any means necessary."

Free Venice accomplished several important things at that meeting: they got the commissioners to delete from the city plan any reference to a new freeway. They stopped the plan for rezoning Oakwood, where Blacks had lived since the 1920s, which would have reduced the Black population there. They got the commissioners to agree not to pave any of the beach for parking lots. But on the big issue—letting the community develop its own plan—the commissioners turned them down. Then, they voted unanimously for the remaining portions of the Master Plan.[16]

The Roundups in Oakwood

Black Venice had its own battles with the police. In Oakwood in the Sixties, many people belonged to families that had been there for forty years. Oakwood was a "Black ghetto," and commentators thought it looked something like Watts—tiny old houses rather than tenement apartments. The developers considered the very existence of an Oakwood to be an affront to real estate values: Why should poor Black people get to live near the beach? And like the young people of Watts, the young people of Oakwood were hassled regularly by the LAPD. There was the night of July 25, 1969, when police raided a dance at St. Mark's Center, a Catholic church and parochial school, and arrested forty young Black people—along with twenty-five other young people arrested the same night elsewhere in Venice. Some were released; the rest were charged with curfew violations, drunkenness, narcotics possession, and violations of the open bottle law.

Later that week, 120 people—the *Times* described them as "angry residents" and "minorities"—met with police officials to protest the harassment of young people and submitted a petition demanding "a psychiatric examination of Lt. Richard Tackaberry, Venice Night Watch commander, to determine his competence as a police officer"— the one who had declared the "unlawful assembly" at the *Freep*'s free concert. They also called for "a full and immediate investigation of conditions between police and the Venice community." Leading that protest were Bob Castile, director of the Venice Community Improvement Union (VCIU); and Vermont McKinney, director of Community Activity Aides. The Venice police commander told the *Times* there would "be no changes made in law enforcement policies in the Venice Division" as a result of the meeting.[17]

The police in Venice were brazen in their treatment not only of young Black people but also of Black community leaders. A "roundup of suspected narcotics peddlers" early in December led to the arrest of forty-four people on drug charges—and twenty others "incidental to the roundup." The twenty, it turned out, included many community leaders who had been trying to monitor the police sweep of their neighborhood. They included the director of the Community Activity Aides, a youth program; the director of the Neighborhood Youth

Association; and the education director of the Venice Community Improvement Union, funded by the federal anti-poverty program. When word of the arrests got out, a crowd gathered outside the jail. "Is this the way you do community relations?" a local political figure asked. The police captain for the Venice Division, Robert Sillings, replied "Yeah. We put people in jail."[18]

The complaints were then investigated by the Community Relations Conference of Southern California, which consisted of representatives of ninety religious, labor and civic organizations. They found "shocking and inexcusable" police conduct. Officers "stopped and frisked persons at random on the streets, invaded homes without warrants, harassed community workers, used abusive racial epithets and, in one instance, used excessive force." The entire raid was a case of "terrorization and intimidation of the Black residents of Venice." The committee recommended investigation by the county grand jury and the US Attorney's office. Five months later, the LAPD announced the results of its own internal investigation, and nine cops were "temporarily suspended or lost days off" as punishment for "misconduct" in the December sweep. Most notable: Captain Robert Sillings, long a subject of complaints, was suspended for eleven working days.[19]

Another measure of the LAPD's performance in Oakwood came from the ACLU's "West Side Police Practice Complaint Center" in the Oakwood Wesley House. Between 1966 and 1969 they filed one hundred complaints against the LAPD on behalf of Oakwood people. Not one was upheld.[20] And sometimes the ACLU went beyond filing complaints. In November 1968, they filed suit in federal district court on behalf of twenty-two Black men, including two from Venice, against LA Police Chief Tom Reddin for a systematic pattern of harassment and intimidation. The two Venice men included a member of the local community patrol. He had been stopped in his car and surrounded by four officers with guns drawn, who said they would shoot him and his five passengers—all Black—if any guns were found in the car.[21]

Oakwood had been peaceful during the Watts uprising, and the federal funding that flowed into L.A. under the post-Watts War on Poverty included Oakwood among the beneficiaries. OEO-funded projects in Oakwood included, in 1968, a citizen street patrol; unarmed, the eight young Blacks were called "the Organizers." As the project director explained: "We decided to do what the Police Department wasn't doing. And that is to have Black people tending to Black people's problems." The police, of course, had what the *Times* called "an unhappy feeling" about "an unofficial police force, beyond police direction or control," and three of the eight had "brushes with the law after the project began—some serious."[22]

Bob Castile was a key leader defending Oakwood from both the police and the developers. He was director of the Oakwood Wesley House, supported by the Methodist Church, which served as the center of much of the organizing in Oakwood. "The tiny four-room house bristles with signs," Carolyn See explained after a visit.[23] The front bedroom was the office and meeting space for twenty workers for VISTA, the "domestic Peace Corps." The back bedroom was the ACLU Police Malpractice Complaint Center. And the VCIU had a space—the organization explained that it had been motivated by "the belief that Venice can be saved for the poor people who live there." All but one of the group's twenty-five-man multiracial staff lived in Venice. Governor Reagan didn't like any of it—he tried to get Bob Castile fired as director of the VCIU when the poverty program in Washington approved a grant of $183,000 to the organization to build new low-cost housing under local control. The feds rejected Reagan's complaint.[24]

The Tucson Five

One more thing: in 1971 the FBI thought there were "Weathermen all over Venice." That's what bureau agent Wesley Swearingen told his superiors during the period when members of the Weather Underground were on the FBI's Ten Most Wanted list.[25] Indeed, Venice was the kind of place where windows would display posters reading "Angela Davis: Sister You Are Welcome in This House" while she was underground. The Internal Security Division of the Department of Justice brought six people before a grand jury in Tucson in October 1970, whom they suspected of harboring Weather Underground leader Bernardine Dohrn. Five of the six lived in Venice in a commune at 2201 Ocean Front Walk.

The FBI was interested in them because one of the five, Terri Volpin, a local activist and contributor to the *Beachhead*,[26] had loaned her car to a guy named John Fuerst, who drove it from Venice to Arizona to buy dynamite, which the Justice Department thought might have been used in an amateurish bombing of a National Guard armory in Santa Barbara. But it's not a crime to buy dynamite in Arizona. The "Tucson Five," as they came to be known, "knew nothing of the whereabouts of the Weatherman underground support people or the Weatherman fugitives," Wes Swearingen later declared.[27] All took the Fifth Amendment—at which point the prosecutor, Guy Goodwin, granted them immunity, and started in again. A typical question from Goodwin was

> Tell the grand jury what period of time you resided at 2201 Ocean Front Walk, who resided there at the times you lived there, identifying all persons you have seen in or about the premises, and tell the grand jury all of the conversations that were held by you or others in your presence during the time that you were at 2201 Ocean Front Walk.[28]

The five believed that nobody should be required to tell the government about all the conversations they had while they lived in a particular place—so they all continued to refuse to answer.

Under federal law, refusing to testify after receiving immunity is a crime—"civil contempt"—and the punishment is imprisonment for the life of the grand jury. So despite the best efforts of Bar Sinister, the left-wing legal collective that defended them—including Ken Cloke, Barry and Paula Litt, and Karen Jo Koonan—all five went to prison for the next four months. In the end the grand jury's term expired without any of them being charged with a crime—because, as Swearingen explained, "it is not a crime to live in a house in Venice, California."[29] Nevertheless, when they were released from prison, "federal marshals met them at the jail door with subpoenas to appear at a new grand jury."[30]

The FBI began breaking into the houses in Venice of people connected to the Tucson Five, looking for traces of the Weathermen. Swearingen was "ordered ... to do a black bag job" on activists Robert

Gottlieb and Susan Sutheim, at their house one block from the beach, "without bureau approval." They also broke into the offices of Ken Cloke, the National Lawyers Guild attorney. They also did black bag jobs on the law offices in L.A. of Barry Litt, of Bar Sinister, and of attorney Leslie Abramson.[31] Despite all its efforts in Venice, Swearingen reported, the FBI found "nothing about any of the Weatherman underground support people or the Weatherman fugitives."[32]

The Canals Festival

Once in a while the police did not show up for a gathering, and people got a glimpse of an alternative Venice, free of LAPD harassment and violence. One such day was the first Venice Canals Festival, in the fall of 1969. The canals had been part of the original Venice real estate development, creating a unique and wonderful neighborhood, which like everything else in Venice had been left alone by the developers for decades but rediscovered in the Sixties. The redevelopment people wanted to raise taxes, upgrade the canals, and drive out the residents, replacing them and their little houses with something more upscale and trendy. Free Venice fought it, but the city assessor agreed to create a special Canals assessment district to raise taxes to pay for redevelopment. The Canals Festival was planned as "a funeral dirge." But both sides were surprised when no one bid on the redevelopment project—so the unimproved canals and their old houses and existing residents would remain, at least for the time being. The festival turned into "a tremendous celebration"—on a Saturday afternoon and evening in September—and most surprising of all, the *Beachhead* reported, was "the pleasing lack of Law Enforcement Officers."

Along the Grand Canal a dozen artists set up exhibits, including sculptor Claire Falkenstein and painter Billy Al Bengston; others exhibited stained glass and photos, while still others offered body painting, astrology readings, clothing, and leather goods—along with "a spontaneous mural by the children from the Nightingale school." Poets from Beyond Baroque, the newly founded arts center, read their work; boat rides down the canal were provided for the kids; and the Song of Earth Chorale sang from a barge—a "singularly ethereal experience." The Venice Library showed slides, and, after sunset, Newsreel, a group of left-wing documentary filmmakers, showed films.

In the nighttime finale, the Grand Canal was lined with flares on both sides, and a barge set off down the canal between the flares with festival organizers on board, all singing. "However, too many people got on the barge," the *Beachhead* reported, and it began to tilt and sink.

> In the end, one long-haired, long-bearded freak stumbled back and forth on the floating edge of the barge, waving a flare, while the dry ice at the other end sank into the water and billows of mist boiled out into the night air. The barge drifted in circles but remained afloat. All the participants, artists and visitors, seemed to have a marvelously gay time ... Altogether the first Venice Canal Festival was a fantastic success.[33]

The most surprising movement victory in Venice during this period was the prevention of the redevelopment of Oakwood. This was accomplished largely under the leadership of Bob Castile, who managed, through nonprofit Project Action, to get federal Section 8 funding in the early Seventies to build fourteen buildings of subsidized low-income housing. The first eight buildings, with 176 units, were all rented to Black residents of Oakwood. Part of the genius here was building many smaller buildings scattered around Oakwood, instead of putting them all together in the traditional housing project style.[34] If they had done that, the rest of Oakwood could have been bulldozed. Smaller low-income rental units spread around the neighborhood discouraged the developers from going after the rest and preserved Oakwood as a Black community.

Although the Venice secession campaign eventually failed, local mobilization succeeded at stopping the new freeways forever, blocking the developers for decades to come. The boardwalk remained basically unchanged through the Seventies—a place of longhairs, buskers, young people of color, and booths selling those candles and sandals. The little houses of Venice would be upgraded but (mostly) not razed. Venice remained, as one writer put it, "L.A.'s democratic libido."[35]

31

Generation Chicano:
Aztlán versus Vietnam (1969)

On April 24, 1969, Governor Reagan was speaking at a banquet at the Biltmore in downtown L.A. when nine fires broke out in rapid succession in the hotel's linen closets and bathrooms. Although the small blazes were quickly extinguished, thanks to an earlier warning from an undercover LAPD officer, it provided DA Evelle Younger with dramatic confirmation of his frequent claim that the Chicano movement was infiltrated by terrorists and Communists. The grand jury soon authorized the arrest of ten young men, mostly Brown Beret members, including Carlos Montes, the group's minister of information, but also Moctezuma Esparza, the UCLA student and future filmmaker who had played a key role in the Blowouts the previous March. Montes and Esparza were also defendants in the "LA Thirteen" case, and now, if convicted in both, faced a possible lifetime in prison. When four of the ten were separated for trial on lesser counts, the defendants were winnowed down to the "Biltmore Six," a case that dragged on for years and, as intended by Younger, consumed immeasurable time and resources from the Berets and the larger defense movement. Montes, who had fled to Mexico, was not captured until 1980, but like all the other defendants, he was eventually exonerated by a jury.[1] The original defense attorney, the flamboyant author-lawyer Oscar Acosta, had successfully undermined the image of the LAPD plant, Fernando Sumaya, as a "hero" (the term the *Times* used repeatedly), convincing two juries that he was an agent provocateur who had solicited various crimes and probably set most of the Biltmore fires himself.[2] In many respects, the case prefigured the vastly larger "conspiracy" that police and sheriffs would orchestrate to delegitimize Chicano activists after the Chicano Moratorium in late August 1970.

But if the atmosphere of repression was steadily darkening, 1969 was also a luminous turning point for young Mexican-Americans. It was the year that a generation, largely native-born, redefined themselves as "Chicanas/os," with epic consequences.

Dialectics of Identity

In his memoir, Bert Corona recalled a conference in 1958 that brought local leaders and organizers from all over the Southwest together to launch a new coordinated political organization. There was general accord on purpose and electoral stategy, but the delegates unexpectedly deadlocked over identity. "The Texans wanted 'Latin American,' the New Mexicans wanted 'Spanish-speaking,' the Arizonans wanted 'Hispanic' or 'Latin American,' the Coloradans wanted 'Hispanic,' and we in California wanted 'Mexican,'" he recalled. Without a consensual name on the bow, the ship couldn't be launched. Two years later Corona and the other organizers gave it a second try. In Fresno the majority successfully compromised on the name "Mexican American Political Association" (MAPA). "The name 'Mexican' *had* to be included," he said. "It was important for the Mexican community to recognize itself. If we didn't recognize ourselves and instead shied away from using our name in order to be more acceptable to Anglos, we would be giving in to all the discrimination and belittling that had characterized our political experience."[3]

"Chicana/o," in contrast, was rapidly embraced, usually with alacrity, by youth across the Southwest and in urban barrios. Its etymology was unclear, but its informal "rude" usage incontestably dated back decades if not generations. But what new meanings did its popularity imply? By the beginning of 1969 an informal consensus was emerging around four general principles. First, the new activists, while honoring the older generation's fight for first-class citizenship, rejected cultural assimilation and sociopolitical integration as movement goals. In their experience, integration had failed, and voting rights had been subverted by gerrymandering. Community control and self-determination were their demands, and "revolution" was abstractly the pathway. Second, they rejected "whiteness" and proudly accentuated the *indio* component of their *mestizo* ancestry. Whereas many of their elders had fought tooth and nail against being racialized as nonwhite, Chicanas/os envisioned themselves as an indigenous people, a brown race.[4] Third, the preference for "Chicana/o" expressed a populist identification with struggles of working-class and poor people as incarnated by the UFW and symbolized by the figures of Zapata and the Adelitas (revolutionary women soldiers). Fourth, while borrowing heroes and symbols from the Mexican Revolution, many considered the greater Southwest as their authentic homeland, rather than the Mexican nation-state. In the case of the Los Angeles movement, the active cadre were almost entirely native born, and surprisingly few spoke Spanish fluently, so their nationalism was diasporic in conception. Long caricatured as *pochos* (a derogatory term for supposedly deracinated border-dwellers) by Mexican intellectuals, Chicanas/os had marginal interest in Mexican politics per se and until the 1970s had little or no contact with the Mexican Left—a relationship, in contrast, that had been very important to the Mexican-American movements of the 1930s and 1940s.[5]

There is no doubt that the evolution of chicanismo was influenced by the template of Black nationalism. Karenga, in particular, had spoken at La Piranya, and at several protests, always applauding the movement's rejection of whiteness and its search for a unifying conception of nationhood. His syncretic amalgamation of West and East African traditions, summarized in Nguzo Saba (Seven Principles of African Heritage), offered a model of invented yet historically grounded identity. The major ingredients for a Chicano ideology, however, were borrowed from Mexican advocates of *indigenismo* as well as from the distinctive historical memory of Hispanos in the upper Rio Grande Valley and Tejanos in the lower Valley. The idea of *la raza*, for instance, echoed José Vasconcelos's famous claim in *La raza cósmica* (1925) that Mexico's ethnic mixtures had produced a superior race with a universal destiny. Vasconcelos, appointed Mexican secretary of education by Álvaro Obregón, the revolutionary and president of Mexico in the 1920s, started a massive school construction program in the countryside, subsidized folk arts, and acted as chief sponsor of the great mural renaissance of the 1920s. He was also something of a border hybrid or proto-Chicano, having gone to school in Eagle Pass, Texas; nurtured a legal practice in San Diego; and, after his defeat for the presidency in 1929, lived as an exile in Los Angeles.

Meanwhile, "Aztlán," the mysterious northern homeland of the Aztecs, had been the subject of studies by the Mexican archeologist Manuel Gamio and his nephew, the celebrated pre-Columbian historian Miguel León-Portilla. The latter's best-selling *La filosofía náhuatl*—translated into English in 1963 as *Aztec Thought and Culture*—captivated the militant San Diego poet "Alurista" (Alberto Urista) who in turn popularized it as essential reading for Chicanos. The idea of the Southwest as an internal colony awaiting liberation had a genealogy going back to the Anglo conquest in 1848. Both Corky Gonzales (of Colorado's Crusade for Justice) and Reies Tijerina (of the New Mexico land rights movement) had been denouncing the "Anglo colonial system" in speeches and rallies since at least 1967. The rediscovery of the insurrectionary Plan de San Diego, written by Tejano revolutionaries in 1915 who hoped to win back the Southwest for Mexico, also had an electrifying effect on Chicano activist-intellectuals.[6]

The synthesis of these different elements into a core ideology took place in Denver in March 1967. The Crusade for Justice, the dynamic Denver-based civil rights movement led by Gonzales, had taken the initiative to unify the different barrio youth movements into a national force by calling the first National Chicano Youth Conference.[7] The organizers, anticipating only a few hundred attendees, were soon overwhelmed by 1,500 young women and men arriving by the busload or crammed into family cars. The large LA contingent included a surprising number of college freshmen, testimony to the ironic success of the Blowouts: while there was little or no improvement in high school conditions, UCLA and other campuses had dramatically increased recruitment of Chicanos. Participants' memoirs recount the excitement and novelty of comparing experiences with local activists hailing not only from Colorado and the Southwest states, but also Chicago and New York, which sent a Puerto Rican contingent. A majority had spent at least part of 1968 striking for better schools and Chicano studies programs, protesting police brutality, supporting the grape boycott, canvasing for Bobby Kennedy, or in the Los Angeles Berets participating in the Poor People's March on Washington. The Northern California delegation, veterans of the long Third World Liberation Front strikes at Berkeley and San Francisco State, brought a distinctly Marxist and pro-Panther outlook to the conference, but they were a minority. Chicano unity and identity, not united fronts and class analysis, were the compelling themes that had brought most of the young people to Denver.

The historic climax of the conference was the presentation of *El Plan espiritual de Aztlán* drafted by Alurista, Jorge González (another San Diego writer), UCLA graduate student and blowout organizer Juan Gómez-Quiñones, and Teatro Campesino's Luis Valdez.[8] In soaring language, reminiscent of Vasconcelos, they wrote: "With our heart in our hands and our hands in the soil, we declare the independence of our mestizo nation. We are a bronze people with a bronze culture ... we are a nation, we are a union of free pueblos, we are *Aztlán*." The *Plan* summarized the resolutions that had emerged from the workshops: nationalism as the basis of unity; an independent political party; "Chicano defense units" to combat police violence; restitution for land and resources stolen during "the brual *gringo* invasion of our territories"; community control of schools; the traditional Chicano family as a moral pillar; and the Southwestern pueblos as both spiritual and political models. A month later at another, well-attended conference in Santa Barbara, a second *Plan* was adopted that reprised the Denver principles, outlined a strategy for making Chicano studies a powerful resource for communities, and founded the Movimiento Estudiatil Chicano de Aztlán (MEChA) as an umbrella organization for renamed UMAS chapters and other campus groups.

On both occasions cultural nationalism was affirmed as the essential foundation for collective self-consciousness, political action and ultimate liberation. The LA filmmaker Jesús Treviño, who documented the Denver conference, later recalled the excitement he felt after the reading of *El Plan*, especially the revelatory invocation of Aztlán:

> Now we declared that we were no longer outsiders in a foreign land, but a prodigal people returning to the ancient homeland of our ancestors ... The battle for landed sovereignty had been lost over a hundred years ago. But we were still a nation of Chicanos. We were united by race, culture, and language in a country that despised us. [But] working together we might create a parallel government in the United States.[9]

Treviño was also pleased by the central role that was assigned to poets, writers, performers and artists of all kinds in the elaboration of this identity. The Denver conference called for nothing less than a Chicano renaissance.

The two manifestos together were widely seen as the Chicano Declaration of Independence and were fulsomely embraced by most of the movement. Critiques, however, were soon forthcoming from several sides. References in *El Plan* to the "call of our blood" and the "foreigner *gabacho*" struck some as either historically naïve or even sinister. The explicit statement that culture and nation came before class set off alarms on the left and brought comparisons with the supposedly "counterrevolutionary" politics of Karenga and US. For those with a knowledge of pre-Columbian cultures, moreover, the Chicano narrative that equated Mexico with the odyssey of the Aztecs was a gross simplification of a history that included many magnificent indigenous civilizations. (How did Zapotecs from Oaxaca or Mayans from Chiapas, for instance, fit into the Aztlán story?) Traditional nationalists and older leftists were also unsettled by the supremacy assigned to Aztlán as ur-homeland and crucible of identity. As Jorge Klor de Alva slyly notes, "In effect, not only were the Chicanos redefining themselves as primordial Americans, but also as the original Mexicans!"[10] This left little room for immigrants, documented or undocumented, who retained a profound identification with *la patria*. While celebrating indigenous roots, the new ideology also appropriated the history and identity of native peoples in the fracture zones of *el norte* who did not see themselves as having Aztec ancestors. In the case of the upper Rio Grande Valley, for instance, colonizers had been colonized; hispano/ mestizo violence against Pueblo people yielded to gringo violence against both hispanos and Indians.

But as Jorge Mariscal has argued, only a small minority of activists ever embraced a totally exclusivist interpretation of nationalism. "Cultural nationalism" was less an ideology than one of several shifting frameworks for debating identity and ideology. Its political impact, however, was focused. "Reduced to its fundamental organizing function, Chicano cultural nationalism was a necessary corrective for ethnic Mexicans in the United States who had either opted for the path of traditional assimilation or felt trapped in an economic and cultural system that positioned them as inferior."[11] Moreover, the post-Denver wave of barrio nationalism pumped huge energy into the most internationalist of causes: ending the genocide in Southeast Asia.

Chale con el Draft!

In July 1965 George Brown (D–Monterey Park), one of the earliest congressional opponents of Johnson's escalation in Vietnam, polled his Eastside constituents on their attitudes toward the war. Ninety percent expressed some degree of support.[12] Brown couldn't have been too surprised, since the community's record of military service and unquestioning patriotism, despite Anglo calumnies to the contrary, was remarkable. In greater proportion than any other ethnic group in the Southwestern states, they had enlisted in frontline units (especially the Marines), been wounded or killed, and received decorations for valor. For older groups, especially the GI Forum, such sacrifices had cemented the hyphen in "Mexican-American," and they had fought for the monument at Cinco Puntos, a major intersection in the heart of the barrio, that commemorates Mexican-American Congressional Medal of Honor winners and other heroes of World War II and Korea. However after four years of Vietnam and hundreds of body bags labelled "Hernandez," "García," and "Pérez," young Chicanos began to rise in rebellion against the traditions that had made them disposable and forgettable cannon fodder.[13] In white middle-class neighborhoods of L.A., where student deferments and diagnoses from family doctors shielded a majority of young men from the draft or at least from combat, deaths in the family were rare. On the Eastside and Southcentral, as well as in the tough blue-collar white communities east of Alameda and at the harbor, Vietnam was an intimate tragedy. Garfield High walkout leader Harry Gamboa, later celebrated for his role in Asco, the legendary Chicano arts collective, told Mario García: "If you look at my high school yearbook, it's like looking at the book of the dead because of Vietnam."[14]

All this weighed heaviest on Chicano activists facing the draft: Should they serve, or resist? A decisive step was taken when Rosalío Muñoz, recently graduated from UCLA, where he had been student body president, decided to refuse induction. In a conversation with his friend and fellow activist Ramses Noriega, one of them had said: "What we need in the Chicano movement is someone like Muhammad Ali who publicly resisted induction based on his opposition to the war." Bizarrely or fortuitously, the Selective Service ordered Muñoz to report on Mexican Independence Day, September 16, 1969. After seeking advice from Corky Gonzales, Cesar Chavez and many others, he decided to take the leap. In front of the Armed Forces Induction Center in downtown L.A., with a hundred supporters chanting and holding picket signs, he read a statement to reporters that ended with the call: "Chale con el draft!" (To hell with the Draft!) This became the name of the informal draft resistance collective that grew up around Muñoz's case and quickly linked up with other Chicano anti-war activists across the country.

Meanwhile some veterans of Eugene McCarthy's primary campaign were proposing to pressure Congress to end the war by organizing an escalating series of one-day campus strikes and community actions. The "Vietnam Moratorium," as they named it, soon won widespread support from student government leaders across the country and, more grudgingly, from the major anti-war coalitions. On September 15 (a weekday, to emphasize "no business as usual"), there were dozens of local demonstrations, often in areas with little past history of protest, as well as a monster rally of 100,000 people in the Boston Commons. A second, even larger Moratorium was scheduled a month later in San Francisco and Washington, DC. Muñoz was invited to speak at the San Francisco event but placed last on the speakers' list. When the organizers attempted to end the program before he had an opportunity to speak, the popular Cree Indian folk singer Buffy Sainte-Marie, who was supposed to close the event, told them: "I'm not singing until this guy gets to speak." That evening Muñoz and Noriega watched the news coverage of the demonstration.

> My rap, of course, wasn't covered, but what we noticed and what bothered us was how the other Chicano speakers, such as Corky and Dolores [Huerta], were also ignored. It was like Chicanos weren't there that day. We talked of how even though it was important to have Chicanos speak at these national moratoriums, it wasn't a successful way to reach Chicanos on the issues of the draft and the war. "We need our own Chicano antiwar moratorium," we told one another.[15]

Beret leader David Sanchez had the same idea for the same reasons and quickly convened a community meeting to form a Moratorium Committee with an initial demonstration on the Eastside slated for the week before Christmas. Muñoz and Noriega soon climbed on board, although both were also helping Corky Gonzales and Bobby Elias (another LA activist) organize a Chicano anti-war summit on December 6–8. The 150 or so activists who met in Denver agreed to let L.A. temporarily take the lead in demonstrating, with a final decision on a national action to be taken the following March at the second Youth Conference. In the meantime most of the actual work for the December "March against Death" was coordinated by Gloria Arellanes. Hailing from El Monte and the only female Beret minister, she was admired for her role in setting up and administering the Berets' highly successful El Barrio Free Clinic, which had opened in May. But her increasingly outspoken demand that women be treated as full equals and not just as the movement's "housewives" was provoking resistance from the male leadership and would soon lead to her resignation and an exodus of Beret women.[16]

The December demonstration, taking place less than two weeks after the LAPD's military assault on the Black Panther headquarters, was a venture into the unknown in terms of community support and the cops' reaction. In the event, several thousand people, led by pall-bearers carrying a silver coffin representing the Chicano war dead, marched from the Cinco Puntos memorial to Obregon Park, where the speakers included Sanchez and Oscar Acosta, the movement's flamboyant defense attorney.[17] Muñoz, for his part, was delighted with the turnout, but even more enthused by its diverse composition and affable solidarity. The big national anti-war umbrella groups—the Student Mobilization Committee, the New Mobilization Committee, and the Vietnam Moratorium—were all wracked with conflict at the time over whether to limit protests strictly to the demand for withdrawal or broaden the agenda to include other issues such as the conspiracy trials and the government campaign against the Panthers. This was not a problem for Chicanos. As Muñoz observed,

> The Moratorium Committee had put together a true coalition. People spoke about the war and how it was damaging the Chicano community. They integrated their political issues, such as the farm-workers' struggle, the schools, police abuse, welfare rights ... to the protest against the war. What was impressive to me was that these different movement groups were comfortable fitting these issues in with the antiwar issue. This held the key to the future organizing of the Chicano anti-war movement.[18]

To maintain momentum the committee decided to organize another moratorium as soon as possible. They selected a date in February, not realizing that a major El Niño would be directing rivers of rain to the West Coast that month. When the day arrived it was indeed lashing outside, and the organizers feared that only a few diehards would turn out, but an estimated 3,000 people, including supporters from the Peace Action Council, showed up in wildly improvised rain gear, ready to march. One contingent made a particularly dramatic impression: twenty or so women dressed in black and wrapped in dark rebozos, the traditional garments of mourning. A few days earlier the women had resigned from the Berets and now marched behind a huge pink rain-battered banner announcing "Las Adelitas de Aztlán." They sang a traditional corrido about the Revolution's legendary *solderas*. "At my suggestion," Arellanos remembered, "we also carried white crosses with the names of some of the Chicano men from L.A. killed in the war. My cross had the name of my cousin, Jimmy Basquez, who was killed in Vietnam."

Jesús Treviño was present with a crew from KTLA, the local PBS affiliate, and shot footage of the Adelitas as well as a short speech by Muñoz at the conclusion of the march. It was edited into a short film, *The March in the Rain*. Father Luce of the Church of the Epiphany in Lincoln Heights bought twenty copies and gave them to the Moratorium Committee, which eventually screened them across the country to build support for a National Moratorium.[19]

Self-documentation was a major innovation of the emergent Chicano movement. While Black radicals had come to expect comprehensive misrepresentation of their ideas and actions in the white media, Chicanos insisted on taking control of the narrative. Aside from Treviño, at this point an experienced professional with a regular half-hour segment on public television, several Chicano film students also contributed surprisingly high-quality short documentaries. The Eastside's alternative press comprised a half dozen papers, but none excelled *La Raza*, which was now a magazine edited by Raul Ruiz. In addition to writing news and editorials, he had also become an excellent and daring photographer. One of his photographs—of sheriffs shooting into a bar during the August National Moratorium—would haunt Los Angeles for decades.

In the meantime, Roosevelt High School, which had been represented by a large contingent at the February march, was hissing steam and ready to explode. Although it had gained a Mexican-American principal, Alfonso Perez, none of the reforms advocated by the Blowouts had been seriously implemented. Moreover, Perez, a lieutenant colonel in the Air Force Reserve, seemed to regard his role as prison warden first, and educator second. A profile of him in the *Times* reported that when the school bells sound a special signal, all teachers must lock their doors. Other teachers patrol the halls, "sweeping up" students and taking them to the teachers' cafeteria where their names are recorded ... To further insure security Perez has initiated the unpopular policy of locking many campus buildings during the hours when students are free for lunch and snack breaks. He ordered the doors leading off campus chained and he instituted increased teacher patrols during non-class hours.[20]

Student anger was molded into a new wave of protest by a charismatic seventeen-year-old senior, Jorge Rodriguez. He had grown up in the tough Boyle Heights Flats with his brothers and had helped to transform (temporarily) the feared Quatro Flats gang into a movement social club called Carnalismo (Brotherhood). At Salesian High, a Catholic school a few blocks from Roosevelt, he had been elected student body president and had founded a UMAS chapter, but following a fight with white students after a football game, he was forced to transfer to Roosevelt—where he became Perez's nightmare.[21]

On Friday, March 5, the second anniversary of the original Roosevelt blowout, Rodriguez led 300 or 400 kids out of their morning classes and held a rally on the lawn in front of the school, where they were joined by some college MEChA members who were recent alumni. After the Blowouts, the board, prodded by Julian Nava, had created the Mexican-American Education Commission, chaired by Vahac Mardirosian, as an official advisory body. The commission interpreted its mandate to include acting as first responders and mediators in the event of new walkouts or student protests.[22] Perez, however, ignored the commission and called the cops, who responded exactly as they had two years earlier: by sending a riot squad of seventy officers to push and prod kids, and bust heads when they refused to go back to class. Seven students were hurt and thirty-two arrested, along with a few of the supporters. The following week, a skirmish on Tuesday grew into an authentic riot on Wednesday involving nearly 800 students, 150 supporters, and 120 cops. Dozens were taken to jail, bringing the total of student arrests to 110.[23]

Community outrage about police conduct rose to a level not seen since the infamous "Bloody Christmas" beating of jailed Mexican-Americans in 1951.[24] "Television cameras showed police beating protestors with nightsticks and dragging young Mexican-American girls across the high school campus by their hair," historian Edward Escobar writes. KMEX, the Spanish-language television station, interviewed one mother who said that she had kept her boy home from school because she feared the police would kill him. In the aftermath of the demonstrations, the Barrio Defense Committee attracted more than a thousand people to a meeting to plan ways of counteracting the police actions." The *Times* published an article by Ruben Salazar that criticized LAPD Chief Edward Davis for his dismissive attitude toward Chicano concerns about the events at Roosevelt; the article left the chief and his associates enraged. Davis's personal assistant, Lieutenant Bob Walter, "promised that his boss would tear 'the hide right off [Salazar's] back,'" and the department opened a file on the journalist.[25]

Meanwhile, Chicano students at other high schools, including Lincoln, Huntington Park and South Gate, held rallies or set up picket lines that echoed the demands made at Roosevelt. The most surprising support, however, came from kids at Beverly Hills High, where hundreds boycotted classes at midday in response to leaflets that had urged solidarity with "our Chicano brothers and sisters at Roosevelt High."[26]

The Roosevelt crisis was still unresolved when LA activists left for Denver in late March. The second Youth Conference was a huge event with several thousand participants; it made two decisions that set the course of the movement for the next several years. First, it endorsed the expansion of the Raza Unida Party that been founded by Tejano activists in January. Second, it voted to mobilize for a National Chicano Moratorium in Los Angeles at the end of the summer. A debate over the exact date for the demonstration highlighted the extent to which Chicano separatism had now drawn a border between itself and traditional Mexican nationalism. As Muñoz recalls:

Several supported September 16, Mexican Independence Day, because it would allow us to build on this widely celebrated event. It would provide us with a ready-made audience. I could see their argument, but I didn't buy it. "Look," Ramses pointed out, "the sixteenth of September is a Mexican holiday. We're Chicanos. We need our own history." The distinction between Mexican nationalism and Chicano nationalism made a difference. We ruled out September 16. [27]

As they returned from Colorado, the LA Moratorium Committee plunged into the hectic but exciting work of recruiting support for the demonstration now scheduled for August 29. David Sanchez, however, resigned as co-chair: the first public indication of a bitter and deepening conflict between the Crusade for Justice's assertion of national leadership and the Berets' attempt to build chapters across the country. But Moratorium organizers, including Arrelanes and her efficient Adelitas, had little time to worry about the incipient dispute. Spring 1970 arrived as an unexpected hurricane of strikes, protests, rioting and police violence.

Teamsters, Teachers and MEChA

April saw two of the largest and most protracted strikes in LA County since the epic confrontation of the Conference of Studio Unions with the movie industry's moguls back in 1945. Both strikes brought ferment to the Eastside and had important consequences for Chicanos. First to go out—unofficially—were the Teamsters. The regional administration of the union, Joint Council 42, was the largest and most powerful labor organization in Southern California, and out of its dozens of locals the most militant were the two that represented most of the 14,000 drivers and warehouse workers in the freight industry. The industry was covered by a national contract, and when the major freight companies balked at signing a new agreement, there were spontaneous walkouts across the country. The Mob-connected president of the International since the disappearance of Jimmy Hoffa, Frank Fitzsimmons, ordered the membership back to work on April

2, but drivers in Ohio and Southern California refused and continued their wildcat strike.[28] When the LA freight companies summarily fired the strikers, Joint Council 42 did nothing—because it shared a common interest with the companies in stripping power from the shop stewards who led the rebellion.

As a result, the strike spun into chaos, with tremendous militancy on the picket lines, but poor coordination between strike committees in different "barns," few allies apart from some UCLA students and members of the Liberation Union (the ex–Friends of the Panthers), and no real strategy for victory.[29] The companies, most of them located in industrial parts of Eastside like the "Hole" below Brooklyn Heights, City of Commerce and Pico Rivera, brought in strikebreakers and a private army of Pinkertons and Wackenhuts. When picketeers tried to stop trucks driven by strikebreakers, they also had to deal with a regiment of sheriffs drafted from all over the county. On one memorable occasion the latter tried to break up a strike rally at Legg Lake near Whittier only to face a fierce barrage of bottles and beer cans. As arrests mounted, some of the barns began to surrender, while the others became more desperate. There were bombings, sniper attacks on scab trucks, and, under controversial circumstances, a strikebreaker and a striker were killed.[30]

Although the collapse of the wildcat brought only victimization and a suspension of union democracy, one of its unforeseen consequences was the acceleration of an ethnic transition in the industry. Chicanos already had a substantial foothold, and the strike groomed a new leadership that eventually took charge of the locals after a long period of trusteeship. But as routes to power opened up inside Joint Council 42, some of the new Chicano business agents became loyal partisans of the reactionary policies of the International. (Fitzsimmons supported Nixon in 1972, and the union provided security at many of his campaign rallies.) A sad result was the contingent of brawny Chicano Teamsters from L.A. who went out to the Coachella Valley in 1973 to terrorize grape strikers.

Two weeks after the start of the Teamster wildcat, thousands of LA schoolteachers hit the bricks. After years of frustrated courtship, the two major teachers' organizations had merged in January to become United Teachers Los Angeles (UTLA). After futile talks with the acting superintendent of education, Robert Kelly, they set up picket lines on April 13.[31] The new union garnered broad support from parents, at least on the Westside and in minority communities, because its demands emphasized quality-of-education issues, especially a reduction of class sizes and the hiring of teachers' aides. (Indeed, at the end of the strike, teachers would show their mettle by voting to trade a 5 percent salary increase for additional funding for remedial education.) The LAUSD administration claimed to agree with some of the demands but deflected blame to Sacramento, where Governor Reagan had been beating up on school kids since 1967. In addition to ruthless cuts in state funding for both K-12 and colleges, Reagan regularly intervened in local elections to oppose school bond measures that attempted to make up the shortfall in state aid. But the board was culpable nonetheless because of its refusal to use reserve funds and its preference for funding majority-white schools while older inner-city campuses felt the brunt of austerity and decay. And one key demand—giving teachers an integral role in shaping curricula and school policies—required only a majority vote on the board.[32]

Many high school students, politicized by previous struggles, keenly understood what was at stake and embraced the strike. Officially schools were open and all students were required to attend, but at Belmont and Grant in Van Nuys, they walked out, chanting, "We don't want babysitters." At Fairfax, on the Westside, where the Red Tide (the high school affiliate of International Socialists) was especially active, 250 kids blocked the main entrance and urged their schoolmates to go home. Meanwhile at Franklin High in Highland Park, hundreds of students joined their teachers' picket line. Although the principal described the situation as "orderly," the LAPD dispersed the pickets anyway. By the end of the second week, huge numbers of kids, 50 percent or more at many high schools, were playing hooky, and one state senator from the Valley was calling for strikers to be fired and their leaders imprisoned. The strike would grind on until mid May, with Sacramento unmoved but LAUSD forced to recognize UTLA—a resolution that was totally upended when a Reagan-appointed judge ruled that teachers had no right to bargain collectively, nor did the board to recognize UTLA.[33]

But while teachers and Teamsters were still out on the streets, Nixon blew up campuses across the country. Although there had been little reaction from the peace movement earlier in April when South Vietnamese forces invaded Cambodia, the president's decision to send 30,000 American troops across that border—an escalation that turned the Vietnam War into the Indochinese War—lit a fuse. The largest student protest in American history followed: before the month was out, an estimated 4 million students participated in prolonged strikes on at least 450 campuses. Forty ROTC buildings were set afire or bombed, and six student protestors, four at Kent State in Ohio and two at Jackson State in Mississippi, were shot dead by the National Guard and state police. Scores more were wounded or seriously injured, and thousands were arrested. At UC San Diego, a 23-year-old history student, George Winne, distraught over the war, set himself on fire during a campus protest and died ten hours later. "'He asked me to write a letter to President Nixon,' his mother later told reporters. 'This was his way of calling attention to the terrible things going on in the world today.'"[34]

Earlier in the week UCLA had declared an unprecedented state of emergency after several thousand students, including members of its national champion basketball team, attempted to shut down the campus. They broke windows, tried to set the ROTC building ablaze, and scuffled with university police, who in turn called for help from the LAPD. Chief Davis, an avid supporter of Governor Reagan's zero-tolerance policy toward campus protest, sent in more than 500 of his troops to take back UCLA from the anti-war movement. Aside from the usual promiscuous use of nightsticks (twelve students were hospitalized), squadrons of motorcycle cops roared onto campus to chase down protestors. Meanwhile, other cops were battling and arresting students at Cal State Fullerton, which had already experienced several months of convulsions after the administration had cracked down on campus radicals. The escalation of violence against college anti-war protestors in Southern California and the rest of the country only promoted the expansion of the movement to campuses and communities that had little or no previous tradition of active dissent. In the ten days following Nixon's announcement, there were strikes or boisterous rallies at the Claremont Colleges, Valley State, Occidental, Citrus College, Whittier, UC Irvine and, perhaps most surprisingly, at famously cloistered Cal Tech.

MEChA chapters and individual Chicanos, of course, were active in all of these protests, which provided innumerable opportunities to publicize the National Moratorium. The planned Eastside protest, moreover, took on additional importance as a hot spring turned into a strangely cold summer. In early May, when 1.5 million college students were on strike and 100,000 protesters were camped next to the Lincoln Monument, it was easy to believe that this was a culminating confrontation: Congress would either force an end to the war, or a large part of the country's higher education system would shut down. But Congress postponed decisive action, AFL-CIO President George Meany and the conservative unions such as the construction trades and the Teamsters rallied to Nixon's side, and the administration, promising that all troops would be out of Cambodia in two months (and 150,000 more out of Vietnam altogether in a half year), successfully quelled the upsurge. Meanwhile, the peace movement on a national level had splintered into two hostile factions, one advocating business as usual—that is to say more peace marches—and the other calling vaguely and rather desperately for "disruption." Neither was a realistic strategy for moving protest forward, and the liberal wing that had championed the original Moratorium left the streets altogether in order to lobby Congress and work behind the scenes with anti-war Democrats.

As Fred Halstead writes in his history of the anti-war movement: "There was one major exception to the relative ebb in demonstrative antiwar activity during the summer of 1970. This involved the Chicano community and the actions were organized under the name of the Chicano Moratorium."[35] Buoyed by the successes of local moratoriums in places as diverse as Houston and Oxnard, the national organizers no longer fretted about the size of the turnout. The real problem now was, where would they find housing for so many amigas and amigos?

32

War on the Eastside: The Chicano Moratorium (1970)

August 29 was hot, smoggy and exhilarating. All week long contingents had been arriving from every point of the compass where people of Mexican descent lived. They spanned generations and represented scores of grassroots groups—MAYO (Mexican American Youth Organization) from Texas, the Black Berets from San Jose, Denver's Crusade for Justice, and so on. Over the summer, moreover, the Moratorium had gained support and financial aid from a broad united front of home-ground organizations. Particularly important were the endorsements from MAPA, CSO (Community Service Organization, which had trained Cesar Chavez and Dolores Huerta), the Congress of Mexican American Unity, local UAW locals, and the Peace Action Council. On the left, Angela Davis and the Che-Lumumba Club were active supporters as well as an array of campus anti-war groups. Muñoz was particularly excited by the participation of "older grassroots activists from the zoot-suit days ... such as Rudy Tovar, Rudy Salas, Carmen Vera, and Lillian Villegas."[1] The only sour note during the buildup was the refusal of José Ángel Gutiérrez, the leader of Texas's Raza Unida Party, to play an active role in the mobilization, presumably because of his enmity toward Corky Gonzales, but other members of the party were avid supporters.

In order to encourage ordinary Eastside residents, especially families with children, to attend the Moratorium, the organizers had given careful attention to keeping the event peaceful. Esteban Torres of the UAW (twelve years later a member of Congress) provided experienced union stewards to train MEChA members as monitors, while the organizers and older allies reached out to law enforcement. That meant Sheriff Peter Pitchess—since the march route, starting in Belvedere Park and heading south on Atlantic before turning west on Whittier Boulevard, was entirely under his jurisdiction. Pitchess, elected in 1958, had won his reputation as the head investigator for the FBI's LA office in the period of the Hollywood blacklist and saw enforcement problems in East L.A. through a Red Scare lens that attributed an outsize role to secret Communist infiltration of the Chicano movement. Moreover, his department was easily as ruthless in quelling protest as the LAPD on the other side of the city-county line. Earlier in the summer, sheriff's deputies had shot and critically wounded a Chicano high school student during a protest about four suspicious "suicides" in the holding cells of the East Los Angeles station. Muñoz and others were thus naturally apprehensive about how the department, and specifically its seemingly out-of-control East LA unit, would react to the Moratorium. They were surprised and reassured when the sheriffs readily agreed to keep a low profile as long as the organizers retained control of the marchers.

However, Ruben Salazar, now news director for Spanish-language television station KMEX while retaining a regular column in the *Times*, warned that it might be a ruse. He was writing a book on police abuse and had developed some confidential contacts who provided information on law enforcement plans.[2] The night before the march he asked Bert Corona and two others to meet with him at the Century Plaza Hotel on the Westside. Corona later wrote that

> Ruben came right out and told us that he really feared there was going to be police action against us. He had reason to believe that agent provocateurs had infiltrated both the moratorium committee and the Brown Berets and that we had better be on alert. He believed that the provocateurs would cause incidents to "justify" police repression of the moratorium. Ruben also said that he knew from some of his sources that top officials in Washington, including President Nixon, were quite concerned about the moratorium,

since it would be the first large minority-sponsored demonstration against the war … the word out of Washington was, "What the hell is going on in Los Angeles? Why have officials there allowed things to reach this point?" … Ruben concluded by telling us that he had all his evidence, including tapes, in his car. [Someone had gone through his desk at the station.] "And when this is all over, when it's history, I'll be able to share it with you guys."[3]

The march certainly was history. Twenty to twenty-five thousand people—Muñoz later estimated it was 85 percent Chicano and 15 percent from other communities—marched down Whittier Boulevard, East L.A.'s main drag and "cruising" strip, in a colorful sea of banners and protest signs, chanting "Raza si, guerra no!" The atmosphere was charged with that special excitement that occurs when a group of people can see and visibly measure their potential power for the first time. Coalitions might be disintegrating in other parts of the country, but in East L.A. that Saturday, the anti-war movement crossed a new threshold as thousands of ordinary working-class people from one of the most patriotic communities in the United States marched for immediate withdrawal, thereby adding to the White House's ever-increasing paranoia.

And the march was almost entirely peaceful. The sheriffs, seemingly true to their promise, diverted traffic and otherwise laid low on side streets along the route. As the marchers arrived at Laguna Park, the rally site located on the city-county borderline, they found a group of families and older people already gathered, those who had forgone the rigor of the four-mile march. "What struck me," remembers Muñoz, "was that the people who hadn't marched seemed to be families with small children … [which] only added to the festive atmosphere. It seemed typical of a weekend in the park in East L.A., when families go to have a picnic or barbeque and let the kids enjoy the open spaces." On the stage, while marchers continued to arrive, musicians were warming up the crowd with revolutionary corridos while a group of girls in traditional costumes danced.

The Murder of Ruben Salazar

What happened next would destroy this triumphal mood and open a long season of unequal warfare between police and sheriffs on one side and activists and barrio youth on the other. There are several confused accounts of how it all started, but one of this volume's coauthors (MD) was present at the scene and can recall the main details.

My wife and I were with the young grandsons of Sam Kushner, the *People's World* correspondent who, despite being blacklisted for his left-wing views, was widely admired by other journalists for his in-depth reportage on the farmworkers' strike and the Chicano movement.[4] Sam was elsewhere on the route and was apparently one of the last people to talk to Ruben Salazar. Meanwhile we had found a place to sit on the periphery of the rally, and I went to get sodas for the kids. Someone told me there was a liquor store around the corner, on the city side of Whittier Boulevard. The store was packed with thirsty people, and there was some kind of confusion; a window was broken, which I assumed was just an accident. Rather than waiting in line, I decided to fetch the kids and take them for an ice cream back in Echo Park where we all lived.

I was on the sidewalk outside the Green Mill Liquor Store when dozens of squad cars came roaring down the street at about fifty miles per hour. It was both astounding and terrifying. (I remember thinking that this was LAPD Metro Squad, but reading other accounts, they were more likely sheriff's deputies.) Scores, and eventually hundreds, of riot-ready helmeted cops and deputies poured out of the vehicles and jogged into the park clutching their riot batons. After a desultory warning that the rally was an "unlawful assembly," they began pushing, prodding and—where there was any resistance—beating people. Our little group, like most of the families, immediately retreated to our cars. Our evacuation was covered by a steadfast group of monitors and MEChA members, who tried to talk to the deputies, and when that failed, took blows that otherwise might have fallen on our heads.

Other youth defending the speakers' stand threw rocks that were answered with volleys of tear gas. The next day, the *Times* printed the claim from the Sheriff's Department that their response was justified since at "about 1:30 p.m. 300 persons stormed inside [the Green Mill] and began looting shelves." This was utter fiction meant to excuse an obviously well-prepared and blatantly massive attack designed to generate headlines about "rioters" and the subversive groups that controlled them.

Police and Sheriff's supervisors exercised little tactical control over their troops, whose ranks soon went berserk. Skirmish lines disintegrated as deputies chased rock throwers, attacked unresisting people leaving the park, and then launched furious forays into the neighborhood streets on both sides of Whittier. Residents, including elderly women and men who had nothing to do with the Moratorium, were attacked in their front yards and even on their porches when they failed to obey orders to go inside their homes. Tear gas saturated the streets, and eventually three square miles of the Eastside was transformed into a combat zone.[5] Police barriers were quickly erected to cordon off the area, and thirty-year-old Gilberto Diaz was shot and killed by deputies when he attempted to drive through one of the barricades. A fifteen-year-old Brown Beret from El Monte, Lyn Ward, was initially reported by the *Times* as critically injured by a gas canister, but after he died the Sheriff's Department claimed the cause was actually a homemade bomb. The Berets' angrily contested this new account and acclaimed Ward as their first martyr, but his death was overshadowed by that of a third victim, also killed by tear gas projectile.[6]

While cops and deputies continued to stoke community rage by skirmishing with residents and invading their homes, some of the afternoon's anger coalesced into window breaking and arson along Whittier Boulevard's business strip. It soon became the Eastside's equivalent to Watt's 1965 "charcoal alley." Jesús Treviño, who had filmed the march for KCET, left the rally before the attack to drop some friends at their car back in Belvedere Park. As he drove down Atlantic to Whittier, he was astonished by what he saw.

As I looked west along Whittier, I saw a most incredible sight: the
huge plumes of black smoke had increased, filling the sky. There
was smoke as far as the eye could see, and flames crackled in nearly
all the buildings within view. This was the scene later depicted by
Chicano artists Willie Herrón and Gronk in a famous mural in the
Estrada Courts housing project.[7]

Hundreds had tried to escape Laguna Park by backtracking along
Whittier, only to encounter a pitched battle between local youth and
angry sheriffs who made little distinction between window breakers
and people just leaving the area. The KMEX news team—Ruben
Salazar, Guillermo Restrepo, Hector Franco and Gustavo Garcia—
were among these refugees. They ducked into a bar-café called the
Silver Dollar to make some phone calls, use the toilets, and get drinks.
The disruption of the Moratorium had eerily confirmed Salazar's pre-
diction to Corona, and he was nervous, suspecting that they were being
followed. "About a block before we get to the Silver Dollar," Restrepo
later testified, "he says to me, 'Guillermo, I'm getting very scared.'"[8]
Soon after they entered the bar, deputies with drawn guns ordered six
people who had been standing outside watching the inferno to go back
inside. A little later Franco and Gustavo tried to step outside to check
on the action but were shooed back inside by a deputy with shotgun.[9]
For the time being, all the people in the Silver Dollar were trapped.

Across the street, meanwhile, Raul Ruiz and Joe Razo had arrived
and were observing the deputies in front of the Silver Dollar. Denied
press passes and long harassed by the sheriffs, the two *La Raza* editors
were risking injury and arrest in order to document the conduct of
deputies. Their curiosity was focused on a big deputy crouching next
to the bar's open doorway with what looked like a rifle with most of
its barrel sawed off. It was a tear gas gun in the hands of Thomas
Wilson, a sergeant from the Montrose Station who had volunteered for
duty at the Moratorium. He would later explain that another deputy
told him that a witness had seen two men with guns go inside the
Silver Dollar. (The "witness"—crucial to the Sheriff's later defense
of the shooting—turned out to be a former LAPD reserve officer,
bareshirted and wearing a red vest, who was helping deputies direct

traffic.)[10] Wilson claimed that he repeatedly yelled for the people inside the Silver Dollar to come out, but eleven of them later testified that had they never heard such an order.[11] After shouting the order, or not, Wilson got up and stood in front of the entrance with his weapon leveled at the open doorway, the interior shaded by a curtain. Ruiz snapped a photograph. An instant later Wilson fired through the curtain, reloaded, and fired again. Wilson left, and another sheriff's car arrived at the scene, having heard the account of gunmen inside but apparently unaware that the bar had already been cleared. Three more projectiles were fired through the tattered curtain. Incredibly, neither Wilson nor the deputies in the second car bothered to enter the Silver Dollar to find out the result of their attacks.[12]

Wilson's first round, in fact, was a high-muzzle-velocity tear gas projectile known as a "Flite-Rite," which was nine inches long with fins and a weighted nose. It was specially designed for so-called "barricade" situations and was able to penetrate a door or a wooden wall. Flite-Rites were labeled by the manufacturer "not for crowd control" and contained toxic CS gas, secretly developed by the British Army in the 1950s and later banned in many places because of its lethality. Salazar was sitting closest to the entrance, nursing a beer. The projectile entered his head from the left and came out on the right, blowing up his brain. The others in the bar, their eyes and faces burning from the gas, fled out the back door. The KMEX crew was later interviewed by the *Free Press*'s Sue Marshall, and she summarized their account of what happened after they stumbled out the back of the Silver Dollar:

> They were met in the back parking lot area by sheriff's deputies who had by now surrounded the bar. The crew showed the police their official press passes and Restrepo told them that the news director was inside and hurt … The newsmen were unable to get co-operation from either the sheriff's deputies or firemen at the scene, and no went in to help Salazar. The news crew was prevented from going in to get him at gunpoint by the deputies.

Restrepo then phoned his station manager Danny Villanueva, who, over the course of the next several hours, made ten separate calls to the sheriff's department, begging them to look for Salazar. They kept telling him they were too busy. Ambulances were sent to the scene, only to be turned back by deputies. Finally at 7:45, more than three hours after the shooting, a deputy in a gas mask entered the bar and found the body. At 10:30 they finally identified the victim as Salazar.[13]

Salazar's friends at the *Times* and KMEX were well aware that he had been threatened by the LAPD and was undoubtedly under surveillance, perhaps by multiple agencies. His repeated warnings that both the Moratorium and he himself were in some sort of danger were unsettling, especially in light of the LA Thirteen and Biltmore cases. Eastside leaders called for a federal grand jury to investigate his possible assassination. The sheriff's homicide bureau meanwhile conducted a hasty internal investigation, preliminary to the coroners' inquest. The records of this inquiry, kept secret and stored for years in the County Administration Building, were finally revisited in 2011 by the Office of Independent Review, a body established by the board of supervisors in 2001 after innumerable accounts of abuses by sheriffs in jails and elsewhere. Their report focused on two key issues: first, the original investigation's finding after testimony by "the Department's expert on tear gas and firearms" that Sergeant Wilson had acted properly in using a Flite-Rite; and second, the failure of the homicide detectives to explore claims that Salazar was under surveillance or even targeted. On the first count, the 2011 investigators were incredulous. "The obvious follow up question about whether it was appropriate to fire into a darkened building through a door blocked by nothing more than a curtain was never asked."

As for the second issue:

The failure to focus on any aspects of the incident beyond the immediate question of how Mr. Salazar died ... opened the door for decades of speculation about what the Department may have been trying to hide ... [Detectives] asked no questions about the more sinister theory being expounded, namely, that Mr. Salazar was targeted. As a result, responding deputies were not asked if they knew or had heard of Mr. Salazar, whether they knew he had been observing the March earlier, whether they had been assigned to follow him, and whether they knew he was inside the Silver Dollar at the time of the incident. [And] because the incident was not subjected to any sort of internal administrative review … no one was held accountable for performance that did not meet Department expectations.[14]

The desultory investigation of Salazar's death by the Homicide Bureau contrasted with the high-powered campaign immediately launched by Pitchess to convince the public that the Moratorium was violent from the beginning and under the control of violent left-wing groups. "Hundreds of provocative acts were committed by known dissidents who came to the location to incite and foment trouble," he told the board of supervisors. The board's conservative members echoed the charge: "The Mexican community was ripe for exploitation by confrontation-seeking agitators" (Supervisor Ernest Debs) and what resulted was "a very bad revolutionary situation … a well-planned conspiracy" (Warren Dorn). Moreover, the sheriff had captured a notorious instigator, Corky Gonzales. He and twenty-five members of the Crusade riding in a big truck had been stopped by deputies as they were leaving the Eastside and charged with carrying concealed weapons and suspicion of robbery. Although the charges were soon dropped and the Crusade people went home, the sensation generated by the arrests contaminated the public view of what had happened. Meanwhile the FBI readily accepted Pitchess's invitation to help hunt down other subversive forces behind the "riot." His office soon publicized another telling piece of evidence: a seditious leaflet from the Progressive Labor Party. (Eyes rolled in the movement: the PLP routinely leafleted *every* demonstration and had exercised no role whatsoever in the Moratorium.)

The sixteen-day-long inquest into Salazar's death was broadcast live by a rotation of local television stations. The hearing officer, Norman Pittluck, gave the sheriffs home-court advantage. For three days they were allowed to present carefully prepared and scripted testimony on the violence of the Moratorium and the role of "outsiders" in fomenting attacks on law enforcement. The department's press officer showed a film that had been carefully edited to emphasize rock throwing and vandalism by protestors without a hint of the official violence to which these acts were the reaction.

Eastsiders at the hearing were outraged, and Joe De Anda from the new Chicano studies program at Valley State got up and protested: "This inquest was supposed to be confined to the circumstances directly surrounding Ruben Salazar's death. Instead, an attempt is being made to inculcate the public with the idea that the sheriff's deputies were justified in all their actions." The Chicanos in the audience, led by future Congress member Esteban Torres, twice walked out. When Raul Ruiz was finally called to the stand, Pittluck showed astonishingly rude disinterest in his testimony, repeating questions that already been answered and looking away in obvious boredom as Ruiz showed his photos to the jury and explained the sequence of events at the Silver Dollar. This was too much for Oscar Acosta, who began shouting at Pittluck, who in turn ordered Acosta removed from the courtroom—a process that involved considerable use of force by marshals after the stoutly built lawyer refused to budge from his seat. Salazar's family and his media colleagues were appalled by the conduct of the proceedings and the toothlessness of the verdict. A majority of jurors ultimately found for "death at hands of another," a rebuke to the sheriff's case for mere "accident," but the categories were vague and the verdict had no legal consequence. Still, it could have been used to support indictments for negligent homicide or manslaughter if Younger had been so inclined. He wasn't. The general election was imminent, and he was mining gold in the conservative white suburbs through his demonization of the Chicano movement. As a result, neither Wilson nor any of the other deputies involved in the deaths of Salazar, Diaz and Ward ever suffered so much as a departmental reprimand, much less criminal charges for what they did that day.

The Labyrinth of Repression

August 29 was immediately followed by a curfew and the systematic harassment of the Moratorium Committee and other Chicano activists and community workers. Offices were raided, often without warrants, and individuals were arrested on bogus charges and then released after interrogation. The FBI increased its surveillance of the movement, while both the LAPD and the sheriff's department planted more informers and agents provocateurs. A plan to follow up the Moratorium with a national meeting at Cal State LA had to be abandoned because of the arrests of Gonzales and the Crusade people, as well as the sudden hostility of the school's administration. When Gonzales was finally released, Muñoz asked his advice about how to maintain the momentum of the Moratorium in the face of growing repression. "You have to get the Chicano middle class involved so that there's a more general community reaction to what the cops did," he answered. "They're going to try to isolate you guys as violent and responsible for what happened. But if you can get the businessmen and the professionals to support you, this will help against those charges."[15] Accordingly the Moratorium decided to ask permission to march as a contingent in the traditional Mexican Independence Day celebration on September 16. All agreed that the highest priority was to put the movement back on streets with a show of support from older and more moderate community leaders. The organizers of the event, however, were under heavy pressure from Pitchess to cancel the entire parade. With Esteban Torres as their forceful advocate, the Moratorium, reiterating its commitment to nonviolence, finally persuaded them to hold the march and allow them to participate under their own banners.

On that particular Independence Day, Raul Ruiz was taking the stand at the coroner's inquest—while fifty miles away, a hundred young prisoners were shouting "Viva La Raza!" and battling guards at a Chino juvenile facility. Thirty-three of them escaped.[16] Several thousand Moratorium supporters, meanwhile, formed the largest contingent at the Eastside demonstration, peacefully reclaiming the streets they had been driven off of three weeks earlier. "We literally took over the Sixteenth of September parade and transformed it into an antiwar and anti-police march," said one organizer. At the end of the event, as marchers and monitors were dispersing, sirens, flashing lights and what sounded like gunfire alarmed the crowd still remaining at Belvedere Park. Some neighborhood youth pelted several passing sheriff's cars and were quickly met, according to one of the legal observers, by "a great show of force by the deputies," about fifty strong, seemingly beginning a sweep of the avenue. The crowd headed toward them, hurling rocks, bottles and anything else that could be picked up. "The monitors were doing a hell of job," one of the lawyer-observers told the *Times*. "They might have succeeded if it hadn't been for the police presence."[17]

This "mini-riot" illustrated the intractable dilemma faced by the Moratorium Committee: no matter how much effort they made to ensure the peaceful character of their demonstrations—including bringing in outside lawyers, law students and clergy—as long as the sheriffs treated protests as incipient riots and conspicuously displayed ranks of deputies visored and clutching their riot batons, some violence was inevitable. One of the successes of the Chicano awakening had been the politicization of many gang members and *pintos* (ex-convicts) who, as a matter of honor, would fearlessly fight cops and sheriffs—even when the odds were overwhelmingly against them. Given an instigation by deputies or police—or provocateurs—spontaneous combustion was assured.[18]

The next demonstration, on January 9, became such a self-fulfilling prophecy. The Moratorium had been having trouble with the Eastside Berets, who had waved guns and forced them to surrender their office. David Sanchez was out of town, absorbed in building new chapters across the country, and the local leadership was assumed by someone whom Muñoz and others believed to be both psychotic and working for the FBI. Moreover, his own group was splintering in an outburst of factionalism incited by its official chair Frank Martinez, later to be exposed as an undercover ATF agent. The Berets and the Moratorium had been sparring over the question of whether the LAPD or the sheriffs should be the principal target of a new mobilization against police abuse. In the end, two protests were planned. The first, called by the Berets and reluctantly supported by the Moratorium group, took place at the Civic Center and was broken up by the LAPD with forty arrests.

This afforded Chief Davis, who loved to play one-upmanship with Sheriff Pitchess, an opportunity to advance an even more startling explanation of the sinister forces behind the Chicano movement.

Speaking to the Chatsworth Chamber of Commerce, the chief said that "Communist agitators *and* action by the Attorney General's Office were responsible for the disturbance."[19] Back in July 1970, Ruben Salazar had enraged Davis with an exposé of the LAPD's execution of two unarmed immigrant laborers, the Sanchez brothers. Searching for a murder suspect in a Skid Row flophouse, cops had broken down the wrong door and immediately opened fire on the innocent brothers. It was such an egregious killing that John Mitchell, Nixon's superconservative attorney general, was forced to issue an indictment of the officers involved. Davis, proving himself to be one of Chief Parker's more demented protégés, declared this to be nothing less than collusion with Eastside rioters. As for the Berets and their red puppeteers, Davis claimed that it was Father Luce who had "spawned" a group of "Bolsheviks" who were clearly identified in police photos of the Civic Center protest. He didn't mention that they were all over sixty years old.[20]

The next demonstration by the Moratorium returned the focus to Sheriff Pitchess and his department. A series of spirited local marches organized by neighborhood Beret groups in San Pedro, Venice, and San Fernando preceded the main event. To avoid the danger of a collision with deputies, "La Marcha para Justicia" on January 29 was planned to terminate in Belvedere Park rather than the nearby sheriff's station. Once again a well-monitored march went off smoothly, and at its end Rosalio Muñoz begged the 5,000 to 7,000 protestors to "disperse peacefully." "I hope you're going to respect those who came a long way," she told marchers. "Don't go to the police [*sic*] station unless you want to get involved in a suicide." But a large minority, frustrated by the protest's failure to confront the sheriffs, took the risk and marched to the station on the east side of the lake, just across the Pomona Freeway. Some tore down a section of the chain-link fence surrounding the deputies' parking lot and broke a few car windows. Then, as the two *Times* reporters on the scene reported, "it seemed for a moment that the situation might be saved when the crowd began to respond to a rally monitor's requests to "'go home, get away from here.' The monitors and two young priests helped to put the fence back in place."[21]

But the more angry or hotheaded members of the crowd broke away and, throwing rocks at the station as they passed, advanced on Whittier Boulevard. Deputies headed them off and, in the confrontation that followed, did not hesitate to open fire on the protesters. Raul Ruiz, as usual, was on the scene documenting the confrontation. "Lots of people got shot," he reported afterward. "The cops fired live ammo. I was with the demonstration but when I saw the contingent of deputies waiting for us as we turned into the substation, I left to a position where I could take better photos. I thought at the time that it was a wise decision, but it wasn't." He too was shot, although only a flesh wound on his back.[22] Altogether, twenty people were wounded, and a young Austrian student, enrolled in a Hebrew course at East LA College, caught a shotgun pellet or slug in the heart and died. Muñoz later said that the deputies' action could only be characterized as a "firing squad," while Ruiz, reminiscing years later, compared the riot to a "Palestinian intifada."[23]

The Belvedere Park bloodshed was a death knell for the Moratorium and future attempts at peaceful mass demonstrations. Although the organizers, as the *Times* reporters had repeatedly underscored, were blameless for the violence, they nonetheless felt the wrath not only of the law enforcement establishment but also of conservative forces within their own community who equated protesters with gang members. "The attitude of the press changed noticeably," wrote Acuna. "Salazar's death was forgotten and the daily press dwelled on the violence ... The *Sun* printed a letter from a 'disgusted ELA mother,' who defended the police and condemned the marchers."[24] To make things worse—that is to say, to make the campaign against the movement more credible—a clandestine group calling itself the Chicano Liberation Front began bombing everything in sight, including Roosevelt High School, seven banks, two supermarkets, a Chevron facility and city hall. The group also warned that it had stolen rifles from a ROTC facility. The explosions were mostly small-scale and there were no injuries, but the aura of incipient urban terrorism was a splendid gift to the enemies of the movement. The falling plaster also dovetailed with the indictment of "Los Tres," a trio of activists involved in a community campaign against drug sales, who were accused of shooting and paralyzing a notorious dealer who it turned out was a special agent for the Justice Department division that preceded the DEA.[25]

Alarmed by the prevalence of touts and provocateurs, and convinced that any new protest would only repeat a tragic pattern, Eastside activists turned to new arenas of activity. Muñoz and the Moratorium veterans, allied uncomfortably with the Berets, initiated La Marcha de la Reconquista from Calexico to Sacramento, carefully avoiding the City of Los Angeles. Conceived as a protest against the Reagan administration that would also advertise the infant Raza Unida Party, it quickly pushed relations between the two groups to the breaking point. David Sanchez, suspicious of the role of Marxists within the new party, refused to support the RUP and adopted a distant attitude toward the march. His followers on the march, meanwhile, grew menacing, waved guns, and generally intimidated Muñoz and the Moratorium people. It was their last collaboration, and the exhausting march produced negligible results.

In the fall elections, however, a great burst of enthusiasm accompanied Raul Ruiz's campaign as an RUP candidate against Democrat Richard Alatorre and Republican Bill Brophy in the Forty-Eight Assembly District in East L.A. There was also a PFP candidate. Ruiz came in third with almost 3,000 votes, a credible effort, but he and the Anglo PFPer subtracted 4,000 votes from Alatorre and ensured the election of the Republican. Corona, although supportive of Ruiz, thought the RUP's rigid principle of never endorsing even the most progressive Democrats was a parochial error that arose from generalizing the situation in South Texas, where the party had first emerged. In the Rio Grande Valley, Tejanos were an overwhelming majority, and the Democrats had long operated as a machine representing Anglo growers and corrupt politicians. (In some areas there were actually two Democratic parties: "old" and "new.") In many ways it was an ideal situation for the emergence of a third party of the majority that refused to play plantation politics. The situation in urban California was obviously different and, as Corona attempted to point to his younger amigos, required an "inside-outside" strategy that combined independent candidacies with support for authentic allies among the

Democrats. But a friendly internal debate about RUP strategy was excluded by an explosive polarization between the supporters of José Ángel Gutiérrez, the Texas leader of the original party, and those of Corky Gonzales.

Although important issues were at stake in their rivalry, including differences over the relationship between electoral politics and community organizing, Raul Ruiz thought the essence of the conflict mirrored the political history of Mexico: regionally based caudillos fighting for control of a national movement that never transcended the sum of its geographical components.

> I had the utmost respect for both Corky and Jose Angel. Both had done great work in their communities. But, at the same time, I had my doubts about both of them as national leaders ... [They] were trying to be national leaders but in fact weren't operating nationally. They were quite sectional in their operations and in their perspectives. Curiously, the same thing could be said of Cesar Chavez. He focused almost exclusively on farmworkers in California. We really had no national leaders.[26]

The bitter leadership contest soon percolated down to the base in California, where it drove a wedge between many former compañeros and accentuated the political inexperience of a movement still in its early twenties. The RUP's trajectory was much like that of the Peace and Freedom Party: both were the products of extraordinary campaigns (Bob Scheer's near-defeat of a powerful establishment Democratic congressman in Berkeley, and the Texas RUP's clean sweep of political offices in the middling farmtown of Crystal City) that generated hopes that such successes could be repeated elsewhere. In both cases, however, the state or national third parties that were formed ignored the special local circumstances of these initial victories; and they treated far too cavalierly the risk of playing the role of spoiler in elections where their voters could tip the balance in favor of much more reactionary Republicans.[27] As a result, both parties soon stumbled, lost their initial élan, and ended up squandering their unity in endless internal squabbles. Whereas the PFP ended up in a decades-long state of suspended animation, with a line on the ballot but no pulse, the RUP totally collapsed in the mid Seventies, and Chicanos lost their best hope for a unifying national-action framework.

In 1972 one Chicano movement was in steep decline, while another, both more and less radical than its predecessor, was emerging. The social forces shaping a new phase of Chicano politics included: (1) an acceleration of undocumented immigration that was countered by a sharp rise in local nativism and INS repression; (2) the successful institutionalization of Chicano studies on a number of campuses and the creation of an array of new publications; (3) the embrace of hard-core Leninism or Maoism by a large cohort of 1968–69 activists, who were organized in two competing organizations (CASA and the August Twenty-Ninth Movement); and (4) the accretion of power by a union-funded economic development corporation (TELACU) that would soon spawn a new Eastside Democratic political machine. The last three stories properly belong in another narrative: a movement history of L.A. in the 1970s. But La Hermandad Mexicana Nacional, another project associated with the leadership of the indefatigable Bert Corona, deserves at least a callout since it started planting roots in Los Angeles from 1968 onward. It marked a debut of sorts for new immigrants as major social actors.

Corona, who left the leadership of MAPA feeling that it was being taken over by "middle-class lawyers," turned his attention toward the struggles of immigrant workers. In San Diego, the Hermandad Mexicana Nacional, formed in the aftermath of deportations in the early 1950s, had been successfully aiding the undocumented for years. It was a hybrid of a traditional mutual aid association—popular safety nets in immigrant communities of many nationalities—with a legal defense group. Corona, together with crack union organizer Soledad "Chole" Alatorre, persuaded its leaders to let them expand the franchise to L.A. and elsewhere in California. By 1972 the new branches in East L.A., the harbor, and elsewhere counted several thousand dues-paying members and provided a constituency of more than 60,000 people with services ranging from legal aid to food and shelter. Hermandad's community centers were known as Centros de Acción Social Autónomos (CASAs) and welcomed volunteers with activist backgrounds. Corona and Alatorre, although focused primarily on grooming leadership among young immigrants, hoped that the new movement could also provide some of the Blowout and Moratorium veterans with a path toward class politics. Indeed, their work within the original CASAs soon inspired the creation of the short-lived but seminal Marxist party, the Hermandad General de Trabajadores, which was the first of the Chicano New Left formations to build a serious relationship with the Mexican Far Left.[28] The name of its paper, *Sin Fronteras*, became an enduring slogan, but also signified a new strategic vision of the "combined and uneven development" of the Chicano and Mexican revolutions.

Meanwhile the Brown Berets, the targets of ceaseless infiltration, surveillance, and prosecution, made a final attempt to reinvigorate their image by raising the Mexican flag on Catalina Island, twenty-six miles offshore. At the beginning of Labor Day weekend, twenty-five Berets led by David Sanchez and dressed in casual clothing took a crowded holiday ferry to Avalon, an old-time resort town, then marched to the top of the bluff that overlooks the legendary Casino. They changed into combat fatigues, raised their flag, erected tents, and began digging latrines. A rumor spread that the Mexican Army had landed, but the Berets, although stern-faced, were anything but menacing. "Sanchez exchanged greetings with passing tourists, the mayor of Avalon, and the local youngsters," the *Times* reported. He told the interviewers that Catalina and the other Channel Islands had never been ceded to the United States by the Treaty of Guadalupe Hidalgo in 1848—a claim that had some historical justification—and that they were liberating the island in order to bring attention to the problems of Chicanos on the mainland. They had not brought any provisions and were short of cash, so townspeople began to donate food, and some of the local Chicano families, traditional employees of the Santa Catalina Island Company, invited them home for dinner. The "occupation" lasted for more than three weeks and was tolerated by the sheriffs (Catalina was officially part of LA County) after they established that the Berets were peaceful and unarmed. Their camp became a popular stop for the Island's tour buses. As Sanchez had hoped, the action garnered much media coverage, but he was bitterly disappointed that it was mostly devoted to the comic opera aspects of the adventure rather than the substantive issues. After twenty-four days, the mayor, backed up by the sheriffs and the company's private guards, issued an ultimatum to leave. The Berets, who for five years had been portrayed as fierce revolutionists and likely terrorists, made no protest and quietly departed.[29]

A month later the Berets' national office expelled Sanchez, claiming that he had "killed another member, committed rape, and stole money from the organization." He immediately retaliated by dissolving the national office and the rest of the organization. "All legitimate and official capacities of the Brown Beret national organization," he told a press conference, "have been dissolved. As prime minister … and founder of the Brown Berets, I resign my post, as well as membership." He said that factionalism within the organization, largely instigated by police agents, was on the verge of turning violent, as had happened to the Panthers. He denounced the collapse of discipline and leadership in the dissident chapters, a phenomenon he labeled "hippie-ism," and deplored what that had done to the group's prestige.[30] Although some chapters outside of L.A. fought to survive as independent collectives, the Berets otherwise quickly disappeared, shocking Chicano activists and surprising the police agencies who had used the group as an invaluable prop in their scare campaigns. The formal certificate of death was an FBI memorandum the following summer telling local offices that since there had been no evidence of any Beret activity for the previous six months, they should end their investigations.[31]

Part VIII

Other Liberations

33

The Many Faces of Women's Liberation (1967–74)

On September 20, 1972, seven LAPD officers and three state medical examiners raided the Women's Self-Help Clinic on Crenshaw Boulevard. They had warrants for the arrest of two staff members, Carol Downer and Colleen Wilson. The charge: practicing medicine without a license. The women weren't there; the police seized rubber gloves, syringes, IUDs, hypodermic needles, menstrual extraction devices; equipment for blood tests, Pap tests, and urine analysis; and patient charts and records. The warrants charged Carol Downer with "diagnosing a women's illness as a yeast infection and treating it with yogurt." Colleen Wilson was charged with eleven counts, including "performing a menstrual extraction, giving pelvic examinations and testing for pregnancy."[1] The right of women to know their bodies had been declared illegal by law enforcement officials.

Feminist activist and author Barbara Ehrenreich explained the origins of this movement: the "humiliation and helplessness" women felt when doctors called them "difficult" for "asking questions," or diagnosed them as "neurotic" for "possessing a symptom for which the doctors did not yet have a disease." She remembered the "secrecy and shame"—and then the excitement of hearing that two Los Angeles women, Carol Downer and Lorraine Rothman, had taught themselves to do cervical self-examinations, and that Downer was starting the first Feminist Women's Health Center. "It began to seem possible," she recalled, "that, with enough organizing, studying, and—especially—sharing, we might just achieve 'the right to control our own bodies.'"[2]

Carol Downer's defense became a national cause célèbre. Her supporters included Congresswoman Bella Abzug, Gloria Steinem, Robin Morgan, and Dr. Benjamin Spock. The prosecution case rested on the testimony of three undercover agents who had gone to the clinic posing as patients—two female LAPD officers and a high school guidance counselor. The clinic collective decided that Wilson, who had so many charges against her, should plead guilty, and Downer should demand a trial, where the case for women's self-help could be presented to a jury. Wilson made a deal, pled guilty to one count, and was sentenced to a fine of $250, twenty-five days in jail (suspended), and two years of probation.[3]

In the campaign leading up to the trial, Downer argued that the center "does no more than teach vaginal self-examination ... We don't diagnose and we don't treat," she said. "We're in health education ... We realize that women do not know their own bodies and haven't been given the kind of information they need to take care of themselves." The investigator for the state's department of consumer affairs replied that "the case has nothing to do with women's liberation."[4]

The trial lasted for five days, and the courtroom was packed every day. Downer's supporters gleefully called it "the great yogurt conspiracy," pointing out that the police had seized, among the other items, yogurt from the refrigerator. Medical experts for the defense testified that yogurt was used to cure yeast infections "because bacterial agents in the dairy product work to combat bacterial agents spawned by the yeast infection." Downer's attorneys, Diane Wayne and Jeanette Christy, argued that "application of the home remedy was no different than applying eye drops to an eye infection or a Band-Aid to a bruised knee." The deputy city attorney of L.A. replied, "Who are they to diagnose a yeast infection and prescribe yogurt for it?"[5] Everything they were doing at the center, he said, should have been done by a physician.

The jury—eight men and four women—found Downer not guilty. Women's self-help had won a huge victory. The trial and verdict also galvanized local feminists. One wrote,

What man would be put under police surveillance for looking at his penis? What man would have to spend $20,000 and two months in court for looking at the penis of his brother? This case is a clear-cut version of the position of women in America—the lengths to which we must go and the obstacles which must be overcome to be FREE.[6]

As the women's self-help movement grew, historian Ruth Rosen explains, "male doctors became proxy figures for all male authority." Women refused to be passive patients, learned to be assertive, and to do their own research. As a result, the women's health movement "turned women into feminists."[7]

The year after the Downer trial, in 1973, Simon & Schuster published *Our Bodies, Ourselves* by the Boston Women's Health Book Collective—featured at first at places like Sisterhood Bookstore, founded in 1973 in Westwood by two sisters-in-law, Adele Wallace and Simone Wallace. Within a few years, the book became a national bestseller. 1973 was also the year the Supreme Court issued its ruling in *Roe v. Wade*. The course of history had changed over the space of a couple of years.

Chicana Feminism

Meanwhile, a different kind of battle over women's health was underway, with a different constituency: instead of a fight for abortion rights, it was a fight against forced sterilization; and instead of a mostly white constituency, this movement was mostly Chicana. But the underlying issue was the same—women's right to control their own bodies.

"Eleven Latin Women File Suit on Sterilization" read the page-one headline in the *LA Times*; "Claim They Were Coerced or Deceived into Having Operation at Medical Center." The case was a shocker: Dolores Madrigal, a married mother of two who didn't speak English, said she told the doctor and nurse and County-USC Hospital "no" when they suggested in 1973 that she submit to sterilization. "But then, under the severe pain of labor, she said, she signed the consent form"— after being "assured that 'the operation could easily be reversed.'"[8]

There were more: Rebecca Figueroa said that in October 1971, when she went to County-USC to deliver her baby and was bleeding profusely before delivery, nurses told her that "birth control pills caused her sickness and that sterilization was the only alternative to death." She signed the consent form. Maria Figueroa said that she refused to have her tubes tied in June 1971, but in the delivery room and subjected to "repeated solicitation and pressure," she agreed—"provided the baby delivered was a boy"—because she already had a daughter. It was a girl, but the doctor performed a tubal ligation anyway. A total of eleven women told similar stories.

The court case had been preceded by more than a year of organizing, demonstrations, and publicity, organized by the leading Chicana feminist group in California, the Comisión Femenil Mexicana Nacional. It held its first conference in 1973 in Goleta, outside Santa Barbara. More than 800 women participated, representing farmworkers, garment workers, trade unions, college campuses, grassroots communities, and professional groups. One of the key organizers of the Comisión, and later president, was Yolanda Nava, who had been a leader of MEChA at UCLA. The Comisión, Nava later explained, "focused on grassroots activism in poorer communities ... rather than consciousness-raising." Their first projects involved childcare, job training, and a rape hotline.[9] And they discussed abortion, which members regarded as "a fact of life" and "a personal decision." That was a controversial position within the Chicano movement, where Cesar Chavez and other male leaders argued that "smaller families would only diminish the numerical power of the poor" and that "the race" should "multiply" in order to "progress."[10]

But the group's biggest and best-known effort was a campaign to stop forced sterilization. It began in 1973, when Bernard Rosenfeld, a medical resident at County-USC General hospital, had gone to the Center for Law and Justice, a legal aid center in L.A., with confidential hospital records documenting forced sterilization. Antonia Hernandez worked at the center—she had just graduated from UCLA Law School—and, along with attorney Richard Navarette, she set out to find the women in Rosenfeld's documents, hoping to recruit plaintiffs for a class action suit. The attorneys for the class decided they needed an additional plaintiff—a larger group of women who received medical care at County-USC. They turned to the Comisión as the organization that could represent that class of Latinas. Comisión President Gloria Molina and Antonia Hernandez, from their base at the Comisión's Chicana Services Action Center in East L.A., raised funds, organized demonstrations, and distributed press releases to the media.[11]

When the case was finally filed in 1975, the *Times* ran a story featuring a photo of two women: a stern and determined Gloria Molina, and a tearful Dolores Madrigal. The judge eventually ruled in favor of the doctors and the hospital, but the Comisión had won the political fight: the governor and the state legislature strengthened protections against unwanted sterilizations, providing for consent forms in languages other than English, a seventy-two-hour waiting period for patients under twenty-one, and a requirement that women be informed that their welfare benefits would not be terminated if they refused sterilization.

The *Madrigal* case "galvanized an emerging Chicana feminist movement," says historian Vicki Ruiz. And it drew some lines between men and women activists.[12] But the women led this fight and defined the issues.

While these battles over women's health were being fought in Los Angeles, other strands of the new women's activism also emerged in L.A., with distinct constituencies and issues. The earliest, beginning in 1963, was welfare rights organizing among Black women in public housing.

Welfare Rights Organizing

Black women's organizing in L.A. in the Sixties has its own history, beginning in Watts with the remarkable Johnnie Tillmon, who helped found the first grassroots welfare mothers' organization in the country. She explained what it was about in a memorable article in *Ms.* magazine: being on welfare, she said, was like being in a "supersexist marriage." "You trade in 'a' man for 'The' Man," she wrote.

But you can't divorce him if he treats you bad. He can divorce you, of course—cut you off—any time he wants. But in that case, "he" keeps the kids, not you. "The" Man runs everything. "The" Man, the welfare system, controls your money. "He" tells you what to buy and what not to buy, where to buy it and what things cost ... In ordinary marriage, sex is supposed to be for your husband. On A.F.D.C. [welfare] you're not supposed to have sex at all. You give up control of your body. It's a condition of aid.[13]

Johnnie Tillmon was born in Arkansas in 1926 to a family of share-croppers. She left her husband behind when she moved to California in 1960 as a single parent with six children. She got a job in a laundry—doing work she had done in Arkansas—and became the union steward for Local 52 of the Laundry and Dry Cleaning Workers Union. She applied for welfare in 1963, she later said, so she could stay home with her children, the oldest of whom had been skipping school while she was at work. She joined the community group in the housing project in Watts where she lived, the Nickerson Gardens Planning Organization —Nickerson Gardens was the largest public housing project west of the Mississippi, with 1,054 units. She also became active in local politics, working to elect Augustus Hawkins as California's first Black member of Congress in 1962.

The turning point for Tillmon came one Sunday when she heard a neighborhood churchgoer disparage women on welfare as lazy. She organized six women to go to the managers' office to complain, and there, she says, she "noticed a stack of folders on his desk marked "ANC," identifying the women in the housing project who were receiving welfare." (Aid to Needy Children was the official name of the welfare program.) The manager agreed to give them the list, and they talked to more than 300 women—and formed an organization they called "ANC Mothers Anonymous." It was the first organization of women on welfare in the nation, and it was all Black. It was "anonymous" because they didn't want their social workers to know they were members.[14]

At first, ANC Mothers Anonymous worked to help women who were denied assistance or who wanted to complain about their social workers—especially about midnight raids on their apartments, where social workers searched for men staying the night. Any woman on welfare found with a man would not receive a check that month. The group also "tried to help people being evicted, people not being able to get all their aid, people being cut off for whatever reason," Tillmon later explained.

> We began finding out that we could appeal. A lot of people were afraid to. We encouraged folk, if what you need is not met, then these are the places that you write to. And then we found out that we could go with the recipient to ask for a fair hearing. We developed some resources where we could contact a person, maybe on the board of supervisors, or a person in the top administration, because most of your trouble comes from down at the bottom.[15]

And, they demanded respect from caseworkers. The ANC Mothers quickly gained supporters throughout Watts.

L.A.'s first Black TV journalist, Louis Lomax, featured Tillmon and her work with ANC Mothers on his show—the beginning of her rise as a national figure. Similar groups of welfare mothers soon formed in the Bay Area, and others in other parts of L.A. The groups formed the California Welfare Rights Organization, with Tillmon as the group's first president. At an April 1966 conference in Washington, DC, she declared, "When the poverty program is over, the rich will be rich, the poor will be poor, and I will still get a welfare check." That got national publicity, and when Tillmon and women from welfare rights organizations in other states formed the National Welfare Rights Organization in August 1966, she became a national leader.[16]

Then Republicans, led by Ronald Reagan (then a candidate for governor), started attacking welfare recipients, calling them "welfare queens," as the centerpiece of their campaign (along with attacks on Berkeley's Free Speech Movement). Reagan won the election that November. The battle lines had been drawn. While much of the national welfare rights movement focused on defending the right to public assistance, Johnnie Tillmon had a different political agenda: poor women, she argued, needed training to get good jobs so they could support their children, and they needed childcare. She never wanted poverty program funding for ANC Mothers Anonymous and relied instead on private fundraising. Also, while ANC Mothers Anonymous was a Black group, Tillmon thought Black and white poor women should belong to the same organization. She also welcomed lesbians to welfare rights groups. She always said the struggle for welfare rights was not between women and men, but between women and "The Man."

L.A. NOW

The LA chapter of the National Organization of Women formed in 1967, a year after the foundation of the national organization. A media-savvy group in one of the world's media capitals, L.A. NOW had a high-profile presence and from the start organized news-grabbing events. At their first demonstration, on Lincoln's Birthday in February 1969, they picketed the Polo Lounge in Beverly Hills, which refused to serve women at lunch or dinner unless they were escorted by a man. (The assumption at the time was that an unescorted woman at the Polo Lounge was probably a prostitute.) The pickets made it a point to dress fashionably and look respectable to make it clear that they were suitable customers for the place. A week later, four members of NOW staged a sit-in at the Polo Lounge, demanding to be served—a demand that was met, once the news media showed up. The next month, NOW staged a sit-in at the bar at Trader Vic's in Beverly Hills.[17] Nine years earlier, Black students in the South sat-in at lunch counters to protest segregation; women in NOW in L.A. were following their example—but in a way that opened them to the criticism that their action excluded almost all women, who didn't have lunch at the Polo Lounge on their calendars.

The key person organizing L.A. NOW was Toni Carabillo. Many of the founders and organizers of the different strands of women's liberation came out of the Left; after years in the civil rights and anti-war movements, they concluded that women's liberation should be their first priority. But several others had not started out as leftist activists, and had no background in organizing. Carabillo was one of them.

But, after moving to L.A. in the early Sixties as a single, thirty-year-old college-educated woman, she faced discrimination in her career in public relations. She had read Betty Friedan's *Feminine Mystique*, and in 1966 she saw an article in the *LA Times* about the formation of NOW. She wanted to join an organization that dealt with sex discrimination, although, she later recalled, she had "no intention of getting involved"; she "just wanted to give money and have them deal with the problems" she was facing. The next year, she went to a meeting called to set up an LA chapter—one of the first five local chapters. One hundred women were there. Carabillo came out of the meeting as head of the speakers bureau, the recording secretary, and the PR chair, and she soon started the L.A. NOW newsletter. She later said the reason she did not attend the sit-in at the Polo Lounge was that she did not want to risk her job by appearing in public. She went on to serve as president of the LA chapter in 1969 and 1970; during that time the chapter grew from 30 members to 300.[18]

In June 1969, L.A. NOW held an anti–Mother's Day event. The leaflet called it "a general protest against hypocrisy which celebrates 'Mother's Day' one day a year and exploits her year round." Their demands included "a living wage for all women, equal pay for equal work, free child care centers, rehabilitation programs for imprisoned women, ending the special oppression of black and brown women," and also "a world without wars."[19] Clearly they had moved beyond demanding to be served at the Polo Lounge.

L.A. NOW also organized demonstrations that confronted enemies of feminism. On New Year's Day 1971, they picketed the Rose Parade in Pasadena, that international symbol of the glories of Southern California, protesting the presence of Billy Graham as grand marshal. He had recently published a piece in the *Ladies' Home Journal*, "Jesus and the Liberated Woman," where he made the familiar argument that "the word of God teaches that the primary duty of a woman is to be a homemaker."[20]

NOW's biggest efforts in L.A. (and nationwide) focused on job discrimination. In March 1971, L.A. NOW demonstrated outside AT&T as part of a nationwide campaign against the Bell System, the largest employer of women in America, which discriminated in hiring and promotion (and two years later agreed to a $38 million settlement with the Equal Employment Opportunity Commission that benefited 13,000 female employees.)[21] In August 1973, L.A. NOW joined a march in support of Chicana workers striking against Farah pants, the second largest employer in El Paso with 4,000 workers, all of whom were Latino and 80 percent women.[22] A third initiative targeted opponents of the Equal Rights Amendment, which was before Congress in 1972; that August, L.A. NOW protested the AFL-CIO's opposition to the ERA by picketing their convention downtown at the Biltmore Hotel.[23]

NOW's less public work focused on lobbying for equal rights and equal pay. *NOW News*, published by the LA chapter, consistently featured legislative issues and campaigns. In May 1970, for example, NOW brought fifty women from L.A. to Sacramento in support of four education bills: one to require hiring more women faculty and administrators at the state colleges and universities, and another that would provide free, full-time day care centers on campus for children of students, staff, and faculty. The third required elementary schools to adopt textbooks that portrayed women and men in non-stereotypical ways.[24]

NOW had been the starting point for Carol Downer, arrested at the Self-Help Clinic in 1972. Her political life had begun on Mother's Day 1969, when Betty Friedan and other founders of NOW demonstrated outside the White House, at the same spot to which suffragettes had chained themselves fifty years earlier. The NOW group was demanding passage of the Equal Rights Amendment—their slogan that Mother's Day was "Rights, not roses."[25] Downer, living in L.A., had six children and a sick husband; hoping to "dig herself out of the hole" in which she found herself, she "went to a meeting not knowing what to expect and was very pleasantly surprised to find that the women there were very happy and ordinary."[26]

At her first NOW meeting in L.A., she signed up for the group's abortion task force—an obvious choice, given her experience: she had had an illegal abortion, and also a legal one. To get the legal one, however, she had had to claim that without it she would commit suicide. Then she volunteered at the Crenshaw Women's Center, which had been founded in 1970. At the Women's Center, Downer helped women get abortions at an illegal clinic in Santa Monica—women's right to abortion had been established in California by the state supreme court in 1969, but the law required that they be performed only by doctors and only in hospitals. Indeed, at that point only doctors could dispense the Pill or provide women with contraceptive devices. At the Santa Monica clinic Downer learned to use a speculum and to look at her own cervix. Her first idea was that a women's self-help clinic should run its own abortion service—at that point, abortion was still illegal in forty-four of the fifty states, and *Roe v. Wade* would not become law for two more years. But she decided on another route, which turned out to be more radical: consciousness raising, meetings for women to learn about their bodies and about how to avoid relying on the medical profession.[27]

On April 7, 1971, Carol Downer made history at an event at Every Woman's Bookstore in Venice by inserting a speculum into her vagina and inviting the other women who had come to this event to observe her cervix.[28] That was the beginning of women's self-help medicine. NOW invited her to do the same demonstration at their national meeting five months later in L.A., and then she did a national tour. Within a year, more than 2,000 women had attended similar self-help sessions at women's clinics across the country.[29]

Lorraine Rothman, one of the founders of the clinic, also went on that national tour, demonstrating the procedure called menstrual extraction, which allowed women to perform very early abortions—up to two weeks after a missed period—"by inserting a small plastic cannula into a woman's uterus and gently extracting the contents of the uterus into a small bottle attached to the cannula."[30] Rothman called the menstrual extraction kit the "Del-Em," and patented it—a unique move in the women's movement. With Downer, she then started the Feminist Women's Health Center in 1972.

Rothman, like Downer, had neither been an activist not come to the women's movement out of the Left. Raised in an Orthodox Jewish family who moved to L.A. when she was twelve, she traced the beginnings of her feminist consciousness to her refusal to have a bat mitzvah—on the grounds that women were treated unequally in Jewish religious practice. As a young adult, Rothman had attended

Cal State LA, receiving her teaching credential, then worked as a substitute teacher and raised a family while her husband worked as a biology instructor at Cal State Fullerton. In 1968 she had joined a consciousness-raising group on campus there, and then joined the Orange County chapter of NOW. In 1971, she helped form the Crenshaw Women's Center, and with Carol Downer visited the illegal abortion clinic run by Harvey Karman on Santa Monica Boulevard in West L.A. to "learn how Karman performed abortions." It was there that she had decided that Karman's manual vacuum aspiration equipment should be available for home use.[31]

The Crenshaw Women's Center

The local NOW chapter became the first organization of Sixties feminism in L.A. in 1967; radical women, who wanted to go beyond NOW's focus on legislating equality, trace their organizational beginnings to an unlikely moment: Immaculate Heart College's hosting of a feminist conference in fall 1969. It led to the formation, in 1970, of the Crenshaw Women's Center, funded for its first six months by UCLA. The center organized consciousness-raising groups, provided abortion counseling, ran a legal clinic, published a newsletter (later, *Sister* magazine), and in February 1971 started a food co-op and a free store for clothing exchange.

The most lasting contribution of the Crenshaw Women's Center, after launching the women's health movement, was its work on rape, started by Joan Robins. She had come to L.A. as a student at UCLA, where her "goal," she said, "was just to be an anti-war activist." She started working at the *Free Press*, and traces the development of her feminist consciousness to an interview she did for the *Freep* with prominent Chicago feminist Marlene Dixon in 1969.[32] Robins went to her first women's liberation meeting with Nancy Hollander, an early SDS organizer and feminist, and then with Dorothy Bricker she formed "Women's Liberation One," a consciousness-raising group that met at the Haymarket, the leftist coffeehouse. She helped found the Crenshaw Women's Center, and edited and wrote for *Sister* magazine throughout its existence.

After a friend was raped while hitchhiking, Robins organized the "Anti-Rape Squad" in the summer of 1971. Their goal, she said, was "to find rapists and confront them"—by spray-painting their names on walls at the Venice boardwalk. They also launched a campaign to encourage women to pick up female hitchhikers, distributing bumper stickers that declared, "Sisters give rides to sisters." In 1973 they set up a rape hotline at the Westside Women's Center, staffed by volunteers, and named themselves the LA Commission on Assaults against Women (LACAAW). That June, they held a conference on rape, which was attended by 200 women. Their position from the beginning, she explained, was that rape was "a political act of violence, not primarily sex, but men demonstrating their power over women when they might feel powerless in other areas."[33]

The Crenshaw Women's Center closed on December 31, 1972, after some of its members and much of its energy shifted to the Westside Women's Center, which had opened its office that September. Sherna Gluck was one of the founders of the Westside Center and a key figure in the women's movement in L.A. Unlike Carol Downer and Lorraine Rothman, she came to the women's movement from the Left. Born in Chicago, she had gone to Berkeley in the Fifties and joined the Student Civil Liberties Union, fighting to bring Communist speakers on campus. While there, Gluck also became part of an anarcho-pacifist group, which demonstrated against ROTC—she later called it "a precursor of SLATE and Free Speech Movement." She moved to L.A. to attend graduate school at UCLA, where she promptly joined "an anti-militarism demonstration during an air-raid drill on campus." Then in 1965 she took part in an anti-war demonstration organized by the Women's International League for Peace and Freedom—work which also led her to get involved with SDS. Gluck's turn toward the women's movement began in 1970 with her work on a radio program for KPFK called "Feminism in Your Living Room." In 1971 she went to work with the Crenshaw Women's Center, where she did abortion counseling. She also wrote frequently for *Sister* magazine, and in 1972 founded the Feminist History Research Project, conducting oral histories with women activists from earlier eras. Later she recalled that her decision to participate in the Women's Movement was "intellectual," and only later became personal.[34]

The LA Women's Union

Jackie Goldberg followed a similar trajectory: "Some of us," she recalled, "were first leftists and then became feminists." A native Angeleno, she had gone to college in Berkeley, became a leader of the Free Speech Movement in 1964, and returned to L.A. in 1967. "I was one of the left women who was going to go into these feminist organizations and raised their political consciousness," she recalled in a 2015 interview:

> Certainly there were women who were oppressed, I didn't deny that. But compared to African Americans and poor people and Vietnamese at the time—really, we said, come on! We needed consciousness raising. And that's what happened to me. Joan Anderson, who had been in the legal collective Bar Sinister, grabbed me and said "you need to come to this group." It worked. I began to think: maybe we shouldn't wait to do this until after the revolution. Maybe we need to do this right now![35]

Goldberg had already read "Wages for Housework" by Selma James—"that really did impress me," she said. So she got involved in the Crenshaw Women's Center. She taught a class on women's economics and the law. Then a group of women organized a one-day conference at UCLA to set up a citywide organization around women's issues. She went—and, as she remembered, "a brilliant woman named Susan Rabinovitch laid out a vision of what a women's liberation union might be able to do if we could actually organize across race and class lines."[36]

So they started the LA Women's Union. Another leader was Jan Breidenbach; she would later describe the group's members as "feminists who were coming out of the Left but didn't want to reject the Left." There were three socialist feminist women's unions in the country at the time, she recalled: Chicago, Oakland and L.A., "all formed about the same time, all with the same mission—to combine socialism and feminism."[37]

At its height, Goldberg said, the LA Women's Union had a membership of 200. They organized different chapters. She and Breidenbach were part of an agitprop street theater group they called "Bread and Roses"—they performed at schools, universities, churches, unions, and conferences. Interviewed almost fifty years later, she could still sing a few verses of one of their songs—to the tune of "Maria" from *West Side Story*: "Stagflation—I just met a thing called stagflation …" "We did a fashion show of blouses from the oppressed nation of your choice," she recalled. "We did a cheer, 'Smash Guilt!,' with pompoms."[38] At performances they passed out a leaflet that read "We know that a Guerrilla Theater alone is not sufficient. Bread and Roses Theater gives voice to our anger, our values, and our goals. It gives visibility and force to the voices of women now being raised against the sexism and degradation of people. It is our hope to be part of 'the rising of the Women.'"

Another Women's Union chapter, called "Nine to Five," agitated around workplace issues. "We were bold and audacious," Goldberg recalled.

> We would call major companies in L.A. and tell them they had a problem with the way women were treated in their organization. We got some companies to meet with us—I don't know why, maybe because it was the right time and the right place. We showed them that women got paid less than men for the same jobs. We showed them that women had a harder time getting promoted. Some companies actually did something about it.

And they started doing International Women's Day events. "That was the best thing we did," she recalled—"reaching out to Black groups and brown groups; marching downtown and stopping outside the offices of corporations that oppressed women."[39]

In early 1974, they helped set up the Coalition of Labor Union Women. They argued that not only did women need to be in the leadership of unions, but also that women's concerns needed to be part of contract negotiations. They worked with the women in the Steelworkers and the Oil and Chemical Workers and the Building Trades "because they were being harassed. Sometimes we were helpful; sometimes we did more harm than good, because we gave them a higher profile." They had a Women against the War chapter. "And of course, we started a million consciousness raising groups. This was a tremendous life-changing thing for huge numbers of people."[40]

The First West Coast Lesbian Conference

Lesbian feminists began organizing in L.A. around 1970, when lesbians in the Gay Liberation Front decided they had more in common with women—even straight ones—than they did with gay men; they differed with gay men especially on promiscuity. Meanwhile, lesbians in groups on the left decided they had more in common with other lesbians than they did with male radicals. Lesbian feminists worked in the women's health movement and the rape crisis centers, and they helped organize the historic West Coast Lesbian Conference at UCLA in April 1973. Two thousand women showed up, coming from twenty-six states and several other countries—it seemed to have been the largest single gathering of lesbians in history at that point.[41] UCLA had provided the space as a result of the work of Sheila Kuehl—a dean there at the time, though still in the closet.

The conference was organized by, among others, a new magazine, *Lesbian Tide*, edited by Jeanne Córdova—its masthead declared it was "maintained by the pride, time, and efforts of a working collective of gay women."[42]

The big blowup that everyone remembers came in Robin Morgan's keynote address, when she attacked a trans woman in the audience, singer and activist Beth Elliot. Robin Morgan labeled her "an opportunist, an infiltrator, and a destroyer—with the mentality of the rapist."[43] The conference then voted on whether to allow Elliott to remain; two-thirds voted in favor, but, according to historian Susan Stryker, "the antitranssexual faction refused to accept the popular results and promised to disrupt the conference if their demands were not met." Elliott sang her song and then left.[44]

The idea that trans women did not belong in "women-only" spaces, and in particular in lesbian spaces, Stryker reports, "spread widely after the conference," and Robin Morgan's speech is recalled today as the opening of the bitter battle between some radical feminists and the trans movement. Trans women say that they are women because they feel female. Mainstream feminists accept that, but some radical feminists, following Robin Morgan, argue—as Michelle Goldberg explained in the *New Yorker* in 2014—that "anyone born a man retains male privilege in society; even if he chooses to live as a woman—and accept a correspondingly subordinate social position—the fact that he has a choice means that he can never understand what being a woman is really like." When trans women seek to be accepted as women, "they are simply exercising another form of male entitlement." In response, trans women and their allies—starting at that UCLA conference—"point to the discrimination that trans people endure; although radical feminism is far from achieving all its goals, women have won far more formal equality than trans people have."[45]

The LA Council of Women Artists

Many cities had NOW chapters, and many had radical women's centers and clinics, rape crisis hotlines, and welfare rights organizations. L.A. was distinctive for two contributions to the national women's liberation movement—not only the women's self-help health movement started by Downer and Rothman, but also the feminist art movement centered around Judy Chicago, who, with Miriam Schapiro, started the Feminist Art Program at Cal Arts in 1971. Chicago and others organized the Women's Building, a mecca for feminist artists, in 1973, and Judy Chicago created *The Dinner Party*, an epic feminist artwork, starting in 1974. That story has been told often and well,[46] but there was also an earlier chapter that has received far less attention: the story of the LA Council of Women Artists. Joyce Kozloff explained their beginnings: she was an aspiring artist, the mother of a one-year-old, and a faculty wife—she had come from New York with her husband, critic Max Kozloff, who was to teach at Cal Arts in its first year. She recalled a faculty party in 1971 where the wife of another faculty member said to her, "I'm starting a consciousness-raising group, would you like to join?" She replied, "What's that?"[47]

The group was formed at the Westside Women's Center in Santa Monica. "It wasn't a group like some of my friends' groups in New York," Kozloff recalled, "with other artists. These were women who had different ages, different professions, different experiences. But it didn't matter. The basic consciousness-raising process works." She explained:

> You choose a subject for the night, and you go around, and each addresses it from her own experience. Then when everyone's done speaking, there's a discussion. And what you find out is the commonality of your experience. Your basic subjects: How do you feel about your body? How do you feel about your mother? Very, very basic. And within a couple of months we were all totally radicalized.

Because of the work in the CR group, "I was angry all the time," Kozloff said. "I was unpresentable at dinner parties. Some man would say something that would just tick me off, and I couldn't control myself. I would just blast the guy. I think that happened to a lot of women."

She was invited by a friend to an all-women brunch, with women she had never met. Each of them described the project they were working on. "When it came to me, I didn't have a project," she recalled. Her friend "started yelling at me and saying, 'All you do is talk about consciousness raising but you're not doing anything.' I remember holding back the tears. She said 'Put up or shut up, I'm tired of this already.' So I said, 'What do you want me to do?'" She was told, "'You're going to organize the women artists of Los Angeles.' Well, I didn't know any except the ones in that room. But everybody gave me lists. And everyone I called gave me more names. I believe I called sixty-five women."

They held their first meeting in her small apartment in Ocean Park, Santa Monica. Everyone introduced themselves. "I was told afterward that a lot of these women didn't know that some of the other women were artists. They knew them as wives of male artists. And some of them introduced themselves with their own names, and the others had only known them with the names of their husbands."[48]

Ten consciousness-raising groups were formed out of that meeting; one of them would last almost twenty years.[49] One group decided to take on the LA County Museum—"it was the only game in town" at that point, Kozloff later said. "Somebody brought the catalogue of their new Art and Technology show," an expensive multiyear project. The cover of the catalogue had a grid of sixty-four faces of the artists in the show; all were men. The women, Kozloff recalled, "were absolutely enraged." The first action of the new "Los Angeles Council of Women Artists" was thus to publish a report on the exclusion of women artists from LACMA and to demand their inclusion. They counted the works by men and women on the walls of the museum, and in past shows—5 out of 800 were by women. The only solo show by a woman in LACMA history had been that of Depression-era photographer Dorothea Lange, decades earlier.

"We are not seeking token acceptance into museums," the council's statement declared. "We want to change the structure ... Our efforts are part of the efforts of women throughout this country to give full, meaningful status to women in every area of our society." They presented twelve demands: among them, that exhibits of contemporary art be fifty-fifty women and men; they demanded the same for the board of trustees, and for all jobs at LACMA. Finally they demanded that LACMA do a show of women artists of the past. "We had a lot of media-savvy people in the group," Kozloff recalled. "We had a press conference. It was on the radio, it was in the newspapers, it was on the evening TV news. I think it was embarrassing for the museum. They were taken by surprise. And that's why they met with the group."[50] The museum did agree to one of the demands: the exhibition *Women Artists 1550–1950*, curated by Linda Nochlin and Ann Sutherland Harris. Though it took five years, it eventually opened in 1976.[51]

Women's Equality Day, 1973

The LA women's movement, like the national movement, was divided among liberals, radicals, and socialist feminists, and efforts to overcome race and class divisions were not consistently successful. But an impressive show of unity came in August 1973, when twenty-five LA feminist groups joined together to celebrate the newly established "Women's Equality Day" with a fair in Rancho Park celebrating the fifty-second anniversary of women's suffrage.[52] "Great Guts" awards were presented to Helen Reddy (who sang "I Am Woman"), tennis star Billie Jean King, and Representative Shirley Chisholm, the first Black woman elected to Congress. Sponsors of the event included the LACAAW, La Comisión Feminil Mexicana, the Feminist Women's Health Center, Womanspace (a women's art gallery) and the League of Women Voters, as well as several local chapters of NOW. The entertainment featured a guerilla theater presentation and an example of a consciousness-raising group by the Long Beach chapter of NOW. And, in keeping with the 1973–74 National NOW action against poverty, the booths included one where attendees could write representatives in Washington and Sacramento in support of a minimum wage bill and other crucial legislation. The "Great Guts" awards were followed by the presentation of "Class Awards" to women who had voted in 1920, fifty-two years earlier, and then to "those who have filed sex discrimination grievances against employers."[53] That day connected past, present, and future.

Taking part in the beginning of the women's movement in L.A. was "an incredible experience," Joyce Kozloff of the LA Council of Women Artists said. "I've always felt I was very lucky to have participated in that moment. It doesn't leave you. It was a moment of such optimism and enthusiasm and energy. We thought we could change the world. The world doesn't change that fast. But we did change some things."[54]

34

"Everybody Wanted It": The Free Clinic (1967–70)

The counterculture famously celebrated sex, drugs, and rock 'n' roll. The kids listened to Bob Dylan's exuberant "Everybody Must Get Stoned," and the Rolling Stones' irresistible "Let's Spend the Night Together." And some of the young people who got stoned and spent the night together ended up as patients at the LA Free Clinic.

On a typical evening at the Free Clinic, on Fairfax, volunteers at the reception desk interviewed walk-ins, all young and white. One worried he had a venereal disease, another said he had crabs, and one guy said he feared the drugs he had taken contained rat poison. One wanted his rash looked at, another was concerned that he had had sex with somebody who had hepatitis. And one woman wanted a pregnancy test. Rock music was playing, and free cans of Coke were handed out. The hallways were packed with people. In an examination room, a guy with long, curly hair played his guitar and sang while a volunteer doctor waited patiently to begin the examination.[1]

The first free clinic of the Sixties had been organized in Haight-Ashbury, during the summer of 1967. The LA Free Clinic was the second in the nation, opening a few months later. Dozens and then hundreds would follow. In 1969 the clinic saw more than 1,200 medical patients a month, and counselors saw almost 200 people a month. Every night thirty volunteers came in to work at the medical and legal clinics.[2] The professional staff—doctors, lawyers, and psychologists—worked at the clinic mostly at night, after putting in eight hours in their straight jobs. Young people came because of the Free Clinic's philosophy—the staff called it "nonjudgmental," but behind that term was a worldview. David Smith, founder of the Haight-Ashbury Free Clinic, explained that "the 'Free' in Free Clinic refers more to a state of mind than to the absence of a cashier. Free means an entire philosophy of service … free of red tape, free of value judgments, free of eligibility require-ments, free of emotional hassles, free of frozen medical protocol, free of moralizing, and last and least, free of charge." At the Free Clinic, addiction was not seen as a moral weakness and certainly not viewed as a crime. Gonorrhea was not a punishment for sexual activity. One of the hallmarks of the clinic: "You can't tell the doctors from the patients." Their policy was to renounce "impersonal standards such as credentials and uniforms as a way of relating to people."[3] Finally, in the words of Smith, in 1967, healthcare at free clinics was seen as "a right, not a privilege."[4]

"Free" also meant free of legal problems for the patients. The clinic had anticipated searches of patients' medical records—by subpoena, which was legal. They understood that they would fail if young clients knew their medical records could get them in trouble with the police or the courts, so the clinic set strict limits on record keeping, especially on counseling records, which as a matter of policy made no reference to drug use or to the identity of underage runaways whose parents might be searching for them.[5]

But that freedom for patients also meant that the staff were some-times breaking the law—on abortion, on medical exemptions for the draft, and on the enforcement of drug laws. And these acts of civil disobedience were particularly risky at a time of widespread hostility toward longhairs and hippies—not just from parents, but from Mayor Yorty and Governor Reagan (who famously said, "A hippie is someone who looks like Tarzan, walks like Jane and smells like Cheetah"), and of course, from the LAPD and the sheriffs—especially in the era of riots on Sunset Strip, just a few blocks up the hill from the clinic. Nevertheless, the Free Clinic became one of the counterculture's biggest and most successful institutions in L.A.

The beginning, however, was not auspicious. The Free Clinic had its first encounter with the LAPD three weeks after it opened, in

November 1967—but the staff agreed with the police on that one. The clinic had opened that month on Fairfax near Santa Monica Boulevard, founded by John Duke and Leonard Malcolm. They called it the "Albert Schweitzer Memorial Clinic," and the *Times* wrote a friendly piece about the new clinic and its founders, reporting that Duke and Malcolm were psychology PhDs. Malcolm was quoted saying that the homeless kids they saw "don't want to be dirty." As if he was replying directly to Reagan, he called that idea "another myth," explaining that "they're dirty because there are no facilities for them."[6]

The favorable press brought many new volunteers, including psychologist Murray Korngold, who taught at Cal State LA—the oldest volunteer, at forty-seven; pediatrician Barry Liebowitz, thirty-one, who worked for Kaiser in the San Fernando Valley, and lawyer Phil Deitch, thirty-seven. None were movement activists, and none had any experience with social work.

There was another person who read the article in the *Times*; he called the reporter, Noel Greenwood, and said he had been a cellmate of John Duke's at Soledad prison in California and that Duke's claim to have a PhD was a lie. Greenwood investigated and then called Korngold, who later described the phone call in an interview with historian Rebecca Baird: Greenwood, Korngold recalled, told him that "these guys" were "lying their heads off, they're peddling dope, fucking young girls who come in for treatment … Very nasty stuff."[7] The LAPD, he said, was about to arrest Duke for dealing in drugs while on parole for grand theft auto, forgery, and check fraud.

On November 22, 1967, the police arrived at the clinic. They were met by Korngold, who let them in, and they arrested Duke for parole violation; Malcolm promptly fled the city, and the clinic closed. In the previous couple of weeks Duke and Malcolm had made swift progress, recruiting fifty volunteers, including doctors, lawyers, and psychologists. The clinic had been seeing between seventy and one hundred patients a night, and had been open less than a month. "It was all lies," Korngold told Baird, "but at the same time it was a great idea!"[8]

The motivation of Duke and Malcolm has never been clear. There wasn't much money in the clinic, so fraud seems unlikely. They had worked really hard to build it into something substantial. And they had gone to the trouble of getting "Doctor of Social Psychology" degrees from the Science Progressive Life Association in Kansas City—they said they actually had to take a written exam to receive that "doctorate." Malcolm, who had recently earned a BA from Cal State, had described himself as a "staff member" of Gateways Psychiatric Hospital, run by a Jewish welfare agency; his job in fact was caretaker—he didn't treat or advise any patients. The *Times* reported that the two were "well mannered and dressed conservatively in brown or charcoal gray suits" and were "well received before civic and medical groups where they gave talks on hippie medical problems." Duke wasn't available for comment after his arrest, but Malcolm told the *Times*, "I can walk down Fairfax Ave. and 100 kids will recognize me ... I know their problems. I enjoyed working with the kids. I wish this had not happened and I'm sorry it did. I feel I was an effective worker."[9]

Liebowitz, Korngold and Deitch decided it was up to them to reorganize and reopen the clinic as a registered nonprofit. All of them had full-time jobs, and none had any experience running nonprofits or doing fundraising. Korngold later said he felt like Charlie Chaplin in *Modern Times*, where he picks up a red flag that has fallen off the back of a lumber truck, and, trying to return it, inadvertently ends up leading a Communist parade.

The clinic's founders didn't want a board of directors, because they wanted policy decided democratically. But to comply with the law, a board was formed: Korngold, the psychologist, who was an LSD researcher and enthusiast; Liebowitz, the pediatrician, who was more conservative and conventional; and Deitch, the attorney. Korngold said he had dropped acid more than one hundred times, with dosages ranging from 25 to 500 micrograms. At the clinic, administrator Marsha Getzler told Baird, Korngold "dressed in flowing robes like a guru." Liebowitz was the opposite—he dressed and acted more like a traditional professional. But, Deitch said, Liebowitz was "the guiding light of the clinic—everybody really respected him."[10]

When the clinic reopened in early December, eighteen doctors and five clinical psychologists were working under Liebowitz and Korngold. Favorable press from the *Times*—Korngold was quoted saying that volunteers shared "a certain anguish at turning away anybody who is in trouble"—helped recruit more volunteers.[11]

But what they needed most was the right building in the right place. A building was for rent a few blocks down on Fairfax, across from CBS Television City—prime real estate that cost $800 a month. Liebowitz met the landlord down the block at Canter's Deli, and, drawing on their shared Jewish heritage and the Jewish traditions of the neighborhood, he persuaded the landlord to do a mitzvah—a good deed—and rent the space for $200. The clinic moved into its new space just a few weeks after its brief closure.

One of the first priorities of the newly reorganized clinic was to persuade the LAPD not to arrest anyone inside; indeed, the police knew that many of the people who came to the clinic "would be in possession of drugs." The more ominous problem was that the police saw the clinic as a magnet for people selling drugs. And the neighbors didn't like drug dealers, especially people at the Jewish Senior Center next door, and the store owners on the block didn't want stoned kids hanging around, much less dealers—so the neighbors sometimes called the cops. And sometimes someone visiting the clinic became violent or threatened staff members. Even in that situation the clinic was "extremely hesitant to call police," the executive director, Leonard Somberg, explained at the time. The policy was to consider "the welfare of the individual against the welfare of the Clinic." And if the clinic was in danger, the preferred solution was to get the threatening person to "leave the immediate area of the Clinic."[12]

So the clinic organizers told the police they should stay out—because "if the kids felt free of harassment at the Clinic, they would feel more inclined to seek help, rather than hide their problems." And, Somberg wrote in a 1971 history, "committee members also made clear that any harassment by public authorities would be met with as much adverse publicity as the clinic could muster in return."[13]

In a surprising move, the LAPD "grudgingly agreed to a moratorium on arrests on the Clinic premises," with one condition: "no flagrant violations." And over the next many years the LAPD stuck by their agreement. They violated it only once—and it wasn't to arrest a drug dealer. In late summer 1968, eight LAPD officers knocked on the front door of the clinic at four in the morning, saying they had received a call from a neighbor reporting a burglar on the roof. They were told that the "burglar" on the roof was actually the night watchman. Nevertheless, they came in and "began looking through desk drawers, medical files and cabinets." They found a girl "who was living here while we were trying to find a place for her to live," the clinic spokesman told the media the next day. When she refused to show the police an ID, they told her, "'You'll have to go to jail.' They grabbed her and handcuffed her and roughly threw her down into a chair." Then they went through her purse. They handcuffed a second guy who had been "outside hanging around" and was "freaked out on acid or something." One cop "was laughing at him and thrusting his gun at him." The guy "was screaming because he was scared to death. They handcuffed him to the railing outside and they were going to leave without freeing him." But finally they gave the key to the cuffs to a clinic staffer, and no arrests were made. The clinic filed a formal complaint—searches of a building are not permitted unless the police have a warrant or are in "hot pursuit"—but of course the LAPD did nothing.[14]

Volunteers

Two hundred fifty volunteers made up the warm heart of the clinic—all worked for no pay. They included MDs and PhD clinical psychologists and other trained professionals, as well as ordinary people who wanted to help. Many came, Somberg explained at the time, because they were "attracted by the excitement, controversy and glamour of a significant new social movement." And there was another reason: many professional and lay volunteers, Somberg calmly said, "were interested in 'turning on' ... Many hoped to find someone who could introduce them to the psychedelic experience on a first-hand basis."[15] So there was more to volunteering than worthy social service. The Free Clinic served as a meeting ground for the straight world and the counterculture, where a middle-aged suburban do-gooder could encounter a real-life hippie, where "ordinary people" who were curious might find a guide to help them relax and float downstream.

Of course, the kids were not looking for curious adults. In the beginning they came in seeking help for drug overdoses and sexually transmitted diseases. The medical services included birth control information and free access to the Pill (donated by the pharmaceutical companies or by doctors in private practice),[16] and prenatal services, along with pregnancy and abortion counseling. Over the next two years the clinic added a dental office—a huge undertaking. The equipment was donated by the widow of a dentist, after staffers found his obituary in the paper and contacted her.[17] Legal help, mostly draft counseling, was available five days a week. They also offered free food every day—they called it a "feed-in"—and classes at what they called a "free school" seven days a week.[18] Many of the kids coming in were runaways who needed help finding places to stay. At the other end of the spectrum, the clinic also had clients who were "ambulatory psychotic," so they set up programs for them as well.[19]

Drugs and the drug culture, of course, were a central factor in the Free Clinic's daily work. In the beginning, 1967–68, this meant psychedelics—which meant providing treatment for "bad trips," sometimes caused by strychnine in LSD—because "it is similar to and often is contained in improperly manufactured LSD." To help kids avoid bad LSD, the clinic set up an "anonymous testing drop-off bin" for suspect drug samples, one user recalled, "sort of like getting your photos developed." But instead of appearing in person to get your results, you would check the *Free Press* for your receipt's number, next to which the paper would print an analysis of "what was really in your sample." One writer found that his "magic mushrooms" were actually "grocery store dried mushrooms laced with junk acid no one would take normally."[20]

The biggest problem drug of the early years was speed. It was much worse than heroin, Korngold said, because "the effects on the central nervous system are absolutely damaging and ultimately lethal." "If the Establishment would stop lying about LSD and pot," he argued, "they could inspire the trust of young people, and warn them instead about the amphetamines, we'd be a lot better off."[21] Somberg added that he told the kids speed had "virtually no emotional or spiritual value."[22]

By 1970 the Free Clinic's work with "drugs of abuse" shifted to heroin and barbiturates. The clinic view of the shift was that young people were turning to other drugs that "serve to help combat or avoid anxiety." The biggest problem was the Nixon administration's war on marijuana, "Operation Intercept," which seized tons of pot coming in from Mexico. "The shortage of a relatively mild psychedelic," wrote Somberg, "only led these frustrated people to use more dangerous drugs."[23] The problem was exacerbated by the fact that methadone treatment for heroin addicts, available in New York and Chicago, was not available in L.A. in 1971.

As for barbiturates, the clinic blamed the drug companies, whose ads told kids, in Somberg's words, that "that a tiny pill or two solve big problems immediately," and also parents, whose medicine cabinets made pills readily available to their children, and "made hypocrites out of mothers and fathers who cry out against any and all drug use. Picture the effect on a child whose mother gets upset talking to her son about drugs and then pops a tranquilizer to calm herself." The clinic's approach was to focus not on the drugs, but rather on "the feelings of the person involved." If these feelings changed, Somberg wrote, "a decline or abandonment of symptomatic drug abuse often follows." The clinic's drug counselors also distinguished between use and abuse. A person who used marijuana, who was aware of the legal dangers and was doing okay in life, was usually not considered in need of treatment. If he were, Somberg said, then "80–90 per cent of all the staff and 'patients' would be lined up for counseling."[24]

Draft counseling was also a big part of the work of the legal department. Mostly, Phil Deitch later said, people didn't come in until they had already been drafted—so the question for them concerned the legal consequences of refusing induction. They were told that could get them up to a year in prison—it all depended on the judge.[25] When clients needed more help, they would be given the phone number of local Quakers. Those who had not yet received an induction notice, but only been summoned for a draft physical, often came in to ask the doctors for letters that would get them a 4-F medical exemption. Of course, it was a violation of medical ethics to make false statements in such letters, and the practice was controversial on the medical staff. Nevertheless, Liebowitz later told Baird, clinic doctors did it "on a fairly regular basis"—"even the conservative ones."[26]

The job co-op focused on short-term employment, often one-day jobs. One that was frequently available was work in a local horseradish factory. Although the pay was good, a staff member explained, the "smell made it less appealing."[27] The clinic's free school ran seven days a week, with free classes in guitar and ceramics, among other things—Stephen Stills of the supergroup Crosby, Stills, Nash and Young showed up to teach at the guitar workshop at least once.[28] And the Free Clinic workshop aimed to "rehabilitate the jobless and directionless youth" of the area with classes aimed to teach skills that could get them jobs. The first were a photography lab, a sewing clinic, and a sandal-making shop.[29]

Money was a huge problem, even though only a handful of staff were paid. The monthly budget was between $4,000 and $5,000. The only paid staff were a clinic administrator, four assistant administrators and the night watchmen—but, as Somberg admitted in 1971, even the minimal salaries offered by the clinic were sometimes not paid.[30] And the stress of managing 250 volunteers and thousands of clients meant the turnover in paid staff was great—few lasted more than two years. The clinic by definition provided services without charge, so the money to run the place had to come from somewhere else. The city of L.A., the county and the State of California were all suspicious of the clinic and unwilling to provide support. And the clinic staff were suspicious of contributions by individuals "interested in their own self-aggrandizement," refusing any funding that would set conditions or "compromise the Clinic's receptive atmosphere of the confidentiality of its clientele."[31]

The initial funding came from the Monterey Pop Festival of 1967: $5,000. And there were many benefit rock concerts: at the Kaleidoscope, a short-lived club on Sunset Boulevard, the 1969 bill included Linda Ronstadt, Frank Zappa and the Mothers of Invention, Chicago, and others;[32] and a September 1968 benefit concert at the Rose Bowl had an astounding lineup: Joan Baez, the Everly Brothers, Big Brother and the Holding Company, the Byrds, Country Joe, Junior Wells with Buddy Guy, and Wilson Pickett. But the Rose Bowl concert lost money, despite the fact that the musicians all performed for free. Not even enough tickets were sold to pay the union crews.[33] And celebrities contributed: James Coburn threw a fundraising party at his Hollywood Hills home; the Smothers Brothers contributed, and so did George Carlin. The LA premiere of *Hair* was a clinic benefit. The greatest moment, though, came when Elvis stopped by with a check for $10,000.[34]

End of the Carnival

By 1971, four years after the Free Clinic's founding, the clientele was changing. Originally virtually all white and all young people, by 1971 almost a third of the patients were Black. And the clientele was shifting away from those "identified with the youth culture"; increasingly it was people who were simply poor. Somberg explained why that had happened: the end of the "carnival" on Sunset Strip brought a decline in public youth culture. "The glory of the creation is over," Somberg said, "and a lot of hard work remains for those who are really committed to the new values and life styles." Many of those "really committed" young white people had moved to rural areas to build communes. More poor people, more Black people, and older people were coming in for the dental services—according to Somberg, because they saw that the clinic understood that they had "the right to be heard," and that clinic staff were "listening and responding understandingly and appropriately"—which indeed was what the clinic did.[35]

Part of the clinic's success was due to changes in the law. In the beginning, 1967–68, the clinic helped thousands of young people who had contracted STDs, were pregnant, or wanted birth control pills—all of which, by law, required parental consent. Thus, the clinic policy of treating them without parental consent amounted to civil disobedience. But the California legislature changed the law in the fall of 1968 to eliminate the parental consent requirement, after which two dozen private and public clinics in L.A. began treating kids for those afflictions.

Abortion was another area of legal change. In June 1967, Governor Reagan signed the Therapeutic Abortion Act, which liberalized abortion in California by permitting abortions when a doctor determined that pregnancy endangered the physical or mental health of the mother. Before that, abortion had been a crime unless the life of the mother was in danger. The clinic was one of the few places, by then including the Crenshaw Women's Center, that provided information about abortions and abortion law.[36]

By the end of 1970 the Free Clinic could claim some amazing successes. Murray Korngold later recalled that

> there was no such thing as a gradual growth, little by little. One day there was nothing, a few months later they were around the block and we were talking on the phone to people who wanted to start a free clinic in Long Beach or Simi Valley ... It wasn't something that one had to labor for. Everybody wanted it.[37]

The Brown Berets opened the Barrio Free Clinic in East L.A. in May 1969, modeled on the one on Fairfax, with the help of the LA chapters of Psychologists for Social Action and Physicians for Social Responsibility. The Peace and Freedom Party helped start the Long Beach Free Clinic in July, and in December 1970 the Panthers opened a clinic in South L.A., headed by Marie Branch (a Black professor of nursing at UCLA) and Terry Kupers (an activist doctor who was white), both members of the Medical Committee for Human Rights. The Panthers named it "The Alprentice Bunchy Carter Free Clinic," after the LA Panther who had been shot and killed at UCLA by US members a year earlier. The Panther clinic was two doors down from the Party's LA headquarters, the scene of the massive police attack on December 8; despite lingering traces of LAPD tear gas, the clinic opened on December 27. The *Free Press* quoted Terry Kupers as saying the clinic would "educate people to what kind of health care they are entitled to."[38]

The first county-run free clinic for young people opened in December 1968, a few blocks from the Fairfax Clinic. It was expected to treat some of the people who had been going to the Free Clinic, and also to provide drugs to the Free Clinic, and possibly some medical staff. County Supervisor Ernest E. Debs, the clinic's key backer, told the *Times* that "for a politician, this isn't easy, you know. The sentiment is all against the hippies."[39] By 1971 the Southern California Council of Free Clinics had fifteen members, and in addition, LA County sponsored close to a dozen tax-supported public clinics, which used the Free Clinic's nonjudgmental approach. Equally amazing, the LA County Board of Supervisors adopted a declaration commending the Free Clinic for its work.[40] And in 1971, the clinic won recognition as a place where conscientious objectors could do alternative service.[41]

Also by 1971, both Korngold and Liebowitz, the founders of the revived clinic, had departed—by mutual agreement, in the interest of promoting democratic decision making by the staff.[42] Korngold moved to San Francisco in the fall of 1969, where he continued his private practice. Liebowitz left the clinic in 1970, moving to New York City to work at a health center on the Lower East Side providing services to heroin users and the homeless.[43]

By 1971 the Free Clinic was seeing 42,000 patients annually.[44] In the decades that followed, the clinic not only survived but moved into the mainstream. That move was completed in 2008 when Cheryl and Chaim Saban—Israeli-American philanthropists and major Democratic Party donors—gifted $10 million to the clinic, which was renamed in their honor. By its fiftieth anniversary in 2017, the Saban Community Clinic had 220 paid employees and an annual budget of $22 million, and saw more than 100,000 patients a year.[45] The flowering of the Free Clinic into the Saban Community Clinic provides a neat encapsulation of how some projects from the Sixties brought the margins into the mainstream—and also allowed figures like Saban to sprinkle their Establishment profiles with countercultural stardust.

35

Gidra: Asian American Radicalism (1969–74)

Asian American radicals started out in the Sixties supporting organizations rooted in other ethnic groups: Shinya Ono, born in Japan, attended Columbia and then joined the Weathermen; Wendy Yoshimura, born in the Manzanar internment camp, went to Berkeley and then joined the Symbionese Liberation Army; Grace Lee Boggs, a Chinese-American, got a PhD from Bryn Mawr and then spent her life working with the Black Left in Detroit.[1] Organized, self-conscious Asian American radicalism appeared for the first time, dramatically and unmistakably, in 1968 at the San Francisco State student strike for the first ethnic studies program. In L.A. several months later, a group of Japanese-American students at UCLA started publishing a monthly newspaper they called *Gidra*.[2] It became the voice of the Asian American movement.[3]

Gidra was "an odd name for a newspaper," historian William Wei later wrote, because at the time "it had no known meaning. The absence of meaning gave it an existential appeal." (Some, however, knew "Gidra" to be the three-headed dragon in Japanese films who was the archenemy of Godzilla.)[4] *Gidra* number one, the first issue of the first Asian American movement newspaper, dated April 1969, led with a quotation from John F. Kennedy: "Those who make peaceful revolution impossible make violent revolution inevitable." The front page described a new kind of group on college campuses, bringing together Afro-Americans, Mexican-Americans, Asian Americans and other people of color to form what they called "Third World organizations." Writing as students, the authors declared that "we will not be educated to sustain, rationalize, or justify an expansionist, capitalist, imperialist society." Thus, from the start *Gidra* identified not only as Asian American but as part of a multiethnic, revolutionary, anti-capitalist "struggle for self-determination."[5]

"Truth is not always pretty," *Gidra* declared in its first editorial. "Not in this world." When it comes to disturbing realities, Americans "try hard to keep from hearing about the feelings, concerns, and problems of fellow human beings." "That is why *Gidra* was created. *Gidra* is dedicated to truth. The honest expression of feelings or opinions, be it profound or profane, innocuous or insulting, from wretched or well-off—that is *Gidra*."[6]

Gidra had been conceived in February 1969 by five students, led by Mike Murase, who were all third-generation Asian Americans and volunteers at UCLA's Asian American Studies Center office.[7] They tried to get school funding for "a community-oriented publication" featuring "the sentiments and ideas of the students," one that would both address "socially relevant topics" and also provide "a vehicle for creative expression." But the administration didn't buy it. So they decided to start their own paper, even though none of the five had any actual experience in journalism. On March 31, 1969, the maiden issue of *Gidra* rolled off the presses, a modest four-page tabloid that had "consumed the full energies of ten people for over a week."[8] They went on to publish sixty issues over the next five years, with almost 250 people working on the paper over that period. It became the largest-circulation Asian American movement publication in the nation, inspiring other movement publications and setting a high standard for writing and reporting that was nonsectarian, politically engaged, and sometimes visionary.

If the lead article in the first issue of *Gidra* advanced a revolutionary Third World perspective, the second article on page one did the opposite: it was a defense of L.A.'s celebrity coroner, Thomas Noguchi, who had just been fired—charged with sixty-two counts of wrongdoing, including charges that he smiled at news of disasters, and that he had botched Robert Kennedy's autopsy.[9] *Gidra* argued he had been a victim of racism—as did many others, including Noguchi himself.[10] Noguchi had been in the news a lot, as "coroner to the stars." He had done the autopsy on Bobby Kennedy in June 1968, and on Marilyn Monroe in 1962. In 1969, the charges against him included "drug abuse" and "mental instability," and he was appealing his termination to the county board of supervisors. *Gidra*'s point was that even the most prominent Japanese American professional could have his career destroyed by racism, and that Noguchi was setting an example—and disproving a stereotype—by refusing to accept his fate.

What was missing from *Gidra* number one was even more striking than what was there: the first issue, and several that followed, had nothing about Vietnam. Nixon had taken the oath of office three months earlier; by April 1969, US combat deaths in Vietnam exceeded the total for all of the Korean War—33,000—and more than 50 percent of Americans thought the war was a mistake. Indeed, April was the month the number of US troops in Vietnam peaked (at 543,000). The war and the anti-war movement were everywhere else in the mainstream media and the alternative press.[11] *Gidra*'s claim to be part of Third World Liberation made its initial silence on Vietnam all the more puzzling.

Gidra number two, dated May 1969, also had nothing on Vietnam, but it did bring up the San Francisco State strike, with a report that seventy-five students from UCLA, USC and Cal State Long Beach picketed S. I. Hayakawa, the right-wing head of San Francisco State who had tried to crush the strike there. He was the featured speaker at the Japanese American Citizens League (JACL) conference in Anaheim. To the delight of the pickets, Hayakawa, in his speech to 600 people, held up a copy of *Gidra*—and denounced it as "errant nonsense."[12]

Vietnam did not appear in *Gidra* until issue number eight, in November 1969, in a news report on the Vietnam Moratorium Day events at Cal State Long Beach. *Gidra* correctly described the national Moratorium day, October 15, as "the largest anti-war demonstration in the history of the US," and declared that the peaceful demonstration was "a form of protest that has thus far been ineffective in changing US military policy in Vietnam." The *Gidra* piece didn't talk about the effect of the war on the Vietnamese, but rather its effect on Japan—it quoted Warren Furutani of the JACL, who said that on account of the Vietnam War, the United States had made Okinawa the "largest military base and ammunition depot in the Pacific." He declared "we must cut off the ugly tentacle of imperialism that reaches to the Far East."[13] That focus reflected the fact that the *Gidra* collective was overwhelmingly Japanese American.

The next issue, however, in December 1969, explained the situation with *Gidra* and Vietnam: "No Asian American group in Los Angeles" had "come out publicly against the war" until very recently, when Asian Americans for Peace made its first public appearance, on November 15 in San Francisco, at the second nationwide Vietnam Moratorium Day. Three hundred Asian Americans marched together, *Gidra* reported in its lead article, and "history was made" that day—with the group "breaking the characteristic silence of Asian Americans."[14] The paper announced that the organization would soon make its first public appearance in L.A. at a march in Little Tokyo.

The first rally in L.A. of Asian Americans for Peace was held on January 17, 1970, and *Gidra* led its February issue with a report: "The silence of the 'quiet Americans' was broken … when over two hundred Asian Americans marched through the business district of Little Tokyo … to petition the government 'to cease the illegal and immoral military action in Vietnam immediately.'" Their signs read "No Vietnamese Ever Called me a Fat Jap," "Asia for Asians," and "Remember Manzanar." One of the speakers, Yuji Ichioka, associate director of UCLA's Asian American Studies Center, recalled how an Iowa housewife said that the recent My Lai massacre involved a "bunch of worthless Asians in a part of the world that's already over-populated anyway. It's no real loss."[15] Ichioka said "a lot of people felt that way when the bomb was dropped on Hiroshima"—the Japanese connection once again. The same commentator also noted "a significant shift in the theme" of this march compared to previous ones: an emphasis on Vietnamese casualties.[16]

Comix

Gidra followed the example of the rest of the underground press and included comix and humor in every issue. Each of the first several issues had a four-panel strip, *Stereotypes*, with wonderful cartoon characters: "One Japanese is a gardener; two Japanese is a karate match; three Japanese is a sneak attack; four Japanese is a relocation camp." In issue number two, the *Stereotypes* strip read "One Chinese is a laundry; two Chinese is a restaurant; three Chinese is an immigration quota; four Chinese is a population explosion."[17]

Indeed, much of the material published in *Gidra* critiqued stereotypes: "The very existence of a publication like *Gidra*," the editors declared, "belies the stereotype of the Asian American as a taciturn, unfeeling and unresponsive individual."[18] Articles attacked Asian Americans who pursued the "model minority" image ("'Jap,' 'Chink'; and 'Gook' are racist words and some of you Uncle Toms are saying what a great nation we live in").[19] And a lot of *Gidra* was about Asian American studies at UCLA. For instance, the battle for office space for Third World student groups was covered closely. The students demanded, and eventually got, Campbell Hall—but the negotiations revealed the administration's "reactionary, colonialist mentality" through its "lies and obstruction."

The paper also critiqued the creation of an Asian American Studies Center with a first-year budget of $100,000. *Gidra* had several complaints: the center was "not a department, not a separate college," and thus subject to annual renewal. It was under the control of the faculty and administration, rather than the students. And, they noted, UCLA got an Asian American Studies Center without a struggle, whereas at San Francisco State no center had been established despite a lengthy strike. "Obviously UCLA is benefiting from the sacrifice of the northern strikers," *Gidra* declared. This was "intended to split the movement for state-wide student power unity." UCLA students should have "demanded equal financial treatment ... of all campuses"[20] —a unique demand in this era.

Thomas Noguchi continued to receive regular coverage in *Gidra*—each of the first six editions carried an update on his battle to get his job back. Perhaps this was not surprising: the issue became a huge one in the Japanese American community in L.A. Activists had presented the county board of supervisors with a scroll 200 feet long containing 7,000 signatures in support of Noguchi, *Gidra* reported in August 1969.

The spokesman for the Noguchi defense committee, Japanese United in Search of Truth, reminded the county civil service commission that "110,000 Japanese Americans were sent to concentration camps during World War II," concluding, "We will no longer be a meek and silent minority." JUST placed a full-page ad in the *Times* in July, which *Gidra* described as "blasting the county's handling of the Noguchi case," and concluding "This is a time when silence is betrayal."[21]

Then, in August 1969, Noguchi won his appeal and got his job back. It had taken seven weeks of hearings by the board of supervisors, followed by another five weeks of deliberations by the county civil service commission, which ended up voting unanimously to restore him to his former position. The September 1969 issue of *Gidra* featured a front-page story about a testimonial dinner celebrating the victory, attended by 500 people, at the Biltmore Bowl—the banquet hall in downtown L.A.'s most luxurious hotel that had been the site of the Academy Award ceremonies throughout the 1940s. The master of ceremonies was George Takei, already famous for TV's *Star Trek* and for episodes of *The Twilight Zone* and *Mission Impossible*. *Gidra* quoted Takei as telling Noguchi's attorney, Godfrey Isaac, "You have helped create a new Japanese American community, actively involved in the democratic process."[22] Subsequently *Gidra* drew on the Noguchi defense campaign as a model of political mobilization, writing in December 1969: "The Asian community has shown once before—during the Noguchi hearings—that it is no longer a 'quiet' minority. It is hoped that all Asian Americans opposed to the war in Vietnam will join the march ... and not support 'the silent majority' of President Nixon."[23]

Already by issue five, the mostly Japanese American *Gidra* collective was trying to expand its focus, running articles on the history of the Chinese, Koreans, and "Filipino Immigrant" in L.A., along with a directory of community organizations for each group and statistics on population, education and income. (In L.A. and Long Beach in 1965, there were 81,000 Japanese—more than any other city in the United States—30,000 Koreans, 20,000 Chinese, and 13,000 Filipinos.) The list of members of the *Gidra* collective for that issue, however, was again about 90 percent Japanese names. The statistics in the piece itself suggest why the *Gidra* collective was mostly Japanese American: they were by far the biggest Asian immigrant group in L.A., and the only group where the median number of school years completed exceeded twelve. That was higher than the median for whites, and significantly higher than for Chinese Americans. The UCLA Asian American student population from which the *Gidra* collective was drawn was overwhelmingly Japanese American.[24]

As *Gidra*'s first year came to an end, the editors changed its focus: "from the campus to the community, from Asian identity to Asian unity, and from 'what happened' to 'what we can do.'"[25] The change included moving from UCLA's Campbell Hall to an office in the Crenshaw district. Political events played a big role in the shift: May 1970 was the month of Nixon's invasion of Cambodia and the national student strike, during which four students were killed by national guardsmen at Kent State. At UCLA, a massive police force came on campus for the first time that May, clubbing and arresting dozens of students whose only offense had been demonstrating in support of the student strike. *Gidra* people became leaders of the student strike and, for the first and only time, missed their next scheduled issue (June 1970) as a result.

By its second year *Gidra* was reporting on the full spectrum of activism across Southern California: Angela Davis's speech in Oceanside at the GIs against the War march, the Valley State building occupation and trial, the Panthers, the campaign to free the Soledad Brothers, the Chicano Moratorium, the grape strike. It also featured serious coverage of Asian issues: "US War Crimes in the Philippines," incipient fascism in South Korea, the American military's occupation of Okinawa, the revival of Japanese militarism. And every issue had beautiful art on the cover.

The Manzanar Pilgrimage

Gidra focused a lot of its reporting on the World World II internment of Japanese Americans, at a time when Manzanar and the other camps were not well known, even on the left. One of *Gidra*'s first big pieces on Manzanar was written not by a member of the collective, but an academic authority—sociologist and UC Davis assistant professor Isao Fujimoto. As a child he had been sent from his home in rural Washington state to the camp at Heart Mountain, Wyoming, with his family; he was eight years old. After that he had been taught by his parents to "make the most of a bad situation and push ahead"—to refrain from speaking about their wartime experiences.[26]

Then he met Dorothy Day, the anarchist founder of the *Catholic Worker* newspaper. She told him she had protested the internment and picketed one of the urban assembly centers, where Japanese Americans were held before being shipped to remote camps. "I had never met anyone who had done this," Fujimoto recalled. He asked where. When Day replied, "Outside the Portland Livestock pavilion," he wrote, "I looked at her and felt a strange bond of comradeship. My family and I had been inside the Portland Center," detained there for several weeks, with thousands of other Japanese Americans from Oregon, living in livestock stalls—their first stop on the way to Heart Mountain.

In the same essay, Fujimoto also lodged a cutting critique of the 1967 revision of the McCarran Internal Security Act, which included a provision for the establishment of new detention camps in the event of a "national security emergency" declared by the president. The Japanese American experience in World War II, he argued, showed how quickly the government could round up and hold a hundred thousand people, and, equally important, how few Americans protested the denial of basic democratic rights.

The first anniversary of *Gidra* marked a historic moment for the Japanese American community of Los Angeles: the first Manzanar pilgrimage. On December 27, 1969, 150 people, ranging from the ages of three to eighty, traveled to the camp in a caravan of one bus and twenty cars, both to pay tribute to the memory of those who had been interned there, and to dramatize the efforts of the JACL to repeal the detention camp section of the Internal Security Act. All that was left of the camp, abandoned in 1945, was two guard towers, six graves, and a monument. The pilgrims, *Gidra* reported, immediately set to work: one group "cleared the fenced-in area of dead trees and shrubbery with hoes, knives, shovels, rakes and hands," while another refurbished the huge monument. Others "planted and watered trees, restored the graveyards, and placed flowers and wreaths on the graves and on the monument." Then food was served, followed by a Buddhist ceremony. One of the pilgrims remarked, "When people ask me, 'how many people are buried in this cemetery?' I say 'A whole generation is buried here.'"[27]

The centerfold of that issue was a photo of the Manzanar monument, a white obelisk in the desert with tall mountains in the distance. Photographer Bob Nakamura surrounded that image with the faces of pilgrims. That *Gidra* photograph "was later reproduced as a poster," historian Karen Ishizuka reports, which "wallpapered the dorm rooms, hallways and offices of Asian America."[28]

Women's Liberation

Gidra published a "Women's Liberation" issue in January 1971.[29] That issue opened with a declaration in which the authors identified themselves as "Third World, Asian Sisters" who were "united to oppose this capitalistic society which confines the role of women to a cheap labor force, or to mindless bodies completely influenced by Madison Avenue propaganda." They pledged that they would "resist the degrading images that a racist society has imposed on both ourselves and our brothers" and "struggle with our brothers against male chauvinism." The declaration concluded, "In no way is our struggle different from the struggle for the liberation of all people."[30] The women of *Gidra* made no mention of the subordination of women in traditional Asian and Asian American cultures; it all came from capitalism and Madison Avenue.

Gidra's women's liberation statement was missing one big thing. In nearly every racialized group, historian Ruth Rosen writes, women discovered that "their status in New Left or liberation or independence movements was one of subordination."[31] Of course, that came first of all in the work of white women, who emphasized that women were oppressed not just by capitalism or by Madison Avenue; women were oppressed by men, including men in the movement. The women of *Gidra*, in contrast, did not embrace that idea: "rather than condemning, putting down, separating from, fighting with ... men, we should instead direct our energy towards giving constructive criticism to the brothers" because "it is the existing system"—capitalism—"which perpetuates the oppression and exploitation of women." The piece quoted from Engels in *Origins of the Family*, Marx in *Capital*, and the *Quotations from Chairman Mao* on women, concluding that male chauvinism came from "the ruling class which exploits and oppresses" men as well as women. The way to abolish women's oppression thus was to abolish the system of "private ownership."[32] Thus *Gidra*'s feminism came from orthodox Marxism, rather than from the new women's liberation movement.

The *Gidra* women's issue opened with a piece on "GIs and Asian Women" in Vietnam, two articles on working-class Asian immigrant women in sweatshops, one on war brides, and a lot on demeaning stereotypes of Asian women as submissive. One piece, by Wilma Chen, argued that some Asian American men "feel they have been so 'emasculated' by white racism that they cannot stand to see women in roles of equality or leadership in the movement." This view was critiqued as a "rather subjective understanding," and the author quoted Lenin and Mao on the objective importance of women in liberation struggles. The concern about emasculation of men of color in a white-dominated culture was characteristic of minority women's liberation. "The women hesitated to further threaten their sense of manhood," Rosen writes, "but they were also not willing to turn themselves into mere followers ... Wanting to support their men, but unwilling to defer to them." Creating and then sustaining egalitarian relationships in these movements, she reports, "proved extremely difficult."[33]

The issue included a "Male Perspective," arguing that "the woman's struggle is so much more than simply women's liberation. The women's struggle is the liberation of MEN." Men, the author said, "won't have to be tall, dark, strong, aggressive, competitive, rugged or independent, any more than women will have to be small, delicate, passive, artistic or dependent."[34] Robin Morgan was familiar with that argument: "In the long run," she wrote in "Goodbye to All That" in 1970, one of the defining works of the era, "Women's Liberation will of course free men—but in the short run it's going to COST men a lot of privilege, which no one gives up willingly or easily."[35]

Perhaps the most original and remarkable thing in the women's liberation issue was the photograph of the contributors and editors as a group, which filled half of page three. The other half reproduced an advertisement for a book about "how to meet Japanese girls in the US," including "how to obtain Japanese ladies and girls for maids, domestics, housekeepers, cooks, female servants." Below that was the photo of ten *Gidra* women, looking directly at the camera, serious, determined, unsmiling, and one of them giving the finger—apparently to the ad, but also to the viewer, presumably male. Of the image, historian Laura Pulido wrote, "The fact that the women even *thought* to have a picture of themselves taken reflects a higher level of collective feminist consciousness than existed in either [the Latina] CASA or the [Black] BPP."[36]

Connecting with Vietnamese women was an obvious goal for the women of *Gidra*. The May 1971 issue included a multipage report on a weeklong conference in Vancouver where 200 women from across the western United States, including 120 Asian Americans, met with six Indochinese women at the Anti-Imperialist Women's Conference, held at the University of British Columbia. The Indochinese women came not only from North Vietnam but also from the Patriotic Women's Association and the Women's Union for the Liberation of South Vietnam. *Gidra* published statements from the conference by the vice commander in chief of the Armed Forces of Liberation of South Vietnam, and from a woman who spent six years imprisoned in the tiger cages of South Vietnam, both recounting how they became revolutionaries.

Asian American women from L.A. who attended the conference also wrote about it for *Gidra*, including one Nisei (born in the US of Japanese parents) who said she was one of three "oldsters" who "formed our own caucus for self-preservation—in other words, we needed more than [the] three or four hours of sleep on which the 'youngsters' thrived." She described the six Indochinese women as "physically small, sincere, friendly, often appearing extremely tired. Yet, whenever one spoke, it was with such clarity and with a background of personal involvement that the meaning of a people's revolution became a reality."[37] One of the "youngsters" later wrote:

> One weird feeling I had in Vancouver was that I was so much ashamed of being from the United States ... Meeting Indochinese women who had seen their land destroyed, their people suffering, and their families die because of the US, I now see the importance of our struggle—being in the belly of the monster itself—and I am only ashamed when I know I am not doing all that I can for the liberation of mankind.[38]

A year after those meetings, in May 1972, *Gidra* was invited to send one of its staffers to China as part of an official Asian American People's Delegation. Evelyn Yoshimura was selected, and when she came back in the fall she spoke to many community groups and wrote a series of articles for *Gidra*. China at the time was in the middle of the Cultural Revolution. Her first report began with a street scene in Shanghai, where, waiting for the delegation bus, she found herself being stared at by about two dozen children, curious about the unusual sight of a foreigner:

> Then a far out thing happened. A small, but very determined looking girl about eleven, with a red arm band, came over to the crowd of kids and began dispersing them ... telling them that it was impolite to stare at foreign guests, and that they should leave me alone because it would make me feel uncomfortable. The children slowly began to disperse ... except for one boy about seven or eight. He turned and said something and raised his hand threateningly ... The Little Red Guard ... took hold of his arm, ignoring the threat, and took him aside. Some other children came over and began to explain very calmly and seriously how the little girl was right, and that he should learn to listen and to think of others, not only himself.[39]

The women's liberation issue was the first of a series of topical issues. One of the most remarkable was a "street" issue that came out of work by high school students whom *Gidra* had hired and paid—the only paid staffers in the five-year history of the paper—because of a poverty program grant through the Neighborhood Youth Corps. Probably the most powerful of the special issues was on the "middle generation." It amounted to "a public avowal" that the radicals of *Gidra* had, in the words of William Wei, "finally come to appreciate their parents' struggles."[40]

Shinya Ono's "Asian Nation"

One of the most remarkable things *Gidra* published was an unsigned 1971 essay titled "Asian Nation" written by Shinya Ono. Born in Tokyo just before Pearl Harbor, he said he had "a very American Nisei mother and a liberal Japanese father who was killed in the war." He was older than the rest of the *Gidra* collective, and new in L.A. when the piece appeared. He had a long history of leftist study and activism, starting in 1960 at Columbia, where he went to classes at the New York School of Marxist Studies taught by the CP's Herbert Aptheker. Then in 1963 he joined the editorial board of *Studies on the Left*, the first New Left journal in America, where he worked with Eugene Genovese, Staughton Lynd, Tom Hayden, William Appleman Williams, and other leading Left historians and intellectuals of the period. He organized in Chinatown with the teachers' union, and then in 1969 joined the Weatherman faction of SDS, taking part in their ill-fated "Days of Rage" in Chicago, which led to his six-month imprisonment in the Cook County Jail.

It was during that time in jail that he wrote "Asian Nation." When he got out in January 1971, he moved to L.A., where he decided to "serve the people" "for at least ten years." That included joining the *Gidra* collective. One of the longest pieces *Gidra* had ever published, "Asian Nation" appeared with a line at the end: "written and revised by two members of the collective."[41] Ono identified himself as the author only in 2001.[42]

"Asian Nation" opened by explaining how Asian Americans were both united and divided. United because they were all targets of racism in America, and all had "roots back across the Pacific," where "people are carrying out a fierce and valiant struggle against the same white, imperial Amerika." And divided because in fact they came from diverse national backgrounds, making them a group "with opposition and contradiction a part of its character"—Chinese, Japanese, Korean, Filipino, Indian (he did not list Vietnamese, Thai, or Cambodian— they would arrive in the United States during the Seventies); speaking many different languages; some recent arrivals, and some coming from families that had been in the United States for several generations. And, he wrote, "historically the differences have been greater than the unity."[43]

His central arguments were against "sectarianism" and in favor of building "parallel and alternative institutions." He was against the sectarian idea that there was a single correct strategy for organizing Asian Americans. The sectarian, he wrote, "becomes destructive to our movement, and to himself—he will make the 'less advanced' or 'less committed' people feel trashed, and cause splits and make people want to drop out of things ... I speak here from personal experiences, having been a sectarian myself." He argued that the Asian American Left should "affirm and embrace all activities ... because, he said, "every form of activity, struggle, and digging each other ... makes us feel more powerful and human." His examples were wide-ranging: "everything from a dignified peace vigil, a scholarly teach-in, Asian studies, community cultural festivals like Nisei Week," and even "family softball games, martial arts, dances, and even trying to relate to people at Holiday Bowl"—a famous Japanese American bowling alley and coffee shop in the Crenshaw district.[44] "It will be a long time before we could even guess which of these different seeds we plant would bear the largest number of fruits." The only people who should be excluded from this broad effort, he wrote, were "those Asians among us who have actively participated in strengthening the oppression we are being subjected to, and who refuse to turn over a new leaf after sincere efforts to warn them."[45]

Thus the biggest task of the Asian American movement, Shinya Ono argued, was to "create a new culture" that would "bring peace to our soul" while also "serving as a valuable tool for our movement." It should build "parallel institutions and alternative institutions" in the media, the professions, and social services. His list was long and rich: "legal, medical and social service clinics"; "day-care centers and liberation schools," food co-ops, garages to repair cars and trucks, "pioneer centers where our grandparents can share their experiences and skills with the rest of us," community newspapers, magazines, radio, TV shows, films, art centers and theaters; and "last but not least, our own farm-communities in the country where we can learn agricultural skills—from, yes, Issei and Nisei gardeners and farmers, where we can grow our own organic crops," along with "rest and rec-reation centers for brothers and sisters working in the cities, and where our children can dig on a righteous and real nature trip." Obviously he had been thinking about the counterculture's rural communes and urban food co-ops and the underground press. The essay concluded that building an alternative culture also meant "releasing all that anger, hurt, frustration and love that we have been holding in for so long."[46] It was probably the richest and most far-reaching political statement *Gidra* published in its five-year life.

The Finale

Most of the Sixties underground and alternative press faded away in the early Seventies, or disintegrated after factional fights, or was transformed into something else. *Gidra* was different: it planned and scheduled its final issue, dated April 1974, a massive eighty pages filled with essays and personal statements about the life of the publi-cation and its successes and failures. One of the things that wasn't at all evident from reading the regular monthly issues of the paper was the behind-the-scenes debates and efforts among the editorial staff about defeating hierarchy. They took the *LA Free Press* as a negative example—it had a publisher, Art Kunkin, and a management system not too different from capitalist publications. *Gidra* tried different things to promote "equality within the staff": at one point, they decided that "high ranking members ... would not participate in the decision making process." That failed, so in an effort to "develop leadership and organizational qualities" among everybody, "a system of rotating monthly 'coordinators' was set up" in July 1971—and they stuck with that until the end.[47]

Of course, the staff debated the political direction of the publication: some readers complained that the paper was too grim, that the staff was "too negative" in their "interpretation of history" and "too subjective" in their "analysis of current conditions." Some readers wanted articles with "a more tolerant and hopeful outlook."[48] The editors agreed, but the result, Murase wrote, was "a hodge-podge ... of recipes for ethnic foods, directions for a vegetable garden, tips on how to buy a used car, and instructions for sewing your own pants." They thought they were pursuing the idea that "the skills and knowledge within society ought to be shared for the benefit of the people." But other readers "scowled" at these articles, "labeling them petty boojiwah or calling them imitations of white hippie counterculture."[49]

The Gidra editorial staff continued to meet regularly after they stopped publishing—at first, twice a week. They considered publishing a new weekly focused more narrowly on community issues; they also considered publishing a series of pamphlets on specific issues, or a literary anthology, or starting an Asian American news service. They didn't do any of those things, but they did publish a twentieth-anniversary issue in 1990—a remarkable achievement for a movement publication started in the Sixties.[50]

36

L.A.'s Black Woodstock: Wattstax (1972)

t was the biggest all-Black gathering in American history: 100,000 people at the LA Coliseum in August 1972.[1] The event was not a civil rights rally; instead it was a "celebration of Blackness" on the seventh anniversary of the Watts uprising: the Wattstax music festival. Organized by Stax Records, the Memphis soul label, it featured The Staple Singers, doing a stirring version of "Respect Yourself"; the irresistible Rufus Thomas, wearing a pink cape, pink shorts and shiny white disco boots, for whom thousands of people poured out of their seats and onto the football field to "Do the Funky Chicken"; and for the finale, the brightest star of Stax, the Blacksploitation superstar Isaac Hayes, wearing gold chains over his naked chest and singing "Shaft": "Who is the man / That would risk his neck for his brother man?"

It had been a bad seven years for Black L.A. "Charcoal Alley"—103rd Street, seven miles south of the Coliseum, remained in ashes, and some of the main streets around the stadium, especially Vermont Avenue and Broadway, also still had deep scars at sites that had been torched in August 1965.[2] The LAPD campaign to kill the Panthers that had started three years after Watts had been vicious and effective. The effort of liberals to elect a Black mayor, Tom Bradley, had been defeated. In 1972 Sam Yorty remained mayor, and the LAPD continued its reign over the streets.

So the first requirement of the Wattstax festival was that the LAPD wouldn't be allowed inside the Coliseum. And the organizers, led by

Al Bell and Larry Shaw of Stax Records, insisted that the security force inside had to be all Black—and unarmed. Al Bell later said the thing he was proudest of was that there were "no guns. No guns inside. Security with no guns. And no incidents."[3]

Tickets cost $1 for the six-hour festival, which meant virtually all of Watts could afford to go. The event opened with the national anthem, but in the stands virtually no one stood, or sang; most people were talking or just sitting. Then came a speech by Reverend Jesse Jackson. In 1971, the year before Wattstax, he had founded Operation PUSH (People United to Serve Humanity) in Chicago.[4] Onstage at the Coliseum, with a big Afro and wearing a dashiki, he declared, "This is a beautiful day … It is a day of Black people taking care of Black people's business. Today we are together … 'Cause when we are together, we've got power." Then he declared, "In Watts, we have shifted from "Burn, baby, burn," to "Learn, baby, learn."

He called on the audience to stand, raise their fists, and repeat after him:

I am—somebody!

I may be poor, but I am—somebody!

I am Black—

beautiful—

proud!

Then came a call and response:

When we stand together, what time is it?

Nation time!

When we say no more "Yessir, boss," what time is it?"

Nation time!

Next, Jesse announced that "Sister Kim Weston" (whose "Take Me in Your Arms" had topped the R&B charts) would sing "the Black national anthem." What followed was a stirring and powerful performance: "Lift every voice and sing / 'till earth and heaven ring / Ring with the harmonies of liberty …" While Jesse, Al Bell and Larry Shaw stood silently behind her with raised fists, thousands in the stands stood and joined in singing. The uniformed security officers in the stands had taken their hats off for the national anthem; Homer Banks, a Stax producer who sat in the stands, recalled that when they did not do the same for the "Black national anthem," people in the audience asked them, "Would you please pull your hat off?" "It was amazing."[5]

The concert was the finale of a seven-day festival that had been held annually since the uprising, founded by Ted Watkins of the Watts Labor Community Action Committee, who had been a UAW activist. The concert had been preceded by a parade featuring Isaac Hayes as grand marshal, plus other Stax stars, actors and activists Ossie Davis and Ruby Dee, as well as local marching bands. The festival—described by the *LA Times* as "the only event sponsored for black people by black people"—included booths in Will Rogers Memorial Park selling food, clothes, jewelry and art, along with organizations like the Veterans Council and Guidance Center, where activists passed out literature about racism in the military—challenging the nearby recruiting booths of the Army, Navy, Marine Corps, and Air Force—and a Tehachapi prisoners' organization booth.[6]

During the six-hour concert at the Coliseum, Stax presented more than two dozen groups. Some, like the Staple Singers, brought an explicit message of Black empowerment. Booker T. Jones of Booker T. and the MGs later explained that "Respect Yourself" "became an anthem for every black ghetto in America, like a ship come to save drowning dark-skinned sailors from self-loathing." Released the previous year, it had reached number two on the Billboard R&B chart. The Staple Singers had started out as a gospel group, and then crossed over, but always with a political message—"before it was commercial," Robert Christgau reminds us.[7]

The music had started with gospel: Jimmy Jones, who had performed at the Newport Jazz Festival, sang "When I Am Lonely and Filled with Despair," followed by a big group singing "Gimme That Old Time Religion." Then announcer Richard Roundtree, who had played "Shaft" in the 1971 movie, said "we all know what we're here for ... We're here to commemorate a revolution that started a movement, and was one of the milestones in Black pride." He was talking about the Watts Rebellion. "Some folks may find it a little strange that we laugh, we sing, and we joke. But we're doing our thing, the Black way, to commemorate."

Later, Rufus Thomas came onstage, in that pink cape with pink shorts and high boots. He sang "Do the Funky Chicken." Many people in the stands were dancing, and some kids jumped the chain-link fence protecting the football field. Rufus said, "Now when I tell you to get on the field, then you get on the field. Then I just might get out on the field with you. All right, here we go!"

Thousands charged onto field, dancing wildly—the field where the Rams were to play a game the next night. The organizers had promised to keep people off the playing field as a key provision of the insurance policy negotiated with Lloyds of London, so this was a moment of anxiety for the concert promoters. This was quickly explained to Rufus Thomas, who stopped the music and changed his tone: "Wait a minute," he said. "We all together out here, we all gonna have some fun, but you ain't supposed to have your fun on the ground, you're supposed to be in the stands ... All of you, will you please, please go to the stands, Please, with a capital "P" ... Might be a little slow, but you just got to go. So, how about it, brother? Power to the people that go to the stands!"

For the finale Jesse Jackson introduced Isaac Hayes. As he strode onto the stage with his shaven head, dark glasses, cape, gold chains, and bare chest, his band started into the unmistakable hi-hat riff and the wah-wah rhythm guitar from the theme from *Shaft*. Already a triumphant anthem of the soul era, the song had spent two weeks at number one on the Billboard Hot 100, then won a Grammy, followed by the Academy Award for Best Original Song.[8]

No doubt many in the audience remembered the moment the previous year when Hayes had won the Oscar. "For many African-Americans," writes historian Rob Bowman, "that was an event comparable to Joe Louis's knockout of Max Schmeling in 1938. It was a victory for all of black America." At the ceremony, when his name was announced as the winner, he walked down the aisle with his 79-year-old grandmother; the audience gave the two of them a standing ovation. After the Academy Awards ceremony, Hayes and his grandmother went to Chicago, invited by Jesse Jackson. Oscar in hand, and press in tow, they spoke at an Operation PUSH meeting and then went around to hospitals and jails, "taking the Oscar to the

CHARGED WITH 1,730 FELONIES: *These 24 students of San Fernando Valley State College in California are on trial in the Superior Court, Los Angeles, for acts allegedly committed during campus disturbance last November: From left, front row—Lidwina Apo (Hawaiian), Arnold Boyd, George Brady, Benjamin Caraveo (Mexican-American), Archie Chatman and Jethro Collins; second row—Vaye Crockett, Eddie Dancer, Deardis Davis, Robert Dyer, Larry Hardison, Arrinita Holloway; third row—La Frida Jamison, Howard Johnson, Arthur Judge Jones, Jr., Schelton Jones, Marian Kindle, Robert Lewis; fourth row—Linda Nichols, Marita E. Pette, Yvonne Robinson, Leaman Scott, Michael Wrice and Sharon Emory. All are being defended by NAACP attorneys.*

The Crisis, November 1969, published by the NAACP.

In Los Angeles, unlike the Bay Area, the most politically active campuses were not the big universities but rather state and community colleges. Valley State in the almost all white West Valley was the regional epicenter. Demanding a Black Studies program, Black students occupied the administration building, leading to what the *LA Times* called "the first mass prosecution in this country of campus activists on felony charges."

MEChA silent march at Valley State protests burning of Chicano House, May 6, 1970. While Black students at Valley State found themselves tied up in felony trials with their leaders sentenced to prison, Chicano students focused on efforts to establish their own community-oriented Chicano Studies department. The campus Chicano House burned on May 6, 1970—the cause was never found—but the campaign eventually succeeded at building one of the strongest Chicano Studies departments in the country.

The Doors on the Venice Beach Boardwalk—December 20, 1969. Venice, a vibrant counterculture community since the Fifties, with a black neighborhood that went back to the twenties, fought high-rise developers and frequent LAPD sweeps of the beach and boardwalk.

Photo by Allen Zak.

Chicano Moratorium, August 29, 1970. With 25,000 marchers in East L.A., the anti-war movement crossed a new threshold as thousands of ordinary working-class people from one of the most patriotic communities in the US chanted "Raza si, guerra no!" And the march was entirely peaceful—until it was attacked and broken up by sheriff's deputies.

Chicano Moratorium, August 29, 1970.

In Los Angeles, Black and Chicano junior and senior high school students were the most important social force behind the great protest wave of 1967–71. Here, youth from the Florencia barrio of South Central Los Angeles arrive at Belvedere Park for La Marcha Por La Justicia, January 31, 1971.

Artist: Carol Clement.

Wonder Woman defeats the AMA and "Pro-Life" Christians: *Sister Magazine*, July 1973, cover. To overcome the "humiliation and helplessness" women felt when doctors called them "difficult" for "asking questions" (in the words of Barbara Ehrenreich), Carol Downer and Lorraine Rothman taught women to do cervical self-examinations, and started the first Feminist Women's Health Center in L.A. in 1972. The goal: women's right to control their own bodies.

George A. Wiley Papers/Wisconsin Historical Society. WHi-8771.

Starting in a Watts housing project, Johnnie Tillmon built a pioneer welfare rights organization that became a model for other cities. Being on welfare, she said, was like being in a "supersexist marriage: You trade in 'a' man for 'The' Man," but you can't divorce him if he treats you bad. He can divorce you, of course—cut you off—any time he wants. But in that case, 'he' keeps the kids, not you." Here she addresses Mother's Day March, with welfare rights leader George A. Wiley sitting beside her and Ethel Kennedy looking on, Washington, D.C., circa 1968–1969.

Photo by Mike Murase.

Japanese-American students at UCLA started publishing a monthly newspaper in 1968—they called it Gidra, and it became the voice of the Asian American movement. Their Women's Liberation issue in January 1971 included a half-page photo of the women on the staff—suggesting, Laura Pulido wrote, "a higher level of collective feminist consciousness" than existed in either the Chicana movement or the Black Panthers.

Courtesy Wattstax and the Saul Zaenz Company 2004.

The biggest all-Black gathering in American history (up to that point) took place in L.A. One hundred thousand people met at the Coliseum in 1972 in "celebration of Blackness" on the seventh anniversary of the Watts uprising for the Wattstax music festival, organized by Stax Records. The festival opened with Jesse Jackson leading a call-and-response "I Am Somebody!" (Al Bell of Stax Records to his right).

people," "letting them see and touch it," symbolically giving the Oscar "back to the people."[9]

Later the Staple Singers told the story behind their appearance at the Coliseum. Although they were one of Stax's top acts, they had not been on the program for L.A., because they were performing two shows a day in Las Vegas as the opening act for Sammy Davis Jr. But Davis told them he was canceling one day's shows in order to campaign for Richard Nixon, who was running for reelection that fall. When he got the news, Pops Staples, patriarch of the family group, called Al Bell and told him "We can make it to Wattstax." Mavis Staples later said, "They got us there. We flew in, did our songs, stayed a while, and flew back to Las Vegas. That was the biggest crowd any of us had ever seen."[10] (As for Sammy Davis Jr., that was the day he hugged Nixon on live TV.)

The concert was filmed, with legendary documentary producer David Wolper providing financial backing—he later produced the TV show *Roots*—and instead of a narrator, director Mel Stuart used man-on-the-street interviews. He explained that "we hired a whole bunch of very gifted young Black cameramen, and they went into the barbershops and the schools and the churches." Wattstax had songs about gospel, so they asked about gospel. Wattstax had songs about love, so they asked about love. "And slowly, from that footage emerged a soulful expression of the Black experience."[11] In the film the interviews were interspersed with the onstage performances.

In the film's opening scene, three Black men on the street are talking about the Watts uprising seven years earlier:

The first man recalls, "That's what we did in 1965: we all got crazy and went out, and started burning up our own neighborhood and shit. That brought the man on our own land, man."

The second replies, "The thing about it was, it did something constructive for the whole community."

"That's the only beautiful thing that went off. Thank you, whitey. That's the only way we communicate with whitey, man. You've never seen in the community as many markets. They've opened up a Dr. Martin Luther King Hospital. There's more black people in Watts, that were formerly on county and state aid, that are employed right now. Like your mama! Your mama got a job for the first time in 10 years."

"Dumb-ass motherfucker."

"I'm talking about black people—like you, nigger ..."

The third interjects: "Shit ain't getting better. They're still putting officers into the area, man, shit."

"But look, brother: you'd be surprised how much that building, that particular building will satisfy so many niggers."

"Pacify them a little."

"Make them think—make them think it's progress."

"Up until the point that we had a riot, everybody said, 'Those niggers are all right, they're doing fine.' Then when we had a riot, then the white man said: 'Something's wrong, 'cause these suckers are burning down my store. Now I got to give these niggers something, because I thought they was happy.'"

"But what did he give them?"

An older Black man offers his conclusion: "They've changed some for the best; in an awful lot of cases, for the worst; and some they have not changed at all. There's no difference in Watts now than Watts '65."

Epilogue

Sowing the Future

The Yorty era ended with a whimper in the May 1973 general election. A year earlier the mayor, who had already run for more offices than any politician in American history, had astounded political observers by launching his twentieth campaign—this time for the Democratic presidential nomination. Utterly unknown in most of the country, he campaigned on promises to stop school busing, continue the war in Vietnam, and make George Wallace his running mate. The *Times* disgustedly accused him of making L.A. "a national joke."[1] In the event, he won only 1.4 percent of California's votes cast, coming in far behind Shirley Chisholm, the first Black woman to contest a presidential primary. Elsewhere Yorty was almost invisible; in Rhode Island, for instance, he received exactly six primary votes. Despite his buffoonery and exorbitant malapropisms (in a national debate he introduced himself as "mayor of the third-largest city in Los Angeles"), he still managed to win a majority of white votes in his mayoral rematch with Tom Bradley. But Bradley increased his own proportion of the white vote from 37 percent in 1969 to 46 percent in 1973 and won 51 percent of a Chicano vote that had gone strongly for Yorty in 1969. The result was a four point victory over Yorty.[2]

In key respects, however, this was a different Bradley than the progressive candidate of 1969. Although the core cadre of the old coalition—middle-class Blacks, Jews and Japanese Americans from the Tenth Council District—remained influential as allies and advisors, the conduct of the campaign itself was turned over to a clique of powerful white business leaders and political professionals. Nelson Rising, a corporate lawyer and future mega-developer who had managed John Tunney's sensational 1970 Senate race, became campaign chair, while Max Palevsky, the fabulously rich founder of computer firm Scientific Data Systems, coordinated the finances, including his own series of large loans to the campaign. Together they convinced Bradley to hire David Garth, who had invented the modern television-based political campaign in 1965 on behalf of New York's John Lindsay.[3] Garth's strategy, as Raphael Sonenshein later explained, inverted the key elements of the 1969 crusade: "It had become more professional and less ideological. The emphasis would be on mass media, backed by grassroots campaign, rather than the other way around."[4] The ad blitz focused on Bradley's police career and his political moderation. A very reserved and well-spoken man, Bradley radiated strength and conciliation while Yorty simply acted berserk.

His attempts to race- and red-bait Bradley gained less traction than in 1969, in part because the streets and campuses were tranquilized. The last big anti-war demonstration, protesting Nixon's second inauguration, was held downtown on January 20; a week later a ceasefire was called in Vietnam. At the same time, the Nixon administration suspended the draft. Robert Hahn, an education professor at Cal State LA, announced he was ending the silent vigil that he had conducted weekly for seven years in protest of the war.[5] Meanwhile, the LA Panthers, US, SNCC, SDS, the Brown Berets, Che-Lumumba, the Chicano Moratorium Committee, and even the Peace Action Council were now either extinct or moribund.[6] The threat of school busing, on the horizon as the federal court finally moved toward resolution of the ACLU's 1963 Crawford lawsuit, roiled white voters, particularly in the Valley, but Garth ensured that the Bradley campaign steered clear of controversies about school integration. Likewise when Bobby Seale in Oakland endorsed Bradley, the candidate publicly rejected his support.[7]

Bradley's victory was unique and would remain so for many years: a Black mayor elected by a multiracial coalition in a city whose Black population share was actually declining. The greatest rewards, however, did not go to the neighborhoods or jobless youth as the 1969 campaign had promised, but to white men in office towers gathered around ambitious plans for downtown redevelopment and multibillion-dollar expansions of LAX and the port. Bradley's election ended the organic crisis of elite governance that had arisen in the wake of Yorty's surprise victory in 1961 and the schism between liberal West-side and conservative downtown power structures. With his electoral base stabilized by liberal rhetoric and patronage (mediated by his arch-supporter Reverend Brookins), his relationship with Westside moguls, big developers, major banks, and the *Times*'s Otis Chandler grew more intimate—and eventually more corrupt—over the course of twenty years in office. In historical retrospect, Bradley's greatest accomplishments were not his attacks on residential segregation or direction of public investment to have-not neighborhoods, but rather the rebirth of downtown property values and the creation of a state-of-the-art infrastructure for the globalization of the metropolitan economy in the 1990s.

Despite public expectations, he was no more successful than the early Yorty in controlling the LAPD or changing its leadership, which continued to be passed on dynastically to protégés of Chief Parker such as Daryl Gates. Moreover, the department continued to blackmail politicians and occasionally destroy their careers, as in the case of Maury Weiner—Bradley's progressive conscience and deputy mayor who was arrested in 1975 for supposedly groping an undercover vice officer in a Hollywood theater. Weiner's real sin was not that he was gay but rather that he was still urging the mayor to tame the cops.

Although Bradley made a number of key Chicano hires at city hall, he was soon accused of betraying his Eastside supporters by not endorsing Chicano candidates for the city council, particularly for Roybal's old seat, at the time held by Gilbert Lindsay. (Only in 1985 and running in another, white-voter-majority district would Richard Alatorre finally restore a Spanish surname to the council roster.) Instead of fully integrating Chicanos into his coalition, the new mayor gave priority to meshing his policies with the plans of the major power players in the business community, who in turn guaranteed the campaign finances that made Bradley's tenure unassailable. Otherwise he might have been more vulnerable to political challenges within the

Black community that arose from his "invasion" of the turf controlled by allies of Mervyn Dymally (now lieutenant governor) and Jesse Unruh. Their respective political bases in 1973 were roughly defined by Vermont Avenue. West of Vermont, Bradley support was rooted in stable Black working- and middle-class neighborhoods whose relative prosperity was based on expanding public employment opportunities, for which the mayor claimed much of the credit. East of Vermont, in the 1965 riot zone, Dymally loyalists represented a population that was more likely to be badly housed, dependent on low-wage private employment, and served by the worst schools.[8]

Far from experiencing a community renaissance under the new regime, the riot zone neighborhoods in the 1970s lost the little ground they had gained through the War on Poverty and temporary youth employment schemes. Watts, in particular, once a symbol of hope and Black pride, was now a pit of despair. In 1975, on the eve of the tenth anniversary of the uprising, *Times* reporters surveyed the district and came to the grim conclusion that conditions were considerably worse than in 1965. "Unemployment is now higher in the Watts area, welfare rates are climbing and housing continues to deteriorate." Ron Karenga, interviewed in prison, told the *Times* that "people view the '60s as a failure when in fact the '60s were not a failure but a transitional period in our long struggle … We can't look at the temporary disarray that we find ourselves in and be dispirited." Yet most of the people who talked to the *Times* were dispirited and expressed little hope that the Bradley administration, particularly in the absence of federal support, would reverse the decline. As Walter Bremond, the former chair of the Black Congress, put it: "The system whipped the shit out of us."[9]

During the 1980s, moreover, a wave of closures shuttered the auto assembly plants, aluminum mills, steel plants and tire factories that had symbolized greater L.A.'s prowess as the nation's second-largest manufacturing center. Although thousands of older white workers were victims of this industrial collapse, it hit especially hard at the young Blacks and Chicanos, many of them Vietnam veterans who, thanks to federal consent decrees, had recently acquired access to more of these unionized high-wage jobs, and in some cases risen to union leadership. Many leftists in the 1970s had envisioned the big plants as the new power bases for continuing the Black and Chicano liberation struggles. Deindustrialization, whether or not an inevitable response to global competition, was the asteroid that destroyed Marxist dreams. City hall, so proactive on behalf of exporters, land developers and financial sector, did nothing to stanch the hemorrhage of good jobs. (Bradley and the council, for instance, could have led a coalition of the region's industrial cities and suburbs to pressure Sacramento and Washington.)

Meanwhile, gang violence, largely quelled in the wake of the '65 rebellion, returned to the streets of South Central in a new and more deadly form. A few months after Bradley's inauguration, investigators were warning his office of the existence of twenty-seven "chapters" of a new, heavily armed gang nation that called itself the Crips. Twelve additional gangs—later to be known as Bloods—had been formed in self-defense against the expanding Crip empire.[10] Gang membership would steadily increase through the 1970s, then grow exponentially in 1980s as crack cocaine, imported from Colombia and retailed by neighborhood gangs, became the ghetto's alternative economy. The connection between the decline of Black radicalism and rising gang violence may have escaped the notice of the white media, but it was widely acknowledged and mourned in the community. The Crips were indeed, as Cle Sloan titled his film made in the wake of the 1992 uprising, the *Bastards of the [Black Panther] Party*.

But it was LAUSD that remained ground zero in the struggle for equal opportunity. Waves of immigration from Mexico as well as Central America and South Korea reshaped the city's demography and added their own baby boom to the school-age population. But new immigrants were typically years away from citizenship, so a chasm opened up between the active electorate and voteless immigrant parents. White voters, their children now grown, had little inclination to vote for school bonds but were enthusiastic for Proposition 13 in 1978, which ended the financing of schools through local property taxes and inaugurated an era of permanent fiscal stress and declining quality of education. The conservative Valley was the cradle of this statewide tax revolt and soon became the principal school desegregation battleground. The Valley-based New Right activists—who in 1976 organized the BusStop anti-busing group, claiming 30,000 members—went on to win positions on the school board and even a seat in Congress. They also helped lead the rebellion of local home-owners' associations against apartment construction, and in 1994 they were catalysts in the passage of anti-immigrant Proposition 187 ("Save Our State")—ultimately ruled unconstitutional—which among other provisions ordered school districts to expel undocumented children. Their underlying political raison d'être, reincarnated today in the Trump administration, was to deny immigrants and children of color the opportunities that high levels of public spending on education in 1950s California had provided for their own kids.

The fires of April 1992 that followed the not-guilty verdicts in the trial of the cops who beat Rodney King illuminated the city's con-tinuing landscape of inequality. South and East L.A. were still policed ruthlessly by the LAPD, but the uprising of angry Black youth and poor Latinos also presented a price tag for the failures of reform in the 1960s. From this perspective one might conclude that all the dreaming, passion, and sacrifice of that era had been for naught. But the Sixties in Los Angeles are best conceived of as a sowing, whose seeds grew into living traditions of resistance. Movements rose and fell to be sure, but individual commitments to social change were enduring and inheritable. Thousands continued to lead activist lives as union organizers, progressive doctors and lawyers, schoolteachers, community advocates, city employees, and, perhaps most profoundly, as parents. Memories of Black Power, draft resistance, the high school Blowouts in South Central and the Eastside, the grape boycott, *Gidra* and the Asian New left, the Free Angela movement, the mass arrests at Valley State in the struggle for Black studies, the Black Cat Tavern "riot," the women's movement, the 1970 Teamster wildcat, the endless battles to free Venice and free the Strip—all of this was transmitted intergenerationally, sometimes providing icons of protest during the massive renewal of labor activism and immigrant rights organizing in the 1990s.

The turning point came after California voters approved Prop 187 in 1994. It won almost 60 percent of the votes statewide, passing in LA County by a twelve-point margin.[11] But it spurred a massive

Latino backlash. Miguel Contreras, a son of migrant farmworkers who had picked grapes as a child, became the first Latino head of the county federation of labor. He set to work making unions a vehicle for mobilizing L.A.'s vast Latino community. A massive door-to-door registration drive was followed by a get-out-the-vote operation in support of progressive candidates allied with Latino labor. They reshaped the city council and L.A.'s delegations to the state legislature and Congress. In L.A., labor also organized the Living Wage campaign, which in 1997 became one of the first in the nation to succeed at raising the incomes of workers on publicly funded projects. Next came the Latino-led Justice for Janitors campaign, which, after protracted struggle, mass arrests and police beatings, won a huge citywide strike in 2000.[12]

And the LAPD was finally required to change its ways—in 2001. After decades of litigation by the ACLU and protests organized mostly by activists in South L.A., the federal courts forced dozens of major reforms on the department and imposed a court-appointed monitor to supervise compliance. The decree wasn't lifted until 2013. And history was made in the streets: on May Day in 2006, half a million people marched down Wilshire Boulevard demanding rights for undocumented immigrants. Most of them were Latino, and most were young. The march had been called by labor unions and immigrant rights groups, and endorsed by the pro-immigrant Cardinal Roger Mahony and the city's first Latino mayor, Antonio Villaraigosa. And then on January 21, 2017, the day after Trump was inaugurated, an estimated 750,000 protested downtown at the LA Women's March—perhaps the largest in California history.

But the 2019 LA teachers' strike was perhaps the most dramatic example of the renewal of activism. A coalition of the classroom and the community, it focused on the same issues of overcrowded schools and educational disinvestment (now aggravated by the drain of resources to charter schools) that had contributed to the student uprisings in 1967–69. Moreover, thousands of the Latino students who boycotted classes and joined teacher picket lines were proudly aware that they were following in the footsteps of Sal Castro, Gloria Arellanes, Bobby Elias, Carlos Muñoz and all the others who had made time stop in March 1968. The union then capped its victory by recalling from retirement L.A.'s most irrepressible Sixties veteran, Echo Park's Jackie Goldberg, and electing her to the school board where she had fought so hard for integration and quality education thirty years earlier.

For more than a half century, the Right has waged a relentless campaign against the goals and achievements of the Sixties' movements for racial, social and economic equality. From Reagan to Trump, there has been an endless hammering away at caricatures of dopey hippies, traitorous peace protestors, bra-burning feminists, dangerous Black radicals, and commissars of political correctness.

However, as this book's two authors have discovered in myriad conversations with their students and other young comrades, this rewrite of history from the standpoint of wealthy white men has had minimal impact on the social consciousness of the young people of color who are Los Angeles's future. If anything, their own experiences of nativism, discrimination, sexual harassment and blocked mobility ensure that they will be genuine successors to grandmothers and grandfathers who so long ago raised their clenched fists and demanded power to the people. To keep that circle unbroken, this book was written.

Acknowledgments

The indispensable source for the history of radical movements in L.A. is the Southern California Library for Social Research—our deep thanks to Michele Welsing for all her help. We thank the UCLA Library Center for Oral History Research for access to their collection on "Women's Activist Lives," especially their Dorothy Healey interviews, and also UCLA's Young Research Library Special Collections for help with the Don Kalish papers, and with the *LA Times* Photographic Archive. The ONE National Gay and Lesbian Archives at USC is the indispensable source on L.A.'s LGBTQ history—thanks to Michael C. Oliveira and Loni Shibuyama there. The LA Public Library holds the Los Angeles Resistance Archive collected by Bob Zaugh, and also the *LA Herald Examiner* Photo Collection. At Cal State Northridge, the Oviatt Library University Archives has a valuable collection of interviews with activists in the SDS and BSU protests there—thanks to April Feldman, Archivist, for assistance. Cal State Long Beach has an extensive Oral History Archive, "The Sixties: Los Angeles Area Social Movements/Activists," and "Women's History" in the Virtual Oral/Aural History Archive, assembled in part by Sherna Gluck. Cal State LA has a Peace and Freedom Party Collection—Azalea Camacho, University Library Archivist, provided assistance there. Swarthmore College hold the Women Strike for Peace Records—thanks to Wendy E. Chmielewski, Curator of the Swarthmore College Peace Collection, for guidance there.

We relied on the Activist Video Archive for the stories of many LA people—thanks to Julie Thompson and Brogan de Paor for that. And Lenna Poulatian, Director of Development at Friends of the Saban Community Clinic, provided archival help, including a copy of the UCLA student video made in 1968 by Bob Eberlein and Paul Deason.

Interviews with Sixties activists were an essential part of our research—special thanks to Rudy Acuña, Gordy Alexandre, Jan Breidenbach, Ellen Broms, Marc Cooper, Ed Cray, John Densmore, Bill Garaway, Sherna Gluck, Jackie Goldberg, Levi Kingston, Mark Kleiman, Paula Litt, Leo Mouton, Spencer Olin, Irving Petlin, Paul Rosenstein, June Solnit Sale, Sabina Virgo, Jack Weinberg, and Bob Zaugh, who provided not only an interview but also access to the archives of the draft resistance movement in L.A., and even free xeroxing. Marilyn Katz and Karen Jo Koonan wrote wonderful memoirs for us of their LA movement days. Victor Cohen provided a copy of his extensive interviews with Ed Pearl. We had research assistance from Jonas Oppenheim and Alex Jacoby; from Renee Reynolds, who did magnificent work on our photo section; and from Amanda Beebe at the Swarthmore Women Strike for Peace collection.

At Verso Books, Andy Hsiao did superb work editing our chapters and generally keeping ducks in line. Sam Smith is a great copy editor. Thanks to production editor Duncan Ranslem and the rest of the Verso team: Anne Rumberger, Ben Mabie, and Julia Judge.

Jon Wiener thanks Judy Fiskin for editing all of his chapters and telling the truth (gently) about which ones needed more work. And Mike Davis apologizes to his daughter Roisin for breaking his promise "to stop talking about the goddamn Sixties."

About the Authors

Mike Davis

From shortly before the Watts Rebellion in August 1965 until late October 1966, I was the Los Angeles regional organizer for Students for a Democratic Society. My assignments from the Chicago national office were to help build a draft resistance movement in the city (I had burnt my own draft card the previous March and was waiting to see whether or not I would be prosecuted), and to assist two brilliantly eloquent SDSers—Margaret Thorpe at USC and Patty Lee Parmalee at UC Irvine—in raising hell on local campuses. The most hell was generated by a wonderful group of high school activists from Palisades, University and Hamilton High Schools—one of whom, Mark Kleiman, would later become SDS's national high school organizer. The teenagers, along with some recently minted college SDSers (Ross Altman from USC, Walt Crow and Doug Layfield from Pasadena City College, Doug Norberg from Whittier College, and others), met regularly at the ramshackle SDS office-cum-crash pad that Margaret and I had rented near USC. Betty Carstens, a veteran of "Freedom Summer" who was finishing a degree at UCLA, soon moved into the house and made us a trio. We all shared the astute mentorship of Levi Kingston, a former merchant seaman and coffeehouse manager, who was then organizing the "Freedom Draft Movement" in South Central L.A. Bob Duggan, the charismatic leader of the local Du Bois Clubs, would show up episodically to lead forays, including a trip to the notorious Imperial Valley to meet beleaguered farmworkers and a late-night raid on USC that left the conservative campus spray-painted from stem to stern with anti-war graffiti. As new SDS chapters sprouted at surprising speed, regional-scale actions became possible, kicked off by a rather nightmarish anti-war march from the Claremont Colleges to Cal State LA that included a stoning by pro-war locals. This was followed by the first major protest against the manufacture of napalm at Dow Chemical's plant in Torrance. As a new crop of local SDSers took over regional leadership, I left L.A. in 1967 to work briefly with SDS in Texas, returning to California later that year to begin real life as an apprentice butcher in San Diego and later as a heavy-duty truck driver in East L.A. While in Austin I missed the Century City "massacre" and most of the Sunset Strip battles, although I marched in the final and exultant Strip protest in 1968.

I joined the Southern California branch of the Communist Party that year because of its bold opposition to the Soviet murder of Prague Spring, as well as its multiracial membership. Thus began years of dueling with Dorothy Healey, who, despite our chronic disagreements over the Democratic Party, Trotsky, and other issues, became the major and enduring intellectual and moral influence in my life. In the remaining years covered by this volume, from late 1968 until 1973, I was active in the Teamster rank-and-file movement, and a face in the crowd (and sometimes in jail) in almost all of the big protests of the period. In the course of the Sixties I witnessed tragedies, but also social miracles and innumerable instances of unheralded courage and defiance. It is fitting to acknowledge some of my local heroes of that era: Franklin and Kendra Alexander, Tommy Ashton (murdered at the University of Texas in 1966), Rudy Acuña, Art Carstens, Mary Clarke, Ken Cloke, Angela Davis, Ben Dobbs, Jimmy Garrett, Tim Harding, Ray Hewitt, Jonathan Jackson, Karen Koonan, Hugh Manes, Roger McCready, Ed Moritz, Ed Pearl, Nelson Peery, Judy Perez, Ron Ridenour, Sue Romo, Paul Rosenstein, Barry Sanders, John Shannon, Paul Shinoff, Frank Spector, Gary Vogan, Adele Wallace, Gene, Judy and Ron Warren, Devra Weber, Sabina Virgo, and Edith and Milt Zaslow. From 1968 onward, Ron Schneck has been a compadre in many reckless but character-building adventures.

Jon Wiener

Like so many others, my Sixties began when Black students started sitting in at Woolworth's lunch counters in the South in 1960. I was a student at Central High School in St. Paul, and joined my first picket line outside a Woolworth's downtown. For reasons I've never understood, I got recruited by Princeton, and the first month of freshman year brought the Cuban Missile Crisis, when I joined my first protest march. Then, with Mike Lipsky, a grad student, we organized Friends of SNCC, honoring our heroic classmates who went to Mississippi—especially the wonderful Bob Cover—and after Mississippi Freedom Summer, we organized a memorable fundraiser featuring the parents of Mickey Schwerner, who had been killed a few months earlier in Neshoba County. At Princeton I had some great left-wing teachers: Maurice Zeitlin, a sociologist who had just gotten back from Cuba; Arno Mayer, a historian who lectured about the counterrevolution; Everett Gendler, the amazing town rabbi who had been part of the movement in Birmingham and Selma; and, most of all, Michael Walzer, who had organized that national Woolworth's boycott and now taught Marx and worked on *Dissent*—an activist and writer. I decided that's what I wanted to be.

A turning point came when we organized Princeton SDS and brought Tom Hayden down from Newark to talk strategy. Then came Vietnam: with Bob Edelman and others, we went to the first anti-war March on Washington, organized by SDS in spring 1965; we made a banner that said "Even Princeton." I wrote my first activist/journalist piece for *New Left Notes*, the National SDS newspaper, about the Madame Nhu / Vietnam War protest at Princeton. Then LBJ came to campus in spring '66, and we ended our college years with a big anti-war march, wearing suits and ties for the occasion. (After that LBJ didn't appear on campus again.) Then to Harvard for grad school—where during the first month of classes, Robert McNamara visited the school but refused to appear in a public forum—so we (800 SDS members) surrounded him as he was leaving a secret appointment and demanded he answer questions. I wrote about that for *New Left Notes*, too. The next fall, on the spur of the moment, Dave Rubenstein and I drove down to DC for the March on the Pentagon. And then my main Cambridge mentor, the brilliant student organizer Mike Ansara, hooked me up with *Ramparts* magazine and its activist/journalist editor Robert Scheer to do research for their exposé on CIA funding of cultural organizations. Michael Walzer (now at Harvard) recruited me to help organize the Cambridge Neighborhood Committee on Vietnam, which aimed at getting the anti-war message off campus and into the community—and we got an initiative on the ballot calling for immediate withdrawal, and ran a door-to-door precinct campaign. (We got 39 percent—not enough). Then Mike Ansara put me to work on the *Old Mole*, one of the more political underground papers of the era, alongside two inspiring guys, Nick Egelson and Vernon Grizzard, and my dear friends Linda Gordon and Danny Schechter "the news dissector," another great example of an activist-journalist. And when Harvard students went on strike against the war and for Black studies, occupying the administration building, we published some interesting correspondence of the dean's, "liberated" from the office of the university president—under the triumphant title "Reading the Mail of the Ruling Class."

I arrived in L.A. the summer of 1969, thanks to my girlfriend and political partner Temma Kaplan, who had gotten a job teaching history at UCLA despite having been arrested in the Harvard Strike. We became immediate friends and comrades with Bob and Johanna Brenner. Bob also taught history at UCLA, and brought us into the political scene. My ambition was to write about L.A. for *Liberation News Service* (*LNS*), which provided twice-weekly packets to more than 200 underground and college newspapers around the country. There was plenty to write about: a few weeks after we arrived, the regents fired Angela Davis. Then came reporting on the LAPD campaign to kill the Panthers, campus anti-war mobilizations, GI organizing at Camp Pendleton, the Teamsters' wildcat strike, and the battle for Venice Beach—with unforgettable acts of heroism and moments of exaltation. For one of my first *LNS* articles, about the arson attacks by *gusanos* (right-wing Cuban exiles) on movement centers, I interviewed a local organizer named Mike Davis. He was intense, eloquent, and a little intimidating. We didn't become friends until more than a decade after that.

Notes

1 Setting the Agenda

1 E. P. Thompson, "At the Point of Decay," in Thompson, ed., *Out of Apathy* (London: New Left Books, 1960), 5.

2 A. J. Muste, "Niebuhr on the Brink of War," quoted in Robert H. Craig, *Religion and Radical Politics* (Philadelphia: Temple University Press, 1995), 210.

3 The ground had been prepared by the two Youth Marches for Integrated Schools in Washington, DC, in October 1958 and April 1959, both spectacularly successful: the first attracted 10,000 students and the second, 25,000. Bayard Rustin, the principal organizer, hoped to open a second front for the Southern struggle on Northern campuses and put pressure on liberal Democrats: John D'Emilio, *Lost Prophet: The Life and Times of Bayard Rustin* (Chicago: University of Chicago Press, 2003), 272–5.

4 United States Commission on Civil Rights, *Hearings before the United States Commission on Civil Rights: Hearings Held in Los Angeles, California, January 25, 1960, January 26, 1960; San Francisco, California, January 27, 1960, January 28, 1960* (Washington, DC: US Government Printing Office, 1960) (hereafter, *Hearings*). The spades and shovels incident is related in the *California Eagle*, July 28, 1960. As the incidents continued, the LAPD finally established surveillance of the Holmes home and arrested one of the rock throwers in May 1960. His conviction for disturbing the peace, according to the district attorney's office, was "the first criminal case in the state where racial discrimination is the probable root of the offense" (*Los Angeles Times* [hereafter, *LAT*], July 28, 1960).

5 The most prominent member of the commission, University of Notre Dame president Father Theodore Hesburgh, bluntly acknowledged that it had been established as "a substitute for action": "As I look back to 1957," he wrote later, "there is little doubt in my mind that creation of the Commission was—in part, at least—a 'cop out.' In fact, there were many at the time who were convinced that the Commission would do less than an honest study and would, in fact, perform a 'whitewash' job and gloss over the deep civil-rights problems confronting the nation." In fact, until the Reagan presidency, the hearings and reports of the commission were invaluable weapons in the hands of activists and civil rights lawyers (Theodore Hesburgh, "The Commission on Civil Rights—and Human Rights," *Review of Politics* 34:3 [July 1972], 291–2).

6 *Hearings*, 6–7.

7 *Hearings*, 118–20, 335, 426.

8 The *Eagle*'s statement of principles was concise: "We oppose: 1. Jim Crow in all forms. 2. Communists and all other enemies of democracy." With this shrewd disclaimer, Miller consistently published sympathetic articles about the Cuban Revolution throughout the early 1960s.

9 *Hearings*, 253, 255, 260–3. For recognition of Miller's role at the time, see R. J. Smith, *The Great Black Way: L.A. in the 1940s and the Lost African-American Renaissance* (New York: Public Affairs, 2006), 236.

10 *Hearings*, 130.

11 Douglas Flamming, *Bound for Freedom: Black Los Angeles in Jim Crow America* (Berkeley: University of California Press, 2005), 378.

12 *LAT*, May 8, 1960. West Covina had only 9 acres of industry; La Puente, none at all.

13 *Hearings*, 130.

14 "Civil rights policy has substantially dismantled neighborhood level, or 'intrajurisdictional,' mechanisms of segregation. But federal court policy has reinforced devices which support interjurisdictional racial segregation. If neighborhood level segregative mechanism are removed while municipal level segregative mechanisms are left intact, municipal borders would gradually become racial and class borders as well. A change in patterns of segregation of this sort would entail no necessary change in the overall level of segregation" (Gregory Weiher, *The Fractured Metropolis* [Albany: SUNY Press, 1991], 88).

15 Winston Crouch and Beatrice Dinerman, *Southern California Metropolis: A Study of Government for a Metropolitan Area* (Berkeley: University of California Press, 1963), 383; Michan Connor, "Public

Benefits from Public Choice: Producing Decentralization in Metropolitan Los Angeles, 1954–1973," *Journal of Urban History* 39:1 (2013). See also Tom Hogen-Esch, "Fragmentation, Fiscal Federalism, and the Ghost of Dillon's Rule: Municipal Incorporation in Southern California, 1950–2010," *California Journal of Politics and Policy* 3:1 (2011).

16 Discrimination in public accommodation had been illegal in California since 1905, but it was still common for bars, restaurants, gyms and especially motels to refuse service to Blacks. Glendale was particularly notorious. See *LAT*, July 16, 1963.

17 I rely here on accounts of the Luau incident in the biographies by Horne's daughter, Gail Lumet Buckley: *The Hornes: An American Family* (New York: Knopf, 1986), 242–3; and James Gavin, *Stormy Weather: The Life of Lena Horne* (New York: Simon & Schuster, 2009), 295–7. Gavin emphasizes the emotional cost of Horne's lifelong struggle to overcome the stereotypes of her light-skin beauty. He also provides a rich account of her friendships on the left, her valuable contributions to the Southern movement, and her admiration for Malcolm X. For King's visit to L.A., see *LAT*, February 25, 1960.

18 *California Eagle*, June 2, 1960. Otis emphasized the issue of drug addiction and the need for a state agency to rehabilitate young addicts. Although he won a majority of the Black vote in the district, he lost the election.

19 *LAT*, June 25, 1958.

20 *California Eagle*, March 11, 14 and 17, 1960. The "White Citizens' Council" seems to have been a real group, notorious for the racist leaflets it distributed throughout LA County. See *Chicago Daily Defender*, March 30, 1960.

21 Scott Greer, *Last Man In: Racial Access to Union Power* (Glencoe, IL: Free Press, 1959), 39, 51, 171–3 (table 1); Herbert Northrup, *Negro Employment in Basic Industries* (Philadelphia: University of Pennsylvania Press, 1970), 68, 360.

22 Anthony Chen et al., "Explaining the Contemporary Alignment of Race and Party: Evidence from California's 1946 Ballot Initiative on Fair Employment," *Studies in American Political Development* 22:2 (fall 2008).

23 *LAT*, January 8 and February 9, 1958.

24 *LAT*, April 29, 1960.

25 Northrup, *Negro Employment*, 543.

26 On the other hand, Unruh's chief financial backer was Howard Ahmanson, a moderate Republican whose giant Home Savings of America was deeply implicated in housing segregation and would be

picketed by CORE in 1963. Ahmanson and his cronies provided the financial resources that enabled Unruh to develop his own powerful Democrat faction in Sacramento and Los Angeles: Eric Abrahamson, *Building Home: Howard F. Ahmanson and the Politics of the American Dream* (Berkeley: University of California Press, 2013), 188.

27 Mark Brilliant contrasts the success of the NAACP in legislating its agenda to the failure of the Community Service Organization, its Mexican American counterpart, to win support for a minimum agricultural wage and an end to the bracero program. Apparently, farmworkers were at the bottom of Brown's liberal agenda: *The Color of America Has Changed: How Racial Diversity Shaped Civil Rights Reform in California, 1941–1987* (New York: Oxford University Press, 2010), 165–70.

28 See Alex Abella, *Soldiers of Reason: The Rand Corporation and the Rise of the American Empire* (Boston: Houghton Mifflin Harcourt, 2008), 54. Paula Dinnerstein, the daughter of a prominent Rand scholar, was a founder of the first high school SDS chapter (at Pacific Palisades High) in 1965.

29 Rod Janzen, *The Rise and Fall of Synanon: A California Utopia* (Baltimore: Johns Hopkins University Press, 2001), 13.

30 Frank Bardacke, *Trampling Out the Vintage: Cesar Chavez and the Two Souls of the United Farm Workers* (London and New York: Verso, 2012).

31 *LAT*, February 20, 1960.

32 SLATE, which had played a leading role in the anti-HUAC demonstrations, sponsored a statewide conference in late July to discuss the coordination of student action.

33 The students linked up with the local "Ad Hoc Committee on the Chessman Case," led by Dr. Isidore Zifferstein, a UCLA psychiatrist and prominent peace activist; Phil Kerby, publisher of *Frontier* magazine, who later moved to the *Times*; and Dr. William Graves, a former medic at San Quentin.

34 *Independent Student*, June and September 1960, from the files of Ellen (Kleinman) Broms. See also *LAT*, May 1 and October 27, 1960; *California Eagle*, May 26, 1960.

35 *LAT*, June 26 and August 28, 1960.

36 "Brown lost face, and Unruh, who had mostly been a loyal servant to the governor, became the Kennedys' lieutenant in California": Ethan Rarick, *The Life and Times of Pat Brown: California Rising* (Berkeley: University of California Press, 2005), 202.

37 *Chicago Daily Defender*, July 12, 1960.

38 See Gilbert Estrada, "If You Build It, They Will Move: The Los Angeles Freeway System and the Displacement of Mexican East Los Angeles, 1944–1972," *Southern California Quarterly* 87:3 (fall 2005), 287–315.

39 *LAT*, September 30 and October 16, 1955 (fight over routing of Santa Monica Freeway); April 11, 1966 (number displaced). Adding Orange County, David Brodsly estimates more than a quarter of a million people were moved: *LA Freeway: An Appreciative Essay* (Berkeley: University of California Press, 1981).

40 *LAT*, September 18 and 25, and October 2, 1960.

41 John Arthur Maynard, *Venice West: The Beat Generation in Southern California* (New Brunswick, NJ: Rutgers University Press, 1991), 107–13.

42 *LAT*, May 21, 1959, and October 21, 1960; *Hearings*, 73.

43 Paul Bullock, "Watts: A View from the Outside," in *Watts: The Aftermath: An Inside View of the Ghetto* (New York: Grove, 1969), 238, 246.

44 *LAT*, November 4 and 15, 1960.

45 In 1960 there were 629,292 Spanish-surname residents of Los Angeles and Orange Counties, versus 461,546 Blacks. But the Black population of the city of Los Angeles, 334,916, was considerably larger than the Mexican, 260,389: US Census Bureau, *US Censuses of Population and Housing: 1960 Census Tracts Los Angeles–Long Beach, California SMSA* (Washington, DC: US Government Printing Office, 1962).

46 *LAT*, January 8, 1961.

47 *LAT*, December 2, 1960; January 13, 1961; April 27, 1961.

48 *LAT*, March 25, 1960. COPE disingenuously claimed to be "opposed to all incorporations," when in reality it had made little or no protest against the earlier incorporation of several dozen segregated Lakewood Plan cities.

49 *LAT*, February 27, 1963.

2 Warden of the Ghetto

1 United States Commission on Civil Rights, *Hearings Before the US Commission on Civil Rights, Hearings Held in Los Angeles, January 25, 1960* (Washington, DC: US Government Printing Office, 1960), 325, 327, 330–1.

2 *LAT*, January 29 and February 3, 1960.

3 Joe Domanick, *To Protect and Serve: The LAPD's Century of War in the City of Dreams* (New York: Pocket Books, 1994), 95.

4 *LAT*, June 20, 1959.

5   Domanick, *To Protect and Serve*, 146. See also John Buntin, *L.A. Noir: The Struggle for the Soul of America's Most Seductive City* (New York: Broadway Books, 2010), 170. It is claimed that Parker later went on the wagon: Alisa Kramer, "William H. Parker and the Thin Blue Line: Politics, Public Relations and Policing in Postwar Los Angeles," PhD diss., American University, 2007, 84. This is the only actual biography of Parker and thus very useful, but Kramer does depend heavily on Domanick.

6   Domanick, *To Protect and Serve*, 133.

7   Kramer, "William H. Parker," 73–4.

8   Ibid., 78.

9   Ibid., 184.

10   Ibid., 29.

11   Kramer, "William H. Parker," 103, n260, citing her interview with David Dotson.

12   Kramer, "William H. Parker," 62. The LAPD as well as the LA County Sheriffs had very high rates of felony arrests that were subsequently dismissed by the district attorney's office (18,934 out of 49,311 in one period). The LAPD, however, kept the dismissed records on file and shared them with other agencies. It was therefore easy for the police to attach a "record" to anyone without evidence (*LAT*, November 13, 1959).

13   *LAT*, November 13, 1959; Robert Gottlieb and Irene Wolt, *Thinking Big: The Story of the Los Angeles Times, Its Publishers, and Their Influence on Southern California* (New York: Putnam's, 1977), 257–8, 270, 360–3.

14   Kramer, "William H. Parker," 103.

15   The hunter, however, was also being hunted. In 1953 Parker confided to another police chief that he was being tracked by ten to fifteen FBI agents. Hoover rightly regarded the LA chief as his chief competitor and would-be replacement in a new administration. Moreover, Hoover had always discounted the importance, even the existence, of organized crime, but Parker saw it everywhere, and his view was confirmed by the Senate hearings led by Senator Estes Kefauver in 1950–51. Parker, a conservative Catholic, later became friends with Robert Kennedy, who publicly shared his views about organized crime, and privately those about Hoover. At the 1960 DNC, Parker ostentatiously welcomed JFK with a police detail befitting a sitting president. After the election, however, the Kennedys' plan to bring Parker to Washington was scuttled after confidential meetings with Hoover, who presumably had an impressive collection of tapes

certifying the young president's satyriasis. See Kramer, "William H. Parker," 145.

16 Like many radical liberals of the period (Reverend Stephen Fritchman of the First Unitarian Church was another), Wilkinson worked with and respected members of the party, but was unlikely to have ever accepted its discipline (MD personal knowledge).

17 Domanick, *To Protect and Serve*, 157. His source is unclear.

18 *LAT*, May 23, 1956; Kramer, "William H. Parker," 131.

19 Buntin, *L.A. Noir*, 280. In 1960 Governor Brown helped unseat Ziffren from his DNC membership just a few months before the Convention. Ethan Rarick, *California Rising: The Life and Times of Pat Brown* (Berkeley: University of California Press, 2006) suggests that the mob rumor contributed to his downfall (194).

20 Kramer, "William H. Parker," 190–1. Her account is based on Charles Rappleye and David Robb, "The Judge, the Photos, and the Senate Race," *LA Weekly*, March 4–10, 1994.

21 Bruce Tyler, "Black Radicalism in Southern California, 1950–1982," PhD diss., Department of History, UCLA, 1983, 130–4. Parker is often given credit for building the LAPD around a Marine Corps model of training and command. As Kramer points out, however, he inherited the paramilitary paradigm from his predecessor, Marine Major General Worton, although Parker enhanced it with veteran Marine drill instructors at the police academy. His true innovation, influenced by Wilson, was shifting the force from foot beats into squad cars, with a large gain in efficiency counterbalanced by a loss of intimacy with neighborhoods and the public (50–4).

22 *LAT*, October 12, 1995.

23 Almena Loman, column in *California Eagle*, May 17, 1962.

24 *California Eagle*, July 16, 1960.

25 *LAT*, April 28, 1960; Kramer, "William H. Parker," 237, n78.

26 *LAT*, July 1, 1960.

27 *California Eagle*, April 7, 1960.

28 Buntin, *L.A. Noir*, 196–7.

29 Yorty's "downtown machine" strategy is discussed in John Bollens and Grant Geyer, "The Politics of Rubbish," in *Yorty: Politics of a Constant Candidate* (Pacific Palisades, CA: Palisades Publishers, 1973), chapter 15; and Charles Mayo, "The 1961 Mayoralty Election in Los Angeles," *Western Political Quarterly* 17:2 (June 1964), 325–37.

30 See Celes King, "Black Leadership in Los Angeles Oral History: Celes King III," interview transcript, July 14, 1985, UCLA Library Center for Oral History Research, 384–5 (tape 10, side 1).

31 *LAT*, June 10, 1961; Kramer, "William H. Parker," 197.

32 Mike Davis, "As Bad as the H-bomb," in *Dead Cities and Other Tales* (New York: New Press, 2002), 214–15.

33 Kramer, "William H. Parker," 196.

34 *LAT*, February 18, 19 and 20, 1963. Kramer, "William H. Parker," 197. Kramer interviewed the veteran *Times* city editor Bill Boyarsky, who is a connoisseur of the paper's legends and secrets. More compelling is Raphael Sonenshein's interview with Tom Bradley. The mayor confirmed that Parker "did threaten Sam Yorty" but not in person. "One day Parker sent a message over with a package. And they showed that to Yorty and told him he wanted him to shut up and stop criticizing the chief and laid out all of these bits of information that they had gathered on him" (Sonenshein, *Politics in Black and White: Race and Power in Los Angeles* [Princeton: Princeton University Press, 1993], 68).

35 *LAT*, August 21, 1963.

3 L.A. to Mississippi, Goddamn

1 "Like a seed, a real core, it would germinate and radiate its equality in wider and wider circles until it encompassed the whole nation" (James Farmer, *Lay Bare the Heart* [Fort Worth: TCU Press, 1985], 105).

2 See the very useful chronology and roster of the Rides in Raymond Arsenault, *Freedom Riders: 1961 and the Struggle for Racial Justice* (New York: Oxford University Press, 2006), 533–87. Greater New York City (including Long Island and New Jersey on the west bank of the Hudson) contributed about seventy volunteers.

3 August Meier and Elliot Rudwick, *CORE: A Study in the Civil Rights Movement*, 1942–1968 (New York: Oxford University Press, 1973), 31, 42–3, 59.

4 Martin Luther King Jr., Martin Luther King Jr. Papers Project, letter of September 19, 1956, Montgomery, AL. Although the Mobilization was basically a pipe dream, it did lead to a major Supreme Court decision that stills weighs significantly in legal battles over anonymity on the Internet and in political contributions. In 1958 Talley, who had been handing out his boycott fliers, was cited for violating a city ordinance that required handbills to include the name and address of their author or distributor. He contested the law, and two years later the US Supreme Court ruled in a 6–3 decision that anonymous speech was protected. See the entry "Talley vs. California" in John Vile, David Hudson, and David Schultz, eds., *Encyclopedia of the*

First Amendment (Washington, DC: CQ Press, 2008). Talley also won a second victory in the Supreme Court. With the able counsel of the ACLU's A. L. Wirin, he and two other wartime draft resisters—Katsuki Otsuka and John Abbott—sued for restoration of their right to vote, which had been taken away after their original convictions for violating the Selective Service Act. The case went on for years, but the Supremes eventually ruled in their favor (Supreme Court of California Resources, *Otsuka v. Hite*, 64 Cal.2d 596, 1966, available at: scocal.stanford.edu/opinion/otsuka-v-hite-27340).

5   See accounts in *LAT*, September 10, 1962; September 15 (representing CORE in protests against the Hoover Redevelopment Project) and October 11, 1965. Later, Talley made two almost whimsical attempts at running for office. *LAT, May* 13, 1984.

6   Meier and Rudwick, *CORE*, 74, 109, 121–2, 125–7, 151.

7   Arsenault, *Freedom Riders*, 97.

8   Ibid., 164. Patterson, who had been officially endorsed by the Klan, was one of the few Southern governors to support Kennedy in 1960. He also assented to a White House request to have the Alabama National Guard secretly train exile flyers for the Bay of Pigs invasion.

9   Ibid., 282–3.

10   Meier and Rudwick, *CORE*, 139–40.

11   Robert Farrell recalls that when he joined, several dozen other people were on the CORE waiting list to become Riders.

12   *California Eagle*, February 9, May 4 and June 8, 1961.

13   I don't know of any instance in local history when the LAPD has ever exaggerated the size of a crowd—and they claimed there were 10,000 people unable to get into the Sports Arena—MD. This would support an estimate of at least 30,000 (*LAT*, June 19, 1961; *Washington Post*, June 20, 1961). The event was officially organized by the Western Christian Leadership Council (Reverend Maurice Dawkins) and cosponsored by CORE, the ISU, the Jewish Labor League, the CSO, and others.

14   Taylor Branch, *Parting the Waters: America in the King Years, 1954–63* (New York: Simon & Schuster, 1988), 480–5.

15   Ellen (Kleinman) Broms, interview by MD; see also Broms, "When MLK Thrilled L.A.—and Me: A Rally in the Sports Arena Changed Me from Picketer to Freedom Rider," *Zocalo Public Square*, January 18, 2013.

16   *Hamilton v. Alabama*, 376 U.S. 650 (1964).

17   Arsenault, *Freedom Riders*, 372; Anne Valk, *Radical Sisters: Second-*

Wave Feminism and Black Liberation in Washington (Champaign: University of Illinois Press, 2008), 22–3.

18. Taylor Branch has an interesting vignette concerning Henderson's early warnings to the young lions King and Abernathy about the dangers they faced, both physical and reputational: the elder minister especially warned them that "white women can be lures. You must exercise more than care. You must be vigilant indeed" (Branch, *Parting the Waters*, 242).

19 Arsenault, *Freedom Riders*, 373–5.

20 Fulton Lewis Jr., "Washington Report: Reds Take Part in Freedom Ride," *Lakeland Ledger*, September 4, 1961.

21 Arsenault, *Freedom Riders*, 346.

22 Between the second and third LA Rides, two more locals, James Dennis from Cal State LA and Candida Lall from Long Beach State, were arrested as members of other contingents.

23 See Singleton's remarks during a panel discussion by Freedom Ride veterans: "A Salute to UCLA Freedom Riders," *UCLA Newsroom*, February 9, 2015, newsroom.ucla.edu.

24 A year after the bombing, the Klan kidnapped a random Black male and castrated him as a "message to Shuttlesworth": "I want you to tell him to stop sending nigger children and white children to school together or we're gonna do him like we're fixing to do you." Their leader—Joe Pritchett—"plopped the scrotum in a paper cup to take home for a souvenir." Diane McWhorter, *Carry Me Home: Birmingham, Alabama: The Climactic Battle of the Civil Rights Revolution* (New York: Simon & Schuster, 2002), 124–5. For Shuttlesworth's visit, see *California Eagle*, August 1961.

25 Thomas G. Smith, *Showdown: JFK and the Integration of the Washington Redskins* (Boston: Beacon, 2011), 126–7, 150–1, 165–7; *California Eagle*, August 17, 1961. Threat of protests also led to the cancellation of a planned reenactment of the city's founding that excluded Blacks in the cast, although more than half of the pobladores were Afro-Mexicans (*California Eagle*, August 24, 1961).

26 Annie Lu, "Steven McNichols, Former Freedom Rider, Remembered for Civil Rights Activism," *Daily Bruin* (UCLA), May 31, 2013.

27 *California Eagle*, August 31, September 21, October 26, and November 9, 1961. Rank-and-file groups of any kind, but especially those protesting discrimination, were anathemas to local Teamster leadership, who fired Williams from his job as an administrator with freight Local 208.

4. "God's Angry Men"

1 James Carr, *Bad: The Autobiography of James Carr* (New York: Herman Graf Associates, 1975), 91–4. We've been unable to find newspaper references to this episode in 1958–59, and it's likely that Carr has wildly scrambled the order of events. In February 1963 Booker Johnson, described in the *Los Angeles Times* as the "leader" of the Muslims inside San Quentin, was killed in the exact circumstances described by Carr (*LAT*, February 27, 1963).

2 In 1960 California corrections authorities ruled that the Muslims were not a "bona fide religious sect" and encouraged wardens to break up their activities (*LAT*, March 4, 1961 and May 20, 1962). The result was years of riots, attacks and excessive punishment.

3 C. Eric Lincoln, *The Black Muslims in America*, 3rd ed. (Grand Rapids: Eerdmans, 1994), 141.

4 Manning Marable, *Malcolm X: A Life of Reinvention* (New York: Viking, 2011), 148–9. Among the attendees were Hank Ballard and Sam Cooke: Hakim A. Jamal, *From the Dead Level: Malcolm X and Me* (New York: Random House, 1972), 152.

5 See Alfred Ligon, "All the Lights the Light," oral history transcript, ca. 1984, UCLA Library Center for Oral History Research; and Yael Tamar Lewin, *Night's Dancer: The Life of Janet Collins* (Middletown, CT: Wesleyan University Press, 2011), 18–19. Collins was Young's niece and made history in 1951 when she became the first Black member of the Metropolitan Opera's ballet corps.

6 Elizabeth Pat Alexander, interview by R. Donald Brown, April 8, 1967, African American History Collection, Center for Oral and Public History, CSU Fullerton, 4–11. Thanks to Stephanie George for making the transcript of this interview available to us. In this interview, Alexander also makes disconcerting claims about her family history.

7 *Herald-Dispatch*, February 27, 1958; Louis Decaro, *Malcolm and the Cross: The Nation of Islam, Malcolm X, and Christianity* (New York: NYU Press, 2000), 141. The paper was published from 1952 until 1977.

8 Lincoln, *Black Muslims*, 124–6; *LAT*, August 20 and 22, 1964; *LAT*, July 2, 1965; *Jet*, July 22, 1965, 24. There was a second bombing a year later, which Alexander did not blame on the NOI but speculated was retaliation for the paper's "patroniz[ation of] Negro business."

9 FBI file, New York 105–8999, March 20–October 10, 1958. On the other hand, at a meeting at Normandie Hall, Malcolm told the

audience (at least as the FBI reported it) that California might be the ideal location for an independent Black nation, since Elijah Muhammad "does not want his state to be where it is too cold nor too hot, nor where there is no water outlet to an ocean or gulf." A first step would be the establishment of a NOI farm colony (15).

10 *California Eagle*, February 11, 1960.

11 Jamal, *From the Dead Level*, 213.

12 The documentary conferred fame on two hitherto-unknown journalists, Mike Wallace and Louis Lomax. Wallace, of course, would end up on CBS while Lomax became familiar as a commentator on Black-white relations.

13 Speech at Princeton University, October, 1959, quoted in Karl Evanzz, *The Messenger: The Rise and Fall of Elijah Muhammad* (New York: Vintage, 2001), 208–9.

14 Dorothy Healey, interview by Maurice Isserman, March 5, 1973, Center for Oral History Research, UCLA, tape xii, side 2.

15 Johnny Otis, *Upside Your Head! Rhythm and Blues on Central Avenue* (Hanover, NH: Wesleyan University Press, 1993), 44–5. Otis, the olive-skinned son of immigrants from Crete, was comfortably accepted by almost everyone, including Malcolm X, as a Black man, regardless of his heredity. In the language of the period, he was not a "white Negro" but a Negro who happened to be biologically white. George Lipsitz's biography, *Midnight at the Barrelhouse: The Johnny Otis Story* (Minneapolis: University of Minnesota Press, 2010) explores all the dialectical aspects of this fascinating man's identity.

16 Lipsitz, *Midnight*, 74–5. After Dymally's election to the California State Assembly in November 1962, Otis became his deputy chief of staff.

17 Marable, *Malcolm X*, 139–40.

18 John Buntin, *L.A. Noir: The Struggle for the Soul of America's Most Seductive City* (New York: Crown, 2009), 295. He does not cite his source.

19 *LAT*, September 3, 1961; Marable, *Malcolm X*, 206.

20 Marable, *Malcolm X*, 207. He mistakenly describes Parker as the "city's police commissioner."

21 *LAT*, November 20, 1962 (testimony from preliminary hearing); a remarkably detailed reconstruction of the incident can be found in Taylor Branch, *Pillar of Fire: America in the King Years, 1963–65* (New York: Simon & Schuster, 1998), ch. 1. Branch hired Jonah Edelman, a Rhodes Scholar and son of one of King's chief aides, to interview almost a dozen survivors of the mosque attack.

22 *California Eagle*, May 16 and 30, 1963.

23 *Chicago Daily Defender*, May 25, 1963.

24 *LAT*, May 3, 1963.

25 *LAT*, May 14 and 17, 1963 (court testimony); *Chicago Daily Defender*, May 18, 1963 (court testimony); *Pittsburgh Courier*, May 19, 1962; and *Militant*, June 3, 1963 (court testimony).

26 LAPD injuries included several concussions, many bruises, and a broken thumb. *LAT*, April 29, 1962. See also *LAT*, October 12, 1962; *Pittsburgh Courier*, December 15, 1962; and *Militant*, June 3, 1963 (court testimony of Troy Augustine). In Malcolm's May 5 speech at Stokes's funeral, he shocks the mourners by revealing that two of the victims "had been shot in the penis."

27 Marable, *Malcolm X*, 209. Marable interviewed Farrakhan.

28 Jamal, *From the Dead Level*, 219–23.

29 Interview by Dick Elman, 1962, WBAI Radio, transcript available at theblackamericanmuslim.com/1962-police-brutality.

30 A film of this powerful speech is available at theroottv.theroot.com/video/Malcolm-X-Los-Angeles-Ronald-St.

31 *LAT*, May 14, 1962.

32 *California Eagle*, May 17, 1962. Malcolm nonetheless severely tested his new alliances when he described a plane crash in Paris that killed 121 wealthy white Atlantans as "a very beautiful thing," Allah's revenge for the death of Stokes (Marable, *Malcolm X*, 212).

33 *LAT*, June 16, 1962.

34 *LAT*, August 4, 1962.

35 Evanzz, *The Messenger*, 246.

36 Marable, *Malcolm X*, 208–9.

37 Ibid. Malcolm, while disagreeing over tactics, admired the courage and audacity of CORE and SNCC (227–8).

38 Taylor Branch, *Parting the Waters: America in the King Years, 1954–63* (New York: Simon & Schuster, 1988), 13; Marable, *Malcolm X*, 209.

39 *LAT*, May 10, 1962; *California Eagle*, May 17, 1962.

40 *LAT*, May 10, 1962. In July Yorty attended a *Reader's Digest*–sponsored conference in New York, only to discover Malcolm waiting for him in the audience (*New York Times*, June 27, 1962).

41 *LAT*, May 21, 1962.

42 Buntin, *L.A. Noir*, 299.

43 *LAT*, May 18, 1963.

5 "Not Tomorrow—but Now!"

1 City ordinances criminalized integration even in the most trivial pursuits. It was illegal, for example, for whites and Blacks to play checkers together (David Oppenheimer, "California's Anti-Discrimination Legislation, Proposition 14, and the Constitutional Protection of Minority Rights," *Golden Gate University Law Review* 40 [2009], 121).

2 Bayard Rustin, "The Meaning of Birmingham," *Liberation* (June 1963), reprinted in Paul Goodman, ed., *Seeds of Liberation* (New York: George Braziller, 1964), 317–18.

3 *New York Times*, June 12, 1963.

4 *New York Times*, July 31, 1963.

5 Malcom X, "Message to the Grassroots," in *Malcolm X Speaks: Selected Speeches and Statements*, ed. George Breitman (New York: Grove Weidenfeld, 1965).

6 "[Burke] Marshall and [Robert] Kennedy did not want responsibility for effecting a revolution in race relations with military or police power. This was their political lesson from the Freedom Rides and Ole Miss." Taylor Branch, *Parting the Waters: America in the King Years, 1954–63* (New York: Simon & Schuster, 1988), 721.

7 See, for example, *Greyhound v. Boire*, June 11, 1962, United States District Court S. D. Florida, Tampa Division, Civ. No. 4414; *Eastern Greyhound Lines v. Fusco*, December 4, 1962, United States Court of Appeals, Sixth Circuit, 310F.2d 632.

8 Los Angeles County Commission on Human Relations, *A 25 Year History 1944–1969*, Los Angeles, 1969, n.p.

9 Quoted in *California Eagle*, October 5, 1961.

10 *LAT*, February 23, March 6 and April 6, 1962.

11 *Independent* (Long Beach), October 24, 1962.

12 *LAT*, October 23 and November 17, 1962; *Independent* (Long Beach), October 31, November 3, and November 5, 1962; August Meier and Elliott Rudwick, *CORE: A Study in the Civil Rights Movement, 1942–1968* (New York: Oxford University Press, 1973), 186; *California Eagle*, October 18 and November 1, 1962.

13 *California Eagle*, February 7, 1963.

14 Housing figure from Sam Gnerre, "Marlon Brando Comes to Southwood," *South Bay History* (blog), March 13, 2012, blogs.dailybreeze. com. Excluding the rich Palos Verdes Peninsula—an island unto itself—the South Bay includes the communities of Inglewood, Gardena, Torrance, Carson, Lawndale, Lomita, Harbor City, Wilmington, San Pedro, Hermosa Beach, El Segundo, Manhattan Beach,

Redondo Beach, Carson, Compton, and unincorporated Rancho Dominguez.

15 For a Torrance example, see *LAT*, August 12, 1962.

16 Wilson would describe Centerview as an "interracial experiment," but CORE claimed that was a euphemism for Mexican-Americans—a group also apparently excluded from Southwood. Although Jews and Japanese-Americans (but not necessarily Filipinos or Chinese-Americans) generally found it easier to buy into the postwar suburbs, Latinos were discriminated by appearance and social class. If working-class Mexican-Americans and newer Mexican immigrants were more dispersed residentially in Southern California, it was because of the prior existence of widespread citrus, earth materials and railroad colonias—almost always "south of the tracks" and with rigid boundaries. Segregation of Mexican-Americans unwilling or unable to "pass" as light-skinned "Spanish-Americans," in other words, was almost as universal but more geographically fine-grained than that of Blacks.

17 Andrea Gibbons, *Segregation in Search of Ideology? Hegemony and Contestation in the Spatial and Racial Configuration of Los Angeles*, PhD diss., Department of Geography, London School of Economics, 2014, 191. Gibbons's thesis is a splendid and long-overdue history. She reproduces CORE's "Los Angeles Has a Hate Wall" leaflet on 193.

18 Mildred Pitts Walter, interview, March 2013, Civil Rights History Project, Smithsonian Institution National Museum of African American History and Culture and Library of Congress, loc.gov.

19 *California Eagle*, October 4, 11, 18 and 25, 1962, and March 14, 1963 (Valley-to-Compton march); *Sentinel*, January 17, 1963 (community support at Centerview).

20 Court of Appeals of California, civ. no. 27491, second district, division 1, September 11, 1963. In July Wilson's lawyers went before the three-judge Court of Appeals where they found a sympathizer in Associate Justice Walter J. Fourt, a notorious critic of the Supreme Court's integration rulings who shared the John Birch Society's view that Earl Warren—a follower of "a Swedish Socialist" (social scientist Gunnar Myrdal)—and the other Supremes were "plotting to usurp the policy-making powers of the nation" (*Oxnard Press-Courier*, May 13, 1958). While Deputy Attorney General Robert Burke was attempting to explain that his office had spent nine months trying to persuade Don Wilson to change his sale policies, Fourt cut him off: "You asked Wilson to abide by the law but did you advise them

[CORE] not to go out there in a semi-violent manner, distributing inflammatory leaflets and interrupting business in the tract office?" (*Independent* [Long Beach], July 25, 1963).

21 *Torrance Press*, July 7, 1963, quoted in Gibbons, *Segregation*, 188; *LAT*, April 28, 1963 (profile of Wilson). He was equally "Mr. Norwalk," having constructed 10,000 homes in this southeastern LA County community that had recently been sugar beet fields and Dutch dairies. Wilson was the first Southern California developer to build entire tracts of two-story ranch-style homes with patios aimed at mid-market commuters (*LAT*, June 10, 1962). When the protests began in Dominguez, he ordered the installation of new bathroom and kitchen features as an apparent bonus to homebuyers willing to cross CORE picket lines (*LAT*, November 11, 1962).

22 *Torrance Herald*, January 17, 1963. 1962, however, was the climax of the postwar single-family home boom in the Los Angeles area; henceforth, apartment construction outpaced detached houses. Just as Blacks and Chicanos had gained access to the aerospace industry only in the aftermath of restructuring and the loss of tens of thousands of semi-skilled jobs, they likewise were fighting to enter a suburban real estate market that was already pricing out the white working class or driving it to seek homes inland, further away from jobs.

23 See Margaret Crawford, *Building the Workingman's Paradise: The Design of American Company Towns* (London and New York: Verso, 1995), 89–93; and Robert Phelps, "The Search for a Modern Industrial City: Urban Planning, the Open Shop, and the Founding of Torrance, California," *Pacific Historical Review* 64:4 (November 1995), 503–35.

24 "Decency Group Given City Status," *Daily Breeze*, July 9, 1960.

25 Hal Keating, "Pushers, Bookies find Torrance Closed Down," *LAT*, December 5, 1965; Sam Gnerre, "Wade Peebles and the 1963 Torrance Corruption Scandal," *South Bay History* (blog), April 19, 2013, blogs.dailybreeze.com. See also *LAT*, March 17 and October 1, 1964, and March 4, 1965; and Torrance Public Library Historical Newspaper Archive, library.torranceca.gov/services/archive-search—a splendid collection of the *Torrance Herald* and the *Express* for the period 1962–65.

26 *LAT*, March 31, 1963; Jo Freeman, *At Berkeley in the Sixties* (Bloomington: Indiana University Press, 2004), 68–70; Ethan Rarick, *California Rising: The Life and Times of Pat Brown* (Berkeley: University of California Press, 2006), 259–67.

27 Oppenheimer, "California's Anti-Discrimination Legislation," 121–2.

28 The Rumford bill, targeted at the private housing market, was intended

to close the circle of state civil rights legislation that included a trio of important 1959 bills: the Fair Employment Practices Commission, the Unruh Act (public accommodation), and the Hawkins Act (publicly subsidized housing). California, it should be emphasized, was not in the vanguard of such legislation but rather was trying to catch up with northeastern liberal states, above all New York. The historiography of the civil rights movement has focused primarily on the interaction between Southern protest and federal law making, neglecting the importance of battles over state and municipal laws.

29 Branch, *Parting the Waters*, 727–38; Diane McWhorter, *Carry Me Home: Birmingham, Alabama—The Climactic Battle of the Civil Rights Revolution* (New York: Simon & Schuster, 2001), 290–310.

30 Branch, *Parting the Waters*, 755.

31 The proposal, however, did not include direct federal enforcement but only a statutory pathway for victims of discrimination to seek court orders with the help of the Justice Department. Hugh Davis Graham, *The Civil Rights Era: Origins and Development of National Policy, 1960–1972* (New York: Oxford University Press, 1990), 80.

32 *California Eagle*, January 2, 1962.

33 Thomas Sugrue, *Sweet Land of Liberty: The Forgotten Struggle for Civil Rights in the North* (New York: Random House, 2008), 302. The NAACP, according to Roy Wilkins, counted 2,000 demonstrations during the course of the year (*California Eagle*, January 2, 1964).

34 Fern Eckman, *The Furious Passage of James Baldwin* (Lanham, MD: Evans & Co., 1966; repr. 2014), 180.

35 Branch, *Parting the Waters*, 854.

36 Meier and Rudwick, *CORE*, 226.

37 *California Tech*, May 9, 1963; Barbara Dimmick, "CORE's Corner," *Sentinel*, September 5, 1963.

38 *LAT*, May 16, 1963 (Bull Connor) and May 27, 1963; *Chicago Daily Defender*, June 4, 1963. Dr. King's speech, recorded by KPFK-Pacifica, is available via the Pacifica Archive.

39 *LAT*, June 23, 1963. In this piece and others, *Times* reporter Paul Weeks used anonymous interviews to focus on frictions within the UCRC and to advance the views of the most conservative leaders.

40 *LAT*, May 31, 1963. Marnesba Tackett, a NAACP leader and chair of the UCRC's education committee, claims in her oral history that Dawkins's declaration was made without consultation with Taylor, who read the news in the paper. Dawkins soon began to follow an eccentric course that eventually led him to become a lobbyist for Apartheid's puppet governments in southern Africa.

41 *LAT*, June 1, 1963.

42 Eason Monroe, "Safeguarding Civil Liberties," interview by Joel Gardner, 1974, transcript, Center for Oral History Research, UCLA, 146.

43 *LAT*, June 1, 1963; *New York Times*, June 5, 1963.

44 *LAT*, June 4 and 6, 1963.

45 *LAT*, June 7 and 8, 1963; *Independent* (Long Beach), June 7, 1963. Earl Walter of CORE chaired the direct action committee; Florence Vaughn, housing; Marnesha Tackett, education; Tom Neusom, police practices; and E. J. Franklin, employment.

46 *California Eagle*, August 18, 1960.

47 In addition to images of the slain NAACP leader, at least one marcher "carried a sign protesting the recent conviction of 11 Black Muslims" (*LAT*, June 17, 1963; and *Sentinel*, June 13, 1963).

48 *LAT*, June 3 and 15, 1963. Southern California CORE chapters sent several caravans to Sacramento to reinforce the protest inside the capitol.

49 *LAT*, June 9 and October 22, 1963; *Independent* (Long Beach), June 12, 1963; and Becky Nicolaides, *My Blue Heaven: Life and Politics in the Working-Class Suburbs of Los Angeles: 1925–1965* (Chicago: University of Chicago Press, 2002), 318–19.

50 *LAT*, June 22, 1963.

51 In a dramatic prelude to the historic statewide Democratic victory of 1958, the liberal slate of Mary Tinglof and Ralph Richardson, backed by the Committee for Better Schools (a coalition of teachers, the UAW, progressive Protestants, Jewish groups and the NAACP), defeated two John Birch Society–oriented board of education incumbents, Edith Stafford and Ruth Cole. In a futile but vicious campaign to prevent the election of Tinglof and Richardson, the *Times* accused their supporters of being "the advocates of one-world government, UNESCO protagonists and other ultra-liberal thinkers" ("The Watchman," aka Kyle Palmer; *LAT*, March 24 and 31, 1957). Together with Georgiana Hardy, the sole liberal member of the previous board, the two new members comprised a vocal but still largely impotent minority. (Until 1979 the seven members of the board were elected district wide not by subdistricts, and minority clout was accordingly reduced.) By the summer of 1963, however, only Tinglof was considered a reliable ally of the UCRC. Indeed, Tackett thought that Tinglof "was far ahead of her time" in arguing that busing be used not only to relieve overcrowding in ghetto schools but also to bring white students to formerly all-Black campuses. "Marnesba, the bus runs

two ways … We need to send blacks to the white schools, but we've got to send whites back over the other way" (Marnesba Tackett, interviews by Michael Balter, 1982 and 1984, transcripts, *Black Leadership in Los Angeles Project*, Center for Oral History Research, UCLA, 79–83).

52 *LAT*, June 9, 1963.

53 Clayborne Carson, *Martin's Dream: My Journey and the Legacy of Martin Luther King Jr.* (New York: Palgrave MacMillan, 2013), 32. Carson is quoting from an article he wrote about Coleman shortly before the Watts Rebellion.

54 *LAT*, June 23, 1963.

6 Jericho Stands

1 "Nation's Cops Prepare to Handle Race Fights," *Chicago Daily Defender* (national edition), August 3, 1963. The Harlem attackers were first alleged to be Muslims, but in fact they were members of a Baptist congregational, disgruntled with nonviolence (Taylor Branch, *Pillar of Fire: America in the King Years, 1963–65* [New York: Simon & Schuster, 1998], 115).

2 *LAT*, June 27, 1963.

3 *Independent Press-Telegram* (Long Beach), June 30, 1963.

4 *Independent Press-Telegram*, July 1, 1963.

5 *LAT*, July 12, 23 and 28, 1963.

6 *Independent Star-News* (Pasadena), July 28, 1963.

7 *Independent Press-Telegram*, August 1, 1963; *LAT*, August 2, 1963.

8 *LAT*, August 2 and 4, 1963.

9 *Independent Press-Telegram*, August 18, 1963. The disrupters were identified as Birch members by the Torrance city prosecutor, C. H. Catterlin.

10 *LAT*, August 10 and 11, 1963.

11 *LAT*, September 8, 1963.

12 *LAT*, August 14, 1963.

13 *LAT*, August 5, 1963. Picketing on a small scale did continue, however, at Wilson's Centerview tract in Dominguez Hills, and in the fall there was a CORE sit-in at Home Savings & Loan.

14 For a timeline of early events, see *Independent Press-Telegram*, October 20, 1963; for a historical overview of the scandals, see Sam Gnerre, "Wade Peebles and the 1963 Torrance Corruption Scandal," *South Bay History* (blog), April 19, 2013, blogs.dailybreeze.com. See also *LAT*, October 12, 1963; March 5, March 17, September 12 and October 1,

1964; April 1 and August 8, 1965; *Torrance Herald*, September 8, 12 and 19, 1963; and *Press* (South Bay), September 11, 1963.

15 "Integrationists March," *LAT*, August 9, 1963; *Independent* (Long Beach), August 9, 1963.

16 The Stars for Freedom concert organized by Davis, Sinatra and Martin was held in December and featured appearances by Roy Wilkins, Martin Luther King and Thurgood Marshall (*California Eagle*, December 12, 1963). Other Hollywood icons who rallied to the civil rights struggle included Bobby Darin, Billy Wilder, Ed Wynn, Steve Allen, and Ricardo Montalbán. Sidney Poitier and Eartha Kitt were already involved at the national level.

17 *Los Angeles Sentinel*, September 5, 1963.

18 "Mexican-Americans Now Back Negro Campaign," *LAT*, August 29, 1963.

19 "L.A. Protests Threatened," *LAT*, June 19, 1964. Vice President Johnson, speaking to a large luncheon of Chicano leaders at the Statler Hotel in early August, had urged them to use the President's Committee on Equal Employment Opportunity to fight for jobs. He pointed out that of "4,300 complaints processed in two and one-half years, only 99 had come from 'Spanish-speaking' people" (*New York Times*, August 10, 1963).

20 *Chicago Daily Defender*, July 17, 1963.

21 *LAT*, September 6, 12, 14 and 16, 1962. Baldwin Hills Elementary was another target of the campaign, and twenty Black students were turned away when they attempted to enroll, but the administration quickly surrendered after a week of protests (*California Eagle*, September 13, 1962).

22 *LAT*, June 9 and October 22, 1963; *Independent* (Long Beach), June 12, 1963; Becky Nicolaides, *My Blue Heaven: Life and Politics in the Working-Class Suburbs of Los Angeles: 1925–1965* (Chicago: University of Chicago Press, 2002), 318–19.

23 *Los Angeles Sentinel*, July 11, 1963.

24 Marnesba Tackett, interview by Michael Balter, March 19, 1984, Center for Oral History Research, UCLA, tape 4, side 1.

25 *LAT*, September 15, 1963.

26 *LAT*, September 14, 1963.

27 *LAT*, September 21, 1963.

28 *LAT*, September 20, 1963.

29 *LAT*, October 23, 1963.

30 *LAT*, October 11, 1963.

31 *LAT*, October 26, 1963.

32 *LAT*, December 7, 1963.

33 John Caughey, *To Kill a Child's Spirit: The Tragedy of School Segregation in Los Angeles* (Itasca, IL: Peacock, 1973), 23.

34 August Meier and Elliott Rudwick, *CORE: A Study in the Civil Rights Movement, 1942–1968* (New York: Oxford University Press, 1973), 310. Many chapters splintered during the winter of 1963–64, but the reasons were diverse and unsynchronized by any national caucus or faction.

35 Ibid., 258.

7 Equality Scorned

1 *California Eagle*, January 9, 1964; *LAT*, January 8, 1964 (editorial). What Los Angeles *did* have was a Citizen's Police Commission, which was sometimes confused with a police review board. This powerless body was strictly limited to forwarding complaints to the LAPD's Internal Affairs Division and making recommendations to Chief Parker. Otherwise the LAPD remained completely self-governing.

2 *LAT*, February 24, 1964.

3 *LAT*, March 10, May 5 and August 13, 1963.

4 August Meier and Elliott Rudwick, CORE: *A Study in the Civil Rights Movement, 1942–1968* (New York: Oxford University Press, 1973), 384.

5 James Downs, speaking to California Real Estate Association, *LAT*, September 25, 1964.

6 *California Eagle*, May 14, 1964.

7 *LAT*, January 9, February 17, and October 1 and 2, 1964. In Pasadena during this period, Municipal Judge Joseph Sprankle was offering men convicted of nonpayment of child support the choice of jail or sterilization. "Millions of dollars," he claimed, "are being wasted through society's failure to deal firmly with profligates and irresponsible parents." Most of the targets for sterilization were unemployed and Black or Latino (*LAT*, September 17, 1964).

8 *California Eagle*, January 16 and March 5, 1964.

9 *Independent Press-Telegram*, March 31, 1963; *LAT*, April 1, 1963.

10 *LAT*, April 11, 1964; *Los Angeles Sentinel*, April 16, 1964; *California Eagle*, April 16, 1964. Another incident occurred before dawn Sunday morning, this time in East L.A., when, following a quarrel between highway patrol officers and a motorist parked in his own driveway, fifty sheriff's deputies raced to the scene and began sapping and arresting members of his extended family. Nineteen-year-old

Yolanda Medina was thrown to the ground and booked for suspicion of being under the influence of dangerous drugs. She was, in fact, totally blind (*LAT*, April 14, 1964).

11 *LAT*, April 16, 1964.

12 *California Eagle*, April 30, 1964. For the police account, see *LAT*, April 24, 1964.

13 *LAT*, April 27, 1964.

14 *LAT*, April 28, 1964. Earlier in February, pro tem Senate President Hugh Burns, a conservative Democrat opposed to Rumford, denounced CORE's 1963 demonstrations as "mob rule." He went on to make an insane comparison between CORE and Lee Harvey Oswald: "There is little difference, if any, between the violent actions of a deranged mob seeking its own particular end and the equally violent actions of one individual with a rifle, bomb or deadly weapon, seeking to satisfy his personal desires – and we have so recently seen the tragic result of legislation by individual violence" (speech to California Taxpayers' Association, *LAT*, February 7, 1964).

15 *Los Angeles Sentinel*, July 2, 1964.

16 *LAT*, May 7, 1964.

17 Quoted in *LAT*, April 27, 1964.

18 *California Eagle*, March 26, 1964; *LAT*, May 27, June 10 and July 22, 1964. Later that summer, the mainline civil rights groups—the NAACP, Urban League, and so on—called for a national moratorium on protests out of fear that continued militancy would drive white voters to Goldwater. CORE refused to join the moratorium and was subsequently scapegoated. Dawkins would go on to become a leading Reagan supporter, a lobbyist for South African puppet governments, and a Republican senatorial candidate in Virginia.

19 *LAT*, May 22, 1964.

20 *LAT*, June 10 and 17, 1964.

21 *LAT*, July 5, 1964.

22 Alisa Kramer, "William H. Parker and the Thin Blue Line: Politics, Public Relations and Policing in Postwar Los Angeles," PhD diss., American University, 2007, 200–1, 205.

23 *New York Times*, August 5, 1964.

24 Neil McMillen, *The Citizens' Council: Organized Resistance to the Second Reconstruction, 1954–64* (Champaign: University of Illinois Press, 1994), 200.

25 *LAT*, January 23 and August 6, 1964. Shearer would go on, in 1968, to cofound the American Independent Party as a vehicle for George Wallace's presidential campaign.

26 *LAT*, July 1, 1964

27 *LAT*, July 2, 1964.

28 I heard the story first at my San Diego high school in June; then again in the fall while I was briefly a college student in Portland, Oregon. It reappeared during the 2008 presidential race and presumably still lurks in some racist sewer—MD.

29 *LAT*, May 24, 1964.

30 "Will no one rid me of this meddlesome priest?"—Henry II of England.

31 "Why Prop 14 Deserves a YES vote," *LAT*, editorial, October 18, 1964.

32 Darren Dochuk, *From Bible Belt to Sun Belt* (New York: Norton, 2010), 248. Although idiosyncratic in some respects, especially Dochuk's conflation of liberal Pat Brown and leftist Dorothy Healey as "Social Democrats," this is a genuinely groundbreaking study.

33 *LAT*, September 12, 1964.

34 John Donovan, "The 1960s Los Angeles Seminary Crisis," *Catholic Historical Review* 102:1 (Winter 2016), 75.

35 *LAT*, May 18 and June 11, 1964; "Cardinal McIntyre's Los Angeles," *Ramparts*, November 1964, 35.

36 Francis Weber, "Ecclesial Confrontation in Los Angeles: Father DuBay and the Batman Syndrome," *Southern California Quarterly* 78:4 (winter 1996), 323. Weber, later the author of a two-volume biography of McIntyre, was his chief hagiographer and apologist. This article is a rambling, unscholarly defamation of DuBay.

37 *LAT*, June 12, 1964.

38 William DuBay, telegram, quoted in *New York Times*, June 12, 1964; and *California Eagle*, June 18, 1964.

39 *LAT*, June 16, 1964.

40 *LAT*, June 20, 1964.

41 *New York Times*, July 29, 1964.

42 Weber, "Ecclesial Confrontation," 324.

43 Referring to the November victory of Proposition 14, Coffield said: "I was hopeful that silent acceptance of the injustice to me and my parishioners would help to defeat 14. I was so wrong. I should have fought it openly. On Saturday, November 14, I was ordered to maintain silence on racism. I chose instead a self-imposed exile from the diocese as a gesture of protest against, rather than be a part of, the continuing evil of silence." One thousand supporters turned out at farewell event for Father Coffield. Dubay, meanwhile, submitted to his punishment for a year and then, in 1966, reemerged as a public

critic, calling for the unionization of priests and the abolition of tax exemptions for churches. He soon left the priesthood altogether, although the seeds of conscience that he had planted would bloom again when the Sisters of the Immaculate Heart battled McIntyre in the late 1960s.

44 Daniel HoSang, *Racial Propositions: Ballot Initiatives and the Making of Postwar California* (Berkeley: University of California Press, 2010), 80–2.

45 Raymond Wolfinger and Fred Greenstein, "The Repeal of Fair Housing in California: An Analysis of Referendum Voting," *American Political Science Review* 64:3 (September 1968), 753–69 (esp. 757 and 762). The only two white communities, both heavily Jewish, to reject Prop 14 were Beverly Hills and Lake Elsinore (a favorite bolthole for aging Communists).

46 Meier and Rudwick, *CORE*, 358.

8 From "Ban the Bomb" to "Stop the War"

1 On November 1, 1961, the *LA Times* reported 4,000 demonstrators; on November 2, the *Times* revised that figure to 2,000. Other demonstrations by Women Strike for Peace were held the same day in more than sixty American cities: Amy Swerdlow, *Women Strike for Peace* (Chicago: University of Chicago Press, 1993), 16.

2 Sophia Wyatt, "One Day's Strike for Peace," *Guardian*, December 4, 1961, 2.

3 Swerdlow, *Women Strike*, 20.

4 Leaflets in Southern California Women Strike for Peace Records, Swarthmore College Peace Collection (hereafter "WSP Records, Swarthmore").

5 "Speech by Wallace Thomson," WSP Records, Swarthmore.

6 "Telegram from Governor Brown to Women Strike for Peace," November 1, 1961, WSP Records, Swarthmore.

7 Ibid.

8 Wyatt, "One Day's Strike"; "Who Are We?," leaflet, WSP Records, Swarthmore.

9 Swerdlow, *Women Strike*, 9, 51.

10 Dennis Hevesi, "Dagmar Wilson, Anti-Nuclear Leader, Dies at 94," *New York Times*, January 23, 2011.

11 Women Strike for Peace FBI file, appendix 14, unpublished, in collection of June Solnit Sale.

12 June Solnit Sale, interview by JW, January 18, 2019.

13 *La Wisp* 1:1 (March 1, 1962).

14 Ibid.

15 *LAT*, March 8, 1962.

16 "IF there is testing," *La Wisp* 1:2 (April 7, 1962).

17 *LAT*, July 13, 1962; "Nevada Trip," report, WSP Records, Swarthmore.

18 *LAT*, October 27, 1962.

19 "World Travelers Report Back," *La Wisp* 1:7 (November 7, 1962).

20 Andrew Brown, *J. D. Bernal: The Sage of Science* (Oxford, UK: Oxford University Press, 2005), 423.

21 Lawrence Wittner, *Rebels against War: The American Peace Movement, 1933–1983* (Philadelphia: Temple University Press, 1984), 316, 318.

22 Ibid., 318; Virginia Kahn, "A Page from the Moscow Congress," *La Wisp* 1:7 (November 7, 1962).

23 LA FBI file on WSP, quoted in Swerdlow, *Women Strike*, 102.

24 *La Wisp* 1:8 (December 7, 1972).

25 Ibid.; *LAT*, December 14, 1972; Russell Baker, "HUAC Booboos," *New York Times*, December 15, 1962.

26 Jon Coburn, "Making a Difference: The History and Memory of Women Strike for Peace, 1961–1990," PhD diss., Northumbria University, 2015, 91, available at nrl.northumbria.ac.uk.

27 *LAT*, June 13, 1963.

28 Ibid.

29 *Women's Day*, November 1963, quoted in Swerdlow, *Women Strike*, 95–6.

30 Events calendar, *La Wisp* 2:8 (November 1963).

31 Although the American press gave only minor notice to Hertz's death, "she became a revered and legendary figure, particularly in North Vietnam. To honor her deed the country held a silent vigil following the reports of her death. Schoolchildren composed poems in her memory while others wrote and sang songs detailing her lifelong commitment to peace. The government renamed a street 'Rue Herz' in the heart of Hanoi" (Coburn, "Making a Difference," 128).

32 Ibid., 130.

33 Clarke interview in Mary Hershberger, *Traveling to Vietnam: American Peace Activists and the War* (Syracuse: Syracuse University Press, 1998).

34 "10 Americans Join Vietnam Reds," *New York Times*, July 19, 1965.

35 Hershberger, *Traveling to Vietnam*, 10.

36 Ibid., 11.

37 Ibid.; *La Wisp*, November 1965.

38 Mary Clarke, "Meeting in Jakarta," *La Wisp*, October 1965.

39 Women Strike for Peace, *Peace de Resistance: A Cook Book* (Los Angeles, n.d). Advertised in *La Wisp*, March 1966.

40 Swerdlow, *Women Strike*, 240–2.

9 From Bach to "Tanya"

1 Eleanor McKinney, *The Exacting Ear: The Story of Listener-Sponsored Radio* (New York: Pantheon, 1966), 64–6.

2 McKinney, *Exacting Ear*, 78–9.

3 William Mandel, testimony, US House of Representatives Committee on Un-American Activities, *The Northern California District of the Communist Party: Structure, Objectives, Leadership* (Washington, DC: US Government Printing Office, 1960), 2066; for a transcript of the Pacifica program, see McKinney, *Exacting Ear*, 86.

4 Maurice Isserman and Dorothy Healey, *Dorothy Healey Remembers* (New York: Oxford University Press, 1990), 164, 172.

5 "History of Pacifica Radio," KPFK official website, kpfk.org; "KPFA Chief Leaves to Face Probers," *San Francisco News-Call Bulletin*, January 8, 1963, reprinted in *Pacifica Foundation: Hearings before the Subcommittee to Investigate the Administration of the Internal Security Act and Other Internal Security Laws of the Committee of the Judiciary* (Washington, DC: US Government Printing Office, 1963) (hereafter "*SISS Hearings*"), 6. Cited in Matt Lasar, *Pacifica Radio: The Rise of an Alternative Network* (Philadelphia: Temple University Press, 1999), 284, n38.

6 "Closed KPFK Quiz Protested," *San Francisco Examiner*, January 7, 1963.

7 William H. Honan, "Roman L. Hruska Dies at 94; Leading Senate Conservative," *New York Times*, April 27, 1999.

8 "Senate Red Probers Look at KPFA," *San Francisco Examiner*, January 5, 1963, reprinted in *SISS Hearings*, 3–4.

9 *SISS Hearings*, 19.

10 Ibid., 21, 36.

11 Ibid., 20.

12 *SISS Hearings*, 46, 51.

13 Lasar, *Pacifica Radio*, 202.

14 Lasar, *Pacifica Radio*, 203–4.

15 See "Pacifica Foundation Mission Statement," Pacific Foundation official website, pacifica.org.

16 See Ferlinghetti's account in the *Guardian*: Nicholas Wroe, "Last of

the Bohemians," *Guardian*, June 30, 2006, theguardian.com; Wolfgang Saxon, "Kenneth Rexroth, 76, Author; Father Figure to Best Poets," *New York Times*, June 8, 1982. For a description of this show, see Lasar, *Pacifica Radio*, 119. In the Sixties Rexroth lived in Santa Barbara and taught at UCSB.

17 "Ed Cray, Professor Emeritus," USC Annenberg official website, https://annenberg.usc.edu/faculty/journalism/ed-cray.

18 *KPFK Folio*, July 26–August 8, 1959, Pacifica Radio Archives, available at archive.org.

19 Spencer Olin, interview by JW, July 23, 2014.

20 John Anderson, email to Spencer Olin, July 24, 2014.

21 Ed Cray, interview by JW, July 23, 2014.

22 Alan W. Watts, *Beat Zen, Square Zen, and Zen* (San Francisco: City Lights, 1967); Lasar, *Pacifica Radio*.

23 Ron Tepper, "KPFK 'Cultural Bomb' Will Explode Today," *LAT*, July 29, 1959. All other quotes of media comments on KPFK reprinted from *KPFK Folio* 1.

24 *KPFK Folio*, June 26, 1960, Pacifica Radio Archives.

25 *KPFK Folio*, May 1–16, 1961, Pacifica Radio Archives. The fairgrounds for that first year were at Haskell's Ranch, on Vineland near Cahuenga in North Hollywood.

26 Daniel E. Slotnik, "Phyllis Patterson, Who Revived 16th Century, Dies at 82," *New York Times*, June 11, 2014; "The Original Pleasure Faire and May Market," *KPFK Folio* 4:1 (April 29–May 12, 1963), Pacifica Radio Archives.

27 Lasar, *Pacifica Radio*, 219.

28 *KPFK Folio*, May 25–June 7, 1964, Pacifica Radio Archives.

29 *KPFK Folio*, January 1969, Pacifica Radio Archives, 6.

30 *KPFK Folio*, March 1970, Pacifica Radio Archives.

31 Jack Jones and Mike Goodman, "Phone Call Turns KPFK's Day Upside Down," *LAT*, June 8, 1974; Robert A. Wright, "Miss Hearst on Tape Says Fight by SLA Continues," *New York Times*, June 8, 1974. For audio of the interview, see "Patty Hearst's Chilling Eulogy for Fallen SLA Members," Smithsonian Channel, YouTube, youtube.com.

32 Robert Rawitch, "KPFK Manager Jailed after Failing to Give Up SLA Tape," *LAT*, June 20, 1974.

33 Jack Jones, "Justice Douglas Orders KPFK Manager Freed," *LAT*, July 5, 1974.

34 John Kendall, "Pacifica Radio: Different Tune on the FM Dial," *LAT*, July 5, 1974, A1.

10 A Quarter of a Million Readers

1 Abe Peck, *Uncovering the Sixties: The Life and Times of the Under-ground Press* (New York: Citadel, 1985, repr. 1991), xv.

2 *LAT*, August 14, 1965, 1.

3 *LA Free Press*, August 20, 1965, 1.

4 On the fiftieth anniversary of Watts, the *LA Times* editorial closely mirrored what the *Freep* had been saying in 1965: "Watts Riots, 50 Years Later," editorial, *LAT*, July 28, 2015.

5 Charles Hillinger, "Burning Buildings Symbolize Spirit of Hate Underlying Violent Rioting," *LAT*, August 14, 1965, 2.

6 Bob Freeman, "CORE Leader Observes Ghetto Fighting," *LA Free Press*, August 20, 1965, 1. Other Black reports about Watts in the *Freep* include Herb Porter, "Attorney Analyzes Causes of Watts Demonstrations," *LA Free Press*, August 20, 1965, 6; "Los Angeles Groups Comment on Riots," *LA Free Press*, August 27, 1965, 7; "Discussions Unlimited: Public Hearing Gets Eyewitness Testimony from Watts," *LA Free Press*, October 1, 1965, 2–3.

7 Art Kunkin, quoted in Peck, *Uncovering the Sixties*, 27. The *Times* lacked Black reporters, but it did find "two Negro free-lance photographers" who said, about the people in the streets, "They're just destroying themselves and their cause." "'No Gain, No Purpose': Negro Photographers See Pathos in Havoc," *LAT*, August 14, 1965, 12. Watts wasn't the only historic LA event on which the *Times* was wildly right-wing and the *Freep* a voice of reason. The Century City protest against the Vietnam War provides another vivid example.

8 Sean Stewart, ed., *On the Ground: An Illustrated Anecdotal History of the Sixties Underground Press in the US* (Oakland: PM Press, 2011), 95.

9 William Murray, "The *L.A. Free Press* Is Rich," *Esquire*, June 1970, 54, quoted in Peck, *Uncovering the Sixties*, 22.

10 John Bryan, quoted in Peck, *Uncovering the Sixties*, 23.

11 Art Kunkin, memoir, in *LA Free Press*, September 17, 1964, reprinted in Stewart, *On the Ground*, 10–14.

12 Arthur Kunkin, "Why We Appear," *LA Free Press*, July 30, 1964, 1.

13 Dori Schaffer, "Bank of America vs. CORE: A Duel of Accusations," *LA Free Press*, July 30, 1964, 1. The sculptor charged with obscenity was Connor Everts. His first trial ended with a hung jury. The DA tried again, and the second jury, in 1965, acquitted him. "The verdict and the support Everts received from the LA art community set a precedent for the freedom of expression for artists" (Norton Simon Museum, "Studies in Desperation: A Suite by Connor Everts," press release,

August 2012, available at http://www.nortonsimon.org/assets/Uploads/Studies-in-Desperation-Press-Release.pdf).

14 Art Kunkin, interview in Stewart, *On the Ground*, 95.

15 Tom Nolan, "The Free Press Costs 15 Cents," *LAT*, October 2, 1966, W36.

16 Mary Reinholz, "Violence Breeds Counter-Violence: Marcuse," *LA Free Press*, May 23, 1969, 7; Jean-Paul Sartre, "Why the War Crimes Tribunal?" (speech at the opening of the War Crimes Tribunal in Stockholm), *LA Free Press*, August 11, 1967, 3; Susan Sontag, "Inventing and Sustaining an Appropriate Response" (speech at the dedication of the Peace Tower), *LA Free Press*, March 4, 1966, 4.

17 John Simmons, "He Who Votes for Lesser of 2 Evils Forgets That He Is Voting for Evil," *LA Free Press*, September 9, 1966, 1.

18 Peck, *Uncovering the Sixties*, 150.

19 Ibid., 157.

20 Harlan Ellison, "23 Inches Worth of Introduction," in *The Glass Teat* (New York: Open Road, 2011), 23.

21 "Maharishi's Take on Vietnam," *LA Free Press*, October 6, 1967.

22 The *New Yorker* described the *Freep* as "the newspaper of the New Left": Renata Adler, "Fly Trans-Love Airways," *New Yorker*, February 25, 1967, 122.

23 Kunkin, quoted in Peck, *Uncovering the Sixties*, 187.

24 Marvin Garson, Max Scherr, quoted in Peck, *Uncovering the Sixties*, 210, 208.

25 "Free Press Critics Have Their Say," *LA Free Press*, April 3, 1970.

26 "Is Mexican Abortion Dangerous?," *LA Free Press*, October 6, 1967.

27 David McBride, *On the Fault Line of Mass Culture and Counterculture: A Social History of the Hippie Counterculture in 1960s Los Angeles*, PhD diss., UCLA, 1998, 358.

28 "Free Press Meeting Hears Views on Watts," *LA Free Press*, September 24, 1965, 1.

29 Marty Liboff, "When the Music's Over," *Free Venice Beachhead*, November 1, 2014, freevenicebeachhead.wordpress.com. *Freep* hand-bill available at http://shadwell.tripod.com/colbast.html.

30 Adler, "Fly Trans-Love Airways," 124.

31 John McMillian, *Smoking Typewriters: The Sixties Underground Press and the Rise of Alternative Media in America* (New York: Oxford University Press, 2011), 132.

32 "Deputies Seize 80 Free Press Stands," *LAT*, January 22, 1968, A1.

33 Peck, *Uncovering the Sixties*, 132.

34 FBI file, "Typical Advertisement for Pornography Appearing in the

Los Angeles Free Press," from the November 13, 1970, issue of the *Freep*.

35 FBI LA Field Office, file 145–1403, March 18, 1971.

36 "Obscenity Commission Hears Freep," *LA Free Press*, May 22, 1970, 6.

37 Murray, "The L.A. Free Press Is Rich," 58. Other reports said Bryan quit in protest against the introduction of a time clock in the *Freep* office—"mandated by the Labor Relations Board," Kunkin's defenders said.

38 David McBride, "Death City Radicals: The Counterculture in Los Angeles," in *The New Left Revisited*, eds. John McMillian and Paul Buhle (Philadelphia: Temple University Press, 2003), n25.

39 *Open City*, May 5, 1967, 2:1, (the first issue—for some perverse reason Bryan started with "volume 2"), quoted in Gaye Sandler Smith, "The Underground Press in Los Angeles," MA thesis, UCLA, 1968, 12; Carl Nolte, "John Bryan—Writer, Editor, Valued Underground Press," *San Francisco Chronicle*, February 11, 2007; Pico Iyer, "Celebrities Who Travel Well," *Time*, June 16, 1986. Bukowski's columns for *Open City* were later collected and published by City Lights.

40 Smith, "Underground Press," 16–17. Other journalistic highlights included an outstanding series of reports on L.A.'s Skid Row; a special issue devoted to marijuana and drug issues, which was reprinted by underground papers throughout the country; and a groundbreaking report on jailhouse rape: "Open City," *San Francisco Public Library Herb Caen Magazines and Newspapers Center* (blog), July 21, 2010, sfplmagsandnews.blogspot.com.

41 Art Seidenbaum, "The Los Angeles Cleaners vs. the Underground Press," *LAT*, August 5, 1968, B5; McMillian, *Smoking Typewriters*, 127.

42 Kunkin, *LA Free Press*, quoted in "Open City," *SF Public Library Magazines and Newspapers Center*. Other short-lived underground papers in L.A. included *Los Angeles Underground*, started by Al Mitchell, owner of the Fifth Estate coffee house on Sunset Strip, which published in 1967, circulation 18,000; the *Oracle*, a psychedelic and New Age religious monthly with a circulation of 60,000, second only to the *Freep*; *Provo*, a "hippie/anarchist" paper that was an offshoot of the Dutch collective; and *Free Venice Beachhead*, an opponent of development, published in late 1968. See Smith, "Underground Press," ch. 30; and McBride, "Death City Radicals."

43 Peck, *Uncovering the Sixties*, 187.

44 And "aside from a surprisingly small amount of telephone harassment, nothing happened to the agents or their families." Ibid., 190.

45 Ron Einstoss, "Editor of Free Press Fined for Receiving List of State

Agents," *LAT*, August 29, 1970, A1; Gene Blake, "'Free Press' Case—New Threat to Free Press," *LAT*, September 20, 1970, D1.

46 Supreme Court of California, *People v. Kunkin*, no. 16387 (April 2, 1973), available at http://law.justia.com/cases/california/supreme-court/3d/9/245.html.

47 Peck, *Uncovering the Sixties*, 190.

48 "Manson Can Go Free!," *LA Free Press*, January 19, 1970. The *Freep* later published its entire archive of Manson coverage: *The Book of Manson, 12/12/1969–7/31/1970*, available at losangelesfreepress. com.

49 David Felton and David Dalton, "Charles Manson: The Incredible Story of the Most Dangerous Man Alive," *Rolling Stone*, June 25, 1970. One notable achievement: the paper's Manson trial reporting came from New York poet Ed Sanders; the book that came out of his *Freep* work, *The Family*, became a bestseller.

50 Peck, *Uncovering the Sixties*, 191, 288; Kunkin, in Stewart, *On the Ground*, 123–4.

11 Before Stonewall

1 Although the signs spoke of "our rights," none of the signs used the terms "gay" or "homosexual." Moira Rachel Kenney, *Mapping Gay L.A.* (Philadelphia: Temple University Press, 2001), 165.

2 Lillian Faderman and Stuart Timmons, *Gay L.A.: A History of Sexual Outlaws, Power Politics, and Lipstick Lesbians* (Berkeley: University of California Press, 2006), 155.

3 "Press Release Regarding the Raid of the Black Cat Bar—New Year's Eve, 1966," Tavern Guild of Southern California, January 5, 1967, reprinted in Jim Willis, *1960s Counterculture: Documents Decoded* (Santa Barbara: ABC-CLIO, 2015), 160.

4 John Bryan, "Police Outrages Help Create LA Homosexual Rights Drive," *LA Free Press*, March 10, 1967, 5; quoted in Kenney, *Mapping Gay L.A.*, 165–6.

5 Faderman and Timmons, *Gay L.A.*, 155.

6 Ibid., 112.

7 Ibid., 113.

8 Dorothy Healey and Maurice Isserman, *Dorothy Healey Remembers* (New York: Oxford University Press, 1990), 129–30.

9 Quoted in Faderman and Timmons, *Gay L.A.*, 115.

10 Ibid., 116.

11 Ibid., 120.

12 Paul Welch, "Homosexuality in America," *Life*, July 27, 1964, 66–74.

13 The organized gay liberation movement in L.A. was white and male during this early period; Faderman and Timmons found the first signs of gay Black organization in L.A. in 1977: *Gay L.A.*, 290–4. Lesbian feminists in L.A. began organizing around 1970: Faderman and Timmons, *Gay L.A.*, 390.

14 The founding editors of the *Advocate* were Bill Rau (under the name "Bill Rand"), Aristide Laurent and artist Sam Winston.

15 Jerry Joachim, "The Man and the Many Meet," *LA Advocate* 1:1 (September 1967), 7.

16 Faderman and Timmons, *Gay L.A.*, 83.

17 "Mariposa de la Noche," *LA Advocate* 1:1 (September 1967).

18 Lesser-known groups included: the National League for Social Understanding, Inc.; *Pursuit and Symposium* magazine; and the Southern California Council on Religion and the Homophile. Leaflet available at http://tangentgroup.org/mediawiki/index.php/ Griffith_Park_Gay-In.

19 Kight, interview in Kenney, *Mapping Gay L.A.*, 169–70.

20 "Gay-In," *LA Advocate*, May 13–26, 1970, 1.

21 Patrick Range McDonald, "L.A. Gay Pride Co-Founder Morris Kight Remembered," *LA Free Press*, June 11, 2010.

22 "Interview with Morris Kight," in *Growing Up Before Stonewall: Life Stories of Some Gay Men*, eds. Peter M. Nardi, David Sanders and Judd Marmor (New York: Routledge, 1994), 24, 5.

23 Ibid., 31, 32.

24 Ibid., 32–3.

25 Ibid., 34.

26 Jim Kepner, "Gays Liberate Police Stations," *LA Free Press*, May 22, 1970.

27 Anti-war leaflets, n.d., Gay Liberation Front records, ONE National Gay and Lesbian Archives, Los Angeles, box 1, folder 3, Coll2012.031 (henceforth, "ONE archives").

28 Ibid.; GLF Demands: *LA Free Press*, October 23, 1970.

29 "To All Gay Activists," leaflet, n.d., GLF records, ONE archives.

30 GLF records, ONE archives; "United States Senate Candidates," Peace and Freedom Party official website, peaceandfreedom.org.

31 Carl Wittman, "A Gay Manifesto," *LA Free Press*, Gay Liberation supplement, August 14, 1970.

32 Dick Michaels, "'Patch' Raids Police Station," *LA Advocate*, September 1968, 5; "Editorial: Courage Catches On," *LA Advocate*, September 1968, 5; Faderman and Timmons, *Gay L.A.*, 158.

33 Faderman and Timmons, *Gay L.A.*, 158.

34 "Former Long Beach Resident Lee Glaze—a Pioneer in the Fight for Gay Rights—Dies at 75," *Out in the 562* (blog), February 4, 2014, blogs.presstelegram.com/outinthe562.

35 Troy D. Perry, *Don't Be Afraid Anymore* (New York: St. Martin's, 1990), 35.

36 Faderman and Timmons, *Gay L.A.*, 260; "Our Churches," Metropolitan Community Churches official website, http://mccchurch.org/overview/ourchurches.

37 Perry, *Don't Be Afraid*, 38; Faderman and Timmons, *Gay L.A.*, 260–1.

38 Faderman and Timmons, *Gay L.A.*, 166, citing Jim Kepner, *Pursuit Letter* 1, April 28, 1969, in the Paul Lamport file at the ONE archives.

39 Ibid.

40 Ibid., citing *Hollywood Citizen-News*, May 16, 1969.

41 "Agencies Aid Hippie Invasion, Lamport Says," *LAT*, June 21, 1967, A1.

42 Morris Kight, interview by Kenney, in *Mapping Gay L.A.*, 170–1.

43 Kenney, *Mapping Gay L.A.*, 168; Perry, *Don't Be Afraid*.

44 Troy Perry, interview in *LAT*, June 13, 1970.

45 "History of Christopher Street West / LA Pride," LA Pride official website, lapride.org.

46 "Court Okays Christopher West Parade: Permit Hassle Fails to Kill Celebration of Gay Pride," *LA Advocate* 4:10 (July 8–21, 1970), 1.

47 Perry, *Don't Be Afraid*, 165.

48 Ibid., 165–6.

49 There had been an earlier sort of gay parade in L.A. on May 12, 1966—a parade of cars campaigning to end the ban on gays in the military. They displayed signs reading "Ten Percent of All GI's are Homosexual" and "Write LBJ Today!" They started in downtown L.A. and followed a twenty-mile route to Hollywood. Four other cities held coordinated actions, but L.A. was the only city with a parade. It had been organized by Don Slater, founder of *Tangents* magazine, with Harry Hay, founder of the Mattachine Society, serving as president of the parade (Don Slater, "Protest on Wheels," *Tangents*, May 1966, quoted in Faderman and Timmons, *Gay L.A.*, 261).

50 Morris Kight, "The Great Parade," *LA Free Press*, August 14, 1970, 51. The *Freep*'s report on the parade described it as "a political Mardi Gras" and reported that marchers and onlookers both "shed tears of joy ... carried along in a sea of love and emotion, the 1,200 gays sang, danced, marched, rode on floats and encouraged their brothers and

sisters to … join in the celebration" (Angela Douglas, "Gays March on Hollywood Boulevard," *LA Free Press*, July 3, 1970, 5, quoted in Kenney, *Mapping Gay L.A.*, 168).

51   Andrew Colville, dir., *Live on Tape: The Life and Times of Morris Kight, Liberator* (Los Angeles: Liberator, 1999), film.

52   Faderman and Timmons, *Gay L.A.*, 94, citing "Mayor Fletcher Bowron against Slacks for Women at City Hall," *LAT*, April 22, 1942, 1.

53   Faderman and Timmons, *Gay L.A.*, 184. Separate lesbian organizing appeared in L.A. for the first time in October 1970 with the formation inside the LA Women's Center of a "Gay Women's Liberation" group, a split from the Gay Liberation Front ("New Gay Women's Liberation Office at the Women's Center," *Women's Liberation Newsletter*, October 1970, cited in Faderman and Timmons, *Gay L.A.*, 390, n53).

54   Martin Duberman, *Stonewall* (New York: Dutton, 1993), 184–5.

55   Faderman and Timmons, *Gay L.A.*, 1.

56   Joanna Lin, "Bar Still Symbolic in the Gay Community: Protests at Silver Lake's Black Cat in 1967, Prompted by Police Brutality, Were a Turning Point," *LAT*, November 16, 2008.

12   Sister Corita and the Cardinal

1   Andrew Greeley, quoted in Anita M. Caspary, *Witness to Integrity: The Crisis of the Immaculate Heart Community in California* (Collegeville, MN: Liturgical Press, 2003), back cover.

2   "Among religious women in the US, and maybe in the whole world, no community was more anxious than the Immaculate Heart Sisters to begin the renewal authorized and encouraged by Vatican II" (Francis J. Weber, *His Eminence of Los Angeles: James Francis Cardinal McIntyre*, vol. 2 [Archdioceses of Los Angeles, 1997], 420). McIntyre's "displeasure was often personalized in Sister Corita": Julie Ault, *Come Alive! The Spirited Art of Sister Corita* (London: Four Corners, 2007), 14. See also "Fighting Nuns," *Newsweek*, April 1, 1968, 100.

3   *LAT*, June 24, 2015.

4   Cardinal McIntyre had been after Corita and the IHMers for a long time. It had begun almost ten years earlier, in 1957, when the cardinal warned the head of the order that "work from the art department bordered on blasphemous." Liz Mahoney, one of the IHM sisters, later recalled, "That 'blasphemous' absolutely put a dagger in her heart." McIntyre then told the head of the order to "direct Corita to 'refrain

from representations of our Savior, Our Lady and the saints that are not obviously reverential'" (Ian Berry, ed., *Someday Is Now: The Art of Corita Kent* [New York: Prestel USA, 2013], 42; Caspary, *Witness to Integrity*, 36).

5 Caspary, *Witness to Integrity*, 38.

6 Ault, *Come Alive!*, 23.

7 Marvin Gettleman, ed., *Vietnam and America*, 2nd ed. (New York: Grove, 1995), 305–6.

8 Quoted in Berry, *Someday Is Now*, 77.

9 Mike Davis, *City of Quartz*, 1st ed. (London and New York: Verso, 1990), 333.

10 Maurice Ouellet, "The Uncomfortable Christ," sermon, available at summerinselma.blogspot.com/2013/05/the-uncomfortable-christ_27.html.

11 Robert Howell, "45 Years after March, Selma Priest Remembers Bloody Sunday," *CNN*, March 8, 2010, cnn.com.

12 Dan Berrigan himself said that talking to the sisters, what struck him most was their anguish. Rose Pacatte, *Corita Kent: Gentle Revolutionary of the Heart* (Collegeville, MN: Liturgical Press, 2017), 65.

13 Mark S. Massa, *The American Catholic Revolution: How the Sixties Changed the Church* (New York: Oxford University Press, 2010) 75, 77; Jesuits quoted 80, Caspary quoted 76.

14 Ibid., 93.

15 Harvey Cox, "Corita: Celebration and Creativity," in Sister Mary Corita Kent, *Sister Corita* (Philadelphia: Pilgrim Press, 1968), 18, 17.

16 Quoted in Berry, *Someday Is Now*, 77.

17 Murray Polner and Jim O'Grady, *Disarmed and Dangerous: The Radical Lives and Times of Daniel and Philip Berrigan* (New York: Basic Books, 1997), 163. Francine du Plessix Gray, writing in the *New York Review of Books*, suggested that the two had an affair, but both denied it, as do his biographers. See Gray, *Divine Disobedience: Profiles in Catholic Radicalism* (New York: Vintage, 1971), 96.

18 Quoted in Ault, *Come Alive!*, 24–5.

19 Ibid., 120.

20 Jeffrey M. Jones, "Latest Poll Shows High Point in Opposition to Iraq War," *Gallup*, July 11, 2007, gallup.com.

21 *LAT*, December 23, 1966.

22 Quoted in Caspary, *Witness to Integrity*, 69.

23 Massa, *American Catholic Revolution*, 98.

24 "The Nun: Going Modern," *Newsweek*, December 1967.

25 *Newsweek* wasn't alone in covering the dispute between the IHM

sisters and Cardinal McIntyre; in March 1968, it made headlines in the *New York Times*. Their report, "Criticism of Nuns' Innovations Is Widened by McIntyre," noted that "the order's best known member" was Corita, who "has gained international note as an artist" (Gladwin Hill, "Criticism of Nuns' Innovations Is Widened by McIntyre Paper," *New York Times*, March 25, 1968). See also "Coast Nuns Seek 'Modernization,'" *New York Times*, March 17, 1968: the order's "star artist," Corita, "has gained international note in secular as well as church circles."

26 Letter quoted in Caspary, *Witness to Integrity*, 165–6.

27 Ibid., 193.

28 Massa, *American Catholic Revolution*, 118.

29 Caspary, *Witness to Integrity*, 189.

30 "Nun, 'Op-Pop' Artist, Resigns from Order," *New York Times*, November 22, 1968; *LAT*, November 22, 1968.

31 Helen Kelley, in *Someday Is Now*, 82–3.

32 Ault, *Come Alive!*, 25.

33 Massa, *American Catholic Revolution*, 120. A week after he disappeared, Berrigan "suddenly appeared before ten thousand students" at Cornell "celebrating a 'Freedom Seder'" in his honor. The weekend was called "America is Hard to Find." That was also the title of an LP record released in 1970, featuring poetry from Berrigan that he wrote while underground. Corita did the cover for the LP (black bars of brushstrokes with her familiar script in between them).

34 Caspary, *Witness to Integrity*, 211. In her words, they were "forced to abandon" the church as the result of an "effort to defeat and disempower one group of women devoted to the Church" (220).

35 Massa, *American Catholic Revolution*, 82.

36 Caspary, *Witness to Integrity*, 211.

37 Ault, *Come Alive!*, 27, citing Mert Guswiler, "Corita Kent's 'Time of Conversation,'" *LA Herald-Examiner*, March 13, 1971.

38 Ault, *Come Alive!*, 26–7.

39 *LAT*, March 6, 1971.

40 Berry, *Someday Is Now*, 162. Corita did turn out more political work: in 1972 she did a poster for the McGovern campaign: "Come Home America," featuring a quotation from Jesuit philosopher Teilhard de Chardin: "But some day, after mastering the winds, the waves, the tides and gravity, we shall harness for God the energies of love, and then, for the second time in the history of the world, man will have discovered fire." (These were the closing words of Sargent Shriver's speech accepting the vice presidential nomination to run with George

McGovern.) In 1980 Corita did a new poster for Dan Berrigan and the Plowshares Eight, an anti-nuke group that attacked nuclear missile nosecones with hammers that September: "beating swords into ploughshares." The silk screen presents crocuses and the text "we are filled with hope," which was from a statement of Berrigan's—that they were "going to confront nuclear warheads and go on trial and risk prison" as acts of "hope, not despair." In 1983 she did a billboard for Physicians for Social responsibility—she called it "the most religious thing I've done up till now" (Berry, *Someday Is Now*, 165, 16).

41 *LAT*, September 20, 1986.

42 *LAT*, March 8, 2000.

13 The Midnight Hour

1 Malcolm X, "After the Bombing," speech, February 14, 1965, Detroit, available at malcolm-x.org.

2 For the encounter in L.A., where Malcolm visited two of the plaintiffs in a paternity suit against Elijah Muhammad, see Taylor Branch, *Pillar of Fire: America in the King Years, 1963–65* (New York: Simon & Schuster, 1998), 572–3.

3 UCLA Institute of Industrial Relations, *Hard-Core Unemployment and Poverty in Los Angeles*, report for the US Department of Commerce (Washington, DC: US Government Printing Office, December 14, 1964).

4 Carstens, whose daughter Betty was one of the forty-seven Freedom Summer volunteers from L.A., became the chairman of Californians for Liberal Representation, an offshoot of the Independent Progressive Party, and later was almost elected to Congress from the Valley as an anti-war candidate. Although nothing at UCLA commemorates his life, he left an indelible stamp on the institute and an entire generation of LA trade union activists.

5 Paul Bullock, *Watts: The Aftermath* (New York: Grove, 1969).

6 UCLA Institute of Industrial Relations, *Hard-Core Unemployment and Poverty*, 111, 146.

7 Quoted in *LAT*, October 19, 1962.

8 Paul Jacobs, *Prelude to Riot: A View of Urban America from the Bottom* (New York: Random House, 1966), 237–8.

9 *LAT*, July 4, 1965.

10 John Constantinus Bollens and Grant B. Geyer, *Yorty: Politics of a Constant Candidate* (Pacific Palisades, CA: Palisades Publishers, 1973), 142–8. Roosevelt was denounced as an "Eastern outsider" and

"carpetbagger," despite that fact that he had lived in L.A.—apart from time spent on Guadalcanal with Evans Carlson's Rangers—since 1938.

11 *New York Times*, August 19, 1965.

12 *LAT*, July 7, 1965.

13 Robert E. Conot, *Rivers of Blood, Years of Darkness* (New York: Bantam, 1967), 209.

14 —an anonymous man in mechanic's overalls.

15 *New York Times*, August 17, 1964.

16 Quoted in Conot, *Rivers of Blood*, 101.

17 J. Gregor Payne and Scott Ratzen, *Tom Bradley: The Impossible Dream* (Santa Monica: Roundtable Publishing, 1986), 70–1.

18 Alisa Kramer, "William H. Parker and the Thin Blue Line: Politics, Public Relations and Policing in Postwar Los Angeles," PhD diss., American University, 2007, 267. See also Joe Domanick, *To Protect and To Serve: The LAPD's Century of War in the City of Dreams* (New York: Pocket Books, 1994), 182.

19 *LAT*, August 13, 15 and 18, 1965, my emphasis. The *Times*'s coverage of the rebellion was curiously schizophrenic. The editorials and some of the commentaries were hysterical as they parroted fantastic claims and lies by LAPD brass and rank and file. On the other hand, its reportorial team in the field, with a single Black journalist (Robert Richardson), conscripted from classified ads, interviewed scores of residents and in most cases accurately represented their counter-narratives. (They would later win Pulitzers.) The headlines on their stories, however, were crafted elsewhere: for instance, "Get Whitey, Scream Blood-Hungry Mobs."

20 *New York Times*, August 17, 1965; and August 16, 1965 (European headlines).

21 The team behind the 1974 study found most "intriguing, the existence of several, distinctive mini-riots discernible within what had appeared to be a single, large-scale event … it suggests complex inner dynamics in riot processes not adequately accounted for in previous work" (Margaret Stark, W. Paine, S. Burbeck, and K. Davison, "Some Empirical Patterns in a Riot Process," *American Sociological Review* 39 [December 1974], 869). However instead of using complex Fourier analyses and time-space simulations to establish this thesis, they might simply have interviewed some of the experienced observers who had been on the scene, such as Woodrow Coleman and Danny Gray of N-VAC, or Ron Wilkins (later "Brother Crook"), who was a key broker of gang unity.

22 Magnificent Montague with Bob Baker, *Burn, Baby! Burn! The Autobiography of Magnificent Montague* (Urbana: University of Illinois Press, 2003), 123–4. That evening's performance was recorded and issued as a record, and years later as a CD: *Stax Review: Live at the 5/4 Ballroom*, compact disc, compiled by Roger Armstrong (London: Ace Records, 1991).

23 Conot, *Rivers of Blood*, 40. "LSMFT" was a well-known cigarette commercial: "Lucky Strike Means Fine Tobacco."

24 Conot, *Rivers of Blood*, 15–16; Jerry Cohen and William S. Murphy, *Burn, Baby, Burn! The Los Angeles Race Riots of August 1965* (New York: Dutton, 1966), 37.

25 Conot, *Rivers of Blood*, 21.

26 Cohen and Murphy, *Burn, Baby, Burn!*, 47–58.

27 *LAT*, August 13, 1965.

28 *LAT*, July 31 and October 12, 1965; and *Jet*, August 12, 1965.

29 *Jet*, October 14, 1965.

30 Nelson Perry, *Black Radical: The Education of an American Revolutionary* (New York: New Press, 2007), 212–13. Perry, a charming and charismatic figure, later founded a small but extremely active LA group, eventually called the Communist Labor Party, whose members, many of them recruited from SDS, founded the famous Midnight Special Bookstore in Venice, fought for the rights of prisoners and their families, and were active in several unions, especially the ILWU at San Pedro. Along with Dorothy Healey, he was the most impressive working-class intellectual that I've ever encountered—MD.

31 J. K. Obatala, "The Sons of Watts," *LAT Magazine*, August 13, 1972.

32 *LAT*, August 13, 1965.

33 *New York Times*, August 14, 1965.

34 *LAT*, September 14, 1965.

35 Bullock, *Watts*, 134.

36 *LAT*, August 14, 1965.

37 Montague, in Cohen and Murphy, *Burn, Baby! Burn!*, 131. The "Sons of Watts" were first known as the "Sons of the Stronghold."

38 Cohen and Murphy, *Burn, Baby, Burn!*, 286.

39 Conot, *Rivers of Blood*, 218–19, 232–3.

40 Bullock, *Watts*, 34–6, original emphasis.

41 Cohen and Murphy, *Burn, Baby, Burn!*, 153–4.

42 Calculated from descriptions in Conot, *Rivers of Blood*.

43 Perry, *Black Radical*, 225.

44 Conot, *Rivers of Blood*, 313.

45 Cohen and Murphy, *Burn, Baby, Burn!*, 163.

46 Conot, *Rivers of Blood*, 325.

47 "The Negro Revolt in LA—From the Inside," *Movement* (San Francisco), September 1965, 6.

48 Cohen and Murphy, *Burn, Baby, Burn!*, 230–1. In their "Acknowledgments" they note, "The Los Angeles Police Department refused to allow the authors to interview any officers who participated in suppressing the riot, and declined to permit the examination of records which are normally available to accredited representatives of any news media" (19).

49 Perry, *Black Radical*, 223–4.

50 Conot, *Rivers of Blood*, 339; Cohen and Murphy, *Burn, Baby, Burn!*, 195.

51 *New York Times*, August 16, 1965; *LAT*, August 17, 1965.

52 *New York Times*, August 17, 1965.

53 Conot, *Rivers of Blood*, 278.

54 I was walking next to Levi, but the sniper was clearly aiming at him, not me—MD.

55 *LAT*, August 17, 1965.

56 *New York Times*, August 18, 1965.

57 Taylor Branch, *At Canaan's Edge: America in the King Years, 1965–68* (New York: Simon & Schuster, 2006), 294–8.

58 Martin Luther King Jr., "Watts," in *The Autobiography of Martin Luther King Jr.*, ed. Clayborne Carson (New York: Warner, 1998), ch. 27.

14 Whitewash

1 *LAT*, September 15, 1965.

2 *LAT*, August 19 and 22, 1965.

3 *LAT*, August 15 and 30; September 14 and 16, 1965; Alisa Kramer, "William H. Parker and the Thin Blue Line: Politics, Public Relations and Policing in Postwar Los Angeles," PhD diss., American University, 2007, 307. Stanley Crouch, a Jefferson High graduate who later became an acclaimed jazz critic and novelist, was working for SNCC in Watts and told Tom Bradley that he had watched as police at the Seventy-Seventh Street Division issued bullhorns to volunteers (*LAT*, September 17, 1965).

4 *LAT*, September 7, 1965.

5 "Younger Defends Action against Black Muslims: Evidence of Assault 'Seemed Sufficient,'" *LAT*, September 10, 1965.

6 *LAT*, November 23, 1965.

7 *LAT*, August 19, 1965.

8 *LAT*, September 9, 10, 19 and 21, 1965; February 2, 1966. In 1967, after Parker's death, the LAPD staged a third raid on the Broadway mosque, again based on a secret informant's claim that "submachine guns, rifles, dynamite and grenades" were hidden there. Nothing was found, of course, but the police had a new pretext to gratuitously wreck the inside of the much battered and fired-upon building. Billy Mills was incensed and demanded that the LAPD seek a perjury complaint against the informant, but the department refused to comply, convincing many that such an informant never existed (*LAT*, August 1, 1967).

9 Joe Domanick, *To Protect and to Serve: The LAPD's Century of War in the City of Dreams* (New York: Pocket Books, 1994), 193.

10 Paul Jacobs, *Prelude to Riot: A View of Urban America from the Bottom* (New York: Random House, 1967), 238, 240–1, 287. Jacobs's chapter on the McCone Commission is a small masterpiece of investigative journalism.

11 Jacobs, *Prelude to Riot*, 244, 290–9; Sally Denton, *The Profiteers: Bechtel and the Men Who Built the World* (New York: Simon & Schuster, 2016), chs. 5 and 6; Robert Gottlieb and Irene Wolt, *Thinking Big: The Story of the Los Angeles Times* (New York: Putnam, 1977), 380, 399. "An executive committee was appointed to make all the important decisions about the hiring of staff and the conduct of the investigation: the committee consisted of McCone, Asa McCall and Warren Christopher, and this small group made decisions on a day-to-day basis, generally without consulting the other commission members" (Jacobs, *Prelude to Riot*, 248).

12 McCone Commission transcript, 11:35, quoted in Kramer, "William H. Parker," 305.

13 Jacobs discovered that the eleven-volume archival version of the commission's hearings and research had been heavily censored and important material destroyed (Jacobs, *Prelude to Riot*, 282).

14 Governor's Commission on the Los Angeles Riots, *Violence in the City—An End or a Beginning?*, Los Angeles, 1965, 3.

15 Governor's Commission, *Violence in the City*, 1, 70–2.

16 David O. Sears and John B. McConahay, *The Politics of Violence: The New Urban Blacks and the Watts Riot* (New York: Houghton Mifflin, 1973), 29.

17 *Violence in the City*, 1; House Un-American Activities Committee, *Subversive Influences in Riots, Looting and Burnings, Part 1: Los Angeles—Watts* (Washington, DC: Government Printing Office, 1967), 719, 775.

18 Governor's Commission, *Violence in the City*, 85.

19 Robert Fogelson, *Violence as Protest* (New York: Doubleday, 1971), 191–9.

20 Ibid.

21 *LAT*, November 23, 1965.

22 Fogelson, *Violence as Protest*, 193–5.

23 Summary in *LAT*, August 13, 1967.

24 Bayard Rustin, "The Watts," *Commentary*, March 1966, original emphasis.

25 *New York Times*, December 8, 1965; *LAT*, December 14, 1965; Kramer, "William H. Parker," 313. On the "Freedom Budget for All Americans," which targeted white as well as Black poverty, see Thomas J. Sugrue, *Sweet Land of Liberty: The Forgotten Struggle for Civil Rights in the North* (New York: Random House, 2008), 376–7.

26 *New York Times*, August 24, 1965.

27 For details on Garron's death, see *People v. Stephanson*, crim. no. 12927, Second District, division 2, February 20, 1968; and *People v. Aubrey*, crim. no. 12914, Second District, division 4, August 25, 1967.

28 Susan Welch, "The Impact of Urban Riots on Urban Expenditures," *American Journal of Political Science* 29:4 (November 1975), 743–4; Sears and McConahay, *Politics of Violence*, 160.

29 Mexican Americans polled held similar view to those of whites (Sears and McConahay, *Politics of Violence*, 164–5).

30 *LAT*, March 16, 18 and 20, 1965

31 See Patrick Phillips, *Blood at the Root: A Racial Cleansing in America* (New York: Norton, 2016).

32 *LAT*, May 29, 1965 (previous complaint against Bova).

33 Johnnie Cochran, *A Lawyer's Life* (New York: St Martin's, 2003).

34 *LAT*, May 17, 1966.

35 Peter Bart, "Police Alerted in Watts Unrest: 11 Negroes Arrested after 2 Reporters Are Injured," *New York Times*, May 19, 1966.

36 Richard Bergholz, "Yorty Cites Watts Violence as Proof Reds Are Election Issue," *LAT*, May 19, 1966.

15 Cultural Revolution

1 Daniel Widener, *Black Arts West: Culture and Struggle in Postwar Los Angeles* (Durham: Duke University Press, 2010), 164–5; Plagens quoted 163.

2 Malcolm X: "Our cultural revolution must be the means of bringing us closer to our African brothers and sisters. It must begin in the

community and be based on community participation ... We must work toward the establishment of a cultural center in Harlem which will include people of all ages, and will conduct workshops in all of the arts, such as film, creative writing, painting, theatre, music, Afro-American history, etc." (Organization of Afro-American Unity, "Statement of Basic Aims and Objectives," *The Portable Malcolm X Reader*, ed. Manning Marable [New York: Penguin, 2013], 350).

3 Other important contributions include James Smethurst, *The Black Arts Movement* (Chapel Hill: University of North Carolina Press, 2005), ch. 5; Curtis Carter, *Watts: Art and Social Change in Los Angeles, 1965–2002* (Milwaukee: Haggerty Museum of Art, 2003); Sanid Sheffey-Stinson, "The History of Theater Productions at the Inner City Cultural Center, 1965–1976," PhD diss., Kent State University, 1979; and Victor Walker, "The Politics of Art: A History of the Inner City Cultural Center," PhD diss., UC Santa Barbara, 1989.

4 Ben Ratliff, *Coltrane: The Story of a Sound* (New York: Farrar, Straus & Giroux, 2007), 97.

5 Steve Isoardi, *The Dark Tree: Jazz and the Community Arts in Los Angeles* (Berkeley: Univ. of Calif. Press, 2006), 85.

6 Smethurst, *Black Arts Movement*, 62. See LeRoi Jones (Amiri Baraka), *Blues People: Negro Music in White America* (New York: Praeger, 1980).

7 Isoardi, *Dark Tree*, 100.

8 Quoted in Widener, *Black Arts West*, 129.

9 Isoardi, *Dark Tree*, 101.

10 Max Harrison et al., *The Essential Jazz Records*, vol. 2, *Modernism to Postmodernism* (London: Mansell, 2000), 505–7.

11 Horace Tapscott, *Songs of the Unsung: The Musical and Social Journey of Horace Tapscott* (Durham: Duke University Press), 120.

12 Isoardi, *Dark Tree*, 95–8; Widener, *Black Arts West*, 149–51.

13 Budd Schulberg, "Introduction," *From the Ashes: Voices of Watts* (New York: New American Library, 1967), 6.

14 Mike Sonksen points out that the WWW's classes were open to members of the public who were not formal members of the workshop. He cites the example of Wanda Coleman, later one of L.A's most distinguished poets.

15 Widener, *Black Arts West*, 112.

16 Mervyn Dymally, "Oral History Interview," California State Archives —State Government Oral History Program, vol. 1, 1996–1997, 204. Charles Drew Post-Graduate Medical School (later University) and Martin Luther King Hospital were the two most important legacies of

the 1965 rebellion and the subsequent community struggles following white voters' rebuff of Proposition A in 1966. In addition to addressing the acute shortage of medical care and hospital space in the greater Watts area, King-Drew also became the area's major employer and source of living-wage jobs.

17 J. Alfred Cannon, "Re-Africanization: The Last Alternative for Black America," _Phylon_ 38:2 (1977), 203–10.

18 _Black Panther_, January 16, 1970, 12; Dymallly, "Oral History," 205.

19 _LAT_, October 17, 1967; May 29, 1968.

20 _LAT_, March 2, 1968.

21 _LAT_, July 19, 1966; October 17, 1967.

22 _LAT_, March 31, 1991.

23 Nathan Rosenberger, "Art in the Ashes: Class, Race, Urban Geography, and Los Angeles's Postwar Black Art Centers," PhD diss., Department of History, CSU Long Beach, 2016, 207.

24 Cecil Smith, "The Ghost of WPA Theater Walks Again," _LAT_, August 27, 1967.

25 Michael Denning, _The Cultural Front: The Laboring of American Culture_ (London and New York: Verso, 1997).

26 Rosenberger, "Art in the Ashes," 199, 235.

27 Ibid., 201, 241.

28 Ibid., 222.

29 See, for example, the attempt to defund the ICCC by Rep. Glenard Lipscomb (R-Santa Barbara): _LAT_, September 18, 1968.

30 Quoted in Christopher Miller, "The (Revised) Birth of Negritude: Communist Revolution and 'the Immanent Negro' in 1935," _PMLA_ 125:3 (2010), 746–7.

31 Peniel Joseph, "Black Studies, Student Activism, and the Black Power Movement," _Journal of African American History_ 88:2 (2003), 187–8 (the Warden quote comes from former AAA member Les Lacey); and Scot Brown, "The Politics of Culture: The US Organization and the Quest for Black 'Unity,'" in _Freedom North_, eds. Jeanne Theoharis and Komozi Woodard (New York: Palgrave, 2003), 225–6.

32 Peniel Joseph, _Waiting 'Til the Midnight Hour: A Narrative History of Black Power in America_ (New York: Holt, 2007), 217.

33 Amiri Baraka, _The Autobiography of LeRoi Jones_ (New York: Freundlich Books, 1984), 248, 253. But Baraka could never completely reconcile US's ersatz Africa. "The 'revolutionary culture we must bring to the masses," he wrote in his later Marxist phase, "is not the pre-capitalist customs and social practices of Africa, but heightened expression of the lives and history, art and sociopolitical patterns of

the masses of the African American people stripped of their dependence on the white racist society and focused on revolution" (255). In 1974 Baraka, announcing that he was a Marxist-Leninist, broke all ties with Karenga.

34 Elaine Brown, *A Taste of Power* (New York: Pantheon, 1993), 109. Baraka adds: "When brothers went by, the women were supposed to 'salimu' or 'submit,' crossing their arms on their breasts and bowing slightly ... Karenga also had wild stuff in his doctrine about how women ought to dress, and how what they should wear should always be 'suggestive.' He said they should show flesh to intrigue men and not be covered up so much. I could never adjust to Karenga's thing with women either on paper or in the flesh. He was always making 'sexy' remarks to women, calling them 'freaks' and commenting loudly on their physical attributes" (Baraka, *Autobiography*, 275).

35 Douglas Glasgow, "Sons of Watts," in *Black Power in the Belly of the Beast*, ed. Judson Jeffries (Urbana: University of Illinois Press, 2006), 116–34.

36 *LAT*, July 15, 1966; Nathaniel Freedland, "Big Ol' Stan Out Front," *LAT Magazine*, October 15, 1967.

37 Schulberg, *From the Ashes*, 16.

16 Black Power

1 Peniel Joseph, "Introduction," *The Black Power Movement: Rethinking the Civil Rights–Black Power Era* (New York: Routledge, 2006).

2 A typical interrogation of Carmichael that completely ignored his responses took place on CBS's *Face the Nation* (June 19, 1966), available at youtu.be/2GrZPISpnAw.

3 Stokely Carmichael, "What We Want," *New York Review of Books*, September 22, 1966.

4 "Carmichael was faced with the choice of building political institutions such as he had created in Lowndes County or following the example of the Atlanta Project and becoming preoccupied with rhetorical appeals for the unification of black people on the basis of separatist ideals. His expressed preference was to move in the former direction, but events that occurred soon after his election drew him toward the latter" (Clayborne Carson, *In Struggle: SNCC and the Black Awakening of the 1960s* [Cambridge: Harvard University Press, 1981], 206).

5 Stokely Carmichael, "Black Power Speech," October 29, 1966 available at americanrhetoric.com.

6   *LAT*, October 31, 1966.

7   *LAT*, November 27, 1966.

8   *LAT*, November 26 and 27, 1966.

9   Stokely Carmichael, "Watts Speech," November 26, 1966, transcript available at crmvet.org.

10 The Deacons, based in Bogalusa, Louisiana, organized a Lowndes County chapter to protect campaign rallies. See Lance Hill, *The Deacons for Defense: Armed Resistance and the Civil Rights Movement* (Chapel Hill: University of North Carolina Press, 2004), 213.

11 Carson, *In Struggle*, 201.

12 See *The Story of SNCC*, pamphlet, 1966, available at crmvet.org/docs/sncc66.pdf.

13 "Stokely Carmichael on Puerto Rico, Cities, the Draft, Blackness and More," *Movement* 3:2 (February 1966), 4.

14 *LAT*, July 19, 1966. A few years later Jamal moved to London, then to Jamaica, where he and his lover, Gale Benson, the daughter of a Conservative Party MP, joined a commune run by Black Power leader Michael X. Under sordid circumstances, Benson was murdered by members of the commune. Exonerated of any involvement in the crime, Jamal returned to the United States and was himself assassinated in Boston in 1973, most likely by followers of Elijah Muhammad.

15 *LA Free Press*, July 21–22, 1967. Levi worked closely with the SDS regional office in 1965–1966, when I was one of the organizers, and thanks to him we were enlightened about the irony of providing a new privilege (access to draft alternatives) to the already privileged—MD.

16 Martha Biondi, *The Black Revolution on Campus* (Berkeley: University of California Press, 2012), 35.

17 *LAT*, January 25 and 28; February 28; March 4 and 17, 1967.

18 *LAT*, June 11, 1966.

19 *LAT*, June 20, 1966.

20 Daniel Widener, *Black Arts West: Culture and Struggle in Postwar Los Angeles* (Durham: Duke University Press, 2010), 197.

21 Louis Gothard, "How to Organize a Community Alert Patrol," *Movement*, February 1967, 11.

22 The plan added to the original city limits Watts neighborhoods in unincorporated Willowbrook and Florence-Firestone districts as well as in adjacent parts of L.A. Its proposed borders were the Harbor Freeway on the west; Alameda Street on the east, Vernon Avenue on the north and El Segundo Boulevard on the south—a population of about 250,000.

23 "Declaration of Purpose," quoted in *LAT*, June 24, 1966.

24 *LAT*, June 17, 24 and 27, 1966.

25 *LAT*, July 6 and 8, 1966; *Crisis*, August–September 1966, 365.

26 John Baker, *Vice: One Cop's Story of Patrolling America's Most Dangerous City* (New York: St. Martin's Press, 2011), 14–15. This is an account of eighteen years on the Compton police force. Although torqued up in parts, it is an interesting memoir because Baker, a Latino, went to grade school in Watts and then high school and college in Compton. He recounts without apology the extralegal and usually brutal conduct of white cops in an increasingly Black city.

27 Emily Straus, "The Making of the American School Crisis: Compton, California and the Death of the Suburban Dream," PhD diss., Brandeis University, 2006, 92, 102–3.

28 *LAT*, December 29, 1965.

29 Baker, *Vice*, 31–5.

30 These paragraphs are reproduced from Mike Davis, "Fear and Loathing in Compton," *The Nation*, 1994, reprinted in *Dead Cities and Other Tales* (New York: New Press, 2002), 275–83.

17 The Cat Arrives

1 Donald Wheeldin, "The Situation in Watts Today," *Freedomways* 7 (winter 1967).

2 *LAT*, August 13, 1970.

3 *LAT*, January 10 and 14, 1966.

4 *LAT*, February 11, 1968.

5 *LAT*, August 30, 1970.

6 *LAT*, January 4, 1969.

7 Dennis McDougal, *Privileged Son: Otis Chandler and the Rise and Fall of the L.A. Times Dynasty* (Cambridge, MA: Perseus Publishing, 2001), 270.

8 *Wall Street Journal*, July 26, 1968.

9 *LAT*, May 27 and 29, 1967.

10 Quoted in Elaine Brown, *A Taste of Power: A Black Woman's Story* (New York: Pantheon, 1993), 101–2.

11 Ironically, Brown, a young and little-known organizer, had been elected chairman as part of an effort by SNCC staff to tone down Carmichael-style rhetoric while strengthening urban organizing projects. Clay Carson argues that Brown was emotionally overwhelmed by the violence directed at Black students on Southern campuses and youth in Northern ghettos in the months after his election. He became

a lightning rod, not a candle (Clay Carson, *In Struggle* [Cambridge, MA: Harvard University Press, 1981], 251–6).

12   *LAT*, August 14, 1967; *LA Free Press*, August 18–24, 1967, 3. Another showpiece event for Karenga and US was the Western Region Black Youth Conference held in L.A. in November.

13   James Forman, *The Making of Black Revolutionaries* (Seattle: University of Washington Press, 1997), 458–9.

14   Lenin, *Collected Works*, vol. 23 (Moscow: Progress Publishers, 1964), 163, original emphasis.

15   Dorothy Healey and Maurice Isserman, *Dorothy Healey Remembers: A Life in the American Communist Party* (New York: Oxford University Press, 1990), 208–9.

16   Here again I (MD) interpolate my personal experience. I joined the SCDCP in 1968 because of its bold stand *against* the Soviet invasion of Czechoslovakia and quickly acquired a lifelong admiration for younger members such as Bob Duggan, Paul Rosenstein (future mayor of Santa Monica), Cliff Fried, Sabina Virgo, Adele Wallace (founder of Sisterhood Books), and Ron Ridenour (radical journalist based in Havana and Copenhagen). But the commanding figures, in part because of their absolute seriousness, were the Alexanders. Kendra, in particular, was a superb agitator and organizer, little inclined to rhetoric but keenly focused on the "next link in the chain." Franklin was her rock.

17   Angela Davis, "Eyes on the Prize II Interviews," May 1989, Henry Hampton Collection, Washington University Libraries, St. Louis.

18   Angela Davis, *Angela Davis: An Autobiography* (New York: International Publishers, 1974), 160–3.

19   Huey Newton, *Revolutionary Suicide* (New York: Harcourt, 1973), 132.

20   *LAT*, February 20, 1967.

21   Brown, *A Taste of Power*, 103–6, 112.

22   Davis, *Autobiography*, 164.

23   Brown, *A Taste of Power*, 124.

24   Forman, *Making of Black Revolutionaries*, 524, 528.

25   Davis, *Autobiography*, 165–6.

26   I (MD) can attest to Hewitt's acumen. In 1969 while I was running the SCDCP's bookstore in the MacArthur Park area, he often stopped by to pick up books for Panther study groups and argue with me about white New Left politics. He was a truly formidable thinker, and our conversations reinforced my belief that the best minds on the left (Hewitt, Healey, Nelson Peery, the Boggses in Detroit, and so on)

were those whose knowledge came from disciplined self-study and full immersion in struggle, not from college classrooms. They were certainly the most peerless agitators and tacticians.

27 Brown, *A Taste of Power*, 127.

28 James Forman, *Making of Black Revolutionaries*, 526.

29 Brown, *A Taste of Power*, 127–8.

30 Davis, *Autobiography*, 167–8.

31 Dorothy Healey, interview, October 25, 1973, Center for Oral History Research, UCLA, tape xx, side 1.

32 Davis, *Autobiography*, 172.

33 *LAT*, March 9, 1968.

34 Davis, *Autobiography*, 175.

35 *LAT*, December 19, 1970.

36 Davis, *Autobiography*, 180.

37 Ibid., 186.

18 "Unlawful Assembly"

1 LBJ got 1.6 million votes in LA County in 1964; New York City's five counties provided a total of 2.1 million. Chicago's Cook County produced 1.5 million.

2 *LAT*, June 22, 1967.

3 Ibid.

4 *LAT*, Jun 23, 1967.

5 *LAT*, June 24, 1967.

6 Ibid.; "LBJ Talks Peace; L.A. Pickets Battle," *LA Herald Examiner*, June 25, 1967, 1.

7 Peace Action Council mailing list, 1967, in Donald Kalish papers, UCLA Library Special Collections, box 223, folder 5 (hereafter, "Kalish papers").

8 Ibid.

9 *LAT*, June 24, 1967; "LBJ Talks Peace."

10 *LAT*, June 24, 1967.

11 Ibid.

12 Ibid.

13 *LAT*, July 2, 1967.

14 *LAT*, June 24, 1967.

15 *LAT*, July 2, 1967.

16 James Shafikh, "Police Riot Mars Peace March," *LA Free Press*, June 26, 1967, 1.

17 Sherwin Shane, *LA Free Press*, June 26, 1967, 3.

18 *LAT*, July 2, 1967.

19 ACLU of Southern California, *Day of Protest, Night of Violence: The Century City Peace March*, report (Los Angeles: Sawyer Press, July 1967) (hereafter, "ACLU report").

20 ACLU report, 19.

21 FBI memo, June 21, 1967, "Demonstration Protesting US Intervention in Vietnam," 2, 5.

22 Student Mobilization Committee, Peace Action Council, "Duties and Responsibilities of Monitors," in ACLU report, appendix B, 44.

23 Martin Luther King Jr., "Letter from Birmingham Jail," April 16, 1963, first published in *Liberation*, June 1963.

24 ACLU report, 2.

25 "Declaration of Donald Kalish," *Century City v. Peace Action Council*, LA Superior Court no. WEC 12240, July 5, 1967, Kalish papers, box 227, file 17.

26 *LAT*, June 16, 1967.

27 FBI teletype, "Confidential: Demonstration Protesting United States Intervention in Vietnam, Information Concerning," FBI director to White House, June 23, 1967.

28 "Injunction," June 23, 1967; ACLU report, appendix A, 43.

29 *LAT*, July 2, 1967; "Declaration of Donald Kalish."

30 ACLU report, 3.

31 Shafikh, "Police Riot Mars Peace March."

32 ACLU report, 6.

33 ACLU report, 6; Danny Faragher, "A Blur of White Helmets—The 1967 Century Plaza Police Riot and Brutality in the Summer of Love," *Danny Faragher* (personal blog), dannyfaragher.com.

34 Ali departed after the rally and did not join the march (Shafikh, "Police Riot Mars Peace March," 1). H. Rap Brown had said the same thing at a press conference earlier in the day, when he told reporters: "Whether or not a demonstration is violent is determined by the law enforcement officers themselves. All demonstrations begin peacefully, but if the police come down with billy clubs, there will be violence" (Jeffrey C. Alexander, "In the Shadow of the Glassboro Summit, Policemen Stir Up the Anti-War Movement," *Harvard Crimson*, September 27, 1967).

35 "Protestor Arrested in Assault," *LA Herald Examiner*, June 24, 1967.

36 ACLU report, 9.

37 Alexander, "In the Shadow."

38 "Introduction," ACLU report.

39 Ibid.

40 Ibid.

41 Ibid. Ten years later, Chief Ed Davis conceded on this point, telling the *LA Times* that at Century City, the police "whacked" people over the heads for "a full block." He said that "he felt pushing the demonstrators so far back in 1967 had been unnecessary." That was "the first time a high police official had so much as intimated that the police may have used undue force in the 1967 events" (*LAT*, October 26, 1977).

42 Cliff Blackburn, "Legion Charges Reds Directed LA Protest," *LA Herald Examiner*, June 29, 1967, 1.

43 *LAT*, June 29, 1967.

44 *LAT*, June 23, 1997.

45 Dorothy Healey and Maurice Isserman, *Dorothy Healey Remembers: A Life in the American Communist Party* (New York: Oxford University Press, 1990), 193.

46 FBI Los Angeles, urgent teletype to director, June 22, 1967.

47 "War Protest Mars LBJ's Visit," *LA Herald Examiner*, June 24, 1967, 1.

48 *LAT*, July 2, 1967.

49 *LAT*, June 23, 1997.

50 James R. Jones, "Behind LBJ's Decision Not to Run in '68," *New York Times*, April 16, 1968; Robert Dallek, *Flawed Giant* (New York: Oxford University Press, 1999), 524. Dallek relies in part on his 1997 interview with Lady Bird (722, n86).

51 *LAT*, March 8, 1969.

19 Eldridge Cleaver for President

1 Signature gathering for the Peace and Freedom Party began in the Bay Area in mid July, led by the Berkeley Committee for a New Politics. Their ticket: King-Spock. Robert Hurwitt, "CNP Launches King-Spock Here," *Berkeley Barb*, July 14, 1967, 7.

2 Martin Luther King Jr., "The Three Evils of Society," address delivered at the National Conference on New Politics, August 31, 1967, unpublished, in Pacifica Radio Archives.

3 Taylor Branch, *At Canaan's Edge: America in the King Years, 1965–68* (New York: Simon & Schuster, 2006), 637–8.

4 The fullest report on the New Politics conference is Renata Adler, "Letter from the Palmer House," *New Yorker*, September 23, 1967, 56–88. She found it "a travesty of radical politics."

5 Beverle Houston, "Black New Politics Delegate Opens Eyes of

White Liberal," *LA Free Press*, September 15, 1967, 1, 15.

6 Marvin Garson, "The Whites: A Clown Show," *LA Free Press*, September 22, 1967, 1, 13. Dorothy Healey agreed; she later wrote that the sense of the convention was that "no matter what else happened, white radicals had to meet the demands of Black militants" (Dorothy Healey and Maurice Isserman, *Dorothy Healey Remembers* [New York: Oxford University Press, 1990], 206).

7 Michael Hannon, "CP, Blacks Disrupt Peace and Freedom Meeting," *LA Free Press*, October 6, 1967, 5.

8 Paul Rosenstein, interview by JW, January 31, 2018. Fifty years later, Jack Weinberg called that "an 'Organizing 101' mistake": "Too many clubs were formed to be sustainable," he said. "And there was an underlying problem, which was that the rank and file in LA at the clubs was much more liberal, while the leadership was much more radical. And we were very democratic in those days. Any decision that was made at the citywide meetings had to go back to all those little clubs for ratification. The clubs would debate and come up with questions they needed answers to, and they brought those back to the citywide meeting" (Jack Weinberg, interview by JW, February 8, 2018).

9 "Registration Campaign—Last Days," *Peace and Freedom News*, March 4, 1968, 7, Peace and Freedom Party Collection, California State University, Los Angeles.

10 Dick Yanowitz, "Early History of the California Peace and Freedom Party (1968)," January/February 1968, *Richard D Daynowitz* (personal blog), richardyanowitz.com; Gene Youngblood, "Peace and Freedom Party Now on Calif. Ballot," *LA Free Press*, January 5, 1968, 1.

11 State steering committee, "Statement on McCarthy," *Peace and Freedom News*, March 1968, 1.

12 McCarthy didn't get a majority of the vote—he got 42 percent to Johnson's 49—but he did win a huge majority of the convention delegates—twenty out of twenty-four.

13 "Counties Report on Structure, Candidates," *Peace and Freedom News*, March 4, 1968, 8.

14 Bruce Headlam, "For Him, the Political Has Always Been Comical," *New York Times*, March 13, 2009.

15 "Kennedy and McCarthy, Part of the Sickness," *LA Free Press*, March 22, 1968, 24.

16 Wallace Turner, "Convention of New Left Coalition Sets '68 Goals," *New York Times*, March 19, 1968.

17 John Kifner, "Eldridge Cleaver, Black Panther Who Became GOP Conservative, is dead at 62," *New York Times*, May 2, 1998.

18 Turner, "Convention," *New York Times*.

19 Kathleen Cleaver, Peace and Freedom Party statement, n.d., Peace and Freedom Party collection, California State University, Los Angeles.

20 Betsy Barnes, "Report on Peace and Freedom Party National Convention," report to the SWP, 1968, available at Marxist Internet Archive, marxists.org.

21 Eldridge Cleaver, interview by Henry Louis Gates Jr., "The Two Nations of Black America," *Frontline*, PBS, February 10, 1998, available at pbs.org.

22 David Hilliard, *Huey: Spirit of the Panther* (New York: Basic Books, 2008), ch. 10. Hilliard was "chief of staff" of the Panthers at that point.

23 John Gunther et al., "Violence in Oakland," *New York Review of Books*, May 9, 1968.

24 *LAT*, May 20, 1968; Matthew Harrison Tedford, "Mr. Kennedy and the 1968 Battle for California," *Oakland Standard* (blog), Oakland Museum of California, April 4, 2012, theoaklandstandard.museumca. org.

25 Joseph A. Palermo, "Here's What RFK Did in California in 1968," *Huffington Post*, May 25, 2011.

26 *LAT*, May 14, 1968.

27 The judge focused on the revocation of Cleaver's parole, which he said had been an error because it "stemmed from … his undue eloquence in pursuing political goals—goals which were offensive to many of his contemporaries" ("Eldridge Cleaver, a Black Panther, Is Freed on Coast," *New York Times*, June 13, 1968).

28 "Cleaver Wins Majority: Peace & Freedom Party nominating conventions," *Freep*, August 9, 1968, 5. The vote in San Francisco was 77 percent for Eldridge and 17 percent for Dick Gregory.

29 Barnes, "Peace and Freedom Party."

30 The nomination of Cleaver was not binding on state organizations. California's PFP was running Cleaver, but in three states, Peace and Freedom parties ran Dick Gregory as their presidential candidate, while still others followed Gregory in splitting from Peace and Freedom to form a "Freedom and Peace" party, which ran Gregory for president in New York, New Jersey, Pennsylvania, and Virginia. Cleaver was the presidential candidate of the PFP Party in seventeen states.

31　Of course, other parties on the left ran write-in campaigns; the SWP ran Fred Halstead; the SLP (Socialist Labor Party) ran Henning A. Blomen—and the CP ran Charlene Mitchell, a Black woman from L.A., its first presidential candidate since 1940. The local CP had had impressive success when Dorothy Healey ran for LA County tax assessor two years earlier and got an astounding 86,000 votes—more than any CP candidate had gotten in any election in California since the 1930s; the hope was that Charlene Mitchell might also do well (Healey and Isserman, *Dorothy Healey Remembers*, 207, 194–6). Charlene Mitchell was the sister of Deacon and Franklin Alexander and sister-in law of Kendra Alexander, who became leaders of the Free Angela campaign.

32　The PFP also ran candidates for other offices in California in 1968: Paul Jacobs ran for Senate, and PFP ran candidates for Congress in nine California districts, including four in LA County: Jack Weinberg ran in Hollywood; Hugh Manes, a defense attorney known as "the dean of police misconduct cases," ran in Sherman Oaks; and Sherman Pearl, a journalist and brother of Ed Pearl, owner of the Ash Grove, ran in Santa Monica (*LAT*, June 6, 1968).

33　Nora Sayre, *Sixties Going on Seventies* (New Brunswick: Rutgers University Press, 1996), 45; Charles E. Jones, ed., *The Black Panther Party (Reconsidered)* (Baltimore: Black Classic Press, 1998), 33.

34　Theodore H. White, *The Making of the President, 1968* (New York, Athenaeum, 1969), 302.

35　Jack Weinberg, "PFP Plans Free-Huey March," *LA Free Press*, September 13, 1968, 4.

36　"200 March in Hollywood Last Friday in Effort to Free Huey Newton," *LA Free Press*, September 20, 1968, 2.

37　Fred Hoffman, "3,000 March to Free Huey, Strip," *LA Free Press*, October 4, 1968, 1, 3.

38　*LAT*, September 15, 1968.

39　William H. Honan, "If You Don't Like Hubert, Dick, or George, How About Lar, Yetta or Eldridge?," *New York Times Magazine*, October 27, 1968, 110.

40　Joan and Fred Hoffman, "Choice Not Chance: Pick a Name," *LA Free Press*, November 1, 1968, part 2, 1. The *Freep* also listed as write-ins the candidates of the CP and the SWP, as well as Dick Gregory and Dr. Spock.

41　The six for whom the state announced it would count write-in votes were Charlene Mitchell of the CP, Fred Halstead of the SWP, Henning A. Blomen of the Socialist Labor Party, Dick Gregory, Gene

McCarthy, and Kent Soeters of the "Berkeley Defense Group." *LA Free Press*, November 1, 1968.

42 Rennie Davis and Tom Hayden, "Vote in the Streets—Vote with Your Feet," *LA Free Press*, November 1, 1968, 29. Then it had one strikingly contradictory line: "While boycotting Humphrey, Nixon, and Wallace, we vote for independent candidates." That was sort of the opposite of boycotting the elections.

43 *LAT*, November 6, 1968.

44 "History," Peace and Freedom Party official website, peaceandfreedom. org.

45 Among the "qualified" write-in votes in LA County: Gene McCarthy, 6,604; Dick Gregory, 776; Charlene Mitchell, 119. LA County Registrar of Voters, official 1968 results, general election, available at lavote.net.

46 Statewide, the Peace and Freedom ticket got 27,707, and Dick Gregory received 3,230 write-in votes for president. Some of the PFP candidates did get some votes on Election Day. They included PFP's Senate candidate, Paul Jacobs, who got almost 93,000 votes statewide—about 1.3 percent of the total, and far more than the 27,700 the party's presidential ticket got, and more votes than anyone else in the party (although it was less than the 113,000 who had registered for the party during the signature-gathering campaign). Jack Weinberg's Congressional campaign in Hollywood got 6,400 votes, 4 percent of the total. John Haag ran for the state senate in Venice and got 4,800 votes, about 3 percent of the total. Both of them finished ahead of party registration in those districts. However, the fiasco of Peace and Freedom's presidential campaign in California in 1968 didn't mean the party was finished—far from it. They ran candidates again in 1970 (Ricardo Romo for governor) and 1972 (Dr. Spock for president), and remained on the ballot in California fifty years later.

47 Pat Thomas, *Did It: From Yippie to Yuppie—Jerry Rubin, an American Revolutionary* (Seattle: Fantagraphics, 2017), 58.

48 Bar Barnes, "Eldridge Cleaver, Author and Black Panther Leader, Dies," *Washington Post*, May 2, 1998.

49 Jack Weinberg, interview by JW, February 8, 2018.

20 "Time to Stand Up"

1 This framing of the alternatives is based on Bruce Dancis, *Resister: A Story of Protest and Prison During the Vietnam War* (Ithaca: Cornell University Press, 2014), 1–3.

2 Ibid. Dancis was sentenced to six years, of which he served nineteen months in federal prison in Ashland, Kentucky.

3 Michael S. Foley, *Confronting the War Machine: Draft Resistance During the Vietnam War* (Chapel Hill: UNC Press, 2003), 9.

4 This was part of a protest, not about Vietnam, but against Johnson's invasion of the Dominican Republic in April and the overthrow of the country's social democratic president. Jim Petras, the activist Latin American scholar who was then a graduate student, was the ringleader, while MD, working briefly for SDS in Oakland, was one of the arsonists.

5 *LAT*, October 17, 1967.

6 *LAT*, October 18, 1967.

7 Bob Zaugh, email to JW, September 26, 2019.

8 *LAT*, March 6, 1968.

9 Sterling Hayden, *Wanderer* (New York: Norton, 1977), quoted in Victor Navasky, *Naming Names* (New York: Viking, 1980), 151.

10 Seymour Korman, "Student Foes of War Bailed by Hutchins," *Chicago Tribune*, May 18, 1969, 7. Christian Hayden was put on trial in September 1968 but was acquitted by Judge Warren J. Ferguson, who ruled that the draft board had failed to process his appeal for CO status. In May 1969, he refused a second order to report for induction, and was tried for a second time, resulting in a conviction and a sentence of forty-two months in prison. See *LAT*, September 25, 1968; "Judge Acquits Actor's Son of Draft Evasion," *Chicago Tribune*, September 25, 1968, 54; *LAT*, December 16, 1969; Associated Press, "Seafaring Actor Dies at 70," May 23, 1986, available at AP News Archive, apnewsarchive.com.

11 *LAT*, October 7, 1968. Maizlish did not finish his history PhD, but became a "mediation coordinator" who spoke at an anti-draft event at UCLA in 2005: "UCLA Hosts Panel to Discuss Likelihood of Draft," *Daily Bruin*, February 27, 2005. In 2013 he was active in "Justice Not Jails" in Los Angeles; see his articles for Justice Not Jails at justicenotjails.org/author/joseph-maizlish/.

12 Bill Garaway, interview by JW, March 9, 2015.

13 Monroe H. Freedman, "Jury Nullification: What It Is, and How to Do It Ethically," *Hofstra Law Review* 42:4 (2014), 1125.

14 Bob Zaugh, Amber Zellebaugh, email to JW, March 10, 2015.

15 Bill Garaway, interview by JW, March 9, 2015; Garaway, interview by Cristian Markovitch, n.d., "The Sixties: Los Angeles Area Social Movements/Activists," Oral History Archive, California State University, Long Beach, symposia.library.csulb.edu. After a year in

Arizona, Garaway joined Struggle Mountain, the intentional community in Northern California founded by Joan Baez and David Harris.

16 Bob Zaugh, interview by JW, August 24, 2014.

17 Bob Zaugh, interview, Activist Video Archive, activistvideoarchive. org.

18 *LAT*, January 19, 1969.

19 *LAT*, April 20, 1969.

20 Robert S. Vogel, "Sanctuary at Orange Grove Meeting," *Friends Journal*, April 1, 1969, 215; "Orange Grove Friends Meeting, Dec. 18, 1968," meeting minutes, in JW's possession; Dave Chapple, "Stories of the Los Angeles Resistance," compiled by Sherna Berger Gluck and Winter Dellenbach for the reunion of the LA Resistance, October 24, 2009, in JW's possession.

21 *LAT*, April 20, 1969.

22 Robert S. Vogel, "Sanctuary at Orange Grove Meeting," *Friends Journal*, April 1, 1969, 215.

23 *LAT*, January 15, 1969.

24 Art Seidenbaum, "Friends and Resistance," *LAT*, January 15, 1969.

25 "Orange Grove Monthly Meeting, Jan. 8, 1969," meeting minutes, in possession of JW.

26 Vogel, "Sanctuary," 216.

27 Ibid.; Beach Langston, "Orange Grove Friends Meeting—State of Society Report, April 3, 1969," in JW's possession; see Leonard Brown, "Pasadena Sanctuary Triggers More Action," *LA Free Press*, March 21, 1969, 15–16.

28 Bob Zaugh, interview by JW, August 24, 2014.

29 *LAT*, March 21, 1969.

30 The sergeant who kicked Craig Murphy in the face was charged by the Marines with assault and battery for using "excessive force" in what the sergeant said was his duty as a noncommissioned officer of taking into custody another Marine who was breaking the law. The charges were dropped after Murphy declined to testify (*LAT*, April 19, 1969).

31 *LAT*, March 28, 1969.

32 *LAT*, April 4, 1969; Steve Davis, "Whittier Sanctuaries," *Resistance Newsletter*, April 14, 1969.

33 Associated Press, "Young Church Group has Anti-War Commune," *Sarasota Journal*, June 6, 1969.

34 *LAT*, May 16, 1969.

35 Associated Press, "Anti-War Commune."

36   Robert S. Vogel, "A Quaker Wedding at Fort Ord," *Friends Journal*, September 1, 1969, 505.

21   Riot Nights on Sunset Strip

1   *LAT*, December 10 and 11, 1966.

2   *LA Free Press*, December 16, 1966.

3   See *LAT* and *LA Herald Examiner*, December 11 and 12, 1966.

4   *Chicago Tribune*, December 28, 1966.

5   See Mike Davis, "As Bad as the H-Bomb," *Dead Cities and Other Tales* (New York: New Press, 2002), 207–25.

6   Teenage prostitution predictably soared during the war years, but all independent girls and young women were branded indiscriminately with the scarlet letter. See Marilyn Hegarty, *Victory Girls, Khaki-Wackies and Patriotutes: The Regulation of Female Sexuality During World War II* (New York: NYU Press, 2010).

7   Edgar Friedenberg and Anthony Bernhard, "The Sunset Strip," *New York Review of Books*, March 9, 1967, 8.

8   Brian Carr, report in *LA Free Press*, October 28, 1966; Friedenberg and Bernhard, "The Sunset Strip," 10.

9   Renata Adler, "Fly Trans-Love Airways," *New Yorker*, February 25, 1967.

10   *LA Free Press*, November 18, 1966; *New York Times*, November 13, 1966.

11   *LAT*, November 13 and 15, 1966.

12   *LA Herald Examiner*, November 15, 1966.

13   *LAT*, November 15, 1966.

14   *LA Free Press*, November 18, 1966.

15   Ibid.

16   Ibid. Vostell, a Rabelaisian giant of the postwar European art world, had organized the first Happening in Paris in 1958. Kaprow brought this genre of improvisational street performance to New York in 1960. He moved to L.A. in 1966 to teach at Chouinard, and the anonymous leafletters were probably his students.

17   *LA Free Press*, November 25, 1966.

18   *LA Free Press*, December 2, 1966.

19   Ibid.

20   *LAT*, November 28 and December 4, 1966.

21   *LAT*, November 28; *LA Free Press*, December 2, 1966

22   *LAT*, November 27, 1966.

23   *LA Free Press*, February 17, 1966. For a history of police harassment

of the alternative press, see *Los Angeles Underground*, July–August 1967, microfilm, underground press collection, Wilson Reference Collection, University Microfilms International, Anne Arbor, MI.

24 *LA Free Press*, February 17, 1967.

25 *LA Underground*, April 1, 1967.

26 *LA Free Press*, February 10, 1967.

27 *LA Free Press*, February 17, 1967.

28 Ibid.

29 *LA Underground*, April 1, 1967.

30 *LA Underground*, July–August 1967; see *LA Free Press*, February 17, 1967 for other complaints about the media blackout.

31 *LAT*, September 1 and 8, 1967. See also "Hippies Hurt More Than Riots in Los Angeles," *American City*, July 1968, 47.

32 Recalled by MD.

22 The Blowouts

1 School board statistics show that Wilson was 76 percent "Hispanic" in 1968: LA Unified School District, "Historical Racial Ethnic Data, 1966–1979," cited in Delores Delgado Bernal, "Chicana School Resistance and Grassroots Leadership: Providing an Alternative History of the 1968 East Los Angeles Blowouts," PhD diss., University of California, Los Angeles, 138n24.

2 "Mexican-American" is used until the Blowouts; afterward, "Chicano," in order to emphasize the abrupt generational redefinition of identity.

3 Mario T. García and Sal Castro, *Sal Castro and the Chicano Struggle for Educational Justice* (Chapel Hill: University of North Carolina Press, 2011), 149. The Chicano movement has many excellent historians but only one great biographer, García. He has combined oral history, selected documents, and his own research to create book-length portraits "closer to a Latin American *testimonio,* involving the collective authorship of scholar and activist than to a personally written autobiography or biography" (Mario T. García, *Memories of Chicano History: The Life and Narrative of Bert Corona* [Berkeley: University of California Press, 1994], 341). In more than twenty books, his subjects have included Ruben Salazar, Raul Ruiz, Gloria Arellanes, Rosalio Muñoz, Sal Castro, Bert Corona, Dolores Huerta, Father Luis Olivares, Frances Esquibel Tywoniak, Cesar Chavez, Luís Leal, Father Virgil Cordano, Raymond Telles, and Richard Cruz—a staggering and unique accomplishment by any measure.

4 García and Castro, *Sal Castro and the Chicano Struggle*, 149.

5 Ibid.

6 There were, of course, other important Mexican-American communities throughout Los Angeles County, many of them urbanized agricultural colonias, but unfortunately, as explained in the introduction, space constraints exclude the broader canvas.

7 "There is no Mexican-American equivalent of the Urban League, and no single organization which can legitimately claim to speak for a large segment of the community. Fragmentation and internecine warfare have rendered many Mexican-American groups impotent. Furthermore, those identified as 'leaders' are often detached from those most in need of assistance and either cannot or will not back strong demands for action" (Paul Bullock, "Employment Problems of the Mexican-American," *Industrial Relations* 3:3 [May 1964], 50).

8 Most outrageous was Westside liberal councilwoman Roz Wyman's proposed raid on the Eastside's green space. She and others, including Yorty, wanted to transform Hazard Park into a VA facility in order to free up park space at the Soldier's Home in Westwood. Wyman had also been the key facilitator of the Dodgers' move into Chavez Ravine. As the first Jew and second woman elected to the council, she was certainly familiar with discrimination and in her early years had been allied with Roybal, but they split far apart as she increasingly became the tribune of "homeowners' rights and a middle-class, suburban and anti-communist vision of metropolitan development centered on leisure and culture" (Barbara Soliz, "Rosalind Wiener Wyman and the Transformation of Jewish Liberalism in Cold War Los Angeles," in *Beyond Alliances: The Jewish Role in Reshaping the Racial Landscape of Southern California*, ed. George Sanchez [West Lafayette, Indiana: Purdue University Press, 2012], 79–80). Would it be far-fetched to see in Wyman's career the emergence of the wealthy liberal lifestyle wing of the California Democratic Party?

9 *LAT*, May 14 and 17, 1965. The proposed district would have included Boyle Heights, City Terrace, Lincoln Heights, Belvedere–East Los Angeles, Pico Rivera, and Montebello.

10 Quoted in Matthew Dallek, *The Right Moment: Ronald Reagan's First Victory and the Decisive Turning Point in American Politics* (New York: Oxford University Press, 2000), 218.

11 *LAT*, July 11, 1967.

12 Shana Bernstein, *Bridges of Reform: Interracial Civil Rights Activism in Twentieth-Century Los Angeles* (New York: Oxford University Press, 2011), 142.

13 Rodolfo F. Acuña, *Anything but Mexican: Chicanos in Contemporary Los Angeles* (London and New York: Verso, 1996), 131.

14 Bert Corona and Mario T. García, *Memories of Chicano History: The Life and Narrative of Bert Corona* (Berkeley: University of California Press, 1994), 224–5.

15 *LAT*, March 29, 1966. At a dinner a month later at the LA Statler Hotel to honor the Albuquerque delegation, Bert Corona proposed a day of protest where students would stay home from schools and "we would refuse to speak English—at least those of us who can still speak Spanish." "His shout, '*Viva la causa* (cause), *viva la raza* (race), *y viva la unidad* (unity),' brought the crowd up with a roar" (*LAT*, May 8, 1966). Thus Corona, an instigator and pioneer in so many things (MAPA, for instance), probably deserves credit for planting the seed of what became the legendary "Day without Mexicans."

16 See, for example, "Income Decline Found in Watts," *New York Times*, March 9, 1966.

17 US Bureau of the Census, "Special Census Survey of the South and East Los Angeles Areas: November 1965," *Current Population Reports—Technical Studies*, series P-23/#7, 23 (Washington, DC: US Government Printing Office, March 1966), 16. Rudy Acuña, analyzing US Census data and statistics from the LA Department of City Panning, emphasizes that Boyle Heights (median income $5,928) was considerably poorer in 1970–74 than more suburban East Los Angeles ($7,622) (Acuña, *Anything but Mexican*, 184).

18 However, MAPA, now under the presidency of Bert Corona, did not in any sense accept a subordinate role in a liberal coalition. It was becoming increasingly critical of the Brown administration's failure to appoint Mexican-Americans to important posts or support them in elections. But it did not see, as some groups did, an alternative in either Reagan or Yorty. It was also less "integrationist" and more rooted in union organizing traditions than LULAC, the Mexican-American equivalent to the NAACP.

19 Billy Mills, usually the most radical voice among the city's Black elected officials, surprised and angered others by supporting Yorty, who in turn appointed him to the EYOA board. As Robert Bauman points out in his history of four iconic community agencies originated in this era, Mills, an advocate of a New Deal–sized solution to the inner-city jobs crisis, was legitimately critical of the modest scale of the proposed LA programs. But Mills was also one of Jesse Unruh's condottiere in the civil war within the California Democratic Party, and Unruh was temporarily aligned with Yorty for opportunistic

reasons (Robert Bauman, *Race and the War on Poverty: From Watts to East L.A.* [Norman: University of Oklahoma Press, 2008], 25–6, 48–9).

20 See, for example, "Latins Ignored, Yorty Agrees," *LAT*, September 27, 1966.

21 *LAT*, October 21 and November 8, 1965.

22 *LAT*, September 16 and 19, 1966.

23 *LAT*, October 10, 1965. The article quoted Ralph Guzmán, a UCLA researcher who claimed that because "it has become fashionable to hire colored people, employers are beginning to turn loose Mexican-Americans." Seventy Eastside community leaders quickly signed a letter denouncing the headline and its imputation of racism.

24 *LAT*, December 18, 1966.

25 In 1969 EYOA had one hundred Black staff members but only thirty-seven Mexican-Americans (Rodolfo F. Acuña, *A Community Under Siege: A Chronicle of Chicanos East of the Los Angeles River, 1945–1975* [Los Angeles: Chicano Studies Research Center Publications, UCLA, 1984], 185).

26 Bradley's biographers write: "Surprisingly, Hispanic areas, which Humphrey had won easily against Nixon less than a year before, had gone overwhelmingly to Yorty" (J. Gregory Payne and Scott C. Ratzan, *Tom Bradley: The Impossible Dream* [Santa Monica: Round-table, 1986], 109).

27 The history of educational discrimination against Mexicans in the Southwest is explored in several studies, but see especially Gilbert Gonzalez, *Chicano Education in the Era of Segregation* (Philadelphia: Balch Institute Press, 1990; Denton: University of North Texas Press, 2003).

28 Quoted in George Sanchez, *Becoming Mexican American: Ethnicity, Culture, and Identity in Chicano Los Angeles, 1900–1945* (Oxford, UK: Oxford University Press, 1995), 96.

29 On the long road toward equal education—a goal that remains ago-nizingly distant today—two of the landmark legal cases with national implications that resulted from grassroots struggles were *Alvarez v. Lemon Grove School District* (1931), the first desegregation court decision in American history; and *Mendez et al. v. Westminister School District* (1947), which became the largely unacknowledged template employed by Thurgood Marshall in *Brown v. Board of Education* (1954).

30 In his memoir, Sal Castro vividly describes the mechanics of a Catholic education that offered no higher aspiration to its Mexican-American

students than becoming a craftsman or soldier (García and Castro, *Sal Castro and the Chicano Struggle*, 46–50).

31 Cited in *LAT*, May 1, 1968.

32 *LAT*, October 22, 1962; May 8, 1966.

33 *New York Times*, August 22, 1966; *LAT*, August 18, 1966.

34 The committee was chaired by radical Episcopal bishop James Pike and included attorney Stephen Reinhardt, who later became a Carter appointee to the US Court of Appeals and, because of his progressive rulings, a favorite target of the Reaganite Right. Adding to his notoriety, he was married to Ramona Ripston, the executive director of the ACLU. In the 1968 press conference Reinhardt expressed some of the optimism of the period by claiming that the report "provides a first step in the direction this state must go—to become a bilingual, bicultural state" (*LAT*, May 1, 1968).

35 See Walter Fogel, "Education and Income of Mexican-Americans in the Southwest," *Advance Report 1*, Mexican American Study Project, November 1965, vii.

36 *LAT*, May 9, 1966. Guzmán is quoted in the first part of a series— "Revolt in the Barrios"—written by Jack Jones, who had previously published a similar series on South Central L.A., "The View from Watts."

37 Los Angeles County Commission on Human Relations, *A 25 Year History 1944–1969 and Biennial Report 1967–1969* (Los Angeles, 1969).

38 "Carlos M. Haro Interviews Sal Castro at UCLA, October 6, 2004," video, UCLA Chicano Studies Research Center, YouTube, youtube. com.

39 In 2004 Castro was interviewed extensively about the role of the Kramer conferences in crystallizing the Chicano movement in L.A.: ibid.

40 The Episcopalian congregations in Los Angeles had the most progressive history of any of the Christian denominations. For instance, during the great war between the *Times* and organized labor at the beginning of the twentieth century, the Episcopalian clergy very demonstrably became paid-up members of the Labor Council. At the beginning of the 1960s, and thanks to the crusading work of a young priest, Nicholas Kouletsis, Epiphany and two other churches, basing themselves on the famous model of the East Harlem Protestant Parish, joined together as the Parish of East Los Angeles with a mission of social reform and support for civil rights. John Luce was brought out from East Harlem to lead the work at Epiphany. Unsurprisingly there was great opposition from some wealthy Anglo Episcopalians,

one of whom, LAPD chief Ed Davis, had earlier complained about Kouletsis: "I should have indicted him for protecting Epiphany." See Will Wauters, "The Borderland Cultures Encounter the Church and a Church Gave Birth to a New Chicano Culture," *Anglican and Episcopal History* 82:4 (December 2013), 396–8.

41 García and Castro, *Sal Castro and the Chicano Struggle*, 144.

42 Raul Ruiz, quoted in Mario T. García, *The Chicano Generation: Testimonios of the Movement* (Berkeley: University of California Press, 2015), 39.

43 Ibid., 108–11.

44 The Northern group included the Mexican American Student Confederation from San Francisco and Oakland, and the Student Initiative from San Jose.

45 Muñoz, in Mario T. García, *Chicano Generation*, 226.

46 García and Castro, *Sal Castro and the Chicano Struggle*, 147.

47 Of all of the movements and protest events of 1960s Los Angeles, the Blowouts alone have garnered continuous attention in memoirs, scholarly publications, a TV series and even a feature-length film. See *Taking Back the Schools*, part 3 of the documentary film series *Chicano! History of the Mexican American Civil Rights Movement*, prod. Susan Racho (Los Angeles: NLCC Educational Media, 1995); and *Walkout!*, feature film, dir. Edward James Olmos, prod. Moctezuma Esparza (New York: HBO Films, 2005), 120 mins.

48 "With me in the 'plot' was a who's who of later key activists and adult leaders: Moctezuma Esparza, Al Juarez, Susan Racho, Carlos Vasquez, Monte Perez, Hank Lopez, Juan Gómez-Quiñones, and a few others" (García and Castro, *Sal Castro and the Chicano Struggle*, 153).

49 *LAT*, March 6, 1968.

50 *LAT*, March 6, 14 and 16, 1968.

51 *LA Free Press*, March 8–10, 1968. Strangely all the dates of events in this cover piece are misreported as a day earlier than their actual occurrence.

52 García and Castro, *Sal Castro and the Chicano Struggle*, 158–9.

53 Carlos Muñoz, interview by Nick García, 2002–3, transcript, in "Carlos Muñoz: Latino Leader and Scholar," Regional Oral History Office, Bancroft Library, University of California, Berkeley, 44.

54 García and Castro, *Sal Castro and the Chicano Struggle*, 169.

55 *LAT*, March 8, 1968.

56 García and Castro, *Sal Castro and the Chicano Struggle*, 173; *LAT*, March 9, 1968 (Jefferson); *LAT*, March 17, 1968 (Fran Spector quoted). Spector's older brother Morgan was a local SDS leader.

57 García and Castro, *Sal Castro and the Chicano Struggle*, 155.

58 Quoted in Ian López, *Racism on Trial: The Chicano Fight for Justice* (Cambridge, MA: Harvard University Press, 2003), 24. In January 1969, a Roosevelt teacher called a student a "dirty Mexican," sparking 600 students to walk out. EICC picketed the school, but thirty-five teachers sent a letter to the Board supporting the teacher (Acuña, *Anything but Mexican*, 191).

59 García and Castro, *Sal Castro and the Chicano Struggle*, 179.

60 Ruiz, quoted in García, *The Chicano Generation*, 147–8.

61 García and Castro, *Sal Castro and the Chicano Struggle*, 180–1. The photo is available at "Parish History," Epiphany Conservation Trust official website, epiphanyconservationtrust.org. Harry Gamboa, at Kennedy's right, gives the "V" sign. See also "Protestant Clergy Leads Fight for Mexican-American Goals," *LAT*, April 5, 1968.

62 García and Castro, *Sal Castro and the Chicano Struggle*, 184–6; *LAT*, March 8, 1968.

63 *LAT*, March 14, 1968. This was a case where the political clout of Black elected officials—particularly an intervention by Tom Bradley—made a significant difference in the outcome.

64 *LAT*, March 13, 1968.

65 It would reclaim that distinction in 1994 with a new, even larger wave of campus walkouts against viciously anti-immigrant Proposition 184.

66 *LAT*, March 17, 1968.

67 García and Castro, *Sal Castro and the Chicano Struggle*, 188–9.

68 *LAT*, March 17, 1968. For Castro's critique of integration that only leads to internal campus segregation, see "Carlos M. Haro Interviews Sal Castro at UCLA."

69 *LAT*, March 27, 1968.

70 John Caughey, *To Kill a Child's Spirit: The Tragedy of School Segregation in Los Angeles* (Itasca, IL: Peacock Publishers, 1973), 255.

71 *LAT*, March 15, 1968 (Rafferty and Venice High); and March 28, 1971 (Wallace).

72 Steven Roberts, "Crackdown in California," *Change* 2:4 (July/August 1970), 7–8.

73 *LAT*, June 2, 1968. The head of the team was Richard Hecht, a deputy DA who in 1962 had played a key role in the arrest and prosecution of Lenny Bruce.

74 1968 Grand Jury, *Final Report to the Board of Supervisors*, mimeograph, n.d., 75. The grand jury also urged an investigation of the Economic Opportunity Program, which supported the enrollment of minority and low-income students on local campuses. It claimed such

programs needed to be closely examined "to determine if qualified persons are being required by any persons or organizations to commit themselves to engage in militant campus activities as a condition precedent to acceptance into such college program" (76).

75 *LAT*, June 22, 1968. The arrests also had a somewhat capricious character, as several of the most active organizers of the walkouts—including Raul Ruiz, Paula Crisostomo, and Vickie Castro—escaped indictment. See Ruiz, in García, *The Chicano Generation*, 49.

76 *LAT*, June 2 and 22, 1968.

77 Younger was defeated by Jerry Brown in 1978.

78 *LAT*, October 8 and 16, 1968.

79 Ruben Salazar chronicled Castro's long struggle in the *Times*: see, for example, October 7, 1969; and January 26, March 20 and July 24, 1970. Salazar was murdered by a sheriff a month later.

23 The Children of Malcolm X

1 Martha Biondi, *The Black Revolution on Campus* (Berkeley: University of California Press, 2012), 2.

2 See Robert Cohen and David J. Snyder, eds., *Rebellion in Black and White: Southern Student Activism in the 1960s* (Baltimore: Johns Hopkins University Press, 2103); on Texas Southern, see Alex LaRotta, "The TSU Riot, 50 years later," *Houston Chronicle*, May 16, 2017.

3 *LAT*, April 22, 1988.

4 Mike Stivers, "Ocean Hill–Brownsville, Fifty Years Later," *Jacobin*, September 12, 2018, Jacobin.com.

5 Jeanne Theoharis, "'W-A-L-K-O-U-T!': High School Students and the Development of Black Power in L.A.," in *Neighborhood Rebels: Black Power at the Local Level*, ed. Peniel Joseph (New York: Palgrave Macmillan, 2010), 109–10.

6 Deborah Soloman, *Jackson Pollock: A Biography* (New York: Cooper Square Press, 2001), 41–2.

7 Joseph McBride, *Frank Capra: The Catastrophe of Success* (London: Faber & Faber, 1993), 51. Capra was a notorious reactionary who zealously collaborated with Hollywood's union busters and anticommunist witch-hunters.

8 Tom Adam Davies, *Mainstreaming Black Power* (Berkeley: University of California Press, 2017), 114–15.

9 "Manual Arts High Typifies Problems in Negro Schools," *LAT*, October 27, 1967. This is a characteristically thoughtful report by

Jack Jones, a white reporter assigned to the "Black beat." As Bill Boyarsky accurately noted in Jones's obituary: He "was a reporter with a real social conscience, and he felt a deep obligation to the poor people he was covering. He just pursued it because it was the right thing to do" (*LAT*, May 15, 2011).

10 *LAT*, September 12, 1967.

11 *LAT*, September 12, 15 and 19, 1967.

12 *LAT*, October 27, 1967.

13 Quoted in K. Adam Powell, *Lyman Bostock: The Inspiring Life and Tragic Death of a Ballplayer* (Lanham, MD: Rowman & Littlefield, 2016), 14. Bostock, one of the most promising ballplayers in the city, was recruited to Valley State College, where he became one of the BSU activists charged with multiple felonies after the occupation of the administration building in 1969.

14 Ibram Rogers, *The Black Campus Movement* (New York: Palgrave Macmillan, 2012), 83; Jonathan Rogers, "A Step to an Olympic Boycott," *Sports Illustrated*, December 4, 1967.

15 Fred Hoffman, "Local High Schools in Turmoil," *LA Free Press*, December 20, 1968.

16 *LAT*, February 22 and March 4, 1968.

17 *LAT*, December 12, 1968.

18 Hoffman, "Local High Schools."

19 Ibid.

20 Ibid.

21 *LAT*, December 12–18, 1968.

22 *LAT*, January 6, 1969.

23 "History of Los Angeles Southwest College," Los Angeles Southwest College official website, lasc.edu.

24 A separate junior college district had not yet come into being.

25 *LAT*, March 16, 1969.

26 *LAT*, February 27, 1969.

27 *LAT*, March 16, 1969.

28 *LAT*, March 8, 1969.

29 *LAT*, March 10, 1969.

30 *LAT*, March 7, 1969.

31 *LAT*, March 12, 1969.

32 Ibid.

33 Bruce Franklin, *M.I.A., Or, Mythmaking in America* (New Brunswick: Rutgers University Press, 1993), 55–6.

34 *LAT*, March 13, April 6, and April 17, 1969; *LA Free Press*, June 13, 1969.

35 *LAT*, March 13 and 14, April 11, and November 29, 1969; *LA Sentinel*, March 20 and April 17, 1969.

36 See Nathaniel Turner, "A 'Lil Joe' Bio," *ChickenBones*, nathaniel turner.com/liljoebio.htm.

37 *LAT*, March 14, 1969.

38 *LAT*, March 13, 1969.

39 *LAT*, March 22, 1969.

40 *LAT*, March 15, 1969.

41 *LAT*, May 29, 1969.

42 *LAT*, October 11, October 18 and November 14, 1969. In his 1980 bestseller *The Last Mafioso*, Ovid Demaris detailed the ties between San Bernardino officials, including Ballard and Police Chief Louis Fortuna, with Mob hit man Joseph Dippolito, aka "Joe Dip." Dippolito was a practitioner of the "Italian rope trick," in which he gave his intended victim a bear hug while an accomplice garroted him from behind. The cadavers were then used as fertilizer in Dippolito's vineyard in Cucamonga. See the account by Joe Blackstock: "Back in 1969, Mafia Leader Got Support from San Bernardino Officials," *Daily Bulletin*, January 1, 2018, dailybulletin.com.

43 *LAT*, July 2, 1969.

24 A "Movement Crusade"

1 Quoted in Raphael J. Sonenshein, *Politics in Black and White: Race and Power in Los Angeles* (Princeton: Princeton University Press, 1993), 93, 95.

2 Quoted in ibid., 88.

3 Campaign literature, "Bradley for Mayor" file, Southern California Library, Los Angeles.

4 *LAT*, March 6, 1969; Milton A. Senn, "Speaking Frankly," *B'nai B'rith Record*, April 1969; "Bradley for Mayor" file, Southern California Library, Los Angeles.

5 Campaign literature, "Bradley for Mayor" file.

6 Ibid.

7 "Street Racers 'Do Their Thing' for Tom," *Bradley Beat*, May 1969, "Bradley for Mayor" file; Bob Kholos, "1969: Tom Bradley and the Man Who Made Him Mayor," *Saigon Bob* (personal blog), saigonbob. typepad.com.

8 Campaign literature, "Bradley for Mayor" file.

9 Ibid. The Labor Committee to Elect Tom Bradley included leaders of the LA County Federation of Labor, the Longshoremen, and Farm

Workers, and the Auto Workers—among them Paul Schrade, western regional director of the UAW, who had been with Bobby Kennedy when he was killed, and himself had been shot at the Ambassador. Bradley's supporters in the labor movement included the striking workers at the *Herald Examiner*—the Pressmen, the Typographers, and other employee unions.

The Women's Committee for Bradley was headed by Doris "Dodo" Meyer, whose father had been the first head of Universal Studios. She had been one of the key organizers of the Black-Jewish coalition that helped elect Bradley to the city council; the *Times* called her "the engine behind the campaign in the Valley." The Women's Committee leadership included the wives of board members from Cedars Sinai Hospital and Hillcrest Country Club. It also included Joan Palevsky (wife of Max), a key left-liberal Democratic fundraiser who would play a pivotal role three years later in the McGovern campaign. The Women's Committee focused on "confronting urban problems"—a euphemism for fighting racism and poverty.

10 *LA Herald Examiner* headline quoted in Bob Kholos, "1969."

11 *LAT*, April 24, 1969.

12 Rothenberg, *Politics*, 91–2; Tom Bradley, interview by Bernard Galm, "The Impossible Dream," oral history transcript, Center for Oral History Research, UCLA, 162–3, available at oac.cdlib.org.

13 *LAT*, May 14, 1969.

14 *LAT*, April 23, 1969.

15 *LAT*, April 25, 1969.

16 Bradley, "The Impossible Dream," 162.

17 *LAT*, May 18, 1969.

18 *LAT*, April 28 and May 18, 1969.

19 Their leader was Leonard K. Firestone, the tire company magnate and member of Reagan's "kitchen cabinet." Members included Thomas P. Pike, Ike's assistant secretary of defense; Taft Schreiber, another member of Reagan's kitchen cabinet; and Laughlin Waters, onetime state Republican Party chairman (Rowland Evans and Robert Novak, "Inside Report: Strange Bedfellows in Bradley Camp," *LAT*, May 8, 1969).

20 *LAT*, May 18, 1969.

21 "Will Your Family Be Safe?," ad in *Hollywood Citizen-News*, May 24, 1969, 104.

22 Campaign literature, "Bradley for Mayor" file.

23 Forman's "Black Manifesto" was reprinted in the *New York Review of Books*, with an introduction by Murray Kempton. "We are demanding

$500,000,000 from the Christian white churches and the Jewish synagogues," Forman wrote. "This total comes to 15 dollars per nigger" (Black National Economic Congress, "Black Manifesto," *New York Review of Books*, July 10, 1969). Forman himself disrupted services at the Riverside Church in Manhattan on May 4, 1969, demanding reparations: George Dugan, "Year-Old 'Reparations' Demand by Blacks Echoes in Churches," *New York Times*, May 4, 1970.

24 *LAT*, May 24 and 26, 1969.
25 "Siege of the City: Yorty Emphasizes Danger," *Hollywood Citizen-News*, May 25, 1969, 1.
26 Bradley, "The Impossible Dream."
27 Sonenshein, *Politics*, 93, table 6.3.
28 Ibid., 93.
29 Ibid., 99.
30 Bradley, "The Impossible Dream."

25 Living in the Lion's Mouth

1 Kathleen Cleaver, "Back to Africa: The Evolution of the International Section of the Black Panther Party," quoted in Charles Jones, ed., *The Black Panther (Reconsidered)* (Baltimore: Black Classic Press, 1998), 236.
2 Senate Select Committee to Study Governmental Operations with Respect to Intelligence Activities, *Final Report*, April 29, 1976 (Washington, DC: US Government Printing Office) (henceforth "Church Committee report"), book II, 15.
3 In the aboveground chain of command, Bunchy's "deputy ministers" were Shermont Banks and John Huggins. Ronald Freeman and "Long John" Washington were field secretaries for Southern California as a whole. There were also several "captains" who ran crews: Roger "Blue" Lewis and Frank "Franco" Diggs. The latter was actually the head of the LA Panther underground. As the result of the assassinations of Diggs, Carter and Huggins in January 1969, Elmer "Geronimo" Pratt would assume, first, command of the underground, then of the entire chapter (Wayne Pharr, *Nine Lives of a Black Panther: A Story of Survival* [Chicago: Chicago Review Press, 2014], 84–5).
4 Elaine Brown, *A Taste of Power: A Black Woman's Story* (New York: Pantheon, 1993), 142.
5 Pharr, *Nine Lives*, 111; Brown, *A Taste of Power*, 142–3; Earl Anthony, *Picking Up the Gun* (New York: Dial Press, 1970), 162.
6 In this period, according to Wayne Pharr, the "underground"

consisted only of "a small squad of three to four people" led by Diggs and Long John Washington (Pharr, *Nine Lives*, 102).

7 *LAT*, August 7, 1968.

8 *LAT*, August 11, 1968; Brown, *A Taste of Power*, 139, 151–2; Anthony, *Picking Up the Gun*, 174–5.

9 *LAT*, August 6 and 7, 1968. For a hearsay account by a contemporary LAPD officer, see D. E. Gray, *The Warrior in Me* (self-published, 2010), 62. FBI documents related to Steve Bartholomew were destroyed in 2004.

10 Anthony, *Picking Up the Gun*, 173.

11 "Exclusive Interview with Earl Anthony," *LA Free Press*, August 9, 1968. There were other witnesses. Two service station attendants caught a few glimpses of the battle, including a Black person standing over a wounded officer, but their testimony in itself did not support or refute either side. See Edward Jay Epstein, "The Black Panthers and the Police: A Pattern of Genocide?," *New Yorker*, February 13, 1971. Epstein, in an article seeking to discredit Panther charges of victimization, relied on police testimony for his description of the event.

12 *LAT*, August 8, 9 and 11, 1968.

13 *LAT*, August 8, 1968.

14 Anthony, *Picking Up the Gun*, 130–1. See also Jasmyne Cannick's interview with Carter's eldest brother, "Interview with Bernie Morris," *Los Angeles Sentinel*, March 28, 2010.

15 Jack Olsen, *Last Man Standing: The Tragedy and Triumph of Geronimo Pratt* (New York: Doubleday, 2000), 39.

16 This was a follow-up and retrospective to previous Kerner-sponsored secret meetings in Virginia in January and February that strategized responses to the unrest foreseen for summer 1968 (*LAT*, October 3, 1968). The assassination of Martin Luther King in April disrupted the planning process, and President Johnson was forced to deploy the regular Army on an unprecedented scale.

17 "Police: The Thin Blue Line," *Time*, July 19, 1968.

18 "Attack Teams" sounded too "aggressive," so the definition of the acronym was changed to "Special Weapons and Tactics" (Clyde Haberman, "The Rise of the SWAT Team in American Policing," *New York Times*, September 8, 2014).

19 Paul Clinton, "Daryl Gates and the Origins of LAPD SWAT," *Police Magazine*, April 16, 2010.

20 *LAT*, February 15 and March 11, 1968. The department did have Thompson submachine guns, a favorite of former police chiefs, in storage.

21 In 1978 the Citizens Commission on Police Repression obtained an official list of organizations under surveillance by the LAPD's Public Disorder Intelligence Division. It contained almost 200 groups, including the SCLC, the National Organization for Women, MAPA, the Gay Community Services Center, and, Reddin's particular *bête noire*, the National Council of Churches (*LAT*, July 19, 1978).

22 Given the competition and enmity between the LAPD and the FBI throughout the Parker years, it's unclear how successful Reddin was in mending relations with Hoover or to what extent their parallel campaigns against the Panthers were based on shared intelligence and coordinated action. Clearly, in some cities—Chicago and San Diego were notable examples—the FBI used the local police as willing henchmen; whether that was also true in L.A., 1968–70, requires further research.

23 Church Committee report, book III, 7, 9, 27.

24 Ibid., book III, 4, 9, 190. A parallel FBI project in Chicago incited the Blackstone Rangers, the Southside's major street gang, against the local Panther chapter.

25 Ibid., 46.

26 Pharr, *Nine Lives*, 103.

27 Ibid., 102–4.

28 This was not just an idealist delusion. In the Chicano studies department at Northridge, chaired by Rudy Acuña, this vision was substantially realized, and the program became a backbone for several generations of political and social activism. Moreover, the industrial relations program at UCLA had provided invaluable research and training, not only to the local labor movement, but also to community groups in Watts and the Eastside.

29 Its primitive first iteration, ARPANET, sent its first message (to Stanford) from UCLA's Bolter Hall in October 1969.

30 As Mike Levett, editor of the *Daily Bruin* in 1969, complained to *Times* columnist Art Seidenbaum: "As soon as we run up against a real issue here, all of a sudden Chuck Young, the chancellor, comes out and says something like, 'before any problems arise, here is my proposal for …' Meanwhile, people are rioting on some other campus over exactly that issue" (Art Seidenbaum, "UCLA: 'Berkeley with Mothers,'" *LAT Magazine*, July 6, 1969).

31 Brown, *A Taste of Power*, 161.

32 Quoted in Olsen, *Last Man Standing*, 45.

33 Brown, *A Taste of Power*, 164.

34 Ibid., 165.

35 *Daily Bruin* (UCLA), February 21, 2015; *LAT*, June 18, 2008. This agrees with the account given by Watani Stiner after his release from San Quentin in 2015, with the exception that Stiner says that Huggins pistol-whipped Jones (*Mercury News*, February 3, 2015).

36 Ward Churchill and Jim Vander Wall, *The COINTELPRO Papers: Documents from the FBI's Secret Wars against Dissent in the United States* (Boston: South End Press, 1991), 42; Churchill, "'To Disrupt, Discredit and Destroy': The FBI's Secret War against the Black Panther Party," in *Liberation, Imagination and the Black Panther Party*, Kathleen Cleaver and George Katsiaficas, eds. (New York: Rout-ledge, 2001), 93; Floyd Hayes and Francis Kiene, "'All Power to the People': The Political Thought of Huey P. Newton and the Black Panther Party," in Jones, *Black Panther Party*, 169; Joshua Bloom and Waldo Martin, *Black Against Empire: The History and Politics of the Black Panther Party* (Berkeley: University of California Press, 2013), 219. The LAPD has spread and continued to purvey misinformation about the Stiners' role. In 2007 *LA Weekly* published a sympathetic portrait of Larry "Watani" Stiner as he awaited his ninth parole hearing. Matthew Fleischer, the reporter, was shown a letter from Chief William Bratton's office that influenced the board to reject his previous application in 2005. "Stiner," the letter reminded the board, "murdered two victims by shooting them with a firearm for unknown reasons." "Of course," exclaimed Fleischer, "Watani was never accused of shooting anyone, leading one to wonder whether Bratton's office even reviewed Stiner's file before finding him unfit for parole" (Fleischer, "Children of the Revolutionary," *LA Weekly*, August 22, 2007).

37 Angela Davis, *Angela Davis: An Autobiography* (New York: Interna-tional Publishers, 1974), 194.

38 *Black Panther*, January 25, 1969.

39 Pharr, *Nine Lives*, 114. The *Times*'s first accounts of the trial also give the impression that there were more than two shooters. Only later did the DA and the newspaper clarify publicly that Hubert and Huggins were the only ones to discharge their guns. See *LAT*, August 12 and 26, 1969.

40 *LAT*, January 22, 1969.

41 Olsen, *Last Man Standing*, 46.

42 *LAT*, February 16, 1969

43 *LA Sentinel*, July 10, 1969.

44 *LAT*, July 24, 1969.

45 *LAT*, September 4, 1969.

46 The Panther press, falsely claiming that Karenga wanted the director-
ship of the program for himself, ranted against the "US plot": "Pork
Chop Nationalism is as guilty as Cain, as scurvy as Brutus, as low lifed
and trifling as Judas," and so on (*Black Panther*, January 25, 1969; see
also *LAT*, January 25, 1969). Unfortunately the Party's press releases
and newspaper articles failed to provide any concrete information or
firsthand testimonies on what actually happened. Geronimo would
reveal years later that he had believed all along that the shooting was
spontaneous, not a carefully concocted plot.

47 Amiri Baraka, *The Autobiography of Leroi Jones* (New York: Lawrence
Hill, 1997), 391. CFUN later became the Committee for a Unified
New Ark.

48 See profile of Swearingen, *LAT*, March 21, 1979.

49 Huey P. Newton, "War against the Panthers: A Study of Repression
in America," PhD diss., Department of History of Consciousness,
UC Santa Cruz, June 1980, available at ouleft.org. Newton, who,
significantly, makes no charge against Karenga, footnotes a 1980
Penthouse article on "Othello" and affidavits by Perry submitted to
Charles Garry and another lawyer. Newton quotes Perry at length
from the Garry affidavit, although he notes that "after approving
both affidavits, Perry failed to show up at the agreed-upon time at the
office of either attorney to execute his sworn statements."

50 Garry affidavit, as quoted in ibid.

51 After five years of repeated attempts on their lives at Quentin, the
Stiners managed to escape from a family visiting center. They fled
to Guyana, and then Larry moved on to Surinam. Like Hubert,
George Stiner never returned home, but Larry, penniless, eventually
extradited himself as part of a deal to allow his new family to settle
in the States. After serving eighteen years of hard time, he finally
emerged, only to tell the same story once again: he and his brother
were not conspirators, Hubert acted alone, and the death of Carter
was a tragedy for all concerned. The Orange County robbery and
any possible connection between it and the later Bank of America
holdup for which US leader James Tayari was convicted—that is to
say, the existence of a secret armed fundraising operation similar to
the one conducted by the Panther underground—are not topics that
Stiner or anyone else has ever addressed in public. On Larry Stiner,
see Julie Caine, "47 Years after Black Panther Killings a Correspondence Heals Old Wounds," *Crosscurrents*, KALW radio, San Francisco,
September 21, 2016, kalw.org.

52 *LA Sentinel*, October 30, 1969.

53 Scot Brown, *Fighting for US* (New York: NYU Press, 2003), 122.

54 It's fascinating that Karenga and Amiri Baraka, in this period allies and staunch anti-Marxists, shared a virtually identical critique of the Panthers with Dorothy Healey. "The Panthers," wrote Healey, "picked up the Maoist slogan 'All power grows out of the barrel of a gun' and made an ideological fetish out of it. That phrase has to be one of the stupidest things Mao ever said, because what power really grows out of is the organized consciousness of millions of people ... revolutionaries are always going to be outgunned by forces defending the old order." Similarly, Baraka scoffed that the Panthers "were misguided dudes who think by saying 'Pick Up the Gun,' that the devil will wither up and die." Karenga and Healey both thought the Panthers' "survival programs" were naïve. "That's not a revolutionary act," said Karenga, "to set up a kitchen and put out food for people, the welfare does that, the bureau of public assistance." Healey agreed: "They function as a kind of freelance social welfare agency, providing free food, clothes, and health care services to the community. We obviously didn't have anything against people receiving those kinds of services, but our idea had always been that the role of radicals was to organize people to demand that such benefits be provided by the government. Radicals shouldn't be in the position of competing with the churches as dispensers of charity" (Baraka and Karenga, in Brown, *Fighting for US*, 108, 112; Dorothy Healey and Maurice Isserman, *Dorothy Healey Remembers: A Life in the American Communist Party* [New York: Oxford University Press, 1990], 211).

55 *LA Sentinel*, March 20, 1969; *LAT*, May 16, 1969.

56 *LAT*, July 3, 1969. Details of their trial are discussed in the ruling on their unsuccessful appeal to the Ninth Circuit: Federal reporter, second series, *Doss v. United States*, 431 F2d 601, September 1970.

57 *LAT*, January 3, 1970. Reddin, in a move that surprised the city, resigned from his post to become the news anchor on KTLA TV, then in 1973 ran for mayor. He performed dismally in the primary and left politics and television to run his own successful security company.

58 Kenneth O'Reilly, *Racial Matters: The FBI's Secret File on Black America, 1960–1972* (New York: Free Press, 1989), 307.

59 "When Black Panthers Roamed San Diego," *San Diego Union-Tribune*, March 4, 2018; and Church Committee report, 32, 192–3, 194–5.

60 Brown, *Fighting for US*, 125.

61 Trial testimony, *LAT*, May 13, 1971.

62 Trial testimony, *LAT*, May 14, 1971.

63 But Karenga's ultimate fate, in contrast to that of Huey Newton, was not a Shakespearean tragedy. After four years in the California Men's Colony in San Luis Obispo, he emerged determined to rebuild both his reputation and US. His success in achieving both goals (he's currently a respected academic, and US is modestly thriving) is testament to a truly remarkable personality.

64 Assemblyman Leon Ralph charged that Reagan's real goal was to keep Blacks out of the studio unions (*LAT*, June 8, 1971).

26 Killing the Panthers

1 *LA Sentinel*, August 14, 1969. Pharr claims that Banks was expelled from the Party: Wayne Pharr, *Nine Lives of a Black Panther: A Story of Survival* (Chicago: Chicago Review Press, 2014), 118.

2 Jack Olsen, *Last Man Standing: The Tragedy and Triumph of Geronimo Pratt* (New York: Doubleday, 2000), 55.

3 Angela Davis, *Angela Davis: An Autobiography* (New York: International Publishers, 1974), 193–4.

4 SWAT would be folded into Metro in 1972.

5 Pharr, *Nine Lives*, 144–8, 160; Elaine Brown, *A Taste of Power: A Black Woman's Story* (New York: Pantheon, 1993), 196.

6 *LAT*, April 26, 1969.

7 *LAT*, August 7, 1969.

8 *The Black Panther*, October 3, 1970.

9 *LAT*, July 4, 1969.

10 Pharr, *Nine Lives*, 160.

11 Ibid., 160–9.

12 *LAT*, July 22, 1969; Joshua Bloom and Waldo Martin, *Black against Empire: The History and Politics of the Black Panther Party* (Berkeley: University of California Press, 2013), 300–1.

13 In March four white supporters of the Panthers, three of them members of the Cal State Fullerton SDS chapter, had been arrested in the desert near Twentynine Palms, and charged with burglarizing twenty-nine firearms from a Corona sporting goods store. The nonstudent in the group was Stanley Quast, a conscientious objector and draftee from Anaheim who had just completed a two-year sentence at Leavenworth for refusing to wear his uniform. At a preliminary hearing one of the defendants confessed that the stolen weapons had been turned over to the Panthers. Several of the stolen guns were identified in the cache seized in the attack on the Panther's Central Avenue office in December. See *LAT*, March 21 and December 9,

1969, and January 28, 1970; and *Corona Daily Independent*, February 19, 1970.

14 Brown, *A Taste of Power*, 209–10. See also David Hilliard, *Huey: Spirit of the Panther* (New York: Thunder's Mouth Press, 2006), 178–9. Other Hollywood allies included Elliot Gould, Barbra Streisand, and Shirley MacLaine.

15 Duncan Campbell, "How the FBI Used a Gossip Columnist to Smear a Movie Star," *Guardian*, April 22, 2002.

16 Gossip columnists were publishers' hired assassins, and Norman Chandler unleashed Hopper against the Left in Hollywood—particularly against their shared nemeses, Dalton Trumbo and Charlie Chaplin.

17 *LAT*, July 19, 1970.

18 *LA Free Press*, July 10, 1970; *LAT*, October 3, 1969, and March 4, 1970. On the Geronimo/Jarrett connection, see the special report by Roy Haynes in *LAT*, June 21, 1970.

19 *LAT*, March 4 and June 21, 1970; *LA Free Press*, July 10, 1970; Frank Donner, *Protectors of Privilege: Red Squads and Police Repression in Urban America* (Berkeley: University of California Press, 1990), 262–3.

20 Pharr, *Nine Lives*, 163; *LAT*, September 4, 1969.

21 *LAT*, September 9, 1969; *LAT*, May 5 and June 21, 1970; and Romaine "Chip" Fitzgerald, available at prisonersolidarity.net.

22 *LAT*, January 23, 1970. At the time of the raid, however, the LAPD gave the press a different legal justification for their actions: ten days earlier the acting commander of the Newton Division had gone to the headquarters to ask the Panthers to turn down the volume on a loud-speaker and was supposedly threatened by two gun-toting members (*LAT*, December 9, 1969).

23 Pharr, *Nine Lives*, 6.

24 Matthew Fleischer, "Policing Revolution: How the LAPD's First Use of SWAT—a Massive, Military-Style Operation against the Black Panthers—Was Almost Its Last," *LA Times Magazine*, April 2011.

25 *LAT*, December 9, 1969; Matthew Fleischer, "Policing Revolution."

26 *LAT*, January 21 and April 2, 1970.

27 *LA Free Press*, December 12, 1969.

28 *Sentinel*, December 11, 1969.

29 *LA Free Press*, December 19, 1969.

30 *LAT*, December 12, 1969.

31 *Sentinel*, December 11, 1969.

32 *LAT*, April 26, 1970.

33 I (MD) was there and vividly recall the extraordinary demonstration of power that took place: there was a general sense, shared by nervous cops and officials, that if the crowd had decided to seize city hall, nothing could have stopped them.

34 Quoted in Bloom and Martin, *Black against Empire*, 345.

35 Akinyele Umoja, "Repression Breeds Resistance: The Black Liberation Army and the Radical Legacy of the Black Panther Party," in *Liberation, Imagination, and the Black Panther Party*, eds. Kathleen Cleaver and George Katsiaficas (New York: Routledge, 2001), 10.

36 Errol Henderson, "Shadow of a Clue," in Cleaver and Katsiaficas, *Liberation*, 205.

27 Free Angela!

1 Ironically, the department's reputation was primarily as a world-class center for mathematical logic; hence the visiting professorships given to the field's giants—Russell and later Rudolf Carnap. Kalish was a logician.

2 Appropriately, UCLA later designated Meyerhoff Park as the campus's free speech area.

3 Dorothy Healey and Maurice Isserman, *Dorothy Healey Remembers: A Life in the American Communist Party* (New York: Oxford University Press, 1990), 215.

4 *LAT*, October 3, 1969.

5 *LAT*, September 19, 1969.

6 *LAT*, October 9, 1969.

7 *LAT*, October 3, 1969.

8 *LAT*, October 4, 1969.

9 "DB Editorial: Don't Riot—Yet," *Daily Bruin* (UCLA), October 6, 1969.

10 It was the same slogan used the previous year when a guest lecture by Eldridge Cleaver had been canceled at Berkeley—testimony to the statewide level of organization of the BSU.

11 *LAT*, October 7, 1969.

12 UCLA Student Legislative Council to UCLA Academic Senate, October 7, 1969, in Leon Letwin archive, leonletwin.wordpress.com.

13 *LAT*, October 9, 1969.

14 *LAT*, October 21, 1969.

15 Pacht's ruling was overturned on appeal, when the Ninth Circuit ordered the venue moved to Alameda County, legal home of the regents. The court there also ruled in Angela's favor.

16 *LAT*, October 10, 1969.

17 *LAT*, October 15, 1969.

18 *LAT*, December 15, 1969.

19 "Red UCLA Teacher Flays Regents for 'Racism,'" *Independent* (Rancho Park), October 9, 1969, in Leon Letwin archive.

20 Angela Davis, *An Autobiography* (New York: International Publishers, 1974), 226.

21 *LAT*, December 9, 1969, 1; Jon Wiener, "Police Lay Siege to Los Angeles Panther Office," *Liberation News Service* 217, December 10, 1969, 13. *Liberation News Service* declared the Panthers had succeeded at their strategy of holding off the police from 5:30 a.m. to almost 10:30 to allow time for the community and the media to gather as witnesses, who would deter the police from killing them when the Panthers surrendered. Jon Wiener, "Los Angeles Blacks Speak Out against Pig Attack on Panthers," *Liberation News Service* 218, December 13, 1969, 21.

22 Davis, *Autobiography*, 238; the *LA Times* said "5,000 or more": *LAT*, December 13, 1969.

23 Davis, *Autobiography*, 238; *LAT*, December 13, 1969.

24 Davis, *Autobiography*, 240; *LAT*, December 13, 1969.

25 *LAT*, January 8, 1970.

26 *LAT*, April 19, 1970.

27 *LAT*, May 14, 1970.

28 Wallace Turner, "California Regents Drop Communist from Faculty," *New York Times*, June 20, 1970.

29 *LAT*, June 20, 1970.

30 Ibid.

31 Julius Lester, "Black Rage to Live," *New York Times Book Review*, November 20, 1970.

32 Davis, *Autobiography*, 251.

33 Healey and Isserman, *Dorothy Healey Remembers*, 217.

34 See, for example, *Liberation News Service*, October 26, 1970, available at Duke University Library, Women's Liberation Movement Print Culture collection, library.duke.edu.

35 *Life* Magazine, September 11, 1970.

36 Bettina Aptheker, *The Morning Breaks: The Trial of Angela Davis* (Ithaca: Cornell University Press, 1977), 27.

37 Sandra E. Garcia, "Aretha Franklin, Civil Rights Stalwart," *New York Times*, August 17, 2018.

38 Aptheker, *The Morning Breaks*, 28.

39 James Baldwin, "An Open Letter to My Sister, Miss Angela Davis,"

November 19, 1970; *New York Review of Books*, January 7, 1971.

40 Aptheker, *The Morning Breaks*, 28.

41 *LAT*, January 3, 1971. According to Wikipedia, there were "more than 200 local committees" in the United States as of February 1971.

42 The Stanford University Library bought the letters collection from Angela in 1974; the Stanford archives description notes that "many are form letters," and reports that, "when the collection was received by Stanford University, the majority of the letters had never been opened" (Stanford Libraries, "National United Committee to Free Angela Davis records, circa 1970–1972," searchworks.stanford.edu).

43 Sol Stern, "The Campaign to Free Angela Davis," *New York Times*, June 27, 1971.

44 Healey and Isserman, *Dorothy Healey Remembers*, 218.

45 *Black Panther*, August 21, 1970, 1.

46 Aptheker, *The Morning Breaks*, new introduction.

47 Healey and Isserman, *Dorothy Healey Remembers*, 219.

48 "Remember August 7," *Free Angela* 1:10 (August 1, 1971).

49 "Plot Denied," UPI report, August 15, 1970.

50 *LAT*, November 23, 1970.

51 *LAT*, August 29, 1970.

52 All fundraising info above: Southern California Library, Angela Davis Collection, box 1, series 2, folder 1.

53 *LAT*, June 6, 1971.

54 *LAT*, March 5, 1972.

55 *LAT*, June 10, 1972.

56 Davis, *Autobiography*, 398.

57 Ibid.

58 *Guardian*, July 29, 1972, quoted in Healey and Isserman, *Dorothy Healey Remembers*, 221.

59 Davis, *Autobiography*, xv.

60 Healey and Isserman, *Dorothy Healey Remembers*, 219–20.

28 The Ash Grove and the Gusanos

1 The Shell bombing seems to have been a mistake—"the company does not engage in trade with Cuba," the *Times* reported, so "why Shell Oil Co. was struck remains a mystery to police and Shell officials" (*LAT*, October 29, 1968).

2 *LAT*, March 13, 1970; "Three Cubans Hunted in Coast Bombing," *New York Times*, August 1, 1968.

3   *LAT*, October 29, 1968.

4   Marilyn Katz, undated memoir (2017), in authors' possession.

5   Jon Wiener, "Los Angeles Movement Center Attacked, Burned by Cuban Exiles," *Liberation News Service*, April 15, 1970, 2–3.

6   "Cuban Rightists Target SWP," *Militant*, June 10, 2003, themilitant. com.

7   Ed Pearl, interview, n.d., Activist Video Archive, activistvideoarchive.org; Rebecca Kuzins, "The Last Coffeehouse," *Los Angeles Magazine*, February 1985, 216.

8   *LAT*, September 9, 1969. *LAT*, January 24, 1967; *LAT*, September 26, 1969. The playlist is typical, rather than specific to their opening night.

9   *LAT*, July 4, 1968.

10 Alan Bershaw, "Liner Notes," *The Chambers Brothers at the Ash Grove*, Bill Graham Archives, available at concertvault.com.

11 *LAT*, December 5, 1993; Linda Ronstadt, interview in *Los Angeles Times*, December 5, 1993, available at ronstadt-linda.com/artlat93.

12 John Einarson, *Mr. Tambourine Man: The Life and Legacy of the Byrds' Gene Clark* (Montclair, NJ: Backbeat Books, 2005), 43.

13 Dave Alvin, interview, ca. 2007, *The Ash Grove*, documentary film, Ash Grove documentary, available at ashgrovefilm.com/quotes. html/.

14 The 1963 performance was recorded—they played Big Bill Broonzy, Mississippi John Hurt, and Leadbelly, and did a great duet on "Betty and Dupree." See Alan Bershaw, "Jackie DeShannon and Ry Cooder," *Paste*, June 9, 2011, paste.com.

15 *LAT*, June 29, 1965; Denise Sullivan, *Keep on Pushing: Black Power Music from Blues to Hip-Hop* (Chicago: Lawrence Hill, 2011), 38. Wikipedia reports that "They were early contemporaries of the famous LA band the Byrds and fans often wondered, before Tambourine Man hit, which band would be the biggest success. Their recorded material became widely bootlegged and nearly three decades later was eventually released by Columbia Records under the title *Rising Sons Featuring Taj Mahal and Ry Cooder* (New York: Columbia, 1992). Ry would soon become one of the greatest guitar players of the era, and had a monster worldwide hit in 1997 with the *Buena Vista Social Club* album and film, recorded and filmed in Cuba with old-time Cuban musical masters. Taj Mahal became one of the young American heroes of blues and world music.

16 Bob Dylan, *Chronicles*, vol. 1 (New York: Simon & Schuster, 2005), 60.

17 *LAT*, February 8, 1962; *LAT*, June 20, 1967.

18 Cash's performance took place in March 1964: Gordy Alexandre, interview by JW, August 19, 2014; Peter F. Feldman, "Old Time Hits the Big Time in Hollywood USA," *Old-Time Herald* 5:8 (summer 1997), oldtimeherald.org.

19 Ed Pearl, interview by Victor Cohen, February 15, 2009, typescript in JW's possession.

20 Ash Grove official website, ashgrovemusic.com.

21 FSM benefit at the Ash Grove, December 10–16, 1964. See Free Speech Movement Archives, fsm-a.org. Anti-nuclear protest also made the agenda: In June 1967, after white blues singer Barbara Dane sang Tom Paxton's song "Lyndon Johnson told the nation / 'Have no fear of escalation,'" she closed with her own version of the Fugs classic, "Nothing." When Tuli Kupferberg sang it, it went "Monday nothing, Tuesday nothing, Wednesday Thursday nothing." But Dane changed the words: "Monday napalm, Tuesday napalm, Wednesday Thursday napalm" (Alan Bershaw, "Liner Notes," *Barbara Dane at the Ash Grove: June 30, 1967*, concertvault.com).

22 Ed Pearl, interview by Victor Cohen, February 7, 2009, typescript in JW's possession.

23 *LAT*, June 13, 1967.

24 See "Jayne Cortez," Poetry Foundation official website, poetry-foundation.org. Before her Ash Grove work, she had been married to Ornette Coleman—they divorced in 1964. Following her death in 2012, the Spring 2013 issue of *Black Scholar* (v. 43, no. 1/2), was dedicated to her memory and work. See also Daniel Widener, *Black Arts West: Culture and Struggle in Postwar Los Angeles* (Raleigh: Duke University Press, 2010).

25 Ed Pearl interview, n.d., Activist Video Archive.

26 *LAT*, May 27, 1969.

27 *LAT*, June 9, 1969.

28 *LAT*, August 17, 1969.

29 Gordy Alexandre, interview by JW, August 19, 2014.

30 Alex LaRue, "Ash Grove: Folk's L.A. Stomping Ground," *Daily Bruin* (UCLA), April 16, 2008.

31 Dennis Levitt, "Ash Grove Firebombed; Cuban Exiles Strike Again," *LA Free Press*, June 12, 1970.

32 The *LA Times* spelled their names "Renaldo Castro," "Mario Pelaz," and "Renaldo Gonzales": *LAT*, June 8, 1970.

33 Dennis Levitt, "Ash Grove Arson Hearing; Four Cubans Charged," *LA Free Press*, July 10,1970. See also *LAT*, June 8, 1970.

34 Memo, US Department of Justice to FBI, "Cuban Representation

in Exile (RECE)," Miami, FL, July 13, 1965, available at nsarchive2. gwu.edu.

35 Plan Torrente: "Cuban Exile Terrorism," Cuban Information Archives, cuban-exile.com; Círculo Güinero: "Traitors' Gallery," Círculo Güinero de Los Ángeles, circuloguinero.org.

36 Bail had been set at $18,000 for each of the three arsonists, a total of $54,000—requiring a payment to the bail bondsman of 10 percent, $5,400 (*La Actualidad Politica*, July 1970, quoted and cited in Della Rosa, "Cuban Terrorists Jump Bail," *LA Free Press*, November 6, 1970). The magazine was edited by Salvador Rodríguez Santana.

37 Forty-two years later, in a 2012 interview, Ed Pearl said that "they were caught years later during Watergate, in Florida, in Miami, in New York and Connecticut, and they were hauled back to Los Angeles, and they went to San Quentin." No print source supports this statement. Ed Pearl interview, n.d., Activist Video Archive.

38 *LAT*, April 23, 1971.

39 *LAT*, September 3, 1971; "Mechicano Art Center," *Departures* blog, November 7, 2011, KCET, kcet.org/socal/departures. See also Barry Schwartz, interview by Victor Franco, July 1972, Smithsonian Archives of American Art, aaa.si.edu.

40 *LAT*, October 29, 1971.

41 *LAT*, April 29, 1972.

42 *LAT*, June 12, 1972.

43 *LAT*, December 20, 1973.

44 Harry Shearer, email interview by JW, November 21, 2014.

45 Dennis Levitt, email interview by JW, August 30, 2014.

46 Harry Shearer, email interview.

47 *LAT*, June 8, 1970.

48 Ed Pearl has said in several more recent interviews that he believes the third fire was "planned in the basement of the White House" in 1972 to sabotage left-wing efforts to organize demonstrations at the 1972 Republican National Convention, which was originally planned for San Diego. "They wanted to take care of all the gathering spots in Los Angeles," he said, and that's why the Ash Grove was burned. This doesn't make sense on the face of it. The third fire was Nov. 11, 1973, a full year after Nixon had been reelected. If the plan was to sabotage demonstration plans for the Republican convention, they were 15 months too late. (Ed Pearl, interview by Victor Cohen, March 7, 2009, transcript in JW's possession; Feldman, "Old Time Hits the Big Time").

49   Ed Pearl, interview by Victor Cohen, January 17, 2009, transcript in JW's possession.

29 "The Last Place That Sort of Thing Would Happen"

1   In 1972 the name was changed to California State University, Northridge—"Cal State Northridge," or "CSUN." The most thorough history is in Jean-Paul deGuzman, "'And Make the San Fernando Valley My Home,'" PhD diss., UCLA, 2014.

2   Marc Cooper, interview by JW, January 5, 2017.

3   *LAT*, September 15, 1969.

4   Police in Houston arrested 488 students at Texas Southern on May 17, 1967, charging five with conspiracy and incitement to riot. All five were exonerated because of "insufficient evidence" (Alex LaRotta, "The TSU Riot, 50 years later," *Houston Chronicle*, May 16, 2017). In protests on LA college campuses, other felony charges included five SDS members at UCLA who were charged in 1970 with false imprisonment for sitting-in seeking the rehiring of a Black cafeteria worker ("Trial Today in Brugger Case," *Daily Bruin* [UCLA], May 19, 1970). The five—including Jim Prickett—defended themselves in Santa Monica Superior Court and were eventually found guilty of false imprisonment and conspiracy, and sentenced to probation with severe restrictions on campus political activity. They appealed, and the probation conditions were modified (*People v. Arvanites*, 17 Cal. A3d 1052 [Cal. Ct. A1971]).

5   At UCLA the largest was seventy-four arrests on May 5, 1970, after the invasion of Cambodia and the Kent State killings ("Activism through the Years," *Daily Bruin*, February 22, 1996). At San Francisco State, 449 people were arrested in the strike for Black Studies on January 23, 1969. At Berkeley, 800 were arrested in the Free Speech Movement on December 3, 1964.

6   *LAT*, January 29, 1970.

7   Marc Cooper interview.

8   Kirkpatrick Sale, *SDS* (New York: Random House, 1973), 302–3.

9   Ibid., 468.

10 Ina Schneider, "200 'walkout' to attend forum," *Daily Sundial* (San Fernando Valley State College), October 19, 1967; Pat Bryant, "CIA Recruit Visit to VSC Called Off," *San Fernando Valley Times*, November 15, 1967, both quoted in deGuzman, "'And Make the San Fernando Valley,'" 179.

11 *LAT*, May 26, 1967.

12 *LAT*, September 21, 1998.

13 Sale, *SDS*, 486.

14 Mike Lee, oral history, October 20, 1977, California State University Northridge, Oviatt Library, Urban Archives General Oral Histories Collection, 1967–2004, series 1B: Reel-to-Reel Tapes, 1968–1986, box 3, item 1 (hereafter, "Mike Lee Oral History").

15 *LAT*, November 5, 1968.

16 Ibid.

17 *LAT*, November 7 and 8, 1968. Torgerson was later killed in Honduras covering the Sandinistas: Barbara Crossette, "Two American Journalists Killed at Border, Honduran Army Says," *New York Times*, June 22, 1983.

18 *LAT*, December 21, 1968; David Nevin, "Uneasy Peace at Valley State," *Life Magazine*, March 4, 1969.

19 "NAACP Defends College Students," *Crisis*, November 1969, 368–70.

20 *LAT*, November 8, 1968.

21 "Reagan Praises Blomgren," *Daily Sundial*, November 6, 1968.

22 "Senate Revokes BSU Charter," *Daily Sundial*, November 6, 1968.

23 Mike Lee oral history; Cliff Fried, oral history, November 9, 1977, California State University Northridge, Oviatt Library, Urban Archives General Oral Histories Collection, 1967–2004, series 1B: Reel-to-Reel Tapes, 1968–1986, box 2, item 11.

24 Mike Lee oral history.

25 Ibid.

26 *LAT*, November 16, 1968.

27 *LAT*, November 28, 1968.

28 *LAT*, December 11, 1968.

29 *LAT*, January 8, 1968.

30 *LAT*, January 9, 1969.

31 D. T. Oviatt, "A State of Emergency Has Been Ordered by the Acting President," January 9, 1968, ACLU-SC Records, quoted in deGuzman, "'And Make the San Fernando Valley,'" 202.

32 Marc Cooper interview.

33 Mike Davis, email to JW, November 25, 2017.

34 *LAT*, January 10, 1969; "VSC Campus Blood Bath Plan Bared," *San Fernando Valley Times*, January 14, 1969, cited in deGuzman, "'And Make the San Fernando Valley,'" 202.

35 *LAT*, January 16, 1969.

36 *LAT*, February 2, 1969.

37 *LAT*, January 26, 1969.

38 Quoted in Greenwood, "How Valley State Moved."

39 *LAT*, January 24, 1969, quoted in Martha Biondi, "Student Protest, 'Law and Order,' and the Origins of African American Studies in California," in *Contested Democracy: Freedom, Race, and Power in American History*, eds. Manisha Sinha and Penny Von Eschen (New York: Columbia University Press), 269.

40 *LAT*, February 2, 1969.

41 *LAT*, January 18, 1969.

42 Mike Lee oral history.

43 Petition quoted in Biondi, "Student Protest," 269.

44 Biondi, "Student Protest," 270.

45 *LAT*, April 11, 1969.

46 *LAT*, September 15, 1969.

47 *LAT*, November 6, 1969.

48 *New York Times*, quoted in Biondi, 270.

49 "How to Play Valley State," *LA Free Press*, October 3–10, 1969, 1 (repr. from Valley State College *Sundial*). The same issue featured Mike Lee, "Valley State Black Students' Trial Begins," also on 1.

50 *LAT*, November 19, 1969.

51 *LAT*, November 20, 1969.

52 *LAT*, January 31, 1970.

53 Rodolfo F. Acuña, *The Making of Chicana/o Studies* (New Brunswick: Rutgers University Press, 2011), 48.

54 Ibid.

55 Ibid., 50, 52.

56 Ibid., 51.

57 Ibid., 52.

58 Ibid., 66.

59 Ibid., 92.

60 Ibid., 95.

61 Ibid., 98.

62 Ibid.

63 Ibid., 97.

64 Marc Cooper interview; Stu Simmons, "MECHA Loses Campus Home," *Daily Sundial*, May 11, 1970. Acuña says only that a silent march took place, which "solidified the group" and "gave it an identity" (98).

65 *LAT*, May 7, 1970.

66 Rudy Acuña, email to JW, December 12, 2017.

67 Marc Cooper interview.

68 Sale, *SDS*, 468.

69 Marc Cooper interview.

70 One result of "the all-out invasion of SDS by the Progressive Labor party" in 1967–68, Kirkpatrick Sale reports, was that "UCLA's SDS chapter was wholly PL controlled" (Sale, *SDS*, 468).

71 Mike Lee, oral history.

72 Earl Anthony, *The Time of the Furnaces: A Case Study of Student Revolt* (New York: Dial Press, 1971), 32–3.

73 Biondi, "Student Protest," 261; Anthony, *Time of the Furnaces*, 26–7, 21–3.

74 Harry Edwards, *The Revolt of the Black Athlete* (New York: Free Press, 1969).

75 Biondi, "Student Protest," 261.

76 Ibid., 259–60.

77 *LAT*, June 24, 1969.

78 Ibid.

79 Acuña, *Making of Chicana/o Studies*, 96.

30 The Battle for the Last Poor Beach

1 *LAT*, November 5, 1967.

2 Miami and Waikiki as models for a future Venice Beach were discussed by a member of the Santa Monica Redevelopment Agency: Carolyn See, "Venice: The Last Poor Beach," *LAT*, November 5, 1967. See also *LAT*, March 12, 1967; July 14, 1968; and July 28, 1969.

3 Gary Kavanagh, "Santa Monicas That Weren't," *Streetsblog LA*, August 2, 2013, la.streetsblog.org.

4 *LAT*, March 28, 1965.

5 John Haag, "Free Venice!," *Free Venice Beachhead* 1:1 (December 1, 1968), 3.

6 "Venice Political Activist and Poet John Haag Dies," *Argonaut*, April 6, 2006.

7 Haag, "Free Venice!"; John Arthur Maynard, *Venice West: The Beat Generation in Southern California* (New Brunswick: Rutgers University Press, 1991), 162–3.

8 "A Parade Was Planned," *Beachhead*, July 1969, special, 6.

9 Ibid.

10 Ibid.

11 Lynn and Walter Davis, "Meanwhile, Back at the Front …," *Beachhead*, July 1969, special, 8.

12 Carol Fondiller, "Hog Wild Weekend," *Beachhead*, May 1969, 3.

13 *LAT*, April 21, 1969.

14 John Haag, "Do Not Co-operate with Organized Crime," *Beachhead*, May 1969, 4.

15 Yitzak Gershman, "Open Letter to the People of Venice," *Beachhead*, May 1969, 4.

16 John Haag, "Free Venice from the Master Plan," *Beachhead*, June 1969, 1; *LAT*, June 1, 1969.

17 *LAT*, August 3, 1969.

18 *LAT*, December 7, 1969.

19 *LAT*, December 17, 1969; May 7, 1970.

20 *LAT*, November 2, 1969. The ACLU also transported people to court, helped arrested people win release on their own recognizance (instead of having to pay bail), took people to visit relatives in other jails, worked with employers of arrested people to try to keep their jobs— and ran frequent know-your-rights sessions, often at high schools.

21 *LAT*, November 3, 1968.

22 *LAT*, October 31, 1968.

23 *LAT*, November 5, 1967.

24 *LAT*, November 30 and May 21, 1969. The head of the OEO at that point was Donald Rumsfeld: Frank Gannon, "21 April 1969: RN + DR = OEO," Richard Nixon Foundation official website, April 21, 2011, nixonfoundation.org.

25 M. Wesley Swearingen, *FBI Secrets: An Agent's Exposé* (Boston: South End Press, 1995), 71.

26 Terri Volpin, "Community Law," *Beachhead*, June 1969, 4.

27 Swearingen, *FBI Secrets*, 77.

28 Tim Findley, "Farewell to the Fifth Amendment," *Rolling Stone*, December 7, 1972.

29 Swearingen, *FBI Secrets*, 75.

30 Findley, "Farewell."

31 Abramson was later played by Edie Falco in a TV show about the Menendez Brothers trial, in which she had been a defense attorney.

32 Swearingen, *FBI Secrets*, 78.

33 Robin Hembel, "First Annual Venice Canal Festival," *Beachhead*, October 1969, 1.

34 Andrew Deener, *Venice: A Contested Bohemia in Los Angeles* (Chicago: University of Chicago Press, 2012), 52–5.

35 Mike Davis, in Deener, *Venice*: quoted on back cover.

31 Generation Chicano

1 For Montes's story, see Ben Ehrenreich, "Never Stop Fighting," *Los Angeles Magazine*, March 1, 2012.

2 See, for example, "Hotel Fire Indictments Reveal Heroism of Rookie Policeman," *LAT*, June 7, 1969. Under heavy cross-examination by Acosta, Sumaya "admitted that he once participated in the fire bombing of a Safeway store in East Los Angeles and was not arrested, though the bomb thrower was (based on information supplied by Sumaya)" (*LAT*, August 5, 1971). At various times there were four other undercover agents, LAPD and a sheriff's deputy, inside the Berets. See Jennifer Correa, "Chicano Nationalism: The Brown Berets and Legal Social Control," MA thesis, criminology, Oklahoma State University, 2006, available at academia.edu. Correa studied all 1,200 pages of the Berets' FBI file and offers a fascinating account of law enforcement provocations used to brand the group as violent.

3 Mario T. García, *Memories of Chicano History: The Life and Narrative of Bert Corona* (Berkeley: University of California Press, 1994), 197–9, original emphasis.

4 On the perpetuation of Mexico's colonial caste hierarchy and the internalization of anti-Indian racism within Mexican-American families and communities, see Rodolfo F. Acuña, *Anything but Mexican: Chicanos in Contemporary Los Angeles* (London and New York: Verso, 1996), 8–10.

5 This caesura, of course, was never complete, and the 1968 Mexican student movement, in particular, had some impact on Chicano thinking. Moreover, the CASA group that emerged at the beginning of the 1970s out of a support movement for undocumented immigrants led by Bert Corona had important contacts with both the Mexican Left and the Puerto Rican Socialist Party. It celebrated *mexicanidad* and heavily criticized the "separatist" strain in Chicano ideology.

6 Ramon Gutierrez, "'Internal Colonialism': An American Theory of Race," *Du Bois Review* 1:2 (2004), 288; Juan Gómez-Quiñones, "Plan de San Diego Reviewed," *Aztlán* 1:1 (1970), 124–32.

7 For background see Ernest Vigil, *The Crusade for Justice: Chicano Militancy and the Government's War on Dissent* (Madison: University of Wisconsin Press, 1999).

8 The special contribution of Alurista was acknowledged by all. In preparation for the Denver conference, he had focused on a chapter in León-Portilla: "Alurista immediately grasped the significance of the text: the alleged geographical location of Aztlán and its potential

as a unifying metaphor. Above all, he felt elated at having found a common denominator with the claims of the *locos, pochos, pachucos, cholos,* and other mestizos. The socioeconomic debate was awarded a spiritual dimension and a dynamism that were sadly lacking" (Eyette Benjamin-Labarthe, "The Vicissitudes of Aztlán," in *Aztlán: Essays on the Chicano Homeland,* eds. Rudolfo Anaya, Francisco A. Lomelí, and Enrique R. Lamadrid (Albuquerque: University of New Mexico Press, 2017), 185.

9   Jesús Treviño, *Eyewitness: A Filmmaker's Memoir of the Chicano Movement* (Houston: Arte Público Press, 2001), 106.

10 Jorge Klor de Alva, "The Invention of Ethnic Origins and the Negotiation of Latino Identity, 1969–1981," in *Challenging Fronteras: Structuring Latina and Latino Lives in the U.S.,* eds. Mary Romero, Pierrette Hondagneu-Sotelo, and Vilma Ortiz (New York: Routledge, 1997), 60.

11 George Mariscal, *Brown-Eyed Children of the Sun: Lessons from the Chicano Movement, 1965–1976* (Albuquerque: University of New Mexico Press, 2005), 45, 63.

12 Rodolfo F. Acuña, *A Community under Siege: A Chronicle of Chicanos East of the Los Angeles River, 1945–1975* (Los Angeles: UCLA Chicano Studies Research Center Publications, 1984), 137.

13 In 1971 Ralph Guzmán, one of the founders of the Community Service Organization, published "Mexican American Casualties in Vietnam," a summary of his research in official casualty lists. It fully confirmed community perceptions that Chicanos were paying a disproportionate price for the war. Roughly 10 percent of the population, they constituted one-fifth of the dead and wounded (published in *La Raza* 1:1 [1971]).

14 Quoted in Mario T. García and Sal Castro, *Blowout!: Sal Castro and the Chicano Struggle for Educational Justice* (Chapel Hill: University of North Carolina Press, 2011), 123.

15 Muñoz, quoted in Mario T. García, *The Chicano Generation: Testimonios of the Movement* (Berkeley: University of California Press, 2015), 249.

16 The revolt of Beret women is analyzed in Dionne Espinoza's important article, "'Revolutionary Sisters': Women's Solidarity and Collective Identification among Chicana Brown Berets in East Los Angeles, 1967–1970," *Aztlán: A Journal of Chicano Studies* 26:1 (Spring 2001).

17 *LAT,* December 21, 1969.

18 Muñoz, quoted in García, *Chicano Generation,* 253.

19 Ibid., 249.

20 *LAT*, March 29, 1970.

21 The fight occurred after a football game between Salesian and Bell Gardens High. "Rodriguez got involved when a friend was attacked. He admitted wielding a crowbar. 'There were 100 of them and two of us,' he said" (*LAT*, March 29, 1970).

22 *LAT*, March 20–1, 1970. When commission members went to Roosevelt to investigate conditions, they were turned away by Perez. The following February the entire commission resigned after the board refused to consider letting Sal Castro return to an Eastside high school (*LAT*, February 19, 1971).

23 *LAT*, March 7 and 11–13, 1970.

24 The seven—five young Mexican-Americans and two whites—all suffered major injuries including broken bones and ruptured organs in what was apparently considered a sporting event by the cops involved. An inaccurate and racist portrayal of the attack is one of the early scenes in the 1997 film *L.A. Confidential*, based on a novel of the same name by James Ellroy.

25 Edward Escobar, "The Dialectics of Repression: The Los Angeles Police Department and the Chicano Movement, 1968–1971," *Journal of American History* 79:4 (March 1993), 1499.

26 *LAT*, March 14, 1970; *LA Free Press*, March 27, 1970.

27 Muñoz, quoted in García, *Chicano Generation*, 261.

28 The long-distance or over-the-road freight drivers, something of a Teamster aristocracy, belonged to a third local and were only marginally involved in the wildcat in Southern California.

29 See the important study by Samuel Friedman, *Teamster Rank and File: Power, Bureaucracy, and Rebellion at Work and in a Union* (New York: Columbia University Press, 1982).

30 As a unionized high-wage industry (at least until deregulation by President Carter), freight was particularly attractive to Chicanos, and they were already a substantial minority in the two locals. They also contributed some of the most militant fighters and strike leaders. For instance, of eight strikers arrested for an alleged sniping incident on the "Grapevine," five had Spanish surnames (*LAT*, May 1, 1970). (MD was an active Teamster in this period, albeit in a non-striking local, and friends with several of the strike leaders. In particular he relishes the memory of Mike "Scotty" Napier, who brought some of the spirit of the Red Clydeside to Local 208.)

31 An estimated 60 percent of teachers actually walked out; those who remained in classrooms tended to be older and more conservative.

32 See John Donovan, "A Tale of Two Strikes: The Formation of United

Teachers—Los Angeles and the Los Angeles Teacher Strikes of 1970 and 1989," *Southern California Quarterly* 81:3 (fall 1999).

33 *LAT*, April 14, 15 and 21, 1970; May 17, 1970.

34 *LAT*, May 12, 1970.

35 Fred Halstead, *Out Now! A Participant's Account of the Movement in the U.S. against the Vietnam War* (New York: Pathfinder, 1978), 661.

32 War on the Eastside

1 Muñoz, quoted in Mario T. García, *The Chicano Generation: Testimonios of the Movement* (Berkeley: University of California Press, 2015), 265–7.

2 Ruben Salazar, ed. (introduction by Mario T. García), *Border Correspondent: Selected Writings, 1955*–1970 (Berkeley: University of California Press, 1995), esp. 32–3. García was given access to Salazar's FBI files by the newsman's wife, Sally.

3 Mario T. García, *Memories of Chicano History: The Life and Narrative of Bert Corona* (Berkeley: University of California Press, 1994), 278–9.

4 Sam, with many others (including MD), had left the Communist Party after the national leadership launched a purge of the Southern California District for its opposition to Brezhnev's murderous Prague Spring. His book *The Long Road to Delano* (New York: International Publishers, 1975) was widely praised as the classic account of the first decade of the UFW.

5 "Roughly Indiana St. on the west, Atlantic Blvd. on the east, the Pomona Freeway on the north, and Olympic Blvd. on the south" (*LAT*, August 30, 1970).

6 Ian Haney López, *Racism on Trial: The Chicano Fight for Justice* (Cambridge: Harvard University Press, 2003), 195–6.

7 Jesús Treviño, *Eyewitness: A Filmmaker's Memoir of the Chicano Movement* (Houston: Arte Público Press, 2001), 144.

8 Ibid., 163.

9 Los Angeles County Office of Independent Review, *Review of the Los Angeles County Sheriff's Department's Investigation into the Homicide of Ruben Salazar*, report, February 22, 2011, 14 (hereafter "Independent Review").

10 The man in the red vest, Manuel Lopez, not only directed traffic, but also moved a bus bench to block a lane of Whittier Boulevard, chased bystanders away from a burning carpet store, and "stood in the boulevard near the Silver Dollar and directed a group of sheriff's deputies toward the tavern." On a day when ordinary Mexican-American

citizens were harassed and sometimes beaten on sight by deputies, Lopez could assume this role only if he was well-known to some of the sheriffs. Was he also in their employ? See *LAT*, September 12, 1970, for the testimonies of two subpoenaed witnesses who owned a record store across the street from the Silver Dollar and repeatedly observed Lopez that afternoon.

11   Moreover, some of them had a few minutes before been ordered inside —a glaring contradiction that was never explored or resolved, either in the Sheriff's internal investigation or during the coroner's inquest.

12   At the inquest, the department insisted that the deputy in Ruiz's photograph was not Wilson but a member of the other team. Yet the second deputy testified that he fired projectiles while standing behind the door of his squad car across the street.

13   Sue Marshall, "Silver Dollar Scenario," *LA Free Press*, September 18, 1970; Independent Review, 13–14.

14   Independent Review, 11 and 15–16. For a detailed and compelling critique of the official "so sorry but it was an accident" account of Salazar's murder, see the video of Raul Ruiz's talk, "Mapping Truth: Following the Paper Trail in the Murder of Ruben Salazar (three parts)," UCLA Chicano Studies Research Center, August 29, 2012, at chicano.ucla.edu.

15   Gonzales to Muñoz, quoted in García, *Chicano Generation*, 283.

16   *LAT*, September 18, 1970. Ruiz bitterly recalls his experience with the inquest. "I testified for two straight days for a total of about sixteen hours … None of the inquiries dealt with my eyewitness account of the Silver Dollar incident. Instead, all the questions had to do with the demonstration itself and with the intent of casting doubts on my legitimacy as a journalist and on the reliability of my photos" (Ruiz, quoted in García, *Chicano Generation*, 81).

17   Quoted in García, *Chicano Generation*, 286.

18   In addition to the Berets, who had many *batos* in their membership, two groups directly emerged from the streets and prisons: La Junta (led by Cruz Olmeda and "Shorty" Martinez) and La Lucha (Moe Aguirre). They later fell into warfare with one another, and Martinez was shot and wounded by Aguirre. (MD was friends with Martinez, a wonderful character.)

19   *LAT*, January 11, 1971. See also *LA Free Press*, January 29, 1971. Davis named Sam Kushner as one of the main infiltrators and called him a "swimming pool Communist," an appellation that must have provoked a belly laugh from the crusty old newspaperman and former union organizer.

20 *LAT*, January 15, 1971.

21 *LAT*, February 1, 1971 (the reporters were Paul Houston and Ted Thackrey Jr.).

22 Ruiz, quoted in García, *Chicano Generation*, 85.

23 *LAT*, February 2, 1971; Ruiz, quoted in García, *Chicano Generation*, 85.

24 Rodolfo F. Acuña, *A Community Under Siege: A Chronicle of Chicanos East of the Los Angeles River, 1945–1975* (Los Angeles: UCLA Chicano Studies Research Center Publications, 1984), 214.

25 Ibid., 216–17.

26 Ruiz, quoted in García, *Chicano Generation*, 167.

27 "Black Power," at least as originally conceived by SNCC, had a more sophisticated approach to ethnic electoral politics. Through organizing as an independent third party or third force, Black radicals hoped to unify their communities around demands that would form the basis for negotiations with Democrats or others seeking their vote. The key thing was to accumulate political clout and never give it away for free.

28 The doubling of names has always made for confusion between the old Hermandad and the new. Likewise, members of the new party usually referred to it as "CASA," thereby risking further mistaken identity with the service centers.

29 *LAT*, August 31; September 1, 12 and 23, 1972.

30 *LAT*, November 2, 1972.

31 Jennifer G. Correa, "Chicano Nationalism: The Brown Berets and Legal Social Control," MA thesis, Texas A&M University, July 2006, 96.

33 The Many Faces of Women's Liberation

1 *LAT*, October 3, 1972. There is no published history of the women's movement in L.A. (as of 2019)—not even an article. Writers have relied on the UCLA senior thesis written by Michele Moravec, "In Their Own Time: Voices from the Los Angeles Feminist Movement, 1967 To 1976."

2 Barbara Ehrenreich, "Body Politic: The Growth of the Women's Health Movement," *Ms. Magazine* 12:2 (May 1984).

3 Sandra Morgen, *Into Our Own Hands: The Women's Health Movement in the United States, 1969–1990* (New Brunswick: Rutgers University Press, 2002), 23.

4 *LAT*, October 3, 1972.

5 *LAT*, December 6, 1972.

6   Quoted in Ruth Rosen, *The World Split Open: How the Women's Movement Changed America* (New York: Penguin, 2006), 177.

7   Ibid., 178.

8   *LAT*, June 18, 1975.

9   Yolana Nava, "Chicana Feminists," oral history, Virtual Oral/Aural History Archive, California State University Long Beach.

10 Virginia Espino, "Forced Sterilization and Chicana Resistance," in *Las Obreras: Chicana Politics of Work and Family*, ed. Vicki L. Ruiz (Los Angeles: UCLA Chicano Studies Research Center, 2003), 70, citing Thomas B. Littlewood, *The Politics of Population Control* (South Bend: University of Notre Dame Press, 1977), 85.

11 *Madrigal v. Quilligan*, Central California Court of Appeals for the Ninth Circuit, 639 F.2d 789, 1975; Vicki L. Ruiz and Virginia Sanchez Korrol, eds., *Latinas in the U.S.: A Historical Encyclopedia* (Bloomington: Indiana University Press, 2006), 416–19; Espino, "Forced Sterilization," 75.

12 Espino, "Forced Sterilization," 71.

13 Johnnie Tillmon, "Welfare Is a Women's Issue," *Ms.*, spring 1972.

14 Johnnie Tillmon, "Welfare Mothers, Welfare Rights," interview by Sherna Gluck, Virtual Oral/Aural History Archive, California State University, Long Beach.

15 Nick Kotz and Mary Lynn Kotz, *A Passion for Equality: George A. Wiley and the Movement* (New York: W. W. Norton, 1977), 211.

16 M. David Forrest, "Johnnie Tillmon," *American National Biography*, October 2014, anb.org; Nick Kotz and Mary Lynn Kotz, *A Passion for Equality*.

17 Moravec, "Voices," 56; "Founding Feminists," Today in Herstory, *Feminist Newswire*, June 24, 2015, feminist.org; Stephanie Gilmore, "Rethinking the Liberal-Radical Divide: The National Organization for Women in Memphis, Columbus, and San Francisco," PhD diss., Ohio State University, 2005, 89.

18 Toni Carabillo, interview by Michelle Moravec, December 28, 1988, Activists: Feminist History Collection, Virtual Oral/Aural History Archive, California State University, Long Beach, library.csulb.edu.

19 *LAT*, May 11, 1969.

20 Billy Graham, "Jesus and the Liberated Woman," *Ladies' Home Journal*, December 1970. Earlier that year 200 women organized by NOW held a daylong sit-in at the *Journal*'s offices in New York protesting the piece; as a result, the *Journal* published a nine-page feature, "'The New Feminism': A Special Section Prepared for the *Ladies' Home Journal* by the Women's Liberation Movement," *Ladies Home*

Journal, August 1970; Grace Lichtenstein, "Feminists Demand 'Liberation,'" in "Ladies Home Journal Sit-In," *New York Times*, March 19, 1970.

21 "NOW Pickets AT&T," *NOW News* 3:3 (April 1971); Marjorie A. Stockford, *The Bellwomen: The Story of the Landmark AT&T Sex Discrimination Case* (New Brunswick: Rutgers University Press, 2004).

22 Farah workers won union recognition after two years and a national boycott.

23 Moravec, "Voices," 57.

24 Louise Ramsdell, "Women Lobby in Sacramento," *NOW News*, June 1970.

25 Carol Downer, "Feminist Health Movement," oral history, Virtual Oral/Aural History Archive, California State University, Long Beach, library.csulb.edu; Betty Friedan, *It Changed My Life: Writings on the Women's Movement* (Cambridge, MA: Harvard University Press, 1998), 137.

26 "Carol Aurilla Downer," in *Feminists Who Changed America, 1963–1975*, ed. Barbara J. Love (Urbana: University of Illinois Press, 2006), 123; Downer oral history.

27 Downer oral history.

28 The story has been told many times, notably in Sheryl Burt Ruzik, *The Women's Health Movement: Feminist Alternatives to Medical Control* (New York: Praeger, 1979), 53.

29 Ruth Rosen, *World Split Open*, 176.

30 Jennifer Nelson, *More Than Medicine: A History of the Feminist Women's Health Movement* (New York: New York University Press, 2015), 63.

31 "Lorraine Rothman," in Love, *Feminists*.

32 Robins reprinted her interview with Dixon in her book: "On the Beginnings: An Interview with Marlene Dixon," in *Handbook of Women's Liberation* (North Hollywood: Now Library Press, 1970), 103–8.

33 Joan Robins, interview by Dara Robinson, February 11, 1984, Activists: Feminist History Collection, Virtual Oral/Aural History Archive, California State University, Long Beach, library.csulb. edu.

34 "An Oral History Interview with Sherna Berger Gluck," interview by Mary Rothschild (2004), in *Women and Social Movements in the United States* 23:1 (March 2019); Love, *Feminists*, 176–7. She taught for many years in the Women's Studies program at Cal State Long Beach, where she was director of the Oral History Program. She published

many books, notably *Rosie the Riveter Revisited* (Woodbridge, CT: Twaine, 1987).

35　Jackie Goldberg, interview by JW, October 22, 2015; see also Jackie Goldberg and Sharon Stricker, oral history, Activist Video Archive, activistvideoarchive.org.

36　Jackie Goldberg interview.

37　Jan Breidenbach, interview by JW, September 15, 2015.

38　Jackie Goldberg interview.

39　Ibid.

40　Ibid.; see also Jackie Goldberg and Sharon Stricker oral history.

41　Lillian Faderman and Stuart Timmons, *Gay LA* (New York: Basic Books, 2006), 190.

42　Marcia M. Gallo, *Different Daughters: A History of the Daughters of Bilitis and the Rise of the Lesbian Rights Movement* (Emeryville: Seal Press, 2007), 180. The cover of the *Lesbian Tide* issue on the UCLA conference is reproduced at womenslibrary.org.uk.

43　Quoted in Joanne Meyerowitz, *How Sex Changed: A History of Trans-sexualism in the US* (Cambridge, MA: Harvard University Press, 2002), 260.

44　Susan Stryker, *Transgender History: The Roots of Today's Revolution*, 2nd ed. (New York: Seal, 2017), 127, 168. In her memoir of the events, Elliott described Morgan as a "queen bee feminist hustler": Beth Elliott, "Fear and Loathing in Westwood," in Geri Nettick with Beth Elliott, *Mirrors: Portrait of a Lesbian Transsexual* (Oakland, CA: CreateSpace, 2011), 258.

45　Michelle Goldberg, "What Is a Woman? The Dispute between Radical Feminism and Transgenderism," *New Yorker*, August 4, 2014.

46　Sue Mayberry, *Doin' It in Public: Feminism and Art at the Woman's Building* (Los Angeles: Otis College of Art and Design, 2012), an exhibition that was part of the Getty's 2011 initiative Pacific Standard Time. See also the extensive bibliography at Otis College of Art and Design official website, www.otis.edu/old-ben-maltz-gallery/womans-building-suggested-readings.

47　"Otis Presents Pioneers of the Feminist Art Movement: Joyce Kozloff," interview by Anne Swartz for *Doin' It in Public*, October 7, 2011, available at youtube.com.

48　Ibid.

49　"Los Angeles Council of Women Artists," *Everywoman* 2, 17:28 (December 17, 1971).

50　See Dorothy Townsend, "Women Artists Say Museum Discriminates," *LAT*, June 16, 1971; the original "Los Angeles Council of

Women Artists Report," June 15, 1971, was exhibited as part of the Getty's Pacific Standard Time series of shows in 2011. It is available via the Getty Research Institute, getty.edu/research.

51 Ann Sutherland Harris and Linda Nochlin, *Women Artists 1550–1950* (Los Angeles: LACMA, 1976).

52 Women's Equality Day was established by Congress that year, 1973, in response to a push by lawyer and activist Bella Abzug.

53 "LA Feminists to Meet Sunday at Rancho Park," *Long Beach Independent*, August 24, 1973, 24, available at newspapers.com.

54 Joyce Kozloff interview. The changes were not limited to the legalization of abortion and the prohibition on forced sterilization, nor to the opening of many careers to women. The women's movement in Los Angeles produced leaders for the next decades: Carol Downer became a lawyer and author of books on the women's health movement, and practices immigration law in L.A. Gloria Molina went into politics and became the first Latina elected to the California State Legislature, the Los Angeles City Council, and the Los Angeles County Board of Supervisors. Antonia Hernández went on to become President of the Mexican American Legal Defense and Education Fund (MALDEF) and then the CEO of the California Community Foundation, a $1 billion nonprofit supporting community organizations in LA County. Johnnie Tillmon left L.A. in 1971 for Washington, DC, and became executive director of the National Welfare Rights Organization, which campaigned for a guaranteed adequate income and challenged stereotyped portrayals of the poor. When the NWRO folded in 1974, she returned to L.A. and community organizing of welfare recipients. Jackie Goldberg also went into politics—elected to the LA School Board, then the city council, then the state legislature, returning to the school board in 2019 to fight the charter school advocates. Sheila Kuehl went on to become the first openly gay member of the California State Assembly, the first woman elected speaker of the state assembly, and then an LA County supervisor. And Sherna Gluck became a historian of the women's movement, interviewing many leaders and activists, starting the Feminist History Research Project, publishing widely, and directing the Oral History Project at Cal State Long Beach—a key source for this chapter.

34 "Everybody Wanted It"

1 The scenes appear in a 1968 UCLA student film: Bob Eberlein and Paul Deason, dirs., *The Free Clinic*.

2 "Kids Who Can't Cope," *Los Angeles Magazine*, May 1969, 33; Noel Greenwood, "One of a Kind Medical Facility Never Gives Its Patients a Bill," *LAT*, June 29, 1969.

3 Leonard Somberg, "The Los Angeles Free Clinic, 1967–1970: A Folk History," typescript, 1971, 9. Somberg was executive director when he wrote this twenty-three-page document.

4 Jan Spence, "Health Care—A Right, Not a Privilege: Interview with Dr. David E. Smith," *Share International*, May 1993, shareintl.org.

5 Somberg, "Clinic," 3. One kind of contact with the police was unavoidable: some people with drug overdoses had to be sent to hospital emergency rooms via ambulance, and city policy required police to accompany city ambulances. The LAPD "occasionally" displayed their "moral disapproval," Somberg wrote, "in their rough handling, even handcuffing, [of] people with drug overdoses."

6 *LAT*, November 19, 1967.

7 Murray Korngold, interview by Rebecca Therese Baird, in "Shelter from the Storm: The Los Angeles Free Clinic, 1967–1975," PhD diss., Arizona State University, 2016, 112. This is the most important scholarly study of the subject.

8 Baird, "Shelter," 103.

9 *LAT*, November 23, 1967.

10 Marsha Getzler and Phil Deitch, interviews in Baird, "Shelter," 138.

11 Noel Greenwood, "Free Clinic on Fairfax Picking Up the Pieces," *LAT*, December 3, 1967.

12 Somberg, "Clinic," 3.

13 Ibid., 3.

14 Paul Eberle, "Police Invade Free Clinic; Clinic Asks Return to Peace," *LA Free Press*, November 1, 1968, 1; Somberg, "Clinic," 3–4.

15 Somberg, "Clinic," 9.

16 Baird, "Shelter," 112.

17 Kelly Hodel, interview in Baird, "Shelter," 127. Hodel had been a medical corpsman with the Marines in Vietnam.

18 Somberg, "Clinic," 5.

19 Korngold, interview in Baird; "Shelter," 112.

20 Mycrofft, "Not Going There Again," post on *EMTLife* (web forum), March 19, 2012, emtlife.com.

21 Noel Greenwood, "Young People's Free Clinic Is Busier Than Ever, but It's Almost Broke," *LAT*, June 27, 1968.

22 Somberg, "Clinic," 14.

23 Ibid., 14–15.

24 Ibid., 16.

25 Phil Deitch, interview in Baird, "Shelter," 114.

26 Korngold, Liebowitz, interviews in ibid., 144.

27 Frances Helfman, interview in ibid., 114.

28 Kelly Hodel, interview in ibid., 132.

29 Joan Hoffman, "Loitering Legal at Free Clinic Workshop," *LA Free Press*, September 13, 1968, 19.

30 Doug Shuit, "'Hip Subculture's' Clinic in Debt and Faced by Collapse," *LAT*, December 14, 1970.

31 Ibid.

32 "6230 Sunset Blvd, Hollywood, CA: The Kaleidoscope 1968 Performance List," *Rock Prosopography 101*, rockprosopography101. blogspot.com.

33 Part of the problem was that "the Rose Bowl was too far away and no one could find it, and also that Cream was playing at a venue in town for $5 less than the clinic's concert" (Hodel, interview in Baird, "Shelter," 124).

34 Liebowitz, Mizrahi, Helfman, interviews in Baird, "Shelter," 126; "50 Years of Redefining Community Health," Saban Community Clinic official website, sabancommunityclinic.org.

35 Somberg, "Clinic," 11–12.

36 Nancy Reagan privately urged her husband to sign the new law, and to talk about it with her father, the right-wing but pro-abortion Chicago physician Loyal Davis (Lou Cannon, "California's Abortion Law: A Road Not Taken," *RealClearPolitics*, April 4, 2013, realclearpolitics.com).

37 Korngold, interview in Baird, "Shelter," 130–1.

38 Jenna M. Loyd, *Health Rights Are Civil Rights: Peace and Justice Activism in Los Angeles, 1963–1978* (Minneapolis: University of Minneapolis Press, 2014), 99–100; Paul Cabell, "Long Beach Free Clinic Serves Area's Medical Needs," *LA Free Press*, July 4, 1969, 19; Dennis Levitt, "Panthers Open Free Clinic," *LA Free Press*, January 2, 1970, 3.

39 Noel Greenwood, "County to Open Its First Free Health Clinic for Young People This Week," *LAT*, December 29, 1968.

40 Somberg, "Clinic," 21.

41 Ibid., 22.

42 Somberg stayed, but on November 3, 1975, he was shot and killed in a holdup at the clinic (*LAT*, November 4, 1975).

43 Baird, "Shelter," 151.

44 Somberg, "Clinic," 21.

45 "50 Years," Saban Clinic official website.

35 Gidra

1 Laura Pulido, *Black, Brown, Yellow, and Left: Radical Activism in Los Angeles* (Berkeley: University of California Press, 2006), 106.

2 William Wei, *The Asian American Movement* (Philadelphia: Temple University Press, 1993), 102.

3 Brian Niiya, "Gidra: Now Available Online," *Densho Blog*, densho. org. The complete *Gidra* archive is available at ddr.densho.org.

4 Wei, *Asian American Movement*, 102. The dragon's name appeared as "Ghidrah" in some sources, but was trademarked as "Ghidorah."

5 Dr. Juan Martínez of Stanford, quoted in Kanji, "The Third World: A Response to Oppression," *Gidra*, April 1969, 1.

6 *Gidra*, April and May 1969.

7 In addition to Mike Murase, the founders were Dinora Gil, Laura Ho, Tracy Okida, and Colin Watanabe.

8 Mike Murase, "Toward Barefoot Journalism," *Gidra*, April 1974, 1, 35 (final issue of the original run).

9 *LAT*, January 29, 1999.

10 S. Hayashi, "A Commentary on the Noguchi Firing," *Gidra*, April 1969, 1; Thomas I. Noguchi, *Coroner* (New York: Simon & Schuster, 1983), 113.

11 For example, the *Freep* front page in mid April 1969 featured a report that "GI's Against the War held massive peace demonstrations in L.A. and other cities on the first anniversary of Martin Luther King's death." The week before, the *Freep* reported on "thousands of people marching for peace" on Easter Sunday in L.A. See Fred Hoffman, "GIs Lead LA Peace March, Park Rally," *LA Free Press*, April 11–17, 1969, 1; and Leonard Brown, "Thousands to March Easter," *LA Free Press*, April 4, 1969, 1.

12 "S. I. Rips Gidra!," Laura Ho, "Pigs, Pickets, and a Banana," *Gidra*, May 1969, 1.

13 Alan Ota, "Moratorium Day," *Gidra*, November 1969, 2. Furutani soon became *Gidra*'s first regular columnist. In 1969, Okinawa was scheduled to be returned to Japan in 1972 after its use as a US military base since World War II.

14 Mike Murase, "A Los Angeles First: Asian Americans to March for Peace," *Gidra*, December 1969, 2.

15 The statement was reported by Ron Ridenhour, who received it in a letter after he exposed the My Lai massacre: Lloyd Shearer, "Ron Ridenhour: He Broke the Story of the Mylai 'Massacre,'" *Oakland Tribune*, January 18, 1970.

16 Alan Ota, "A Commentary: The Asian American March," *Gidra*, February 1970, 8.

17 Mike Murase "created the 'Stereotypes' cartoons," according to Karen L. Ishizuka, *Serve the People: Making Asian America in the Long Sixties* (London and New York: Verso, 2016), 63.

18 *Gidra*, editorial, July 1969.

19 Anonymous, "A Brother Speaks," *Gidra*, May 1969, 2.

20 Eddie Wong, "Shuck 'n Jive," and Irene Miyagawa, "UCLA Sells Out," both in *Gidra*, September 1969, 5.

21 "Noguchi Receives Support," *Gidra*, August 1969, 2. Noguchi, in his memoir published fourteen years later, says the Japanese American community initially refused to support him because "they believed the charges against me … were true," and felt he had "embarrassed" them. He writes that JUST was formed only toward the end, when the county's case collapsed. He doesn't mention the full-page ad or the celebratory banquet (Noguchi, *Coroner*, 114, 119).

22 Audre Miura, "Isaac Honored," *Gidra*, September 1969, 1.

23 "March for Peace," *Gidra*, December 1969, 2.

24 Stats from charts in *Gidra*, August 1969, 8–9.

25 Murase, "Barefoot Journalist," 36.

26 Isao Fujimoto, "The Failure of Democracy," *Gidra*, September 1969, 6–8.

27 Carol, James, Seigo and Victor, "Remember 1942?," *Gidra*, January 1970, 2. The pilgrimage was the project of the Organization of Southland Asian American Organizations.

28 Ishizuka, *Serve the People*, 154. The Manzanar pilgrimage became an annual event, and it was featured in *Gidra* every year.

29 Ruth Rosen, *The World Split Open: How the Modern Women's Movement Changed America*, rev. ed. (New York, Penguin, 2006), 285. The previous year, 1970, saw the publication of *Sisterhood Is Powerful, An Anthology of Writings from the Women's Liberation Movement*, ed. Robin Morgan (New York: Vintage); and *Our Bodies, Ourselves*, published by the Boston Women's Health Book Collective as a newsprint booklet. It also saw the founding of the Comisión Femenil Mexicana by Chicana feminists, and Toni Cade's publication of *The Black Woman* (New York: Pocket).

30 *Gidra*, January 1971, 2.

31 Rosen, *World Split Open*, 276.

32 Linda Iwataki, "Women's HerStory," *Gidra*, January 1971, 12.

33 Wilma Chen, "Movement Contradiction," *Gidra*, January 1971, 8, 276.

34 Mike Yamamoto, "Male Perspective," *Gidra*, January 1970, 13. Thirty

years later, Yamamoto transitioned from male to female, "emerging as Mia in 2003" (Ishizuka, *Serve the People*, 202).

35 Robin Morgan, "Goodbye to All That" (1970), Reprinted in Rosalyn Baxandall and Linda Gordon, eds., *Dear Sisters: Dispatches from the Women's Liberation Movement* (New York: Basic Books, 2000), 53.

36 Pulido, *Black, Brown, Yellow, and Left*, 210. The photographer was one of the key *Gidra* men: Mike Murasake.

37 Kiku Uno, "From the Vancouver Conference," *Gidra*, May 1971, 12.

38 Candace Murata, "From the Vancouver Conference," *Gidra*, May 1971, 12.

39 Evelyn Yoshimura, "Not Enough Can Be Said about So Much," *Gidra*, November 1972, 6–7.

40 Wei, *Asian American Movement*, 110–11.

41 [Shinya Ono], "Asian Nation," *Gidra*, October 1971, 16–19.

42 Shinya Ono, "Finding a Home Community," in Steve Louie and Glenn Omatsu, eds., *Asian Americans: The Movement and the Moment* (Los Angeles: UCLA Asian American Studies Center Press, 2014), 263–73. At the time the essay was written, in 2001, he had moved to Japan with his wife and two daughters and was working as a translator.

43 Ibid., 263.

44 The revived *Gidra* in 2001 lamented the closing of Holiday Bowl, which it called an "irreplaceable treasure": Scott Kurashige, "Game Over for Holiday Bowl?," *Gidra*, summer 2001.

45 "Asian Nation," 18.

46 "Asian Nation," 19. Ono himself worked for six years at Resthaven Community Mental Health Center as a counselor. The larger project was "the struggle for community control" at the federally funded downtown LA clinic, where his group focused on "the need to develop alternative approaches to mental health that are suited to Asian Americans, Latinos, African Americans, Native Americans, and poor and elderly whites." They also carried out a successful unionization drive for one hundred staff members. "The demand for 'community control,'" he later wrote, "was criticized by many Marxist-Leninist groups as 'narrow' and 'reformist.'" But "instead of saying that sweeping changes will be realized AFTER people win the revolution, some meaningful changes were actually won and implemented in the course of struggle—here and now—which gave us a foretaste of what a revolution can bring" (Ono, "Finding a Home Community," 169).

47 Murase, "Barefoot Journalist," 37, 38. Another remarkable thing:

no one on the staff received a paycheck in the entire five years of publication.

48 Ibid., 38.

49 Ibid., Murase, 39.

50 Wei, *Asian American Movement*—he interviewed and corresponded with the editors in 1985 and 1986.

36 L.A.'s Black Woodstock

1 Of course, the March on Washington in 1963 had more people, but it included many whites; two decades after Wattstax, the Million Man March, in 1995, had an estimated 837,000, making it the largest Black gathering ever. See "Million Man March," Boston University Center for Remote Sensing, bu.edu/remotesensing.

2 See the McCone Commission map: "Mapping the Watts Riots," *Maps Mania*, August 12, 2015, googlemapsmania.blogspot.com.

3 Rob Bowman, quoting Al Bell: on DVD extras for Mel Stuart, dir., *Wattstax*, documentary film (Los Angeles: Stax Records, 2004).

4 "Rev. Jesse Jackson Bio," Rainbow PUSH Coalition official website, rainbowpush.org.

5 Rob Bowman, *Soulsville, USA: The Story of Stax Records* (New York: Schirmer Books, 1977), 278. The security guys refused.

6 *LAT*, August 21, 1972; Stuart, dir., *Wattstax*.

7 Robert Christgau, "Staple Singers," *Christgau's Record Guide*, robert-christgau.com.

8 Donald Clarke, ed., *Penguin Encyclopedia of Popular Music* (New York: Puffin, 1991), 528.

9 Bowman, *Soulsville*, 278, 231, 233.

10 Robert Gordon, *Respect Yourself: Stax Records and the Soul Explosion* (New York: Bloomsbury, 2012), ch. 23.

11 Mel Stuart, "Filmmaker Interview," *POV*, Public Broadcasting Service, n.d., pbs.org.

Epilogue

1 *LAT*, March 9, 1972.

2 John C. Bollens and Grant B. Geyer, *Yorty: Politics of a Constant Candidate* (Pacific Palisades: Palisades Publishers, 1973), 204–9; Robert Halley, Alan Acock and Thomas Greene, "Ethnicity and Social Class: Voting in the 1973 Los Angeles Municipal Elections," *Western Political Quarterly* 29:4 (December 1976), 526; Harlan Hahn, David

Klingman, and Harry Pachon, "Cleavages, Coalitions, and the Black Candidate: The Los Angeles Mayoralty Elections of 1969 and 1973," *Political Research Quarterly* 29:4 (December 1976), 507–20.

3 Garth, returning to Gotham, would go on to work his media magic on behalf of the mayoral campaigns of Koch, Guiliani and Blumenburg.

4 Raphael Sonenshein, *Politics in Black and White: Race and Power in Los Angeles* (Princeton: Princeton University Press, 1993), 105. This is the indispensable overview of the Bradley era.

5 *LAT*, January 21 and February 1, 1977.

6 For the national scene, see Christopher Lehman, "Civil Rights in Twilight: The End of the Civil Rights Movement Era in 1973," *Journal of Black Studies* 36:3 (January 2006), 415–28.

7 Hahn, Klingman and Pachon, "Cleavages," 517–18.

8 Sonenshein, *Politics*, 115–23.

9 *LAT*, March 20 and 23, 1975.

10 See "'Horror Stories' Told: L.A. Warned of 'Gang Crisis,'" *LAT*, November 30, 1973.

11 *LAT*, November 10, 1994.

12 *LAT*, November 8, 2014.

Index